HEGEL

To KAREN
who came in at the beginning
and thought it would never end

HEGEL

Charles Taylor

Professor of Philosophy and Political Science
McGill University, Montreal

CAMBRIDGE
UNIVERSITY PRESS

PUBLISHED BY THE PRESS SYNDICATE OF THE UNIVERSITY OF CAMBRIDGE
The Pitt Building, Trumpington Street, Cambridge, United Kingdom

CAMBRIDGE UNIVERSITY PRESS
The Edinburgh Building, Cambridge CB2 2RU, UK   http://www.cup.cam.ac.uk
40 West 20th Street, New York, NY 10011-4211, USA   http://www.cup.org
10 Stamford Road, Oakleigh, Melbourne 3166, Australia
Ruiz de Alarcón 13, 28014 Madrid, Spain

© Cambridge University Press 1975

First published 1975
First paperback edition 1977
Reprinted 1978, 1983, 1984, 1987, 1988, 1989, 1991, 1993, 1995, 1996,
1998, 1999

Printed in the United States of America

Typeset in Caledonia

A catalog record for this book is available from the British Library

Library of Congress Catalog card number: 74-25642

ISBN 0 521 29199 2 paprback

Contents

Contents

Preface and Acknowledgements

This is another attempt to expound Hegel. I suppose that it would be superfluous and very possibly self-defeating to try to justify it at the outset. But it is worth looking at the difficulties which beset all such attempts.

The enterprise can easily go awry in one of two opposite ways. Either one can end up being terribly clear and sounding very reasonable at the cost of distorting, even bowdlerizing Hegel. Or one can remain faithful but impenetrable, so that in the end readers will turn with relief to the text in order to understand the commentary.

The reader will have to judge whether I have succeeded in avoiding either or both of these pitfalls. But I should like to explain now how I have tried. Part I of this book is an attempt to expound the central lines of Hegel's conception without confining myself to his own terms. I recognize that this is a hazardous undertaking. But I hope to remain faithful to Hegel's intentions by placing this outline of his philosophy in relation to the main aspirations of his generation, which his philosophical vision was intended to meet in its own unique way.

Chapter I is thus devoted to an attempt to describe the aspirations of the generation of young Romantics of the 1790s, from which Hegel sprang and against whom he defined himself. After a brief chapter on Hegel's development, I then try in chapter III to present an outline of his central ideas.

In the rest of the book I fill out this skeletal portrait by using it to expound the major phases of Hegel's work. Part II is devoted to the *Phenomenology of Spirit*. In Part III, I attempt to give an account of the Logic. This is the longest, the hardest, and for those not interested in the detail of Hegel's arguments, the most unrewarding part of the book. A reader interested in the general sweep of Hegel's thought, or more specifically in Hegel's political theory, or philosophy of history, or conception of modern culture, might skip this part. But for anyone who wants to understand how Hegel's philosophy was authenticated in his own eyes, and indeed, how this philosophy and its authentication are inseparable for Hegel, the Logic remains indispensable.

Part IV gives an exposition of Hegel's philosophy of history and politics, and of the insight Hegel had, in my view, into the dilemmas of modern societies. In Part V I look briefly at Hegel's philosophies of art and religion and his conception of the history of philosophy. And in the concluding chapter try to show in what way Hegel's philosophy is an essential part of the recapitulative conflict of interpretations through which we try to understand ourselves as a civilization.

My thanks go first to Isaiah Berlin, Stuart Hampshire and A. J. Ayer who set me going on this enterprise many years ago, more than I can remember or would like to recall. And I am very grateful to Isaiah Berlin for his comments on part of the manuscript and for the benefit of his wide knowledge and understanding of the whole phase of German thought and sensibility from which Hegel sprang.

I should also like to thank Bernard Williams who made some valuable suggestions for changes, of which I have perhaps not taken sufficient account; and Professors Hermann Boeschenstein and Harold Sarf, and Geoffrey Chambers, for their comments on parts of the manuscript.

References Given in Abbreviated Form

ABBREVIATION	WORK	COMMENT
SW	*Sämtliche Werke*, Jubilee edition by Hermann Glockner, in xx volumes, Stuttgart, 1927–30.	
Nohl	H. Nohl (Ed.) *Hegels Theologische Jugendschriften*, Tübingen, 1907.	Collection of unpublished MSS of the 1790s.
Knox	T, M. Knox (Ed.) *Early Theological Writings*, Chicago, 1948.	Translation of some of the contents of Nohl.
Differenz	Hegel, *Differenz des Fichte'schen und Schelling'-schen Systems der Philosophie*, ed. G. Lasson, Leipzig, 1928.	Hegel's first published philosophical work, July 1801.
SdS	*System der Sittlichkeit*, in G. Lasson, (Ed.), *Schriften zur Politik und Rechtsphilosophie*, Leipzig, 1923.	Unpublished work of the Jena period.
Realphilo II	*Jenaer Realphilosophie*, ed. J. Hoffmeister, Hamburg 1967.	Hegel's Jena lectures of 1805–6, published by Hoffmeister for the first time in the 1930s.
PhG	*Phänomenologie des Geistes*, G. Lasson edition, Hamburg, 1952.	The *Phenomenology of Spirit* published by Hegel in 1807 at the end of his Jena period.
WL	*Wissenschaft der Logik*, G. Lasson edition, Hamburg, 1963.	The *Science of Logic*, published by Hegel 1812–16 in his Nürnberg period, also known sometimes as the 'Greater Logic'.
EL	*System der Philosophie*, erster Teil. Die Logik, SW VIII.	These three were originally published by Hegel in 1817 under the title, *Encyclopaedia of the Philosophical Sciences in Outline*, with second and third editions in 1827 and 1830. The first part is sometimes referred to as the 'Lesser Logic'. The text referred to here is based on the third edition, with additions based on students' lecture notes. The references to these works are to paragraph numbers (§...). Hegel's paragraphs consisted of a
EN	*System der Philosophie*, zweiter Teil. Die Natur-philosophie, SW IX.	
EG	*System der Philosophie*, dritter Teil. Die Philo-sophie des Geistes, SW X.	

ix

References

| | | principal statement, sometimes followed by an explanatory remark, sometimes in turn followed by an addition inserted by the later editors. Where useful I distinguish in my references between the principal statement and the remark, and where remark or addition are very long, I give the page reference in the SW edition. |

PR   Grundlinien der Philosophie des Rechts, ed. J. Hoffmeister, Hamburg, 1955, or *Hegel's Philosophy of Right*, trans. T. M. Knox, Oxford 1942.   References to this work, first published in 1821, are also to paragraph numbers (§...). Here also the main text of a paragraph is sometimes followed by an explanatory remark (sometimes referred to with an 'E' after the paragraph number), and also sometimes by an addition inserted by later editors on the basis of lecture notes. I have usually quoted the text of Knox's edition, but the references to paragraph number makes it easy to find the texts in the German edition as well. Where remarks or additions are long, I have given page references to the Knox edition.

VG   *Die Vernunft in der Geschichte*, ed. J. Hoffmeister, Hamburg, 1955.   The introductory part of Hegel's lectures on the philosophy of history, put together from various cycles of lecture notes after his death.

GW   *Die Germanische Welt*, ed. G. Lasson, Leipzig, 1920.   This is the concluding part of Hegel's lectures on the philosophy of history, put together in the way described above.

I & I   *Die Idee und das Ideal*, ed. G. Lasson, Leipzig, 1931.   Introductory part of Hegel's lectures on aesthetics, again put together from lecture notes after his death.

BRel   *Begriff der Religion*, ed. G. Lasson, Leipzig, 1925.   The first part of Hegel's lectures on the philosophy of religion, put together posthumously from lecture notes.

NatRel   *Die Naturreligion*, ed. G. Lasson, Leipzig, 1927.   The second part of Hegel's lectures on the philosophy of religion, put together posthumously from lecture notes.

RelGI   *Die Religionen der geistigen Individualität*, ed. G. Lasson, Leipzig, 1927.   The third part of Hegel's lectures on the philosophy of religion, put together posthumously from lecture notes.

AbsRel   *Die absolute Religion*, ed. G. Lasson, Leipzig, 1929.   The fourth and concluding part of Hegel's lectures on the philosophy of religion, put together posthumously from lecture notes.

GPhil   *Geschichte der Philosophie*, ed. J. Hoffmeister, Leipzig, 1940.   The introductory part of Hegel's lectures on the history of philosophy, put together posthumously from lecture notes.

Glossary of German Words Used in the Text

WORD	TRANSLATION	COMMENTARY
an sich für sich an und für sich	in itself for itself in and for itself	As Hegelian terms of art, cf. discussion in Chapter III. 7.
Aufhebung	Abrogation or suppression	In Hegel's special usage, the term combines its ordinary meaning with a rarer sense, of 'setting aside' or 'preservation'. It thus serves to designate the dialectical transition in which a lower stage is both cancelled and preserved in a higher. Cf. Chapter III. 8.
Aufklärung Aufklärer	Enlightenment man (men) of the Enlightenment	
bei sich	at home	Exactly translates into French as 'chez soi', and carries also a connotation of presence to self.
Dasein	existence, or existent	Used by Hegel to designate the category of the Logic which emerges from the dialectic of Being and Nothing. In this sense, usually translated 'Determinate Being'. Cf. Chapter X. I.
Ding-an-sich	Thing-in-itself	
Geist	spirit	Used by Hegel to designate subjectivity as it returns to itself out of its embodiment; hence also used of the cosmic spirit, or God.
Moralität	morality	Used by Hegel in contrast to *Sittlichkeit*, to designate the morality which holds of us as universal rational wills, independently of our belonging (or not belonging) to a community. Cf. Chapter XIV.
sittlich Sittlichkeit	ethical ethics	As Hegelian term of art designates the morality which holds of us in virtue of being members of a self-subsistent community, to which we owe allegiance as an embodiment of the universal. Cf. Chapter XIV.

Glossary

WORD	TRANSLATION	COMMENTARY
Sein	Being, to be	
Sollen	ought to	
Verstand	understanding	
Vernunft	reason	
Volk	people	
Volks-geist(er)	spirit(s) of people(s)	Cf. Chapter xv. 1.
Volks-religion	religion of a people	Cf. Chapter ii.
Vorstellung	representation	As a Hegelian term of art used of a mode of thought which relies on images instead of being purely conceptual. This is the mode of thought proper to religion. Cf. Chapter xvii.
Wirklichkeit	reality	Used of the real in the ordinary sense only in so far as it is there in fulfilment of the Idea. Cf. Chapter xi. III.

PART I

THE CLAIMS OF SPECULATIVE REASON

Aims of a New Epoch

Hegel was born in 1770, at the moment that German culture was entering the decisive shift known as the *Sturm und Drang*, and when the generation which would revolutionize German thought and literature at the turn of the century was being born. Hegel belongs to this, the 'Romantic' generation, as it has been called, a bit loosely. In fact such party labels are misleading; there were certain pre-occupations which captured the thinkers and artists of this generation, whether they qualify as Romantics or not, pre-occupations which were shared even by sharp critics of the Romantics, as Hegel was. We cannot really understand what he was about until we see the basic problems and aspirations which gripped him, and these were those of the time.

It was a revolutionary time, of course. This has become to us a hackneyed phrase, because revolution in the world is become almost a constant of our experience. But in the 1790s Revolution had its full impact, as the shock waves from Paris spread across Europe; and its impact was all the stronger for being bi-valenced: enthusiasm followed by perplexed horror, among the young intelligentsia of Germany. Much in the writings of Hegel and his contemporaries can be explained by the need to come to terms with the painful, perturbing, conflict-ridden moral experience of the French Revolution. But we have also to understand something of the medium in which this epochal event reverberated, the climate of thought and feeling in which the rising generation of young educated Germans was formed and evolved.

Perhaps the most economical way of sketching this climate, or those aspects of it which will most help us in understanding Hegel, is to delineate a central problem, which insistently demanded solution of the thinkers of this time. It concerned the nature of human subjectivity and its relation to the world. It was a problem of uniting two seemingly indispensable images of man, which on one level had deep affinities with each other, and yet could not but appear utterly incompatible.

1

Both these views arose as reactions to, and hence partly as developments of, the main stream of radical Enlightenment thought as this had developed through the seventeenth and eighteenth centuries in England and France. By this I mean the line of thought which begins with the epistemological revolution which was part inspirer, part beneficiary of the seventeenth-century scientific revolution. It develops through such diverse thinkers as Bacon, Hobbes, Descartes, Locke; and authenticated by the science of Galileo and Newton, it entrenches its hold in the eighteenth century not only as a theory of knowledge, but as a theory of man and society as well. In the hands of its more radical protagonists it develops towards a thoroughgoing atomism and mechanism, sometimes going as far as materialism, in its account of man and society, and it becomes a radical utilitarianism in ethics. Helvétius, Holbach, Hume, Bentham can be thought of as representatives of different currents of this broad stream.

Now there are many ways of reading this movement of ideas; the most common is the one just mentioned: that we see it as primarily an epistemological revolution with anthropological consequences. But it will be more relevant to our purposes if we try to concentrate on the notion of the subject which underlay this revolution from the start.

As epistemological innovators, the moderns of the seventeenth century directed their scorn and polemics against Aristotelian science, and that view of the universe which had become intricated with it in Medieval and early Renaissance thought. Final causes and the related vision of the universe as a meaningful order of qualitatively differentiated levels give way first to a Platonic–Pythagorean vision of mathematical order (as in Bruno, Kepler, and partly too, in Galileo), and then finally to the 'modern' view of a world of ultimately contingent correlations, to be patiently mapped by empirical observation. From the modern point of view, these earlier visions betrayed a deplorable if understandable weakness of men, a self-indulgence wherein they projected on things the forms which they most desire to find, in which they feel fulfilled or at home. Scientific truth and discovery requires austerity, a courageous struggle against what Bacon called the 'Idols of the human mind'.

We are all 'moderns' enough to have bought a good deal of this story. It is with a mixture of condescension and embarrassment that we read a passage like the following, an early seventeenth-century 'refutation' of Galileo's discovery of the moons of Jupiter.

There are seven windows given to animals in the domicile of the head, through which the air is admitted to the tabernacle of the body, to enlighten, to warm and to nourish it. What are these parts of the *microcosmos?* Two nostrils, two eyes, two ears, and a mouth. So in the heavens, as in a *macrocosmos*, there are two favourable stars, two unpropitious, two luminaries, and Mercury undecided and indifferent. From this and from many other similarities in nature, such as the seven metals, etc., which it were tedious to enumerate, we gather that the number of planets is necessarily seven.[1]

1 Quoted from S. Warhaft (Ed.) *Francis Bacon: A selection of his works*, Toronto, 1965, p. 17.

4

What seems to underlie this reasoning as an 'anthropomorphic' assumption is the vision of meaningful order. It can be called a meaningful order because the notion is that different elements in creation express or embody a certain order of ideas – this is why the apertures in the head, the planets, the metals, and other phenomena 'which it were tedious to enumerate' can all be put in relation with each other. They all embody the same idea reflected in different media, rather as 'it's hot' and 'il fait chaud' express the same statement in different languages. And because of this correspondence, we can conclude to the nature of one from the other just as I know from learning that someone said, in French, 'it's hot' that he said 'il fait chaud'. The idea of a meaningful order is inseparably bound up with that of final causes since it posits that the furniture of the universe is as it is and develops as it does in order to embody these Ideas; the order is the ultimate explanation.

Understanding the world in categories of meaning, as existing to embody or express an order of Ideas or archetypes, as manifesting the rhythm of divine life, or the foundational acts of the gods, or the will of God; seeing the world as a text, or the universe as a book (a notion which Galileo still makes use of) – this kind of *interpretive* vision of things which in one form or another played such an important role in many pre-modern societies may appear to us the paradigm of anthropomorphic projection onto the world, suitable to an age in which man was not fully adult. And if this is our only way of seeing this transition in our intellectual and cultural history, then we must interpret the revolts against mechanism of the late eighteenth century, the vision of Goethe, the Romantic imagination, the philosophies of Nature of a Schelling or a Hegel, simply as a failure of nerve, a nostalgic return to earlier, comfortable illusions.

This way of seeing things is not uncommon, but it very much misses the point of these reactions, as well as obscuring the way in which the issues raised then remain central today. Instead of seeing the issue between Galileo and the Paduan philosophers, between modern science and medieval metaphysics, as a struggle between two tendencies in the self, one deploying comforting illusions, the other facing stern realities, we might see it as a revolution in the basic categories in which we understand self. This is not to say that it was understood in this way at the time, but that this formulation is best suited to help us understand the movements of the late eighteenth century.

The moderns' reading of their predecessors and opponents as caught in a web of illusion which they themselves have spun, self-indulgently projecting meanings devised in the mind onto the facts, arose understandably out of the struggle of innovators to free themselves from a venerable orthodoxy. But it persists partly because the very completeness of the modern revolution militates against our understanding the view it replaced. The very modern notion of the self, which is the locus for this struggle between indulgence and austerity, really only comes to be in the seventeenth century, although the epicurean view foreshadows it to some extent.

The essential difference can perhaps be put in this way: the modern subject is self-defining, where on previous views the subject is defined in relation to a cosmic order.

Any account of the human subject has to cope with certain universal facets of experience: that at times we can be 'in touch' with ourselves, with our central concerns, we can be clear about who we are and what our purposes are; while at other times we are confused, unclear, or distraught, torn this way and that, or obsessed with the inessential, or just giddily forgetful. Many concepts and images can be used to describe these opposed conditions: harmony vs. conflict, depth vs. superficiality, self-possession vs. -loss, self-centring vs. dispersal. And of course none is neutral, in the sense that each proposes an interpretation of what is at stake which can be contested. For different notions of the subject suggest very different interpretations.

If we pick 'self-presence' as against 'distraction' or 'dispersal' as provisional terms to designate the oppositions here, then we can say that the view of the subject that came down from the dominant tradition of the ancients, was that man came most fully to himself when he was in touch with a cosmic order, and in touch with it in the way most suitable to it as an order of ideas, that is, by reason. This is plainly the heritage of Plato; order in the human soul is inseparable from rational vision of the order of being. For Aristotle contemplation of this order is the highest activity of man. The same basic notion is present in the neo-Platonist vision which through Augustine becomes foundational for much medieval thought.

On this view the notion of a subject coming to self-presence and clarity in the absence of any cosmic order, or in ignorance of and unrelated to the cosmic order, is utterly senseless: to rise out of dream, confusion, illusion *is just* to see the order of things. We might say that on this view, there is no notion of the self in the modern sense, that is, of an identity which I can define for myself without reference to what surrounds me and the world in which I am set. Rather, I am essentially vision of...either order or illusion.

Now the shift that occurs in the seventeenth-century revolution is, inter alia, a shift to the modern notion of the self. It is this kind of notion which underlies Descartes' *cogito*, where the existence of the self is demonstrated while that of everything outside, even God, is in doubt. Similarly, it is this notion which underlies the emancipation from meaning. If man only comes to self-presence in a rational vision of cosmic order which is an order of ideas; and if science as the highest mode of consciousness presupposes self-presence, then science must be founded on a vision of meaningful order. Not deployed as an argument, but rather as an unspoken boundary to thought, this must have underlain the argument of Galileo's opponents. If there *had* to be a meaningful order, then the set of correspondences they deploy are pretty convincing, granted other current assumptions. But at base there had to be an order because this was a condition of the rational grasp of the world we call science, on the assumption that rationality = vision of this order. Of course, it would be anachronistic to place this as an *argument* in the mouths of contemporaries. For it is we post-Kantians who can cast it as a transcendental argument from the fact of science. But it is not incoherent or illegitimate to think of it as an inarticulate limit of thought.

But plainly the obverse relation holds as well, and to dispense with the notion of meaningful order was to re-define the self. The situation is now reversed: full self-possession requires that we free ourselves from the projections of meanings onto things, that we be able to draw back from the world, and concentrate purely on our own processes of observation and thought about things. The old model now looks like a dream of self-dispersal; self-presence is now to be aware of what we are and what we are doing in abstraction from the world we observe and judge. The self-defining subject of modern epistemology is thus naturally the atomic subjectivity of the psychology and politics which grow out of the same movement. The very notion of the subject takes on a new meaning in the modern context, as a number of contemporary writers have pointed out.[1]

Of course, as mentioned above, this modern notion of the self was not without precedents. The Epicureans and Sceptics among the ancients presented a view of the self which was defined in abstraction from any order; and it is not surprising that this minority tradition among the ancients provided some of the fuel for the modern revolution, or that many figures of the Enlightenment felt great affinity for Epicurus and Lucretius. But the modern subject provided a significantly new twist.

The Epicureans and Sceptics achieved a notion of self-definition by withdrawal from the world; their weapon was scepticism about cosmic order, or a plea for the irrelevance of the Gods. By contrast the modern shift to a self-defining subject was bound up with a sense of control over the world – at first intellectual and then technological. That is, the modern certainty that the world was not to be seen as a text or an embodiment of meaning was not founded on a sense of its baffling impenetrability. On the contrary, it grew with the mapping of the regularities in things, by transparent mathematical reasoning, and with the consequent increase of manipulative control. That is what ultimately established the picture of the world as the locus of neutral, contingent correlations. Ancient sceptics while denying our ability to know the nature of things, had claimed that men had enough immediately relevant grasp on their situation to go about the business of life. While sometimes taking

---

[1] E.g. Heidegger: 'Die Zeit des Weltbildes' in *Holzwege*, Frankfurt a.M., 1950, 81–5.

up the same formulae, the seventeenth century changed their content radically. The immediately relevant knowledge which was not to be compared with knowledge of final causes came to enjoy a higher and higher prestige. It came to be understood as the paradigm of knowledge.

This control over things which has grown with modern science and technology is often thought of as the principal motivation behind the scientific revolution and the development of the modern outlook. Bacon's oft-quoted slogan, 'knowledge is power' can easily give us this impression, and this 'technological' view of the seventeenth-century revolution is one of the reasons why Bacon has often been given a greater role in it than he deserves, alongside Galileo and Descartes. But even in Bacon's case, when he insists on the nullity of a philosophy from which there cannot be 'adduced a single experiment which tends to relieve and benefit the condition of man',[1] we can read his motivation in a different way. We rather see the control as valuable not so much in itself as in its confirmation of a certain view of things: a view of the world not as a locus of meanings, but rather of contingent, de facto correlations. Manipulability of the world confirms the new self-defining identity, as it were: the proper relation of man to a meaningful order is to put himself into tune with it; by contrast nothing sets the seal more clearly on the rejection of this vision than successfully treating the world as object of control. Manipulation both proves and as it were celebrates the vision of things as 'disenchanted' (entzaubert) to use Max Weber's famous phrase.

Technological progress has so transformed our lives and produced so many things we could barely do without, that we easily think of the 'pay-off' of the seventeenth-century revolution in terms of these benefits (if such they unambiguously are). But in the seventeenth century itself, this pay-off was very slim. For Bacon and the other men of his time, control was more important for what it proved. In the very passage quoted above where he speaks of relieving and benefitting the condition of man, Bacon says: 'For fruits and works are as it were sponsors and sureties for the truth of philosophies.' And later he makes an explicit comparison of the relative importance of the two considerations: 'works themselves are of greater value as pledges of truth than as contributing to the comforts of life'.[2] We have no reason to think of this as false scientific piety.

Bacon later defines this goal which 'is in itself more worthy than all the fruits of inventions' as 'the very contemplation of things as they are, without superstition or imposture, error or confusion'.[3] My suggestion is that one of the powerful attractions of this austere vision, long before it 'paid off' in technology, lies in the fact that a disenchanted world is correlative to a self-defining subject, and that the winning through to a self-defining identity

---

[1] Novum Organum, Book I, LXXIII. [2] Op. cit. Book I, CXXIV.
[3] Book I, CXXIX.

was accompanied by a sense of exhilaration and power, that the subject need no longer define his perfection or vice, his equilibrium or disharmony, in relation to an external order. With the forging of this modern subjectivity there comes a new notion of freedom, and a newly central role attributed to freedom, which seems to have proved itself definitive and irreversible.

In the preceding pages we have been speaking of a transformation in philosophical outlook, which as such could only touch a minority in seventeenth-century Europe. But the modern notion of the subject has left no one untouched and unchanged in European society, or indeed the world. In part we can see this as the result of changes, political, economic, social which spread under the influence of minorities first over Western society as a whole, and then over alien societies. But in the European case there was another powerful influence at work which seems to have moved in the same direction. For the majority of non-philosophical men the sense of being defined in relation to a larger order is carried by their religious consciousness, and most powerfully for most men in most ages by their sense of the sacred, by which is meant here the heightened presence of the divine in certain privileged places, times and actions. Catholic Christianity retained the sacred in this sense, both in its own sacraments and in certain pagan festivals suitably 'baptized'. But protestantism and particularly Calvinism classed it with idolatry and waged unconditional war on it. It is probable that the unremitting struggle to desacralize the world in the name of an undivided devotion to God waged by Calvin and his followers helped to destroy the sense that the creation was a locus of meanings in relation to which man had to define himself. Of course the aim of this exercise was very far from forging the self-defining subject, but rather that the believer depend alone on God. But with the waning of Protestant piety, the desacralized world helped to foster its correlative human subjectivity, which now reaped a harvest sown originally for its creator.

In any case, under the impact of philosophical revolution and religious reformation, we can discern the development in these countries of a modern notion of the subject, which I have characterized as self-defining, and correlative to this a vision of things as devoid of intrinsic meaning, of the world as the locus of contingent correlations to be traced by observation, conforming to no a priori pattern. I have spoken above of this vision of the world as 'disenchanted' using Weber's term, or as 'desacralized' in speaking of the religious development. Perhaps I can introduce the term of art 'objectified' here to cover this denial to the world of inherent meaning, that is, the denial that it is to be seen as embodied meaning. The point of using this term is to mark the fact that for the modern view categories of meaning and purpose apply exclusively to the thought and actions of subjects, and cannot find a purchase in the world they think about and act on. To think of things in these terms is to project subjective categories, to set aside these categories is thus to

9

'objectify'. This marks a new, modern notion of objectivity correlative to the new subjectivity.

The new notion of objectivity rejected the recourse to final causes, it was mechanistic in the sense of relying on efficient causation only. Connected with this it was atomistic, in that it accounted for change in complex things not by gestalt or holistic properties, but rather by efficient causal relations among constituents. It tended towards homogeneity in that seemingly qualitatively distinct things were to be explained as alternative constructions out of the same basic constituents or basic principles. One of the most spectacular results of the new physics was to collapse the Aristotelian distinction between the supra- and sub-lunar to account for moving planets and falling apples in the same formula. Thus this science was mechanistic, atomistic, homogenizing, and of course saw the shape of things as contingent.

But this notion of objectivity could not be confined to external nature. Man is also an object in nature, as well as the subject of knowledge. Hence the new science breeds a type of understanding of man, mechanistic, atomistic, homogenizing and based on contingency. Hume gives us a prime example of this kind of view of man, in its first mode where the medium of observation was introspective; but the same notions underlie later 'behaviouristic' attempts at a science of man. The attempts at such a science of the radical Enlightenment, of a Helvétius, a Holbach, a Condorcet, a Bentham were founded on this notion of objectivity, and the age of Enlightenment was evolving an anthropology which was an amalgam, not entirely consistent, of two things: the notion of self-defining subjectivity correlative to the new objectivity; and the view of man as part of nature, hence fully under the jurisdiction of this objectivity. These two aspects did not always sit well together. They reinforced each other in support of atomism, an atomistic science of nature matching a political theory whose starting point was the individual in a state of nature. But they seemed to conflict on an issue like that of determinism, for example, where the freedom of man as subject seemed compromised by the strict causal necessity under which he lay as part of nature. And this was reflected in diverging notions of the relevance of nature to practical reason. For Kant, for instance, the promptings of nature stood in contrast to the demands of freedom. While for the mainstream of the Enlightenment, nature as the whole interlocking system of objective reality, in which all beings, including man, had a natural mode of existence which dovetailed with that of all others, provided rather the basic model to man as a natural, desiring being, the blueprint of reason for happiness and hence good.

But in spite of tensions the amalgam held, and these two perspectives, partly converging partly conflicting, combined in different ways to generate a wide gamut of views, from the mildest deism which stressed the spiritual nature and destiny of man to the most radical materialism; from the deepest pessimism about the common man's capacity for enlightenment to the wildest Utopian hopes of a world rebuilt by science. These were the views of the era we know of as the Enlightenment.

2

This anthropology was the point of attack, or perhaps recoil would be a better term, of two major tendencies in German thought whose reconciliation was the key problem of Hegel's generation. But this is not to say that the radical, mechanistic, materialist Enlightenment was strong in Germany. Quite the contrary. If we think of the French materialists as the fully developed form, then the Enlightenment unfolds in Germany in a mitigated version.

In so far as the radical Enlightenment presupposed a tremendous confidence in human subjectivity and human powers, we can perhaps understand the German variant as a result of German backwardness, the legacy of the Thirty Years War: internal division into a crazy-quilt of often absurdly minuscule states, the slow development of a middle class which could stand on its own, the economic backwardness relative to West Europe, the late cultural development in the vernacular. And obviously some good part of the explanation for the form the Enlightenment took in Germany lies in its religious background. The Lutheran churches never got to the point of head-on opposition, of a knock-down, drag-out fight with the Enlightenment, that French Catholicism so quickly reached. In this respect Germany resembled rather Protestant England. But beyond this, both the Enlightenment in Germany and the reaction to it was shaped in part by an important movement of religious revival, generally referred to as Pietism.

Pietism – which had some affinities to Methodism in the English-speaking world – was a movement of renewal in spiritual life. Starting in the seventeenth century it reached its culmination in the eighteenth. It reacted against the formalism of official Lutheranism, its stress on right beliefs and its concern for the established structures. All this was made secondary to the main point; the inward, heartfelt relation to Christ. Pietism was in this sense another outgrowth of the old German spiritual tradition, going back to the medieval mystics Eckhart and Tauler, and passing through Boehme – a tradition on which Luther himself had drawn – which made central the inner encounter of the soul and God.

It turned to a religion of the heart, one of enthusiastic devotion, of a renewal (Wiedergeburt) in which men are filled with the fire of the Spirit. The result was that it found itself allied with the Enlightenment on certain important points, for all the profound difference in spiritual basis between them. Thus Pietism too tended to denigrate the concern with dogma and confessional differences. It too ended up defending the individual, his sincere convictions and his freely chosen community against the larger official structures of state and church which commanded allegiance. It too tended to galvanize men towards works of improvement, education and social welfare. Indeed, the Pietists with their stress on a religion of the heart paid initially less heed to differences of class and education than the *Aufklärer*.[1]

Alongside this agreement, there was of course also a spiritual gulf fixed between Pietism and the spirit of the *Aufklärung*. This latter shared with Pietism's orthodox opponents that stress on adherence to the right *propositions*, on the truth as correctly *stated* and *proved*, at the expense of the spontaneous response of the heart. Thus Pietism, as we shall see later, was a very important factor in the reactions to the *Aufklärung*.

But even before these arose it coloured the atmosphere and tone of the German Enlightenment. Intensely suspicious of reasoning as many Pietists were – 'He who wishes to comprehend God with his mind', declared Zinzendorf, leader of the Herrnhuter, 'he becomes an atheist'[2] – nevertheless Pietism helped shape the thought of some of Germany's greatest *Aufklärer*, e.g., Lessing and Kant. Lessing's *Nathan*, which greatly influenced the young Hegel as we shall see, is a plea for a rational and humane religion beyond differences of dogma and independent of 'cold booklearning'[3] which owes something both to Enlightenment reason and to Pietist spirituality. With this kind of interweaving, religion and Enlightenment could never be two opposed camps, as in France.

But whatever the reasons, the German *Aufklärung* developed its own intellectual climate. This was much more receptive to deism than it was to radical materialism. Eighteenth-century deism of course reflected the new sense of the self and its relation to the world. And it reflected this at its clearest in its notion of God, as supreme architect of a universe constructed to run according to objective causal laws. The cosmic order so built was not an order of meanings, that is, an order in virtue of its embodying ideas, but rather in virtue of its elements meshing perfectly in their reciprocal effects. Hence the image of the universe as clock. And what God was as super-subject, man was destined to approach as he grasped more and more of the laws of the universe and became more and more able to second the order of nature with his own artifice.

But European deism took on a different, characteristic form in Germany, that of Leibniz's system, which as interpreted by Christian Wolff dominated the philosophical world of Germany in the eighteenth century. This philosophy

[1] I.e., the men of the Enlightenment. German is lucky in having a single word where in English we need four. For this reason, I shall sometimes use the German word in the text, as also, for variety, the German term for the Enlightenment, *Aufklärung*.

[2] Quoted in Koppel S. Pinson *Pietism as a Factor in the Rise of German Nationalism;* Columbia University Theses, 1934, v. 23, p. 52.

[3] Kalte Buchgelehrsamkeit, Act v, scene 6, the words are Recha's.

can be seen from one point of view as a kind of half-way house between a philosophy of cosmic order and the radical Enlightenment, although from another and more fruitful viewpoint, it is clearly the seed of the important post-Enlightenment departures which created the climate of Hegel's time. Leibniz does indeed present us with a cosmic order, where the ultimate explanation is in terms of final causes, that this world is 'the best of all possible worlds'; and yet the order is made up of beings, monads, who develop out of themselves, who are really subjectivities in the modern sense. The Leibnizian order of things is not there to instantiate a certain order of ideas, but rather to realize the greatest variety compatible with the greatest amount of order or harmony. This means that we are to understand things not by attempting to interpret the world like a text, but rather by seeing how the purposes of monads dovetail with each other, and this is a framework of understanding which can consort well with a mathematical physics. (Another such half-way house, Shaftesbury's harmonious order of natures, influenced ultimately by the Cambridge Platonists, was very popular in Germany as well.)

In any case, on the basis of this German variant, and proceeding pari passu with a reaction against the presumption shared by the French and many Germans that the French Enlightenment was the paradigm to be followed, and that French culture was the model to be copied, there develops in Germany a post-Enlightenment climate, at once critical of some of the main themes of the modern revolution, and yet striving to incorporate much of it. In this schematic background sketch, I want to single out two strands.

The first comes to expression in the decade of the 1770s, the period of the so-called *Sturm und Drang*, a revolution in German literature and criticism which was decisive for the future of German culture. Perhaps the man whose thought is most worth singling out here is Herder, the major theoretician and critic of the *Sturm und Drang*, who greatly influenced Goethe in the crucial formative years of his life.

Herder reacts against the anthropology of the Enlightenment, against what I called above the 'objectification' of human nature, against the analysis of the human mind into different faculties, of man into body and soul, against a calculative notion of reason, divorced from feeling and will. And he is one of the principal of those responsible for developing an alternative anthropology, one centred on the categories of expression.[1]

I would like to try to examine a bit more closely what is involved in a theory of man based on these categories because these are central to any understand-

---

[1] 'Expression' here is necessarily a term of art, but I am following here Isaiah Berlin in his 'Herder and the Enlightenment' in Earl Wasserman (ed.) *Aspects of the eighteenth century*, Baltimore 1965 where he identifies one of Herder's innovative ideas by the term 'expressionism'. I think I am making the same point in somewhat different form, though to avoid confusion with the twentieth-century movement, I shall rather use the term 'expressivism' – a term also suggested by Berlin (Private Communication).

ing of Hegel or indeed of this period. The central notion is that human activity and human life are seen as expressions. Now we saw above that the model of a self-defining subject brought along with it an objectifying of things, that is, it debarred notions like 'meaning', 'expression', 'purpose' as inappropriate descriptions of objective reality and confined them rather to the mental life of subjects. For instance the theories of linguistic meaning which run from Hobbes through to Condillac see meaningfulness as an external relation which certain marks, sounds, things or ideas (representations) have for us. That is to say, this relation is in the mind of subjects and consists in the marks, sounds, etc. being thought or used by us to refer to something else. That there be some things in the world about which we can speak in categories of meaning requires that there be other things to which these categories cannot apply, for the first (signs, words, ideas, etc) only fit these categories because of their relation of reference to the second. Further, that some things can be described in meaning-categories is not an 'objective' fact about them, that is, one that holds independently of the particular contents and beliefs in men's minds; the connections which make meaning are subjective. This theory of linguistic meaning is a thoroughly 'objectifying' one in the sense above; it rigorously segregates meaning from being. It makes the medieval and early Renaissance view of the world as text incapable of coherent statement. The notion of things in the world as expressing some ideal order, and this regardless of whether we grasp the order or not, makes no sense. This early modern theory is an uncompromising extension of medieval nominalism to its farthest conclusion.

Does then the anthropology of expression mean simply a return, a reversal of the modern revolution of subjectivity? As mentioned above, many have thought so; but this is a serious misreading. For a different notion of expression is at stake here. In talking of the reigning model which inspired Galileo's opponents above, I said that we could see the corresponding terms – apertures in the head, planets, metals, etc. – as corresponding because they express or embody the same ideal order. Here we speak of expression as of an ideal which the expression presents. This is the sense of the term, or related to the sense of the term, in which we talk about expressing our thoughts in speech. But there is another sense in which we speak of expression as giving vent to, a realizing in external reality of something we feel or desire. This is the sense in which we might speak of my expressing my anger in cursing, or striking the man who provoked me. Now in the latter sense what is expressed is a subject, or some state of a subject, or at the minimum some life form which resembles a subject (as when we speak of animals expressing feeling).

Now in saying that the central notion in this new anthropology was of human action or life as expression, I was using the term in something closer to this latter sense. Though in fact as we shall see something of the first is incorporated as well. On the anthropology developed by Herder and those who followed him, there is certainly a rehabilitation of some basic Aristotelian concepts; to see life as an expression is to see it as the realization of a purpose, and in so far as this purpose is not meant to be ultimately blind, one can speak of the realization of an idea. But this is also understood as the realization of a self; and in this respect the notion is modern, it goes beyond Aristotle and shows a filiation to Leibniz.

To talk about the realization of a self here is to say that the adequate human life would not just be a fulfilment of an idea or a plan which is fixed independently of the subject who realizes it, as is the Aristotelian form of a man. Rather this life must have the added dimension that the subject can recognize it as his own, as having unfolded from within him. This self-related dimension is entirely missing from the Aristotelian tradition. In this tradition a proper human life is 'my own' only in the sense that I am a man, and this is thus the life fit for me. It was Herder and the expressivist anthropology developed from him which added the epoch-making demand that my realization of the human essence be my own, and hence launched the idea that each individual (and in Herder's application, each people) has its own way of being human, which it cannot exchange with that of any other except at the cost of distortion and self-mutilation.

But what more precisely is added to the Aristotelian notion of the realization of a form when we also see it as the unfolding of self? There are two related strands here which are worth tracing a little further.

First, realizing the human form involves an inner force imposing itself on external reality, perhaps against external obstacles. Thus where Aristotelian philosophy saw the growth and development of man and the realization of human form as a tending towards order and equilibrium constantly threatened by disorder and disharmony, the expressivist view sees this development more as the manifestation of an inner power[1] striving to realize and maintain its own shape against those the surrounding world might impose. Thus the ideal realization is one which not only conforms to the idea, but is also internally generated; indeed these two requirements are inseparable in that the proper form of a man incorporates the notion of free subjectivity.

It is evident that Rousseau played an important role in the development of this theory in that he virtually reinterpreted the traditional opposition of virtue and vice into the modern opposition of self- versus other-dependence. But the corresponding theory of man is barely hinted at, and not even consistently, in his writings. It was left to German thinkers, and particularly to Herder, to develop the anthropology around the notion of the self-unfolding subject.

Leibniz too is obviously of central importance, whose notion of the monad

---

[1] Cf. Herder's '*Kräfte*'.

15

was seminal for that of a self-unfolding subject. But Herder and those of his generation and the succeeding one were also greatly influenced by Spinoza. This may be surprising in that Spinoza was the great philosopher of the anti-subject, the philosopher who more than any other in the Western tradition seems to take us beyond and outside of subjectivity. But the age in receiving him imposed a certain reading on Spinoza. His philosophy was not seen as denying an understanding of human life as self-unfolding; rather the Spinozan notion of a *conatus* in all things to preserve themselves was read in this light. What Spinoza seemed to offer, why he drew Goethe, and tempted so many others, was a vision of the way in which the finite subject fitted into a universal current of life. In the process Spinoza was pushed towards a kind of pantheism of a universal life force. In other words he was re-interpreted to incorporate the category of self-unfolding, now seen as the act of a universal life which was bigger than any subject, but qua self-unfolding life very subject-like. Why such a strong need was felt for a relation to this universal current of life, I shall return to below.

The second important strand in expressivism is the notion that the realization of a form clarifies or makes determinate what that form is. If we return to our guiding analogy, the way in which an action or gesture can express what is characteristic about a person, we can see that there are two aspects which can be united in this idea. Something I do or say can express my feelings or aspirations in the sense of making these clear to others or to myself. In this sense we can speak of a person expressing himself when he finally gets out and thus makes determinate, perhaps for the first time, what he feels or wants. In another sense we can speak of someone's actions as expression of his feelings or desires when they carry out what he wants, or realize his aspirations. These two aspects can be separated: I can bring my desires to verbal expression without acting, I can act and remain an enigma to myself and others; but they often do go together, and frequently we are inclined to say of ourselves or others, that we did not really know what we felt or wanted until we acted. Thus the fullest and most convincing expression of a subject is one where he both realizes and clarifies his aspirations.

It is this fuller model of subjective expression which underlies what I have called here the expressivist theory. If we think of our life as realizing an essence or form, this means not just the embodying of this form in reality, it also means defining in a determinate way what this form is. And this shows in another way the important difference between the expressivist model and the Aristotelian tradition: for the former, the idea which a man realizes is not wholly determinate beforehand; it is only made fully determinate in being fulfilled. Hence the Herderian idea that my humanity is something unique, not equivalent to yours, and this unique quality can only be revealed in my life itself. 'Each man has his own measure, as it were an accord peculiar to him of all his feelings to each other'.[1] The idea is not just that men are different; this was hardly new; it was rather that the differences define the unique form that each of us is called on to realize. The differences take on moral import; so that the question could arise for the first time whether a given form of life was an authentic expression of certain individuals or people. This is the new dimension added by a theory of *self*-realization.

Thus the notion of human life as expression sees this not only as the realization of purposes but also as the clarification of these purposes. It is not only the fulfilment of life but also the clarification of meaning. In the course of living adequately I not only fulfil my humanity but clarify what my humanity is about. As such a clarification my life-form is not just the fulfilment of purpose but the embodiment of meaning, the expression of an idea. The expression theory breaks with the Enlightenment dichotomy between meaning and being, at least as far as human life is concerned. Human life is both fact and meaningful expression; and its being expression does not reside in a subjective relation of reference to something else, it expresses the idea which it realizes.

This provides a new interpretation of the traditional view of man as a rational animal, a being whose essence is rational awareness. This idea is now formulated in a new concept of self-awareness. As we saw, our life is seen as self-expression also in the sense of clarifying what we are. This clarification awaits recognition by a subject, and man as a conscious being achieves his highest point when he reconizes his own life as an adequate, a true expression of what he potentially is – just as an artist or writer reaches his goal in recognizing his work as a fully adequate expression of what he wanted to say. And in one case as in the other, the 'message' could not have been known before it was expressed. The traditional view receives a new formulation in expressivism: man comes to know himself by expressing and hence clarifying what he is and recognizing himself in this expression. The specific property of human life is to culminate in self-awareness through expression.

The expressivist anthropology thus sharply breaks with the modern scientific objectification of nature, at least as far as human nature is concerned (we shall see later how it goes beyond this). In seeing human life as expression, it rejects the dichotomy of meaning against being; it deals once more in the Aristotelian coin of final causes and holistic concepts. But in another respect it is quintessentially modern; for it incorporates the idea of a self-defining subjectivity. The realization of his essence is a subject's self-realization; so that what he defines himself in relation to is not an ideal order beyond, but rather something which unfolds from himself, is his own realization, and is first made

[1] 'Jeder Mensch hat ein eignes Maß, gleichsam eine eigne Stimmung aller seiner sinnlichen Gefühle zu einander' *Ideen*, VIII.1 in Bernhard Suphan *Herders Sämmtliche Werke*, Berlin, 1891, XIII, 291.

determinate in that realization. This is one of the key ideas underlying the revolution of the late eighteenth century. But it is more than that; it is one of the foundational ideas of the civilization which has grown up since. In different forms, it is one of the major *idées-forces* which has shaped the contemporary world. It is worth examining further what it involves.

It is evident that a theory of this kind had to break with the Enlightenment accounts of language and meaning. It needed a theory of meaning which was not exclusively concerned with linguistic meaning and did not restrict meaningfulness to the single relation of reference for a subject. It seems clear to us who are heirs of this revolution that art provides us the paradigms needed, for we are familiar with an understanding of art objects as expressing something without necessarily referring beyond themselves.

But in the eighteenth century this understanding of art had yet to be defined. The reigning view of art was in terms of the Aristotelian concept of mimesis; art was principally understood as an imitation or picturing of reality. The expressivist view of man, like all profound changes in thought, had to create its own paradigms. It needed a theory of art as expressive, and a theory of meaning in which linguistic meaning, the meaning of signs, was not sharply marked off from other forms of meaning, but was rather continuous with the expressive meaning of art. But it needed this new understanding of linguistic and artistic expression not just to have models for the understanding of human life as expression; the point was not just to see life as like a work of art, although this is undoubtedly one of the important legacies of this period. If man's life is to be expression in the strong sense, that is both fulfilment of purpose and clarification of meaning, then it is because man is more than just a living being, but one capable of expressive activity. What makes man capable of expression is language and art. Thus these provide not just models for human life as expression, they are the privileged media through which this expression is realized.

There is both a continuity here with the Western tradition and a radical new twist imparted to it. The continuity lies in the fact that language is still central to man, as it has been ever since the ancient definitions of man as the 'rational animal'. The new twist is that language is no longer of crucial importance as the vehicle of the Ideas – indeed, it ceases to be so for some writers of this period, like Herder, who in this respect can be classed as a nominalist – but rather as the expression of self. Consequently, it is now in danger of being supplanted by art as the paradigm human activity. The human centre of gravity is on the point of shifting from *logos* to *poesis*.

These three related transpositions: a new theory of language, a new understanding of art, and a new understanding of their centrality, can all be seen developing through the work of Herder, other writers of the *Sturm und Drang*, and the following 'Romantic' generation. Thus in Herder's important

18

treatise *On the Origin of Language* of 1772, we see a break with the Enlightenment mode of theory about language as this had developed from Hobbes to Condillac. Herder radically displaces the problem. He quotes the Condillaquian account of how language could arise between two children in a desert, as they gradually learn to associate certain signs with certain objects. In a passage which reminds us at points of Wittgenstein combatting a not-dissimilar theory some two centuries later, Herder points out that this account presupposes the really important step as already taken; how do the children get the idea in the first place that some things can stand for others, that there can be such a thing as a *sign*? In other words how do they step from animal to linguistic, hence human consciousness?

Herder does not really answer the question himself, which has led many to comment that the treatise is misleadingly named. But the important point is that Herder has transformed our understanding of language. For his Enlightenment predecessors representative consciousness, the understanding that something stands for or refers to something else, was taken for granted. It arose naturally in the play of associations in the subject's experience. The institution of language, that is, arbitrary signs, only served to put us in control of the flow of association, to allow us to introduce order in our thoughts, to have 'empire sur notre imagination', as Condillac put it.[1] On this view words are a sub-class of signs, their having meaning is simply their being given a relation of reference to things.

But for Herder the existence of this representational or linguistic consciousness is the central question. What is it which makes it possible for us to have this distinct, focussed awareness of things, where animals remain caught in the dream-like, melodic flow of experience? It is language that makes this possible. Hence language must be probed from an entirely different point of view. It is not just a set of signs which have meaning in virtue of referring to something, it is the necessary vehicle of a certain form of consciousness, which is characteristically human, the distinct grasp of things which Herder calls 'reflection' (*Besonnenheit*). In other terms, words do not just refer, they are also precipitates of an activity in which the human form of consciousness comes to be. So they not only describe a world, they also express a mode of consciousness, in the double sense outlined above, that is, they realize it, and they make determinate what mode it is.

This is one of Herder's great seminal ideas. If man is a being who is to be understood under the category of expression, if what is characteristic of him is a certain form of consciousness, *Besonnenheit*, and if this is only realized in speech, then thought, reflection, the distinctively human activity is not something which can be carried on in a disembodied element. It can only exist in a

---

[1] *Sur l'Origine des Connaissances humaines* Part I, Section 2, Chapter IV §46.

19

medium. Language is essential to thought.[1] And if thought or the characteristically human activity can only be in the medium of language, then the different natural languages express each the uniquely characteristic way in which a people realizes the human essence. A people's language is the privileged mirror or expression of its humanity. The study of language is the central and indispensable road to the understanding of human variety. Herder's work is thus at the origin of the great growth in philological studies which begins at this time.[2]

Hence language is understood in a different dimension by Herder than by his Enlightenment predecessors. It is not only referential sign, it is also expression. And in this aspect it is continuous with art. Hence Herder's view that language in its origin was inseparable from poetry and song (not original with him, true, but to which the *Sturm und Drang* gave a new twist.), and that the most adequate language united description of the world and expression of feeling. This notion of language as expression of feeling in the strong sense had no place in the Enlightenment theories of man and meaning – although it was already beginning to appear in some of their writings on art, in particular in discussions about 'genius' of, e.g. Diderot. The idea was current of the cry, for instance, as the natural 'expression' of feeling in the sense of that which gave vent to feeling, its natural outlet, and which later could be chosen as a sign. But the idea of an expression in the strong sense, which also *defines* what the feeling is, only arises with the new theory of man. Language describes the world, but it also has to realize man and through this clarify what he is.

It was in this respect that it was continuous with art, at least with the new understanding of art which was developed by the generation of the *Sturm und Drang*. Where the standard view of the time saw art as primarily either imitative or didactic or pleasing in function, that is as existing either to picture the world, to improve men or to give them pleasure, the *Stürmer und Dränger* evolved a notion of art as expressive, as expressing the profound feelings of the artist, and in the process completing him, expanding his existence; Goethe uses the expression 'purification' (*Läuterung*). As Goethe's term implies, this expression is not just a giving vent to feelings, but a transformation of them to higher form. For the same reason, this expression of feeling is not subjective in the restrictive sense, making no claim to truth. On the contrary, the highest art is so because it is true to Nature; but not in the sense of an imitation, rather as the highest and fullest expression of its potentialities.

Because art was seen as expressive in this new sense, the artist was seen as a creator, and a new impetus was given to the eighteenth-century theme of

[1] Herder did not always see the implications of this idea, but they were of central importance for Hegel, as we shall see later.
[2] Herder was also the originator of the great interest in folk-song and folk culture which starts in this period.

genius, a power for which no formula could be given beforehand, but which could only be revealed in its unfolding.

As the most authentic expression of man, in the eyes of the *Stürmer und Dränger*, art was also the principal way in which men recovered community with other men and communion with nature. I shall return to this below.

Hence the 1770s in Germany saw a new philosophy of language and a new theory of art which formed part of a new developing theory of man. As a result of this art was given a central part to play in the realization of human nature, in the fulfilment of man. It is from this time that art begins to take on a function analogous to religion, and to some extent replacing it. In so far as this quasi-religious function of art is a fundamental feature of contemporary civilization, the 1770s can be considered a watershed in the development of the modern world.

The central importance of art is bound up with an enhanced role for feeling. The realization of man, as we saw, involved an expression, in the sense of a clarification, of what he is; and this is why the highest fulfilment comes in expressive activity. In its highest form, this expression must be recognized by him and be a mode of self-awareness as we saw above, since subjectivity at its highest is self-consciousness. But the life of a subject is also one of feeling, his self-realization or lack of it is not a matter of indifference but is experienced with joy or pain. And the feeling here referred to is not simply a passive state of mind, but is also a disposition of the will. Hence this self-awareness is not just a vision of self, but also a self-feeling, and as such also pregnant with the aspiration to remain or to become oneself, and it is all these inseparably. Thus the highest expressive activity is the vehicle of both vision and feeling together, and this is why language, not only in its origins but in its highest functions, is continuous with art.

Feeling here is not what it was for the mainstream of the Enlightenment, a passive state of affect only contingently linked with what provokes it on one hand, and with the action it motivates on the other. Rather we have a notion of feeling in the pregnant sense as inseparable from thought, just as thought, if it truly engage with reality is inseparable from feeling. Thus Herder: 'All [passions and sensations] can and must be operative, precisely in the highest knowledge, for this grew out of them all and can only live in them.'[1] Only idle speculation can be unaccompanied by feeling. Only 'liars or enervated beings' (Lügner oder Entnervte) can be satisfied with this.

Since we are expressive beings, our life is a unity, it cannot be artificially divided into distinct levels: life as against thought, sentience as against rationality, knowledge as against will. Man is not an animal with reason added, but a totally new indivisible form.[2] Feelings are thus modes of awareness, their

---

[1] *Vom Erkennen und Empfinden der Menschlichen Seele.* Suphan, VIII, 199.
[2] *Über den Ursprung der Sprache*, Suphan, V 28–9.

thought content is internal to them, and they can be qualitatively differentiated by the thoughts or awareness they embody. A hierarchy of feeling is thus inseparably bound up with the hierarchy of self-awareness, and with a hierarchy of dispositions of the will, for 'Impulse (Reize) is the driving force of our existence, and it must remain this even in our noblest knowing.' Hence 'love is, the noblest form of knowing, as it is the noblest feeling'.[1]

Thus an essential component of man's highest realization is a certain quality of feeling, a feeling of self which is also a vision of self, which feeling/vision is expressed in our highest activities, language and art. At his fullest man is realized not only as life but also as a being capable of expressive activity and therefore of achieving self-clarity and freedom. This is what Herder expresses in his notion of 'reflection' (*Besonnenheit*) as the crucial property of man. In this definition of human fulfilment we see once more the filiation and yet the break with the classical tradition. Man is a rational animal: '*Humanität*' is defined by Herder as 'reason and justice' (Vernunft und Billigkeit).[2] But rationality is not a principle of conformity with cosmic order. Rather it is self-clarity, *Besonnenheit*. Achieving this, we become what we have it in us to be, we express our full selves, and hence are free.

Thus essential to our fulfilment is the feeling/vision we have of ourselves at our fullest, as natural and spiritual beings, as subject of natural desires and of the highest aspiration to self-clarity and freedom and expressive form, and all of these in harmonious unity. This is why art, as the vehicle whereby this feeling/vision comes to be, can expand our existence and purify us.

In order to set the stage for the problems of the 1790s, let us look at some of the aspirations which flowed from this new theory of man. The expressivist anthropology was a response to the mechanist, atomist, utilitarian picture of human life. If we can think of the Enlightenment anthropology as recommending itself through the sense of freedom, even exhilaration, of self-definition, the reaction to it experienced this picture of man as dry, dead, as destroying life. For the sense of freedom as a self-defining, reasoning subject was won by objectifying nature, and even our own nature in so far as we are objects for ourselves. It was won at the expense of a rift between the subject who knows and wills, and the given: things as they are in nature. And this realm of the given includes not only external things in the world, but also what is given in the subject, his desires, feelings, leanings and affinities.

The Enlightenment developed a conception of nature, including human nature, as a set of objectified facts with which the subject had to deal in acquiring knowledge and acting. Of course, nature as a harmonious whole whose parts meshed perfectly also represented a model or blueprint for man as well as offering the raw material for its fulfilment. But the rift was still there

---

[1] *Vom Erkennen und Empfinden der Menschlichen Seele*, Suphan, VIII, 199–200.
[2] In *Ideen*, XV. 3 (Suphan, XIV, 230).

between nature, whether as plan or instrument, and the will which acted on this plan.

It was this rift which the originators of the expressivist theory – Rousseau, Herder, later the Romantics – could not tolerate. They experienced this vision of things as a tearing apart of the unity of life in which nature should be at once the inspiration and motive force of thought and will. It was not enough that nature provide the blueprint for the will, the voice of nature must speak through the will.[1]

Thus what is experienced as affirmation of self for one view of the subject is felt as exile or inner cleavage by the other. The objectified world is the proof for one of the subject's self-possession, for the other it is a denial of the life of the subject, his communion with nature and his self-expression in his own natural being.

This experience of an objectified world as exile explains why the expressivist reaction was partly seen, and partly saw itself, as a nostalgia for an earlier time when the world was seen as a text, when nature was the locus of meaning. But as should be clear from the above discussion, the aspiration was not really for a return. Because the expressivist view held on to, even accentuated the idea of subjectivity, communion with the surrounding world was desired not in the form of the contemplation of a cosmic order of ideas, but rather as a communion appropriate to subjectivities, as we shall see below.

Let us look at the aspiration which sprang from this view. First, there was a passionate demand for unity and wholeness. The expressivist view bitterly reproached the Enlightenment thinkers for having dissected man and hence distorted the true image of human life in objectifying human nature; they divided soul from body, reason from feeling, reason from imagination, thought from senses, desire from calculation, and so on. All these dichotomies distorted the true nature of man which had rather to be seen as a single stream of life, or on the model of a work of art, in which no part could be defined in abstraction from the others. These distinctions thus were seen as abstractions from reality. But they were more than that, they were mutilations of man. These false views were more than just intellectual errors. Because man is a self-expressive being, and he realizes himself in part through the definitive shape he gives to his feelings and aspirations in expressions of art and language, such a false view is an obstacle to human fulfilment. A man who sees his feelings as in another category from thought, as facts about him to be

---

[1] Obviously, the Enlightenment view of nature as the model for human action provides one of the transitions to the expressivist notion of the voice of nature. And some of the passages in praise of nature of such radical thinkers of the Enlightenment as Holbach seem to verge on expressivist sentiments. But the people I have called originators of expressivism – Rousseau, Herder, and those who built on them – were the ones who developed a theory of man consonant with this notion of the voice of nature. Of course, the background had also been partly provided by Shaftesbury and the theorists of moral sentiment.

explained mechanistically, cannot rise higher to a transformed expression of them. Hence this intellectual error is to be fought with moral passion, as we find Herder combatting the various theories of faculty psychology.

Along with the attack on dichotomies within man, we find the mainstream Enlightenment sometimes taxed with another kind of abstraction, introducing a false world of representation which cuts man off from the real living sources. This is one of the dominant themes in Rousseau and usually bespeaks his influence. We can see how it flows from the same order of ideas. Man's self-expression is distorted, his life does not express him, but rather an illusory substitute for his real feelings and aspirations.

At this point we can see one powerful thrust of the expressivist theory which is of prime importance for understanding Hegel's work: it is strongly anti-dualist, it strives to overcome the body–soul dichotomy, or the spirit–nature dichotomy, which is the legacy of Descartes. It turns more towards categories of life which straddle this division, and draws on Aristotle in the way we saw above. The rejection of any disembodied spiritual reality is as we shall see one of the basic principles of Hegel's philosophy.

Secondly, expressivist theory makes freedom a, if not the central, value of human life. Freedom becomes an important value with the modern notion of self-defining subjectivity, as we saw. But the expression theory both alters the notion of freedom, and greatly enhances its importance. It alters the notion in that the standard Enlightenment view of freedom was that of independence of the self-defining subject in relation to outside control, principally that of state and religious authority. New freedom is seen as consisting in authentic self-expression. It is threatened not only by external invasion but by all the distortions that expression is menaced by. It can fail through a mis-shaping which is ultimately of external origin, but may become anchored in the self. Rousseau presents us with a theory of this kind.

Freedom takes on central importance because it is synonomous with self-realization which is the basic goal of men. It may be only a, rather than the central value in this sense, that freedom is only one of the ways we can characterize this goal: we can also speak of it as unity, maximum fulfilment, harmony, and so on. Not every author will make freedom his privileged description of the goal, but it always is one available description.

Thirdly, expression theory contained an inspiration towards union with nature which the Enlightenment was held to have jeopardized. We saw above how an objectified nature was experienced as an exile. And indeed the exigencies of life conceived as expression which could not brook the dichotomy between body and soul, between thought and sense, could not stop at the boundaries of the body. If I am not satisfied with an image of myself as a mind confronting internal and external nature, but must think of myself as life in which nature speaks through thought and will, if therefore I as a subject am one with my body, then I have to take account of the fact that my body is in interchange with the greater nature outside. Nature knows no fixed boundary at the limits of the body, and hence I as a subject must be in interchange with this greater nature.

But then, if my life is to be fully reflected in my expressive activity, if the feeling/vision of myself which this expresses is to be adequate to my real existence, then this feeling cannot stop at the boundary of my self; it has to be open to the great current of life that flows across it. It is this greater current, and not just the life of my own body, which has to be united with higher aspiration to freedom and expression, if there is to be unity in the self. Thus our self-feeling must be continuous with our feeling for this larger current of life which flows through us and of which we are a part; this current must nourish us not only physically but spiritually as well. Hence it must be more than a useful interchange of matter. It must be experienced as a communion.

Thus Herder: 'See the whole of nature, behold the great analogy of creation. Everything feels itself and its like, life reverberates to life.'[1] Man, as the image of God, 'an epitome and steward of creation' (ein Auszug und Verwalter der Schöpfung), is called to this, 'That he become the organ of sense of his God in all the living things of creation, according to the measure of their relation to him.'[2]

Thus one of the central aspirations of the expressivist view was that man be united in communion with nature, that his self-feeling (Selbstgefühl) unite with a sympathy (Mitgefühl) for all life, and for nature as living. We can see how the objectified universe, which allowed of only mechanical relations within itself and with the subject, was experienced as dead, as a place of exile, as a denial of that universal sympathy which obtained between creatures.

We can see also how this demand could become confused with that for a return to the pre-modern idea of a world-text, but how this equivalence does not really hold. Both views stand against the modern vision of an objectified universe which is devoid of significance for man. But in one case the world is seen as embodying a set of ideal meanings, our way of contact with it is the contemplation of ideas; in the other case, nature is seen as a great stream of life of which we are part, our way of contact is thus by sympathetic insertion into this stream. What is sought for is interchange with a larger life, not rational vision of order.

We can see this if we look at the most important form of nostalgia for the pre-modern in the period, the admiration, even worship for classical Greece.

---

[1] 'Siehe die ganze Natur, betrachte die große Analogie der Schöpfung. Alles fühlt sich und seines Gleichen, Leben wallet zu Leben.' *Vom Erkennen und Empfinden der Menschlichen Seele*, Suphan, VIII, 200.

[2] 'daß er Sensorium seines Gottes in allem Lebenden der Schöpfung, nach dem Maße es ihm verwandt ist, werde.' loc. cit.

This was one of the most powerful and deeply-felt themes in German letters in the latter third of the eighteenth century. Winckelmann's studies triggered off a deep and lasting response. We can throw some light on this if we see it in the context of the expression theory of man. For the ancient Greeks represented to the men of this age a mode of life in which the highest in man, his aspiration to form and expression and clarity was at one with his nature and with all of nature. It was an era of unity and harmony within man, in which thought and feeling, morality and sensibility were one, in which the form which man stamped on his life whether moral, political or spiritual flowed from his own natural being, and was not imposed on it by the force of raw will. And of course in this age, the great current of life in nature was not alien to the human spirit; on the contrary, it was inhabited by gods of human shape, with whom man sustained communion, and who drew from him his highest feats.

Thus what many *Stürmer und Dränger* saw in the Greeks was less an authentic pre-modern consciousness, man defined in relation to an order that transcended him and was in many ways incommensurable with him, but rather what they themselves yearned for, unity with self and communion with nature. And this communion was one of feeling. In Schiller's *The Gods of Greece*, one of the best known statements of this longing nostalgia, we find:

> Da der Dichtung zauberische Hülle
> Sich noch lieblich um die Wahrheit wand,
> Durch die Schöpfung floß da Lebensfülle,
> Und was nie empfinden wird, empfand,
> An der Liebe Busen sie zu drücken,
> Gab man höhern Adel der Natur,
> Alles wies den eingeweihten Blicken,
> Alles eines Gottes Spur.
> [When poetry's magic cloak
> Still with delight enfolded truth
> Life's fulness flowed through creation
> And there felt what never more will feel.
> Man acknowledged a higher nobility in Nature
> To press her to love's breast;
> Everything to the initiate's eye
> Showed the trace of a God.]

But this communion is now irretrievably destroyed as man stands before a 'Godless nature':

> Unbewußt der Freuden die sie schenket,
> Nie entzückt von ihrer Herrlichkeit,
> Nie gewahr des Geistes, der sie lenket,
> Sel'ger nie durch meine Seligkeit,
> Fühllos selbst für ihres Künstlers Ehre,
> Gleich dem toten Schlag des Pendeluhr,

26

Aims of a New Epoch

Dient sie knechtisch dem Gesetz der Schwere,
Die entgötterte Natur.
[Unconscious of the joys she dispenses
Never enraptured by her own magnificence
Never aware of the spirit which guides her
Never more blessed through my blessedness
Insensible of her maker's glory
Like the dead stroke of the pendulum
She slavishly obeys the law of gravity,
A Nature shorn of the divine.]

What was the ontological foundation for this communion thought to be? Schiller in the above poem seems to imply that there is none, that rather the world of Gods in nature was the creation of poetry (Dichtung). Schiller was in fact very divided in his attitude to the expression theory, as we shall see. But in another famous poem, the *Ode to Joy*, which Beethoven used for the final of his choral symphony, he speaks of Joy as the great unifying course of life flowing through all.

Among those who moved more fully in the orbit of the expression theory, the foundation was variously seen. With Herder, for instance, it does not seem to have gone farther than a notion of universal sympathy, an idea which was already in currency before the *Sturm und Drang*, in, e.g., Shaftesbury. But others went farther towards the notion of a universal life flowing through nature, basing themselves on a Spinoza transposed into life-categories. Goethe seems to have had some view of this kind. Later we see a more far-reaching ontological assumption, endowing this universal life with subjectivity; Hegel's solution will be one variant of this.

In this case we find once again a theory which is reminiscent of the pre-modern world-text view, in that different aspects of nature are seen as embodying different ideas. Thus the philosophies of nature of Schelling and Hegel seem to be returns to the past. But the crucial point is that these readings of meaning in nature are supported by the notion of a cosmic subject; and the meanings themselves are derived from the notion of subjectivity as developed by these authors. In this respect they do not depart an inch from the principle of modern subjectivity.[1]

Fourthly, what has been said of communion with nature applies with the same force to communion with other men. Here too, the expressivist view

---

[1] It might be thought that the case of Hamann does not fit this portrait of the age, that in speaking of nature as a language of God, he is harking back to a pre-modern view of the world as embodiment of Ideas. But apart from the fact that Hamann is far from typical of the movement he helped to inspire in that he remains very much an orthodox Christian, and has no truck with the Spinozistic-pantheist tendencies evident in Herder, and of course still more in avowed non-Christians like Goethe; his language of God in nature is anything but an order of ideas embodied, it is rather the living speech of God to man; it is not *langue* but *parole* de Dieu; in that respect it is put alongside the Bible.

27

responds with dismay and horror to the Enlightenment vision of society made up of atomistic, morally self-sufficient subjects who enter into external relations with each other, seeking either advantage or the defence of individual rights. They seek for a deeper bond of felt unity which will unite sympathy between men with their highest self-feeling, in which men's highest concerns are shared and woven into community life rather than remaining the preserve of individuals.

Here, too, the Greek polis seemed to provide the paradigm which modern man had lost to his sorrow. Many Germans in this period – among them Hegel – saw in the ancient polis a summit of human achievement yet unequalled. They saw in it a society whose public life was the locus of all that was of greatest importance to its citizens. So that not only did these have Montesquieu's *vertu* to the highest degree in that they were ready to give their all for their city; but they also had a hand in shaping its life and found themselves expressed in it. The identification with, and expression in the city were two sides of the same coin. So that the ancient polis united the fullest freedom with the deepest community life, and was thus an expressivist ideal.

These four demands, for unity, freedom, and communion with man and nature, reflect the aspirations of expressivist consciousness. These demands, and the complaints against modern society that go with them, were seen as inextricably connected, and this not just in the ways that have been traced here, but in a number of others.

Thus Schiller in his 6th Letter on the *Aesthetic Education of Man* traces the cleavages which man has suffered in the evolution from ancient Greek to modern society. Modern man has divided up the faculties which were united in the men of classical times; and in doing so, men have become specialized, so that instead of expressing the whole, each is only a fragment (Bruchstück) of humanity. This specialization, fruit of the dichotomies of the understanding, is in turn linked to the division in society between classes, which are each confined to a function. This division into classes transforms the living unity of society into a mechanical interdependence. Running the complex machine of modern society cannot be left to spontaneous initiative of the members, but must follow bureaucratic formulae. Men are treated no longer as concrete beings but as mere intellectual constructs, and in return they can feel no identification with the state, which finally loses all authority and sinks to mere ruling power.

This passage of Schiller makes us aware of how the basic ideas of the theory of expression have continued to recur in different formulations up to the present day. The complaint against the Enlightenment, and the society which had developed in modern times, is now directed against technological society which is in so many ways the heir of the Enlightenment. In our day, too, it is reproached for dividing reason from emotion, thought from feeling, for

28

narrowing men and blunting their creativity, and in the process deforming them and thus dividing them from each other in a class society, and hence negating the community with which men can identify and confronting them instead with naked power which denies them freedom.

Hence in May 1968 in Paris, the aspiration which caught fire was that of a society '*décloisonnée*', one in which the barriers between different aspects of life, work and play, love and politics, are broken down, and by the same act the barriers between classes; while this *décloisonnement* is both carried by and releases a flood of creative energy; so that the ultimate barrier which is overcome is that between art and life. It is evident that the expressivist conception of man is of more than merely historical interest.

We have drawn a portrait of expressivist consciousness as an aspiration to escape from a predicament in which the subject is over against an objectified world, to overcome the gap between subject and object, to see objectivity as an expression of subjectivity or in interchange with it. But does not this imperious desire to unite with the world threaten the existence of the subject? This is the question or dilemma that inescapably arises. Before we try to face it we should see how the notion of subjectivity was also developed in opposition to nature by this age.

3

There was another powerful reaction against the radical objectification of the Enlightenment, this time against the objectifying of human nature and in the name of moral freedom. If man was to be treated as another piece of objectified nature, whether in introspection or external observation, then his motivation would have to be explained causally like all other events. Those who accepted this view argued that this was not incompatible with freedom, for was one not free in being motivated by one's own desire, however caused?

But from the standpoint of a more radical view of freedom, this was unacceptable. Moral freedom must mean being able to decide against all inclination for the sake of the morally right. This more radical view of course rejected at the same time a utilitarian definition of morality, the morally right could not be determined by happiness and therefore by desire. Instead of being dispersed throughout his diverse desires and inclinations the morally free subject must be able to gather himself together as it were and make a decision about his total commitment.

Now the main figure in this revolution of radical freedom is without question Immanuel Kant. Rousseau in some ways foreshadowed the idea, but Kant's was the formulation, that of a giant among philosophers, which imposed itself, then and still today. In a philosophical work as powerful and as rich in detail as Kant's critical philosophy, the tracing of any single theme must

The Claims of Speculative Reason

involve over-simplification, but it is not too great a distortion to say that the revendication of this radically free moral subjectivity was one of the main motivations of Kant's philosophy.

Kant's critical theory takes a new departure, and one which would be immensely influential: in trying to define the subject by transcendental argument. It was taken for granted by Enlightenment thinkers like Hume that the subject could only be studied as another object. True, it was special in that one gained access to it by 'reflection' rather than the ordinary perception which yielded us knowledge of external things; but in either case one was dealing with the given, a set of phenomena which presented themselves to our gaze. It was because Hume was dealing with the self as a set of phenomena that he could say such an outrageous thing as that the self was a mere 'bundle of perceptions' with no visible principle of unity.

By transcendental argument, on the other hand, Kant's aim was to define the subject not as a given to inner attention, but as we must conclude it to be, granted the type of experience of objects we have. Transcendental argument tries to infer from experience back to the subject of that experience: what must we be like in order to have the kind of experience we do? In this way it can claim to say things about the nature of the subject which could never be founded in the objects of experience. The Kantian answer to Hume's bundle theory of the self is to point out that the subject is not exhausted by the phenomena given in introspection, that underlying the observation of self as much as that of the external world is the subject of this observation, who pro tanto as observer is not the observed. But this dimension of the subject can only be reached by inference, by arguing back from what experience is like to what the structure of the subject must be if this experience is to be possible.

This is transcendental argument, and in introducing this dimension Kant was to open a new and as yet unclosed chapter in the history of philosophy. But Kant did not push his new line of argument as far as his successors would, as Fichte, Schelling and Hegel. By transcendental argument he showed that the subject of experience has to be a unity, that of the 'I think' which must potentially accompany all my representations; and that the necessary connections which Hume wanted to deny the phenomenal world must necessarily inhabit it, for they form its indispensable structure. But for Kant this kind of claim about phenomenal necessity could only be made provided one clearly distinguished phenomena from things in themselves, for a claim to prove from the nature of the subject the shape of necessity in things as they are even independent of the subject would be wild and baseless presumption.

Thus the Kantian world of experience was distinguished from the ultimate reality. It took its shape partly from the subject, from the shape of our minds, and these structures could be explored by transcendental argument; but by the very fact that its shape was partly given by us, it could allow us to conclude

30

nothing about the shape of things as they were in themselves. Such things there must be because we as finite subjects are affected, our intuition receives its content from outside of us; but the nature of this ultimate reality is a closed book to us, and that insurmountably.

We shall see directly how this separation from ultimate reality was felt as intolerable by Kant's immediate successors. For them Kant stopped half-way. But for Kant, this position was not just a compromise which enabled him to hunt with the hounds of the Enlightenment in running to ground all the baroque structures of Leibnizian metaphysics, while saving the central unity and freedom of the moral subject. When Kant said that he wanted to demolish claims to speculative knowledge about God to make room for faith, he was not just offering a consolation prize. His principal interest here was in the moral freedom of the subject, and this in a radical sense, that man should draw his moral precepts out of his own will and not from any external source, be this God himself. Thus in the *Critique of Practical Reason*[1] Kant makes the point that it is fortunate for us that our speculative reason cannot take us farther. If we could convincingly see God and the prospect of immortality, we would have always acted out of fear and hope, and would never have developed the inner motivation of duty, which is the crown of moral life.

It is in this second critique that Kant sets out his notion of moral freedom. Morality is to be entirely separated from the motivation of happiness or pleasure. A moral imperative is categorical, it binds us unconditionally. But the objects of our happiness are all contingent, none of them can be the ground of such an unconditional obligation. This can only be found in the will itself, in something that binds us because of what we are, i.e., rational wills, and for no other reason.

Hence Kant argues that the moral law must be binding a priori; and this means that it cannot depend on the particular nature of the objects we desire or the actions we project, but must be purely formal. A formally necessary law, that is, one whose contradictory is self-contradictory, is binding on a rational will. The argument that Kant uses here has been much disputed, and it appears rightly: the Kantian appeal to formal laws which would nevertheless give a determinate answer to the question of what we ought to do has always seemed a little like squaring the circle. But the exciting kernel of this moral philosophy, which has been immensely influential, is the radical notion of freedom. In being determined by a purely formal law, binding on me simply qua rational will, I declare my independence, as it were, from all natural considerations and motives and from the natural causality which rules them. 'Such independence, however, is called *freedom* in a strict, i.e. transcendental sense.'[2] I am free in a radical sense, self-determining not as a natural being, but as a pure, moral will.

---

[1] Book II, sect. IX.   [2] *Critique of Practical Reason* Book I, Part I, sect. 5.

The Claims of Speculative Reason

This is the central, exhilarating notion of Kant's ethics. Moral life is equivalent to freedom, in this radical sense of self-determination by the moral will. This is called 'autonomy'. Any deviation from it, any determination of the will by some external consideration, some inclination, even of the most joyful benevolence, some authority, even as high as God himself, is condemned as heteronomy. The moral subject must act not only rightly, but from the right motive, and the right motive can only be respect for the moral law itself, that moral law which he gives to himself as rational will.

This vision of moral life induced not only the exhilaration of freedom, but also a changed sentiment of piety or religious awe. In fact, the object of this sentiment shifted. The numinous which inspired awe was not God as much as the moral law itself, the self-given command of Reason. So that men were thought to come closest to the divine, to what commands unconditional respect, not when they worship but when they act in moral freedom.

But this austere and exciting doctrine exacts a price. Freedom is defined in contrast to inclination, and it is plain that Kant sees the moral life as a perpetual struggle. For man as a natural being must be dependent on nature, and hence have desires and inclination which just because they depend on nature cannot be expected to dovetail with the demands of morality which have their utterly different source in pure reason.[1] But what is more, one has the uneasy sense that an ultimate peace between reason and inclination would be more of a loss than a gain; for what would become of freedom, if there were no more contrast? Kant never really solved this problem, and he was raked over the coals more than once by Hegel for it. And it is an embarassing problem, since it is part of the duty of a moral man to strive for perfection, that is, to strive to overcome the contrary drive of inclination, hence to aim at a state of holiness, as Kant calls it, where the very possibility of a desire which would spur us to deviate from the moral law would no longer arise, where we would always do the moral law gladly (gerne).[2]

Kant can avoid facing this problem the more easily in that he plainly believed that such holiness was impossible in this vale of tears; that we are faced rather with the endless task of struggling to approach perfection. But for his successors this became a point of acute tension. For they were strongly drawn both by Kant's radical freedom and by the expression theory of man.

On reflection, this is not at all surprising; there were profound affinities between the two views. The expression theory points us towards a fulfilment of man in freedom, which is precisely a freedom of self-determination, and not simply independence from external impingement. But the highest, purest, most uncompromising vision of self-determining freedom was Kant's. No wonder it turned the head of a whole generation. Fichte clearly poses the

[1] op. cit. Book I, Part III, 149.   [2] Loc. cit.

choice between two foundations for philosophy, one based on subjectivity and freedom, the other on objectivity and substance, and opts emphatically for the first. If man's fulfilment was to be that of a self-determining subject, and if subjectivity meant self-clarity, self-possession in reason, then the moral freedom to which Kant called had to be seen as a summit.

But the lines of affinity run the other way too. Kantian freedom of self-determination called for completion, it must strive to overcome the boundaries in which it was set and become all-determining. It cannot be satisfied with the limitations of an inner, spiritual freedom, but must try to impress its purpose on nature as well. It must become total. This is in any case how this seminal idea was experienced by the young generation which received Kant's critical writings in its formative youth, and which was seized with enthusiasm for the idea, however older and wiser heads may have felt.

But along with this deep affinity between the two views which tended to draw the same people into their orbits, there was an obvious clash. Radical freedom seemed only possible at the cost of a diremption with nature, a division within myself between reason and sensibility more radical than anything the materialist, utilitarian Enlightenment had dreamed, and hence a division with external nature, from whose causal laws the free self must be radically independent, even while phenomenally his behaviour appeared to conform. The radically free subject was thrown back on himself, and it seemed on his individual self, in opposition to nature and external authority, and on to a decision in which others could have no share.

For young, and some not so young intellectual Germans of the 1790s these two ideas, expression and radical freedom, took on a tremendous force. It was born partly no doubt of the changes in German society which made the need for a new identity to be felt all the more pressingly. But the force was multiplied many times by the sense that the older order was breaking and a new one was being born which arose from the impact of the French Revolution. The fact that this Revolution began after the Terror to arouse ambivalent feelings or even hostility among its erstwhile admirers did nothing to still the sense of urgency; on the contrary. There was a sense that a great transformation was both necessary and possible and this aroused hopes which at other times would have seemed extravagant. It was felt that a great break-through was imminent, and if because of the situation in Germany and the turn taken by the French Revolution, this hope soon deserted the political sphere, it was all the more intense in the sphere of culture and human consciousness. And if France was the homeland of political revolution, where else but Germany could the great spiritual revolution be accomplished?

The hope was that men would come to unite the two ideals, radical freedom and integral expression. Because of the affinities between them mentioned above, it was almost inevitable that if either were deeply and powerfully felt, the

33

The Claims of Speculative Reason

other would be as well. Members of the older generation could remain aloof from one or the other; thus Herder never warmed to the critical turn of Kant's thought, and the two from having been close during Herder's time of study at Königsberg became somewhat estranged in the 1780s. Herder saw in the transcendental exploration of Kant only another theory which divided the subject. Kant for his part was snooty about Herder's philosophy of history, and seems to have felt little attraction to this powerful statement of the expression theory.

It is true that Kant's third critique shows signs of being moved by the *Zeitgeist*. Part of it is devoted to an examination of aesthetic judgement and this is seen by Kant as mediating between the purely factual and the purely moral judgements, and another part is devoted to the study of teleological concepts which in some way unite matter and form more closely. In his discussion of the beautiful, Kant seems to shift from a view of beauty as founded on the sheer play of our faculties of intuition and understanding, to a view which sees the beautiful object as a shadowy and necessarily fragmentary representation of a higher reality which cannot be fully presented in experience. He even speaks in a passage reminiscent of Hamann of 'the text in cypher [...] by which Nature through its beautiful forms speaks to us in figures'.[1]

But although for this very reason the third critique was immensely important for all those who tried to unite the two ideals, it was the generation of the 1790s which really threw itself into this task. The poles were variously identified. For the young Friedrich Schlegel the task was to unite Goethe and Fichte, the former's poetry representing the highest in beauty and harmony, the latter's philosophy being the fullest statement of the freedom and sublimity of the self. To unite the two, as Schlegel for a time thought he saw them united in *Wilhelm Meister*, would bring men to a new height of consciousness and art. Where the French had revolutionized the political world, the Germans inaugurate a new, higher cultural era.

Others, such as Schleiermacher and Schelling, talked of uniting Kant and Spinoza, the latter being transposed as mentioned above into life-categories and as such a paradigm of that unity of the subject with the All demanded by expression theory.

But one of the most basic ways of stating the problem was in terms of history, as a problem of uniting the greatest in ancient and modern life. We find this in Schiller, Friedrich Schlegel, the young Hegel, Hölderlin and many others. The Greeks as we saw above represented a paradigm of the expressivist perfection. This is what helps to explain the immense enthusiasm for ancient Greece which reigned in Germany in the generation which followed Winckelmann. Ancient Greece had supposedly achieved the most perfect unity

[1] 'Chiffreschrift...wodurch die Natur in ihren schönen Formen figürlich zu uns spricht', *Critique of Judgement*, sect. 42, p. 170.

34

between nature and the highest human expressive form. To be human came naturally, as it were. But this beautiful unity died. And moreover, it had to, for this was the price of the development of reason to that higher stage of self-clarity which is essential to our realization as radically free beings. As Schiller put it,[1] the 'intellect was unavoidably compelled [...] to dissociate itself from feeling and intuition in an attempt to arrive at exact discursive understanding'...and below[2] 'If the manifold potentialities in man were ever to be developed, there was no other way but to pit them against each other.'

In other words the beautiful Greek synthesis had to die because man had to be inwardly divided in order to grow. In particular the growth of reason and hence radical freedom required a diremption from the natural and sensible. Modern man had to be at war with himself. The sense that the perfection of the expression model was not enough, that it would have to be united with radical freedom, was clearly marked in this picture of history by the realization that the loss of primal unity was inevitable and that return was impossible. The overpowering nostalgia for the lost beauty of Greece was kept from ever overflowing its bounds into a project to return.

The sacrifice had been necessary to develop man to his fullest self-consciousness and free self-determination. But although there was no hope of return, there was hope once man had fully developed his reason and his faculties of a higher synthesis, in which both harmonious unity and full self-consciousness would be united. If the early Greek synthesis had been unreflective, and had to be, for reflection starts by dividing man within himself, then the new unity would fully incorporate the reflective consciousness gained, would indeed be brought about by this reflective consciousness. In the *Hyperion Fragment*, Hölderlin put it thus:

There are two ideals of our existence: one is a condition of the greatest simplicity, where our needs accord with each other, with our powers and with everything we are related to, *just through the organization of nature*, without any action on our part. The other is a condition of the highest cultivation, where this accord would come about between infinitely diversified and strengthened needs and powers, *through the organization which we are able to give to ourselves.*[3]

Man is called on to tread a path from the first of these conditions to the second. This spiral vision of history, where we return not to our starting point but to a higher variant of unity, expressed at once the sense of opposition between the two ideals and the demand, flaming up to a hope, that the two be united. The

---

[1] *Aesthetic Education of Man*, 6th letter, para 11.   [2] Para 12.

[3] 'Es gibt zwei Ideale unseres Daseins; einen Zustand der höchsten Einfalt, wo unsre Bedürfnisse mit sich selbst, und mit unsern Kräften, und mit allem, womit wir in Verbindung stehen, *durch die bloße Organisation der Natur*, ohne unser Zutun, gegenzeitig zusammenstimmen, und einen Zustand der höchsten Bildung, wo dasselbe stattfinden würde bei unendlich vervielfältigten und verstärkten Bedürfnissen und Kräften, *durch die Organisation, die wir uns selbst zu geben im Stande sind.*'

prime tasks of thought and sensibility were seen as the overcoming of profound oppositions which had been necessary, but which now had to be surmounted. These were the oppositions which expressed most acutely the division between the two ideals of radical freedom and integral expression.

These were: the opposition between thought, reason, morality, on one side, and desire and sensibility on the other; the opposition between the fullest self-conscious freedom, on one side, and life in the community, on the other; the opposition between self-consciousness and communion with nature; and beyond this the separation of finite subjectivity from the infinite life that flowed through nature, the barrier between the Kantian subject and the Spinozist substance, Deus sive natura, or in Lessing's phrase, the '*Hen kai pan*'.

4

How was this great re-unification to be accomplished? On what could one's hopes be founded? One foundation for the hope was a more and more far-reaching idealism, a total idealism. Fichte inaugurated this. Recognized at first as the most brilliant young disciple of Kant, by the master as well, he moved under the profound pull of the age to transform the whole system. The intolerable thing about kantianism was the division from the thing-in-itself. Fichte rejected the thing-in-itself. Ultimately, there was not a subjectivity meeting a foreign world of reality never to be fully known: rather subjectivity was at the basis of everything; the world of objects was posited by the 'I think' and was thus not ultimately independent of it.

Of course, this is not something the ordinary finite subject is aware of: it has to be won through to by an 'intellectual intuition'. Nor can the subjectivity that posits the world be thought of as identical to finite subjectivity; it is more like the all-encompassing subject of which the finite ones are emanations. Fichte developed this aspect of his thought through the 1800's and up to his premature death in 1814, and God as the ultimate subject took on a greater role. But the crucial point of Fichte's system, what gave tremendous impact to his *Wissenschaftslehre* when this was published in 1794, was the declaration of omnicompetence on behalf of the Kantian moral subject. Not only was dualism overcome, but this was accomplished by throwing down all barriers limiting the subject of knowledge and will.

Fichte's theory was immensely exhilarating. Perhaps the pain of division could be overcome by pushing the initially divisive self-consciousness to its fullest development where it would be seen to englobe its opposition. But in the end it could not fill the bill. Fichte was really too onesidedly Kantian, in spite of spectacular departures from Kant, to unite the two ideals. That is, his interest was still exclusively for moral freedom. Fichte understands the positing of a world by the subject as taking place in order that there may be a subject of knowledge and above all will. The subject of knowledge requires an object known, the will requires an obstacle to work on. The highest activity of the subject is the free will, and this is the ultimate goal of the positing activity of the 'I think'. But then Fichte runs into the same problem as Kant: if we are free only in struggling against the obstacles of nature, then our struggle is an endless one; we never can reach unity of nature and free will, on pain of the disappearance of the latter. Thus although Fichte returns us to monism ontologically, he holds out no prospect of a return to harmony. The perfection in which nature and morality come together is something we always strive after but which never can come to be; we approach it, but can never reach it. It is always in the domain of what ought to be (*Sollen*) never what is. Fichte has not united the two ideals; he cannot satisfy the demand for integral expression.

Another, and equally seminal approach was taken by Schiller in his famous Letters on the *Aesthetic Education of Man*. Schiller was older than the generation to which Hegel, and Hölderlin, the Schlegels, etc. belonged. Perhaps this has something to do with the fact that he did not rush into a monist ontology, and seek a unified foundation in being. Schiller remains with a rough approximation to the Kantian account of subjectivity: we form as subjects the stuff which we receive through the senses. As men we have a 'sense drive' (sinnlicher Trieb) which spurs us to experience the sensible, and a 'drive to form' (Formtrieb) tries to bring order and form to experience. Both these are essential to knowledge, but limit each other; in the practical sphere they oppose each other as desire and freedom.

But Schiller sees the possibility of a third drive which unites these two functions inseparably, where the sensible matter before us itself effortlessly takes on form, and form finds expression in matter, where desire spontaneously meets the exigencies of freedom. The object of this third drive unites life and form, it is living form (*lebende Gestalt*), and this says Schiller is the same as beauty. It is in beauty that the two sides of our nature meet in harmony. The beautiful object is a sensible form, that is, one in which every bit of the sensible content is relevant to the form, the form can only take this content and the content can only have this form; in contrast to the subsumption of some observed reality under a concept, where only some of its properties justify the subsumption, and the rest are only contingently related. This latter subsumption is always arbitrary, as it were, but in the beautiful object, the form demands just this content, the content takes on spontaneously and irresistibly this form in our perception of it.

This third drive takes us beyond the strain of opposition, where form and sensible drives limit each other and reciprocally impose necessity on each other (*nötigen*). This third drive is beyond the seriousness of effort, it is play; and Schiller accordingly calls it the 'play drive' (*Spieltrieb*), pointing out that this far from diminishing its importance shows it to be the perfect realization of man and his freedom. We can recognize here the ideal of the expression theory, an expressive harmony in which natural desires and the highest human forms are effortlessly united in a single élan. This is freedom, in the sense of integral, undivided, unconflicted self-expression. It is all this, the effortlessness, harmony, free creativity, which Schiller wants to convey in the word 'play'.

Hence it is that 'Man only plays when he is human in the fullest sense of the word, and he is only fully human when he plays.'[1]

It will come as no surprise after the above discussion of the expression model, that man recovers his unity in the aesthetic dimension. Schiller obviously here has built on Kant's third critique. But he has obviously gone much farther. The experience of beauty is not just that of the effortless agreement of our faculties, nor just a shadowy vision of the realization of the Ideas of reason in the world, but it represents a recovered unity of the receptive and the spontaneous in us, where they are not just in agreement, but fused. In the play drive, nature and spirit speak with one voice.

Of course the ultimate doctrine of the work on *Aesthetic Education* is not unambiguously clear; Schiller speaks in some passages as though the aesthetic were a stage on the road to moral freedom, a help in getting there, in other passages as though it were an embellishment on moral freedom. But in passages like the one quoted above, it would seem that the unity achieved in the play drive is the perfection and realization of man itself. This is not to say that it replaces moral freedom, rather that moral freedom comes to its fullest when it no longer is in conflict with nature, and it is this overcoming of conflict which the play drive can provide. Realized humanity would live entirely in the creation and love of beauty.

In any case, this is the vision that emerges from the *Letters* for those who hunger to unite freedom and integral expression. But Schiller himself does not give way to extravagant hope. Rather he ends up presenting a rather Kantian perspective, not of a realized humanity, but of a gradual progression towards it.

What Schiller lacks in order to answer the demand for integral unity of the two ideals is what Fichte was beginning to provide, an ontological foundation for this unity.

If the highest spiritual side of man, his moral freedom, is to come to more than passing and accidental harmony with his natural being, then nature itself has to tend to the spiritual. In order even to formulate this demand we have to go beyond Kant's terms. We have to think of nature not as Kant did most of the time, as the object of phenomenal awareness, whose ultimate ontological foundation, the thing in itself, is shrouded in impenetrable mystery; but rather

---

[1] 'der Mensch spielt nur, wo er in voller Bedeutung des Wortes Mensch ist, und *er ist nur da ganz Mensch, wo er spielt*' (15th letter, para 9).

38

following the expression theory, as a set of underlying forces which manifest themselves in phenomena.[1]

Then the requirement of unity is that nature in this sense come to have or come to be seen as having a bent to realize spiritual goals. Of course, the mere aspiration to be at one with the great current of life in nature can be met by a naturalist vision: natural, unregenerate man is such that his spontaneous desires and feelings are in accord with nature. Nature is at one with him and always answers his call. Other living things are bound with him in the same chain of sympathy which runs through the whole.

This kind of vision was not without its protagonists in the late eighteenth century as it is not without its defenders today. But it could not satisfy the Romantic generation whose aim was to bring man back to unity with nature within and without, while maintaining his highest spiritual achievements, consciousness and moral freedom, intact. But it is these which must go in the union envisaged by naturalism. For man depends so much on the great course of nature outside him, that it is he who must adapt to nature in order to achieve harmony. In this unequal union the 'spiritual' being is the lesser partner. He must adapt to unconscious, unreflective forces which are beyond the call of reason; and he can only reach harmony with them by listening to what is most unconscious, unreflective in him, the voice of instinct.

As long as we think of nature in terms of blind forces or brute facts then it can never fuse with the rational, the autonomous in man. We must either choose capitulation, with naturalism; or content ourselves with an occasional partial accord within ourselves, won by unremitting effort and constantly threatened by the massive presence of untransformed nature around us with which we are in constant, unavoidable interchange. If the aspirations to radical freedom and to integral expressive unity with nature are to be totally fulfilled together, if man is to be at one with nature in himself and in the cosmos while being most fully a self-determining subject, then it is necessary first, that my basic natural inclination spontaneously be to morality and freedom; and more than this, since I am a dependent part of a larger order of nature, it is necessary that this whole order within me and without tend of itself towards spiritual goals, tend to realize a form in which it can unite with subjective freedom. If I am to remain a spiritual being and yet not be opposed to nature in my interchange with it, then this interchange must be a communion in which I enter into relation with some spiritual being or force.

But this is to say that spirituality, tending to realize spiritual goals, is of the essence of nature. Underlying natural reality is a spiritual principle striving to realize itself.

Now to posit a spiritual principle underlying nature comes close to positing

---

[1] Kant himself slips into this way of speaking at certain moments of the third critique, e.g., where he speaks of 'nature in the subject' giving 'the rule to art'. *Critique of Judgement*, sect. 46, 182.

39

a cosmic subject. This is where Fichte was going, but he stopped crucially short of there. Like Kant, Fichte's main focus was on man's moral vocation and his freedom. Hence, though the world of nature is posited by the 'I think' in Fichte's radical idealism, this nature is still the object of perception or the raw material of the will. It is not yet an independent reality, the articulation of its own underlying forces. Nature is essentially related to subjectivity. But its relation is to be vis-à-vis, the essential other which a subject needs to realize himself through striving; it is not the bodily expression of a subject. True, Fichte's absolute subject is not identical with the individual; it is rather the universal with which the individual strives to unite. But just for this reason it must be identified with the universal moral subject rather than with a cosmic subject whose life would be visible in the great current of nature. Fichte's theory is still in this respect the transcendental idealism of Kant, but with the *Ding-an-sich* left out, i.e., where the phenomena shaped by the 'I think' constitute the only objective reality. The objective world has, as it were, no depth. It merely provides props for the moral drama.

This conception of freedom and nature can never allow a fully realized unity of the two, as Hegel clearly expounds in his first published philosophical work.[1] For the self posits a not-self which it struggles to overcome. But subjectivity needs to be related to something else in order to be. Consequently, the overcoming of the not-self can never be completed, if the subject himself is not to disappear. It must therefore be seen as an infinite progress of self-realization towards a goal which ought to be realized but never fully is.

This must be the case, Hegel argues, as long as we see Nature, the vis-à-vis of subject, as simply posited as the foil for the subject in his self-realization. A real unity of subject and object can only come about if nature is an expression of subjectivity in its own right, as it were, an independent spiritual reality which can come of its own to realise its unity with freedom.

What is missing in Fichte, the grounding of nature in some cosmic spiritual principle, can be found in Spinoza, who offers union with a cosmic substance. But this system suffered from the opposite fault, that in it finite subjectivity seemed to sink without trace.

If the task was to find an ontological foundation for the unity of freedom and nature in a union of finite subjectivity and a cosmic spiritual principle or subject, then what was needed was a kind of synthesis of Fichte and Spinoza. And this in some form or another (a synthesis of Fichte and Goethe for Friedrich Schlegel, of Kant and Spinoza for Schleiermacher) was the recurrent theme of this generation of the 1790s, the generation of Romanticism.

The young Romantics, the Schlegels and Novalis, for instance, were im-

---

[1] The *Differenz* of 1801, when he was still under Schelling's influence.

mensely excited by Fichte. They draw from him the idea of a free, creative subjectivity, sublimely disengaged even from its own creations (cf. Friedrich Schlegel's doctrine of 'Irony'), which was not entirely consonant with the stern moral purpose of Fichte's philosophy. But they soon came to find this philosophy inadequate. For they were also looking for communion with nature, with the greater life outside man, and following the *Sturm und Drang*, and more recently the leading intuition of Schiller's *Letters*, they saw this communion as something to be realized through art. They draw on Jacob Boehme, Spinoza, and Goethe to develop a vision of Nature as expression, a kind of poetry of cosmic spirit, with which men can unite through their own poetic expression. And this necessarily took them beyond Fichte. They wanted to unite his radical notion of creative subjectivity with their own poetic vision of nature. Schelling was the philosopher who answered this need.

Schelling was a boy wonder. He was five years younger than Hegel (born in 1775), and yet he was the senior partner in their period of collaboration at Jena, where he had Hegel called in 1800. He began publishing in his late teens, and for a decade a spate of books came out.

It is difficult to follow Schelling's evolution in detail, but the general direction is clear. He started off as a Fichtean, but then went on to complement Fichte with Spinoza. He took the Fichtean thesis that subjectivity posits the world and extended it into a view of subjectivity as the underlying principle which expresses itself in nature. In doing this, he gave a shape to the poetic vision of a cosmic spiritual principle and developed it into a philosophy of Nature.

In his *System of Transcendental Idealism* of 1800, Schelling puts forward the view that nature is the unconscious product of subjectivity. But as such it has an inherent bent to realize subjective life. This inner bent explains the articulation of nature into different levels, from the lowest level of inanimate existence in time and space through mechanical laws and chemical bonding to the summit in organic nature. For life manifests subjectivity in the objective world, it shows us nature which is also teleological, directed towards its own goals. It thus realizes at one level the harmony between necessity and freedom.

This is the principle of Schelling's philosophy of nature, that the unconscious subjectivity in nature strives to rejoin full subjectivity. But reciprocally, conscious subjectivity tries to unite itself to its objective counterpart. And this is essential. For the best nature can do on its own is life. But this, although uniting necessity and freedom, does not incorporate consciousness. There must be a higher unity, where conscious subjectivity reaches out to incorporate nature, and this is attained in art.

Schelling has taken up Schiller's vision, and beyond Schiller Kant's third critique, whose two main topics, beauty and teleology, are put at the apex of the system. But Schiller's notion of the aesthetic as the locus of recovered unity between freedom and necessity is now given an ontological foundation. Art is the point where the conscious and the unconscious meet, where conscious activity fuses with inspiration from the depths of unconscious nature in us, and where the two thus reach a harmony beyond opposition. It is therefore the point at which spontaneity and receptivity, freedom and nature are one. And this meeting point is, as it were, foreordained in the ontological fact that nature and consciousness have ultimately the same source, subjectivity.

Subjectivity thus spawns two worlds, as it were, the unconscious world of nature, and the conscious one of moral action and history. Having the same foundation, these two strive to rejoin each other. Nature's hierarchy of being shows the bent of the first towards the second, history the development of the second towards the first. The spiral vision of history mentioned above is given ontological foundation.

Schelling thus gave philosophical expression to the poetic vision of the Romantics, the vision which drew Schlegel and Novalis, of nature as slumbering spirit. He seemed at last to answer the need for the fulfilment together of the two ideals: radical freedom and integral expression; for the self-consciousness of radical freedom could now see itself expressed in the whole of nature, within and without, and could achieve unity with this great current of nature in art.

In this synthesis Schelling, along with the Romantic thinkers, linked up not only with the developing line of post-Kantian thought and the expressivist theory, they also gave a new interpretation to currents of religious thought which had long had popular following without much recognition by the learned. We have already seen that Boehme influenced them. At the same time their spiral vision of history gave a new formulation to the old prophetic scheme of history as divided between the three ages, of the Father, Son and Holy Ghost; and this spiral vision was itself a transposition of the Christian drama of Paradise–Fall–Redemption. These links were not just the fruit of accidental convergence. The Romantics were very conscious of these mystical and eschatological roots, and their use of religious terms both reflected and enhanced their sense that an important transformation was at hand.[1] In this respect, Hegel was at one with the Romantic generation, as we shall see.

But Hegel cannot be called a Romantic. Schiller is not generally classed as a Romantic, although he shared their hunger for unity; and this is partly because he would not take the ontological step, either as philosopher or writer, to a divinized nature, or an absolute subjectivity. But this was not Hegel's disagreement with Romanticism. On the contrary, his system centres on the notion that the Absolute is subject. What sets him apart is a certain rigour and

---

[1] Cf. M. H. Abrams, *Natural Supernaturalism*, N.Y., 1971, Chapters 3 & 4.

consequence in his thought; that he pushed through to the end in a uniquely consistent way the requirements of a unity between radical freedom and integral expression. For in fact the synthesis of Schelling, and even more those of the Romantics, fell far short of fulfilling these requirements.

Hegel's distance from the Romantics, and the great inadequacies of their attempts at solution, can be seen if we examine a little more closely what the desired synthesis of subjectivity and nature entails.

This synthesis requires that we posit a cosmic subjectivity, as we saw. But what is the relation of this cosmic spirit to finite spirits, that is, men? At one end, the cosmic spirit could be thought to be identical with that of man at his highest; so that at its ultimate fulfilment the human ego would be seen to be at the base of all objective reality. This seems to have been Fichte's conception of the absolute ego, with this important reservation, that this ultimate fulfilment never comes, and can never come, but we are always striving towards it.

On the other hand, if nature is to be more than the necessary *point d'appui* of human consciousness and will, and if we think therefore of the cosmic spirit as the inner power which comes to articulated expression in all the varied manifold of nature, including man, then the temptation is strong to adopt some kind of 'pantheistic' view. For if the principle of expressive unity – the unity of body and spirit – is to apply to the cosmic spirit as well, then the whole of nature is his 'body', that is, the expression from which he is inseparable.

But pantheism as this is generally understood will not do. For man is only an infinitesimal part of the divine life which flows through the whole of nature. Communion with the God of nature would only mean yielding to the great current of life and abandoning radical autonomy. Hence the view of this generation, which it drew from Herder and Goethe, was not a simple pantheism but rather a variant of the Renaissance idea of man the microcosm. Man is not merely a part of the universe; in another way he reflects the whole, the spirit which expresses itself in the external reality of nature comes to conscious expression in man. This was the basis of Schelling's early philosophy, whose principle was that the creative life of nature and the creative power of thought were one.[1] Hence as Hoffmeister points out, the two basic ideas which we see recurring in different forms from Goethe to the Romantics to Hegel: that we can really know nature only because we are of the same substance, that indeed we only properly know nature when we try to commune with it, not when we try to dominate or dissect it in order to subject it to the categories of analytic understanding;[2] and secondly, that we know

---

[1] J. Hoffmeister *Goethe und der deutsche Idealismus*, Leipzig, 1932, 10.
[2] So Goethe: Wär nicht das Auge sonnenhaft,
        Die Sonne könnt' es nie erblicken;
        Läg nicht in uns des Gottes eigne Kraft,
        Wie könnt' uns Göttliches entzücken?

nature because we are in a sense in contact with what made it, the spiritual force which expresses itself in nature.

But then what is our relation as finite spirits to this creative force which underlies all nature? What does it mean to say that it is one with the creative power of thought in us? Does it just mean that this is the power to reflect in consciousness the life which is already complete in nature? But then in what sense would this be compatible with radical freedom? Reason would not be an autonomous source of norms for us; rather our highest achievement would be to express faithfully a larger order to which we belong. If the aspiration to radical autonomy is to be saved, the microcosm idea has to be pushed further to the notion that human consciousness does not just reflect the order of nature, it completes or perfects it. On this view, the cosmic spirit which unfolds in nature is striving to complete itself in conscious self-knowledge, and the locus of this self-consciousness is the mind of man.

Thus man does more than reflect a nature complete in itself, rather he is the vehicle whereby the cosmic spirit brings to completion a self-expression the first attempts at which lie before us in nature. Just as on the expressivist view man achieves his fulfilment in a form of life which is also an expression of self-awareness; so here the power underlying nature, as spirit, reaches its fullest expression in self-awareness. But this is not achieved in some transcendent realm beyond man. If it were, then union with the cosmic spirit would require that man subordinate his will to a higher being, that he accept heteronomy. Rather spirit reaches this self-awareness in man.

So that while nature tends to realize spirit, that is, self-consciousness, man as a conscious being tends towards a grasp of nature in which he will see it as spirit and one with his own spirit. In this process men come to a new understanding of self: they see themselves not just as individual fragments of the universe, but rather as vehicles of cosmic spirit. And hence men can achieve at once the greatest unity with nature, i.e., with the spirit which unfolds itself in nature, *and* the fullest autonomous self-expression. The two must come together since man's basic identity is as vehicle of spirit.

A conception of cosmic spirit of this kind, if we can make sense of it, is the only one which can square the circle, as it were, that is, which can provide the basis of a union between finite and cosmic spirit which meets the requirement that man be united to the whole and yet not sacrifice his own self-consciousness and autonomous will. And it was something of this kind which the generation of the Romantics was struggling towards, and which Schelling wanted to define in his notion of the identity between the creative life in nature and the creative force of thought; and in formulae like: 'die Natur ist der sichtbare Geist, der Geist die unsichtbare Natur'.

And it was a notion of this kind which Hegel in the end hammered out. Hegel's spirit, or *Geist*, although he is often called 'God', and although Hegel claimed to be clarifying Christian theology, is not the God of traditional theism; he is not a God who could exist quite independently of men, even if men did not exist, as the God of Abraham, Isaac and Jacob before the creation. On the contrary, he is a spirit who lives as spirit only through men. They are the vehicles, and the indispensable vehicles, of his spiritual existence, as consciousness, rationality, will. But at the same time *Geist* is not reducible to man, he is not identical with the human spirit, since he is also the spiritual reality underlying the universe as a whole, and as a spiritual being he has purposes and he realizes ends which cannot be attributed to finite spirits qua finite, but on the contrary which finite spirits serve. For the mature Hegel, man comes to himself in the end when he sees himself as the vehicle of a larger spirit.

We shall examine Hegel's notion in Chapter III. But it must already be clear that it is not easy (if indeed it is possible at all) to win through to a coherent view of a cosmic spirit on this model, or to maintain clearly in view what it requires. And in fact the Romantics never succeeded in doing so. It requires at least two things: (1) that we be able to give a plausible interpretation of nature as 'petrified spirit', as the precipitate of a cosmic spirit on the way to a fuller realization in self-consciousness. We must find in nature 'the history of *Geist*'.[1] And this means not just that we find in Nature a set of images which allow us to portray it in this light. Rather it must be that this vision of nature as the first incomplete attempts at the self-realization of spirit provide the ultimately true and basic account of nature and why it is as it is. (2) Reciprocally, we must develop a notion of what it is for man to be the vehicle of *Geist* which is not incompatible with his vocation to rational autonomy.

It is the first task into which the Romantics threw themselves with their poetry of nature, the mystical 'physics' of a Ritter, and ultimately with the philosophy of Nature of Schelling. But it is in the second where they went most grievously astray.[2] For what if our conception of the self-awareness of spirit, of

---

[1] Hoffmeister *op. cit.* 18.

[2] A word here would perhaps be in order about Goethe and his relation to the Romantics. In fact he was one of the inspirers, almost the paragon, of the Romantic generation. And there is no doubt that they drew from him the idea of nature as the emanation of a spiritual life in which man could discover the secrets of his own life. 'Suchet in euch, so werdet ihr alles finden und erfreut euch, wenn da draußen, wie ihr es immer heißen möget, eine Natur liegt, die ja und Amen zu allem sagt, was ihr in euch gefunden habt' (Hoffmeister *op. cit.* 7).

But Goethe's classicism was also far removed from the restless striving, the heady enthusiasms of the Romantics. For although Goethe's work had deep roots in the expressivist conception of man, he remained unmoved by the other pole of this younger generation's aspirations – the ideal of radical moral autonomy of Kant and Fichte. That side of Kant which excited Fichte and through him the generation of the 1790s left Goethe cold. The exhilaration of radical freedom was not for him. Not that the ideals of freedom and reason meant nothing to him. On the contrary; only he was not tempted to interpret them in terms of Kantian autonomy, a self-given law of human reason.

Consequently, he was content with a vision of things in which man was not the centre. He could accept without protest the idea that man was related to a larger life which dwarfed him and which he could never fully understand, even if man was in some sense its highest realization. He could envisage an expressive unity of man with the whole without feeling compelled to find a place in it

The Claims of Speculative Reason

which we are the vehicles, in fact pulls us away from conscious self-possession, sinks us more into a stream of life which we cannot fully grasp by reason? Then once more we fall into heteronomy; the careful synthesis veers again towards a pantheistic view in which man sinks himself in a larger whole. And in the end if we follow this road far enough man finds himself once more in face of a God who is complete without and beyond him, more like the God of traditional faith.

And in fact, after going through a more 'pantheistic' phase, most of the Romantic generation ended up more or less orthodox theists: Schleiermacher and Novalis first; but then Friedrich Schlegel converted to Catholicism; and even Schelling made a later comeback as an orthodox Christian.

Whether this development was inevitable or not, the fact is that the Romantic synthesis was inadequate from the start. First, they were deeply attracted to a view of this synthesis, the meeting point of finite and cosmic spirit, as a process or activity which is endlessly inventive, which constantly creates new forms and never takes on a definitive embodiment; rather than as one which reaches a final shape which can be encompassed in a vision of things, or a work of art, or a way of living (or all of these together). This vision of continuous creation was implicit in Freidrich Schlegel's notion of 'Irony', or in Novalis' 'magical Idealism'. In this way, they saw man's vocation as vehicle of cosmic *Geist* as fully consonant with his free subjectivity, for was not original-ity, boundless creative power, the essence of free subjectivity? This in any case was the idea they drew from Fichte, and what excited them in idealism.

But this notion of an endlessly original creative power contradicts the requirements of a complete union of autonomy and expression, of subjecti-vity and nature. A subjectivity which is inspired tirelessly to create new forms is one which by definition can never achieve integral expression, can never find a form which truly expresses itself. This Romantic ideal of infinite change is ultimately inspired by Fichte's philosophy of endless striving and shares the same inadequacy, which Hegel will castigate with the term 'bad infinity'. This romantic notion of Irony, Hegel will argue in his lectures on aesthetics,[1] denies the ultimate seriousness of any of the external expressions of spirit, all of which are of no significance before the endlessly creative 'I'. But this 'I' is at the same

for radical subjectivity. By an irony which may become more understandable below Goethe's serene 'classicism' ends up finding a securer place for reason and self-clarity than the heady visions of the Romantics who were trying at all costs to secure the unrestricted freedom of the subject, the recognition 'daß die Willkür des Dichters kein Gesetz über sich leide', as Fr. Schlegel put it (Haym *Die Romatische Schule*, 256) in his description of Romantic poetry, which he found above all realized in *Wilhelm Meister*.

Only Hegel won through to a comparable equilibrium between creativity and form, and he was generally well seen by Goethe – who, it must be said, appreciated in general the attempts at a philosophy of Nature of the Romantics and Schelling, even though their brand of idealism was not to his liking.

[1] *Die Idee und das Ideal*, 95–102.

time seeking, indeed craves external expression, and thus the triumphal self-affirmation of Irony gives way to the sense of loss, of longing (Sehnsucht),[1] to the withdrawal from the world as abandoned by spirit, which many Romantics experienced and which Hegel characterizes in the portrait of the 'beautiful soul'. On Hegel's view there is an inner link between the Romantic subject's claims to boundless creativity and his experience of the world as God-forsaken, which Hegel constantly combats in the name of his own vision of the rationality of the real.

And when Fichte is thus transposed into the domain of fantasy, as in the Romantic notion of originality, or in Novalis' 'magical Idealism', the difficulty is compounded. For this activity of the subject, this endless originality of the imagination, which operates in the twilight zone between conscious and unconscious life, is something which is not fully understood by the subject himself. But this contradicts one of the main requirements of autonomy, rational self-consciousness. The inexhaustibly fertile flow of fantasy can never be fully grasped, let alone encompassed in a single vision, by Reason. But if Reason is out of its depths in this realm, where it moves rather with the instinct of the sleepwalker then what becomes of moral autonomy, which requires that Reason provide the rule?

This brings us to a second basic issue which divided Hegel from the Romantics and which concerns precisely the place of reason in the synthesis. For the Romantics the unity between subjectivity and nature was achieved by intuition or imagination. Reason was seen as a divisive, dissecting, analytic faculty, one which could only take us further away from union with nature. This ultimate exclusion of reason was in a sense also implicit in Schelling's solution. As long as the highest synthesis was to be found in art, the unity of the conscious and the unconscious, it must remain something not fully understood, not transparent to reason, the object of an intuition which can never be fully explicited. The point about artistic creation, as Kant pointed out, is that we cannot give the formula.[2]

But if we accept this we are sacrificing something in our synthesis. For the full clarity of rational understanding is of the essence of self-determining freedom, which obtains, after all, where pure reason gives the law. To achieve a unity with nature in pure intuition, one of which we can give no rational account, is to lose oneself in the great current of life, and this is not a synthesis between autonomy and expression, but a capitulation in which we give up

---

[1] Ibid, 99.

[2] And later, when Schelling moved beyond the *System of Transcendental Idealism*, he went further from Fichte towards the Spinozan end of the spectrum. He no longer defined the source of both nature and mind as subjectivity, but rather as an absolute which was beyond subject and object, the 'Indifference'. But of this absolute it was even truer to say that free subjectivity was swallowed up in it without trace. Hegel's objections to this – 'the night in which all cows are black' – were the roots of his break with Schelling in 1807.

autonomy. It is a return to the original unity which was broken by reflection, rather than the higher synthesis to which the spiral ascends.

In other words our conception of spirit and its self-realization must have a place for reason if man is to be the vehicle of cosmic spirit and yet retain his autonomy. This is the central insight which Hegel alone of his generation saw in full clarity and worked out to its full conclusion. Without it, the Romantics either fell into the despair of exile in a God-forsaken world, or recovered unity with nature and God only in the twilight zone of intuition and fantasy.

But this is not to say that the Romantics were just guilty of oversight. In fact, our difficulties just begin when we accept the central role of reason; and it was these difficulties which motivated them in turning away from it to fantasy, invention and art.

For if we abandon the view of spirit as endless creative power and see the synthesis of subject and nature as taking some definitive shape, are we not denying some of the essential properties of free subjectivity? For we seem to be positing a final, static condition, while the life of a subject is continuing activity. And in seeing the solution in one encompassable form, we seem to limit the subject unduly, to make him merely finite where the cosmic subject should be infinite.

The requirements of our synthesis seem to put us in a dilemma. Hegel was not unaware of it. But he claimed to have hammered out a solution which avoided both horns. He was pitiless towards Romantic visions of the power of fantasy and endless creativity. He insisted that the final synthesis be one which reason could encompass. But at the same time he had a conception of the subject as essentially activity, and infinite activity. The solution lay in his conception of infinity, which incorporated the finite, and which returned to itself like a circle. Just what this notion involved we shall examine later, but only a conception of this kind can resolve the dilemma of confining infinite activity to encompassable form.

Then again, Hegel agrees as he must with the main Romantic objection to Reason that it (or rather 'understanding' to use his own terminology) divides, analyses, individuates, kills.[1] In other words, rational understanding is not possible without a clear consciousness of the distinction between subject and object, self and other, the rational and the affective. And just because of this, Hegel will insist that the ultimate synthesis incorporate division as well as unity. Once again, Hegel will claim to combine the seemingly uncombinable. He will claim to arrive at the 'identity of identity and non-identity' (*Differenz*, 77), the

---

[1] In the preface of his PhG, Hegel likens this analytic power of the understanding to the power of death, the power to wrench things from the unity of life. But he insists that the way to reconciliation with spirit is not to flee this death as a certain 'powerless beauty' does, but to 'hold it fast', to 'bear it and maintain oneself in it', to 'sojourn' with it. 'This sojourning is the magic power which returns it to being.' (PhG 29–30).

48

unity of the single current of life and the division between subject and object implicit in rational consciousness. This is perhaps the central and most 'mind-blowing' idea of the Hegelian system, which we shall shortly try to tackle. It is what most clearly singles him out from the whole generation whose aspirations he shared.

The synthesis in art is not rejected – Hegel throws nothing away – but it is subordinated as the first stage of absolute spirit to the higher realizations in religion and, at the summit of clarity, in philosophy. Hence reason as conceptual clarity takes the central role in his synthesis. Nor can this be thought of as a matter only of our mode of *access*, through intuition or reason, to what is substantially the same vision. For in fact substance and mode of expression cannot be separated here, as in all expression theories. It is integral to spirit as reason that it come to a full rational understanding of itself. But our understanding of spirit is not in the end distinct from its self-understanding. So that if we could only come to an unexplicited intuition of the synthesis, and spirit's understanding of itself were thus similarly unexplicited and intuitive, then the nature of cosmic subjectivity would be different; it would not incorporate rationality.

Thus Hegel in his mature system developed an original stand vis-à-vis the generation to which he belonged in time and aspiration. He did not slough off their aspirations – to combine the fullest moral autonomy of the subject with the highest expressive unity within man, between men and with nature. He shared the hope that this unprecedented and epoch-making synthesis could be made only if one could win through to a vision of a spiritual reality underlying nature, a cosmic subject, to whom man could relate himself and in which he could ultimately find himself.

But he stood out in his uncompromising attempt to think through the requirements of this synthesis with surprising rigour and a quite impressive thoroughness. And as a result he produced one of the great monuments to the aspiration of his age – a seminal age for modern civilization. Indeed, if it could ever be claimed that these aspirations were met, this claim could only be made on behalf of the Hegelian system. Hegel's notion of the cosmic subject, or *Geist*, his concept of infinity which incorporates finitude, and his insistence on the unmitigated claims of reason mark him as the ultimately serious contender.

With this in mind we can already begin to see why the Hegelian synthesis is of perennial and recurring interest in our civilization. For the two powerful aspirations – to expressive unity and to radical autonomy – have remained central preoccupations of modern men; and the hope to combine them cannot but recur in one form or another, be it in Marxism or integral anarchism, technological Utopianism or the return to nature. The Romantic rebellion continues undiminished, returning ever in unpredictable new forms –

Dadaism, Surrealism, the yearning of the 'hippy', the contemporary cult of unrepressed consciousness. With all this surrounding us we cannot avoid being referred back to the first great synthesis which was meant to resolve our central dilemma; which failed but which remains somehow unsurpassed.

I have tried in the preceding pages to give an idea of the basic objectives which guided Hegel's philosophical thought. But I have presented these in the general form they took for his generation. Before trying to outline how he tried to meet these objectives, it would be useful to look briefly at his personal itinerary, at how these philosophical goals took shape in his mind. This is what the next chapter will attempt.

CHAPTER II

Hegel's Itinerary

1

Hegel as a young man in the 1780s, first at the Stuttgart Gymnasium then at the *Tübinger Stift*, was deeply moved by the expressivist current of his time. The image of a whole, integrated life in which man was at one with himself, and men were at one with each other in society, also assumed its paradigmatic form for him in the classical past of Greece.

But there were two other important poles of his thought and aspiration which were already evident at that time and remained vital to him through many transformations: the first was the moral aspiration of the Enlightenment, that man should at last come to the freedom of self-direction through reason. Later he will come to think of Kant as the paradigm proponent of this aspiration, but at the beginning Mendelssohn and Lessing were more important for him. The second major reference point was the Christian religion. That theology was one of his preoccupations might be thought to flow normally from the fact that he received his higher education in a theology seminary. But his interest in Christianity was much deeper. Indeed, the theology he was taught at Tübingen aroused his opposition. It is one of the negative poles *against* which he defines his position in the early writings. And the fact that his conception of the Christian religion underwent profound changes and yet remained central to his basic views right through to the mature system shows that this orientation was not the result of a passing influence.

These three reference points were potentially in deep conflict and Hegel's mature thought is a heroic attempt to reconcile them. But in his early, Tübingen days he felt that the three corresponding aspirations thrust in the same direction. The age was seen by Hegel and many of his generation as one of division and repression of spontaneity. They longed to restore it to the wholeness of expressive unity, so that men's moral activity and social life would spring out of a living experience of unity and the good, rather than be ruled by dead formulae.

But this expressive aspiration seemed to them at base no different from the demands of *Aufklärung*, that man live by his own reason instead of external, irrational authority based on the prestige of the past. In both cases, it was a matter of restoring man's autonomy against external authority, something

51

living and felt by the self against something external and an object of mere understanding. And in both cases the revolution affected both the life of the individual (who recovered autonomy and wholeness) and the relations between persons in society (relations of domination give way to spontaneous, equal association).

Thus Hegel and the young radicals at Tübingen did not see their longing to restore the Greek ideal as in any way conflicting with their allegiance to the Enlightenment. Pericles, Socrates, Lessing and Kant were thought to stand at base for the same ideals. But these could not but be seen as in conflict with the established Christian religion of their day, grounding its claims on supernatural authority, supporting hierarchies of command, both spiritual and temporal, and preaching a radical division in man between sinful nature and the spirit.

Because of this some of the young radicals of Hegel's day moved to a position of global opposition to Christian faith. This was the case, for instance, of the young Schelling, although he changed his mind later on. But Hegel, and also Hölderlin, however critical they were of established Christianity and even at times of Christ himself, never broke away.

What seemed to them not only compatible but fundamentally identical with the demands of expressive unity and Reason was (what they saw as) the original teachings of Jesus, the teacher who taught that the letter killeth while the spirit giveth life, who came to fulfil the law through the spontaneity of *agape*.

Hegel's period at Tübingen was from 1788 to 1793 – obviously a pivotal one for young Germans. The growth of Enlightenment, the recent recovery of sympathy with the ideals of Greece, the cultural ferment following the *Sturm und Drang* were now capped by the epoch-making events in Paris. It is not surprising that in young minds the spark of hope be kindled that they might see, even bring about a transformation of Germany, a new edition of the Great Age of Athens. The young radicals at Tübingen with whom Hegel associated reflected in their language about themselves and their ideals all three of these reference points. 'Hen kai pan' ('one and all'), one of Hölderlin's great watchwords, expressed the great current of life flowing through all beings with whom men must be reunited. The vision of hen kai pan – a term given currency by Lessing's use of it – was grounded on the expressivist reading of Spinozism referred to in an earlier section. 'Reason and Freedom' was a slogan which needs no comment in the context of the time. But this same group of hellenophile *Aufklärer* referred to themselves as the 'invisible church' and spoke of their goal as the 'Kingdom of God', not more than half in irony.[1]

Thus in the mind of the young Hegel Germany stood in need of regenera-

---

[1] Cf. H.S. Harris: *Hegel's Development*, Oxford, 1972, II, 4.

52

tion, which would at the same time be a triumph of the Enlightenment's autonomous reason, a recreation of what was best in the Greek spirit, and a recovery of the pure teaching of Jesus. Hegel's earliest unpublished writing can be seen as studies motivated by this triple aspiration. And his development through the 1790s up to the early 1800s when his system assumes something like its final form can be seen in part as the response to two pressures: first the external fact of failure, that the hoped-for regeneration did not come; and second the inner tension between the three poles of reference which force a redefinition of all of them and of their mode of relation.

A very early manuscript from his Tübingen period[1] shows how Hegel's vision of regeneration was not that of the secular revolutionaries who were then transforming French society, but involves at its most fundamental level a renewal of religious life. But Hegel's religion is far from that of traditional piety. At this stage it is largely a religion of *Aufklärer* in terms defined by Kant.

After the Kantian fashion religion is seen in the perspective of morality, rather than vice versa. What I ought to do I determine not by my religious faith or the commands of God but by the commands I give myself as a rational being. Indeed, the rational core of religion, the belief in God and immortality, is founded on the requirements of morality, as necessary postulates if the highest good is to be realized. Hegel's early essays resonate with the sense, which we saw in Kant, that man comes closest to the holy when he acts as the subject of a pure moral will.

But religion in the full sense – and not just the holding of the above 'rational' beliefs – is none the less indispensable to man. Man is not just a rational but also a sensible creature. Although we may put as our highest ideal that of man acting in pure respect for the moral law – Hegel does not yet challenge this anchor point of Kantian ethics – this is very far from where men are. In fact men are effectively moved to good by the heart, by a brace of inclinations, interwoven with sensibility, which constitute the different forms of benevolence: love, friendship, compassion (Nohl, 18). In this Hegel is closer to Rousseau.

Now religion, not as nominal belief in a number of propositions about the supernatural, or in the carrying out of external practices, but as living piety, is the great source of motivation towards good for the whole man. Hence Hegel begins this fragment with a distinction between objective and subjective religion. The former is just the theology and the practices seen externally. The latter is the living experience of man of the good and of God as its author, however this expresses itself in belief and cult.[2]

---

[1] Published by H. Nohl as one of the 'Fragmente über Volksreligion und Christentum', Cf. his *Hegel's Theologische Jugendschriften*, Tübingen, 1907, 1–72.

[2] This notion shows the stamp of that pervasive influence of Pietism on much German thought in this period, and of its partial fusion with some of the aspirations of the Enlightenment. This marriage can be seen, for instance, in Lessing; and it seems that Lessing greatly influenced Hegel's thought

The Claims of Speculative Reason

From the very beginning, therefore, Hegel does not take up the standpoint of the austere Enlightenment about religion, that nothing can be believed but what reason licences. He does indeed condemn superstition, where men act in order to bring about a response from the supernatural, say, sacrifice in order to placate an angry God. But he is far from holding, for example, that sacrifice as such has no place in a purified religion, if it is done in a spirit of pious thankfulness, as an expression of grateful dependence on God, rather than a means of avoiding punishment (as Hegel rather unrealistically saw Greek sacrifice, Nohl, 25–6).

Another important distinction in this MS is that between private religion, which touches the life of the individual in his personal and family relations, and a 'religion of a people' (*Volksreligion*) which is woven into the public life of a society. Obviously the most important model of a *Volksreligion* for Hegel was provided by the public religions of ancient Greece, which were an integral part of social life, inseparable from the other aspects of the city's common existence, and essential to its identity.

The importance of these distinctions for Hegel's purposes can be readily grasped. The regeneration he looks for is one in which men achieve the freedom of moral self-determination, while at the same time recovering a wholeness or integrity where reason is not at odds with the passions, or spirit with sensibility, but where the whole man is moved spontaneously to moral goodness.

And this wholeness would not only heal the divisions within men but between them as well. The regeneration Hegel seeks is thus also and necessarily a political one: the recovery of a society in which men are free and undivided, as the Greeks were, in which the public life is an expression, and a common expression, of the citizens, rather than being imposed by unchallengeable authority on subjects. Hegel was thus profoundly in sympathy with the French Revolution in its early years – and in fact the ideals of 1789 remained an important part of his political thinking throughout his life.

In other words, Hegel holds to the aspiration to expressive unity; it is this, of course, rather than a simple calculation of human fallibility which makes him unable to accept fully Kant's separation of reason and sensibility and cleave rather to Rousseau; it is this which will ultimately turn him against Kant.

Now a regeneration of this kind, which involves the whole man, can only be achieved by religion, within the terms of the problem which Hegel has established. But in order to do this, religion must be fully subjectivized: that is, it must be more than an external allegiance to certain doctrines and practices, and become living piety in order to unite man within himself: and it must be

about religion as a student in Gymnasium and University. Cf. above p. 12, Hegel's subjective religion is also defined in opposition to a religion of 'cold booklearning' condemned by Recha in Lessing's *Nathan*, a play often quoted or referred to in Hegel's early writings.

more than the religion of some individuals, it must be woven into the life of the people, and linked with reformed political institutions, if it is to unite men with each other.[1] What is wanted is a subjectivized, folk religion, which is nevertheless not in contradiction to the Enlightenment, not a religion of superstition. These are the three requirements which Hegel sets out towards the end of this early MS: the regenerate religion must be such that

I. Its doctrine must be grounded on universal reason.
II. Fancy, heart and sensibility must not thereby go empty away.
III. It must be so constituted that all the needs of life and the public affairs of the state are tied in with it.'[2]

These requirements plainly express two of the poles of Hegel's thought. The first reflects the allegiance to the *Aufklärung:* religion must teach nothing contrary to the rational doctrines about the supernatural: the existence of God, immortality, their relation to a good which one should seek for its own sake (not in order to placate God). The other two reflect the aspiration to expressive unity. II insists that the whole man, not just reason, but also 'Phantasie', the power to discern higher realities in sensible images, 'Herz', or moral sentiment, and Sinnlichkeit; the sensible side of human nature, should have their

---

1 We can see from this how much Lukács' attack in *Der Junge Hegel* on the standard interpretation of Hegel's early writings as centring around reflection about religion runs the risk of distorting his thought in this period. Lukács speaks of this 'theological' approach to the young Hegel as 'a reactionary legend'. Hegel's early writings should rather be seen as at grips with the problems of political revolution and change.

Of course, particular interpretations of Hegel's early religious views, like those of Haering, Wahl, Kroner, are open to criticism. But Lukács' global objection involves introducing a false dichotomy into Hegel's thought. We cannot oppose a central concern for religion to one for political reform and freedom, when Hegel's thought in the 1790s was precisely characterized by a view of religion nurtured on expressivist theory and inspired by the Greeks in which religious life and social relations were inseparable. Of course, the young Hegel longed to see the restoration of moral autonomy and political liberty, but this was to him inseparable from, hence unrealizable without a profound religious regeneration.

From a different standpoint, Walter Kaufmann also objects to the designation 'theological' applied to Hegel's early writings, and suggests rather the description anti-theological essays (cf. 'The Young Hegel and Religion', in *Hegel*, ed. A. MacIntyre, Anchor 1972, 61–100). But this too is very misleading. Hegel is strongly against theology in the sense of dead formulae as opposed to subjective religion, that is, living piety. But these writings are best understood as an attempt to find out how to restore a relation to God or Spirit or Life or the Infinite (Hegel's designations and also his conception change through this decade) in which this living piety can come again into its own.

It is also a bit quick to ascribe to the young Hegel affinities with the Enlightenment *as opposed* to the Romantics (Kaufman 72–4). He shared the expressivist mistrust of the 'understanding', the attempt to capture the living in abstract formulae and fragment it. This came to him through thinkers like Herder and Goethe who from one point of view can plausibly be called men of the Enlightenment. But this expressivist theory also becomes an essential element in Romanticism. It is very misleading to claim it for one side *against* the other.

2 From Harris, *Hegel's Development*, p. 499, slightly amended.
  I. 'Ihre Lehren müssen auf der allgemeinen Vernunft gegründet sein.'
  II. 'Phantasie, Herz und Sinnlichkeit müssen dabei nicht leer ausgehen.'
  III. 'Sie muß so beschaffen sein, daß sich allen Bedürfnisse des Lebens, die öffentlichen Staatshandlungen daran anschließen.' (Nohl 20).

part. III requires that this uniting of the whole man with reason be a common, public realization, not confined to the private realm or to one side of life, but woven into the business of meeting 'all the needs of life' and into 'the public actions of the polis'. III, in other words, is the demand for a *Volksreligion*, such as the Greeks enjoyed.

But how does this fit with the third pole of Hegel's thought, the Christian religion? Very uneasily, in fact; and this tension will occupy Hegel throughout the 1790s. A number of other unpublished MSS deal with this and connected questions, among them an essay of the Berne period, written in 1795–6, which has been given the title, 'The Positivity of the Christian Religion', and the great MS from his Frankfurt period which has been called 'The Spirit of Christianity and its Fate', written and re-written between 1798 and 1800.

Of course, the institutional Christian religion as it has become, particularly in its Catholic variant, a religion of authority encouraging superstition, is not even a starter. But the question arises how much even original, pure Christianity can meet the three requirements. Hegel thinks that it meets the first requirement well. The picture of Jesus in the MSS of the early and middle 1790s is of a Kantian *avant la lettre*, but one who embodies and teaches wholeness. Against the Jewish morality of law he set a teaching founded on reason and the heart. The principle of his Gospel was the will of God but this was at the same time (zugleich) 'his own heart's living sense of right and duty' (Knox 75).[1]

This Jesus wonderfully manages to combine the demands of Kantian ethics and the expressivist ideal. In setting the 'living feeling of *his own* heart' against a law supposedly handed down as an external command from God (or rather transposing this law into one of the heart, thus 'fulfilling' it) Hegel's Jesus replaces heteronomy with autonomy. But in finding the will of God in 'the living feeling of his own *heart*', he avoids the opposition between reason and sensibility, he lives the moral life as an integral expression of his humanity. He goes beyond the law both qua command, and qua dry, abstract formula. This combination, which we have suggested the writers and thinkers of this generation were struggling to conceive, is here bought much too cheaply; Hegel will not be able to sustain it much longer, as we shall see.

In a sense, the main purpose of the 'positivity' essay is to explain what happened to the religion of Jesus that it degenerated into present-day Christianity. The key concept in the answer is just this one of positivity. A 'positive' religion is one which is grounded on authority, rather than being postulated by our own reason (and supplemented of course, by our response of feeling to what reason has postulated, e.g., the images and cult of our devotion to God). We have a positive religion when we have 'a system of

---

[1] 'das lebendige Gefühl seines eigenen Herzens von Pflicht und Recht'. Nohl, 158.

religious propositions, that is supposed to have the force of truth for us, because we are commanded to believe by an authority to which we cannot refuse to subject our faith' (Nohl, 233). The origin of this term is plainly in the law, where 'positive law' is what reposes on command of authority, and is opposed to 'natural' law.[1]

Now the pathos of Christianity is just that Jesus' teaching could not penetrate an age and people who were so imbued with legalism and oriented to command. So he was forced to rely on the Messiah myth, in terms of which as a great teacher he could not but be perceived by his followers. His response was to try to give the myth a higher sense. But the result was ultimately that men who were incapable of living the full unity of reason and *Herz* preached a religion of Christ, that is another positive religion in which *belief* in Christ, not a recovery of God's will in one's own heart, is the foundation; in which the good must be done because *revealed* in Christ, not out of respect alone for the moral law (Nohl, 212; Knox, 144).

But this story, while it exonerates the original teaching of Jesus, in fact raises deep problems for anyone who would want to see it the basis of a regenerated *Volksreligion* meeting the three requirements. Hegel is very aware of these. First of all, what is gained by preaching a religion of autonomy and wholeness together, when in fact men cannot attain this unity? What one gains on the swings, one loses on the roundabouts. Indeed, more than loses. For not only does the ideal of autonomous integrity once more slip away from men and become something external: a Christ to which men pray, or an after-life beyond this world. But the sense of separation and inadequacy is all the crueller in that the ideal is higher than its predecessors, not just the compliance with a law of external observances, but a purity of intention, against which men must sense uncleanness of the heart, a vice of the will.

This is the point of origin of Hegel's reflection on the theme of the 'unhappy Consciousness', which reaches one of its most powerful expressions in the section of that title in the *PhG*. Hegel begins to measure the depth of the problem in the Berne period. Christianity is in a sense a *failed* religion, once we grasp what the original teaching of Jesus was. The failure can be most dramatically seen in the fact that Jesus had to die, so little was the world prepared to receive his message. Already this marks the subsequent life of Christianity with a certain melancholy, that at the centre of its worship is the Crucified One, and this starkly contrasts with Greek religion in which the divine is woven into the self-affirmation of the community.

But this melancholy can be further understood as springing from a deep division, one continuous with the division that Christianity was meant to heal, the rift between man's spiritual vocation and his life in nature. This idea grows

---

[1] But the opposition of positive to 'natural' religion comes to pose serious problems in Hegel's mind, as he says in a revised (1800) variant of the beginning of this MS.

in Hegel's thought with his consciousness of the depth and importance of this rift, and this cannot but go along with a re-evaluation of Kant, who in a sense made it absolute.

These themes are developed together in the manuscript written during 1799–1800, which has been called 'The Spirit of Christianity and its Fate.' The MS opens with a study of what has become for Hegel the original paradigm of unhappy consciousness, the religion of the Jews as founded by Abraham. Abraham tore himself loose from the original unity with nature and with his tribe. Nature became for him so much neutral matter, which could not be united with spirit, but rather had to be dominated by it. One key term whereby Hegel designates this fateful turn of the human spirit is 'separation' (*Trennung*):

> The first act which made Abraham the progenitor of a nation is a disseverance [Trennung] which snaps the bonds of communal life and love. The entirety of the relationships in which he had hitherto lived with men and nature, these beautiful relationships of his youth he spurned. (Knox, 185)

The other connected term is 'domination' ('Herrschaft'). The spirit that led Abraham was

> The spirit of self-maintenance in strict opposition to everything – the product of his thought raised to be the unity dominant over the nature which he regarded as infinite and hostile (for the only relationship possible between hostile entities is mastery [Herrschaft] of one by the other). (Knox, 186)

Hegel interprets the spirit of Abraham as that we have called above 'objectification', the 'disenchantment' of nature, whereby it ceased to be seen as an embodiment of a sacred or spiritual order in relation to which man must define himself, and came to be seen as raw material to be shaped by human will. Hegel sees the essential connection in this objectification between the separation from nature and our relating to it as something to be dominated. Hegel is thus projecting one of the central strands of modern consciousness back onto the father of the Jewish faith. Historically, this is hard to sustain; but if I am right in holding that Christianity and particularly its Calvinist form had an important role in the forming of the modern consciousness of objectification, Hegel's thesis here may be insightful even if misplaced.[1]

In any case, Hegel was not of course holding that Abraham's consciousness of nature was a modern objectified one. This domination of nature was not

---

[1] Hegel (Nohl, 215) speaks of Christianity as an agent of disenchantment: 'Das Christentum hat Walhalla entvölkert, die heiligen Haine umgehauen, und die Phantasie des Volks als schändlichen Aberglauben, als ein teuflisches Gift ausgerottet...' ('Christianity has depopulated Valhalla, hewn down the sacred groves, and rooted out the phantasy of the people as shameful superstition, as a diabolical poison.')

attributed to man by Abraham (as against Nimrod, the entrepreneur of the Tower of Babel, who came to a sticky end as is known), but was projected onto the pure spirit, God. Men had part in this pure unity over against nature only by cleaving to God, and to this end the chosen people had to separate themselves rigorously from others and from the Gods of nature. But to give oneself to a God of *Herrschaft* (domination) is to submit oneself to his will, it is to become his slaves. Hence man, who is also and inescapably part of nature, had to be on the receiving end of a relation of domination, if he was himself to rule over nature; and nature as 'hostile' (*Feindseliges*) could only be ruled over or rule herself. Man's only choice was between two servitudes, to dead things or to the living God. Hence what God promised the children of Israel was not the expressive unity with nature the Greeks achieved, but rather that it would be at their disposal, would serve their needs, the land 'flowing with milk and honey'.

This was the original wrench which created the 'unhappy consciousness' as Hegel will call it later, the consciousness of separation from nature, a consciousness in which unity and mutuality is replaced by domination and servitude, between man and nature, nature and spirit, and ultimately also as a consequence between man and man. For Hegel as one who held to the aspiration of expressive unity, this consciousness could not but be unhappy, a tearing asunder. The message of Jesus was a call to man to restore the lost unity, to replace the law which commands from outside and divides men from nature and each other with the voice of the heart, that affinity of spirit with nature which comes forward in love.

But as we saw, the message could not be heard. It could not even be integrally understood by the disciples. Hegel's account of this failure follows a significantly different line in the 'Spirit of Christianity' MS than it did in the 'Positivity' essay. There the central idea was that Jesus was forced to assume the Messiah myth, and hence ultimately to set in train the establishing of a new positive authority. Here the central notion is that of retreat, of turning inward.

This new account is set in the context of a new critical appraisal of Kant. Hegel has finally come to see the rift between the Kantian ideal of moral autonomy and the aspiration to expressive unity. We have seen that the Jesus of the earlier MSS, for instance the 'Positivity' MS and that which has been called 'The Life of Jesus', united the two. He was a Kantian *avant la lettre* who also preached a wholeness of moral response, a unity of reason and heart. The conflict with Kant was implicit from the beginning in that Hegel refused to accept the separation of morality and inclination which was central to Kant's position. But now the conflict is out in the open: the Jesus of the 'Spirit of Christianity' is contrasted to Kant just on this central point, that he preaches not 'morality' in the Kantian sense but a spontaneous unity of inclination with the good which thus transcends and 'fulfills' the law.[1]

---

[1] Nohl, 266. Hegel speaks of 'dieser über Moralität erhabene Geist Jesu'.

The Claims of Speculative Reason

Against the Kantian separation of duty and desire, Hegel sees Jesus' vision as that of their union, in which the spirit of reconciliation (*Versöhnlichkeit*, Nohl, 269) replaces, goes beyond and hence fulfils the law with its particular, measured prescriptions. This inclination of the heart, which is no longer particular and egoistic, is life itself coming back into its rights, and as a union of opposites which really belong together it is 'love' (esp. 327). Love is the spirit which restores the unity of man within himself, with other men and with nature.

By contrast the Kantian morality remains one of division. Here Hegel uses a formula which becomes central to his critique of Kant later on: Kantian morality in separating the concept of the right from the reality of my inclinations, expresses simply an 'ought' (Sollen). But the religion of Jesus which unites the two is founded on an 'is' (Sein), a 'modification of life'. (Nohl, 266; Knox, 212.)

But Hegel's main critique of Kant is a cruel ad hominem point. The main *point d'honneur* of Kantian morality is that it alone safeguards autonomy and eschews any 'positive' morality. But Hegel argues, by dividing man and setting up one side, reason, over the other, sensibility or inclinations, Kantian morality retains an 'indestructible residue of positivity'. So that the difference between the believers in a positive religion and the Kantian moral man is not as great as Kant claimed, rather it is simply that the former 'have their lord outside themselves, while the latter carries his lord in himself, yet at the same time is his own slave' (Knox, 211).[1]

Hegel's claim that the moralist is 'his own slave' is more than just a clever ad hominem twist of the argument. It flows from his substantive position. The notion of autonomy refers us to an account of the self to whom it is attributed. The Kantian self is ultimately identified with the faculty which gives laws to ourselves, reason; man is thus free even against inclination. But Hegel holds fundamentally to the expressivist view of man: the self is the inner single source which expresses itself in the unfolding of reason and inclinations alike. Thus the imposition of an alien law on one of these sides of our being is a kind of (partial) slavery.

In a more direct way, this slam at Kant fits into the logic of his argument in this manuscript. At the outset, in his discussion of Abraham he makes the point that separation cannot but lead to relations of domination and servitude. The separation from Nature faces us with the choice of dominating or being dominated by her, and the separation of spirit from ourselves as natural beings makes us slaves of God. Similarly, the rift between reason and inclination makes us slaves of the prescriptions of reason, which in being cut off from the living sense of our situation and relations which we have through sensibility

---

[1] 'Jener den Herrn außer sich, dieser aber den Herrn in sich trägt, zugleich aber sein eigener Knecht ist' (Nohl, 266).

and feeling, are necessarily abstract and rigid. The Kantian moral man is the successor of Abraham who has interiorized his jealous law-giving God and called him 'reason'.[1]

The spirit of the law, from Abraham to Kant, can judge man for his transgressions and mete out punishment. And the punishment meted out by the law is just, whether given by man or God, since its principle is that I forego the right I have transgressed against. But law cannot *overcome* transgression because to be under law is already to be guilty of the essential trespass, that against the unity of life.

Thus when we suffer punishment under law, we never put our sin behind us. For judgement by law is judgement by concept which is abstracted from life and set over against it – and which on the human social level also presupposes an institutional division between men with the power to judge and execute sentence and those which are judged. Hence even to have served our time is not to have reconciled ourselves with that against which we have trespassed, the law. Or if it is internalized, it is present in us as a bad conscience. In either case, the division remains.

Against this vision of man's relation to God, his own conscience and society, Hegel sets an alternative one in this manuscript, whose central notion is 'fate'. Nourished on a study of Greek drama Hegel presents a nation of fate in which what happens to us outside our power, what befalls us in history, should be seen as the reaction onto us of our own trespass against life. The trespass against life is, of course, separation, the dividing of the living whole, within man, between men, or between man and nature. The destruction of life turns it into an enemy, for 'it is immortal and, if slain, it appears as its terrifying ghost which [...] lets loose its Eumenides' (Knox, 229). Thus for instance the fate of the Jewish people, who in separating from nature could allow only relations of domination or servitude with surrounding nature and humanity, was to suffer repeated enslavement.

If we understand our relation to God (and the company of men in history) on this model and not that of the law, then we can see how a reconciliation is possible which quite sets our transgressions behind us. Because the punishment we receive from fate is that of life injured, it offers the road to reconciliation; we can take this by recognizing that our fate is just the other side of our act; and in recognizing this we can restore the unity, cease to act in the way which divides, and therefore cease to call down a seemingly alien fate upon

---

[1] A more unfair slur is that of Pharisaism against the Kantian moralist (Knox, 220). Hegel's notion here of the affinity between the moral philosophy of Kant and the religion of Abraham can also be found in Hölderlin's equating Kant and Moses. 'Kant ist der Moses unserer Nation', he says in a letter to his brother, 'der sie aus der ägyptischen Erschlaffung in die freie einsame Wüste seiner Spekulation führt...' (SW, III, 367). Kant wakes us from slumber but this separation takes us into a desert. Hölderlin sees here that the Kantian separation was necessary, and in this he takes the same position as the mature Hegel.

us. In doing this we restore the oneness of life, we overcome totally the division caused by trespass, and hence trespass and the division from fate are quite set behind us. Fate is punishment, but unlike that from law it is meted out to us by the great current of life. Hence we can be reconciled to it, can come to see it as one with us, can heal the breach altogether as life. 'In fate [...]man recognizes his own life' (Knox, 231), and 'Life can heal its wounds again' (Knox, 230).

Now this conception is very much Greek inspired and not at all Christian. How does it help to understand the religion of Jesus? Because the spirit which recognizes our own life injured in our fate, the spirit which heals wounds and overcomes division, is what Hegel calls love, this is the interpretation of Christian *agape* in this manuscript.

Jesus' teaching was of this love, and his life was lived in the full reconciliation with the whole that love brings. And in this way he in a sense escaped fate. That is, he did not transgress against the unity of life, and hence never encountered hostile fate. Does Jesus then provide the model for the perfect religion, a teaching which is both rational and touches the whole man, and which is now seen to be higher than Kant's divisive reason? No, because in another sense, Jesus cannot escape fate. Fate can catch even the innocent, who is drawn into transgression against his will. Suppose I am attacked, and have to fight for my rights or let injustice be done. In either case I must transgress against the unity of life, by what I do or what I suffer.

The only way to escape this dilemma is to sacrifice my rights gladly, willingly, to withdraw from them, as it were, to be willing to forego everything in order not to be divided from others, and hence from love; to turn the other cheek to the aggressor, go twain with him who would compel me to go a mile, and thus remain 'open to reconciliation' with my malefactor, without the barrier of injured right between us (Knox, 236).

This was the path which Jesus took, that of withdrawal, which Hegel calls 'beauty of soul'.[1] And the withdrawal was not occasional but wholesale. For in fact Jesus' message came in a climate which could not receive it, where the spirit of Jewish legalism reigned supreme, and where the Mosaic law penetrated every aspect of life, not only public life, but family relations as well. The fullness of life Jesus was preaching could not be lived within the bounds of this legalism, and being unable to win the Jews away from this spirit, Jesus himself was forced to forgo the normal expression of a full human life. Not only could his new religious consciousness not find expression in the public life of the Jewish people, so that Jesus had to be content with gathering a small group around him, but he even had to forgo the normal relations of marriage and family, entwined as they were with the legal spirit he wanted to transcend.

[1] The idea here is basically the same as that of the 'beautiful soul' in the *PhG*. Hegel's critical stance towards it there is already foreshadowed in the ambivalence he shows towards it in this study of Jesus and his church.

Jesus in other words was forced to a withdrawal in order to retain the purity of his message; and the logical conclusion of this withdrawal was the supreme renunciation, where he gave up his life to the hostile authorities.

In Hegel's portrait Jesus' withdrawal is meant to be merely strategic, not ultimate. He accepts death, he accepts not to fight by the weapons of his world in the hope that the life thus preserved pure through sacrifice, could flower in a community after. But of course the conditions which forced his withdrawal do not permit this flowering any the more after his death. The community remains a persecuted group, with no place in the public life of the nation, anxiously guarding the purity of its love.

This new account of Christianity's failure does not replace but rather supplements the early one in terms of the creation of a new positivity. The apostles are not only incapable, even as Jesus was, of imparting the new life to their society, they cannot sustain it fully among themselves as he did. They remain dependent on him, now as the departed Christ. Jesus accepted an early death not only as a sacrifice of love which cannot itself use the weapons of division, even in self-defence, but also because he hoped that this passing would cure the dependence of his followers. But in this respect also, his hope was not fulfilled.

From this account we can derive some of the abiding characteristics of the Christian religion. First, unlike that of the Greeks, it is essentially a private religion which was renounced public expression and at its origin marked a distinction between the things of Caesar and the things of God. But second, this division of public and private is just a manifestation of a deeper rift: it springs from the deeper tendency to withdraw from all those multiple aspects of life in which the fullness of love cannot be lived integrally because they are bound up with 'this world', including family and property relations.

The early church tried to escape these by community of property, and Hegel implies that only lack of courage kept them from communal marriage as well. But of course, they cannot forever be escaped, and hence the Christian is doomed to an even more profound unhappy consciousness than the Jew. The Jewish spirit had made nature and the relationships of life into objectified realities. But as such, there was nothing wrong with enjoying them as the fruit of obedience to God. But Christian consciousness demanded that these relations be expressions of love, and being unable still to experience them as anything but objectified it must either renounce them in mortification, or enjoy them with a perpetual bad conscience. The rift remains, and Christian consciousness fails as much as Jewish to recover the Greek mean of beauty (Nohl, 313; Knox, 266).

This rift is what imparts the character of melancholy to Christian worship, and why it centres on a crucified God, thus turning suffering which Jesus saw as a temporary necessity on the way to the Kingdom, and which would be set aside, into something central to the community.

But of course it was already a failure of Jesus' mission, as we saw, that the community had to depend on Christ, either crucified or risen, as an authority and a continuing source. Jesus had meant for the spirit to come to them so that they would be as he was, capable of living the reconciled life independently. This sliding back into positivity is the third important feature of ongoing Christianity.

Hegel hints at the corruption which inevitably came as the Church grew and eventually became 'established' in the world. The positive side of this withdrawal of the early church was that they did live an intense community life, however anxiously they had to guard it against involvement with the world. When the church grew and inevitably became involved with the world, then bad conscience increased with the resulting inevitable increase in hypocrisy. An otherworldly church assuming power in a world it could not but disvalue necessarily corrupted both. The fight of purity against impurity, when the former is already involved with the latter, is something 'horrible' (gräßlich, Nohl, 329). Moreover, this striving for purity, transposed into a positive religion, becomes a battle to keep belief unsullied and gives birth to all the persecutions and heresy-hunts which strew the history of the Church.

Thus Christianity does not really escape fate. Or rather there is a particular fate which awaits those who try to be above fate, try to withdraw from the divisions of the world. And this seems in some ways worse than what it replaces. Christianity seems a failure, and Hegel seems farther than ever from uniting his three poles of allegiance. Not only does the Christian religion appear uncombinable with Greek unity, but Kantian moral freedom is also at odds with both.

2

But some hints towards a new solution, an entirely new synthesis of these three elements, are already present in this manuscript on the 'Spirit of Christianity'.

The need for an entirely new kind of synthesis grows with the insight that this separation of spirit from life is not a gratuitous falling off from the human norm. There is a certain necessity, or at least inevitability about it. Thus that Christianity as a religion of love is essentially a private religion, that it does not consort easily with the web of normal social relations, is not just a function of the incapacity of the Jews two thousand years ago to receive Jesus' message. In a MS from 1797 or 1798 on 'Love' (Knox, 302–8; Nohl 378–82), Hegel points out that property relations, since they essentially attribute exclusive dominion over things, pose a limit to the complete union of lovers. It is the same insight by which he interprets the demand for community of property in the early church. And here he sees that the demands of the church conflict with those of civil society. In a civil society which is coterminous with a church, as was the case in medieval and modern Europe, there cannot but be strains.[1]

Again, Hegel points out in another MS (Nohl 219-30; Knox 151-65) that the decline of pagan religion before Christianity is due obviously to an inner weakness in ancient society; the ancient religions of beauty which united spirit with nature and to whom thus the spirit of domination was foreign declined with ancient freedom. When the polis with which all its citizens could identify gave way to the rule of some classes over others and eventually to the great empires, men could no longer see the state as an emanation of themselves, but they were only its instruments. But when men no longer gave themselves their own law in the political realm, the vision of autonomy disappeared from the divine realm as well. Men accepted a positive religion and along with this a doctrine of their own corruption (Nohl, 225-6). This doctrine was thus not gratuitously accepted in replacement of the old religion; it gained credence because in a sense corruption was the reality, it 'agreed with experience'; a religion of slaves was quite naturally accepted by slaves.

In what way do these hints of the inevitability of separation (*Trennung*) point a way beyond the failure of Christianity? Because they are the germs of the later Hegelian doctrine that the separation of Judaeo-Christianity had to happen because it was essential to the full realization of man, that this realization involved more than a recovery of Greek unity, but rather a synthesis of Greek unity and the freedom of autonomous spirit.

It is not likely that Hegel ever thought the task of the age was simply to recover the lost unity of Greek society, or indeed that he ever thought this recovery possible. From the beginning, as I have said, his thought was polarized as well by the matchless achievement of his own age, the Enlightenment, and by the Christian religion. But this is not to say that he realized all at once at the beginning just what irreversible changes separate us from the ancients and just how profound the opposition was between ancient and modern spirit.

Indeed, the view I am trying to expound here is that this dawned slowly on him as he tried to deepen his vision of a restored society which would combine the expressive unity of the Greeks with the freedom of Enlightenment rationality in the context of a purified Christianity. He gradually took the full measure of the fundamental oppositions between the different poles of his allegiance. In examining how to restore Christianity to its original supposed agreement with the aspirations to expressive unity and autonomy, he began to see how deeply at odds these aspirations were. Thus by the end of his

---

[1] In commenting the evangelical injunction to despise riches, Hegel says: 'the fate of property has become too powerful for us to tolerate reflections on it, to find its abolition thinkable' (Knox, 221).

Frankfurt period he has come to sense that the religion of Jesus, with its uncompromising aspiration to a universal community of love, is somehow incombinable with the confident public religion which sustained the life of the polis. Its demands are too high, and it must rather breed disaffection and withdrawal from the city. The germ is here for the mature Hegel's thesis that Christianity as the attempt to reconcile man with universal spirit had to burst beyond the bounds of the polis where the unity of human and divine was bought at the expense of a certain parochialism.

Similarly, we can see the foreshadowing in this MS on the 'Spirit of Christianity' of the later view that the Greek polis cannot and should not be restored because it is incombinable with the modern spirit of individual freedom, as reflected inter alia in civil society and its property relations. The germ of this is present in the insight that a community founded integrally on mutual love cannot find a place for private property.

And now, most important of all, he sees that the demands of Kantian autonomous morality and those of expressive unity are opposed.

Thus as he came to realize that separation was unavoidable, that men could not help falling away from the beautiful unity of the Greeks, he was also coming to see that this separation was essential, that men had to go through it in order to fulfil their vocation as free rational beings.

Hence the realization that Kantian freedom cannot be combined with Greek expressive unity does not lead him to abandon one of the poles of his thought, the Enlightenment notion of rational freedom as Kant formulated it best of all. On the contrary, Hegel holds firm to his original three reference points. Rather this division, along with those I mentioned earlier, lead him to a basic reformulation of the task.

At the end of 1800 Hegel left his preceptoral job at Frankfurt and went to Jena where he took up a new career as a teacher of philosophy at the University, this under the stimulus and with the help of his younger friend Schelling. In this last period at Frankfurt and the first year or so at Jena, his conception of the predicament of the age altered and assumed something like its final form.

Originally, as we saw, Hegel thought of the regeneration of the age as a recovery of unity within and between men which would at the same time be an achievement of autonomy. These two goals far from conflicting would be identical, that is, different descriptions of the same achievement. But as he begins to see that the demands of radical autonomy based on reason, and the demands of expressive unity or wholeness are opposed, his conception of the task of realizing them together comes to be transformed. Where originally he sees the task as that of recovering unity and overcoming separation, he now comes to see it as one of reconciling opposition. Where earlier separation is simply a falling away, and to be done away with, in the mature system it is seen as inextricably bound up with the development of freedom. Hence there is not just a conflict between the requirements of human fulfilment and man's historical predicament, but there is an opposition between the different requirements themselves of man's realization. Thus the problem cannot be solved by a victory of one side over the other, by a simple undoing of separation in a spirit of unity, rather the two sides must be brought somehow to unity while each requirement is integrally satisfied. This is the task – perhaps an impossible one – which Hegel's mature system is meant to encompass.

In this sense Hegel comes around the turn of the century to a formulation of the problem which I have argued was the central one for the Romantic generation, how to unite expressive wholeness and radical freedom, Spinoza and Kant. He followed his own itinerary getting there, although he touched at most of the stations of the Romantic journey: the enthusiasm for the Greeks, the vogue of Kant, the heady hopes of 1789, the influence of Spinoza, the yearning for a restored Christianity. But he was very definitely to find his own way out. And that is why he is still worth studying.

But at the time of the 'Spirit of Christianity' MS, although Hegel is already exploring the tensions between the three poles of his thought, his conception of regeneration is still one of unity which overcomes separation. Love is this recovered unity and it has no further room for division: 'To love God is to feel oneself in the "all" of life, with no restrictions, in the infinite'...'Love alone has no limits' (Knox, 247).

And even more unequivocally

Since the divine is pure life, anything and everything said of it must be free of any (implications of) opposition. (Knox, 255)[1]

In Hegel's first published work in his new career as a university teacher of philosophy, the *Differenz* of 1801, we see the transformed perspective. Hegel posits that the formal task of philosophy is 'the cancellation of division' (75, die Aufhebung der Entzweiung). But he makes clear that the way to solve the problem is not to 'abolish one of the opposites and raise the other to infinity'. Both separation and identity (Trennung and Identität) must be given their rights. And hence, in a famous formulation,

But the Absolute itself is thus the identity of identity and non-identity; opposition and unity are both in it.[2]

---

[1] Weil das Göttliche reines Leben ist, so muß notwending, wenn von ihm und was von ihm gesprochen wird, nichts Entgegengesetzes in sich enthalten.

[2] Das Absolute selbst aber ist darum die Identität der Identität und der Nichtidentität; Entgegen-setzen und Einssein ist zugleich in ihm. Already in the 'System Fragment', a MS of 1800, Hegel talked of the sought for synthesis, life, as 'die Verbindung der Verbindung und der Nichtverbin-dung' (Nohl, 348).

The Claims of Speculative Reason

In this transformation of perspective all of Hegel's earlier analyses of the rise of separation – his study of the diremption of religious consciousness with Abraham, his hints about the decline of the ancient city – are not set aside; they are woven into the mature position. But they are seen as more than just misfortunes. They are seen as necessary developments, and that in the two senses we outlined above; that is, they are *ineluctable*, but they are also *essential* for the realization of man. They are essential because the realization of man as a spiritual being, hence a free rational being, requires that he break out of the original unity of the tribe. Man becomes a free rational subject by giving himself to rational thought alone and rejecting all other allegiances. And this must mean a break, with other men who are not similarly devoted to reason, with the millenial tradition of one's society, with the parochial custom of one's community which cannot stand up at the bar of universal reason. Men must abandon mythical thought where the images of the divine or spiritual are found in nature, and cleave to the bare concept. And this means a break within man as well, as the criteria of reasoning are shaken free of the matrix of desires and feelings which also motivate us, and reasoning in order to be an autonomous activity has to abstract, to subsume the realities of life under concepts which prescind from much of our lived experience.

Hegel seems to have been slower in taking this point, that separation was essential for freedom, than other thinkers of his generation. This is perhaps because he did not feel the impact of Fichte and the *Wissenschaftslehre* in the middle 1790s with anything like the force that Schelling, or the Romantic thinkers, or even Hölderlin did; perhaps because he was far from its epi-centre, serving as a perceptor in Berne. But having got the point, Hegel thought it through more consistently, rigourously and thoroughly than anyone else in his generation, and this, as we saw in the last section, is what ultimately separated him from the Romantics. And it is in virtue of this that he grows beyond Schelling and parts philosophical company with him at the end of his Jena period, a break consummated in the preface to his *PhG* where he describes Schelling's absolute as an 'abyss' (Abgrund) in which all differ-ences disappear, a night of indistinction, as it were, 'in which all cows are black' (*PhG*, 18–9).

Hegel comes to see separation from nature as both ineluctable and essen-tial. But he saw it as both inseparably. In other words, he developed along with this new perspective a notion of history as the necessary unfolding of a certain human destiny. This is the Hegelian reinterpretation of Providence. As against the blithely optimistic eighteenth-century notion of Providence as the perfect dovetailing of a well-joined universe into the purposes of God for man, a vision which Hegel never ceased to treat with scorn, Hegel developed a view of history as the unfolding of a purpose from within, through tragic conflict to a higher reconciliation. Separation ineluctably occurs because it is essential for man. But men also need unity, with society and with nature within and without. They are thus driven to a tragic conflict in which two incompatible ends claim their allegiance. But if this conflict is ineluctable because essential, then so must the higher reconciliation be in which these two goals are fulfilled together. History moves to heal the wounds it made.[1]

Thus Hegel takes up in his own way a category of thought which we have seen was already current in the Romantic generation: history as a circle, or rather spiral, in which unity gives way to division, and then is recovered on a higher level.[2]

Thus at about the time he moved to Jena, Hegel also moved his perception of the predicament of the age more into line with the dilemma defined by Romantic thinkers. Thus it was that the move to Jena was also one into the orbit of the young Schelling, then at the height of his success. And it brought with it a transposition of Hegel's thoughts into the terms of post-Kantian philosophy.[3] And here we come to a second transformation which would have definitive significance for the final system.

For this transposition is not just one of medium, and not just occasioned by Hegel's new career; it corresponds to another important transformation in Hegel's position. In the early MSS, and still in the 'spirit of Christianity' MS, Hegel believes that the unity recovered in love cannot be adequately expressed in conceptual thought. It is beyond the understanding in this sense. Hegel expresses this clearly in the poem that he wrote for Hölderlin in 1796, 'Eleusis':

> Dem Sohn der Weihe war der hohen Lehren Fülle
> Des unaussprechlichen Gefühles Tiefe viel zu heilig,
> Als daß er trockne Zeichen ihrer würdigte.
> Schon der Gedanke faßt die Seele nicht,
> Die außer Zeit und Raum in Ahndung der Unendlichkeit
> Versunken, sich vergißt, und wieder zum Bewußtsein nun
> Erwacht. Wer gar davon zu andern sprechen wollte,
> Spräch er mit Engelzungen, fühlt' der Worte Armut.*

---

[1] We already see this idea foreshadowed in the notion of fate in the MS on the 'Spirit of Christianity'. What befalls us is the vengeance of life for our transgression against it, but precisely for that reason it opens the possibility of reconciliation. We see another illustration of the importance for Hegel of Greek tragedy in the development of his philosophy of history.

[2] This too is foreshadowed in the 'Spirit of Christianity' MS (Nohl, 318; Knox, 273), where it is a question of unity lost and restored, and Hegel puts the three stages in parallel to the three persons of the Trinity, Father, Son and Holy Ghost, an important theme of his mature work.

[3] Of course philosophical terms are frequent in Hegel's writings of the 1790s. In his analysis of Abraham he speaks of the opposition of unity and multiplicity, while his critique of Kant in the 'Spirit of Christianity' is partly couched in terms of the opposition of universal and individual. And there is much mention of subjectivity and objectivity, nature and freedom, and so on. But what is new in the Jena period is a serious coming to grips with the language of post-Kantian philosophy, with Fichte and Schelling, with the Ego, and its relation to the non-Ego, both theoretical and practical.

* For the initiate, the fullness of the lofty doctrine and the depths of ineffable feeling, were much too holy for him to honour dry signs with them. For thought cannot grasp the soul which forgetting

And again in a fragment of the Frankfurt period, Hegel speaks of the unity of Religion, or love, as 'a miracle we cannot grasp' (Nohl, 377).

But in Hegel's final position, philosophy occupies the highest place, just because it is the only fully adequate expression of the highest unity, the medium in which spirit comes totally to itself, and hence the development of philosophical thought is essential to the perfection of this highest synthesis.[1]

It is true that there is an important thread of continuity which runs through this change. In speaking in the 'Spirit of Christianity' of the limits of the intellect, Hegel speaks of the unity of love being beyond the 'understanding' (*Verstand*), which he equates with 'absolute division, the destruction of life' (Knox, 264)[2] 'Every reflection annuls love' (Knox, 253).

Now these terms continue to designate modes of thought which cannot grasp the unity of opposites right into the mature system. Indeed, the term '*Verstand*' has a remarkable stability throughout the development of Hegel's thought from the earliest beginnings. It represents always the kind of understanding which abstracts from experience, analyses and keeps the elements so abstracted rigidly separated, above all the form of thought which fixes distinctions and makes them unbridgeable, and therefore is incapable of understanding the whole. 'Reflection' designates the mode of thought which describes man and the world under categories of division and opposition, or as applied to a domain of concepts, it designates the domain of paired opposed terms. It is therefore essentially a thought of *Trennung*.

But what changes through this consistency in vocabulary is that Hegel in the early manuscripts does not see a possibility of conceptual thought beyond understanding and reflection. Or perhaps it would be more accurate to say that with the growing intuition that expressive unity and Kantian reason are not combinable ideals, his faith in such a higher mode of conceptual thought vanishes. In the new position which he comes to at Jena, however, that faith triumphantly returns; indeed, he would not agree to call it a 'faith'; it is the

---

itself plunges out of space and time into a presentiment of infinity, and now re-awakens. Whoever wanted to speak of this to others, though he spoke with the tongues of angels, would feel the poverty of words.

[1] That he came so late to this philosophical enterprise, although it put him for a while behind – and under the wing of – the younger but more philosophically versed Schelling, actually helped him surpass Schelling and the rest of his followers. The fact that he had pondered so long on man's religious and social development made him use the categories of post-Kantian idealism with a much richer field of reference and to incomparably greater effect. Fichte and Schelling were thoroughly at home – too much at home – in the jargon of the Ego, the non-Ego, Subjectivity and Objectivity, etc. Schelling also absorbed the poetic vision of nature from Goethe and the Romantics which he transposed in his philosophy of Nature. But with Hegel philosophy is used to illuminate the whole field of human history – political, religious, philosophical, artistic. This was unprecedented. Fichte, for all that he was thoroughly *engagé* as an intellectual, is hardly someone one would turn to to understand the historical significance and philosophical relevance of the great events of his time.

[2] 'die absolute Trennung, das Töten' (Nohl, 311).

cornerstone of his philosophical system, the Hegelian notion of *Vernunft* (Reason).

We can readily understand this change, at least in part, in relating it to the previously mentioned one, Hegel's growing realization that the final synthesis must have a place for separation as well as unity. Separation was essential for rational autonomy. And a synthesis which incorporates rational autonomy has to be expressed in the language of reason, as we noted in the previous section. Hence Hegel gives a new sense to Reason, as opposed to understanding, and seeks the fullest synthesis in philosophy. Hegel saw that a synthesis which reconciled the opposition of freedom and integral expression, as against just returning to the original, undifferentiated unity, *required* philosophical statement. On this he parts company with the Romantics.

A third important change which Hegel's views underwent in this transition period when he was first at Jena displaced the centre of gravity in his thought from man to *Geist*.

We saw in the last chapter how Hegel came finally to a notion of spirit which was neither the transcendent God of theism, nor simply equivalent to the spirit of man. This spirit is a cosmic one, but man is the vehicle of his spiritual life.

Now this represented an evolution on Hegel's part. He started out at Tübingen with a position which was really theistic, since he agreed with the Kantian thesis that God's existence is a necessary postulate of practical reason. But around the middle 1790s he seems to have abandoned, partly under Schelling's influence, the notion of a personal transcendent God, and accepted rather some notion of spirit, or at least life, which at any rate could not be set over against man and the world as the God of theism must be.

But although Hegel nowhere defines his conception of the absolute in this period, and while he does not want to equate it simply with restored man, nevertheless his conception of religion, i.e., man's relation to this absolute, is very man-centered in his Berne and Frankfurt periods. Thus he accepts at first the Kantian notion that the moral law can be totally derived from the demands of man's (that is, ultimately, the individual's) reason; and he sees the restored unity with nature and within man as being identical with this recovery of autonomy. It is a unity in which man remains the centre-piece, drawing his inspiration out of himself rather than seeking to conform to a larger order outside himself. Even with the critical stance towards Kantian morality which appears in the 'Spirit of Christianity' MS, it remains true that the man who has reconnected with love derives his pattern of feeling and action out of himself rather than discovering it in a wider order, even though he is thus connecting with a larger current of life. Jesus is portrayed as self-sufficient spiritually as a man. These aspects of the Gospel which do not fit with this picture – Jesus talking of a 'father' to whom he 'prays', his talk of 'sin' and 'forgiveness' – all this is explained in a 'demythologizing' way, as the lang-

The Claims of Speculative Reason

uage which he had to use to communicate to the people of his time. And Hegel makes very clear that Jesus was not in principle exceptional among men in this regard, although it (Knox, 268) turned out tragically that he was so in fact. His idea was that after his death the community he left behind would become fully independent as he was in their communion with the spirit of love; this was, indeed, one of the reasons why he accepted an early death.

The Hegel of the early theological manuscripts thus has a man-centred view of human regeneration.[1] Indeed, at times it would appear that man is the *only spiritual* being, although he must unite with a larger life to recover wholeness.[2]

The mature Hegel has broken with this view, and adopted a notion of the absolute as *Geist.* Man as a spiritual being is related to a larger scheme of spiritual activity. Kantian formalism, the attempt to derive the content of duty from the necessary form of reason, is constantly attacked as vain and empty, and this precisely because men can only discover the real content of ethical life by seeing themselves as part of a larger scheme. This is not supposed to be a regression to heteronomy in that the larger scheme is that of *Geist* with which man comes to identify as his indispensable vehicle, as we saw in the last section. How well this solution stands up we must examine later. The point is here that while claiming to avoid heteronomy Hegel has broken with his earlier, Kant-influenced, man-centred formulations of autonomy. Freedom is no longer just drawing the law or the inspiration of love from oneself.

It is likely that this shift is bound up with the others we discussed above. In coming to see that the demands of man's autonomy pulled in a different direction from the demands of unity with the whole, he was forced to a re-assessment of the place of man-centred autonomy in his total vision of things. Recovering unity just with a larger current of *life* is now seen to be not enough for a spiritual being. On the contrary, reuniting with the whole must mean regaining contact with a cosmic spirit. But this synthesis must unite the separation essential to man-centred autonomy and the expressive unity with nature. It cannot be simply equivalent to either, but must be higher than both.

[1] After Hegel's death, the dispute between man- and God-centred conceptions broke out again among his intellectual heirs over the interpretation of his system and its import. The 'old Hegelians' pushed his philosophy in the direction of orthodox theism, the 'young Hegelians' towards a man-centred interpretation in which *Geist* became identical with man. This culminated in the works of Feuerbach and the young Marx. Both these twists are of course untrue to the Hegelian synthesis which is meant to be neither theist or atheist; but if I am right the young Hegel had some affinities with the later young Hegelians, which the mature Hegel had shed. This was of course not known at the time since the early MSS were not published until much later. But it is not surprising that Marxists with affinities with early Marx should find the young Hegel an interesting study: cf. G. Lukács, *Der Junge Hegel.*

[2] As seems implied by a description of the goal of unity aimed at as 'To find peace in a non-personal living beauty' (Knox, 301) ('in einer unpersönlichen lebendigen Schönheit Ruhe zu finden', Nohl, 342).

Hence this man-centred autonomy can no longer be the absolute goal. It must be set in a wider synthesis, and this is what the mature Hegel claims to do.

Of course, this development in Hegel's thought cannot be seen as powered simply by these logical connections between his intellectual goals. It is likely that it was also influenced by the train of events in his time. Without our being able to be sure because of the lack of evidence, it is probable that the early Hegel was quite radical politically. In the early days at Tübingen young radicals followed the progress of events in Paris with interest and enthusiasm. And while it is not likely that they wanted simply to re-edit the French Revolution in Germany, and certainly not its Jacobin phase – for all that the reactionaries dubbed them all with the title 'Jacobin' – nevertheless it is probable that they favoured far-reaching political change in the direction of equality and popular representation. Even in 1798 Hegel wrote a pamphlet as an intended contribution to the debate on the constitutional future of his native Württemberg (it was never published) which seems to have advocated election of the *Landtag* by at any rate a larger franchise.

The mature Hegel on the other hand was not a political radical at all. It is easy, however, to misconceive the change. It is too simple and misleading to see it simply as a shift from left to right. First, it is probable that the 'organic' notions of the state, derived from the Greeks, the distrust of the 'mob' acting outside any institutional framework, the stress on differentiated function, these ideas which are so important to his later political theory were there at the beginning. And reciprocally, the mature Hegel incorporates a great deal of the principles of 1789, more than were incorporated in the Prussian state of his time of which he is so often accused of being the apologist, and more in some respects than many contemporary bourgeois writers if one thinks of his prophetic mistrust of the thrust of a capitalist economy.

The change rather lies in his conception of the role of willed action to political change. The regeneration he looks for in the 1790s is something which seems largely to have to be *done* by religious and political transformation. In the later system the fulfilment of man's destiny is something which is *in train*; it is incumbent on men to recognize and live in relation to it. Of course, here too we can easily misconceive the difference. To recognize one's connection with *Geist* is *ipso facto* to change oneself and the way one acts and in important respects. A change of consciousness cannot just be opposed to a change in reality; they are bound up together; and this link between the two was important from the beginning of Hegel's thought, for which religious transformation was central. But there is a difference nonetheless between a view which sees widespread willed social and political transformation as something to be *done* by those who would achieve regeneration and a view which sees the relevant social and political transformations as needing to be *discerned* and hence accepted and lived in the right spirit.

The Claims of Speculative Reason

This is the fourth major change which came over Hegel's position and which came to maturity somewhat later than the others. But although maturing at a different pace, it is clearly linked with the third. The man-centred conception of regeneration naturally goes with the prospect of a willed transformation of institutions to realize the desired end. But with the development of a notion of *Geist* as a subject greater than man, Hegel developed a notion of historical process which could not be explained in terms of conscious human purposes, but rather by the greater purposes of *Geist*. The transformations in political, social, religious institutions which must come about if man is to fulfil his destiny are no longer seen as tasks which men must consciously accomplish; on the contrary, although they are carried through by men, these do not fully understand the part they are playing until after they have come about. This is the mature Hegelian doctrine of the 'cunning of reason' and the retrospective understanding of history which Hegel expressed in that famous phrase of the Preface to the *Philosophy of Right*, that 'the owl of Minerva spreads its wings only with the falling of the dusk'.[1]

In other words the notion that man is related to a larger, cosmic subject went along with a displacement of the subject of history in Hegel's thought, who is no longer simply man – if indeed, he ever clearly conceived it as such – but *Geist*. What needs to be *done* in the sense of carried through by intentional action is thus not the institutional transformations of history, for these can no longer be intentionally encompassed in this sense, but rather the recognition of what *Geist* has *in train* and the connecting of oneself to it. It is this, of course, that the young Marx was protesting against when he complained that 'philosophers' had only interpreted the world, whereas the task was to change it. The young Hegel would have been closer to agreeing with him than the mature philosopher.

Thus these four transpositions in Hegel's position which take place around the time he goes to Jena and carry through the Jena period into his mature position, are related: the acceptance of separation as part of the ultimate unity, the shift to philosophy as the crucial medium, the shift from a man-centred theory to one centred on *Geist*, and the notion that man's realization is not planned by him, but can only be recognized post hoc. The first two are linked through Hegel's sense of the connection between separation and autonomy, autonomy and rationality; the opposition between autonomy and expressive unity leads him to a notion of *Geist* as greater than man, and *Geist* as the subject of history transforms his view of history. Man's task is now to recognize, and to recognize clearly, not by a cloudy intuition which would deny his vocation to rational autonomy; and thus the apex of human realization, which turns out to be the realization of *Geist*, lies in philosophical awareness.

From this vantage point, we can see more clearly that this complex shift in

[1] *PR*, 13.

Hegel's Itinerary

Hegel's thought was also probably motivated by the political events of the time. In the early 1790s many young radical Germans had hopes of revolutionary developments in their homeland. By the end of the decade, these had faded: the ancien régime in Germany was plainly proof to any transformation within. The main hope of change remained the French Army, and later its leader Napoleon. Hegel seems to have been one of those Germans who judged favourably the results of Napoleonic hegemony in the 1800s. But the changes wrought thereby were not as radical as those dreamt of in the early 1790s, nor did this revolution from without induce a sense of self-activity. In the late 1790s and early 1800s Germany seemed incapable of rising to the challenge of the dissolution of the Empire under the blows of the French Revolutionary Army and of finding a rejuvenated form. It was not a vantage point from which it was easy to believe that men consciously and deliberately make their own history.

Of course, this is not the whole story as far as Hegel was concerned. There was another moment of hope, after Napoleon shattered Prussia at the battle of Jena, and a spirit of renewal seemed about to take hold of Germany, spearheaded by the reforms of Baron vom Stein. Hegel seems to have been relatively unmoved by this. Perhaps he had already set in a certain mould; in this realm early experiences are more important than later ones. In any case, the movement of renewal was squashed after the Restoration.

Let us now turn to examine Hegel's mature position.

CHAPTER III

Self-positing Spirit

1

I have been trying to present in the preceding chapters an idea of the fundamental problems and aspirations which Hegel's philosophy was addressed to. And I have suggested that we can best see these in the light of the yearning of his time to find a way of life and thought which would unite two powerful aspirations, which were both connected yet opposed. One is to that unity with nature, other men and himself which man demands as an expressive being; the other is to the radical moral autonomy which reached paradigm expression in Kant and Fichte.

I have suggested that Hegel by the early 1800s had come to realize how deeply these two aspirations were opposed to each other. In particular, he had come to see that freedom required the breaking up of expressive unity, of the original undivided wholeness within man and communion with other men and nature, which he like many contemporaries attributed to an earlier age – principally that of ancient Greece. The sense of fragmentation within, and of exile in a dead, mechanical universe and society, which so many writers of the age had experienced and testified to, was not an inexplicable and unmitigated loss of an earlier paradise. Rather it was the result of an ineluctable development, essential for the full realization of man as rational and free agent.

But the story was not to end there. This necessary division was to be healed in a higher reconciliation. This reconciliation was already in train, fruit of a rational unfolding of purpose which history exhibits, and which required to be discerned and grasped by philosophy, and hence completed – since this reconciliation, incorporating reason, could only be adequately formulated in the language of reason. Hegel along with many contemporaries believed that his age was the axial period which would see the dawning of this reconciliation. 'It is surely not difficult to see that our time is a time of birth and transition to a new period' (*PhG*, 15).[1] And Hegel goes on to speak in this passage of a 'qualitative leap' (ein qualitativer Sprung).

Thus the major task of philosophy for Hegel can be expressed as that of over-coming opposition.[2] The oppositions are those which arise from the

---

[1] Quoted from the Walter Kaufmann translation, *Hegel: texts and commentary*, New York, Anchor books, 1966, p. 20.

[2] 'die Aufhebung der Entzweiung' as he puts it in *Differenz*, p. 75.

breaking up of the original expressive unity. Hence first, man as knowing subject is separated from nature, which he now sees as brute fact, not expressive of some idea or purpose. Nature is thus other than mind in not exhibiting any rational necessity or expressive form. And when we push this distinction to its furthest conclusion we have to agree with Kant in attributing whatever degree of necessary form we find in experience to our own understanding rather than to the reality which comes to impinge on this understanding. Since some degree of necessary form is essential to experience, we have to admit that reality as it is in itself, that is, unaltered by any structures that we impose on it, is forever beyond our ken. Man's estrangement from nature makes the world ultimately a *terra incognita* for him.

This separation which arises with man's developing self-consciousness about his own thought, becomes an opposition in the sense that nothing is allowed to mediate or bridge the gap between mind and world, everything is either on one side or the other.[1] But it is also an opposition in the stronger sense that this separation between mind and world runs counter to the nature and purpose of knowing mind. Thus Hegel will often protest that the Kantian idea of a thing in itself is incoherent, in that the philosopher in using this term is positing something out of the reach of his mind, but which at the same time cannot be out of reach in that *he* is positing it. (Of course, a Kantian will protest that this ignores the distinction between what can be experienced and what can only be thought, but Hegel's point is just to challenge this distinction.) Hence the opposition sharpens here. It comes to lie between two requirements laid on the knowing subject, that he come to distinguish himself from his object in full self-consciousness of what he is doing, and that he also know it thoroughly, to its core as it were.

A similar opposition arises within men between their rational will and their own nature, their desires, inclinations, affinities. Once more men come to distinguish the rational determinants of their will in the process of growing self-consciousness, and this seems essential to the growth of rationality itself and freedom. And this separation becomes an opposition in which reason and nature are not only considered to be watertight categories without any intersect, but also are in conflict as they vie for the control of our will. But this conflict is the reflection of an opposition between two requirements which hold of us as agents. On one side we are called on as rational agents to be free, and hence follow reason. On the other side, freedom means acting out of motives which flow from the self rather than being externally imposed or induced. But

---

[1] Of course, Kant made some tentative steps towards mediation in his third critique. But Kant was careful never to commit himself beyond the bounds of dualism. Thus the teleological understanding of living things is a way we have of ordering phenomena 'as if' they served final causes. Kant's successors, including Hegel, went beyond this.

since I am also a natural being, a conception of freedom which excludes and even opposes natural inclination must be defective.

This opposition between nature and freedom can also be presented in a theoretical mode, as between two kinds of explanation of what men do, by natural necessity and by freely chosen goals, which seem both inescapable and yet in conflict.

Thirdly, the growth of self-consciousness leads the individual to distinguish himself from his tribe or community. And this growing sense of individuality again leads to a practical opposition, a conflict of interest, between man and society, which in turn is based on conflicting requirements of freedom. Man to be free must be his own master, and hence not subordinate to any others. But at the same time man on his own is weak and necessarily dependent on outside help. The freedom of the bare individual is thus a very circumscribed and shadowy thing. But what is more, man as a cultural being only develops a mind and purposes of his own out of interchange with others; the very aspiration to individual freedom is nurtured on this interchange, and can be dulled and perverted by it. So that integral freedom cannot be attained by an individual alone. It must be shared in a society which sustains a culture that nurtures it and institutions which give effect to it. Freedom seems to require both individual independence and integration into a larger life.

The individual man is part not just of a larger social whole, he and his society are in turn set in a wider frame, mankind, and the whole of nature, with which they are in interchange and on which they depend. The development of self-consciousness has meant a separation from these larger frameworks, formerly seen as meaningful orders, now looked on as a set of de facto limits and conditions of our action. We saw above how this separation gives rise to an opposition for the knowing subject. But it creates one for the subject as a free expressive being as well. My freedom is limited by my dependence on the greater framework of nature. But just as with the relation of my reason to my own desires, or my freedom to my society, this dependence creates a dilemma. Or rather it does on the assumption of an expressive theory of man, according to which men seek communion with the larger order of nature. For to be true to ourselves, we seem to have both to separate from and integrate into this larger framework.

We saw in the last chapter how this double requirement of integrating into nature while remaining a spiritual being seemed to many to be met in the conception of a cosmic spirit underlying nature. But we also saw that this merely displaces the dilemma, which now centres on man's relation to this cosmic spirit. The opposition now lies between the self-dependence and autonomy of finite spirits, which seems to be enjoined on them as rational, hence free agents, and the demands of union with cosmic spirit, without which they remain merely fragmentary beings in opposition to their own vocation to integral expression.

The fourth opposition can thus be described as one between finite and infinite spirit, between the demands of human autonomy and those of participation in the current of infinite life. Hegel saw the solution to this in his notion of *Geist*, as we saw in the last chapter and shall examine shortly. But this opposition can also be expressed in terms of the concept of fate. From the standpoint of the autonomous, finite subject, the larger course of events which affects him is distinguished from what he does as what happens to him; his fate. This fate is quite distinct from himself, in the sense that it is not at all an expression of him, something one can only find in what he does. From this point of view, that of separation, the injunction of an earlier time to reconcile oneself to fate, to come to see its necessity and hence make peace with it, can only be understood as a call to surrender, not as an invitation to deeper insight.

But the course of things is in some sense an expression of cosmic spirit; and hence to see it as quite other is to define oneself in opposition to cosmic spirit. On the other hand, to be united to infinite spirit, even more to see oneself as its vehicle, would be to recognize in one's fate an expression of a reality from which one could not dissociate oneself.

The opposition between finite and infinite spirit can therefore also be described as the opposition between the free man's need to affirm himself against fate, as expressed in Dylan Thomas' words: 'do not go gentle into that good night/Rage, rage against the dying of the light'; and the requirement to reconcile oneself with fate, so that in Nietzsche's words, we can 'change each "thus it was" into a "thus I would have it"'.[1]

These then are the oppositions which philosophy must overcome, between the knowing subject and his world, between nature and freedom, between individual and society, between finite and infinite spirit, or between free man and his fate. For philosophy to overcome them is of course for it to discern how the oppositions are overcome of themselves. And 'overcome' here does not mean simply 'undone'; there is no question of returning to the primitive consciousness before the separation of subject and nature. On the contrary the aspiration is to retain the fruits of separation, free rational consciousness, while reconciling this with unity, that is, with nature, society, God and fate.

But how can these oppositions be reconciled when each term only comes to be in its opposition to the other? For this is in fact our problem. Man only attains his self-conscious, rational autonomy in separating off from nature, society, God and fate. And Hegel sees this very clearly, which is why he repudiates any attempt simply to undo the oppositions and return to primitive unity.

[1] *Thus spake Zarathustra*, Everyman Edition, 126.

Hegel's answer is that each term in these basic dichotomies when thoroughly understood shows itself to be not only opposed to but identical with its opposite. And when we examine things more deeply we shall see that this is so because at base the very relations of opposition and identity are inseparably linked to each other. They cannot be utterly distinguished because neither can exist on its own, that is, maintain itself as the sole relation holding between a given pair of terms. Rather they are in a kind of circular relation. An opposition arises out of an earlier identity; and this of necessity: the identity could not sustain itself on its own, but had to breed opposition. And from this it follows that the opposition is not simply opposition, the relation of each term to its opposite is a peculiarly intimate one. It is not just related to *an* other but to *its* other, and this hidden identity will necessarily reassert itself in a recovery of unity.

That is why Hegel holds that the ordinary viewpoint of identity has to be abandoned in philosophy in favour of a way of thinking which can be called dialectical in that it presents us with something which cannot be grasped in a single proposition or series of propositions, which does not violate the principle of non-contradiction: $\sim (p.\sim p)$. The minimum cluster which can really do justice to reality is three propositions, that A is A, that A is also $\sim$A; and that $\sim$A shows itself to be after all A.

To grasp this truth of speculation is to see how free subjectivity overcomes its opposition to nature, society, God and Fate, Hegel claims. This is a rather staggering thesis. So much of moment to man seems to ride on what looks very much at first like verbal legerdemain. What does it mean to play fast and loose with 'identity' and 'opposition', 'identity' and 'difference'? What exactly does the thesis assert, and how does one back it up? Or are we just meant to take Hegel's word for it?

2

In order to see what Hegel is talking about here we have to understand his notion of *Geist,* or cosmic spirit. What seems bizarre in the abstract, when we talk of 'identity' and 'difference' *tout court,* may seem less so when we apply it to *Geist.* Now the basic model for infinite spirit is provided for the mature Hegel by the subject. We saw that earlier he tried to account for the reality which overcame separation in terms of Love, or Life. But in his mature view, the crucial term for understanding the Absolute is 'subject'.[1]

Before seeing how this term applies to *Geist* it is worth examining what Hegel's notion of subject was. And this is the more worthwhile in that his notion is important philosophically in its own right, that is, as a conception of the human subject which breaks with the dualism which had become dominant in philosophy since Descartes among both rationalists and empiricists. Hegel is in

---

[1] Cf. the preface to the *PhG,* p. 19.

fact one of the important links in a chain of thought in modern philosophical anthropology, one which is opposed to both dualism and mechanism, and which we see continued in different ways in Marxism and modern phenomenology.

Hegel's conception builds on the expressivist theory, which was developed by Herder and others. As we saw, this brought back Aristotelian categories in which we see the subject, man, as realizing a certain form; but it also added another dimension in that it looks on this realized form as the expression, in the sense of clarification, of what the subject is, something which could not be known in advance. It is the marriage of these two models, of Aristotelian form and modern expression, which enables us to speak here of *self*-realization.

Hegel's theory of the subject was a theory of self-realization. And as such it was radically anti-dualist. For this expressivist theory is opposed to the dualism of post-Cartesian philosophy (including empiricism), and that on both sides of its ancestry. This dualism saw the subject as a centre of consciousness, perceiving the outside world and itself; which centre was immaterial, that is, heterogeneous from the world of body, including the subject's own body. The 'spiritual' functions of thought, perception, understanding, etc., are attributed to this non-material being. And this 'mind' is sometimes thought of as perfectly self-transparent, that is, able to see clearly its own contents or 'ideas'; (this seems to have been Descartes' view).

Now, first, this view leaves no place for life as understood in the Aristotelian tradition, that is life as a self-organizing, self-maintaining form, which can only operate in and therefore is inseparable from its material embodiment. This kind of life disappears in dualism, since its whole nature is to straddle the gap dualism opens. It is material, and yet in the maintenance of form it exhibits the kind of purposiveness and even sometimes intelligence which we associate with mind. We feel tempted to think of living things as 'taking account' of their surrounding precisely because of the intelligent adaptation which they can make to novel situations.

Dualism on the other hand attributes all these functions of intelligence to a mind which is heterogeneous from body; so that matter is left as something which is to be understood purely mechanistically. In this way, Cartesian–empiricist dualism has an important link with mechanism. Descartes tended to give mechanistic explanations of physiology, and modern mechanistic psychology is closely affiliated historically to empiricism; it is dualism with one term suppressed.

But the modern temptation to dualism arises in a very different philosophical climate from Aristotle's. It is fed in part by a notion of the will which comes to us from Judaeo-Christian roots and is foreign to Greek thought; it grows with the modern idea of a self-defining subject which we discussed in the first chapter. In short it is bound up with the modern pre-occupations with pure rationality and radical freedom. And as we saw, Hegel has no desire to sweep these aside and return to an earlier phase.

And it is in fact when we focus on pure thought, on the reflective activity of the mind when it is pondering some problem in science or mathematics, when it is deliberating on some principle of morals, that the mind seems to be freest from external control – in a way it does not appear to be, for instance, in our emotional life. It is in this realm that the thesis of dualism seems to be most plausible. While I might hesitate to locate my rage at the enemy, which I can 'feel' in my body, in some disembodied haven, where else can I place my purely inner reflections on a problem in logic, or a question of moral conduct?

This is where the other aspect of expressive theory becomes relevant. We saw in the first chapter how Herder developed an expression theory of language along with, and indeed, as an essential part of the expression theory of man. On this theory words have meaning not simply because they come to be used to point or refer to certain things in the world or in the mind, but more fundamentally, because they express or embody a certain kind of consciousness of ourselves and things, peculiar to man as a language-user, for which Herder used the word '*Besonnenheit*'. Language is seen not just as a set of signs, but as the medium of expression of a certain way of seeing and experiencing; as such it is continuous with art. Hence there can be no thought without language; and indeed, the languages of different peoples reflect their different visions of things.

Hence this theory of expression is also anti-dualist. There is no thought without language, art, gesture, or some external medium. And thought is inseparable from its medium, not just in the sense that the former could not be without the latter, but also in that thought is shaped by its medium. That is, what from one point of view might be described as the same thoughts are altered, given a new twist, in being expressed in a new medium, for instance, translated from one language to another. To put the point in another way, we cannot clearly distinguish the content of a thought from what is 'added' by the medium.

Thus where the Aristotelian conception of the relation of matter and form, or hylomorphism, as it has been called, gives a notion of living beings in which soul is inseparable from body, so this theory of expression gives us a view of thinking beings in which thought is inseparable from its medium. And hence it takes just those functions, of pure thought, reflection, deliberation, which one would be most tempted to attribute to a disembodied mind, and reclaims them for embodied existence as necessarily couched in an external medium.

Thus expressivist theory as a marriage of hylomorphism and the new view of expression is radically anti-dualistic. And so was Hegel's theory of the subject. It was a basic principle of Hegel's thought that the subject, and all his functions, however 'spiritual', were inescapably embodied; and this in two related dimensions: as a 'rational animal', that is, a living being who thinks; and as an expressive being, that is, a being whose thinking always and necessarily expresses itself in a medium.

This principle of necessary embodiment, as we may call it, is central to Hegel's conception of *Geist*, or cosmic spirit. But before we go on to look at this notion of *Geist*, let us see how this expressivist theory of the subject already gives us some basis for speaking of a unity of identity and opposition.

We can see that Hegel's expressive theory does not see the hiatus between life and consciousness which we find in Cartesian–empiricist dualism. For the latter, the vital functions are relegated to the world of extended, material being, and are to be understood mechanistically; while the functions of mind belong to a separate, non-material entity. Hence Descartes could look on animals as complicated machines. But for any follower of Aristotle, this kind of dichotomy is untenable. For a living thing is a functioning unity and not just a concatenation of parts. More, in maintaining a certain form through changing conditions it shows a sort of proto-purpose, and even a sort of proto-intelligence in adapting to novel circumstances, akin to what self-conscious beings show in explicit form in their striving for goals and their ability to take account of self and surroundings in doing so. The living thing is, in other words, not just a functioning unity, but also something in the nature of an agent; and this places it in a line of development which reaches its apex in the human subject.

In this way Hegel restored the sense of the continuity of living things which was damaged by Cartesianism. But there is not just continuity between ourselves and animals, but also within ourselves between vital and mental functions, life and consciousness. On an expressivist view these cannot be separated out and attributed to two parts, or faculties, in man. Hegel agrees with Herder, that we can never understand man as an animal with rationality added; on the contrary, he is a quite different kind of totality, in which the fact of reflective consciousness leaves nothing else unaltered; the feelings, desires, even the instinct for self-preservation of a reflective being must be different from those of other animals, not to speak of his bearing, bodily structure, the ills he is subject to, and so on. There is no other way of looking at things for whoever sees living beings as totalities, i.e., entities in which each part is what it is only in relation to others and to the whole. And both Aristotelian hylomorphism and the theory of expression makes us look on them as totalities.

This view thus holds not only to a continuity of living things, but also to qualitative discontinuities. Man as a living being is not radically different from other animals, but at the same time he is not just an animal plus reason, he is a quite new totality; and that means he has to be understood on quite different principles.[1] Hence along with the idea of continuity we have that of a hierarchy of levels of being. We can speak of a hierarchy here and not just different types, because the 'higher' ones can be seen as realizing to a greater degree what the lower ones embody imperfectly.

Hegel holds to such a hierarchy of being which reaches its apex is conscious subjectivity. Lower kinds of life exhibit proto-forms as it were of subjectivity; for they show in ascending degree purpose, self-maintenance as life-forms, knowledge of what surrounds them. They become in short more and more like agents, and with the highest animals only want the power of expression to be selves. Hegel extends this hierarchy, as we shall see later, beyond living beings to the whole of creation. We can see a hierarchy among inanimate phenomena which points to the higher stage of life, just as animals point beyond to human subjectivity. Thus just as the living is a proto-form of consciousness, so the unity of, say, the solar system is to be seen as a proto-form of the living.

So far, Hegel's theory is not very different from that of other expressivist thinkers, Herder for instance. But he also builds into it a contribution from Kantian idealism. Consciousness is not only continuous/discontinuous with life in the way described; it also in a sense 'negates' life. For man as a conscious, knowing, rational being aims as we saw at a clarity and self-sufficiency of rational thought which he only attains by separating himself from nature, not only without but also within. Hence he is induced to separate rational thought, to insulate it as it were, from his desires, leanings, affinities; to try to free it as much as possible from the unconscious drift of inclination. Rational consciousness has a vocation to divide man, to oppose itself to life, and it is this of course which finds expression, inter alia, in the theory of Cartesian dualism.

Man is thus inescapably at odds with himself. He is a rational animal, which means a living thinking being; and he can only be a thinking being because he is alive. And yet the exigencies of thinking carry him into opposition to life, to the spontaneous and natural in him; so that he is led to divide himself, to create a distinction and a discord within himself where originally there was unity.

Developed rationality and hence discord is not something man starts with, but something he comes to. And this means two things: first beyond the hierarchy of forms of life, there is a hierarchy of modes of thought. As man's

---

[1] This notion of a hierarchy of forms is the negation of reductivist explanation, which looks forward to being able to account for the higher functions of organisms with the same explanatory concepts and principles by which one accounts for the lower ones, and indeed, would extend this homogeneity of explanation downwards to the inanimate.

If anything a theory like Hegel's is the exact inverse of a reductivist theory. For to the extent that one level illuminates others, it is the higher which casts light on the lower, being a fuller realization of what the lower is aiming at. But we cannot take this too far, for the lower cannot be accounted for by the principles of the higher which are richer and more complex. They are related to the higher by impoverishment. Hence they are different kinds of entity, and not just applications of the same basic principles, as on the reductive hypothesis.

rational consciousness of himself grows, so his mode of expression of this self-consciousness must alter. His language, art, religion and philosophy must change; for thought cannot alter without a transformation of its medium. Thus there must be a hierarchy of modes of expression in which the higher make possible a more exact, lucid and coherent thought than the lower.

The concept of a hierarchy of this kind plays an important role in Hegel's thought. It is best known in connection with the distinction between art, religion and philosophy. These are vehicles for understanding spirit, but they are of unequal rank. In a sense we express the same truths in these three modes, only at different levels of adequacy; which is like the other kind of hierarchy where the lower levels contain proto-forms of the higher, that is, they exhibit an impoverished version of the same kind of unity.

Secondly, that rationality is something man achieves rather than starts with, means that man has a history. In order to come to clarity man has to work his way with effort and struggle through the various stages of lesser, more distorted consciousness. He starts as a primitive being and has to acquire culture and understanding painfully and slowly. And this is not an accidental misfortune. For thought or reason can only exist embodied in a living being, as we have seen. But the processes of life itself are unconscious and dominated by unreflecting impulse. To realize the potential of conscious life therefore requires effort, internal division and transformation over time. We can thus see that this transformation over time involves more than the ascent up a hierarchy of modes of consciousness. It requires also that man struggle with impulse and give a shape to his life which moulds impulse into a culture which can express the demands of rationality and freedom. Human history is thus also the ascent up a ladder of cultural forms.

Perhaps we can now cast some light on the puzzling claims made at the end of the last section, that identity and opposition are linked, that they can hold of the same pair of terms. Hegel's notion of the subject begins to make sense of this.

The thinking rational subject can only exist embodied. In this sense we can truly say that the subject *is* his embodiment, that, e.g., I as a thinking being am my living body. And yet at the same time this embodiment in life has a tendency to carry us along the stream of inclination, of impulse towards unreflecting unity within ourselves and with nature. Reason has to struggle against this in order to realize itself. And in this sense his embodiment is not only other than the thinking rational subject, but in a sense his opposite, his limit, his opponent.

Thus we can say that the subject is both identical with and opposed to his embodiment. This can be because the subject is not defined by Hegel in one dimension, as it were, as a being with certain properties, but in two. He has certain conditions of existence, those of embodiment; but at the same time, the subject is characterized teleologically, as tending towards a certain perfection, that of reason and freedom, this in line with both Aristotle and expressivist theory. And the demands of this perfection run counter, at least at first, to his conditions of existence.

It is this inner complexity which makes possible its double relation to its self/other. In order to be at all as a conscious being, the subject must be embodied in life; but in order to realize the perfection of consciousness it must fight and overcome the natural bent of life as a limit. The conditions of its existence are in conflict with the demands of its perfection; and yet for it to exist is to seek perfection. The subject is thus necessarily the sphere of inner conflict, may we say, of contradiction? Hegel did not hesitate.

Thus both relations, identity and opposition can be said to hold together. But since one is founded on the unchanging conditions of existence, while the other comes from the requirements of the subject's realization which it achieves over time, we can think of the two relations as linked in a temporal pattern. Primitive identity must give way to division which inevitably arises since the subject cannot but contain the seed of division within himself.

But how about the third stage in this temporal pattern, the reconciliation? I said at the end of the last section that Hegel held that opposition fully understood shows the recovery of unity. And this too can be seen in Hegel's theory of the subject. Man does not remain forever at the stage of opposition between thought and life, reason and nature. On the contrary, both terms are made over to come to higher unity. Raw nature, the life of impulse, is made over, cultivated, so as to reflect the higher aspirations of man, to be an expression of reason. And reason, on its side, ceases to identify itself narrowly with a supposedly higher self fighting to hold nature at bay. On the contrary, it sees that nature itself is part of a rational plan, that division had to be in order to prepare and cultivate man for a higher union. The rational subject identifies himself with this larger reason, the rational plan underlying the whole, and as such no longer sees himself as opposed to a nature which has itself been made over to be an apt expression of rationality.

Human history thus does not end with division. It moves beyond it to a still higher cultural form, in which our nature, that is, our individual and collective life in interchange with our surroundings, expresses a larger rational plan than that of the autonomous individual; and to a still higher mode of consciousness in which we come to see this larger plan and identify with it. Hegel reserves the term 'reason' (*Vernunft*) for this higher mode, and calls the vision of things as divided or opposed 'understanding' (*Verstand*).

This unity is very different from the undifferentiated one of the beginning. It is 'mediated'; it preserves the consciousness of division which was a necessary stage in the cultivation of nature and the development of reason. It is fully conscious, and (supposedly) quintessentially rational.

Self-positing Spirit

Thus the human subject models Hegel's thesis of the relation of identity and opposition. Not only is he both identical and opposed to his essential embodiment; but this dual relation can be expressed in a temporal pattern: out of original identity, opposition necessarily grows; and this opposition itself leads to a higher unity, which is founded on a recognition of the inevitability and rational necessity of this opposition.

3

But how does this theory of man justify such startling formulae as the 'identity of identity and non-identity'? Even if we grant that Hegel's theory of the subject gives us insight into an inescapable conflict in man, which we might be tempted to call a 'contradiction', how does this justify talking about a link between identity and opposition tout court?

The answer is that this theory of the subject applies not only to man, but to cosmic spirit, or *Geist* as well. And indeed, we already saw at the end of the last section that the resolution of opposition in man required that we refer beyond him to a larger rational plan, which is that of *Geist*.

We saw that for Hegel, the absolute is subject. That which underlies and manifests itself in all reality, what for Spinoza was 'substance', and came for those inspired by the *Sturm und Drang* to be seen as a divine life flowing through everything, Hegel understood as spirit. But spirit or subjectivity is necessarily embodied. Hence *Geist* or God cannot exist separately from the universe which he sustains and in which he manifests himself. On the contrary this universe is his embodiment, without which he would not be, any more than I would be without mine. We can already see why Hegel had to suffer accusations of Spinozism or pantheism. And in this he was in the company of many other thinkers of the period who had been influenced by the *Sturm und Drang* or Romantic thought. In order to appreciate his reply, we have to examine more closely his conception of *Geist*, which was indeed peculiar to him.

We saw that there are two models of embodiment which come together in the expressivist theory of the subject on which Hegel built. One was the Aristotelian-derived notion of a life-form which can only be in a living body. The other is that of the expression of thought which requires a medium. They come together in the notion of a mode of life which properly expresses what I am as a man, or more appropriately from an expressivist point of view, as *this* man, member of *this* community. The mode of living is both a way of carrying out the necessary functions of life, nourishment, reproduction, and so on, and also a cultural expression which reveals and determines what we are, our 'identity'. The marriage relation of a couple, the mode of economic production of a society, can – from an expressivist point of view, must – be seen in these two dimensions. They are modes of interchange which sustain life and reproduction. But they also incorporate definitions of role, of value, of aspiration, success and failure, fairness, and so on. And there could not be anything which we would recognize as a human marriage, or mode of production, which did not incorporate such definitions. Or to put it another way, these relations would be impossible without language.

But although these two dimensions of embodiment are necessary to understand man, they do not overlap totally. There are aspects of man which we must understand simply as life-function, and not cultural expression, his digestion for instance; and we can argue, at any rate, that there are cultural expressions which can be understood without relating them to life-functions (though Marxists and Freudians would disagree). And these have to be set alongside marriage customs or modes of production which must be understood as both.

With *Geist*, however, the two coincide perfectly. The universe is the embodiment of the totality of the 'life-functions' of God, that is, the conditions of his existence. And it also is throughout an expression of God, that is, something posited by God in order to manifest what he is. The universe must therefore both be grasped as something analogous to a life-form, hence understood by the Aristotelian-derived category of 'internal teleology'; and be read as something analogous to a text in which God says what he is.

This perfect coincidence in God of life and expression is what marks him off as infinite spirit from ourselves as finite spirits. We must see the universe as the conditions of existence of God, and also as posited as such. God can be thought of as positing the conditions of his own existence. In this sense the universe can be looked at as if it were designed, as long as we take care to set aside the image of a designer who could exist separately from his creation. The universe has, we might say, a necessary structure. Before we go on to look at this difficult notion of a designed universe without an independent designer, let us see the shape of this necessary structure.

If the universe is posited as the conditions of existence of God or *Geist*, then we can deduce its general structure from the nature of *Geist*. Now *Geist*, or subjectivity, as we saw, is to be understood teleologically as tending to realize reason and freedom and self-consciousness, or rational self-awareness in freedom. We can see how these three terms are linked together in an expressivist theory of the subject. Rational self-awareness is rational awareness of a self which has been expressed in life and thus made determinate. The fullness of self-awareness is reached when this expression is recognized as adequate to the self. If it is not, if it is seen as truncated or distorted and requiring further change, then the self-awareness is not complete, however lucid the perception of inadequacy, for on the expressivist view, what we really are is not known in advance of its expression. The truncated being can only go on to a fuller expression in order then to recognize what he really is.

Self-positing Spirit

But freedom, on the expressivist view, is the condition in which the self is adequately expressed. Hence full self-awareness is impossible without freedom. If we add to this the notion that self-awareness is of the essence of the subject, then the converse proposition is also true: freedom (that is, full self-expression) is impossible without self-awareness. Now Hegel would add to this common basis of expressivist theory, the thesis that the essence of subjectivity is *rational* self-awareness, that self-consciousness must be in the clear medium of conceptual thought and not in cloudy intuition or ineffable vision. Hence rationality, too, is for him a condition of integral expression or freedom, and reciprocally.

Now let us transfer this from man onto *Geist*, and see what it shows us about the necessary structures of the world. If *Geist* as subject is to come to rational self-awareness in freedom, then the universe must contain, first, finite spirits. Geist must be embodied. But bodily reality is external reality, it is partes extra partes, extended in space and time. Hence for consciousness to be it must be located, it must be somewhere, sometime. But if a consciousness is somewhere, sometime, it is not somewhere else, sometime else. It thus has a limit between itself and what is not itself. It is finite.

We can thus show the necessity of finite spirit from the requirement that *Geist* be embodied, and from the nature of embodiment in external, spatio-temporal reality. But there is also another argument, which Hegel frequently employs, from the requirements of consciousness itself. Hegel took over the notion from Kant and Fichte that consciousness is necessarily bi-polar, i.e., that it requires the distinction of subject and object. This plays an important role in Kant's transcendental deduction, which in one form turns on the requirement of objectivity, that is, that there be a distinction between phenomena which are bound together merely in my experience and those which are bound together universally and necessarily. The extraordinary achievement of Kant's first *Critique* is to rehabilitate this distinction between subjective and objective *within* experience considered as distinct from things in themselves. This necessity of an objective pole to experience also underlies Kant's refutation of idealism.

Fichte took up the same principle. The Ego posits the non-Ego because this is the condition of consciousness. Hegel makes this principle his own, and it is part of his general espousal of the view that rational awareness requires separation. Consciousness is only possible when the subject is set over against an object. But to be set over against an object is to be limited by something other, and hence to be finite. It follows that if cosmic spirit is to attain full awareness, it can only be through vehicles which are finite spirits. Hence finite, limited subjects are necessary. The notion of a cosmic spirit which would be aware of itself directly, without the opposition to an object which is the predicament of finite subjects, is incoherent. The life of such a spirit would at best be one of dull self-feeling, there would be nothing in it which merited the name 'consciousness', much less 'rational awareness'. A fitting pantheist vision for the Romantic enthusiasts of intuition, but nothing to do with Hegel's *Geist*. *Geist* is thus necessarily embodied in finite spirits. This is the same in the context of this argument as the thesis that *Geist* returns to himself out of opposition and division; or that his self-consciousness incorporates consciousness. And Hegel frequently does use the word 'consciousness' to refer to this bi-polar dimension in the life of *Geist*.[1] And he will reject any theory of man which tries to avoid this bi-polarity, any theory of consciousness as culminating in self-coincidence.[2]

Thus *Geist* must have a vehicle in finite spirit. This is the only kind of vehicle it can have. Moreover, there cannot be only one such. For *Geist* cannot be confined to the particular place and time of any one finite spirit. It has to compensate for its necessary localization, as it were, by living through many finite spirits.

Geist must thus embody itself in finite beings, in certain parcels of the universe. And these must be such that they can embody spirit. They must be living beings, for only living beings are capable of expressive activity, of deploying an external medium, of sound, gesture, marks, or whatever, in which meaning can be expressed; and only beings capable of expressive activity can embody spirit. Hence we can see that if *Geist* is to be, the universe must contain rational animals, ourselves.

There are finite spirits, who must be living beings, hence finite living beings. Finite living beings are in interchange with a world outside them. Thus the universe must also contain a plurality of kinds of living things, as well as inanimate nature. Other species and inanimate nature are necessary as the background and foundation on which finite life can exist. But one can perhaps discern another argument in Hegel in favour of the necessary existence of many species and inanimate nature. *Geist* to be embodied requires, as we saw, externality, that is, extension in space and time; life; and conscious life. All of these, of course, exist in man. But a universe in which only finite conscious spirits existed, and lived purely in interchange with each other, would not be anything like as rich and varied as one in which life also existed on its own without consciousness, and externality was there on its own without both in the form of inanimate nature. The richest universe is one in which all these levels (and others, which Hegel distinguishes within inanimate nature in his philosophy of nature) exist on their own.

It may seem odd to see this Leibnizian principle, that the real world be the richest possible, recur in Hegel. But in fact it can be grounded on his own

---

[1] As, for instance, in the divisions of the *PhG*.

[2] Or as he puts it, the notion that I = I, a formulation which shows the Fichtean background of his reflections on this subject.

position. The universe, as we saw, is at once the embodiment, i.e., realization of the conditions of existence of *Geist*, and its expression, a statement of what *Geist* is. In this latter respect, there is no doubt about the superiority of a world in which the differences are maximally deployed. It is fuller, clearer as a statement.[1]

The general structure of the universe (about which only the barest indications have been given here, the detail is worked out in the philosophies of nature and spirit) is thus determined by virtue of its being the embodiment and expression of *Geist*. It includes a hierarchy of beings from the lowest inanimate forms through various kinds of living species to man. And then, of course, for the realization of *Geist*, man has to develop, as we saw in the last section. So that there is also a hierarchy of cultural forms and modes of consciousness which succeed each other in time and make up human history. The articulation of the universe in space and time can be deduced from the requirements of a cosmic spirit which must be embodied and expressed in it. Even the different stages of human history can be derived as necessary, from the nature of man's starting point in raw, uncultivated existence and the consummation he is heading towards.[2]

What is it then for *Geist* to come to rational self-awareness in freedom? If the structure of the universe is as it is in order to be the embodiment/expression of *Geist*, then *Geist* comes to self-awareness when this is recognized. Of course, this can only be recognized by ourselves, finite spirits, for we are the only vehicles of awareness. But in recognizing that this is the structure of things we at the same time shift the centre of gravity of our own identity. We see that what is most fundamental about us is that we are vehicles of *Geist*. Hence in achieving full insight our science of the universe is transformed; from being knowledge that we as finite spirits have about a world which is other than us it becomes the self-knowledge of universal spirit of which we are the vehicles.

[1] Cf. Hegel's assertion about the external articulation of the universe at the very end of the *Logic*, the point of transition to the philosophy of nature. The Idea, as freedom, also leaves its embodiment 'free'. It is not embodied in an external reality which it controls tightly but which is left to develop to the full limit of externality, right up to 'the exteriority of space and time, existing absolutely for itself without subjectivity' (*WL*, II, 505).

[2] Hegel missed a trick in not espousing a theory of evolution a half century before Darwin. Instead he holds that while human culture has a sequential development, the whole order of things in nature, including animal species, does not. The linked ascending order of things in nature is to be understood not temporally as with historical forms, but timelessly. Hegel's reason for making this distinction, that only spirit can have a history, sounds 'Hegelian' enough. But in fact he could have found grounds for accepting a theory of evolution if he had believed it to be true on other grounds. Indeed, it fits if anything better, in that all transitions in the philosophy of nature could have been temporal as well. This is another example of how Hegel's philosophy of nature was dependent on (his understanding of) the science of his time as well as other writers in the same field like Schelling; while his philosophies of man and history struck out beyond all contemporaries.

The Claims of Speculative Reason

And in coming to full self-awareness, *Geist*, has also come to its fullest self-expression, hence freedom. It has shaped its vehicle to a perfect expression of itself. And since the essence of that vehicle, man, is to be the vehicle of *Geist*, he too is and knows himself as fully self-expressed, i.e., free.

But the self-expression and -awareness of *Geist* is something infinitely higher than our own. When man comes to full awareness of his perfect self-expression, he recognizes in this something which is ultimately given. Human nature, what is common to all men, is there as a basis or determinable which circumscribes the field for every man's original creation. And even my original creations, the things in my life that seem to express me as against man in general, even these seem to come to me as inspiration which I cannot fully fathom much less control. That is why, as we saw, not all of human life can be seen as expression; but much of what we do and what goes on in us must be understood purely in terms of our life-form, just as we do with animals with no power of expression. And even our expressive activity is conditioned by this life-form.

With *Geist* it is meant to be different. Its whole embodiment is supposed to be an expression of it as well. The universe, as this embodiment, is thought to be posited by *Geist*. *Geist* posits its own embodiment. Hence there can be nothing merely given. I as a human being have the vocation of realizing a nature which is given: and even if I am called on to be original, to realize myself in the way uniquely suited to myself, nevertheless this scope for originality is itself given as an integral part of human nature, as are those unique features of me on which my originality builds. Freedom for man thus means the free realization of a vocation which is largely given. But *Geist* should be free in a radical sense. What it realizes and recognizes as having been realized is not given, but determined by itself.

Hegel's *Geist* thus seems to be the original existentialist, choosing his own nature in radical freedom from anything merely given. And in fact, Hegel laid the conceptual groundwork for all the modern views called 'existentialist', from Kierkegaard to Sartre. But Hegel himself was no existentialist. On the contrary, it is hard to see how Hegel's *Geist* could ever have begun, how he ever could have chosen one world rather than another, if we were to understand his radical freedom in the existentialist sense. For he would not start with a situation as does the human agent.

But for Hegel the radical freedom of *Geist* is not incompatible with a necessary structure of things; on the contrary, the two notions are intrinsically linked. *Geist* in positing the world is bound by rational necessity, the necessary structure of things if *Geist* is to be. But this is no limit on his freedom. For *Geist* as subjectivity is quintessentially reason. And reason is most fully realized when one follows, in thought and action, the line of rational, i.e., conceptual necessity. If one had a line of action which was grounded entirely on rational, conceptual necessity, without reposing on any merely given premises, then we would have a pure expression of subjectivity as reason, one in which spirit would recognize itself as expressed, and hence free, in a total, unadulterated way; something immeasurably greater than the freedom of finite spirits. This is the freedom of *Geist*, which posits a world as its own essential embodiment according to rational necessity.

But there seems to be something amiss here. Now can there be a line of action which is founded *entirely* on rational necessity? Surely there must be some goal which is taken as the starting point, even if everything that is done is determined by strict reasoning from this basic aim. For otherwise how can reasoning by itself come to any conclusion as to what action to take? But then is this basic goal not simply given?

The answer is, in a sense, yes. But not in a sense which need negate the radical freedom of *Geist*. For *Geist* can be thought to have as its basic aim simply that spirit, or rational subjectivity, be; and the rest can be thought to follow of necessity. If the principle of embodiment, which has so far just been stated here without argument, could be shown to be necessarily true; if the arguments which I briefly sketched above from the principle of embodiment to the existence of finite spirits, living things, inanimate nature, etc., hold; then the design of the universe could be shown to flow of necessity from the single basic goal: that rational subjectivity be. We could show in other words, that if a subjectivity which knows itself rationally, i.e., in conceptual consciousness, is to be, then all this is necessary.

But then the only input into this skein of rational necessity would be the goal, let rational subjectivity be. Once this 'decision' is taken, the rest flows of itself. But it cannot be thought of as a limitation on the freedom of *Geist* that this 'decision' is preformed. That subjectivity should be is not a limit on its freedom, but the very basis of it; and that it should be rational, i.e., expressed in conceptual consciousness, is thought by Hegel to belong to the very essence of subjectivity. For what do we mean by subjectivity if we do not include consciousness, self-consciousness and the power to act knowingly? But consciousness, knowledge, can only reach completion in conceptual thought.

Hence once we start with the basic goal, that rational subjectivity be, which is no limit on the freedom of *Geist*, the fact that from then on *Geist's* 'activity' in positing the world follows entirely the line of rational necessity is not a restriction on his freedom. Quite the contrary, it is just that which makes him radically free, in an unlimited, i.e., infinite, way. Because as a rational subjectivity he is following nothing but his own essence in following rational necessity. There is no outside element, no given which determines him. If the basic structure of the world were shown to be contingent,[1] then something else other than rational necessity, that is, the very essence of rational subjectivity, would have determined it to be A rather than B. But then it would not be integrally an expression of the essence of this subjectivity and he would not be infinitely free.

But because everything that is flows by rational necessity out of the first 'decision', we cannot really say that *Geist* is faced with any givens. We can see this by contrasting his lot once more with ours. Man has a nature which is given; it is a fact about the world, along with a great number of others, that we have sexual desire all the time and not periodically like animals, that we can only live within certain temperature ranges, etc. Freedom for us involves assuming this nature and innovating within the range of originality it allows. But for *Geist* nothing is given in this sense, i.e., as a brute fact. The only starting point is the *requirement* that subjectivity be; and the only 'positive' content attached to this subjectivity is that of rationality, and this belongs to its very essence.

For the rest, the whole structure of the world as it exists in fact is generated from this requirement by rational necessity.

We must avoid a misunderstanding which can all too easily arise here. Hegel is not saying that everything that exists and happens comes of necessity. He means to argue that the basic structure of things, the chain of levels of beings, the general shape of world history: these are manifestations of necessity. But within this structure, there is not only room for contingency, but contingency, as it were, necessarily exists. For we have seen that all levels of being exist independently; but one of the distinguishing marks of the lower levels is that they only imperfectly manifest the necessity underlying things, they show it only in a rough external way; there is much in them which is purely contingent. So that many of the properties of matter, e.g. the exact number of species of parrot, cannot be deduced from the concept of the world. (*WL*, ii, 462).[2] Only in the higher realizations of human culture is necessity fully manifest and all manifestation a reflection of necessity.

But this play of interstitial contingency, as it were, does not introduce an element of the simply given, which Geist has not derived from himself. On the contrary, contingency and its place in the universe is itself derived by necessity from the requirements of absolute subjectivity.

[1] We must stress here that it is a matter of the basic structure; Hegel does not hold that the world has no contingency in detail, as it were. On the contrary, there is contingency, and also must be of necessity, according to the structure of things! We shall see this below.

[2] Cf. also *PhG*, 193–5.

4

What is the nature of this rational necessity? Earlier, I used the expression 'conceptual' as equivalent to 'rational' in talking of 'conceptual consciousness' or 'necessity'. This equivalence is important in Hegel but it could easily lead to misunderstanding in the context of contemporary anglo-saxon philosophy. We have developed a notion of conceptual necessity from empiricist and positivist roots, which is by no means the only conception current in English philosophy today – it may even be receding – but it is well-known enough to mislead. This is the notion of conceptual necessity as opposed to contingent, causal necessity, and as reposing on the meanings of words. Certain statements were necessary and others contradictory because they combined words in such a way that they could not but be true or could not but be false in virtue of their meaning. Analytic statements were thought to be true statements of this type; but for those who have doubts about analyticity, logical truths (e.g. 'horses are horses') could stand as examples.

The idea was that these necessary truths held in virtue of the meanings of words as opposed to facts about the world. The meaning of a word was the semantic and syntactical force attributed to a sign. This could of course be changed, and with certain changes, some formerly necessary truths would cease to hold. 'Bachelors are unmarried' holds now, but not if we decided to use the word 'bachelor' to designate people who were not married in church, even though they were civilly married. In all this, nothing need have changed in the world.

This was of course not Hegel's idea of conceptual necessity. We can see this if we look for example at the argument described above, where the aim was to show that such and such structural conditions were necessary for embodied *Geist*, and see what parallels will illuminate it. Like many arguments it can of course be set up in deductive form, but this does not reveal its real structure. This is rather akin to Kant's transcendental deduction. Like Kant, we start with a given – in Kant's case, experience; here, the existence of *Geist* – and argue back to its necessary conditions. But as with Kant's transcendental arguments the necessary conditions are not derived by simple deduction from the terms used in the starting point; nor of course by examining causal relations.

Thus Kant starts from the fact of experience, moves then to the point that we could not have experience of the world unless we had a place for the distinction between what is objectively so and what is only so for us; and then goes on to show how we could not have this distinction unless the categories hold. But the steps of this argument are neither simply deductive nor based on causal reasoning. That experience requires the distinction 'objectively/for us' is not something we derive from the concept of experience, as we derive 'unmarried' from 'bachelor'. The derivation is not analytic in Kant's sense. Of course we could *decide* that we would take 'experience' as incorporating this in its meaning, and turn this argument into an analytic derivation. But this would be to miss the important point about it: that the necessity doesn't repose on the analytic relation, but on something else: that we are here at a conceptual limit, such that we could not form a coherent notion of experience which did not incorporate this distinction. The whole structure of experience as by a subject and of something would collapse. This is fundamentally unlike the 'bachelor, therefore unmarried' case, in that we could tamper with our concept of bachelor, as we saw above, so that the inference would fail. But the transcendental argument claims that no-one can tamper with 'experience' in the relevant way, and go on saying something coherent.

Hegel's argument of the kind we described above, e.g., that *Geist* cannot be without finite spirits, is something of this type. A crucial step here is that *Geist* embodied must be placed somewhere, and hence limited, finite. But this is not derived analytically from 'embodied'. On the contrary it appeals to another kind of conceptual limit whereby we could make no coherent sense of 'embodied but nowhere in particular'.

And yet in both these cases, it is not out of order to speak of 'conceptual necessity'. For it is clear that we are not dealing here with causal impossibilities, but with a conceptual limit. To speak of 'conceptual' necessity stresses this.

Now a conceptual limit of this kind tells us about more than the meanings of terms; it also tells us about the structure of things. Though just what it says is very much open to dispute. It is possible to argue like Kant that it tells us something about the limits of our minds. But Hegel who holds that the world is posited by *Geist* according to rational necessity, i.e., necessity dictated by such conceptual limits, sees these rather as tracing the lineaments of the universe. A world constructed according to conceptual necessity is only adequately revealed in statements of conceptual necessity. In Hegel's terms, the structure of things is to be deduced from the Concept.[1]

If the world is posited out of conceptual necessity, and is only adequately understood in conceptually necessary thought, then the complete self-understanding of *Geist*, which is the same as our fully adequate understanding of the world, must be a vision of conceptual necessity, a kind of seamless garment of rationality.

Now this might be thought impossible, even by those who have followed us this far. Our vision of the world cannot just be one of rational necessity. For we saw that there had to be a starting point in the goal, that rational subjectivity be; and while this may involve no mitigation of the infinite freedom of *Geist*, it

---

[1] Hegel's dialectical arguments, as we shall see below, are of course more complex than the transcendental-type argument in the above example, although they incorporate this latter type. But they rely on the same kind of conceptual necessity.

surely must be seen as a basic premise, not itself established by reasoning, in our final vision of things.

But this is not how Hegel sees it. In the vision which *Geist* has of himself there is no absolute starting point; rather there is a circle. Thus we do not just *assume* as a starting point that *Geist* is to be, and derive the structure of the world from this. We have also to *prove* this proposition. And if we reflect a minute, we can see that this is necessary from more than one point of view. It is not just a matter of attaining to a seamless garment of necessity, but of being able to prove that our thesis is valid.

For it is not enough to show that if *Geist* is to be, the world must have the design which it in fact has, if we want to conclude that this world is posited by *Geist* as its embodiment. The fact that things are arranged as if by design is never enough to prove a designer and hence a designing. The best we could arrive at here would be high probability, and we are concerned with necessity. What more is needed is that we are able in examining this world to show that it is in fact posited by *Geist*.

This Hegel claims to do; indeed, it is the central thread of his major works. He claims to show that when we examine the furniture of the world, we must see that it cannot be except as an emanation from *Geist*. And we show this by dialectical argument. We come to see that the things in the world cannot exist on their own because they are contradictory. Hence we can only understand them as part of a greater or deeper reality on which they lean, or of which they are parts or aspects. The dialectic goes through several stages as we climb successively beyond the unsatisfactory notions of what this self-subsistent or absolute reality could be; until we come to the only satisfactory conception of it as *Geist*, a spiritual reality which perpetually posits the world as its necessary embodiment, and perpetually negates it as well in order to return to itself.

We shall examine dialectical argument below. For the moment it might be helpful to say this, that the argument from contradiction takes hold because of some inner complexity in the reality concerned, so that there can be a conflict between what it is and what it is meant to be. Part of the great ingenuity of Hegel's argument will be to find this kind of complexity in any and every starting point, no matter how apparently simple and impoverished. We shall see a number of examples later on, but we have already seen this kind of conflict in the Hegelian view of the subject, which is in opposition or 'contradiction' with himself because the conditions of his existence clash with his telos.

Thus starting from finite reality, Hegel claims to be able to demonstrate the existence of a cosmic spirit who posits the world according to rational necessity. This, if it stuck, would certainly plug the gap in his proof in that we would no longer be relying on a probabilistic 'argument from design'. But would it bring us any closer to a vision of things based throughout on rational necessity? Surely, we have just displaced our underived starting point. From the existence of *Geist*, which posits the world in order to be, we have moved it back to the existence of some finite thing from which we can come to *Geist* by dialectical argument. But we still have to take this finite thing as given in order to get things started.

But on Hegel's view this starting point is not an ultimate one either. For as we saw, the existence of this finite reality can itself be demonstrated. Does this mean that in proof we are forced to an endless regress? This would certainly not meet our goal of a totally rational vision, because although there is nowhere we would have to stop, we would have to stop somewhere with an underived premise.

But in fact we avoid the endless regress by a circle. We show in our ascending dialectic that finite reality can only be as an emanation of *Giest*, hence that given finite reality, self-positing *Geist* must be. But then we can also demonstrate, as outlined above, that a self-positing *Geist*, that is a cosmic spirit who lays down the conditions of his own existence, must posit the structure of finite things we know. In these two movements, ascending and descending (which are in fact interwoven in Hegel's exposition), our argument returns to its starting point. The existence of finite reality which originally we just took as given is now shown to be necessary. Originally just a datum, it is now swept up in the circle of necessity.

But is this any solution? we might ask. Is not a circle the paradigm of invalid argument? But this reaction is misplaced. The Hegelian circle of necessity has nothing to do with circular argument. We speak of arguing in a circle when conclusions appear in the premises which are essential to derive them. The circle is vicious because the point of the argument is to establish a conclusion by showing it follows from something which is easier to establish directly, or which is already known. Thus when we find that the conclusion only follows if we supplement the premiss with the conclusion itself, we see that the whole enterprise has gone astray, for we are no nearer to establishing this conclusion via its links with another, more accessible truth.

Now Hegel's arguments are not circular in this way; or if they are it is not at all because of the Hegelian circle of argument. The necessity of self-positing *Geist* follows from the existence of finite things in the dialectic without our having to assume *Geist*, or at least purports to do so. And the necessity of finite things flows from the requirements of *Geist* without our assuming finitude. What we have might rather be seen as two non-circular series of arguments which establish each other's starting point, or take in each other's washing.

But in fact even this is not quite right. For the two series of arguments are not really similar and the circle does *not* precisely return to its starting point. We start the ascending dialectic from a finite reality. We close the circle by showing that this finite reality necessarily exists. 'Necessity' has a different meaning in the two phases.

In the ascending dialectic we are dealing with a necessity of inference. If finite things exist, then they are dependent on and posited by *Geist*. This is a hypothetical proposition. Symmetrical to this we might propound another hypothetical proposition to the effect that if cosmic subjectivity is to be, then the furniture of the world must be of a certain sort. But the Hegelian circle involves more than just putting these two together.

For what Hegel claims to show in the ascending movement is not just that granted finite existence, there must be *Geist*. He will show that this finite existence cannot be except as posited by cosmic spirit – a cosmic spirit whose nature is to posit its own essential embodiment. Hence the ascending movement shows us that finite reality is posited by a subject according to a necessary plan. What I have called the descending movement spells out this plan, the full conditions of cosmic spirit, which are thus instantiated in the world. The outcome of the whole circle is that finite reality is shown to be not just contingently given, but to be there in fulfilment of a plan, whose articulations are determined by rational necessity.

But now the notion of necessity has changed. We are not just dealing with a necessity of inference: if A, then B. In saying that what exists, exists in virtue of a rationally necessary plan, we are ascribing necessary existence to it. The necessity with which Hegel's argument concludes concerns the ground of existence of things. It is ontological necessity.

The very concept of ontological necessity may be attacked as incoherent, as Kant did in the Transcendental Dialectic. A final judgement on this would have to await our study of Hegel's detailed argument, particularly in the *Logic*. But there is no doubt that this concept is central to Hegel's conclusion. Hence the end of the Hegelian circle contains more than its starting point. We are not just dealing with two hypothetical arguments symmetrically joined. Rather we return and pick up a starting point initially just given and recuperate it for (ontological) necessity.

Our ascending movement thus starts with a postulate and proceeds by necessary inference. But what it infers to is ontological necessity, the proposition that everything which exists is posited by *Geist* according to a formula of rational necessity. The circle is thus not a single stream of inferences. Rather, it involves a reversal of starting point. We begin with the ascending movement which is a movement of discovery. Our starting point is finite existence which is first in the order of discovery. But what we reveal is a pervasive ontological necessity, and this shows that our original starting point is really secondary. Finite reality is itself posited by *Geist*, God, the Absolute. This is the real starting point in the order of being.

Hence we get beyond the problem of a contingent or merely given starting point by rising above it to a vision of ontological necessity which englobes it. We rise to a vision of seamless necessity, and from this vantage point we see that our original starting point, along with everything which is, is part of the same web. So that nothing is left outside, nothing is merely given; and *Geist* as wholly self-positing is truly free, truly infinite, in an absolute sense that has no parallel with finite spirits.

5

What kind of a notion is it, this Hegelian idea of a self-positing God? We saw this arise inescapably from our application of the Hegelian (and ultimately expressivist) idea of the subject to God: the subject who is necessarily embodied and whose embodiment is both the condition of his existence and the expression of what he is. With God as we saw, the expression is coterminous with the conditions of existence, unlike man, and what is expressed is something totally determined out of God as subject, no part of it is just given.

This idea of God is very hard to grasp and state coherently – if, indeed, it ultimately is coherent – because it cannot fit certain readily available categories in which we think of God and the world. Thus there are two clearly-defined and relatively comprehensible views which could be mistaken for Hegel's.

The first, which we could call theism, looks on the world as created by a God who is separate and independent of the universe. This makes the idea readily understandable that the world is to be seen as designed, as having a structure dictated by purpose. But this cannot be accepted by Hegel, for it violates the principle of embodiment. A God who could exist without the world, without any external embodiment is an impossibility.

Thus although Hegel takes up the notion of creation, as he takes up all Christian dogmas, he re-interprets it, and speaks of the creation as necessary. To say the world was created by God is to say that it exists necessarily so that *Geist* can be. It is to say the same thing as that *Geist* posits a world, and just what this means we shall try to make a little less obscure below. But what it cannot mean is what it means for orthodox theism, that God created the world freely, having no need to do so. Or as he put it in his notes for the lectures on the philosophy of religion 'Without the world God is not God.' (*B Rel* 148.)[1]

The other scheme by which we might try to understand what Hegel is saying is one we can call naturalist. Here we abandon all talk of creation, however interpreted. We think of the world as existing as a matter of fact, but having such properties that beings evolve on it which are vehicles of rational life, and moreover who come to see themselves as vehicles of a rational life which is larger than themselves, but rather that of the whole. This would avoid all

---

[1] 'ohne Welt ist Gott nicht Gott'.

danger of thinking of this rational life, or spirit of the whole, as a God separate from the world. But here too, we have a scheme unacceptable to Hegel, for the existence of such a universe would be ultimately a brute fact. True, it would happen to secrete a rational consciousness which could be called in some sense that of the whole (as for instance if the workings of the human mind reflected not just what is peculiar to man but also what he has in common with all other life, or even with all other beings – an idea which Freud, e.g., seems to have flirted with at one point). But this would be contingent good fortune. The universe would not be there *in order to* embody this rational consciousness. In recognizing the structure of things, this global mind would not be recognizing his own doing, something which was there in order to conform to rational necessity, and hence to his own nature as rational subject; rather he would be recognizing a given, even as we finite minds do when we contemplate our own nature. He would thus not be radically free and unconditioned. We could not speak of him as the Absolute.

Hegel can accept neither of these views. What he needs is some combination of the features of both. Like the theist view, he wants to see the world as designed, as existing in order to fulfil a certain prospectus, the requirements of embodiment for *Geist*. But like the naturalists, he cannot allow a God who could design this world from the outside, who could exist before and independently of the world. His idea is therefore that of a God who eternally makes the conditions of his own existence. This is what I have been trying to express, following frequent use by Hegel, with the term 'posit (*setzen*). This use of the term came in fact from Fichte, who attributed something like the same self-creation of necessary conditions to the ego.

In fact, following this parallel with Fichte, it might be best to express Hegel's idea in this way. Both of the schemes we have compared to Hegel's view repose ultimately on existential propositions: some basic reality exists, and from this everything else can be explained. In one case this is God, in the other, a world with certain features. But what is fundamental in Hegel's conception is not the existence of some reality, but rather a requirement, that *Geist* be. Consequently while both the other views ultimately reach ground in contingency, that of the existence of the world, or of the existence of God, or of his decision to create the world, Hegel's is meant to be grounded in thorough-going necessity. *Geist* not only is, but he has to be, and the conditions of his existence are dictated by this necessity.

There is something in Hegel's philosophy which is irresistibly reminiscent of Baron Münchhausen. The baron, it will be remembered, after falling from his horse in a swamp, extricated himself by seizing his own hair and heaving himself back on his horse. Hegel's God is a Münchhausen God; but it is hard to say in this difficult domain whether his exploits should be treated with the same scepticism as those of the baron.

The Claims of Speculative Reason

In any case, it is clear that Hegel is neither a theist in the ordinary sense, nor an atheist. Whatever the sincerity of his claims to be an orthodox Lutheran, it is clear that Hegel only accepted a Christianity which had been systematically reinterpreted to be a vehicle of his own philosophy. We will trace this in a later chapter. It is little wonder, though, that he was much misunderstood (or perhaps too well understood) in his time, and accused frequently of heterodox views; or that some of his followers could reinterpret him in the direction of orthodox theism. Hegel's position was in a sense on a narrow crest between theism and some form of naturalism or pantheism. The atmosphere was so rarified on top that it was easy to fall off, and remains so.

But how about the accusation of pantheism? This is neither a theist nor an atheist position, and seems at first sight to fit him rather well. Of course, Hegel stoutly denied the charge; cynics might attribute this to the bad effects on his employment prospects if it stuck, even as cynics have explained his protestations of Lutheranism by the impossibility of holding the chair in Berlin otherwise. But in both cases, they fail to do him justice. Hegel did use the term 'pantheist', to apply to a position which indiscriminately attributed divinity to finite things. In this sense Hegel was not a pantheist. The world isn't divine for him, nor is any part of it. God is rather the subject of the rational necessity which manifests itself in the world.

What distinguished Hegel's position from pantheism in his own mind was the rational necessity which, it is true, could not exist without the world as the ensemble of finite things, but which was in this sense superior to the world, that it determined its structure according to its own exigencies. Hegel's *Geist* is thus anything but a world soul, whose nature would be given just as ours is, however great and awe-inspiring. And it is this same insistence on rational necessity which distinguishes his view from that of certain romantics, whose notion of an unfathomable cosmic spirit, or an endless process of creation resembles that of a rationally impenetrable world-soul.

Hegel's theory has also been called by some 'panentheist' or 'emanationist', and likened in this regard to that of Plotinus. There certainly are affinities. And Hegel like the Greeks seems to be committed to something like an eternal universe, once we take seriously his reinterpretation of the dogma of creation. But here too there is no exact parallel. On an emanationist view, finite things arise from a falling away from the One. They emanate from him, perhaps inescapably, as in the famous image the sun's rays from the sun. But they in turn play no essential role in his life, they are not essential to the One as he is to them. For Hegel, however, finitude is a condition of the existence of infinite life. The relationship is not something which could have been thought out before the development of the expressivist theory. It has affinities with very ancient doctrines, but it is a thoroughly modern idea.

102

6

But how does this help us understand the general claims about the identity of identity and difference which Hegel makes? We started to examine Hegel's notion of the subject, in order to clarify this. And we got some indication of what is meant when we saw that the human subject was prey to an inner conflict, in which the conditions of his existence were at odds with his essential goal. And we saw briefly how this might be resolved through a shift to a higher perspective in which man sees himself as vehicle of *Geist* and not simply as finite spirit.

Now the same basic conflict affects the absolute subject. It too has conditions of existence which are at odds with its telos. For it must be embodied in external, finite realities, finite spirits living in a world of finite, material things. And yet its life is infinite and unbounded. Its vehicle is a finite spirit which at first has only the dimmest consciousness of himself and faces a world which is anything but immediately transparent, whose rational structure is deeply hidden. And yet its telos is clear rational knowledge of the rationally necessary. It is the unity of spirit and matter, thought and extension; and yet in the world thinking beings face external reality as something other.

Like finite subject, the absolute subject must go through a cycle, a drama, in which it suffers division in order to return to unity. It undergoes inner opposition, in order to overcome it, and rise through its vehicles to a consciousness of itself as rational necessity. And this drama is not another parallel story to the drama of opposition and reconciliation in man. It is the same one seen from a different and wider perspective. For man is the vehicle of *Geist's* spiritual life.

The two are related in this way, that the greatest opposition in the cosmic subject is the point of departure from which the opposition grows in man. And this opposition grows in man as he strives, albeit without clear knowledge of what he is doing, to overcome this primary opposition of subject and world. The primary opposition, the point of greatest opposition for *Geist* is its being embodied in a world at odds with itself where nothing has yet been done to cancel this opposition. This is the point which is at the beginning as far as men are concerned, where they are still sunk in nature, unconscious of their vocation, as far as possible from a true understanding of spirit. This is the point of primitive unity for man. But in order to play their role in overcoming the opposition of the world to *Geist,* men have to school themselves, become beings capable of reason, break away from a life sunk in nature and dominated by impulse, go beyond their immediate parochial perspectives to that of reason. And in so doing they divide within themselves, oppose spirit to nature in their own lives. The reconciliation comes for both when men rise further beyond this standpoint of opposition, and see the greater rational necessity and their part in it. At that point they are beyond the opposition of spirit and nature because they see how each is necessary for the other, how both spring from the same rational necessity, which determines both their opposition, and then their reconciliation in the recognition of this underlying necessity.

But now we have seen that the absolute, what is at the foundation of everything, is *Geist*, or subject, and this is not just a matter of fact, e.g., that the world is so made that there is a single current of life in it which we can call a world-soul. Rather it is so in virtue of rational necessity. Hence the dialectic of identity and opposition in subjectivity is not of local interest. On Hegel's scheme, it must be of ontological import. If the absolute is subject, and everything that is can only be in being related to this subject, then everything is caught up in the interplay of identity and opposition which makes up the life of this subject. But then in this case, we would not be twisting words or engaging in hyperbole, if we spoke of a necessary relation of identity and opposition *tout court*.

Let us see how this and other Hegelian terms find general application in the context of this view of the world.

The Absolute, what is ultimately real, or what is at the foundation of everything, is subject. And the cosmic subject is such that he is both identical and non-identical to the world. There is identity in that *Geist* cannot exist without the world; and yet also opposition, for the world as externality represents a dispersal, an unconsciousness which *Geist* has to overcome to be itself, to fulfil its goal as self-conscious reason.

The life of the absolute subject is essentially a process, a movement, in which it posits its own conditions of existence, and then overcomes the opposition of these same conditions to realize its goal of self-knowledge. Or as Hegel puts it in the Preface to the *PhG*: 'the living substance is [...] Subject [...] only in so far as it is the movement of positing itself [Bewegung des Sichselbstsetzens], or the mediation between a self and its development into something different [Vermittlung des Sichanderswerdens mit sich selbst]' (*PhG*, 20).[1]

Thus *Geist* cannot exist simply, Hegel would say 'immediately'. It can exist only by overcoming its opposite. It can exist only by negating its own negation. This is the point Hegel makes in the passage in the preface to the *PhG* immediately after the one just quoted, where he says that the Absolute is essentially *Result*, 'that it is only in the *end* what it is in truth'.[2] *Geist* is something which essentially comes to be out of a process of self-loss and return.

But *Geist* is at the root of everything, and hence mediation becomes a cosmic principle. What can claim to exist immediately is only matter, that is, pure externality. But this shows itself on examination to be incapable of separate existence; taken on its own, it is contradictory and can thus only exist as part of the whole which is the embodiment of *Geist*.

---

[1] Walter Kaufmann, translation 28. [2] Walter Kaufmann, translation 32.

Self-positing Spirit

In Hegel's usage, we can speak of something as 'immediate' (*unmittelbar*) when it exists on its own, without being necessarily related to something else. Otherwise it is called 'mediate' (*vermittelt*). If on the level of ordinary talk and not of speculative philosophy I speak of someone as a man, I am speaking of him as something 'immediate', for (at this level of talk anyway) a man can exist on his own. But if I speak of him as a father, or brother, or son, then he is seen as 'mediate', for his being one of these requires his relation to someone else.

Hegel's point is that all descriptions of things as immediate turn out on closer examination to be inadequate; that all things show their necessary relation to something else, and ultimately to the whole. The whole itself can be characterized as immediate, a point Hegel sometimes makes; but he at once adds that this immediacy contains mediacy within it; and this for the obvious reason that the whole cannot even be stated without stating the dualism whose overcoming it is. To state the whole, we have to bring out two terms in opposition and yet in necessary relation (and hence mediate), and characterize the whole as the overcoming of this opposition (and hence also mediate).

Everything is thus mediate. For it cannot exist on its own. But its inability to exist on its own is supposed to spring from inner contradiction. Hence for Hegel contradiction must also be a universally applicable category.

Hegel says in a famous passage (*WL*, II, 58) that contradiction is as essential to reality as identity. Indeed, if he had to choose between these two as to which was more important, he would choose contradiction, for it is the source of all life and movement.

But this may sound itself contradictory. Hegel thinks of contradiction as the source of movement because whatever is in contradiction must pass over into something else, be this passage the ontological one between levels of being which go on existing coevally, or the historical one between different stages of human civilization. But it would seem impossible to have it both ways. If contradiction is the source of passages from one level to another, it is because it is fatal to continued existence, or so one would think from the common-sense principle that nothing contradictory can exist. Hegel seems to be using this commonsense principle when he explains dialectical passages in this way. And yet on the other hand things do go on existing (in the chain of being, if not in history) even after being convicted of contradiction, and indeed contradiction is said to be everywhere. How can we reconcile these affirmations?

The answer is that contradiction, as Hegel uses the term, is not wholly incompatible with existence, and as such perhaps does not really deserve the name. When we say that the whole is in contradiction, we mean that it unites identity and opposition, that it is opposed to itself. Perhaps one might want to amend this way of putting it to get over the apparent paradox. We might want to say, for instance, that 'identity' and 'opposition' are not to be considered incompatible. But to put it this way would miss part of the point, for in a way,

105

Hegel wants to retain some of the force of the clash between 'identity' and 'opposition'. For *Geist* is in struggle with himself, with his necessary embodiment, and only comes to realization out of this struggle. So that we would have to say that 'opposition' is both compatible and incompatible with 'identity'.

The force of using 'contradiction' here is that what is necessary for *Geist* to be at all is an obstacle to its realization as fully self-conscious rationality, as we saw earlier. Perhaps we could use the term 'ontological conflict' for this. Then we could agree with Hegel that this ontological conflict is the source of movement and change; for it is that by which nothing can exist except in struggle, except by developing itself out of its opposite.

Now at the level of the whole this ontological conflict is not fatal because it is that which maintains the whole as *Geist*. But at the level of any part, taken by itself, it is; for this part cannot exist on its own. We could say that there is a contradiction in a stricter sense which attaches to any attempt to characterize any part of the whole – finite spirit, or thing – as self-sufficient. For the partial is essentially related to the whole. It can only be as an expression of the whole and hence of its opposite. Thus in holding only to the self-identity of the finite we are presenting what is essentially in ontological conflict as though it escaped it; and this is a contradiction in a more understandable sense. In Hegelian terms, any attempt by the logic of the 'understanding' to see things as self-identical and hence not in opposition to themselves involves a (fatal) contradiction. Because everything is in contradiction (in the sense of ontological conflict) to try to see things as simply self-identical involves us in contradictions (in a more ordinary sense). In other words, contradiction when we fully accept it is not fatal in the way it is when we still want to stick to our old ideas about 'identity' and 'opposition'.

But the above is still not adequate to Hegel's view. For the implication is still that all that contradiction is fatal to is theories, that is, partial ways of looking at things. Whereas we find in Hegel the idea many times stated that real existences go under because of contradiction. This is true of historical forms, but it is also true of finite spirits, animals, things. But, one might protest, these latter continue to exist, while historical forms disappear. Yes, Hegel replies, they go on existing as types, but the individual specimens go under; they are all mortal; and this mortality is necessary; it is a reflection of the ontological conflict.

We saw above that any attempt to claim independent existence, free from relation to the whole, and hence to its other, on behalf of a finite thing involved contradiction in the strict and thus fatal sense. But Hegel is suggesting that we see the very external existence of a finite thing, material object, animal or finite spirit, as a kind of claim to independent existence. It is the property of matter that it exists *partes extra partes*, and that things that exist materially have a kind of independent existence. Thus it is not just that

106

material existence suggests independence to us; it *is* itself a form of independent existence, a standing claim to be on its own. It is essential that this claim be
made, as we have seen; for *Geist* requires external material existence in order
to be. But it is just as essential that this claim be abrogated, for *Geist* can only be
in a world in which the parts are essentially related in this way. And this is what
determines the fate of finite things. They must come into existence, but at the
same time they are the victims of an internal contradiction which assures that
they will also pass away. They are necessarily mortal. But at the same time, in
going under they have to be replaced by other similar things.

We can now see more clearly the underlying principle of those ascending
dialectics in which Hegel will show that finite things cannot exist on their own,
but only as part of a larger whole. The motor of these dialectics is contradiction; and the contradiction consists in this, that finite beings just in virtue of
existing externally in space and time make a claim to independence, while the
very basis of their existence is that they express a spirit which cannot brook this
independence. The ascending dialectic reveals the contradiction in things and
shows from the nature of the contradiction how it can only be understood and
reconciled if things are seen as part of the self-movement of the Absolute.

Thus contradiction, in the strong sense which involves combining ontological conflict with its denial, is mortal. But since this 'denial' is not just an
intellectual error by us who observe, but is essential to the whole which is in
ontological conflict itself, we can see that contradiction in the strong sense is
what makes things move and change. It is their inherent changeability
(*Veränderlichkeit*); while contradiction in the sense of ontological conflict is the
source of this changeability.

Contradiction is thus fatal to partial realities, but not to the whole. But this is
not because the whole escapes contradiction. Rather the whole as Hegel
understands it lives on contradiction. It is really because it incorporates it, and
reconciles it with identity that it survives. This the partial reality – material
object or finite spirit – cannot encompass. It is stuck with its own independent
existence, and since this independence clashes with the basis of its existence, it
is caught in contradiction and must die. It must die because it is identified with
only one term, the affirmation, and cannot encompass the denial.

Not so the whole. The absolute goes on living through both the affirmation
and the denial of finite things. It lives *by* this process of affirmation and denial;
it lives *via* the contradiction in finite things. Thus the absolute is essentially life
and movement and change. But at the same time, it remains itself, the same
subject, the same essential thought being expressed, throughout this movement. It reconciles identity and contradiction by maintaining itself in a life
process which is fed on ontological conflict. This combination of incessant
change and immobility is described by Hegel in a striking image from
the preface of *PhG:* 'The true is thus the bacchanalian whirl in which no

The Claims of Speculative Reason

member is not drunken; and because each, as soon as it detaches itself, dissolves immediately – the whirl is just as much transparent and simple repose' (*PhG* 39).[1]

In the above we have found it useful to explain a basic point of Hegel's ontology – the mortality of the finite – by using first the language of claim and denial and then moving to ontological analogues of these. In this we are following Hegel himself, who uses logical terms like 'contradiction' to express his ontology. But after the discussion of the previous section, we are better able to understand what has been called Hegel's 'pan-logism'.

For the absolute is subject, a subject who posits its own embodiment, and posits it according to rational necessity. And this means as we saw that the universe should be seen not only as the embodiment of a cosmic life, but also under the category of expression. Its structures express or manifest the lineaments of rational necessity, since it is posited not just to embody spirit, but also to be understood by spirit in its own self-awareness.[2] Hence the universe reflects rational necessity in two ways; it conforms to it, and it expresses it. It can be seen as in a sense analogous to a *statement*.

Of course, the analogy is very incomplete. We think normally of a statement as couched in a medium, a language, which for the most part pre-exists; and as bearing on some extra-linguistic reality to which it refers. Here the 'medium' consists in the various orders of external reality and is coeval with the 'statement' of conceptual necessity made in it. And what is said is not about some reality external to the medium; for rational necessity not only manifests itself in external reality, but comes to be only in this embodiment.

Closer analogies can be found in expressive activity or in a work of art. An original work can partly forge its own medium, or at least profoundly transform pre-existing languages of expression. And the expressive activity of a subject, the way he gives vent to anger, joy, or whatever is in an important sense not 'about' something external. The expression not only manifests the emotion, but helps determine what it is.

Thus is a way unique to itself, although we can illuminate it with these analogues, the universe can be seen as an *expression* of rational necessity. And this is the basis of Hegel's use of logical terminology in an ontological context.

Of course, it is not at all unnatural to extend the use of a word like 'contradiction' out of the purely logical realm of statement and denial into that of purposive behaviour. If someone makes a certain gesture which is

---

[1] 'Das Wahre ist so der bacchantische Taumel, an dem kein Glied nicht trunken ist, und weil jedes, indem es sich absondert, ebenso unmittelbar (sich) auflöst – ist er ebenso die durchsichtige und einfache Ruhe.' Walter Kaufmann, translation 70.

[2] God thus posits the world in order to think himself in it. This notion of God as self-thinking thought shows Hegel's debt to Aristotle, which indeed is evident enough throughout his work. Hegel's God is the lineal descendant of the God of the *Metaphysics*, but extended now to incorporate everything.

aimed at a certain result and which negates it; if he wants to persist in this, then we say that he is behaving in a contradictory fashion. And this is what *Geist* can be said to do, in that it cannot help but posit external finite reality, and yet this negates it and has to be in turn negated.

But the relation becomes even closer when the purpose itself is seen as one of self-knowledge; for in this case the purpose is one which cannot be properly stated without the use of 'logical' language of assertion and denial. If spirit is striving to express itself, then all the partial forms which exist as stages in its growth can be seen as related to assertions. A given form of civilization is linked with a certain view of God and the absolute, and hence a certain form of self-knowledge of *Geist*. But in an analogous way, the very external existence of finite reality can be seen as something like a claim. For it is posited by *Geist* whose basic goal is to come, as it were, to a definitive statement about himself. In positing the world *Geist* is showing what he is. To leave finite matter as truly independent would be thus in effect to say something false. *Geist* is therefore forced to deny it by 'taking it back'. Both existence and mortality of the finite are necessary; and both can be seen in this context quite naturally as assertion and denial; hence the use of the word 'contradiction'.

The notion that the world is posited will allow Hegel to use a language in which he talks not just of things being identical with their other, but of things turning into their other. This is clearly true of the external embodiment, which comes to inner self-consciousness in *Geist*. But because the world is seen as posited, Hegel will speak, not indeed of *Geist* – this word is reserved for the subjectivity returning to itself out of its embodiment – but of the Idea as going out into its other, exteriority. The Idea, as we shall see in the next part, is the formula of the whole as a chain of necessary connections. This shows the whole as necessarily embodied; and it is this necessity which is the basis for Hegel's language of 'positing'. The Idea becomes its other, and then returns into self-consciousness in *Geist*.

7

This is what Hegel means by absolute idealism. This is paradoxically very different from all other forms of idealism, which tend to the denial of external reality, or material reality. In the extreme form of Berkeley's philosophy, we have a denial of matter in favour of a radical dependence on the mind – of course God's, not ours. Hegel's idealism, far from being a denial of external material reality, is the strongest affirmation of it; it not only exists but necessarily exists.

'Idealism' here does not refer us to the 'ideas' of Cartesians and empiricists, i.e., ideas as the content of the mind; but on the contrary to the Ideas of

Plato. Kant had already rehabilitated the term in a Plato-related sense with his ideas of reason; and Hegel follows this use.

Absolute idealism means that nothing exists which is not a manifestation of the Idea, that is, of rational necessity. Everything exists for a purpose, that of the coming to be of rational self-consciousness, and this requires that all that exists be the manifestation of rational necessity. Thus absolute idealism is related to the Platonic notion of the ontological priority of rational order, which underlies external existence, and which external existence strives to realize, rather than to the modern post-Cartesian notion of dependence on knowing mind.

'Negativity' is another fundamental Hegelian term whose use is closely connected with the above discussion of contradiction. Opposites negate each other, and since within everything that exists there is opposition, we can also say that within everything there is negativity. In particular Hegel links negativity to the subject, whose nature is to return to itself (self-consciousness) through its opposite; and in the case of the cosmic *Geist*, to posit its opposite. So Hegel says (*PhG*, 20) that substance is 'as subject [...] pure, simple negativity'.

We can think of the movement which posits and holds other being or external reality as something independent as negativity, as 'the tremendous power of the negative' (*PhG*, 29).[1] And we can also think of the movement by which the particular external forms go under and pass over into others as the work of negativity. For negativity is opposition, and since opposition is essential to everything, everything is in contradiction, contains negativity, and thus is in movement.

This term allows Hegel to link two theses: that all that exists is contradictory and hence mortal (because containing negation), and that all that exists can only be described in concepts which being determinate involve negation. (Hegel takes up the Spinozan thesis here *omnis determinatio est negatio*.) The very use of determinate descriptive concepts involves the negation of others, for these concepts can only have determinate sense against a background of others with which they are contrasted. Hegel will claim that this link between 'negation' and determinate being (*Dasein*) is a manifestation of the negativity which is essentially in and constitutive of *Dasein*.[2]

The use of logical language in an ontological sense which is legitimated by absolute Idealism is also evident in the Hegelian use of the term 'concept' (*Begriff*). Because he sees the world as posited rational necessity, as the external manifestations of the Idea, the concepts which are true of it are not just true of it as a matter of contingent, unexplained fact but provide the ground plan according to which it was posited. So that we move from seeing the concept as a descriptive term correctly applied by us to seeing it as the

---

[1] 'die ungeheure Macht des Negativen', Walter Kaufmann, translation 50.
[2] Cf. Part III in the discussion of the *Logic*.

underlying necessity which brought what it applies to being. When Hegel speaks of *the* Concept, then, the concept of the whole, he often speaks in the mature works of a concept which is also subjectivity, for the rational necessity behind the whole is that of self-knowing subjectivity. This is 'the self-conceiving concept' (der sich begreifende Begriff, *WL*, II, 504).

But there are two other Hegelian uses of 'concept' which are connected with this circle of ideas. Hegel's view is one of reality in development, as we have seen. The Absolute is essentially result; in its true form it is the end-process of growth. Hegel is fond of the analogy of the plant, and uses the Aristotelian language of potentiality and actuality. This latter in particular (*Wirklichkeit*) is a very frequently used Hegelian term. In ordinary German, it could be translated 'reality'; but in Hegel's use it applies not just to any reality but only to that which is the developed manifestation of rational necessity.

But this use of the plant analogy and the recourse to the Aristotelian categories requires a pendant term to *Wirklichkeit* to express potentiality, the germ of inner necessity before it is fully actualized. And for this the term 'concept' also frequently serves. In this second sense, then, things are said to be in their concept, when they are in germ, when they have just started to develop. This use is more frequent than the first earlier on, and seems to be the standard use in the *PhG*. For instance in the Preface to this work, Hegel speaks of our time as one of 'birth and transition to a new period' (*PhG*, 15). This new period is in its infancy; what has stepped forward is only its 'concept'.

As well as being self-knowing subjectivity in the form of rational necessity underlying the developed whole, the concept can thus also be seen as this necessity qua germ in contrast to actuality. And it can easily thence be extended to a third sense in which it is contrasted to reality in the ordinary sense (*Realität*), or rather in the more special sense of external reality before it has been shaped and developed to actuality. For this externality is always there – and this is where the plant analogy is inadequate – even when the 'concept' is in germ; at this stage it is simply not yet properly formed, it is not yet an adequate manifestation of rational necessity: this we can see, for instance, with the early institutions of human history which will later become the law-state based on reason. At this point their 'reality' can be contrasted to their 'concept' in the sense of the plan of their fully developed form. 'Concept' here is thus the formula of their full-fledged stage, towards which they are headed, this is what is only implicit in 'concept' as germ, and which can be contrasted to the raw unformed reality of the present stage.

The stages of development also underlie another set of Hegelian terms which have achieved notoriety. The implicit stage of a process, where the reality concerned is still in germ, is often characterized by the term '*an sich*'.[1]

---

[1] Literally 'in itself', but as it figures in ordinary German it would often best be translated 'by itself' or 'as such'.

Hegel says (*PhG*, 22) that the embryo is '*an sich Mensch*'. By contrast the fully developed form is characterized as '*für sich*'.[1] But sometimes there is a third stage; for as we have seen the basis of things is to be understood as an Idea which posits the external reality necessary for its realization, and then develops to this full realization in the external reality. In this process, the first stage is characterized as '*an sich*', the second as '*für sich*' and the third as '*anundfürsich*'.

The idea behind this language seems to be this: the *an sich* is the implicit, the as yet undeveloped, the self-identical; while the '*für sich*' is the fully deployed, exteriorized, which therefore lies, as it were 'before itself'. In the simpler case of the plant, these represent the only two stages; it is in germ, and then it is fully unfolded (*entfaltet*). But in the case of the full Hegelian theory of reality as posited manifestation of rational necessity, there are three. This necessity in germ, as it were, as yet self-identical, is the Idea. It must be exteriorized, unfolded, and thus *fürsich*. But this means that it loses at first its self-identity; *Geist* is lost in external reality. But in returning to adequate self-knowledge *Geist* realizes a kind of combination of the first two stages, he comes back to self-identity in the opposite of fully developed external reality; and so can be considered as *anundfürsich*.

There are other uses of '*an sich*' in Hegel. Often it carries the sense of self-contained, not dependent on anything outside. Of course, only the whole is truly *an sich* in this sense, although partial realities may appear so at different stages of the dialectic. In this usage '*an sich*' is usually contrasted to '*für anderes*' – 'for another', i.e., dependent on something else. Or else '*an sich*' can be used in a closely related sense, when we consider a thing 'in itself' in contrast to what it is for consciousness (e.g., the contrast of '*an sich*' and '*für das Bewußtsein*' in the introduction of the *PhG*).[2]

This same circle of ideas underlies the Hegelian uses of the term 'universal'. Underlying reality is the rational necessity which links all forms of being to self-knowing subjectivity. Or as Hegel expresses it frequently, underlying 'being' there is 'thought' (*Denken*); being and thought (*Sein und Denken*) are one. This thought is of course the Concept, and 'concept' leads us naturally to 'universal'.

---

[1] Literally, 'for itself'. These terms sound so awkward in English that I propose to go on using the German expressions in the text.

[2] With this latter use we come close to Kant's sense of the term. Kant applied the term '*an sich*' to things outside of their relation to our knowledge of them. The English translation 'thing in itself' seems right for the Kantian '*Ding-an-sich*'. '*An sich*' is opposed here to '*für uns*' (for us). Some of the Hegelian uses are obviously related, and for them too 'in itself' would not be a bad translation. But it is obvious that in Hegel's first sense, the term is very different, for here the point of contrast is with '*für sich*'; '*an sich*' does not mean out of relation to something other (our faculty of knowing), but on the contrary rather 'implicit' (as it has sometimes been translated in English). In other words, for Kant a valid translation of '*an sich*' into English might have been 'by itself', but this would miss the essential point of the Hegelian term.

But like the concept, the universal can take on a different aspect in relation to the different stages of development. As a concept underlying external reality, but taken on its own outside of, or 'before' this reality, the universal is 'abstract'. It is rather like the traditional idea of the universal as a common formula of a given type of thing, arrived at by abstraction from the particular properties of its instances. But of course, as we now know, an abstraction of this kind cannot be; the concept must posit an external reality. And hence we get the concrete universal, the concept embodied in external reality which is there to realize it, to express the idea involved.

But as concrete, the universal can no longer be considered distinct from and merely externally related to the particular (*das Besondere*). It is not just that as instantiated it must occur together at a particular place or time with some other properties, etc. For we could still think of the universal as without any inner relation to the particular features of its instances. But we cannot look at Hegel's concrete universal in this way. For the embodiment of the concrete universal is the manifestation of the necessity contained in the idea concerned, and it is moreover a necessary manifestation, that is, can be seen as posited by it; and for both these reasons Hegel makes us look at the relation between universal and embodiment on the model of that between thought and expression. The concrete universal is the expressed universal or thought. It should not be seen as united indifferently with just any particular features, but these latter should be seen as deployed in order to instantiate it.

The universal is shown here to be in inner relation to the particular (*das Besondere*). Sometimes, however, it is related to the individual (*das Einzelne*); and sometimes to both; for Hegel uses this analysis of the universal in a host of contexts; like many Hegelian terms it expresses a theme with many variations.

One of the variations turns on the close relation between the two dimensions of embodiment, that which relates thought and expression and that which relates life and organism. We have just seen the universal and particular in the first; it is not surprising that they appear in the second. As the abstract universal can be seen as what remains in common to a multiplicity of things when their particular features are pared off, so the 'I' of the subject can be seen as a universal relative to all the particular changing contents of his mind and properties of his character.

And this abstract universal can be said to correspond to a certain stage of human development, that in which man steps back and tries to free himself from all particular contingent attachments, from the simply given facts of his nature and tradition in order to decide by universal criteria. But of course this project is not viable as such, and man can only come to freedom by embodying free rationality in an external mode of being and way of life which is designed for the purpose. This last stage corresponds to the concrete universal, and we can say that the individual cannot attain the universal except through the particular.

In still another, more restricted variant, the universal is set over against the individual as the reality of the collective spirit. The two have to be brought into reconciliation. What corresponds to the 'abstract' stage here is one in which the universal is more '*an sich*', is not yet developed into the set of institutions which effect this reconciliation with the citizens. There is of course a parallel evolution on the part of the individual, which was briefly sketched in the previous paragraph.

The idea that actuality develops within an external reality which exists already, which has thus to be formed to be a proper manifestation of internal necessity, is the basis of a paradoxical reflection on the inner and the outer of which Hegel is fond and which often re-appears in his work.

As reality develops towards actuality, e.g., as political institutions develop towards the law-state or as we pass from inanimate matter to life, we can think of it as progressively 'interiorized', for its different features are more and more closely related to a central plan and it shows a greater and greater unity, which eventually must reach an 'interiority' in the strong sense, consciousness. But at the same time we can see this as an exteriorization; for the necessity which was formerly hidden in the unformed external reality is now 'exteriorized' in the sense of manifested.

By the same token, we can consider the initial stage as one in which everything is 'inner' in the sense of non-manifest, but also as a stage of 'exteriority' in the sense that reality is more *partes extra partes*, that its parts are external to each other in not yet being manifestly bound by any internal necessity. Hence Hegel's oft-repeated statement that a reality which is all internal is also necessarily all external.

One of the most important concepts to which Hegel gave a special twist is that of the infinite. One of the basic motivations of Hegel's philosophy was to reconcile the finite with the infinite, as we saw; and Hegel's thesis is, in fact, that the true infinite is not simply to be opposed to the finite but is in reality one with it; just as one might say that true *Geist* is not simply opposed to external being but is one with it.

This requires obviously a particular, and rather off-beat, conception of the infinite. Hegel's starting point is that the infinite is that which is not bounded, which is pretty unexceptionable; but by bounded he means limited by something outside of it. The finite for Hegel as we have seen is what has something beyond which 'negates' it and thus gives it its determinate nature.

Thus we cannot see the infinite as something separate from, or 'beyond' the finite, as we do for instance when we think of God as infinite life existing beyond and independently of us as finite beings. For this would mean that the infite would be other than, and hence bounded by the finite. The infinite would have something outside of it, the finite, and hence would not be truly infinite.

The true infinite must thus include the finite. Can we then think of the infinite as the boundless, e.g., endless space which includes all the objects in it, or the series of natural numbers which includes each finite series while going on forever? Most definitely not. Hegel rejects this endless progression as the 'bad infinite'. Rather than being a valid model of the infinite, this is rather a nightmarish perpetuation of the finite. For it means that wherever you choose to stop, there is always something beyond, that is, you have a whole which is bounded by something else, namely, the next step in the endless progress. You are always in finitude.

What is needed therefore is something which is not limited, in the sense of bounded from the outside, and yet not simply unlimited in the sense of being endlessly expansible without reaching a boundary; an infinite which is yet a whole one can encompass, or an infinite which is one with the finite.

It seems a tall order, but Hegel claims to have produced just this. For the universe according to Hegel is just such a whole which is not limited from the outside, and yet is not simply without limit. On the contrary, the whole of reality has a definite structure and extent in which each part has its necessary place, in that sense we can say that it has boundaries. But at the same time it is not bounded from the outside, for there is no outside, the universe is turned back on itself like a circle. That is, the boundaries of all existing things are boundaries with other constituents of the universe: each level of being is bounded by, and hence determined, and at the same time negated by, and hence passing over into a higher level. And at the apex is *Geist* which in turn passes into, that is, posits, external reality. Finite objects are limited by others, but they form part of a chain of levels of being which is circular. The universe thus has no external boundaries, only internal ones; and Hegel puts forward on this metaphysical level an idea which bears a strange analogy to certain popularizations of the physics of Einstein.

The proper image of infinity for Hegel is thus not a straight line indefinitely prolonged, but a circle. And we can see that on this conception the finite is not something separate from the infinite; the infinite is an ordered whole. More, the finite turns itself into the infinite; for we have seen that if we start with any partial reality we are referred beyond it, ultimately to the whole system. The finite as a whole is thus one with the infinite; and the infinite finds its only expression in the ordered whole of the finite.

Because reality is a circle, which can only present itself in its true form as the result of a process of development, which process is itself seen as posited by what results from it, we can only present the truth about the absolute in a system. Science itself must be a circle which reflects and gives an adequate account of the linked levels of being which are essential to the whole. As Hegel

The Claims of Speculative Reason

puts it 'it is only as science or system that knowledge is actual (wirklich) and can be expounded' (PhG, 23).[1]

To try to express this philosophy in any one principle or proposition is inherently against its nature. For the nature of reality as grounded on contradiction ensures that the negation of this proposition is also true: Geist is essentially embodied; and it is also opposed to this embodiment. External reality as external is in mutually independent parts; but this independence also contradicts its nature, so that it is inherently perishable. And so on. We can only come close to the truth by seeing how both affirmation and negation fit together and are necessary to each other. Science can only be a system.

The type of thought which underlies this form of science Hegel calls 'reason' (Vernunft); this is the thinking which follows reality in its contradictions, and therefore can see how each level turns into the next one. Reason in this sense is contrasted to understanding (Verstand) which is the habit common to most, of holding fast to the principle of identity. The famous line of Butler, which G. E. Moore inscribed at the beginning of Principia Ethica, 'Everything is what it is and not another thing', this is the quintessence of Verstand. It is obvious that Verstand cannot really come to grips with philosophy as Hegel sees it, with 'speculative' philosophy, but sees the truth as incomprehensible nonsense. Hegel speaks constantly of the fixed rigidity of Verstand. This is an inevitable stage of thought, in which it manages to give itself clarity and rigour as against the vague fluidity of 'representation' (Vorstellung), but it has to be gone beyond to a new fluidity.

Once again we can recognize a Kantian distinction which has been transformed. Reason for Kant was the faculty which tried to think the whole, as against understanding which operated in the immediate context; but Hegel has immensely enriched this distinction with his own theory.

8

We can see now how this system of thought offered the hope of overcoming the oppositions mentioned in the first section, without paying the price which the Romantics were willing to pay in abandoning free rationality. Hegel's notion of the Absolute does give a sense to his thesis of the 'identity of identity and difference'. And this is meant to allow him to have it both ways, as it were; to keep both terms of the opposition in their full force, and yet to see them as one; to see them as coming to unity out of opposition.

The major oppositions which we adumbrated in the first section were those between man and nature, from which he becomes divided both as a knowing subject and an agent; between individual and community; and between finite and infinite spirit. this last opposition is also reflected in man's relation to fate.

[1] Walter Kaufmann, translation 36.

116

Self-positing Spirit

The epistemological gap between man and nature expresses itself in its best known form in the Kantian distinction between phenomena and things-in-themselves. The latter were for ever and in principle unknowable. Hegel directs a powerful polemic against the Kantian thing-in-itself. And the final argument is this: how can there be anything beyond knowledge, that is beyond mind or *Geist*, for *Geist* turns out ultimately to be identical with the whole of reality?

More specifically, the opposition is overcome in the fact that our knowledge of the world turns ultimately into *Geist's* self-knowledge. For we come to discover that the world which is supposedly beyond thought is really posited by thought, that it is a manifestation of rational necessity. And at the same time the thought which was supposedly over against the world, that is, our thinking as finite subjects, turns out to be that of the cosmos itself, or the cosmic subject, God, whose vehicles we are. In the higher vision of speculative philosophy, the world loses its otherness to thought, and subjectivity goes beyond finitude, and hence the two meet. We overcome the dualism between subject and world, between knowing man and nature, in seeing the world as the necessary expression of thought, or rational necessity, while we see ourselves as the necessary vehicles of this thought, as the point where it becomes conscious. (And become conscious it must, for the rationally necessary order of things includes the necessity that this rationally necessary order appear to itself.)

This means that we come to see ourselves not just as finite subjects, with our own thoughts as it were, but as the vehicles of a thought which is more than just ours, that is in a sense the thought of the universe as a whole, or in Hegel's terms, of God.

Hegel's answer to the Kantian doctrine of the *Ding-an-sich* is thus to throw down the barrier between man and the world in having the knowledge of finite subjects culminate in the self-knowledge of infinite subject. But he does not break through the barrier by a Romantic abandonment in which subject and object are felt ultimately to coincide in a kind of ineffable intuition of unity.

Rather Hegel solves the problem of uniting finite to infinite spirit without loss of freedom through his notion of reason. As we saw at the end of Chapter I, none of Hegel's Romantic contemporaries resolved this dilemma. Either they held to the vision of an unboundedly free creative subject, but at the cost of exile in a God-forsaken world; or they sought unity with the divine beyond reason, but at the cost of abandoning their autonomy to a larger order beyond their comprehension. For Hegel too the finite subject must be part of a larger order. But since this is an order deployed by an unconditional rational necessity, it is at no point foreign to ourselves as rational subjects. Nothing in it must just be accepted as brute, 'positive' fact. The rational agent loses none of his freedom in coming to accept his vocation as vehicle of cosmic necessity.

Nor does this union with cosmic spirit only accomodate us as subjects of

117

rational thought at the expense of our lower, empirical, desiring nature; for this too is part of the necessary order of things. The infinite subject is such that in order to be he must have an external embodiment; and who says external embodiment says embodiment in space and time, an embodiment which is somewhere and sometime, in a particular living being, with all that this involves. The infinite subject can only be through a finite one.

Hence nothing of us is abandoned when we come to assume our full role as vehicles of *Geist*. Because the order of which we are a part is deployed by a spirit whose nature is unadulterated rational necessity, and because this spirit necessarily posits us as finite subjects, we can identify with it without remainder. By this vision of absolute reason, ungrounded in the merely given, Hegel believes himself to have resolved the dilemma of the Romantic generation.

Two related essential features of the Hegelian solution follow from this. The first is that the unity of man and world, of finite and infinite subject, does not abolish the difference. Not only is the unity hard-won out of difference, as man struggles to rise to the level where the unity can be grasped; but the ultimate unity retains the difference within it. We remain finite subjects over against the world and God, men with all the particularities of our time, place and circumstances, even as we come to see this particular existence as part of a larger plan, as we come to be vehicles of a larger self-consciousness, that of *Geist*. Spirit's return to unity necessarily incorporates duality.

Secondly, the Absolute must be understood in concepts (*begriffen*) as Hegel insists in the Preface to the *PhG* (13), and not in feeling and intuition (*Gefühl und Anschauung*). Man cannot abandon understanding, the 'frightful power' (*ungeheure Macht, PhG*, 29) by which men analyse their world, divide themselves from nature and fix the distinctions between things. This is in a sense like the power of death which removes things from the stream of life. But we cannot overcome it by fleeing from it, but only by pushing this power of clear thought to the limit, where the division is overcome in the dialectical thought of reason. The great power of understanding is 'to hold onto what is dead' (*das Tote festzuhalten*). The life of the spirit is one which 'endures, and preserves itself through, death'. It finds itself only in 'absolute self-division' (*absolute Zerrissenheit*, 29–30).[1] A certain 'powerless beauty' (*kraftlose Schönheit*) cannot do this, and it thus cannot come to a real vision of unity, for it can never incorporate the 'seriousness, the pain, the patience and the labour of the negative' (20).

Hegel will not abandon the clear distinctions of thought. But he claims to have his cake and eat it through his new concept of reason. This is founded on the ontological thesis that these oppositions themselves proceed from and

[1] Walter Kaufmann, translation 50.

return to identity; so that the thought which marks the clearest distinction is also that which unites. The opposition itself, pushed to the limit, goes over into identity. Man separates from nature in the course of realizing his vocation as a rational being. But it is just this vocation fully realized, just the full development of rationality which shows him to himself as the vehicle of *Geist* and thus reconciles the opposition.

This idea of a duality which is overcome without being abolished finds expression in two key Hegelian terms. The first is '*Aufhebung*'. This is Hegel's term for the dialectical transition in which a lower stage is both annulled and preserved in a higher one. The German word 'aufheben' can in fact carry either of these meanings. Hegel combined them to make his term of art.

Secondly, because the unity does not just abolish the distinction, Hegel often speaks of the resolution as a 'reconciliation' (*Versöhnung*); this word implies that the two terms remain, but that their opposition is overcome.

This term 'reconciliation' comes often to the fore in connection with the opposition between man and God, between finite and infinite spirit, as can well be imagined. As far as the theoretical opposition is concerned, its resolution is already implicit in the foregoing discussion of the duality man–world. For this latter was overcome by our showing the ultimate identity of God's self-knowledge with man's knowledge of the universe. That is, ultimately art, religion and philosophy, what Hegel calls 'absolute spirit', give us the self-knowledge of *Geist*. The idea of God as necessarily hidden and unknowable is therefore overcome, although like the idea of the *Ding-an-sich* it belongs to a necessary stage of human development.

How about the practical oppositions, between man as agent and nature, between man and the state, man and his fate?

Man had to turn against nature within and without, to curb instinct within himself, and to treat the things around him as instruments to be bent to his will. He had to break with an earlier unity and communion with nature.[1] He had to 'desacralize' (*entgöttern*) the world. This was an essential step towards freedom.

But here, too, the opposition, pushed to its limit, leads to reconciliation. The moral agent who strives to act on the dictates of pure practical reason independent of inclination is finally forced by reason itself to a conception of himself as vehicle of *Geist* and hence to a reconciliation with the nature of things, speculatively understood, which is also an expression of *Geist*. This reconciliation does not mean a return to original unity but preserves rational freedom.

---

[1] There was in fact more than one such break in the Hegelian view of history. For the period of 'original unity' par excellence, the one that was the object of the greatest nostalgia in the late eighteenth century – classical Greece – was itself the product in Hegel's view of man's shaping of himself and nature, which culminated in the creation of an art centred on human form. It was preceded by more primitive stages, and was already an achievement.

The Claims of Speculative Reason

At the same time man in acting on external nature to serve his purposes, in working, helps to transform it and himself, and to bring both sides towards the eventual reconciliation. This idea of the crucial importance of work, which is central to Marx's theory, originates with Hegel. He deals with it specifically for instance in the discussion of master and slave in the second part of the *PhG*. But there is an important difference between the two views. It is clear that for both writers man forms himself, comes to realize his own essence in the attempt to dominate and transform nature. But the major difference is that for Marx the actual changes wrought in nature and the consequent man-made environment are of major significance, while for Hegel the role of work and its products is mainly to create and sustain a universal consciousness in man. This of course reflects the fact that for Marx the industrial revolution was the major fact of human history while Hegel's thought is still concerned with what was largely a pre-industrial world. But it also reflects, of course, the (related) major difference between what each writer considered to be the human essence.

As for the opposition between man and the state, we can already see how this will be overcome in Hegel's system. The state plays an important role as an embodiment of the universal in human life. In the formation of the individual as a vehicle of universal reason, the state has an indispensable part. In belonging to it the individual is already living beyond himself in some larger life; and as the state comes to its 'truth' as an expression of universal reason in the form of law, it brings the individual with it toward his ultimate vocation.

Thus in its more primitive forms, the state can be and is in opposition to man who aspires to be a free self-conscious individual. But this opposition is destined to be overcome. For the free individual must ultimately come to see himself as the vehicle of universal reason; and when the state comes to its full development as the embodiment of this reason, then the two are reconciled. Indeed, the free individual cannot realize himself as free outside the state. For it follows with Hegel's principle that there can be no dis-embodied spiritual life that he cannot accept a definition of freedom like that of the Stoics, which sees it as an inner condition of man unaffected by his external fate. A purely inner freedom is only a wish, a shadow. It is an important stage of human development when he comes to have this wish, this idea, but it must not be confused with the real thing. Freedom is only real (*wirklich*) when expressed in a form of life; and since man cannot live on his own, this must be a collective form of life; but the state is the collective mode of life which is backed by the full power of the community; and thus freedom must be embodied in the state.

The last practical opposition is that between finite and infinite life and is brought home most forcefully by a consideration of fate. We can endow human life with as much significance as we wish in considering man, the rational animal, as the vehicle of universal reason. This goes for what man does at the full stretch of his powers. But what about the absurdity of what just happens, including the greatest absurdity of all, death? How do we incorporate this in a meaningful whole? Or to put it in another way, how do we justify the ways of God (laying on him the responsibility of fate) to man?

Hegel is ready to take this on too. He speaks of his philosophy of history as a 'theodicy', and we can see why. Man's fate can be given a place in the skein of necessity just as well as his achievements.[1] Death itself, the death of particular men, is necessary in the scheme of things, as is the death of any animal, and the ultimate disappearance of any external reality; for as external all these things are in contradiction to themselves and must go under.

But more than for the death of men, Hegel in his philosophy of history accounts for the death of civilizations. What seems senseless and ultimately unjustified, the destruction and decay of some of the finest earlier civilizations,[2] is shown to be a necessary stage on the road to realization of *Geist* in the law-state and reason. That is, not only death itself, but the particular incidence of fate in history is shown to be part of the meaningful plan, with which man as reason can be fully reconciled.

One may stop well short of conviction before Hegel's theodicy. It is indeed difficult to see how man can be reconciled to fate, how he can fail to see it as a 'negation'. Even if we accept the general plan of history, and are reconciled to the death of civilization, how do we understand as meaningful the premature death of quite non-world-historical individuals, of children, for instance? One doesn't have to go to the lengths of Ivan Karamazov and give a weight greater than world history to the tears of an innocent child in order to feel that Hegel has not met the difficulty.

But in Hegel's view such instances of individual fate are beneath the sweep of necessity; they fall in the domain of that interstitial contingency whose existence is necessary, as we have seen. We can be reconciled with this as well as with world history if we identify with what we essentially are, universal reason. If we really come to see ourselves as vehicles of universal reason, then death is no longer an 'other'; for it is part of the plan. We are in that sense already beyond death; it is no longer a limit. It is incorporated in the life of reason which goes on beyond it.

This, of course, is the real meaning for Hegel of what is expressed in the mode of 'representation' (*Vorstellung*) in the traditional doctrine of the

---

[1] Hegel's mature 'theodicy' thus develops out of the conception of fate he expounded in the MS of the 1790s, called 'the Spirit of Christianity' which we discussed in the previous chapter. But it now encompasses much more. The destiny with which men reconcile themselves now incorporates division as well as unity.

[2] Hegel speaks in his lectures on the philosophy of history of the melancholy and sorrow we cannot help feeling when we look on the ruins of ancient civilizations, and reflect 'daß die reichste Gestaltung, das schönste Leben in der Geschichte den Untergang finden, daß wir da unter Trümmern des Vortrefflichen wandeln' (VG 34–5).

immortality of the soul. Although Hegel often says that this doctrine is one of the marks of the true religion and could only arise at a high stage of human religious development, he does not actually believe in individual survival after death; if what survives is thought of as disembodied, then this would in any case be an impossibility on Hegel's principle. But the idea of the eternity of personality expresses a profound truth nevertheless; not just the banal idea that although I die, rational life goes on; but the deeper speculative idea that even death is part of the necessary embodiment posited by subjectivity; death is not an external negation of subjectivity, but is part of what is posited by subjectivity, by *Geist*, in order to be.

9

I have given only the briefest outline here of the way in which Hegel believes himself to have resolved the dualisms which aroused the deepest concern in his time and which provided the most powerful motivation of his own philosophical effort; of how in short he thought to answer the aspiration of the age in uniting the greatest rational autonomy with the fullest expressive unity with nature. The discussion of these solutions in detail provides some of the richest passages of Hegel's work. In the next part, I should like to examine some of these.

Up to now, I have just been trying to present the general lines of Hegel's system. But it follows from its very nature as here presented, as a system which claims to reconcile the major oppositions by reason itself, that it cannot just be presented, but has to be demonstrated. Rather, we might say that its only adequate presentation is a demonstration.

What can we consider a demonstration? A demonstration must be able to take us from our ordinary understanding of things, and show that this is untenable, that it must give way to Hegel's vision of things. It will start therefore at the bottom, with the disconnected external jumble which we see as the world, and force us to move to the vision of a system of necessity whose apex is *Geist*.

One obvious path for a demonstration will therefore start from the hierarchy of being which we all observe and show it to be connected systematically in the way adumbrated above. We will show this hierarchy of beings to be the embodiment and manifestation of a formula of rational necessity in which each level has its necessary place. We will start with the lowest and most external level, matter extended in time and space, we will lay bare its underlying concepts and its necessary links to higher levels. In this way we will pass through the various stages of inanimate being, through the various levels of life to spirit, which in turn will show a development in human history.

This is the demonstration which occupies the philosophy of nature and the philosophy of spirit; which is thus laid out in the latter two sections of the *Encyclopaedia,* and in the various works which expand parts of this, such as the *Philosophy of Right,* philosophies of history, religion, history of philosophy, aesthetics, etc.

But we can think of another demonstration which is in a sense prior to this one. The entire chain of being which we run through in the above demonstration is a manifestation of a chain of rational necessity, the formula of which is expressed in the Idea, as we have said. Why not then get at this more directly by a study not of the various kinds of reality as in the above demonstration, but simply of the categories in which we think the world? In examining each of these we shall find that on its own it is contradictory, that it refers us beyond itself, and that ultimately the only category that can maintain itself will be the Idea. We can then conceive of a demonstration which starts with the poorest, most empty category, with 'being', and which shows its internal contradiction, and hence passes on to other categories which are in turn shown to be contradictory, moving always to higher and higher levels of complexity, until we come to the Idea. This is the demonstration which we find in the *Logic,* and hence in the first part of the *Encyclopaedia.*

Is there room for another demonstration? In a sense not, that is, not on the same level. For the two previous ones form a perfect circle. The logic develops our understanding of the categories until we come to the Idea, which shows us that these categories are necessarily embodied in external reality; we therefore turn to examine this external reality, at first in its most 'external' form, and we climb the scale of the philosophy of nature and then that of spirit. At the culmination of this we reach the vision of absolute spirit, of the life of God as the perfect self-knowledge of the whole. But what does God know in knowing himself? Obviously the chain of rational necessity which is laid out in the Logic and which culminates in the Idea. So we have come full circle.

But whatever the value of this reasoning, the fact is that Hegel did give us a third demonstration, that which we find in the *Phenomenology.* We can think of it as a kind of prologomenon, an introduction to the main system. Hegel wrote the work in 1806–7, a number of years before he published the definite form of his system; and one may wonder therefore what role he retrospectively gave it; and this particularly in that the title 'phenomenology' re-appears to designate a section of the philosophy of spirit, and this section does go over some of the ground covered in the earlier work.

But the answer to this can only be speculative (in the ordinary slightly pejorative and not in the Hegelian sense). We do have in fact in the *PhG* the most powerful and exciting of Hegel's works. Its principle is to start not from the forms of being, or from the categories, but from the forms of consciousness. It is in that sense the demonstration which fulfils best one of Hegel's principal goals which is to take us from where we are and bring us to a vision of the system.

The idea is thus to start with the poorest, most elementary notion of what consciousness is, to show that this cannot stand up, that it is riven with inner contradiction, and must give way to another higher one; this one in turn is shown to be contradictory, and we are thus referred farther until we come to the true understanding of consciousness as self-knowing *Geist*, or absolute knowledge.

Hegel is perhaps clearest of all in the Introduction to the *PhG* about his aim to take us by argument from where we are to where he is, not by drawing in any external considerations, or by refutation of our view from the outside, as it were, but purely by taking up the inner logic of our own starting point. The *PhG* is thus a kind of itinerary of our conceptions of ourselves, or perhaps more accurately, a struggle by Hegel to wrench his own conception of *Geist* out of those of his contemporaries, views which arise of necessity in the course of man's spiritual itinerary, but which now have to be set aside and which must be combatted with polemical force. The *PhG* is above all a work of self-clarification, and is shot through with a powerful inner tension, and this is what gives it its extraordinary forcefulness and fascination.

Our next task must then be to go through these three major demonstrations of Hegel's philosophy. And it would be most sensible to go into them in the order of priority which holds between them, in the reverse order, that is, to that in which they have been mentioned here. We should start, therefore, with the prolegomenon to the system, the *Phenomenology*.

PART II

PHENOMENOLOGY

CHAPTER IV

The Dialectic of Consciousness

1

The *PhG*, written at the end of the Jena period (1806–7), can be thought of a kind of introduction to Hegel's system, whose function would be to take the reader from where he is, buried in the prejudices of ordinary consciousness, to the threshold of true science. But this cannot be the whole story. The very nature of Hegel's system of thought is that it shows all partial reality to be dependent on an absolute which in turn necessarily generates this partial reality. From this point of view, there is no reality, however humble and fragmentary, which can be thought to fall outside the system, and no transition between levels of reality whose explicitation could be considered a kind of *hors d'oeuvre*.

And this applies a fortiori to modes of consciousness, in a system where the absolute is spirit. Spirit comes to know himself, and the vehicles of this self-knowledge are finite spirits. The course of *Geist's* development towards self-knowledge lies through the initial confusions, misconceptions and truncated visions of men. These cannot therefore lie outside the system. Rather this initial darkness reflects something essential about the absolute, viz., that it must grow through struggle to self-knowledge. Hence there cannot easily be an introduction to the science of the absolute which is not also part of that science, no mere clearing of the ground which is not also a partial construction of the building.

This goes some way to explaining why there has been so much debate and uncertainty over the status of the *PhG*. Hegel seems to have thought of it as leading in to the Logic, and in this sense as introductory. But at the same time he described the work on the title page as the 'first part' of a 'System of Science'. This was to include the Logic and what later was developed into the philosophies of nature and spirit, first variants of which he had already worked out at Jena. When he came to give these their final form, certain of the things treated in the *PhG* are once more taken up in the philosophy of spirit; and inevitably so, since an account of the development of spirit cannot avoid dealing with forms of consciousness. And to increase the confusion, there is a section of the part of the Encyclopaedia devoted to subjective spirit which is called 'Phenomenology'.

127

But this need confuse us only if we think of the Hegelian system as a perfectly tidy one with a necessary order in which everything falls into place. Hegel rather encouraged this by his presentation of Logic and philosophies of nature and spirit in a great triad as an Encyclopaedia of science. There is indeed some point in presenting these as a triad, but it is not the exclusive order consistent with his philosophical position. The point is, rather, as we described it in the last chapter, that one should be able to start anywhere, and recuperate one's original starting point. There are different ways of laying out the system of necessary connection depending on where one starts.

The *PhG* intends to start with our ordinary consciousness of things (das naturliches Bewußtsein), and to take us from there to the true perspective of *Geist*. The work is called a 'phenomenology' because it deals with the way things appear for consciousness, or with forms of consciousness. But 'appearance' here is not to be contrasted with 'reality'; what is most real, the absolute, is essentially self-appearance. Phenomenology is not a science of lesser things, which can be left behind, but one way of acceding to absolute knowledge, of making the absolute 'apparent'.

Our ordinary consciousness takes us to be individual, finite subjects set over against the world. The perspective of *Geist*, on the other hand, shows us as vehicles of a spirit which is also expressed in the world, so that this world is no longer distinct from us. But how can we induce ordinary consciousness to budge from its perspective and take on the higher one? Just affirming (versichern) our position will do no good, for there is no reason for the plain man to believe us. In fact no argument which is based on a knowledge of the absolute denied to ordinary consciousness will do any good, for it will ipso facto be inaccessible as *argument* to this consciousness.

The kind of argument Hegel proposes to use here is something quite different. It is a form implicit in his system: it is to show how ordinary consciousness carefully examined breaks down in contradiction and itself points beyond itself to a more adequate form. And of course only an argument of this form would be consistent with Hegel's conclusion. If ordinary consciousness had to be shown the way to absolute knowledge from the outside, had to be taught by being given information or insight it could not acquire itself, then it would not be part of that ascending series of modes of understanding which constitute *Geist's* knowledge of himself; it would be outside the Absolute.

In this vein, Hegel starts off the introduction to *PhG* attacking those who begin with a critique of our faculty of knowledge as a tool we use to get at reality or a medium through which reality appears to us. It is not just that this makes the problem of knowledge insoluble, since ex hypothesi we cannot get at reality as it is in itself, untouched by our tool, or unreflected in our medium. It is also that this approach assumes that the absolute, what is to be known, is something which is quite distinct from our knowledge of it, that 'the absolute stands on one side and that knowledge, though it is on the other side, for itself and separated from the absolute, is nevertheless something real' (*PhG*, 65).[1] This, Hegel points out, is to prejudge the issue; something he is the less willing to do in this case since he wants to come to a conclusion diametrically opposed to this common assumption.

The method then is to start in ordinary consciousness, not import anything from outside, and make an 'immanent critique', as this procedure has come to be known in the Hegelian and Marxist tradition. This means that we must follow the dialectical movement in consciousness.

It is important to stress here that Hegel is not proposing the use of a dialectical 'method' or 'approach'. If we want to characterize his method we might just as well speak of it as 'descriptive', following Kenley Dove.[2] For his aim is simply to follow the movement in his object of study. The task of the philosopher is 'to submerge his freedom in [the content], and let it be moved by its own nature' (48). If the argument follows a dialectical movement, then this must be in the things themselves, not just in the way we reason about them.

Now we saw in the last chapter that there is a dialectical movement in things because they are riven with contradiction. Every partial reality is posited by the whole or absolute as a necessary condition of this absolute's existence; for this absolute can only be as embodied in a world of external, physical things and finite spirits. And yet these partial realities, just because they exist externally, each alongside the others, make a standing claim to independence which belies their status as posited vehicles of the whole.

We speak of 'contradiction' in this context because we can give a sense to the language of claim and denial when talking about things. But we can give a sense to this language because we see things not as just there, but as posited in order to embody and express *Geist*. In other words it is the ultimate ontological status of the category of purpose, and expressive purpose, which gives a sense to the theory of ontological contradiction. The whole furniture of the world is there in order to embody *Geist* and to manifest what he essentially is, self-knowing spirit, self-thinking thought, pure rational necessity.

But the inescapable medium of expression of this thought is external reality, and this cannot carry the message integrally. It is bound to distort it, just because this reality is external, its parts are independent of each other, and are subject to contingency. That is why external reality does not express the thought of rational necessity through some stable concatenation of enduring things, but rather through the process in which things come to be and pass away. Pass away they must, because they contradict the very basis of their

---

[1] Kenley Royce Dove translation in Martin Heidegger, *Hegel's Concept of Experience*, New York, 1970, p. 10.
[2] 'Hegel's phenomenological Method' in *Review of Metaphysics*, June 1970, v. xxiii, no. 4.

existence, which is to express rational necessity; but in thus cancelling what it has posited spirit comes after all to say what it wanted. What could not be expressed in external existence is expressed in the movement by which these existents come to be and pass away. The 'distortion' which external reality imposed on spirit's message is corrected by its necessary demise. Spirit never comes to one unchanging expression which says it all, but in the play of affirmation and denial it manifests what it is.

Hence, it is ultimately because we see reality on Hegel's theory as posited in order to say or manifest something, that we can speak of certain of its pervasive and inescapable features – such as existence partes extra partes – as 'distortions', as saying something different from what they are meant to say, and hence as 'contradicting'.

But this insight will not help us in an ascending dialectic such as the one we are now about to embark on. For we agreed that ordinary consciousness was not to be lectured at from outside; rather we were to start with ordinary consciousness and follow its own movement. Instead of showing how all partial realities must be contradictory once we accept the world as embodiment/expression of *Geist*, we have to start by pointing out the contradiction in finite existents and move from there to show how this contradiction can only be made sense of if we see these finite things as part of the embodiment of *Geist*. And as we saw in the previous chapter, an ascending dialectic of this kind is essential to Hegel's position, not just because he wants to convince people, but because the rational vision of *Geist* is supposed to be a seamless tissue of rational argument. It is not enough to show that *Geist* requires finite existents; we also have to show that these require *Geist*. Examined closely, they have to show their dependence on the whole. Otherwise Hegel's conception, which is also *Geist*'s knowledge of himself, is just another vision based on faith, or on over-all plausibility; and this is unacceptable if *Geist* is Reason.

But how can we discover contradiction in finite things? Taken just by themselves, as ordinary consciousness sees them, material objects or finite spirits are just given. We just saw that to see them as in contradiction we have to look on them as posited. But this is just what we are not allowed to do at the beginning without begging the question and violating our method. We seem caught in a vicious circle. How do we get started?

Hegel's claim will be that whatever reality we consider, no matter how circumscribed and seemingly independent, will manifest the inner articulation necessary for contradiction. This inner articulation, as we saw in the last chapter, is one where we can distinguish what the thing concerned is aiming at or is meant to be, on one hand, and what it effectively is on the other. Once this is so, then there can be a clash between effective existence and the goal or standard aimed at, and hence the thing is liable to contradiction. Thus the goal we discern does not have to be that of expressing *Geist* in the first instance. We can start off with a lesser standard, and by showing how effective existence cannot meet this standard, manifest a contradiction.

This is how Hegel accounts for dialectical contradiction in the *PhG*. We start off with something which is intrinsically characterized by the purpose it is bent on realizing or the standard it must meet. We then show of this thing that it cannot effectively fulfil this purpose or meet the standard (and the 'cannot' here is one of conceptual necessity). We are up against a contradiction.

This can take two forms. It can be that the purpose is in fact unrealized in the thing as it is; and in this case the existing reality will necessarily go under or be transformed as the purpose in further pursuing itself cancels its inadequate fulfilment. Or it can be that the standard is already met. And then the contradiction will force us to change our conception of the standard or purpose, or our conception of the reality in which it is fulfilled, in order to give a coherent account of this fulfilment.

And we in fact find dialectics of these two sorts in Hegel. His historical dialectics are of the first form: certain historical forms of life are prey to inner contradiction, either because they are doomed to frustrate the very purpose for which they exist (e.g., the master–slave relation), or because they are bound to generate an inner conflict between different conditions which are equally essential to the fulfilment of the purpose (as with the Greek polis, whose fate Hegel will discuss in chapter vi). These forms are thus destined to go under and be replaced by others.

But Hegel also presents dialectics of the other kind, which we can call 'ontological'. We have an example in the opening section of the *PhG* and also in the *Logic*. Here we are not dealing with historical change, or at least not primarily. Rather we are deepening our conception of a given standard and of the reality which meets it. And essential to the dialectical argument is the notion that the standard is already met. It is because we know this that we know that any conception of the purpose or standard which shows it as unrealizable must be a faulty conception; and it is this which takes us from stage to stage of the dialectic.

This distinction only concerns the basis from which a dialectical argument starts. It has nothing to do with the kind of contradictions it deals with. Thus it would be very wrong to see the distinction as one between dialectics which deal with contradictions in reality, and dialectics which deal with contradictions in our conceptions of reality. For in Hegel's most important ontological dialectic, the *Logic*, we shall see that the contradictory conceptions whose dialectical movement we follow really apply. They correspond to contradictory realities, which as such show their dependence on a larger whole which the higher categories describe. In other words the contradictions in our conceptions of reality will not be overcome by *resolving* them into a vision free of contradiction, but rather by seeing that they reflect contradictions in reality which are reconciled in a larger synthesis.

Similarly, the dialectic of consciousness in the *PhG* will take us through a critique of inadequate conceptions of knowledge considered as a realized standard. But at the same time, all the definitions we examine, even the most inadequate, have been held by men to be true at one time or other (including the present in the case of some men). They have thus necessarily shaped practice. And this means that the perfection of knowledge, where knowledge of the world comes together with self-knowledge, has not always been realized. The practice of knowledge, unlike that of playing hockey, say, cannot be divorced from our conception of it. Knowledge is ipso facto imperfect if it is in error about its own nature. Hence perfect knowledge can only be attained when men reach an adequate conception of it.[1]

Thus the dialectic of theories of knowledge is connected to a dialectic of historical forms of consciousness.

Reciprocally, while historical dialectics deal with the contradiction between certain historical forms and the basic purposes sought in them, this is also bound up with a contradiction in men's ideas. Indeed, the way men conceive the basic purposes of mankind is essential to the characterization of any given historical form and its inadequacy. That men at the beginning of history are incapable of realizing man's potential is bound up with their inability to conceive the goals of man (and *Geist*) adequately.

And it is because the conception of men's basic purposes that goes with a given historical life form is inadequate, that men at this stage are bound to defeat these purposes. This inadequate conception is thus essential to the contradiction; for the contradiction comes not from the fact that men's purposes go awry, but that men defeat them in trying to fulfill them. So that the contradiction in any historical society or civilization can be said to consist in this, that men's basic purposes, conceived in the terms of this society, are doomed to be self-defeating. Thus the play of changing conceptions is as essential to historical dialectics as the change of historical reality, and indeed, the one is bound up with the other.

We can see from this how closely related the two kinds of dialectic are in Hegel's work. Each figures in the explanation of the other. Hegel's philosophy of history refers us to his ontology; and his ontology requires historical development.

I spoke above of dialectical movement as generated by a clash between a

---

[1] This does not mean that there are a number of historical forms of knowledge which are *correctly* characterized as sensible certainty, perception, etc. For the basic properties of these early, inadequate conceptions is that they are in error about themselves. It is this clash between their self-idea and their effective reality which is the motor of the dialectic. But to the extent that they are in error, they are distortions of knowledge, which can be accounted for adequately neither by their own self-image nor by the conception of perfect knowledge.

purpose or standard and its attempted fulfilment. But we can see from the above that we might better understand it as a relation involving not just two terms but three: the basic purpose or standard, the inadequate reality, and an inadequate conception of the purpose which is bound up with that reality. This is clear in the case of the historical dialectics. There is a purpose which is frustrated by the inadequate conception of it which arises inescapably out of a certain historical form of life.

But the ontological dialectics also involve three terms. We start off with an inadequate notion of the standard involved. But we also have from the beginning some very basic, correct notions of what the standard or purpose is, some criterial properties which it must meet. It is these criterial properties which in fact enable us to show that a given conception of the standard is inadequate. For we show that this conception cannot be realized in such a way as to meet the criterial properties, and hence that this definition is unacceptable as a definition of the standard or purpose concerned. But we show the inadequacy of the faulty formula by trying to 'realize' it, that is, construct a reality according to it. This is what brings out the conflict with the standard. So that reality is our third term.

We can illustrate this point, and at the same time show why Hegel calls this kind of argument 'dialectical', by glancing back at Plato. For Plato's argument can sometimes be understood on this model, that is, as the discovery of contradiction in formulae which are put forward as definitions of a certain idea or standard, which formulae are then set aside for more adequate ones.

Thus in *Republic* I, when Cephalos puts forward a definition of justice as telling the truth and giving back what one owes, Socrates refutes it with an example, that of a man whose arms one is keeping, and who asks for them back in a state of madness. This example is enough to set aside Cephalos' definition. This is because the formula 'tell the truth and pay your debts' is put forward as a definition of *justice*. Now we do not yet know the true definition of justice at this stage of the dialogue. But we do know some of its criterial properties. We know for instance that a just act is a good act, one which should be done. When we have shown therefore an act which conforms to the above formula, but which should not be done, as manifestly one should not return his arms to a madman, one makes it untenable as a definition of justice; for to go on maintaining it would involve one in the contradiction of saying that the act was both just and wrong.

What Socrates has done is to show what it would be like to fulfil the standard as defined in Cephalos' formula, that is, what it would be like to act on it across the board. And he shows from this example that Cephalos' principle can't be fulfilled compatibly with the criterial properties of justice. Hence it cannot be a definition of justice.

This dialectic thus involves three terms: it starts with (1) a definition of justice, and (2) certain criterial properties of justice, and shows these to conflict when we try (3) to realize the definition in a general practice. We shall see a parallel with Hegel's dialectical arguments, both historical and ontological, which always operate with three terms, the true purpose or standard, an inadequate conception of it, and the reality where they meet and separate.

We can thus see how a Hegelian dialectic can get started without our having to accept at the outset Hegel's entire vision. We only need to find a starting point whereby some finite reality is to be seen as the (attempted) realization of a goal or fulfilment of a standard. It is not necessary that this goal or standard which we identify at the beginning be that of spirit returning to itself. It is enough that the historical purpose go beyond men's subjective understanding of their own goals, so that the latter can be shown as a self-defeating misconception of the former, or that we have a standard which shares some criterial properties with realized *Geist*.

Then, (provided our arguments hold) a dialectic can get going, in which our first conception (or the first historical form) being shown to be inadequate is replaced by another. Hegel insists on the point, that once a dialectical argument gets going, there is no arbitrary play in it, but each stage is determined by the previous one. Since the contradiction which affects our first stage or conception has a determinate shape, it is clear what changes have to be undertaken to overcome it. And this sets the nature of the next stage. But this second stage itself may be shown to be prey to contradiction, for its realization may be uncombinable with the criterial properties in another way, or fall into contradiction in attempting to embody them; or frustrate the historical purpose in its own fashion. And then the dialectic moves on to a fresh stage. Thus following a dialectical movement is not like deploying a sceptical argument, Hegel claims, where the proof that a form is in contradiction leaves us in the void. Each contradiction has a determinate outcome; it leaves us with a positive result. (*PhG*, 68.)

Hence given a starting point in a reality which is a realized standard or purpose, and granted that all the arguments work, we could climb from stage to stage up to a conception of the whole as *Geist* which alone successfully incorporates contradiction.

But this account may not make us very much more sanguine about the prospects of Hegel's ascending dialectics. For it is not enough that we *be able* to look on something as the realization of an intrinsic goal, that this be one way we *could* look at things. Such a problematic starting point could yield by dialectical argument a view of things which might convince us by its plausibility, but it would not be a binding argument, it would not command our assent in all rigour. To do the work Hegel wants, this starting point has to be undeniable. And this seems a tall order.

But it is one Hegel undertakes to fulfil. We shall see later that it is just the difficulty of sustaining this claim which undermines the whole system. Where his arguments do not work it is usually because they turn on a putative intrinsic purpose or standard which is not irrefutably established. And we shall note later an important distinction to be drawn between different dialectics in Hegel which turns on the nature of the starting point.

But as far as the *PhG* is concerned Hegel can and does vindicate his starting point. For we are dealing with consciousness. And our starting point is going to be the knowing subject. But this, unlike a stone or river, is already something which must be defined in terms of purpose realized, in terms of achievement – even in the eyes of 'natural' consciousness. 'Knowing', as we could put it, is an achievement verb. But then our gross, ordinary conceptions of this consciousness can be the starting points of a dialectic. For supposing we could show that knowledge, as they interpret it, is in fact unrealizable (by necessity), that what fulfilled their formulae could not be called knowledge by their own criteria. We should in this case have uncovered a deep contradiction or incoherence in the ordinary view which would require its amendment.

This is in fact how Hegel presents things in the introduction to *PhG* (70–3). To test the validity of knowledge claims, we need a yardstick or standard (Maßstab). But it would violate the principle of our procedure here if this came from outside, from someone who claimed superior knowledge of how things are. But this, argues Hegel, is not necessary in this case. Knowing consciousness distinguishes (unterscheidet) within itself our knowing from the object known. Consciousness is bi-polar: it is consciousness *of* something; and this means that its contents are not just inert, but bear on something outside. As a knowing subject my thoughts, perceptions, etc., are also knowledge *claims.*

Now we cannot compare the world-as-I-see-it, or the world-as-I-claim-to-know-it with the world-in-itself as yardstick. But what can serve as yardstick is the conception we have formed of what it is for a claim to be successful, i.e., what is veridical knowledge. And this involves no appeal to a standard outside consciousness. We rather appeal to its own conception of truth. 'Therefore, in what consciousness within its own self designates as the *An sich* or the true, we have the standard by which consciousness itself proposes to measure its knowledge' (*PhG*, 71).[1] What we compare with this is its effective knowing. If we can show that this could not meet its own standard, if we can show that in trying to meet this standard, we cannot but produce something incompatible with it, then we have uncovered a contradiction which cannot leave our conception of knowledge unchanged.

In showing that our effective knowing cannot meet the established standard, it may appear that we are showing the inadequacy of this knowing. But in fact the more fundamental critique is of the standard. For if we show that it cannot be met, then either we have got it wrong, or there can never be

---

[1] K. R. Dove translation (amended), p. 20.

knowledge. But the second alternative is one we cannot embrace; we would refute this thesis in formulating it. Knowledge there is, and it is an achievement, the realization of a standard. If the standard we conceive is unrealizable, we have to conceive again. Hence, as Hegel says, 'the test is not only a test of knowledge, but also of its standard' (73).

Hence it is that Hegel has managed here to latch on to a starting point that must be seen as a realized standard, and hence is able to start an ascending dialectic from the most natural and unsophisticated conception of the knowing subject, which he calls 'sensible certainty'. He can make good his promise, at least in the opening parts of the work, not to import any knowledge or insight from outside, but to follow only the movement of ordinary consciousness itself. This movement will arise from the contradictions in ordinary consciousness, which will come to light as its standards are confronted with its effective being.

But we might still be puzzled by this claim to be making an immanent critique. The philosophers who write and read the *PhG* are surely seeing things that many plain men do not. *Something* differentiates them from ordinary consciousness. What is it if not some further insight or knowledge? Hegel's answer is that philosophers are only distinct from the plain man here in holding clearly up to light what is already implicit in what ordinary consciousness recognizes. They make no contribution (Zutat, 72) of their own. Or if one likes, their contribution (Zutat, 74) is only to hold and connect together in a steady gaze what ordinary consciousness experiences without connecting.

For this dialectic is lived and experienced by ordinary consciousness. This is indeed how Hegel defines the term 'experience' in the *PhG*. Contradiction leads to the breakdown of one mode of consciousness and its replacement by another. But what is missing in this ordinary experience and present in the philosopher's account is the connection, an understanding *why* the first form broke down and how it came to be replaced by its successor. Ordinary consciousness experiences change; we philosophers see it as dialectical movement.

Starting from the ordinary conception of knowledge which an unsophisticated finite subject has of himself, Hegel hopes to climb through several stages to a form of consciousness which will no longer be a prey to contradiction, but will be able to hold it reconciled within itself. This will be real, or absolute knowledge.

The itinerary thither will be the phenomenology of Spirit, in which consciousness will fight through and eventually overcome the point of view from which it seems to be involved with what is foreign to it ('mit Fremdartigem behaftet', p. 75), and come to see itself as the self-knowledge of *Geist*. The road through and beyond this appearance (Schein) of isolated dependent existence is the phenomenology, and its stages present us with a series of forms of consciousness (Gestalten des Bewußtseins).

Already it will be clear that this work will have considerable scope. But in reality it stretches still wider than the above discussion implies. Hegel's aim is not just to take us through the various forms of knowing consciousness (*Bewußtsein* in the narrow sense); he must also trace the developing forms of consciousness as subject of action and desire, the subject as it sees itself or as it strives to become (what Hegel calls 'Self-consciousness' – '*Selbstbewußtsein*'). And this is essential to his purpose; for in taking us from a view of the subject as isolated consciousness to one which sees him as a vehicle of the self-knowledge of *Geist*, he has to do more than alter our conception of knowledge, he must also make us change our notion of the self. But some of the crucial transitions which bring about this transformation are not powered by contradictions in our manner of knowing, but rather by those which arise in the claims we make on the world, others and ourselves as agents.

Thus alongside the dialectic of knowing, that of 'consciousness', we see a dialectic of desire and fulfilment, of 'self-consciousness'. The root of this latter is what Hegel calls our 'certainty of self' (*Selbstgewißheit*), a rich concept which designates at once our notion of ourselves and the state for which we strive. This concept can be understood out of the expressivist background to Hegel's thought. Man strives for an external embodiment which expresses him, and is frustrated in this aim when the realities on which he depends in order to be, reflect something alien to him. Certainty of self is the confidence that everything on which we depend is not alien, that we are 'at home' (bei sich) in it. One might think of it as our definition of our integrity in the broadest sense. But since we are beings who live in continuous relation with external reality, and rely on it to be (if only because we need to breathe, eat, stand on something), any notion of self-certainty makes certain claims on this reality; certain things are required of the surrounding world if this self-certainty is to be fulfilled. This men struggle to bring about.

But what if a given notion of self-certainty not only is unfulfilled but cannot be in the nature of things; if the surrounding reality cannot ratify this notion of ourselves? Then action out of this idea is in a sense contradictory; it frustrates what it is meant to fulfil. Our 'truth' (*Wahrheit*), as Hegel calls our real predicament, cannot be made to match our certainty. We have then a dialectic in which our self-certainty plays the role of yardstick and in which our 'truth' is matched against it. If they are in principle non-congruent, then as with knowledge above, the yardstick must change.

The most famous example of a dialectic of this form is that of the master and the slave, which we will come to below. Having shown that man needs the recognition of others to ratify his self-certainty (having, that is, shown the contradictory nature of forms of self-certainty which do not involve recognition), Hegel shows how the attempt to achieve it unilaterally is doomed to failure. For the victorious struggle to wrest it from another ends either in his death or in his enslavement, and in either case the goal of recognition is frustrated.

This dialectic leads thus to a development of our self-notion. And this in the *Phenomenology* is woven into the dialectic of knowledge. The latter occupies the first section on 'Consciousness' (Bewußtsein) the former the second on 'Self-consciousness' (Selbstbewußtsein). The two are then in a sense combined in Chapter v on Reason. For we start again with a dialectic of consciousness, but one which is grounded on the certainty that human reason will meet itself in the world. And after another dialectic of self-consciousness, we go to a higher synthesis in the notion of individuality, which in turn passes over into another much richer dialectic, that of Spirit.

In the *PhG*, this meant what later is called 'objective spirit', and we have here a notion of the self no longer as that of isolated individuals, but rather as inhering in the human community. This in turn makes possible the passage to absolute spirit in the form of religion (Ch. vii), in which we prepare the transition to a notion of consciousness as the self-consciousness of *Geist*. In both these cases, the dialectic can no longer be seen as simply one of knowledge or one of certainty and truth, but integrates the two. It is the dialectic we see at work in history.

The extraordinary sweep of the *PhG* can be seen in this, that it starts with a theory of immediate knowledge and culminates in a brief philosophy of history and of the development of religion. But the latter is implicit in the goal which is introduced with the former, viz. to pass through the different figures of human consciousness until we arrive at a concept which can maintain itself against contradiction. We should therefore not object if en route we discover that those figures of man's consciousness which take him as an individual are radically inadequate, that we have to see him as the vehicle of a wider consciousness, that of a political society, and finally that of *Geist*, if we are to discover a form of man's understanding of self and world which will not collapse from its own weight. For Hegel is claiming that the only consistent view of human consciousness and knowledge is one that sees it as the self-knowledge of *Geist*. There is thus no hope of a defensible result as long as we remain with the lone man facing a world which is other. But once we see man as the vehicle of a supra-individual subject, such as the state, then some of the crucial transitions will be between forms of state organization, and hence in following them we will be tresspassing on the terrain of the philosophy of history. In principle this should not surprise us, since as we saw with Hegel there is no way to isolate phenomenology as a propaedeutic from the main body of his philosophy; the only thing that may surprise is the scope, which makes the *PhG* into an abbreviated version of some of the principal parts of Hegel's system.

But this is not all. Hegel draws his net wider than we might think necessary. Many readers have been struck by the tendency in this, as in all of Hegel's systematic works, to start as it might appear all over again at the bottom with each new section. This is one of the things which makes many of the Hegelian transitions difficult to follow and more questionable than they need be. Having shown the necessity of passing to a new way of regarding the question, Hegel does not remain at the level of conceptual sophistication he has attained, but starts off presenting this new way of approach in its most primitive form, being content to climb back slowly and generate once more in this new domain the sophisticated language he had previously earned the right to use.

Thus Hegel finishes his first section, Consciousness, with a flourish in which he shows that consciousness turns necessarily into self-consciousness. He has in the process deployed some of the language of his advanced speculative theory, such as 'infinity', the division of the self-identical, and so on. Yet he starts the section on self-consciousness without using any of this advanced paraphernalia, at the bottom, as it were, with a study of life and desire. Universality, which was shown to be a necessary part of the baggage of consciousness, must be shown again afresh in connection with self-consciousness.

Or again, Hegel finishes the chapter on Reason with the concept of the self-law-giving individual, and passes over to (objective) spirit, or man's life in the political community. This might be thought to justify our tackling this domain at a fairly advanced level. But Hegel chooses to start with the Greeks. In the chapter on Religion, he starts back with the Persians.

This habit – many examples can be found in all of Hegel's other systematic works – might seem to betray a kind of compulsive encyclopaedism. And it certainly makes Hegel's transitions less rigorous links than he sometimes pretends. But there is method in these seeming meanderings. It must not be lost sight of that the aim of these exercises is to demonstrate from our ordinary consciousness, or our everyday categories, or the existence of finite things (depending on the work in question), that we must end up with the Hegelian notion of self-knowing *Geist* by purely immanent argument, that is, in following a dialectic without presuppositions.

But in fact the starting point of such a demonstration is the one arbitrary thing. Eventually everything will be shown to emanate from the absolute, but in starting the argument one just has to take something as given and proceed from there. Hegel chooses as starting points realities or categories or ideas as distant from his end point as possible so as to strengthen his case. But this judgement of 'distance' is rather approximate and intuitive, at least before the system has been derived.

In order to make his demonstrations convincing therefore Hegel is led to cover all the angles; rather than proceeding on the shortest path to the goal, he is inclined to try to show that given any starting point one will get there. This is the more important in that this demonstration serves not only the purpose of establishing the basic Hegelian notion, but also of showing how everything is a part of it. There is thus a drive towards all-inclusiveness in Hegel's major demonstrative works. Hence the often surprising detours to take in some major idea or phenomenon, and hence the tendency when entering a new domain to start at the bottom.

The image to represent Hegel's system is not a single flow, but rather a river system; starting at the source he travels to the first tributary, then instead of continuing on the main stream he insists on exploring this arm from its headwaters, and so on down; until he can show that all the waters of the vast system flow into the estuary of absolute spirit.

But of course no work can be all-inclusive. There is always some principle of selection. And most readers have found the collection of subjects taken up in the *PhG* baffling, including as it does theories of knowledge and historical civilizations, visions of man of great formative importance to our civilization, like stoicism, and slightly absurd contemporary fads, like phrenology. Some have suggested that the principle of selection is an autobiographical one: these stages represent the theories, attitudes, aspirations or periods of history which Hegel adopted or reflected upon and which enabled him to win through to his mature vision. There is something in this, of course. But the autobiographical interpretation can easily be pushed too far. There is no evidence that Hegel was ever a believer in phrenology. And on the other side, the rich studies of Judaism and the life of Christ are absent from the *PhG*, leaving traces only in the theme of unhappy consciousness.

A much more plausible interpretation would be that Hegel was influenced as to what to include by the currents, beliefs and aspirations of the time. This would make sense in a work designed to take people from where they were to the perspective of absolute science. And this would explain his preoccupation with certain Romantic positions and with the issue of Kantian moral theory.

In fact the *PhG* is much too rich for us to go through systematically, even if we leave aside the detail. In addition, many sections touch on matters which Hegel took up later. What I should like to do is examine certain sections only which throw light on his position, and simply give the general direction of argument in the others in order to show the movement of the whole work. In later chapters, I shall have occasion to refer back to some of the sections which are passed too quickly over here.

2

The opening arguments of the *PhG* are a good illustration of Hegel's immanent critique. The notion of consciousness with which Hegel starts his dialectical critique is one he calls 'sensible certainty'. This is a view of our awareness of the world according to which it is at its fullest and richest when we simply open our senses, as it were, to the world and receive whatever impressions come our way, prior to any activity of the mind, in particular conceptual activity. 'We therefore have to take up a non-mediate or receptive stance, that is, to alter nothing in [this awareness] as it presents itself and to take things in free from conceptualization' (von dem Auffassen das Begreiffen abzuhalten, *PhG*, 79). Now, according to the view called sensible certainty, this pure receptivity is supposed to give us the richest knowledge, as well as the truest, and both these for the same reason, viz. that 'it has as yet left nothing out but has the object before it in its plenitude' (loc. cit.).

This view has evidently a certain resemblance to empiricism. It is not identical with empiricism, since it is not by any means as fully specified. But the idea of consciousness as primordially receptivity, prior to any intellectual (i.e., conceptual) activity, is a recognizably empiricist theme, as is the view that a greater degree of certainty attaches to the deliverances of this receptivity than to any judgements we might make on the basis of it.

Now Hegel's way of entering the dialectical movement here is to ask the subject of sensible certainty to *say* what it experiences. We can see here at work the same basic idea that Herder espoused, that human, reflective consciousness is necessarily linguistic consciousness, that it has to be expressed in signs. But if we are bringing to bear a thesis of this kind, are we not violating our method, and importing ideas, information, theories from outside ordinary consciousness?

Hegel clearly does not think so here. Rather, he treats the ability to say as one of the criterial properties of knowing. And it is hard not to agree with him. For clearly implicit in knowing in the sense relevant here is a certain awareness of what is known. We are after all not dealing with know-how, or with unconscious cunning, or anything of the sort, but with knowledge which we have in waking experience. If we know something in this sense, then we must be able to say what we know, and this even if we have not got the (adequate) words for it, even if we put it stumblingly and badly, and are forced to use words like 'ineffable'. The point is only that what is known be enough of an object of awareness that we can put ourselves to the task of trying to describe it. An experience about which nothing at all could be said, not even that it was very difficult if not impossible to describe, would be below the threshold of awareness which we consider essential for knowledge (in the sense relevant here, i.e., knowledge of the currently experienced). It would have either been lived unconsciously, or else have been so peripheral that we had or could recover no hold on it.

So in asking the subject of sensible certainty to say what he knows we are asking him to produce a bit of effective knowledge gained in this mode of consciousness. And this is where the contradiction arises. Sensible certainty is supposed to be immeasurably rich compared to conceptual consciousness because nothing has yet been selected, or abstracted, or put in a category with other phenomena not now present. The whole scene is there in its richness and particularity. But now we see that in order to know something we have to be able to say something about it; and to say something about it we have to focus on some dimension or other of the reality before us. The great richness of this form of consciousness turns out to be purely apparent: as we 'take in' the scene before us, we might mistakenly believe that we are taking in an inexhaustible richness of detail, because in fact an inexhaustible number of detailed things could be said about this scene. But the requirement that we say what we know shows that what we are really aware of is a selection from this inexhaustible fund, for in grasping things under some descriptions, we exclude (for the present) being aware of them under others. Looking at the objects in my study under their ordinary descriptions as use objects (typewriter, desk, chairs, etc.), I cannot see them as pure shapes; or looking at them as pure shapes, I cannot see them as the juxtaposition of different materials, and so on.

In other words, the exigencies of awareness are that we focus on certain dimensions of the objects before us, make certain ways of seeing them prepotent. Consciousness which is aware is selective. This cannot help coming out as soon as we are asked to say what we know.

Thus, says Hegel, sensible certainty, far from being the richest form of consciousness, would in fact be the poorest, for its very lack of selectivity condemns it to emptiness. To go beyond selection in the attempt to 'take in everything' can only be to fall over into unconsciousness, a trance-like stare. (The references to 'pure Being' evoke parallel arguments in the *Logic*.) Thus the attempt to realize the effective knowledge of sensible certainty clashes with its basic conditions. If there is such a state of unselective, immediate consciousness, then we have to snap out of it in order to know. Hence sensible certainty as a conception or 'yardstick' of knowledge is a prey to contradiction. As soon as we attempt to realize it we must see that it clashes with certain of the criterial properties of knowledge. It is in principle unrealizable.

Sensible certainty not only turns out to be unrealizable in its claim to unselective knowledge, but also in its claim to immediate contact with sensible particulars, without the mediation of general terms. If being aware of something is being able to say something about it, then it involves grasping the objects before us through aspects they have in common or could have in common with other things, rather than in their own particularity. It is this impossibility of bare knowledge of the particular rather than the necessity for selection that Hegel devotes most attention to in this first chapter.

Hegel's argument for the necessary mediation of knowledge through a concept or universal has basically two stages: In the first, he imagines the protagonist of sensible certainty answering the request to say by pure demonstratives ('this' or 'here' or 'now'). Hegel could argue at this point that these must be inadequate expressions of what I am aware of, that a term such as 'this' or 'now', applying as it can indifferently to many different contents, itself functions as a universal, and hence shows that there can be no immediate knowledge of the particular-knowledge, that is, unmediated by general terms. As a matter of fact, in Hegel's particular usage of the term, this likeness of function is enough to class these demonstratives as universals (as he will also class the 'I'). 'Such a simple referential term, which comes about through negation, which is neither this nor that, a *not-this*, and so which can be indifferently either this or that, is what we call a *universal*' (*PhG*, 82).

This stage continues with a consideration of the possible riposte on behalf of sensible certainty: that we can identify the particular time and place meant by 'here' and 'now' by adding that they are the here and now that *I* am contemplating. But 'I' in this context, as Hegel points out, is as much a 'universal' as 'this'. I *mean*, of course, one particular person, but I succeed as little in saying which particular person in saying, 'I', as I do in saying what particular thing in saying 'this'.

But of course this will not satisfy the protagonist of sensible certainty. And Hegel's assimilation of 'I' to the demonstrative terms discussed earlier just brings the malaise to a head. I cannot say who is meant by 'I' or 'this' or 'now' in a way that will be available to anyone regardless of context; and, for the same reason, sentences containing such words cannot be just transplanted from their context and retain the same truth value. But when I say 'I' or 'this', *I* know what I mean, and I can *show* you, if you will just place yourself in the same context.

Here we come to the real idea underlying the notion of sensible certainty. As a pure contact with the particular, it is of course only available in context, and as a knowledge unmediated by concepts, it can of course only be shown. In this second stage of his argument, Hegel is getting down to the real issue:

We have to be *shown* [the object]; for the truth of this immediate relation is the truth of *this* I, who restricts himself to one here and now. If we tried to take this truth in *afterwards* or from a *distance*, it would have no meaning; for we would do away with the immediacy which is essential to it. (*PhG*, 85)

We come across here, in another form, the familiar theme of ostensive definition. This is the nub of the argument.

Hegel's answer is not dissimilar to Wittgenstein's in the *Investigations*, and follows the line sketched above. I cannot know even what I mean in this context if all I can say is 'this' or 'here'. For what do these terms embrace? Take 'now': does it mean this punctual instant, this hour, this day, this decade, this epoch? It can mean all of these, and others in different contexts. But, for it to mean something for me, and not just be an empty word, there must be

143

something else I could say to give a shape, a scope, to this 'now'; let it be a term for a time period, such as 'day' or 'hour', or some description of the event or process or action that is holding my attention and hence defining the dimensions of my present.

And so, Hegel concludes, there is no unmediated knowledge of the particular. Sensible certainty ends up saying the opposite of what it means (88), and this is the proof of its contradictory nature. Any attempt at effective awareness of the particular can only succeed by making use of descriptive, i.e. general, terms. The purely particular is 'unreachable'. What remains beyond description as the 'unexpressible...is nothing other than the untrue, irrational, simply pointed to' (das Unwahre, Unvernunftige, bloss Gemeinte, 88). And by the same token, the particular is the subject of potentially endless description; for at any point, descriptions in general terms will not have captured its particularity, and yet there is nothing further to be done in order to express this particularity other than more description in general terms.

The thesis as here presented will not seem strange, or even wrong, to many contemporary philosophers. But the argument and its conclusion are presented by Hegel in a way that reflects certain major themes particular to his philosophy. Thus the unavailability of the bare particular is not just an epistemological truth; it reflects the ontological one that the particular is doomed by its very nature to disappear, that it is in principle mortal. What is permanent is the concept. So the unsayability of the particular is simply the expression of its ontological status, as that which cannot remain, that which must pass. And reciprocally, external particular existence is impermanent because it cannot be expressed in concepts.

That is why it is astounding, says Hegel, how some philosophers can continue to hold to the sensible reality of the particular as the final ground of knowledge. Even the beasts are wiser than this:

...for they don't remain standing before sensible things as though they existed *an sich*, but, despairing of this reality and in the full certainty of its nullity, they fall right to and consume them. *(PhG, 87)*

But, in Hegel's ontology, if it is true that the particular is mortal, it is also true that it exists of necessity, that the concept, the Idea cannot be outside of its embodiment in (a series of) particulars. The concept reveals itself in the procession of particulars, their coming to be and passing away. The particular can only be understood as a passing vehicle for the concept.

This background of theory makes Hegel present the argument for the unsayability of the particular in a fashion peculiar to himself. The argument reflects not just the impossibility of bare unmediated knowledge of the particular, but also the movement underlying experience itself. As particular sensuous beings, we encounter particular things, we come across them, as it were, with our senses. But as soon as we try to grasp them, they disappear, so to speak; we can hold onto them only by subsuming them under a concept. In Hegelian language, our attempt to grasp things in knowledge first negates them as particulars; then, negating this negation, we recover them by grasping them through mediated conceptual consciousness. The immediate is negated, but it is retained in mediated form.

The term in connection with which Hegel presents this argument is 'now'; and although there are some respects in which this particular example is unrepresentative, the point is plainly meant to be general. The 'now' of sensible certainty could be understood in its most immediate sense as designating the punctual present. But this is no sooner designated than it is past, hence gone, 'negated'; but when we fall back on a description that gives the scope of our present, say 'today' or 'this hour', the immediately fleeting present is recuperated and reintegrated into this larger 'now'; the first negation is negated.

This example is less illuminating than it might be, because the particular fleetingness of time, whose punctual instants vanish in becoming past, cannot be matched easily in the discussion of 'here' or 'this'. But the general point seems to be this: in experience we meet particulars; we can grasp these particular things only by in some sense 'pointing', either literally or by focusing on a thing in a way we could only convey through the use of some demonstrative or related word. But the experience itself of pointing (Aufzeigen) is that, in trying to grasp the thing, we show the fleeting, unseizable nature of the particular, and we can recover it and hold it before our gaze, as it were, only by subsuming it under a universal.

In other words, 'to point something out is to experience that "now" is a universal' (das Aufzeigen ist das Erfahren, daß Jetzt *Allgemeines ist*, *PhG*, 86). And by that terminal 'ist' Hegel means to convey the point that this experience brings us to the ontological truth of the matter, that the particular only is, as a vehicle for the concept. But what is germane from our point of view here is that Hegel has not just argued to the impossibility of unmediated knowledge of particulars and the necessary role of concepts, but wants to present the idea that the argument, as the depiction of an attempt to grasp the particular that fails, reflects our experience itself, as we encounter and reach out for particulars and discover that we can only really hold them through the mediating instruments of universal concepts.

I have tried to set out Hegel's argument in this first chapter in some detail partly because it fits so well his own description of an ascending dialectic, and partly because the points taken up here – the necessity of selection, the fleeting nature of the particular – are basic Hegelian themes. There is unfortunately no space to go into the detail of the argument in the other two chapters which make up this part of the *PhG,* called 'Consciousness'. I shall just give its general direction.¹

The new form which Hegel sees arising out of the dialectic of sensible certainty is a view of the object as a thing with properties. This conception of the object of knowledge, which Hegel calls 'perception', combines our understanding of it as a particular with the insight we have just gained, viz., that it can only be grasped through general descriptions.

This is the starting point for a new dialectic in which Hegel tries to show that experience defined in terms of this object reveals itself once more as contradictory, for the object itself suffers an inner contradiction. In order to get a coherent view of the object of experience we have to go over to a dynamic conception, one which sees the object as the locus of causal force.

Hegel then starts the third chapter with this new conception of the object as the locus of force. The chapter considers a number of ways of understanding an object of this kind. With the introduction of the notion of force, we have a two-tiered conception of the object, one in which its outer, manifest properties can be seen as products of an inner force or forces. Hegel goes through a number of ways of conceiving this inner-outer relation: e.g., characterizing the inner source of phenomena as the 'supersensible', or understanding this source in terms of law. He claims to show that all these break down and lead us inescapably to a notion of the object as the external manifestation of an inner necessity which must manifest itself. Its different features or properties, which are merely contingently linked by natural laws, are shown to be differentiations of an inner identity which necessarily differentiates itself.

We come thus to Hegel's notion of the Concept, the Idea of necessity which necessarily posits its own external manifestation. And since this concept shows itself to have the structure of subjectivity, we have made a transition from consciousness to self-consciousness. In speaking of the identical which divides itself, or the idea which is necessarily embodied, we are using formulae which belong to the subject.

What we have discovered therefore is that the structure of the object known and that of the subject are one and the same. Our consciousness is thus not of a foreign reality, but rather 'consciousness of another, of an object in general, is in fact necessarily *self-consciousness,* reflectedness in self, consciousness of oneself in one's other' *(PhG,* 128).²

The curtain which hid the transphenomenal has thus been pulled away, we discover that what lies behind it is identical with what stood before it

¹ For a discussion of the argument of the second chapter, and the relation of this section of the *PhG* to certain contemporary arguments, see my 'The opening arguments of the *Phenomenology*' in Alasdair MacIntyre (Ed.) *Hegel,* New York, 1972, pp. 151–87.
² 'das Bewußtsein eines Andern, eines Gegenstandes überhaupt, ist zwar selbst notwendig *Selbstbewußtsein,* Reflektiertsein in sich, Bewusßtsein seiner selbst in seinem Anderssein' (p. 128).

(consciousness). 'It becomes clear that behind the so-called curtain which is supposed to veil the Inner, there is nothing to see unless *we* step behind it, not just in order that there be someone who can see, but just as much to have something there to be seen' (*PhG*, 129).[1]

This is obviously an important transition for Hegel. But I do not propose to go into the argument here, for two reasons. First, because this transition is better and more thoroughly done in the *Logic* which moves from the two-tiered concepts of the Essence to the Concept. And secondly, because the argument, whatever its ultimate validity in Hegel's work as a whole, is rather unconvincingly presented here. Thus our ordinary (Hume-influenced) view of natural laws as contingent correlations is judged unsatisfactory and this plays an important role in the argument. It contradicts the 'concept of law' which requires an inner connection between the terms linked. Hegel's grounds for this view are that the law, expressed in a relationship between different terms, must also be seen as the emanation of a single underlying force or necessity. But this is not at all convincingly demonstrated and the reader has the feeling that the argument is circular here, that it is only because inner necessity is assumed as a requirement, that it comes out in Hegel's conclusions about the nature of the object.

Hegel seems here to have fallen prey to one of the dangers which beset dialectical arguments, that of imputing a yardstick or standard to the object under study which in fact is open to question, and which leads us unerringly to our conclusion at the cost of straining credibility at the starting point. In this case the requirement that our conception of natural law must find a place for the notion of inner necessity seems to be such an imputation.

Let us turn now to the second section of the *PhG*.

[1] 'Es zeigt sich, daß hinter dem sogenannten Vorhange, welcher des Innre verdecken soll, nichts zu sehen ist, wenn *wir* nicht selbst dahintergehen, ebensosehr damit gesehen werde, als daß etwas dahinter sei, das gesehen werden kann'.

CHAPTER V

Self-consciousness

1

In the dialectic of consciousness, the tension lay between a certain norm of knowledge and what we actually are able to know in attempting to fulfil it. With self-consciousness, the dialectic will be between our idea of ourselves, what we claim to be, and what we actually are. These are the two moments Hegel calls self-certainty and truth. In the earlier dialectic the key notion was knowledge; here the centre of interest shifts to desire and its fulfilment. In our notion of ourselves, the object of our self-certainty is not something towards which we are neutral; on the contrary we are passionately attached to it. When our truth belies this and forces us on to another model of self-certainty, the transition is not made without pain.

And this transition itself is of a different kind. It must not be seen in intellectual terms, that a certain notion of self becomes untenable and has to be abandoned. Rather it is that the attempt to act out a certain idea of ourselves leads to consequences, in which the original idea is certainly undermined because the goal is not reached, but which give rise to the next stage not so much by refuting the previous self-certainty as by the creation of a new situation for man.

The dialectic of self-consciousness is thus a dialectic of human longing and aspiration, and their vicissitudes. What underlies it? What is the form of aspiration, the self-certainty, which can ultimately be fulfilled and which will bring the dialectic to a close?

What is aimed at is integral expression, a consummation where the external reality which embodies us and on which we depend is fully expressive of us and contains nothing alien. This goal, which we can call a state of total integrity, is identified by Hegel with his conception of infinity, a condition in which the subject is not limited by anything outside. It is this longing for total integrity which for Hegel underlies the striving of self-consciousness, at first after crude and unrealizable versions of the goal, then when man has been educated and elevated by conflict and contradiction, after the real thing.

The real thing can only be attained when men come to see themselves as emanation of universal *Geist*. For it is only then that they will not see the surrounding universe as a limit, an other. And since man depends on this surrounding universe, he can never feel integrity as long as it is seen as other. Because man starts off with a notion of himself as a finite being, and with a raw undeveloped form of life reflecting this, his longing for integrity is doomed to frustration until he can undergo the transformations which will raise him to a grasp of the universal.

The Hegelian notion of *Geist* is thus essential here. Spirit is necessarily embodied. Integrity thus cannot be achieved through an inner retreat, in which self-consciousness would cut itself off from the bodily. But once one admits that I am nothing apart from my body, we have also to count with the fact that my body is dependent on the surrounding world, that my life depends on a series of interchanges with this milieu. Now the integrity which Hegel posits as the goal is the negation of dependence on something other, it is the recognition of self in all that which is essential to me. It follows that there is no strategy of retreat which can give us integrity; there is no circumscribed definition of ourselves, either just as the human race, or just as individual human beings, and above all not as purely spiritual minds, within which we can feel in full possession of ourselves. Or rather, if we do this feeling is necessarily an illusory one. For in actual fact we as so defined are either ontologically or factually dependent on something other; we are at the mercy of foreign reality. All historical solutions which involve a retreat of this kind are branded by Hegel as illusions; this will be seen below with stoicism for instance.

Underlying this extremely far-reaching notion of integrity is the Hegelian preoccupation with fate. The opposition which is seemingly the most insurmountable of all is that between action and fate, between what men make of themselves which has a certain meaning for them, on one hand, and the seemingly senseless things which happen to them, of which death is the ultimate culmination, on the other. Hegel will not be satisfied until this dualism is overcome, and it is this aspiration which the drive for integrity reflects.

With this goal and the Hegelian notion of *Geist* in mind we can already see the kind of inadequacies from which earlier stages of self-certainty may suffer. There is first, the predicament where we depend on an external reality that does not reflect *Geist*. Secondly, there is the situation in which we are temporarily happy in this other dependence because we are unconscious of it; we have too raw and undeveloped a view of ourselves to see the gap. Such is the predicament of the master in the master–slave relation who has his world made over to reflect him by the labour of the slave, but who remains limited in his self-certainty. In another way, the happy stage of the Greek city-state is one in which men feel at home because they have not yet seen themselves as universal. Sooner or later these stages are bound to break apart because of the inner contradiction that man feels at home as a being which he is not.

The third predicament can arise in response to either of the first two; it is one based on retreat. Man achieves the illusion of self-identity by defining himself as an inner spiritual being, by fooling himself that he coincides with himself as a mind or spirit. Hegel refers to this often with the Fichtean formula I = I; the error expressed here being precisely the belief in simple self-coincidence. For we have seen that a subject is necessarily a being who incorporates his other (his embodiment) and 'returns to himself' through this other, that is, comes to self-consciousness in his other. To achieve self-coincidence as spiritual beings is thus ontologically impossible; or otherwise put, its achievement could only be the abolition of the subject. Or, in other terms again, the subject is not only 'self-consciousness'; he necessarily has the structure of 'consciousness' as well, with its inescapable bi-polarity between subject and independent object.

But nevertheless men are often tempted in the course of their long historical development to have recourse to this illusion, often because of the pain of the first predicament, i.e. dependence on an alien reality. But we can also come to this out of the second predicament, complaisance in an external expression which is inadequate to us as subjects. The first realization that a certain form of life in which we have been at home is not adequate to us takes the form of an alienation of certain men from this form; but since their external lives are still bound up in this social form, they may quite understandably define their newly-discovered universal nature in a purely spiritual, internal way. It would appear that both of these developments underlie stoicism, for instance.

Hegel opens the dialectic of self-consciousness with a discussion of its relation to life. We saw in part one why self-consciousness only arises in a living being. Hegel now seems to make this point but in an odd way. The 'object' (Gegenstand) of self-consciousness is a living thing, he says.

This notion of 'object', however, can be interpreted two ways. In the first section of the *PhG*, self-consciousness arose from an inner reality which 'repelled itself from itself'; and the result was an external manifestation or object which in turn must be seen as identical with the inner idea. Following this, one would think of the outer object which self-consciousness must overcome as its own embodiment. It is in connection with a reference back to this earlier notion of self-repulsion (p. 125) that Hegel speaks of the concept which 'splits itself into the opposition of self-consciousness and life' (*PhG*, 135).

But this notion of an object which must be overcome by self-consciousness can also apply to something else, to the object of *desire*. And here is where the famous Hegelian analysis of desire (Begierde) starts. For Hegel the drive for integrity is evident even in lower forms of life in the fact that they seek out what they need from the external world, and devour it, that is, incorporate it in themselves. In so doing they 'cancel its otherness'. This process is essential (causally) to their continued existence. But Hegel assimilates this causal necessity to the ontological predicament of all subjects who to be must cancel the otherness of an external embodiment. And once we accept total integrity as the goal, then this assimilation is right, because I cannot be said to be really at home in my bodily existence if this in turn is dependent on foreign reality. Thus desire reflects not just the factual need for an object, but also the fundamental drive for integrity.

Self-consciousness has thus two objects, its embodiment and the object of desire. Its continued existence involves its overcoming or 'returning to itself out of' both. But these two forms of return are related in that the return out of the first involves overcoming the second. This is what Hegel seems to be saying in the following passage:

From now on, consciousness has as self-consciousness a double object; one immediate, the object of sensible certainty and perception, which however bears for consciousness the character of negativity; and the second, viz. itself, which is the true essence and which at first is only present in opposition to the first object. Self-consciousness presents itself here as the movement whereby this opposition is done away with and its equality with itself becomes real for it.   (*PhG*, 135)

That self-consciousness is only in living beings reflects the fact that life itself is a stage on the road to the kind of unity which is revealed in most perfect form in the subject. The passage which follows on life is resonant of Hegel's earlier view of the Frankfurt period, according to which it was life rather than the subject which provided the paradigm of the identity of the different. Life only exists in an articulation (Gliederung) into existing individual forms (bestehende Gestalten). They seem to be independent, and yet they only exist in the process of life itself. They eventually pass away, and hence lose this independent existence, but this passing away is linked to the creation of new individuals. (This passage leans on the Hegelian idea that death and reproduction are intimately joined.)

Life is thus a process which can only maintain itself in the spawning of individual living beings, and yet which is always more than this external existence; it is never really coincident with these beings, and hence they must of necessity go under. But since life can still only be in living things, they must at the same time be replaced. So life's fullest manifestation is in the continuous cycle of death and reproduction. As an inner reality which can only exist embodied, and yet must also cancel this embodiment in order to be, life is a prefiguration of spirit.

But only a prefiguration; life goes through this process unreflectingly, the negation of the outer embodiment is suffered dumbly by living creatures in their death. Human consciousness, on the other hand, can reach beyond the life of the individual and express in a conscious life form its link with the universal. In other words, the negation of the external embodiment, the return to the universal out of the particular, is effected in a new way by men. Not just in dying but in living consciously in the universal. And this engenders a kind of standing negation, one which does not abolish what is negated, as death does. In living in the universal, men can even be said to live beyond death (this is the meaning which Hegel gives to immortality, which he does not accept in the ordinary sense, as we saw in Part I).

The self-consciousness whose dialectic we shall now examine is a subject, destined for this conscious life in the universal, and also a living thing. This dual nature is essential to the dialectic. The seemingly unclear Hegelian point mentioned above, that the 'object' of self-consciousness is a living thing, must be interpreted to mean both objects. For self-consciousness is embodied in life; and as a living organism, its object of desire is a living being; it feeds on life.

Man cannot remain a simple 'I', simply self-identical, because he needs external things, external life, to live. He is a being of desire. But in consuming what he desires, he seems to overcome this foreign reality and recover integrity. Except that this integrity is not adequate to what he is (second standard predicament above). For the negation of otherness involved here is the simple negation which abolishes; even if it were complete, it would simply return man to the self-identity which is the death of subjectivity; the end of desire would be the end of man. But in fact it is never complete, new desires arise endlessly; so that human life at this level is an alternation between being before another which is wholly foreign, and having incorporated this, being before nothing at all.

Man, as a being who depends on external reality, can only come to integrity if he discovers a reality which could undergo a standing negation, whose otherness could be negated without its being abolished. But the negation of otherness without self-abolition, this is a prerogative of human, not animal consciousness. So that the basic desire of self-consciousness can only be fulfilled by another self-consciousness. 'Self-consciousness attains its satisfaction only in another self-consciousness' (*PhG*, 139).

Here we come to the basic idea, which will be explored in the next section in the dialectic of the master and the slave, that men seek and need the recognition of their fellows. The subject depends on external reality. If he is to be fully at home this external reality must reflect back to him what he is. In the dialectic of desire, we are faced with foreign objects which we then destroy and incorporate; what is needed is a reality which will remain, and yet will annul its own foreignness, in which the subject can nevertheless find himself. And this he finds in other men in so far as they recognize him as a human being (Anerkennen).

This is the real fulfilment of self-consciousness, because it is the real 'unity of oneself in one's other-being' (Einheit seiner selbst in seinem Anderssein; p. 140). This is why the road towards man's recognition that the universe is not other passes through the drama of mutual recognition, the first and basic model of the recognition of oneself in others. And the road to mutual recognition passes through, as we shall see in the following analysis of the master and the slave, the recognition of the universal. And this is why it is this mutual recognition which brings us to the reality of *Geist*. For *Geist* is this

absolute substance which in the perfect freedom and independence of its opposition, i.e., the opposition of different self-consciousnesses each existing *für sich*, is their unity: an 'I' that is a 'we' and a 'we' that is an 'I'. In self-consciousness as the concept of *Geist*, consciousness comes to its turning point, at which it steps out of the multi-colored show of sensible immanence and the empty night of suprasensible transcendence into the spiritual daylight of presence. (*PhG*, 140)

Hegel starts the dialectic of self-consciousness with the famous dialectic of the master and the slave. The contradiction underlying this is the following: men strive for recognition, for only in this way can they achieve integrity. But recognition must be mutual. The being whose recognition of me is going to count for me must be one that I recognize as human. The operation of reciprocal recognition is therefore one that we accomplish together. Each one, says Hegel, accomplishes for himself what the other tries to achieve in relation to him. My interlocutor sees in me another, but one which is not foreign, which is at one with himself; but this cancelling of my otherness is something that I must help to accomplish as well.

The contradiction arises when men at a raw and undeveloped stage of history try to wrest recognition from another without reciprocating. This is at a stage when men have not recognized themselves as universal, for to have done so is to see that recognition for me, for what I am, is recognition of man as such and therefore something that in principle should be extended to all. But here we have man as a particular individual (Einzelnes) who strives to impose himself, to achieve external confirmation.

This leads to armed struggle. And necessarily so, says Hegel. It is not just that men are opposed, since each seeks onesided recognition; it is also that the risk of one's life is part of the very claim to recognition. We have seen earlier that self-consciousness is both a living being and somewhat more; somewhat more because it does not just undergo the life-process unconsciously, but is already beyond it in thought. In the attempt then to win recognition of themselves as self-consciousness men prove that they are beyond mere life by showing that they are not attached to this particular living thing which is themselves, that their recognition as 'beings for themselves' (Fürsichsein) is more important, that they will risk their lives for it.

This struggle easily leads to the death of one or both combattants. And this obviously misses the goal. Even if I remain alive in face of my dead adversary, I have won no recognition. My 'negation' of him has been a natural one, as Hegel says (p. 145), it is a simple negation as we saw earlier, whereas what is needed is a standing negation, one in which my opponent's otherness is overcome, while he still remains in being. The problem is thus that while each is pushed to put his life in hazard, to show that he is above mere attachment to life, this remains essential. The only outcome to the struggle which can even look like a solution is one which takes this into account.

But this is the case with the classical outcome of enslavement. Before it comes to the death, one side gives in, recognizes its attachment to life, and becomes subjected to the other. The victor spares the vanquished in order to make him a slave. Both protagonists then preserve life, but in a very different way. The victor has won his point. That what is essential for him in his *Fürsichsein*, his own sense of self, and that life is subordinate. For the slave, however, it is life which is essential, his sense of self is now subordinate to an external existence which is beyond his control.

The full relation of master and slave has to be understood with the aid of a third term, material reality (Dingheit). Master is related to slave mediately through this reality: the master subjects the slave through this command over things, at the limit through the use of a chain. But at the same time, master is related to material reality through the slave. The relation of the master to what surrounds him is that of a pure consumer; the hard task of transforming things and preparing them for consumption is that of the slave. The master's experience is of the lack of solid reality (Unselbständigkeit) of things; the slave is the one who experiences their independence and resistance as he works them.

But this outcome, although better than a fight to the death, is also vitiated as a solution. The recognition is onesided; slave is forced to recognize master, but not vice versa. But for this very reason the upshot is of no value for the master. His vis-à-vis is not seen to be a real other self, but has been reduced to subordination to things. Recognition by him is therefore worthless; the master cannot really see himself in the other. Rather he is reduced to the parlous condition of being surrounded by beings which to him cannot be self-conscious; so that the surrounding world on which he continues to depend cannot reflect back to him a human visage. His integrity is thus radically undermined just when it seemed assured.

But if this outcome is a failure ultimately for the master, for the slave it prepares the ground for ultimate success, and within the relationship a reversal slowly takes place. The slave at least has before him a being who exists for himself in the master, even if this master does not recognize him. His environment is not reduced to the sub-human, as is the case with the master.

But the important sources of the slave's transformation are the fear of death and disciplined work. The short, three-page (148–50) passage in which Hegel deals with this is one of the most important in the *PhG*, for the themes are not only essential to Hegel's philosophy but have had a longer career in an altered form in Marxism. The underlying idea, that servitude prepares the ultimate liberation of the slaves, and indeed general liberation, is recognizably pre-served in Marxism. But the Marxist notion of the role of work is also foreshadowed here.

But the Hegelian theme which was not taken up in the successor philo-sophy is the role of the fear of death. The vitiated relation of master and slave arises from a struggle between men of limited horizons who are low on the scale of development. They have as yet no inkling of their link to the universal; for all their willingness to risk their external existence in order to impose their sense of self, this self of theirs is still that of a particular individual, a limited one. But in order to come to a real solution to this striving for recognition, men have to see themselves as universal, as we have seen.

For Hegel, a crucial factor in the education of men, in the transformation which brings them to the universal, is the fear of death. The prospect of death shakes them loose, as it were, from all the particularities of their life. Hegel uses the image here of a life which has hardened in a certain form. The menace of death then makes it that consciousness 'has been inwardly dis-solved, has trembled to its depths, and everything fixed in it has quaked'. (*PhG*, 148.)

The same idea recurs in a passage of the *Philosophy of Right*, where Hegel speaks of the necessity of war from time to time to bring men back to the universal. In ordinary life they are too sunk in their day-by-day particular preoccupations, they lose touch with the universal idea represented in the state. War and the risk of death shake them loose from these narrow preoccupations and bring them back to the universal. Needless to say, the passage has done nothing to enhance Hegel's reputation among contem-porary Liberals.

But the role of the fear of death should not be surprising in the light of what we have seen of Hegel's philosophy. The return to the universal *Geist* involves an overcoming of the particular external existence in which it is embodied. This is why as we have seen death comes necessarily to living things. Of course, the highest negation of his external existence is achieved by man in thought, that is, while still alive. But he is helped to this inner negation by coming face to face with death, the final outer negation, for this shows the true status of all the external particularity in his life, it shows it as necessarily passing, as destined to be negated, and thus invites the negation in thought which is the return to the universal. It is not just that the prospect of hanging, as Dr Johnson said, concentrates the mind wonderfully. It is also that it focusses it on the universal.

Now the beginning of the reversal lies here. It is the slave that really suffers the fear of death, for he has been, and still is, at the mercy of another. So it is he that is shaken loose from his particular sense of self, while the master victorious is just hardened in his. But this fear would not be enough, it would have no more than passing effect, if the slave did not transform himself by the work he is forced to do in his service to the master.

And this brings us to the theme which is later one of the central ideas of Marxism. The master we saw above has the advantage that his relation to things is that of simple enjoyment (Genuß); it is the slave who experiences their resistance and independence. But with time, the advantages reverse. The master being in face of a world which offers him no effective resistance tends to sink back into a stupor of self-coincidence. He approaches the stagnant pole where I = I. He is simply a consumer.

The slave however has to struggle with things to transform them, and sooner or later he achieves a mastery over them. And in so doing he imprints his own ideas on them. The man-made environment thus comes to reflect him, it is made up of his creations.

Work thus plays a crucial role in man's struggle for integrity. We saw earlier that the core problem is that the subject is always 'outside himself', he always depends on a surrounding universe; he must therefore come to recognize himself in this surrounding. This is why the principal path to integrity lies through recognition by another; in the human environment a man can recognize himself in others. But now we see another important path; man can come to see himself in the natural environment by making it over in conformity with his own project. For in doing this we achieve another standing negation, a reflection of ourselves which endures.

Achieving integrity involves travelling both of these paths. Ultimately it is mutual recognition which is the most essential. But in order to achieve it we must transform ourselves from limited individuals to self-conscious embodiments of the universal. And this brings us to a second important function of work: in transforming things we change ourselves. By creating a standing reflection of ourselves as universal beings we become such beings.

This idea is deeply rooted in Hegel's whole outlook and in his notion of the subject which as we saw is fundamental to his philosophy. A subject is necessarily embodied; hence any change in the subject, such as the rise from limited individuality to universal consciousness, must be mediated by a change in his embodiment. This is why as we have seen in real historical terms the growth of human thought goes along with a development of his forms of life, of what we call civilizations. But these forms of life involve different man-made environments. As Hegel sees in the description of the master–slave relation, each is related to the other through their relation to things. Hence higher forms of human coexistence, which bring us closer to integrity, each are linked with a characteristic way of relating to things, i.e., a certain form of man-made environment. Thus both paths are complementary, and both are involved in the growth of higher forms of life which embody the higher spiritual status of man.

Thus Hegel's notion here is that the slave becomes a universal conscious-ness through his work. Both the fear of death and the discipline of service were necessary. The fear of death alone would have shaken him loose for a moment from the particular, but would have built no standing embodiment of universal consciousness. But work alone, uninformed by the fear of death, would have produced just particular abilities (Geschicklichkeit), not a uni-versal consciousness of self.

For what the slave achieves through his work, as is evident in the next section, is the grasp of himself as free thought. He recognizes in the power to transform things the power of thought, the power to remake things according to concepts, and thus universal models. It would have been possible to develop particular abilities and skills without awakening this consciousness. But the slave being already brought to the universal by the fear of death sees in his transforming ability the power of a consciousness which thinks and executes, which can create models, archetypes, and then change things to conform to them. He thus sees in the world of objects made by him the reflection of himself as universal, as a thinking being. This passage shows how much Hegel's philosophy of history anticipates historical materialism. The intellectual grasp of things in concepts (a word etymologically related to 'grasp' in both English and German) is seen as arising here out of the physical shaping of things in work. Conceptual thinking arises out of the learned ability to transform things. We learn to know the world of material reality, and ultimately our own minds, in trying to bend this matter to our design. Conceptual thought grows out of this interchange.

The master–slave relation has thus brought about a reversal. The master's prerogative of being only a consumer leads him to stagnant self-coincidence. While the slave who is subject to the refractory existence of matter gradually turns the tables, turns this resistance to account by making it the stand-ing reflection of himself as universal consciousness. The reversal is the more complete in that he owes his transformation to his subjection; only under the discipline of service would he have undertaken the work which has raised him above his original limits.

2

The dialectic of the master and the slave issues in a higher stage, which Hegel identifies with the philosophy of stoicism. Through work, discipline and the fear of death, the slaves have come to a recognition of the universal, of the power of conceptual thought. And this is already to have won through to a certain freedom. For first, man as a spiritual being comes to greater self-realization in becoming capable of universal reflection. And secondly, since thought is the basis of everything, man comes closer to overcoming the alien nature of things when he thinks in universal categories. Conceptual thought, as against representation in images (Vorstellung), is a medium we move freely in because we truly master it ('a concept is for me immediately *my* concept', *PhG*, 152). At the same time, it is truly at the root of things. Thus 'In thought I am free, because I am not in another, but remain quite within my own purview [schlechthin bei mir selbst], and the object which is essence for me is in undivided unity my being-for-self [mein Fürmichsein]' (*PhG*, 152).

But stoic freedom is radically incomplete. For we are still dealing with a philosophy of slaves. Through their commerce with matter they have come to the intuition that thought is the basis of all. But just as they cannot make over their environment, and particularly their society, in order to express this intuition – for a rational political structure and laws will only come at a later stage in history – so they are still incapable of working through their idea in order to show the particular determinations of their world as manifestation of universal, (in the Hegelian sense) conceptual necessity.

These two inabilities, practical and theoretical, go together in Hegel's philosophy of history. Men can only come to see the world as *Geist* or rational necessity manifested in reality, when they are able to shape their own human reality according to this necessity, i.e., to practical reason. The practical experience of achieving the reflection of self in other is essential to the theoretical insight. Once again we see how the thesis that *Geist* is necessarily embodied leads to a partial convergence with historical materialism.

Hegel thus identifies stoicism as a stage of political impotence which is reflected in abstractness of thought. His critique of it is as a strategy of retreat, to use our earlier expression. It is founded on the intuition that consciousness is a thinking essense. But it is still incapable of deriving the determinate shape of the world from this principle. It cannot discern the rationality of things. Its notion of thought is still abstract; it has not yet (and obviously could not have) the notion that thought necessarily 'goes over into' its embodiment from which we can derive (as Hegel will do in the Philosophies of Nature and Spirit) much of the structure of the world.

This leads us into a kind of formalism. Thought underlies reality, but one cannot say in detail how, and so the particular content of the world is necessarily seen as contingent, as just given. Stoicism can only hold onto universal categories, like the true and the good, wisdom and virtue, but cannot derive a determinate content for them.

Now although applied to stoicism, the analysis here is reminiscent of other kinds of formalism criticized by Hegel, and in particular, we are reminded of Hegel's critique of Kant, of the Kantian dualism whereby the forms of experience are derived from the understanding, but the matter is given, and from a source which is forever unknowable. Hegel is clearly also combatting this dualism in his critique of stoicism.

In any case, the reply of stoicism to its inability to derive the content of reality from thought is a strategy of retreat; it is to consider this content as inessential. Thought is free, the subject as thinking is free. But freedom for Hegel means being oneself, 'bei sich' (at home) in one's other, or object. The subject of stoicism cannot be "bei sich" in relation to the determinate reality of the world, for this is something foreign, something that cannot be derived from thought. The strategy is to withdraw from this reality and to redefine the object as simply the object of thought.

The stoic is thus free as a thinking subject in abstraction from the external circumstances of his life, 'whether on the throne or in chains'. 'The freedom of self-consciousness is *indifferent* over against natural existence' (p. 158, italics in original).

But this obviously will not wash. The retreat towards inner self-identity cannot bring freedom for an embodied subject whose real freedom must thus be externally expressed in a way of life. Stoicism is thus in contradiction with itself, it is a putative realization of freedom which is in fact its negation. As such it must go under. The core intuition, that conceptual thought is at the root of things, this is a permanent gain, but the claim to inner freedom collapses.

In accounting for this collapse and the derivation of the next stage, Hegel brings us through another historical philosophy, ancient scepticism. This he paints as the fulfilment of the basic idea of stoicism; where this latter considers the determinate content of things as irrelevant or inessential, scepticism goes over to the attack and calls it into question. It is the polemical consequence of stoicism.

But this just serves to point up more acutely the underlying contradiction. For as embodied subjects we go on living in external reality. We may well declare its non-being, it returns unceasingly and inescapably. So that in fact what we have is an oscillation between a sense of our own self-identity, and an equally acute sense of our dependence on a changing, shifting external reality. As fast as we call this changing reality into question in order to experience ourselves as immutable and self-identical, our own inner emptiness forces us to accept that we are embodied in the mutable and self-external.

But this oscillation occurs in a single consciousness, and putting these two moments together we derive a new dialectical phase, in which the subject has to accept the fact of inner division (Entzweiung), in which the inner self itself is painfully divided, into an ideal immutable and self-identical being on one side and one plunged in a world of confusion and change on the other. This is the stage of the unhappy consciousness, in which the relation of master and slave, which stoicism claimed to have escaped, reappears, but now within the subject, in the relation between these two mutually incompatible sides.

The pages on the unhappy consciousness introduce us to some of the fundamental ideas of Hegel's philosophy of religion. We recognize the themes of Hegel's writings on religion of the 1790s, in particular the theme of separation, where man projects his lost unity into a transcendent spirit to whom he subjects himself absolutely, as in the religion of Abraham.

In the *PhG* Hegel presents the unhappy consciousness as one who is deeply divided because it is both the immutable self-identical subject of thought and the individual who is subject to the changeable world. But this situation as it is lived by the subject is one in which he identifies himself as particular with the inessential and mutable. The immutable is projected into a beyond. His unity with it is felt only in the sense of loss, the sense that he must somehow go beyond his present estate and achieve oneness with this immutable. But since at the present stage, particular and immutable are so defined as to be incompatible, this attempt is perpetually doomed to failure. Since I cannot stop being a particular individual, I can never attain to unity with the unchanging.

As a relationship with a transcendent reality, to which I cannot be indifferent, but with which I must strive to unite myself, the unhappy consciousness can be seen as a religious one.[1] And underlying Hegel's study here is the wealth of his reflections on the historical development of Judaism and Christianity, as well as on the relations of religion and philosophy. We shall look at some of these in our examination of chapter vii of the *PhG*, and return again to a discussion of this matter in chapter xviii below.

But in the passage under study here, Hegel's dialectical development only refers (implicitly) to certain stages of medieval Christianity. We cannot go into its detail here. It includes an interpretation of the Crusades as a vain attempt to recover contact with the historical Jesus, who must as a particular disappear and ever recede from us in time. The failure of this venture forces men to face the real destiny of Christianity which is to make the unity of God and man real in a community (Gemeinde).

Hegel then continues with what is obviously a treatment of the medieval church, though some of the things he says obviously apply to any church which has not yet realized the full unity of man and God. A church life led under the consciousness of division is one where men still see the universal outside them, as something they must be subject to. The hierarchical nature of the medieval church reflects this sense of subordination. But just as with the slave earlier, this servitude under an external discipline forms man and makes him over so that he can recognize the universal in himself. We repeat here in a more

---

[1] We can see here the origin of the Feuerbachian and Marxian conception of religious consciousness as alienated. Not that Feuerbach and Marx had the same notion of religion as Hegel, of course. These successors 'anthropologized' Hegel's Spirit. What replaced Hegel's *Geist* was man, generic man. For Hegel, on the other hand, man must come to see himself as a vehicle of a spirit which was that of a broader reality, whose total embodiment was the universe. So that even at the summit of his development man remains in the presence of something greater than himself.

internalized way the passage from external subjugation to an identification with reason.

This transition takes us beyond unhappy consciousness to a higher stage, and with this transition the 'self-consciousness' section of the *PhG* comes to an end. The higher phase, which Hegel seems to identify in part with the Renaissance, is one in which men have come to see that Reason underlies all reality. In other words, they have come to the insight which was missing in stoic consciousness, the sense that thought is not only a higher reality than external things, but that rational thought *determines* the course of things. Hence they are confident that they will, as rational beings, recognize themselves in reality, that whatever they think or do will be in tune with the rational basis of the universe. A new and higher notion of integrity is born, and will now have to be worked out.

We come here to the end of the chapter on self-consciousness. Just as the first section took us beyond the opposition between the knowing subject and his world; so this section takes the subject of action and desire who at first seems to stand over against a world on which he depends and shows how *this* opposition is overcome. In the first section this required that we develop and refine our notion of the object of knowledge, starting with the most primitive view, that of sensible certainty. Here we had to take the agent from his most primitive stage as a particular individual opposed to others to a realization of his universal nature, which is the same as the universal thought underlying the world. The mutual foreignness of agent and world is thus overcome. But like the first, this section has just established the principle of unity. It remains to trace its development in the sections which follow.

3

I shall just give the briefest indications of the development of this third section on Reason. Its starting point is as we saw where men reach the intuition that rationality, i.e., the principle of their own thought, determines all reality, and hence they are certain to be 'at home' in the world. Or as Hegel puts it in a lapidary phrase, 'Reason is the certainty of consciousness that it is all reality' (Die Vernunft ist die Gewißheit des Bewußtseins, alle Realität zu sein, *PhG*, 176).

The chapter ends in a transition in which the individual consciousness is shown to be an inadequate vehicle for spirit, and this grounds a basic shift in the *PhG*, which will follow henceforth supra-individual embodiments of subjectivity, first political society (chapter VI), then religion (chapter VII). Thus an examination of consciousness which starts with the individual shows the inadequacy of all such conceptions and forces us to shift to a wider spirit.

I

The chapter falls into three sections. The first of these is analogous to the opening part on 'consciousness' in that it deals with different theories of science. And its basic motif is the attempt to make good the promise of reason, that we can achieve a vision of things as fully rationally determined. The search for a rationally necessary science takes 'observing reason' through different modes of scientific thought, from the simple observation of regularities to the search for natural laws. It leads reason to turn its attention from inanimate and focus on animate nature where its instinct tells it – rightly, thinks Hegel – that it will come closer to seeing self-maintaining form. But even here it fails to find thoroughgoing rational necessity.

Hegel makes clear that this is not because of any inadequacy in the sciences of animate or inanimate nature. Contingency is a necessary feature of them, as he makes very clear (esp. 193–5). These sciences are thus perfectly valid forms of knowledge on their level, tracing regularities and laws without trying ultimately to justify them by reason. The hunger of observing reason here will in fact only be filled by speculative philosophy which shows why the world must have the structure it has, including the degree of contingency it contains.

Finally observing reason is led to examine man, as the most likely locus where rational necessity can be seen as work. But this fails because of the nature of observing reason itself, which tries to understand man by looking on him as an object, and cannot grasp his nature as a being who also makes himself. Observing reason cannot really cope with the meshing of the given and the self-made in man, the 'Einheit des vorhandenen und des gemachten Seins' (227), but tries to separate these two aspects from each other. It treats man like a thing, and that is why Hegel sees something appropriate in bringing this section's discussion to a head in an examination of phrenology, which had been in vogue for a time at the end of the eighteenth century. In phrenology man's typically human qualities are related to inert matter, the bumps and hollows of his skull.[1]

Hegel sees, of course, a speculative point in this. It is true that spirit does equal matter, for it must be embodied. But this relation must be expressed in the 'infinite judgement' (253) which affirms both the identity of *Geist* and its embodiment, and their difference; above all which portrays this embodiment as posited by *Geist*. Observing reason lacks an understanding of man as agent, and hence we go over to a phase of reason which parallels 'self-consciousness', where we follow the rational agent.

---

[1] For the relation of Hegel's discussion here to issues of contemporary explanation, cf. Alasdair MacIntyre, 'Hegel on Faces and Skulls', in MacIntyre (Ed.) *Hegel*, New York, 1972, 219–36.

The insight of the universal sovereignty of reason has also transformed man's self-certainty. Just as observing reason was confident of finding rational necessity in nature, so rational self-consciousness is confident of achieving satisfaction in the world.

The dialectic of self-consciousness opens here with the figure of the individual searcher after pleasure. But this is not square one. This individual, unlike the subject of desire in the earlier chapter has behind him the development which brought us to reason, and hence he has reason's certainty that he will find himself in the reality which surrounds him. Man and the world are designed for happiness, man has only to reach out, as it were, and pluck the fruit of happiness. Instead of consuming external reality as in the earlier dialectic of desire, the subject, certain of his unity *an sich* with it, just removes from it 'the form of other-being' (p. 263): The object of pleasure remains an independent being. If the paradigm of the dialectic of desire seems to be consumption, that of this dialectic seems to be sexual pleasure.

The section is full of (as always unstated) references to Goethe's Faust, including an incorrect quote. But Hegel obviously has in mind as well the Enlightenment doctrine of the natural goodness of man. And this is obviously an advanced idea in the sense that it can only come after a long development of human culture. The Enlightenment doctrine of man as naturally good and hence as finding the criterion of right in his own natural desires (whose fulfilment is pleasure) builds on the view of nature as a rational harmonious whole which underlay the scientific enterprise (observing reason). In this regard, Hegel's derivation here makes sense.

But although on an incomparably higher level, this naive figure of self-consciousness will obviously not solve the problem. For man still seeks satisfaction as an individual, even though now he may define himself in universal categories, and see thus that all men are as he is. And as a pure individual he must see the reality which surrounds him, both social and natural, as foreign to him. His self-realization is not a common one with that of other men, but is particular.

But all particulars must go under. Indeed, there is as we have seen an inner connection between the full self-affirmation of a particular thing and its necessary demise. For the external particular, though an essential expression of *Geist* or the universal, nevertheless contradicts it and as such must disappear; and the moment of its fullest flowering is when the contradiction is at its most acute.

Hegel thus sees an inner connection between the individual's fulfilment as a particular in pleasure and his death. Man who defines his fulfilment as that of pleasure experienced by him as a particular faces his inevitable demise as total annihilation. It is not that pleasure brings on death, or that by avoiding the first one can avoid the second. Hegel's point is not that pleasure is to be avoided, and death is, after all, inevitable. The point is rather that defined in such a way that his fulfilment is solely pleasure man experiences this death as an abrupt and total ending.

By contrast a man who so defines himself that his fulfilment lies in a larger, universal goal does not see death as anihilation, for he is identified with something which survives him. But the contrast also goes deeper. For the figure we are studying here death is not just total, but also a blind, external necessity, a fate.

The fate of death is necessarily linked to life for the reason mentioned above. But it is blind only because, defined as a pure particular, man cannot see this inner necessity. Being purely inner, it is purely 'external', that is it seems to him blind and reasonless. Whereas the man who sees himself as the vehicle of the universal not only does not see death as total, but also understands why it must be in virtue of the very universal *Geist* with which he identifies himself. He is thus doubly reconciled to it.

The underlying goal, the reconciliation of man and fate, is described here briefly as a condition in which 'consciousness...would recognize...its own goal and doing in fate, and its fate in its own goal and doing, would recognize its own essence in this necessity' (*PhG*, 265). For the man who defines his fulfilment as pleasure of the particular, there is however only 'a pure leap into the opposed term' (ein reiner Sprung in das Entgegengesetzte, loc. cit.).

This figure is therefore in contradiction. Reaching out for the fulfilment of pleasure he meets the most absolute non-fulfilment. The certainty of finding oneself in reality falls into annihilation. Self-consciousness is thus forced on; and the next step is obviously to incorporate this external necessity in itself. Since this necessity is that linking the particular to the universal, this means incorporating the universal in its own notion of fulfilment, so that instead of desiring simply one's own pleasure, one's spontaneous desire is now seen as aimed at the general good. We have thus a picture of man as spontaneously desiring the good, as having the law of morality in his heart.

Whatever we think of the rigour of this transition, we obviously have here another very important stream of Enlightenment thought (which like all such has been re-edited in different forms since). For alongside and later largely supplanting the utilitarian idea of man as naturally good in his naive egoism, since this fitted into a natural or attainable harmony of interests, came the idea of man as naturally good in being spontaneously altruistic. Certainly this is what many people got out of the writings of Rousseau, and doctrines of this kind had a wide currency at the end of the eighteenth century, although the impact of the French Revolution somewhat dented them. It is obviously this broad movement which Hegel has in mind, although there are a number of (still implicit) references to Schiller's *Robbers*.

In this figure man thus believes in the goodness of his spontaneous feelings. He stands over against a world which is full of suffering and wrong. This must be attributed to the false and unjustified restraints placed on men by society or civilization since man is naturally good. The solution is to free men from these restraints, bring them back to what they really are, and thus make real in the world order the law of the heart.

But this is not going to work either. Man must be lifted to universality so that his aspirations correspond to the universal good; but this requires a long formation and discipline, it requires a hard-won transformation. It is foolish to think that our unreconstructed spontaneous feeling will be one with the universal. The unity here as Hegel puts it is not yet mediated.

The resultant contradiction comes out in two ways. First the world which would result from the imposition on the course of affairs of the law I feel in my heart is not genuinely universal. It is full of ideas and aspirations which are simply mine and which I uncritically project on the universal. It follows that others cannot recognize the law of their hearts in this world. The attempt to reconstruct the world in this way thus leads not to unity and reconciliation, but fanatical struggle between men.

But second, even where the course of things reflects the universal, where, for instance, the structure of society and its laws reflect rational norms, this consciousness cannot recognize it. For the genuine universal is such that man can only reach it by discipline, as we saw. Thus rational laws will always appear as external restraints to those convinced of their own spontaneous goodness. The law of the heart can thus in principle never succeed in reforming the world. For once it does attain some amelioration in things, its work appears to it as foreign, as the enemy, as just another form of the external constraints that it is attacking.

This belief, says Hegel, leads in fact to a fantastic presumption, in which each believes that the world should be reformed according to his instincts. The resultant struggle, suffering and frustration is the exact opposite of the reconciliation which was supposed to be attained. This form of consciousness is thus in acute contradiction with itself. Its struggle to maintain itself in this contradiction Hegel describes as a kind of madness. It desperately tries to blame the evil in the world on priests and despots, and hence to reconcile universal wrong with the supposedly good heart. But the feebleness of this explanation just shows up the underlying contradiction. In fact it has to recognize in the world order 'the law of all hearts', the net result of the struggles of all to realize their aspirations.

But this prepares the ground for a new dialectical reversal. If the world order is the law of all hearts, then it can be considered as potentially capable of expressing the universal. What it would require on this view would be simply to be purged of individual self-seeking. The tables are thus turned. Instead of hoping to save the world by imposing our own individuality on it, our idea now is to purify it by removing all traces of individual aspiration from our actions.

This stance of consciousness Hegel calls the attempts to realize 'virtue'. But he makes it clear that this is not the virtue of the ancients, which was on the contrary to live according to the mores of one's people. This is an individualistic virtue, founded on self-denial; and it will now be evident that Hegel will find it unacceptable.

In fact it is another one of those strategies of retreat of which I spoke earlier, at the beginning of the discussion on self-consciousness. It is reminiscent of stoicism. While the earlier form defined the self as inner freedom by abandoning our outer bodily reality, this present form tries to neutralize it morally. The particular expression of the individual must be suppressed, he must become nothing but the expression of the universal.

The peculiar feature of this kind of phase is man's sense of his own unworthiness, his apologizing for his existence, and his attempt to suppress his particularity, and become nothing but universal will. This is given some importance in the *PhG*, because it comes up three times, first in unhappy consciousness, the second time here, and thirdly at the end of Chapter vi in the section on evil and its forgiveness. This latter is an important stage of the dialectic because it is invoked again in the transition to absolute knowledge.

But the attempt to suppress one's particularity is doomed to failure; and this for the simple reason that the universal cannot be made real unless in the actions of particular men, and men in so acting cannot abstract from what they are as men with particular needs and desires. In other words, man cannot suppress his particularity, and act just as a vehicle of the universal; for he cannot simply act on the motive of conforming his action to universal maxims, setting aside all other motives. To refuse all other forms of action is to do nothing. And this is why we can see this insistence on the suppression of particularity as a form of retreat, a refusal of the very conditions of external, particular existence.

As against the philosophy of self-abnegating virtue, Hegel's is a philosophy of self-realization; becoming the vehicle of the universal is also for man a fulfilment – or at least it will be when he is fully formed. But obviously on the road to this full formation, his 'lower' nature will be in conflict with this universal vocation. Dualistic philosophies reflect this. But more, they justify the discipline and training necessary to achieve the higher integration. We saw this with the piety of unhappy consciousness, for instance.

On the contemporary scene, however, a philosophy of self-denying virtue is no longer justified, and Hegel is harsh and ironic in his dealings with it. His point is that the universal cannot find real expression (Wirklichkeit) except through the lives and actions of particular individuals. But this is made in an elaborate image in which the consciousness of virtue is portrayed as a knight, a sort of Don Quixote, who cannot effectively combat the world of egoistic actors, precisely because this world provides the only conditions of realization of the universal in the name of which he fights. His main concern, Hegel says scoffingly, is to keep his sword immaculate. In short the knight of virtue is condemned by his too pure notion of virtue to inactivity. He cannot intervene effectively in history to realize the good, because this is inseparable from the affirmation of his particularity.

The upshot of this contradiction will be a new phase, the third major phase of this chapter on reason. In the previous figure we learned to see the course of things as the outcome of the self-realizing actions of individuals; here we have learned that the universal can only come to be through such self-realizing actions. So now we step to a higher level in which we see individual self-realization as the expression of the universal. The next stage of the dialectic will thus be a figure of self-consciousness which knows itself as realizing the universal in its actions.

III

In the last section of Reason we come then to forms of consciousness in which the individual sees himself as united with the universal. We have gone beyond the opposition between the individual's goals and the reality over against them. The individual is now united in his action with external reality which therefore reflects reason.

This unity really comes about in objective spirit, that is *Geist* reflected in the life of a people, which Hegel calls ethical substance. But in this last section we tarry awhile among other forms of individual consciousness which give Hegel the opportunity to consider other contemporary ideas and moral beliefs. But this tarrying also makes clear the importance of the transition. In a sense the *PhG* can be thought of as having two parts, whose frontier lies here. In the first, we are dealing with forms of individual consciousness, even if we deal with men in interaction, as in the dialectic of the master and the slave.

But in the chapters which follow, on Spirit and Religion, we are taking spirit as a supra-personal subject, first as the spirit of a people, and then as the self-consciousness of the world-spirit in Religion. This shift in the dialectic is of course necessary if we are to come to absolute knowledge in which *Geist* is united with its world, for only the world-subject can be seen as so united, the individual qua individual can never be.

Thus at a certain point we have to shift our centre of gravity; we have to see the individual no longer as the centre with his social relation as a peripheral fact

167

about him, but rather see the social whole as central, and the individual as a manifestation of it. It is this latter balance which Hegel wants to convey in the frequent use of the term 'substance'. The spirit of the whole society is the underlying reality, from which the acts of individuals emanate. But this is not to say that they are its helpless subordinates, rather they recognize themselves in it (p. 310). Moreover, this spirit is not something separate from them, it cannot exist without them. The 'ethical substance' (sittliche Substanz) can be thought of as 'the essence of self-consciousness; but this in turn is the reality (Wirklichkeit) and determinate existence (Dasein) of the substance, its self and will'. (*PhG*, 312).

Thus the *Geist* of a people can only come to reality in the individual subjectivities. And it follows that it is still not at its fullest development, it is still unconscious and partially deformed when it is not reflected in individuals. But this, of course, is the reality in the whole period between the demise of the Greek city-state and the full flowering of the modern law-state. This latter requires therefore a double development: both the individual and the public expression of *Geist* in laws and institutions must change and grow so that the former can come to recognize himself in the latter.

Hegel seems to have thought that this last transition was happening in his day. The figures he studies here, being all recognizable as contemporary ideas, thus reflect the transition. But, of course, his interest here in the *PhG* is not to derive the final form of the state, but just to show that we cannot understand consciousness without this shift from the individual to the 'substance', whose development we will take up in the next chapter starting from the Greeks.

The figures of this section all reflect a consciousness which is certain of the universal significance of its action. As elsewhere in this chapter, and in the work as a whole, the discussion here reflects Hegel's settling of accounts with the currents of his day. There is not space to follow the argument, but we should look briefly at his treatment of Kant, who is taken to task (unnamed) in the discussion of the last figure of this section, 'law-testing reason'.

In this figure, reason is called on to test laws which could claim to be morally binding by applying a criterion of self-consistency: is there a contradiction in following a given maxim, or not?

The reference to Kant is obvious, and Hegel's reaction not hard to guess. He makes the widely familiar objection that any maxim can be shown to be consistent, but adds this twist, that in a way we can show some, e.g. community of goods, to be contradictory, but in quite the same way the same can be shown of the regime of private property. This contradiction poses no problem for Hegel. He quite agrees with Kant and the whole bourgeois epoch that private property is the right regime; but this cannot be shown from the supposedly greater consistency of acting on this principle.

But in finally going over to *Geist*, we draw from this last figure the following idea, that the free individual who stands over against the society cannot find any real content for his moral reason; he cannot reason consequently to definite conclusions in morals. True, the basis of morality is that one act according to universal maxims, according in other words to the *Geist* which is our real nature, and which is universal (and thus we put together Kant and Aristotle). But if we understand this abstractly, then we have an empty criterion. In the abstract, where reason is just seen as residing in form, in a certain way of thinking, then anything can be justified, any maxim can be universalized. It is only when we see reason as having certain ontological requirements, as calling for an external reality, and a human social reality of a certain kind – in particular one that will express in political institutions the requirement of universal laws – that we can provide a content for practical reason. The shape of our moral duty arises from the nature of the social reality which must come to be for *Geist* to be fulfilled; and *Geist*'s being fulfilled is for us a moral duty, for our nature is precisely this, *Geist*, or to use an older phrase, rational life.

In the end, therefore, the truly moral man is one who does not hope to give himself his own laws purely from his own inner consciousness, but on the contrary he feels the pull of duty from his society. To try to reason purely on one's own is to reason without criteria, hence arbitrarily. 'This immediate law-giving is thus a tyrannical wantonness which makes its arbitrary will into law...' (*PhG*, 309). Hence Hegel seems to reverse totally the verdict of Kant who made of autonomy the very touchstone of all morality.

But really the truth is more complicated. There is a first unreflecting sense of duty which has to be broken into by the universal individual reasoning for himself; and in the subsequent fight between external authority and autonomy, Hegel is not unreservedly on the side of either. Autonomy is right because it is a necessary stage in the formation of man. In the ultimate, however, the two come together in that fully rational man will see his own fulfilment reflected in the law-state to whose institutions he gives his allegiance. But he will then come to see the Kantian vision as one-sided; he will see it as one of the fore-runners of his own; but only as one of the developments that prepared his present achievement. The other necessary condition of this achievement lies in the slow development of the institutions themselves to which the vast run of men never ceased to give their absolute allegiance, in spite of Enlightenment philosophers, be these institutions religious or political.

The break with Kant is thus profound even where Hegel is claiming to 'complete' him. And along with the difference between pure autonomy and a social morality goes another: since the fullest ethic is one lived in a society, is nothing but one's duty to a society, the highest ethic is also one which is fulfilled. It is not just an 'ought', some thing that should be: the norms we follow are those which are being lived out in the institutions which exist in our

169

society, and which we maintain by our allegiance. An ethic which presents us a model which just ought to be always earns Hegel's contempt. This is the basic point of his rejection of both Kant and Fichte's moral philosophy: they present us ethics of pure *Sollen.*

Rather, says Hegel, spirit living in a people shows us laws which are at the same time *Sein,* real existence. We have no room here either for faith; self-consciousness lives within the spiritual reality of *Geist,* which men lost with the demise of Greek city-state, and which they pine to regain. We are now about to recover it in a form consonant with universal reason, but first we return to see it in its original unconscious beauty.

CHAPTER VI

The Formation of Spirit

In entering now the domain of 'Geist', what Hegel will call later 'objective spirit', we are dealing for the first time with real historical forms. Previously we were dealing only with abstracted aspects of these forms: we saw Stoicism, for example, in the development of self-consciousness; now we will come back to the full historical form of which it is an aspect. In this chapter we have whole polities, or phases in the life of a whole civilization, as our stages, and not just a given idea, outlook or ideal (which can ultimately only be understood in the light of *Geist*).

The *PhG* being a non-historical dialectic thus gives a kind a spiralling effect. We return at a higher (or a deeper, if this metaphor be preferred) level to the same phenomena. If from the dialectic of the master and slave to the end of Reason the implicit references had a rough historical order, we now return to the beginning. And at the end of this chapter, we shall again, in the chapter on Religion.

The chapter on Spirit takes us through some crucial passages of the philosophy of history. We start off with the Greeks, with that society of perfect *Beisichselbstsein* which Hegel as many of his contemporaries could not remember without nostalgia. This society, as we remember, was characterized by a perfect unity between citizen and society. The citizens' fullest moral and spiritual aspirations were answered in the common life of the society. This common life was thus like a common substance; as part of it the individual found a meaning and purpose to his life; cut off from it, he withered. But this dependence on the common substance did not make it something quite other to which he could only be subordinate; for the common life was also 'the doing of each and all' (Das Tun Aller und Jeder, *PhG*, 314), it was the work of the citizens. If the substance maintained the individual, then the individual's activity also maintained the substance.

But this early unity has to break down,[1] and this chapter follows this dialectic. The fully universal individual must come to be, and he can only do so by breaking down the parochial walls of the city-state. There follows a long period of alienation, in which the individual stands over against a society which does

---

[1] As Hegel remarks earlier in the *PhG*, 'Die Vernunft muß aus diesem Glücke heraustreten' (258).

not express him. This period of travail is, however, as always in Hegel, a period of formation. From it will emerge a higher stage. In the philosophy of history, this stage is defined as the law-state of modern times. In the *PhG*, however, we pass into the new moral consciousness of contemporary German philosophy, as a prelude to a new philosophically interpreted religious consciousness. The reason for this[1] can perhaps be found in the fact that the *PhG* has different aims than the philosophy of history, even though there is obviously overlap in this chapter; our aim here is to lead consciousness to define itself as ultimately congruent with the world spirit. Hence there is no cause to tarry long in the philosophy of objective spirit; we must be on to what is later called in the *Encyclopaedia* 'absolute spirit'.

1

The first part of the chapter deals with the original unity of the Greek city-state and its breakdown. This is one of the most beautiful passages of the *PhG*, in which the powerful poetic vision that lies at the base of Hegel's philosophy comes through. The power of his images is heightened in that he explicits the inner tension and conflict of Greek society in the medium of Sophoclean tragedy.

In the most general terms the conflict underlying the original unity is this: the individual is perfectly united with his community, man is thus at one with a larger subject, with a universal of which he senses himself to be an emanation. This is as it should be. But this universal is not integrally so. It is the spirit of a people, just one among many. It is parochial. The intuition of genuine universality in man therefore progressively separates him from this community. It leads to a struggle within man and within the community as this public expression of the universal enters into conflict with the very vocation to the universal which underlies it.

The happy unity of citizen with city thus depends on man's being at an early stage of development, 'sunk in nature'. This must pass away. To put it in another way, as a particular existence, the city-state must go under: if it were the expression of a truly universal consciousness, this latter would survive it, would already be beyond it; it would remain itself through the destruction of this expression of it. But as a parochial consciousness the life of the city-state goes under with it, it 'finds...its demise through another' (findet...ihre Aufhebung an einer andern, *PhG*, 342).

---

[1] The explanation has also been given (Cf. Fr. Rosenzweig, *Hegel und der Staat*, Munich and Berlin 1920, I, 217–20, II, 1–5) that Hegel under the impact of Napoleonic conquest abandoned for a time the belief that *Geist* can return to full reconciliation with itself in a modern state, which had been one of his earlier aspirations and was certainly part of his mature system after 1815. On this interpretation, history for Hegel in this period would reach its culmination and Spirit its reconciliation only in religion and philosophy. But this cannot be convincingly established.

The Formation of Spirit

But Hegel through the bulk of this chapter reads the dialectic of society's ethical life, or *Sittlichkeit* as he calls it, on another level, more detailed; whose vocabulary is borrowed from the Greek tragedians. The conflict between the two universals is now seen as one between human and divine law. Human law is the overt, conscious ethic of the state in which the citizens find themselves reflected. Divine law reflects the truly universal, and it thus at this stage appears as unreflective, as an unwritten law, unmade by man, which has always existed.[1] The divine law, as the truly universal, is concerned with the individual as such, not just in his relation to the state. The institution which stands as guardian to this law is thus the family which is also the sphere of immediate unity. The two laws have their paradigmatic expression in these two institutions, and Hegel draws the further conclusion concerning the roles of the sexes: men are mainly concerned with the human and political, women with the divine and familial.

The divine law is concerned with the individual as such, not with any of the particularities of his existence. But since at this stage the monopoly of his effective external life is held by his role in the state, his truly universal existence can only be envisaged as beyond this life, it finds expression in his Shade, where he has left the contingency of life for 'the repose of simple universality' (p. 321).

Hegel then gives a striking interpretation of the death rites of ancient Greece. Death is a natural negation, something which happens to man, a blow struck at him by nature. But we have also seen that death speculatively understood is a necessity, an expression of the true universality of the human spirit which thus cannot leave standing any external expression. The aim of the rites is to raise death from this first to the second reality, to re-interpret it as it were from something that happens to man to some thing done. The rites preserve the body which otherwise would be prey to all the blind forces of nature, would be strewn over the earth by jackals and vultures, and in committing it to the earth make its departure a meaningful act. So that even death is recuperated for self-consciousness.

Of course, being at a primitive stage, the recuperating self-consciousness is not the same as the one negated. At this stage an individual's being beyond his death depends on his family's actions in burying him. At a higher stage, where the truly universal is expressed in the public life of the society, we are all beyond our death as universal consciousness even before we undergo it. But burial is the expression which at this stage the true universality of man must have, and it is thus holy. The stage is set for the tragedy of Antigone.

---

[1] Hegel's words (deliberately) remind us of Antigone's:

> The immutable unwritten laws of Heaven
> They were not born today or yesterday
> They die not; and none knoweth whence they sprang.

173

For state and family, divine and human law must come to conflict. But before exhibiting this Hegel shows how they are bound up with and require each other. The state preserves society, and hence defends the family; but the family forms citizens for the state. Thus the divine forces underlying the family must be fed for the good of the state, and at the same time it is the state that sees to this cult, and thus to the feeding of the Gods. Men thus come from the family fed by chthonic forces into the light of political day; and they are called on to risk their lives for the defence of the state and hence these families, and in falling to return to the earth, to the pure individuality of the shade, to repose in the underworld from which the family continues to draw its strength. And reciprocally, the family, particularly the women, in following the rites bring the chthonic law into the light of day, and give it public expression, and by thus preserving the family play their part in the preservation of the state. The two laws should thus be in perfect harmony.

But they are not. At base they are in conflict, for the human law is not truly universal. And this conflict comes out in historical action. Here we come close to another basic Hegelian theme. To act, in the sense of effecting some important change on the world outside is necessarily to incur guilt. For our action makes real, gives effective expression to our particularity. But this constitutes a kind of defiance of the universal, and hence incurs guilt. Hegel's interpretation of the doctrine of original sin springs from this. The sin is 'original' in the philosophically reinterpreted version only in the sense of being necessary in principle for man; and it is necessary because man is a finite spirit embodied at some point in space and time, and hence cannot but act as a particular; and this in turn is necessary if spirit is to be, as we have seen. But we must nevertheless see this self-affirmation of the particular as 'sinful' because although essential for the existence of spirit it stands in the way of its full realization. It has thus to be overcome; and we have seen that death is one way in which it is surmounted; while the achievement of a fully universal consciousness is the way called for by *Geist*.

Thus sin is necessary for salvation in Hegel's view. This is just another way of putting the basic thesis that spirit can only exist by returning to itself out of its embodiment, that exteriority or alienation is an essential stage in its realization. It follows that any attempt to achieve sanctity or unity with spirit is self-defeating which involves shrinking from action in the world and from the accompanying affirmation of particularity. We are condemned to particular existence as finite spirits. All we can do is to work through our particular existence in order to realize a form of life capable of carrying universal consciousness. We have to work through sin to atonement; sin itself is unavoidable.

Shrinking from action is thus to be rejected; it is another of those strategies of retreat which we have to set aside. And this point has already been taken up in the previous chapter, where the virtuous soul tried to remove his own selfish action from the course of things. We will see it again at the end of this chapter in the section on wrong and its forgiveness. The *PhG* recurs to this theme a number of times. Here Hegel repeats 'thus only inaction is innocent, like the way of being of a stone, but not even that of a child'. (*PhG*, 334.)

But here we have not yet come to this full reconciliation; action in the world on the part of the community is still out of phase with the truly universal. In making effective the particular, action thus opens a struggle within the ethical itself. This struggle is tragic. We who stand outside it can see the conflict; we see Sophocles *Antigone*, and we can understand both Antigone's arguments and Creon's. If we had been there we might well have hesitated which side to support.

But this is for us a conflict of values. We are ultimately in the realm of comedy, because we are not caught up ourselves in the conflict. We suffer such conflicts ourselves, when two goods clash; but we are not caught up in these either, for we have a universal consciousness which can embrace both, which can appreciate the weight and claims of both protagonists. However we chose to arbitrate the dispute we retain this universal consciousness and give expression to it in our actions.

Quite different is the case of the tragic protagonist. He is identified with one side in the struggle, with human or divine law, to the point of not seeing the other, of seeing it only as a 'reality without justification' (rechtlose Wirklichkeit, *PhG*, 332). And this is because at the primitive stage where we are now, men cannot achieve this kind of consciousness, they have an immediate uncritical identity with the law; and since the law is double here, we have two kinds of 'character'; the two laws take expression in different kinds of people (in, say, men and women) each of whom is totally and uncritically identified with his or her part. Hence Antigone and Creon battle out the issue of Polynices' burial, each certain of being totally right.

The tragic character who belongs to this stage of unreflecting *Sittlichkeit* is one who acts only half-conscious of what is at stake. He sees one law; he doesn't see the other which is tied to it, whose violation lies in the realization of the first. He is blind in the very possession of sight, like Oedipus who fails to see his father in the stranger he fights or his mother in the queen he marries (p. 335).

Nonetheless the connection is there. The protagonist having wronged the Gods cannot disown his action. It is really his and he bears all its consequences; he is fully responsible for his action because he did it with full determination even though he could not see its full meaning. But since these consequences were unsuspected by him he experiences the *dénouement* as fate. We see once again Hegel's idea of fate as uncomprehended necessity, as was reflected in the discussion of pleasure in the last chapter. *Moira* plays a big role in Greek thought precisely because men have not achieved universal

175

consciousness, and cannot contain within their purview the whole sweep of necessity, which appears thus as something willed from outside.

In the philosophy of religion Hegel makes the same point in another way. The Greek god is a perfect marriage of the divine with human form, just as the Greek city-state marries the individual and the political. But the price is the same in both cases; man is not ready for reconciliation with the truly universal, so the gods are human at the price of being multiple and particular, as the cities are true ethical substances at the same cost. Conversely, in the same epoch, the people who really grasp the full universality of spirit, the Jews, are those who feel the greatest alienation from the divine. But universal *Geist* must find some expression; and since the Gods are particular, the universal re-appears as a necessity of fate to which even the gods are subject.

But it is precisely this experience of necessity which ultimately does away with the protagonist who is uncritically identified with one law. He goes under, destroyed by his own contradictions; and men achieve from this painful experience a consciousness which can take in the whole conflict. But this is a universal consciousness, that is, one which is no more uncritically identified with a particular society and its ethic, but which thinks in universal terms. In other words the experience of contradiction wrenches men loose from their spontaneous unquestioning allegiance to their particular city. But this must mean the decline of the city itself; for its whole strength reposed on their perfect unity of citizen and ethical substance. Instead now the individuals see themselves as universal, but by the same token as alienated from their society. The city unsupported goes under before the universal empire, which suits this new phase. But this is a phase of alienation: the new empire cannot express in its institutions and mores the deepest values and aspirations of its people; it is too vast and diverse. It simply unites men externally, by making them all subject to the same power. The decline of the city-state leaves nothing comparable in its place; deserted it goes under before the onslaught of the universal empire; but this ushers in an age of alienation in which the individual of universal consciousness stands over against a state which in no way reflects him, which is experienced simply as external power and constraint.

How this breakdown actually takes concrete historical form is left rather vague in this chapter. In other places, the philosophy of history and the history of philosophy, Hegel will comment on the rise of universal consciousness with the Sophists and Socrates. In the next chapter of the *PhG* we will go through the connected evolution of religious forms.[1]

Here Hegel seems little concerned to give a full picture. He is not at much pains to show how tragic conflict leads to historical breakdown. The only

[1] In one of his early unpublished MSS of the 1790s, Hegel gave a Montesquieuian account of the breakdown of the polis in terms of growing polarization between rich and poor. Nohl 214–31.

treatment of this is in a passage of striking poetic power in which he re-affirms that 'the manifest spirit has the root of its power in the lower world' (*PhG*, 339), and that in dishonouring the dead it saps its own power. Then Hegel presents us the image of the dogs and carrion birds defiling the altars of surrounding peoples with the remains of the unburied, and these neighbours taking vengeance on the city. But our admiration for the beauty of this passage fails to blind us to the sketchy nature of the underlying explanation.

Hegel then adds another derivation in which he starts from the battle between the family and the state, between men and women, the institutional and individual protagonists of the two laws. Being repressed by the state, the family and particularly its women take their revenge in subtle forms of corruption. Women induce their menfolk to exercise power for the dynasty rather than for the public weal, they turn the heads of youth away from the wisdom of the elders; and since this youth in turn must be exalted by the state as its defenders, their corruption has disastrous effects.

In any case, by whatever exact steps, the ethical spirit goes under and gives way to an age of alienation. The divine law, previously represented by the individual as shade now comes out into the light of day as the universal 'I' of self-consciousness. But this universal individual now exists in a society which in no way reflects him, which is pure external power. His affirmation of self as universal self-consciousness is therefore an abstract one; the external reality of his life is out of his control, at the mercy of purely external power. True, power in order to be exercised must be concentrated somewhere. At the summit of the state is thus an emperor. But this new universal state has broken with ethical substance, with the underlying sense of limit with which men were totally identified. It has put nothing in its place except sheer power. The reign of the emperor is thus that of uncontrolled capricious will.

The ruler too is a universal consciousness, but at this stage this means only that he has broken with any sense of unquestioned allegiance to a common way of life. The achievement of universality has been won at the expense of the political ethic; the former one has disappeared and a new one has yet to be painfully evolved. We are thus in the realm of sheer power; the self-definition of the subjects as pure individuals over against the state is matched by the naked power of the state which keeps them in line by force and frequently destroys them in the process.

Self-consciousness can thus only maintain its sense of integrity by a strategic retreat; and this is thus the age of Stoicism, which we now see as a full historical form. That is, self-consciousness can only see itself as universal and free by defining itself as a purely inward spiritual reality; the freedom of Stoicism is that of thought which abstracts from external conditions. But just as above in the chapter on self-consciousness, this position of retreat is untenable and must go through the corresponding evolution, through the equivalent of scepticism, to arrive at unhappy consciousness.

The Roman epoch saw the development of individual property rights: legally, we have the beginnings of the recognitions of rights as inhering in a person. But this person, as subject, was at the mercy of the state. Hence the external content he gave to his life, his property, was entirely at the mercy of arbitrary will. Hence the person experiences, as the sceptical consciousness did, his total dependence on the contingent and mutable, his utter lack of integrity.

And the result is, as seen through either dialectic, that the subject comes to place his integrity in something outside himself, to which he feels subordinate and to which he aspires. In other words he 'alienates' his integrity. Under the discipline of this alienation (Entfremdung) he undergoes a formation (Bildung) which will lay the groundwork for a recovery of freedom on a higher level.

2

The next section of the chapter deals with this era of alienation and formation which stretches from the Roman Empire to the contemporary period. But since Hegel is not trying to present a detailed study in the philosophy of history his interest focusses rather on the culmination of this period, the eighteenth century, the Enlightenment and the Revolution. We have here in condensed form a complex and rich Hegelian interpretation of these two epoch-making phenomena, and it is on these that our account will focus.

Alienation consists in this, that men no longer try to define themselves as pure thought, that they accept their identification with external social reality, and in this they are once more like the citizens of the city-state; but unlike these, they experience this social reality as other, they do not feel *bei sich* in it. This alienated identification, as against the happy identification of the Greeks, thus does not express itself in an explicit consciousness of oneness with the society; rather it comes out in the sense that they must aspire to close the gap between themselves and this social reality, that they must give up their individual particularity and come closer to the essential substance of their lives in serving a wider cause, such as the state. This sense that the substance of their lives lies beyond them is the essence of alienation, and the service, discipline and self-transformation which it inspires is what forms men for the next stage.

For this alienation is a necessary stage on the road to the final realization of spirit; and as such it is a mixture of the real and the illusory. In fact men do depend on something greater, on a spirit which is not just that of man, to which men have rather to confirm. But at the same time this *Geist* is one in which man should recognize himself fully, in which he should feel fully at home, once he sees himself qua finite spirit as an emanation and vehicle of *Geist*. The phase of alienation is one in which the dependence relation is clear, while the self-recognition is cloudy and obscure. The sense of being *bei sich* in the Absolute is present only in a veiled form, in religious consciousness, and is displaced out of this world into a beyond.

The phase we are dealing with is thus the same as that we described earlier as the period of unhappy consciousness. It has the sense of a reconciliation which is felt as absent, in another world or long ago and far away, a reconciliation achieved elsewhere on which we essentially depend. This is part of the consciousness of alienation.

We can think of this consciousness as false in failing to see our unity with the absolute. But at the same time it is right to deny this, for at this stage men are not yet ready; they have not yet achieved the universal consciousness which fully reflects their unity with *Geist*. The consciousness of unity as projected in another world is therefore a distorted image of a true fact, that men have yet to transform themselves in order to realize this unity fully. And the function of alienation is to provide the motive for this transformation; it is a kind of tutelage during which men are formed to overcome it.

The basic attitude of alienation is one in which men feel that their substance lies in something outside them, and hence that they can only realize themselves by overcoming their particularity and conforming to this reality. This necessity is felt both by those who willingly accept it and try to act according to it, and by those who resent it and kick against it, what Hegel calls the 'noble' (edelmütig) and 'base' (niederträchtig) consciousnesses respectively. Among external realities to which man can be thus related Hegel mentions state power and 'riches', which is expanded to include the operation of the economy as a whole; but it is understandable from the sequel that other structures can play this role, that of the religious community for instance.

Now the essence of the development under alienation is that men are formed to overcome it. And the result is that out of this alienation eventually arises a consciousness which has 'seen through' these external realities (I am here leaving out a great deal of interesting detail in the dialectic). Men develop to the point where they can grasp these realities for what they are, they can see state power and riches as phenomena in the world like any others, destined to disappear like any other, bound by the same law-like conditions, and suffering the same reversals, as the seemingly good and holy is discovered to be bound up with the evil and base and profane. This 'insight' (Einsicht), which manifests itself at first as a debunking of pretentious claims, reaches its culmination in the Enlightenment.

The Enlightenment represents the beginning of the end of alienation in that the realities towards which the piety of alienated consciousness is directed, and to which it tries to conform, are cut down to size. All external reality is objectified, deprived of spiritual significance and seen as a world of sensible

179

material things spread out before a universal scientific consciousness. State and religious structure are no longer awe-inspiring realities to which man must conform himself, but simply part of the neutral stuff of the world, open to the scrutiny of scientific consciousness, and at its disposal. The significant reality becomes once again man, or rather the universal scientific consciousness who has thus come to dominate the world intellectually.[1]

The self is once again the centre of things, and yet we have a stage very different from that of Stoicism, which also focussed on the self as universal consciousness. For this was a phase of retreat, the self discovered itself outside of and without taking account of external reality; here on the contrary, scientific consciousness claims to have seen through this reality, to have dominated it intellectually – and very soon as we shall see in the French Revolution it will claim to dominate it in act by transforming reality according to universal will. Between Stoicism and the Enlightenment has lain the whole period of alienation and formation in which men have learnt to understand and gain some control over the world, natural and political. The scientific consciousness of the modern age underlies the Enlightenment.

From this notion of the Enlightenment as the insight into reality which cuts it down to size as a world of sensible material things, we can understand two basic features of its ideology which Hegel singles out. First, the absolute or God is reduced to the empty notion of a supreme being (Hegel uses the French expression 'être suprème') to which no further description can be applied. For all particular reality is now seen as merely material and sensible, and all particular descriptions can only be given meaning as interpreted in the light of this reality. So that any attempt to fill out the notion of God by describing him as father, creator, ascribing to him acts in history, etc. are bound to appear totally incongrous, for they depend on our seeing the relationships or acts in question as embodying some spiritual significance. We have to see natural fatherhood as carrying with it (ideally) a relation of love and spiritual care in order to apply this image to God; we have to see God's acts in history also as signs, as a language and not just as a set of material changes. But the Enlightenment consciousness sees the world as an assemblage of purely material sensible things; it therefore cannot find a language to speak of God nor conceive of God as intervening in history. If it thinks of God at all, it is forced to a kind of Deism, a cult of the supreme Being.

Of course, many *Aufklärer* did not believe in God at all, but for Hegel not much separated these materialists from those who believed in a super-sensible reality. For they thought of some abstraction like Nature or Matter as underlying the changing reality of the sensible world. But an abstraction like Matter, which bears none of the particular descriptions of things in the world,

---

[1] Hegel is thus characterizing here what I call in the first chapter the modern 'self-defining' subject.

is indistinguishable from a spiritual substrate; and a spiritual substrate without particular description is indistinguishable from pure being. We have here an echo of Hegel's famous opening dialectic of the Logic, that of Being and Nothing; and the message is the same: in the end all abstractions are alike. Real spirituality is also material.

The second notion of Enlightenment ideology, which Hegel makes one of the central themes of this chapter, is that of the useful, the concept underlying utilitarianism. To think of something as useful is to think of it as without intrinsic significance, rather its significance is to serve the ends of something else. This notion of the useful flows naturally out of the Enlightenment outlook; for this sees the world as made up of material things without any further significance. This neutral world has no meaning for man, either as expressive of something higher, or as embodying a form with which he must conform in order to realize himself. As neutral, the things in the world can only be given significance by serving some human purpose. The only category they can fall under as far as their significance for man is concerned is the useful.

Utilitarianism is therefore the ethic of the Enlightenment. Utilitarianism is an ethic in which acts are judged according to their consequences, that is, their relevance to some extraneous end, hence their usefulness. This is opposed to an ethic which judges an act by some intrinsic quality, such as its embodying a given virtue, or conforming to some moral law. Such intrinsic properties are swept aside by the Enlightenment as nonsense, which accepts only material reality and its law-like connections, and has no place for normative properties, e.g., virtues, or a normative order such as putatively underlies natural law.

But the hidden contradiction in this for Hegel is that the category of the useful has no stopping point, it is universal in application. Some things may be judged useful for my purposes; but I too am a particular reality in the world, there is no reason why my purposes should be considered final ends. I and my purposes in turn can be seen as serving or disserving the ends of others, perhaps that of society in general; and these others, or society in general can be seen as serving or not the purposes of others, say the members of this society, and so on. We have a bad infinite.

Hegel expresses this by saying that each thing can be seen as in itself, but also as for an other, that is, as having just instrumental significance. There is no structure of significant reality which forces us to stop somewhere, which expresses the final purpose; or as Hegel puts it this chain of extrinsic justifications does not return to a self, that is to a subjectivity which would encompass the whole development. Each entity serves another, and so on ad infinitum; and we know now that for Hegel this situation is profoundly unsatisfactory. There must be a final order of things which all partial goals serve, which encompasses them all, and which we can identify with. For only thus can we really be *bei uns* in the universe. In the endless chain of partial purposes of utilitarianism, each one of us plays his part, but we end up serving an extraneous purpose with which we cannot identify – as we can with a spiritual order of the universe of which we are emanations – and we remain thus before a foreign universe.

The basic error of the Enlightenment is to have seized only half the truth. It is right to have debunked the pretensions of kings and churches, to have seen that universal scientific consciousness can penetrate fully external reality, and should thus be considered of greater significance. It is right to perceive that ultimately rational subjectivity is dominant. But it is wrong in thinking that this subjectivity is simply human, in leaving no place for a cosmic *Geist* except the empty slot of the supreme being. For in fact human subjectivity only achieves dominance as the vehicle of this greater subject. Men have to accept that there is significant reality outside them, and in return they can feel fully *bei sich* in so far as they cease to identify themselves just as men, but rather see themselves as vehicles of absolute subject. The basic mistake of the Enlightenment is to refuse this transcendence and try to achieve this consummation on behalf of man alone; it tries to make man's subjectivity alone dominant instead of participating in the dominance of the absolute subject.

Now the Enlightenment is matched by another outlook which is symmetrical with it, which Hegel calls faith (Glaube). This is a form of religious consciousness which projects the true reconciliation of spirit and reality, but in another world. It has grasped the fact that spirit and thought underlies all reality (Hegel is of course here speaking of Christian faith), but it is unconscious of its object as thought. Rather faith understands the Absolute through metaphor and images, a mode of awareness which Hegel calls representation (Vorstellung), and hence it sees as another world of contingently related reality what really should be seen as the necessary structure of this.

Now faith is symmetrical with the Enlightenment, because it is long on the recognition of absolute spirit and our dependence on it, where the Enlightenment is deficient; but it does not see the essential role of human subjectivity which is the central idea of the Enlightenment. Its transcendent world is fixed and impenetrable to active human reason. Reason cannot run easily through its articulations as the Enlightenment claims to do for those of the natural world. These two views thus complement each other. Being blind to this, however, they enter into conflict.

Hegel in setting the stage for this conflict represents faith as well as an outcome of the period of alienation. This may seem strange since this religious consciousness is part and parcel of the phase of alienation itself. Is this 'derivation' then just an artificial device to allow Hegel to discuss the struggle between Enlightenment and faith as one between two forms of the same stage, rather than as a battle of future with past? Two points need to be made before we jump to this conclusion. The first is that religious faith from the very beginning contains a certain element of that debunking of the structure of this world which we saw in the insight of the Enlightenment. Only it robs them of their significance not for the benefit of enlightened human consciousness but rather in favour of the higher otherworldly reality. The second point is that Hegel is here not talking about Christian faith in general, but rather the more spiritualized form of protestant faith which he knew in contemporary Germany and which was already influenced by the Enlightenment to some degree. In a telling passage (387–8), he describes how the spirit of the Enlightenment crept into contemporary theology unconsciously, as theological thinkers began to frame their thought and answer questions in categories posed by the Enlightenment.

This description of osmosis and of dialogue between two contemporary views seems odd to us only because we are much more aware of the French scene where there really was a knock-down, drag-out fight between the Enlightenment as a new ideology and a Catholic Church which prided itself on defending old long-standing ideas (whether its theology really was that old is another matter). The situation was quite different in Germany, and however he introduced it, Hegel could not avoid a discussion of this dialogue.

The dialogue is conditioned for Hegel by the fact that both sides have hold of the same truth, but which they see differently and one-sidedly. The fact that they are at root the same facilitates the penetration of faith by the Enlightenment; and insofar as it not only peacefully penetrates but combats faith, their basic identity makes its shots strike home. But at the same time it opens the Enlightenment to a *tu quoque* reply.

Not recognizing itself in its adversary, the Enlightenment both grasps and misunderstands faith. Its basic effect is to break apart what for faith is essentially united. The religious symbol, the statue, host, altar, or whatever, which is seen by faith both as a material object and as the bearer of something higher, is reduced to its material sensible dimension by the Enlightenment. It accuses faith of worshipping just stones, or bread. Now, of course, this is absurd; and yet the barb goes home; for when faith tries to examine the nature of this unity between the divine and the merely external, it finds that it cannot comprehend it, and particularly that it cannot comprehend it with the intellectual structures of the Enlightenment which it has gradually come to accept. It is thus forced to an even more 'spiritual' religion in which the things of God are more clearly separated from this world.

In a similar manner the Enlightenment reduces the testimony of scripture to the rank of historical documents; and shows that as such they have little probative value. But it does not see that their value lay in the fact that they were recognized by religious consciousness spontaneously as valid, rather than residing in their strength as historical evidence. But this testimony of the spirit itself becomes problematic, and hence uncertain under the onslaught of

Enlightenment categories. In the same way the Enlightenment misunderstands and in so doing transforms faith's idea of sacrifice and mortification. The strength of the Enlightenment in its struggle with faith is that it brings together ideas which faith keeps apart in its consciousness. When it accuses faith of inventing its object, it marks a point Hegel says, in that man recognizes himself in the Absolute, is at home in it, and hence it can be said in a sense to come out of his own subjectivity. This fact makes it hard for faith to rebut the charge of the Enlightenment by rejecting it *simpliciter*. But of course it is also true that the Absolute is beyond man; this is the essential complement without which we have only a half-truth. Strangely enough the Enlightenment hints at this as well when it speaks of faith as something foisted on the people by a scheming priesthood. But this half-truth by itself is even more absurd, says Hegel. In fact a people cannot be deceived on such a fundamental matter (p. 392). It is absurd to think of religion as a pure invention which people are got to believe; unless it awoke some echo in them, they would never accept it. Religion in Hegel's view must always be seen as a veiled, unclear representation of the truth.

But now it is the Enlightenment which fails to put together its ideas about religion. In denouncing the one-sidedness of religion it fails to see its own one-sidedness.

The result for religion is an 'enlightened' theology, where God has become a shadowy supreme being, but which unlike the unbelieving Enlightenment suffers a longing to discover and unite with God. Hegel is obviously referring to the theology of contemporary thinkers like Jacobi and Schleiermacher, who had felt the weight of the Enlightenment critique, and tried to find another path to God through sentiment and intuition.

But Hegel also seems to be claiming a kind of synthesis between the two in the form of a mature Enlightenment which is ready to go over into action in the form of the French Revolution. But this supposedly maturer form is hard to distinguish from the earlier one. It has before it the world as understood in the category of the useful, and this says Hegel provides the independent external reality which was missing previously (412–13); but since the Enlightenment *première manière* was also characterized in terms of the useful, it is difficult to see what has changed.

The point of the passage may be clearer if we ignore this supposed step forward, and focus on the transition of the Enlightenment into revolutionary action. For this is readily understandable: this consciousness sees the world as neutral, as capable of being formed to fit human purposes. There is nothing in it which has intrinsic significance, which demands to be treated with respect and preserved; all can be altered and reformed according to man's needs and goals.

Moreover this consciousness is not that of particular individuals, it is a universal rational consciousness which has won through to this insight; therefore its purpose in reforming the world will be a single, rational and universal one; there is no reason why the world should be the battlefield of different purposes, reason and universality will prevail.

From this springs the idea of creating a definitive, perfect human society by an act of common will, of bringing heaven down to earth (413) and establishing the absolute in the here and now. Now this attempt thinks Hegel is based on the same error mentioned above, that the Enlightenment doesn't recognize significant reality outside man, and the sequel will show how disastrously this contradiction reveals itself.

Hegel plunges here into one of the most interesting passages of the *PhG*. The universal knowing subject who sees the whole world spread out as neutral objects whose workings it thoroughly understands, cannot but be seized by the ambition to transform this world according to universal reason. This is the idea of absolute freedom, freedom untrammelled by any obstacle, not even that of other wills, for the will in question is a universal will, hence that of all men in so far as they are free. 'The world is [for this consciousness] simply its will, and this will is universal' (415).

Moreover, this universal will should not be some putative consensus, arrived at by others for me. In this world of absolute freedom there should be no representation, but all should will together. Hegel is plainly referring here to the Rousseauian doctrine of the general will.

Now this dream of absolute freedom is impossible; and we have seen that the root reason is this, that it does not recognize an independent significant reality outside of its own will, and hence is doomed to self-destruction. The way in which this dialectic is worked out in this passage on the French Revolution is extremely interesting in that it shows the juncture between Hegel's ontology and his political philosophy.

The dream of absolute freedom cannot tolerate any structures and differentiation in society whereby people would have different functions in relation to the state, or whereby the state would be divided into estates. And in fact we see in Rousseau's *Contrat Social* the demand that there be no distinction between citizens as far as the legislative process is concerned, that all participate together and equally. There are, in Rousseau's state no legislative structures (although there are executive structures allowed). But argues Hegel, this means that no working state can be created; because a working state requires that people occupy different functions; and he believes further, that for different functions to be properly filled, there must even be a differentiation into estates (Stände), that is, classes with particular functions and roles in the whole. In other words, to exist really in history, a human political community, even issuing from a general will, must be embodied in some institutions; but institutions

mean differentiation, the inter-relationship of men who are differently related to power.

And this in turn means that each man must accept this structure and give it
his loyalty, even though it exists independently of him to the extent that other
men, other wills over which he has no control are fulfilling other functions
which are equally essential to the whole and which affect his life as well. Not
everything he lives can issue from his will, some things have to be accepted as
given, and accepted with the same loyalty and identification as he would give to
his own creations.

But this is the negation of the idea of absolute freedom; for according to this
each man would will everything that the state did, would thus create by his will
the totality of the political and social conditions in which he lived; and this is
incompatible with the kind of continuing differentiating structure which gives
each man his place and function.

It is obvious that we are on here to a vital debate of modern times which is far
from finished. The Rouseauian ideal returns in our day in the demand for
radical participatory democracy, for 'unstructured discussion', for spontaneous mass action. Nor does the Hegelian side of the argument have to be
linked with particular Hegelian views, such as the belief in the necessity of
estates, which are clearly untenable today.[1] We shall discuss this more fully in
Part IV. What should be pointed out here, however, is that Hegel's view is one
whose roots go deep in his ontology. The need of the human political
community as a general will to be embodied in a differentiated state structure, is a fundamental ontological necessity for man as a vehicle of *Geist*.

As a result of this fundamental notion Hegel sees a necessity by which the
aspiration to absolute freedom engenders the Terror. Since it can come to no
positive realization, its only action can be to destroy: to destroy the existing
constitution and estates first, and then when nothing else of the old remains to
destroy, it is left only with the opposition between the universal will and that of
particular individuals who are not aligned with it. Since its only action can be
destructive it is driven forward to suppress these wills. But since there is no
structure left, there is no mediation between these errant wills and that of the
state, only an absolute opposition; and the state's negation of these wills can be
only the simple unmediated one of liquidation. And moreover this liquidation
is deprived even of its dramatic power to shock, since what is being suppressed is (supposedly) nothing but the utterly inessential particular will.
'It is thus the coldest, flattest death, with no more significance than cutting
through a cabbage-head or throwing back a draught of water' (*PhG*, 418–
19).[2]

---

[1] And nor should we identify it with the baroque end-of-Raj constructions of Hegel's British
follower Bradley with his notion of 'my station and its duties'.
[2] 'Er ist also der kälteste, platteste Tod, ohne mehr Bedeutung als das Durchhauen eines
Kohlhaupts oder ein Schluck Wassers.'

Moreover the existence of material to be liquidated is virtually a necessity. For the absolutely universal will is an abstraction; in fact the government is run by some group, some faction, which is a part of the whole, which has a particular view and which is opposed by others. While this faction reigns all others are declared to be the vehicles of particular wills. And even when there is no overt opposition, the theory of the general will requires that all *will* the actions of the state. It thus becomes a crime even to be alienated from the republic in one's heart. But this alienation can be hidden, so the regime is driven to proceed against people even without overt opposition, but just on suspicion. (Hence Hegel tries to derive the famous *loi des suspects.*)

Hegel's study of the Terror also touches a question that has a relevance beyond his time. The Stalinist terror had some of the same properties as those which Hegel singled out in the Jacobin one: liquidation become banal, the fastening on intentions and other subjective deviations, the self-feeding destructiveness.

In any case, for Hegel the drive to absolute freedom ends in the contradiction of the terror, a kind of destructive fury which destroys the individual it came to liberate. The result is on one level that the organized structured state reconstitutes itself (under Napoleon), although differently because the citizens have had the experience of being close to death, which as we saw above in the dialectic of the master and the slave brings them closer to the universal. From here Hegel could have derived the development of higher forms of the state.

But this is not his interest in the *PhG;* because here his main interest is to go through different forms of consciousness, particularly those which had a certain currency in his time, and show how they develop of themselves into his vision of things. He steps therefore from the Terror, not to another political form, but to a new type of retreat from politics which flows from it.

The Terror can be seen as the final culmination of alienation and formation (Bildung); for it involves a final sacrifice and negation of the self which goes way beyond previous ones in that it is the negation of the self as a reality *simpliciter;* it is not just a transformation of the self, from particular into servant of state power, for instance, but the suppression of the punctual individual himself. Moreover, this suppression does not come about through external necessity but through the universal will which it itself aspires to be.

The step beyond this contradiction which Hegel now takes is the interiorization of this drama. The new form of consciousness accepts that the universal will can only come to be by the suppression of the punctual individual will, and it now proceeds to bring this about inwardly, by resolving to live according to universal reason and hence renouncing its individual particularity.

A reversal has taken place. Instead of striving to ensure that its individual will effectively weighed in the universal, the new form of consciousness calls for a renunciation of one's individual will, its mortification in order to give itself fully to the universal. From the political morality of the *Contrat Social*, we go to the morality of pure will of the *Critique of Practical Reason*.

We have here a transformation like that from the fight to the death to the relationship of master and slave, where the immediate negation of death is substituted for by a standing negation; or perhaps a closer analogy would be the step from the master–slave relation to the interiorization of this relation in Stoicism.

Thus absolute freedom leaves 'its self-destroying reality', and turns inward to a new moral consciousness. But this departure is also a geographical one. Absolute freedom 'goes over into another land of self-conscious spirit' (in ein anderes Land des selbstbewußten Geistes, *PhG*, 422); and clearly Hegel means this in a literal as well as a figurative sense. In the last section of the chapter on spirit we go from Revolutionary France to the awakening moral spirit of German philosophy.

3

The third part of the chapter on *Geist* takes us to Germany and to the movement of thought which started from Kant and developed through Fichte into German Romanticism. We seem to be returning here to figures already familiar from earlier chapters, in particular that on Reason.

But Hegel approaches these now as figures of a higher stage. We have ceased to deal with the subject as an individual only. Throughout the chapter on Spirit we have been dealing with the larger subject, that of a people or society, and with the individual in his relation to this. We are about to pass to the last chapter, on Religion, where we will examine what is really the self-understanding of cosmic *Geist*, although in a veiled and sometimes imperfect form. Here the individual in his religious consciousness is seen as the vehicle of the absolute subject. And there he reaches his fundamental identity, more fundamental than his identity as member of a society or people. For as the citizen is the vehicle of the larger life of the spirit of his people or society, so the different spirits of peoples (Volksgeister) in history can be seen as vehicles of the life of absolute spirit, who comes to self-consciousness in religion (as also in art and philosophy, as we shall examine below).

In this section on morality, we are making this transition from the spirit of a people or society expressed in their laws and institutions, (what Hegel calls later 'objective spirit') to absolute spirit. We are looking at views of the world in which the individual is – perhaps unwittingly – the vehicle of a larger self-consciousness. We are on the threshold of religion.

Hence when the section starts with a discussion of the moral philosophy of Kant and Fichte, which has already been severely dealt with in the previous chapter, it is the moral *world-view* (die moralische Weltanschauung) which is the central theme. This term is peculiarly appropriate to the views of Kant and Fichte, since both held to the primacy of practical reason. For Kant reason in its practical, i.e. moral, use was sovereign. It in no sense had to rely for its maxims on the deliverances of speculative reason. On the contrary, practical reason was able to show the necessity, as postulates, of important truths – concerning God, freedom, immortality – which speculative reason tried in vain to establish. Fichte, more radically, derived the whole structure of things from the demands of practical reason.

So that the world outlook of Kant and Fichte can be called moral. It is grounded on morality and flows from their moral views. But reciprocally, their morality requires completion in a world-outlook. Kant held that the postulates of practical reason concerning the existence of God and the immortality of the soul were inescapable, they were required by the demands of morality.

This need to complete a moral reasoning which is meant to be fully autonomous, which is meant to rely on no facts about the world or the will of God, by a kind of back stairs recourse to a supreme being and personal immortality, shows in Hegel's view the fundamental inadequacy of Kant's notion of the subject. What is on trial in these pages is the Kantian–Fichtean aspiration of radical moral autonomy in its extreme onesided form, where no concessions are made to the aspiration to unity with nature.

Hegel's break with this goes back to the 1790s. In a sense this view was never his, although as we saw he espoused Kant in his early writings on Christianity without understanding fully what was involved. But very early on, while he still accepted Kant's ideal of autonomous morality, Hegel was dissatisfied with the Kantian argument for the postulates of practical reason.[1] For in fact these arguments reflect the profound dualism of Kant's moral philosophy.

We have to postulate the existence of God because this is necessary for the realization of the supreme Good. The supreme good Kant defines as a condition where happiness or fulfilment (Glückseligkeit) is co-ordinated with virtue, that is, distributed among subjects according to their virtue. This notoriously fails to obtain now where the wicked frequently prosper and the good suffer. Nor is there any ground in nature which gives us hope of happiness and virtue coming into phase with each other in the future, for nature and the moral will are quite independent of each other. But we have to believe that the supreme good is possible if we are to be obliged to pursue it. Since only God as a higher power can bring about this harmony of dessert and reward, belief in God is a requirement of morality.

Now this argument is not only grounded on a radical separation of moral will and nature, but also a gulf between virtue and happiness. It is this very

[1] Cf. Nohl 70–1.

189

unGreek dichotomy which offended the young Hegel in the passage referred to above. The ancient warrior gave himself to the life and defence of his polis. This was his true virtue, but it was at the same time his fulfilment. Living beyond himself in the life of polis, living beyond his death through his fame among his people, this *was* happiness. He did not require payment for a virtue which was no reward in itself, some consolation (Trost) or compensation (Entschädigung). The need for this compensation arises from the degeneration (Verdorbenheit) of modern times. The man who has lost political virtue and defines himself as an individual sees death as a total loss. Where the ancient warrior was glad to die for his city and live in its memory, the modern can only envisage dying for the sake of the good as a terrible loss to be made good by the rewards in an after life.

Hence before we even look at Kant's claim that the supreme good requires God, the very notion of the supreme good, of *co-ordinating* happiness and virtue supposes a profound division, in which the good and human fulfilment are utterly distinct and only contingently related. And this division is unacceptable to an expressivist vision of man, which found one of its models in the ancients.

Hegel in this part of the *PhG* attacks Kant's postulates although the Kant–Fichte position is presented here without attribution in a reconstructed form in which the actual postulates identified do not correspond exactly with Kant's. And he attacks them basically by showing how they spring from a profound dualism which Kant's moral philosophy can neither escape nor accept. We start off with a moral will which is utterly distinct from nature, for if it were not, then it would not be fully autonomous, really drawing its maxims from itself. But at the same time, the harmony of morality and nature, of virtue and happiness, is seen as necessary, and hence has to be postulated as the work of God.

But the division is not only between morality and nature outside me, the course of things in the world. My moral will is also in opposition to nature in me, my desires, inclinations, etc. And this, too, is an opposition which must be overcome, since I am called on to fulfil my duty, act it out, make it real. And this will never be complete until my own nature has been made over to conform with the demands of duty, and I have a truly holy will. Hence the postulate of immortality which opens the prospect of endless progress towards a holiness which I cannot attain now in the sensible world.

Here is where the contradiction comes to the fore, Hegel thinks. The postulate of immortality is necessary because we have to surmount our initial predicament where moral will is opposed to nature. But this is not just an initial predicament, it is a necessary one for morality as Kant defines it. For the moral will is defined in opposition to inclination; should it fuse with natural desire, it would disappear.

for if it [sc. complete harmony of moral will and desire] really came to pass, the moral consciousness would be annulled. For *morality* is only a moral *consciousness* as the negative essence, in the face of whose pure duty sensibility has only a negative significance, the significance of what is not in conformity to it. (*PhG*, 428)

Hence the idea of endless progress to perfection reflects a deep contradiction, a division of purpose. This unity of moral will and desire in a holy will seems called for, and yet were it to come it would put an end to morality. The compromise is to refer it to an indefinite future towards which we are always marching without ever arriving there. In the 'dark distance of infinity' (dunklen Ferne der Unendlichkeit), this contradiction is not too clearly discernible.

This is the contradiction of a dualist conception of man. We define what is essential to man, the moral will, in opposition to nature. We are at the farthest point of division. But this cannot be sustained. The subject is essentially embodied, and thus the moral will has to be reconciled with its embodiment, it has to be externally realized. Kant has an inkling of this, hence his doctrine of the supreme good and his postulates of practical reason. But he has debarred himself from bringing it off. For he has defined morality in terms of division, and hence the aspiration to realization of morality has to be contradictory. What would fulfil the moral will would abolish it.

This view is the fruit of the rigid thinking of the 'understanding' (Verstand) which holds fast to division and distinction, and cannot see that the divided terms also recover their unity. The understanding is a mode of thought which holds things fixed, sees them as either unchangingly distinct or identical. It is Reason (Vernunft) which can see how separation springs from identity and returns to it again.

Kant's thought represents understanding in its most uncompromising mood. This is why he remains with division and cannot overcome it. Hence his thought must fall into contradiction with he tries to think the realization of morality. But the contradiction comes out at another point as well, when we try to give a *content* to moral obligation. In order to safeguard autonomy, Kant insists that the moral will be determined only by itself, that it draw its maxims not from some external fact or authority but from itself. Hence Kant argues, what makes a maxim of action morally binding cannot be anything to do with its substantive content, but only its form. It is when it has the form of universalizability, and thus reflects the rational will, that it is obligatory.

Hegel argues in many places that the Kantian formal criterion fails to yield any determinate result. He made this point in the chapter on reason, and also in other places.[1] Many philosophers have, of course, argued that Kant's

---

[1] E.g. in the paper of the early Jena period 'Über die wissenschaftlichen Behandlungsarten des Naturrechts' in *Schriften zur Politik und Rechtsphilosophie*, Ed. Lasson, pp. 349 ff., also PR § 258, and SW, xix, 588–96.

criterion is empty. But for Hegel this defect springs from the same basic cause as the above contradiction, the dualism between moral autonomy and nature. Kant insists that the criterion be formal in order to safeguard the autonomy of the will. The will can turn only to reason as its guide. But Kant's idea of reason is not the true one in which the Idea turns its opposite, Nature, and finds an embodiment which manifests it. Hence Kant's notion of reason is abstract, purely formal. And just because of this cleaving to reason can tell us nothing about how to act. For Hegel, reason is bound up with the ontological structure of things, and this will provide the guidance we need to shape our moral action. But for Kant, reason is utterly distinct from the nature of things, just as moral will is from nature. It is thus purely formal, and just for this reason cannot provide any substantive guidance.

We thus fall into a second contradiction, that of moral duty, which Hegel now draws out. Man is bound by the pure principle of duty, to act according to universal rule. But in order to act, I have to see this general principle of duty instantiated in particular duties, particular acts I must do. But this is the gap that cannot be bridged. No particular act can ever be shown to be binding, because the principle of universalizability in fact can be satisfied by anything. Hegel sees the protagonists of the moral world-outlook here as having to introduce another postulate to bridge this gap, to have recourse to God again, this time to confer on our particular duties the quality of holiness that pertains to pure duty.

This latter postulate is rather dubiously attributable to Kant. But Hegel is not strictly interpreting Kant here (whose name never appears) but rather what he sees to be the inner logic of the moral world-outlook to which Kant and later Fichte gave expression. And his point here as elsewhere is that this vision is shot through with contradiction, in that it is founded on a division which it can neither accept nor overcome. And this contradiction always comes out in two places; when we consider the realization of morality, and when we try to give a determinate content to moral obligation.

The result of this contradiction is that this morality, which started off with the principle of autonomy as its central idea, is forced to have recourse to a deus ex machina. Its fulfilment is placed in a distant future in another world. Its present experience is one of division. It is another form of unhappy consciousness. As Hegel puts it here, we start off with the affirmation that there is moral consciousness. But when we see that this moral consciousness is in principle unreconciled with nature, and incapable of affirming of any particular act that it is really a duty, then we have to admit that among men, who are sensible beings who must realize themselves in particular acts, there is no moral consciousness. Or there is one but only in representation, and representation, moreover, which cannot become clear conceptual thought without showing up its contradictions.

This is the fate of any moral vision which divides morality from nature, which is concerned merely with what ought to be, and is not grounded on what is. How Hegel proposes to go beyond this we shall examine further in Part IV.

After a devastating ten-page passage (434–44) in which he works systematically through the contradictions of the moral world-outlook, and the shifts (Verstellungen) it goes through to avoid seeing them, Hegel goes on to a Romantic theory of conscience which grew in part out of Kant. This figure can be placed here because it grows at least partially out of a sense of what Hegel finds objectionable in Kant's moral theory. The Romantics abandoned the austere Kantian division between inclination and morality, and came to a vision of a spontaneous moral intuition in which the law of the heart and the ethical law are one.

But this is not just a return to the earlier phase of subjective moral certainty described in the chapter on Reason. For here the subject is certain of his intuitions not just as an individual, but as one who is in touch with the universal, with God. For the Romantic conscience is a religious one. It rejoices in having overcome the gap not only between inclination and morality but also between man and God. The community of these consciences is the locus of God's life (460). We thus have a vision which is close to Hegel's.

But we saw in the first chapter how sharply Hegel differed from the Romantics for all the similarity in their aspirations. He could not accept the Romantic notion of an immediate unity with the universal, or the belief in intuition which aspires to a kind of ineffable encounter with God. This unity could only be brought about by Reason, which can bear negation and separation within the unity, and hence maintains clarity of vision.

Hegel's critique of this theory starts from its individual inspirational character, which allows conscience to have any content at all provided someone feels the corresponding inspiration. But this is incompatible with the supposed nature of this conscience as the mouthpiece of the universal, whose inspirations are universally recognized, and thus bring about the universal recognition of the self who identifies with them. On the contrary, the actions which flow from these inspirations clash.

The result is a dialectical shift. We no longer see the expression of the pure conscience in external action, which can be a source of conflict, and which as external reality can always be seen from many points of view and judged from many standpoints. For instance, it can be seen as moral action by some because of one aspect, and as the height of selfishness by others because of another. Instead, the paradigm expression of conscience shifts to speech, which Hegel repeats here, is a form of external existence of *Geist* which nevertheless remains transparent, which doesn't have the obtrusive many-sided nature of external reality which allows us to see something quite other and unintended in the latter. It is the transparent expression of the self, pure identity with self, but posed in objectivity (458).

Hence the spontaneously pure conscience turns from action to talk, to the expression in literature of its own inner convictions, but which it can never act out for fear of losing this sense of its purity and universality. This is the figure of the beautiful soul. It represents of course just another strategy of retreat, and Hegel makes short shrift of it. It brings about its own annihilation, and disappears 'as a formless vapour, which dissolves itself in the air' (als ein gestaltloser Dunst, der sich in Luft auflöst, *PhG*, 463).

But Hegel's attitude towards the beautiful soul – whose portrait seems drawn here especially from Novalis – is much more ambiguous than the above would imply. For this figure reminds us of the Jesus of the Frankfurt MS on the 'Spirit of Christianity', and we thus recall that Hegel did not always judge the beautiful soul this harshly.

Rather, Hegel shows the importance which this phase of thought had for him in all but making the transition of absolute knowledge through a reflection on the dilemma of purity versus efficacy. This occupies the rest of the chapter, and prepares the passage to absolute knowledge, although we will first have to trace this higher, religious vision from its very beginning.

The dilemma of purity arises inescapably out of our relation as particular existents to the universal. Man acts as an individual, and his individuality is inevitably mixed up in his action. Even the most altruistic act with the greatest universal significance is one in which the agent found some kind of satisfaction, and which is coloured in some way with his particular subjectivity. This, we have already seen, is one of the fundamental Hegelian ideas, that all spiritual reality to be must be embodied, and embodiment is in some time and place, hence particular. *Geist* can only be by being embodied in finite spirits which are particular. The price of existence is thus particularization.

To attempt to hold the universal free of the particular in order to maintain its purity, as the beautiful soul does, is to condemn it to non-existence. Universal values have to accept as it were the sacrifice of being embodied in particular lives in order to be realized. But at the same time the particular must sacrifice itself. The particular is the mortal, we have seen; all particular things die or disappear. But the particular man must as it were die inwardly in order to attain the universal; he must recognize that what is essential in his action is the embodiment of universal *Geist*, and recognize that the particular features of its embodiment in his life are what is inessential and hence doomed to pass away. He should be already reconciled to this passing away, that is not putting his essential interest and identification in these particular features.

This reciprocal necessity for sacrifice of universal and particular Hegel

194

presents here in the last pages on *Geist* in the form of a kind of dialogue between two of the stages we have just seen, the pure conscience which is sure of itself and acts, and the beautiful soul which wants above all to maintain the purity of the universal. The passage is called evil and its pardon. Why evil? Because the particular and its affirmation is the essence of evil, for it is that which cuts men off from the universal. But this evil is unavoidable, for *Geist* must be embodied, and this means particularization. This notion of the necessity of evil underlies Hegel's interpretation of the doctrine of original sin. The sin is original not in some quasi-historical sense, but in that particular existence is fundamental to finite spirit, and finite spirits must be for spirit to be, and yet their finitude is what creates the division that has to be overcome; it is the essence of sin which divides man from God. The unity of God with man can thus only be achieved by a reconciliation arising out of a state of sin; there must be evil, particular existence, but this is overcome through man negating it, living beyond it, or in theological terms, asking forgiveness for it; and in so doing, he rejoins the universal life of *Geist*, and is thus pardoned.

This reciprocal necessity is brought out in the dialogue of two consciences: that representing the universal starts out taking the active particular conscience to task for its betrayal of the universal. It accuses it of bending the universal to its own purposes because it can always descry some individual interest in any act undertaken by the active conscience. It thus accuses its interlocutor of hypocrisy, of being moral in word only. This outlook is of course pretty distasteful to Hegel and he comes right back in reply: since the beautiful soul cannot bring itself to embody the universal law in act, which by its nature it demands to be, it is this conscience of which we can say rather that its service to morality is purely verbal, and that it is hypocritical. Hegel makes clear his disapproval of this position by throwing in extra insults – quoting the Napoleonic dictum: 'il n'y a pas de heros pour son valet de chambre'; then adding, not because the first is not a hero, but because the other is nothing more than a valet de chambre (467–8).

The solution is that both sides admit their wrong and their need for the other. The particular agent must ask forgiveness, that is, no longer set store by his particularity. But at the same time the universal must give this forgiveness, that is accept that it cannot be except by this particular agent and hence that it is bound to forgive. The result is a new consciousness, the highest unity in opposition of particular and universal. We are on the verge of passing over into absolute knowledge; for we have a particular subject ready to give up and live beyond his particularity, and a universal which is now seen not as being totally beyond but as needing the particular.

What remains to be done is to set out this ontological vision of *Geist* which must be embodied and return to itself. This speculative philosophy will give us.

But this vision is also contained in a less transparent form in religion. The self-knowledge of the absolute has developed in the religious evolution of mankind. Hence the last chapter before the conclusion will be on religion; and in keeping with the practice of the whole work we will start from the bottom, from the beginning, with the religion of nature.

CHAPTER VII

The Road to Manifest Religion

1

With religion we enter a new point of view from which the development of *Geist* can be read, along with those we have seen earlier: consciousness, self-consciousness, reason and (objective) spirit. But this point of view is not simply on a par with the others. On the contrary, religion is the standpoint of *Geist's* or the absolute's consciousness of itself.

We have seen that for Hegel the ultimate reality which must come to fruition and full self-revelation through history is God or the cosmic *Geist* whose embodiment is the universe, with which he is therefore identical and yet not identical. The fullness of this self-revelation will come in speculative philosophy. But like other aspects of the ultimate fruition of *Geist*, this self-consciousness of the absolute exists and is to be found through history in more rudimentary obscure form.

This form is religion. This self-consciousness of the absolute must, like its ultimate fulfilment in speculative philosophy, be embodied in human consciousness. But Hegel is suggesting that we should see the evolution of religion in human society as more than just the evolution of human consciousness. This of course it is as well, and we have noted various stages of this human religious consciousness in our survey of self-consciousness and *Geist* – e.g. the unhappy consciousness, or the supra-sensible world. But we must also see this evolution as the development of a larger-than-human consciousness. The justification for this comes, of course, with the validation of the ontological reality of the Hegelian notion of *Geist*.

Geist's self-consciousness is inevitably a consciousness of the absolute which underlies all reality. But in its imperfect earlier forms this absolute is not seen as at one with the reality. And in a sense rightly so, for this reality has not yet shaped itself as it will through man's development in history to be an adequate reflection of the absolute. Hence religious consciousness maintains a distinction between the sacred and the secular, and a tension between them. And by the same token this self-consciousness remains unaware of itself as such, since human consciousness, its vehicle, is seen as something separate from and infinitely below the object of religion.

But the greater the felt gap between sacred and secular, the less adequate the conception of the absolute. This is in reality cosmic infinite subject whose life is embodied in that of finite subject. Hence the religion of the incarnation is the only really adequate one, and even Christianity needs to undergo an evolution and a translation into speculative philosophy in order to overcome the remaining alienation which sees Christ alone as the meeting point of finite and infinite spirit, rather than the community (Gemeinde) as a whole. But preceding this religion we have a series of less adequate ones in history, including conceptions of God as Spirit but as utterly other and separate from finite spirit (Judaism, Islam), or of Gods with human form but lacking universality (Greek religion), and extending back to conceptions where the absolute is no longer seen as Spirit. Hence we will start the dialectic of religious development with what Hegel calls 'nature religions', those which see the absolute symbolized through some natural form rather than as free subjectivity.

These lower religions are distinguished as well from the higher in that they have to have recourse to symbolization. Ultimately God is presented to us in the community of finite spirits; there is no symbolization here, God is rather present and evident. This is the hall-mark of what Hegel calls 'revealed religion' (*offenbare Religion*, trading on the connotations of the German word which also means 'manifest' or 'evident'). But when God is not thus evident, then he must be indicated symbolically. The lower stage of religious consciousness the less adequate the symbolization. Before God is even grasped as spirit, men will use natural phenomena as their symbols.

We see here again that the level of religious consciousness is linked with the level of human development. In the early stages man (finite spirit) is a very inadequate reflection of *Geist* (infinite spirit). In the stage corresponding for instance to what we saw as sensible certainty, or the dialectic of the master and the slave, on other levels of description, human consciousness has yet to become a vehicle of universal thought; God must be seen as wholly other. At this stage spirit or subjectivity is not even seen as superior to the blind forces of nature, since it is not conceived as universal. Hence it is natural to picture the absolute by some symbol drawn from nature.

We can see thus that the development of religion will recapitulate the developments we have seen at other levels, from a more all-embracing point of view. Stages of consciousness, self-consciousness and Spirit correspond to stages of religion. The *PhG* thus constantly returns to cover the same ground; but successively from a more central standpoint. Already Spirit represented a shift of standpoint in that we were no longer content to follow the evolution of forms of consciousness in the ordinary sense but saw them embedded in collective life-forms; so that the stages we picked out earlier could be seen as aspects of the stages of spirit. Here again, we shift the standpoint in order to focus on the most fundamental development of all, the growth in self-consciousness of *Geist*. It would seem that for Hegel the other levels of description yield us aspects of this development; for it is on this level that the basic motor of development is revealed, that we can see in other words, the ultimate rationale behind the stages of history – the drive of *Geist* towards rational self-revelation. This is perhaps what Hegel means when he says that the descriptions at these other levels are to the description of religious consciousness as predicates to subject (479).

This relation of 'subject' to 'predicate' should also allow us to understand Hegel's distinction referred to in the last chapter between religion and faith. The latter is a form of human consciousness which senses a reality beyond it with which it is somehow related. Religion on the other hand englobes those facets of our consciousness which can be understood as the (perhaps confused) self-understanding of *Geist*. It follows that the same form of consciousness can sometimes be seen from both points of view, as the faith of the individual who sees himself as far below the absolute and pining after an unseen distant reality, and at the same time as a certain stage of religious consciousness still characterized by the rift between sacred and secular.

But the two are not usually congruent. Religion, for Hegel is more all-englobing thing. What reflects a given stage of the self-consciousness of *Geist* is the whole religious reality, that is, not just the idea of the absolute but also the religious life of the society as lived in their cult. All of this, and not just the theology reflects a certain understanding of the absolute.[1] Faith, as a state of mind of an individual, is thus just one element in the religious life of a community at a given stage of civilization. It is simply an abstract aspect, a 'predicate'. Since the only adequate reflection of *Geist* is by the common life of a plurality of finite spirits, religious life is always the life of a community, whereas faith as a state of soul is a condition of the individual, however many share it.

It can be guessed from this that Hegel is not terribly concerned with the drama of faith. Indeed, faith as the form of consciousness of the individual who sees himself as separated from the absolute (and hence also from the community [Gemeinde] in which the absolute lives) is the reflection of an as yet unfulfilled religious life. In the ultimate religion of the total self-revelation of *Geist*, there would be no room for faith. Ideally religion should transcend faith.

---

[1] This distinction between religion as a whole life-form and theology plays an important role in Hegel's thought from the beginning, as we saw in Chapter II in the discussion of the MS-fragments of his Tübingen period.

2

We start with natural religion, that is, a religion for which the absolute is simply being. As absolute being, it is separate from all particular things; it is the ruler of all and yet untouched by the particularity of things. Thus Hegel sees it represented for instance by early Zoroastrianism, a religion of light and fire: light is pure being in abstraction from all particularity, and fire as that which consumes all particularity.

What is lacking here obviously from a Hegelian point of view is the link between absolute and world, the necessary development of things out of the first principle; without this the world is without necessary structure, just 'an inessential by-play alongside this substance' (ein wesenloses Beiherspielen an dieser Substanz, 484). This is the same thing as saying that this substance is not yet subject, for we have seen that subjectivity has this necessary structure whereby its external reality expresses its inner nature.

However, as negative power (Macht) which destroys all particularity, this substance is already in essence a self, and we thus develop normally into a religion of *Fürsichsein*. But we have not yet got to the idea of a universal self; we are in a stage of many divine beings; and these moreover are very imperfect subjects: men take as their gods plant and animal images.

But the resultant struggle between peoples who follow these different gods leaves nothing in its wake; subjectively as negative power can only destroy. We must therefore move to a higher stage where the transforming power of subjectivity reaches enduring expression through its creations. We have therefore a religion of the artisan. This transition is very reminiscent of that which the slave undergoes in his disciplined work. In effect under external impetus the slave embarks on a course which leads to his own transformation.

And so here with the religion of the artisan, Hegel is here thinking pre-eminently of ancient Egypt.

Instead of just finding the image of his God in nature, the artisan is impelled to form it in stone, in architecture and sculpture. In this way he is already on the road to a higher conception of God since a transformed reality yields us an image closer to that of Spirit than some simply natural being. But in wrestling with his material the artisan is at first not aware that the only adequate image which can satisfy his search is that of free subjectivity. He struggles through a number of intermediate stages in which he represents strange monsters, half-man and half-beast (sphinx) before he finally comes through to the clear representation of spirit which he seeks, viz., the human form. The artisan in struggling with his medium under an impetus which he does not understand is like the slave, and like this latter his transformation of matter is also a transformation of self so that he ends up winning through to higher religion, the religion of art, where men in clarity worship a fully adequate image of spirituality. In other words in transforming their material both slave and artisan reach a higher consciousness which enables them to understand retrospectively the significance of what they were doing, and to work in clear consciousness where before they operated only by instinct or under external compulsion.

This new religion is that of the Greeks, and is the religion of art. We come back here to one of Hegel's most cherished interpretations. The period of the Greeks is a uniquely happy one in that men come into reconciliation with the absolute, with nature and with society. These three levels are obviously linked. Men see the absolute under the aspect of an anthropomorphic being, as eminently representable by a statue with human form. This reflects the fact that they sense the divine not as something utterly other and fundamentally mysterious and incomprehensible. Rather this sense of the strange and the unfathomable is reflected in the monstrous semi-animal forms given to Gods in other earlier cultures. With the Greeks, says Hegel, these animal forms are set aside or are clearly demoted to simple signs. (493–4). But this at the same time reflects a sense of being at home in the natural world; that the divine in human form has bound the earlier images of the numinous which drew on other natural forms to express their otherness. All this is reflected in the victory over the Titans:

> The disordered essence and the confused struggle of the elements' free existence, the non-ethical realm (das unsittliche Reich) of the Titans, is overcome and banished to the borders of a reality which has become clear to itself, to the troubled frontiers of a world which reposes and finds peace in the Spirit. *(PhG, 494)*

But this sense of being 'at home' is closely bound up with the sense of unity with one's society which we discussed at the opening of the chapter on spirit. In fact the individual feels himself fully reflected in his society, feels his activity to be simply an embodiment of its ethos, and this ethos to be the substance on which he depends. Now this sense of one-ness with his society mediates the sense of affinity with the divine, for the God in turn is the god of a given people or city, as well as expressing some cosmic reality. Affinity with city and God go together and strengthen each other. Both reflect a certain form of life, that of the free citizen in the state. We are therefore now about to look at the religious consciousness which goes along with the 'true spirit' of the last chapter.

But both forms of affinity repose on the same condition which is in the end a fatal flaw. Just as man only identifies with the city by circumscribing this to a particular state and hence by being parochial, so he only feels at one with a divinity who is not absolute subject, but just one divine subjectivity among many. The reconciliation of Greek history is not the final reconciliation, but just a foreshadowing of it; it is destined to pass away undermined by the growth of universal consciousness which is the unavoidable next and higher stage on the road to a total reconciliation of *Geist* with itself.

It is this growth of the universal individual whose derivation Hegel shows in this section of the chapter on religion. As we have seen elsewhere, the notion of a parochial universal is closely linked with the idea of fate. Above the Gods, the single absolute which is only half-suspected in this religion appears as a force even greater than they; but necessarily as an impersonal force constraining them from without, viz., fate. This will play a part in the derivation in this section, as also will Greek tragedy.

The basic idea behind these derivations is this: the universal must be embodied in some particular form, as we have seen, but this form is always mortal, so that the universal negates it as well as positing it. The only possible reconciliation comes when the particular form fully understands and identifies with this process; when the particular individual recognizes how its mortality is itself an inseparable part of the order which it aspires to embody. In this case, death does not come from outside, it is not something fundamentally other and incomprehensible which descends on it; but rather is in a sense the willed fulfilment of this embodiment itself.

But in the case of a parochial universal, we have an entity which also must be embodied to be, and hence whose embodiment must go under. But being parochial, this universal cannot comprehend within itself the rationale of its own demise. It is therefore wiped out by something other and ununderstood; it perceives this demise as an inscrutable fate.

For the parochial gods of Greece are identified with certain ephemeral realities, like a given city; they are not fully identical with the universal spirit. If they were, then they would be untouched by the demise of given cities, indeed, would understand this demise as necessary for the unfolding of universal spirit. But a parochial universal goes under with the reality to which he is bound; unlike the real universal *Geist* he does not survive it. Hence the gods are seen as subject to a blind fate, just as men are; whereas later in Christian theology, this will be seen as a divine providence; i.e., 'fate' is no longer blind and God is above it.

Similarly the characters of the tragedy are parochial as we saw in the previous chapter; each expresses only part of the universal; hence they too go under in face of a necessity that they cannot understand. And this parochiality of the characters and hence family and state ethics is itself bound up with the parochiality of the city; for it is only in a city based on universal law that these two sources of right cease to conflict and are reconciled.

The reconciliation of Greek civilization is thus doomed to be rent asunder: and yet it has a special beauty and fascination for Hegel. For unlike the higher solution which will succeed it, it is not dependent on fully explicit rational thought. The universal norms of reason can only be brought to fruition in men's lives by the hard conquest of rational consciousness. True, the reconciliation also exists in representation in the Christian religion which succeeds the Greek; but it cannot come to full expression in history, or even in consciousness without the resources of explicit rational thought.

By contrast the temporary reconciliation of ancient Greece could be embodied completely in spontaneous feeling, and was. Unlike our higher civilization whose basic ideas must be expressed in religion and philosophy, the basis of Greek civilization was expressed in art. Art is the idea in sensuous form; and this is the form which most suited Greek civilization, a reconcilization of *Geist* with itself based on unreflecting feeling. Its religion was thus the religion of art. Previously, religion still contained deep mystery not fully expressible in its art-forms, and later the higher religion is much more adequately expressed in theology and indeed philosophy. Only the Greeks had a religion whose paradigm expression was in art. Hence the undying charm of the age of 'art-religion' (Kunstreligion).

Hegel's analysis follows the stages by which this art religion breaks down, and its images of the divine lose their substance, and are absorbed into the universal *Geist* on one hand and the universal self-consciousness on the other. These two are related developments, but Hegel here separates them: the development of Greek religion is seen as the growth of a self-consciousness which has seen through all the claims of the divine and the related ethical claims of public life (*Sittlichkeit*), and comes to see that human consciousness lies behind all these supposedly higher powers. It reaches an insight something like that of the Enlightenment into the human origin of the gods. This consciousness is that, Hegel thinks, of the comedy of the age of Aristophanes, which treats with irony the claims of gods and demos which were earlier taken as ultimate.

The universal *Geist* on the other hand is exalted in Jewish religion. And here too it demands a reconciliation with subjectivity, which comes in the Incarnation. This is the second step which is necessary after the first represented in the above development of Greek religion. For it is not enough to debunk the false parochial gods in the name of free self-consciousness; this latter alone is empty unless it can find an external reality which fully reflects what it has become and in which it can thus recognize itself. Left to itself it can only sink in the infinite sense of loss of a desacralized world. But the only external reality which it can accept is one which reflects universal spirit and, what is more, universal spirit in unity with self-consciousness. This it finds in the Incarnation.

But this step is reserved for the next section, that on revealed religion. Let us follow first the stages of art religion. The first reality posited is the expression of the divine, this time in human form, say by a statue. This is the image of the divine as free subjectivity to which man feels an affinity. But as it stands it is not enough, for it is simply an object over against the men whose God it is. Men strive to become one with the God through prayer – and here Hegel once again stresses speech as the medium of external existence of the soul; not in the sense of translating some reality already existent inwardly, but rather of embodying an inter-subjective reality which otherwise would not be. The unity of divine form and the hymn of his worshippers make a new reality, an 'animate work of art' (beseeltes Kunstwerk, 496), which is closer to representing the God qua self-conscious subjectivity. We can see here, as was remarked above, how for Hegel religion treats of more than the conceptions of God in theology; here we are dealing with God as lived in the community, God as addressed by his worshippers, rather than just with a static image.

That religion is more than theology is even more evident when we come to cult, which is an essential dimension of religion in Hegel's eyes.[1] Cult is that dimension whereby men strive to become one with God. For all religion contains some inkling that it is the self-consciousness of universal *Geist*, hence that the finite consciousness is both separate from and at one with the infinite one it worships. Hence the necessity of overcoming the separation and returning to the underlying unity. This is the role of cult.

Hegel cites as cult here the sacrifices of Greek religion. Sacrifice exhibits the two-way convergence of all cult; the finite spirit sets aside his finitude to be one with the infinite; but the infinite also steps down from his merely universal and hence unreal existence and accepts his embodiment in finite *Geist*. Both these movements are necessary, for finite spirit can only become the adequate embodiment of infinite *Geist* by overcoming his particularity. The sacrifice of our own to the gods is our act of giving up our particularity; but the god's descent into the victim, and the return of the victim to us for our consumption, is the stepping of the infinite into finite embodiment.

Religion thus goes way beyond conceptions of the divine to forms of experiencing our unity with the divine, of enjoying our affinity with infinite spirit (Genuß, 504). But simply enjoying the sacrifices is not enough. For the consumed sacrifice disappears. Once again we look for something lasting; and this we find in the ongoing cult of the whole people. We came here to what Hegel calls the living work of art, for instance, in the festival of the whole people, or in the frenzy of maenads possessed, or in the athlete.

But this too rapidly gives way to the third stage; for the living work of art still lacks full consciousness, inward awareness; or insofar as there is inwardness, it is the wild confused and mysterious depth of bacchanalian revel. Hence we proceed to a third stage, the 'spiritual work of art', represented by literature.

In this we finally derive the result we have been aiming at, for the three stages of literature, epic, tragedy, comedy, work out the vision and dialectic of what we called above parochial universals to their inevitable outcome.

---

[1] As we shall see below in Chapter VIII. Cf. *BRel.*

In the Homeric epic we have gods whose individuality is largely unreal, since they cannot really impinge on each other, being immortal. The underlying idea that their universality can only become real when embodied in human action comes out in the close interweaving of human and divine action in the epic, so that many results seem to spring from both in such a way that one or the other seems superfluous. The gods are here parochial universals, they lack the concrete reality of individual selves; and so do the heroes who are painted here larger than life. But at the same time they are not identical with the truly universal self; they are thus under the sway of fate, for the reason we saw above.

At the same time the really concrete individual, the bard who sings the epic, is outside the story. The next stage is therefore one in which these two extremes, necessity and the concrete individual, come together. This happens in tragedy where the individual character encounters fate not as something contingent and external, but as necessarily flowing from his action. Here Hegel takes up the analysis of tragedy that we saw in the chapter on Spirit. Each character embodies a basic value, that of the city or the family, which cannot but enter into conflict with the other once it is acted upon. Once again, the general underlying principle is that to be embodied and hence active in history is to suffer eventual dissolution; but when acting on truly universal principles, this disolution is something which flows as it were from the action, and does not negate it. Here, however, this is not the case: action thus not only leads to eventual destruction, but to a destruction which is not consonant with the principles of action, which is unreconciled with the action. Rather the action leads to crime in that it offends another law than the one it serves.

Put in other words, one could say that all action is in some sense guilt-creating in that it is affirmation of the particular, and hence cuts him off from the universal. But in the case of action following some universal principle this element of particularity is cancelled, the fault is atoned for, partly by the fact that we are following the principle, and partly through the inevitable and already accepted demise of the agent and his action. Where we have some parochial principle, however, there is really a crime, in that the action violates right not just in the general way of affirming a particular being's will, but in some specific way. The only atonement possible here is the undoing or renunciation of the act; but since this is enjoined by principle, the agent is in an impossible bind. He goes to a demise with which he is unreconciled, for it signifies the negation of what he stood for not its fulfilment.

Now this external negation is implicit in the parochial act, just as it was in the parochial universals which were the gods of the pantheon. The inner necessity is there all the time, only that in tragedy, it is taken account of; not yet entirely explicitly, but in the sense of necessity expressed in the art form. We cannot quite explain it to ourselves, but we sense the inevitability of the crime. This is also reflected in the dialectic of the known and the unknown. The hero acts on what he knows or is told; but already in his being told, there was an ambiguity which he should have detected. The other side of his action, the right offended by him, is not therefore entirely unknown to him; on some level it is sensed by him, just as we sense the connection; and hence he is not totally blameless.

When this necessity is fully grasped, we rise to a universal subjectivity. But for this subjectivity, the old gods have lost their numinosity. Already tragedy began the process; now they are considered irrelevant. Nature is reduced to what is consumed by the real self-consciousness who enjoys it. Even the claims of city and family to allegiance are undermined when the universal consciousness sees through parochial civic piety, and observe nothing but the ambition of various leaders and the mob. That this is observed is, of course, the fruit not just of a change of consciousness but of an attendant transformation of civic life itself as well.

The religion of art thus ends in the triumph of the self-conscious whose certainty of self makes it master of all it surveys; all universality returns to it, and it recognizes no essence outside itself.

3

Now this cosmic consciousness is at first a happy one; but really it is and will reveal itself to be the unhappy consciousness. We have here the religious consciousness that goes along with the dissolution of the city into the *Rechtszustand*, the universal state which ruled over atomic individuals whose situation was defined by their rights. This also corresponds to the ideology of Stoicism which was examined in the chapter on self-consciousness.

The basic problem in this phase, however described, is that man has achieved self-certainty but only at the cost of retreating into himself. But since man as *Geist* must have an external embodiment to be, a self-certainty which is not expressed in external social and political forms is nothing worth. The free universal individual is in fact the plaything of fortune and of unchained forces of political savagery. His self-certainty is a retreat to an inner citadel, that of I = I, which cannot ultimately be defended, and which hence leads to the unhappy consciousness.

In the religious sphere, this basic predicament can be described in the following way: having desacralized the world outside him, the free self-consciousness is in a parlous condition, because he remains dependent on this outside world, it is this which determines his form of life and hence what he effectively is. Simply reducing the divine to self-consciousness as does the debunking insight of the Enlightenment, and the cosmic consciousness of the Ancients, is a self-defeating action. Self-consciousness cannot sustain the prerogative of the divine, of *Geist*, which is to be fully self in its other, to be the informing necessity underlying a rational world order. On the contrary self-consciousness can only feel abandoned at the mercy of a foreign world, and in so far as it sees salvation describes it from afar, as an unhappy consciousness.

We must therefore return to a renewed sense of the divine as something more than just our self-consciousness. We have to rediscover a cosmic spirit with whom we can be in relation. But we will not simply be returning to our starting point in natural religion; something has been gained, and this is the element of truth behind cosmic consciousness, which is that this cosmic spirit has no other locus of self-consciousness, no other vehicle, than ourselves as finite spirits. He lives in and through us. We are his embodiment. True, as particular individuals we are also in opposition to God or cosmic spirit, we are an embodiment which is also a negation. But this opposition is surmounted in the fact that we are mortal, that each of us plays his part and then dies, while *Geist* goes on. God repairs the imperfection of his embodiment which reposes in the fact that this embodiment is in finite particular beings by casting aside these beings in his path and hence living his eternal life beyond any given one or number of them. God's life is something universal which transcends the individual; hence it is only embodied even at one time in a society, a plurality of men, and it is moreover embodied over time and hence through a plurality of such communities.

The ultimate self-understanding of *Geist* will come in a community which fully understands itself as his vehicle. For this community God will be both separate and above and also not separate and within; and they will be able to grasp both these propositions as true together through speculative reason. This community would also grasp why this has to be so, how God can exist no other way. So that just as man needs God, that is, finite spirits can only achieve integrity through being taken up in his cosmic greater life, so God needs man, that is, infinite spirit is nothing but an abstraction unless embodied in the life of a human community.

It is unclear whether Hegel believed that such a human community based on the total clarity of speculative thought would ever come to be – which is why I used both the future and the conditional in the above passage. But it provides the final term of a process of growth which has to be kept in mind if one is to understand what came earlier. And this is particularly so at the stage we have now reached, for absolute or revealed religion, that is, Christianity, reflects these basic truths albeit in an unclear obscure form, that of 'representation' as against thought. The community is the Christian church which lives the life of God through grace. The flowering of the Christian church is thus at least the penultimate stage of the development of *Geist*, even if we may never fully succeed in going beyond it.

This provides the background for the transition which we now come to.

Universal self-consciousness which arises out of the demise of the religion of art feels the need to rediscover cosmic *Geist*, but cannot simply return to the primitive vision of this *Geist* as a pre-subjective being, and moreover as one which is quite separate from man. At the same time there is another religious form, which Hegel barely mentions in the *PhG* but which has an important place in his lectures in the philosophy of religion, and that is Judaism. This too represents a transcending of parochial universals, but at the cost of an uncrossable chasm between man and God. In a sense Judaism and Greek religion are complements: one achieves the affinity of man and God, but at the cost of parochialness; the other achieves true universality but at the cost of denying all affinity.

But this God as spirit quite separate from man cannot be the final resting place for the divine. To see God as so separate is the very paradigm of the unhappy consciousness (and Hegel saw Judaism as such in his early theological writings); in fact God must live his life through men. Hence the need of post-art-religion man to recover the absolute in a way not unrelated to or destructive of self-consciousness, on one hand, and the need of the pure universal spirit of the old testament to find a vehicle in human history, on the other, meet in the Incarnation. It is because the Incarnation meets as it were the needs of both sides, God and man, that it is seen as springing from the collaboration of God and humankind (through Mary).

Hegel insists on the reality of the incarnation as an historic event, and distinguishes it from the various mystéry religions which merely *imagined* the presence of spirit in the world. By contrast in the Christian Incarnation we have God really present in a particular subject, he is 'a real individual man, given to sensible intuition' (*PhG*, 528). Believers can 'see and feel and hear' the divinity.[1]

One might wonder at first how Hegel can make a distinction of this kind within the terms of his own theory. For *an sich* God is incarnate from the beginning in all men, in this sense, that man is the vehicle of God's self-consciousness. What changes in history between the earliest nature religions and the final understanding in philosophy is that men become aware of this, or God becomes aware of this through man. But then how can one distinguish an incarnation which is merely imagined (in the mystery religions) from one which really happened? As a fact, *an sich*, the Incarnation did not happen, it is always true, and not especially true of one man, Christ. As the realization, *für sich*, that this is so, the Incarnation is indeed an event in human history. How then can we distinguish imagining it as so from its really being so?

But Hegel insists, what is peculiar about the Incarnation is that men did not just come to see it that way, but the substance itself 'for its own part

---

[1] Cf. *AbsRel*, 133, 141, where Hegel also insists that God must take the form of 'immediate, sensible intuition' for men, that he must be 'seen and experienced in the world'.

externalized itself (sich ihrer selbst entäußerte) and became self-consciousness' (PhG, 526).

The Incarnation is unique in this way: where for earlier religions the divine was often seen as in some sense present in the world, inhabiting in some mysterious way different avatars, for Christianity Jesus *is* God, there is an identity between this man and God reflected in the theological proposition that this one person has two natures. Hence what the mystery religions imagined is not the same as what the disciples saw. These earlier religions never came to the crucial insight that God as spirit *is* man; they never got beyond seeing the divine as *appearing* in various epiphanies – and these occurred in animals, places, etc., as well as in men. Hence for Christianity, God *is* really *there*, as a real man in a sense without precedent (527).

Now this point could only be made through the appearance of a unique God-man. In the fullness of speculative thought, we can now grasp the truth that God is identical with each man, and yet non-identical with him as his particularity fails to match the universal nature of God. But at the stage which men then were, the unity of God and man had to be present in immediate sensible intuition. And this point of the identity of man and God could only be made for sensible intuition by a unique God-man, where the singleness of the divine subjectivity is represented in the uniqueness of the Son of God. To see the one God in many incarnations in this stage would be to reduce these to 'masks which Substance puts on and changes in contingent fashion', as we see in 'Indian pantheism' (AbsRel, 137–8).

However, this point could concern the Incarnation only as divine pedagogy, in the way it *appeared* to men. It does not yet make sense of Hegel's claim that something really happened, that substance itself became self-consciousness. To understand this we have to remember that the development of religion in history requires more than that man become aware of his identity with spirit. Or rather, this growth in awareness itself requires that men develop beyond their original raw state, cultivate themselves and acquire a form of life which expresses the universal. Hence for men to be able to see the truth of the Incarnation they had to reach a certain stage of maturity. This is the real happening, the objective correlative of the perception by faith that God has become man. And since this, like all else in history, is the work of *Geist*, the substance of things, we can speak of this substance itself really becoming self-consciousness.

But this is not enough. Because we are not just talking of a realization of the general truth that God and man are one, rather of the perception that this man, Jesus, was God. Can Hegel be talking of *this* as an objective event? This seems hard to credit, especially since, if I am right, he did not even believe in the Incarnation in the ordinary sense, since ultimately Jesus is not God in any sense in which all other men are not.

Here we should recall Hegel's early writings on Jesus. It is very difficult to say for certain, but it is possible that Hegel went on seeing the figure of Jesus as an exceptional and paradigmatic one. In the early writings, Jesus is portrayed as one who manages to unite the divine and the human, the subjective and the external, in a way which is far beyond his time. It is this which leads him to the cross. Can it be, then, that an important part of the objective growth in humanity which Hegel sees as an essential condition of this new religious consciousness consisted in the birth of this exceptional, trail-blazing individual, who really did live in unity with the universal in a way that none other could in his time? Christianity would then require not just a certain maturity among its prospective followers, but also the existence of a man who really was at one with God in a way none of his contemporaries were.

It is very possible that some view of this kind underlay Hegel's treatment of the Incarnation in the *PhG* and probably survived into his mature system, even though the spotlight is no more on the figure of Jesus. And if this is so, we can see the important transformation from the early work, which explains this shift of attention. For we no longer have a man-centered view, but one where the ultimate agent of history is *Geist*. The drama no longer turns on the decisions of the man, Jesus, but on the fact that here Substance becomes self-consciousness.

The Incarnation in this sense is a real event, and also a crucial stage in our religious history. But we have to go beyond it. For while it is true that God is identical with man, as finite spirit, it is also true that he is non-identical with him. And, moreover, God is identical/non-identical with all men, and not just this one individual.

This necessity to transcend the Incarnation is reflected in Christian doctrine itself. For Christ dies, is resurrected, ascends to heaven and sends the holy Ghost. For Hegel all these events belong together. What they reflect is that the unity of God and man cannot be consummated in an individual. For there must always be an opposition between the universal spirit and any particular embodiment. This opposition is resolved, as we saw, when the particular embodiment passes away. Hence the individual must die. But in this case, Christ's death also signifies the transformation of this unity between God and man from a particular to a universal fact. That is why the death and resurrection are indissolubly linked to Ascension and Pentecost, for the whole meaning of the death lies in the coming of the spirit whereby the locus of Incarnation shifts to the community, the 'body of Christ'. The whole movement then from Incarnation to Pentecost can be taken on one level as reflecting the necessary tension in the unity of God and man between his embodiment in particular beings and his continuing life beyond these beings. But on another level, the death of Christ involves something special. It reflects the overcoming of the last separation, the last alienation of spirit from itself. God as a pure abstraction has already taken a giant step toward man in becoming incarnate; but in order to become fully realized in man he has to take the other step, that of dying as an incarnate God and therefore cancelling his inherence in a particular time and place, so that the incarnation of God can become that of the community of men in general.

Hegel's reading of Christian religion and theology can therefore only be understood in the light of this final stage of the community which is the self-conscious vehicle of *Geist*, the community which is the true man-God. But Christianity has not yet fully realized this. Rather it lives this unity implicitly, but by that very token not fully. For the fullness of *Geist*'s unity with itself entails clear self-knowledge, since *Geist* is reason. But Christianity lives this unity still in a muddled and obscure way, in a mode of consciousness which Hegel calls 'representation', that is, a mode of awareness which operates with images and symbols and not in the full clarity of conceptual thought. In other words the Christian church lives this unity without really knowing it, and hence necessarily not fully, and that is why it still lives partly in unhappy consciousness. So that the unity is seen as distant in time, in the future of the Parousia, and in the past of the life of Christ.

But as the religion which has finally expressed the true nature of God and his true relation to man, even in unclear form, Christianity can be called 'revealed religion', for it is the religion in which Geist truly reveals himself, and moreover reveals himself as a being whose essential nature is self-revelation.[1] Thus Hegel sees in Christian theology the whole truth of speculative philosophy laid out in images.

In this section of the chapter Hegel gives one of his interpretations of Christian theology in this sense. The basic notions of speculative philosophy are, as we have seen, that the idea necessarily embodies itself, and then returns to itself out of this estrangement by recognizing itself in this external embodiment. But this is what Christian theology expresses, and expresses moreover on three levels, corresponding each to the three stages of this movement of speculative philosophy.

Now this is doubly fortunate for Hegel himself lays out his system in these three stages: first, one which deals with the idea as a relation of pure categories in abstraction from their embodiment (the Logic), second, a study of the inner necessity visible in external reality (philosophy of nature), and thirdly, the tracing of the return of nature to full self-consciousness through spirit (philosophy of spirit). Corresponding to these, Hegel discerns three levels of theology, which he identifies with the Joachimite messianic language, later taken up by Böhme, of the realms respectively of father, son and holy ghost.

[1] Here again the distinction between religion and faith is relevant. As a total life-form, the Christian religion lived in the Church is here unity of God and man. But the consciousness of faith still sees God as separate.

211

On the first level we have the doctrine of the trinity, representing as it were, God's relation with himself; and this reflects the speculative tri-partite movement: God the father, who begets the son as his other; and who is united with him in love by the Holy Ghost.

But this level calls for another, the exteriorization represented by the begetting of the son calls for a real counterpart, the creation of real exteriority, and this comes in the creation of the world. This includes the creation of finite spirit. But finite spirit, in order to become truly spirit, has to come to self-consciousness (insichgehen, 537). And in doing so he becomes aware of a self over against the rest of the world and infinite spirit. This affirmation of self is original sin, it is the birth of evil. But at the same time it is inevitable, for otherwise there could be no finite spirit. And it is thus in the plan of God, for without finite spirit there would be no infinite spirit. It is necessary for finite spirit, since spirit is necessarily consciousness of self, and since it is embodied in particularity, its self-consciousness will inevitably be a raising to separate consciousness of particularity. The only way of avoiding this would be for man to remain sunk in nature, unconscious of self like an animal, and hence below both good and evil (innocent, says Hegel, but not good, 537). That is why the fall is the moment where men acquire knowledge of good and evil.

So much is the fall in the plan of *Geist*, that the only antidote for the evil of concentration in self is more of the same, a deeper and deeper self-consciousness until men arrive at a grasp of the universal in themselves. But we come here to the third stratum of theology, that which deals with the redemption. And here as we have seen, the reconciliation proceeds from both ends: God strives to be one with men, and men strive to overcome their particularity to be one with God. The reflection of this process comes in the theology of the Incarnation, death, Resurrection, Ascension of Christ, the coming of the Holy Ghost and the continuing life of the church, as we saw. God comes to man through the Incarnation and death, man to God through the self-transformation in his life in the community. But we have as yet not completely consummated this movement, since the separation is still felt, and reflected in the fact that the unity is only grasped by representation, and is put off into the future and the past, instead of being recognized in the present.

But underneath this representation we can recognize the true speculative doctrine. Speculative relations of necessity are deformed by being represented in such images as 'begotten' or 'created'; but nevertheless, these relations are recognized. And in the mutual approach of God and man, the pure universal which must accept unity with the particular in order to be effectively, and the particular which must rise above its particularity to the universal, we recognize the relation of the two consciousnesses which was the culmination of the previous chapter, the relation between evil and its forgiveness, the acting and judging consciousness. The active consciousness incurs evil inevitably, this is the essence of the doctrine of original sin; but the universal which is sinned against cannot exist except at this price; it therefore must accept realization at the hands of the individual, and 'forgive' this individual his particularity, which the latter for his part repents. In this way the two extremes come to unity.

These two extremes are now seen to be, after the development of this chapter, God and man, and we see that the dialectic of evil and its forgiveness is a cosmic one whose resolution gives us the ultimate key to reality. This ultimate reality is a self-knowing cosmic *Geist*, and we have thus also reached the highest form of consciousness – or rather, the threshold of this highest form; for what is represented in revealed religion through representation, must still be expressed in the full clarity of speculative thought. To have achieved this is to have achieved absolute knowledge.

CHAPTER VIII

The Phenomenology *as* Interpretive Dialectic

1

Absolute knowledge can be seen as the combination of our two highest stages. It is the final unity of subject and world, or from another point of view, of finite subject and infinite subject, or of absolute substance and subjectivity. But this union is there implicitly (*an sich*) as religion; whereas the moral consciousness which was the highest stage of the chapter on Spirit contained explicitly (*für sich*) the notion that the subject's will is at one with the universal.

The result is a unity of the self and the essence or substance of things; which unity as always can be seen as a convergence from each direction; the self is lifted up to essence by seeing itself as the vehicle of *Geist*; but the essence or substance 'comes down' to the self in a sense in coming to grasp itself as subject (and therefore needing a finite subject as its vehicle).

When this comes to full consciousness it yields a form of knowledge, which Hegel calls absolute knowledge. What is this? It cannot be expressed in one proposition, for it is simply a grasp of the true nature of things, and this can only be expressed dialectically. Absolute knowledge is the full understanding that substance must become subject, that subject must go beyond itself, become divided, be over against itself as object, in order to return to unity with itself.

Absolute knowledge, one might then be tempted to say, is simply the whole content of the *PhG*; the last chapter has meaning only as a recapitulation of the rest. This is partly true, and we shall see more of this in a minute; but it is only partly so. In fact the insight of absolute knowledge can also be put in a quite different way to that we have followed in the *PhG*. Here the drama has been the split between subject and object, between consciousness and self-consciousness, certainty of self and truth. This is finally overcome at the end of the work.

But we can also present our ascent to the final unity in difference not as a struggle of different forms of consciousness but as a derivation in terms of those basic categorial concepts with which we try to express this ultimate unity in opposition: being, substance, subject, thought, and so on. If we are right, and if each of these can only be understood ultimately in relation to the others, then this should be verifiable by an examination of these concepts themselves. And this, of course, is what the *Logic* will attempt. In this sense the *PhG* can be seen as a kind of introduction to the *Logic*. We will start examining these categorial concepts, starting with 'being', and we shall see that each refers us beyond itself to others, until finally they form a system which expresses the unity in opposition of *Geist* with its world. This system is called the Idea. Hegel announces this (562) in these terms: we will no longer be studying the drama of separation and unity of subject and world; rather we will be taking as our subject concepts, which are already unities of being and self; and just because it contains self and hence negativity in it, each particular concept suffers an 'unrest which pushes it to self-annulment' (seine Unruhe, sich selbst aufzu-heben). This pure science will then follow the inner movement of these concepts as they go over into the Idea. As always, science will not be expressible in a single proposition, but only in a self-developing system; but it will here be presented in a different medium from the one we have been moving in in the *PhG*. *Geist* will be moving 'in this ether of its life' (562), i.e., among concepts which are its own medium.

But this Logic cannot be the whole of science. The basic intuition of *Geist* entails that it must be exteriorized in Nature, hence there must be external, physical, extended reality. And also this *Geist* must return to itself out of this alienation; and this return presupposes another exteriorization, that of time. Moreover this return to self in time, which means through a set of stages which are external to each other in coming one after the other and which are real forms of collective life in history, is itself a precondition of the pure science being achieved; this pure science is the inner *prise de conscience* of *Geist* of its return to itself.

But then this self-consciousness of *Geist* must be more than the pure science of concepts. *Geist* is returning out of alienation in nature through a series of historical stages. In order to complete this return, he must grasp himself in nature and history. And this means that he must see the inner necessity of nature and history; see the necessity underlying the forms of exteriority and hence reciprocal contingency which are space and time.

> Time is the Concept itself which has determinate existence [der *da ist*], and presents itself to consciousness as empty intuition; thus Spirit must necessarily appear in time, and it continues to appear in time as long as it does not seize its pure concept, that is, as long as it does not abolish time. (*PhG*, 558)

Geist's self-knowledge must therefore include this grasp of the inner necessity of nature and history. As always, his final self-knowledge cannot be separated from the way he has followed there; but now the stages of history are interiorized in remembrance.[1] Thus interiorized, nature and history are freed of the form of external contingency, extension and time. And the result,

---

[1] The German word 'Erinnerung' (recollection) permits Hegel this play on words which for him is very significant.

history grasped in concept (die begriffene Geschichte, 564), is the inner reality of absolute spirit. It is on this note, with an (altered) quote from Schiller that the *PhG* ends.

2

How does the *PhG* hold together as an ascending dialectic? Looking back over the extraordinary variety and richness of the figures studied, it is hard to see the uniting thread of argument. And in fact the *PhG* is more impressive and persuasive as interpretation of certain passages of political and religious history than it is as argument.

In order to see why this is so in spite of Hegel's intentions, we should look again at the nature of his dialectical arguments. At the outset of the chapter, we distinguished two types of dialectic, the ontological and the historical.

The first starts from the basis that a certain standard, which we identify only by certain criterial properties, is fulfilled, and moves through different conceptions of this standard to more and more adequate forms. We saw an example of this in the first part of the *PhG*, on consciousness. We start from the basis that there is knowledge, and that knowledge is an achievement. What we do not know, if we can put it this way, is what is involved in meeting the standard. Or rather, all we know about this is certain very sketchy critical properties. Thus we start with the simple but intuitively persuasive idea that knowledge is receiving data, and that the standard to be met is that of maximum openness and receptivity. This is the idea behind sensible certainty. When this involves us in a contradiction, we alter our conception of what knowledge is. This starts a second phase of the dialectic; and so on. The key to dialectical movement here is that since we know that the standard is met, we can conclude that any conception of it which shows itself unrealizable must be wrong.

The historical dialectic, on the other hand, starts from the thesis that a certain purpose is sought after, even though it is *not* yet realized. Here the clash between purpose and effective reality leads not to *our* redefining the purpose, but to the breaking up of the reality concerned and its replacement by a more adequate one (although of course this requires a redefinition of purpose on the part of the *effective agents* in history). This is the kind of development we saw in the section on self-consciousness, for instance in the dialectic of the master and the slave, which predominated in the chapter on Reason, and made up the whole movement of the chapters on Spirit and Religion. Certain historical forms of life are shown to be prey to inner contradiction because they are defeating the purpose for which they exist. The master–slave relation frustrates the purpose of recognition for which it was entered into. The city state fails as a realization of the universal, because its parochial nature contradicts true universality. The revolutionary state destroys freedom because it tries to realize it in absolute form, by dissolving all the articulations of society, without which freedom cannot exist.

Now this distinction is of more than taxonomical interest. For there is an important difference in the grounding of Hegel's dialectical arguments which is interwoven with it. We saw in the first section that the starting point of a dialectical argument must impose itself, as it were, that the conception of the thing concerned as the realization of a purpose must be inescapable. Otherwise the conclusions of the argument are merely hypothetically valid.

Now we saw how Hegel succeeded in the ontological dialectic of consciousness in getting such an unquestionable starting point, since it is hard to resist the view that knowledge is an achievement and involves the fulfilment of a standard. We shall see in the next chapter how he hopes to find a similarly unquestionable starting point for the *Logic* as a science of categories. But historical dialectics pose a much more difficult problem. They involve our imputing a certain purpose or purposes to men in history, or to *Geist* through men in history; and how can any such imputation be undeniable?

Thus we saw how the dialectic of the master and the slave starts with the imputation of the drive for recognition. This is what powers the fight to the death, and this is what in turn makes this outcome unsatisfactory and requires that both protagonists survive in the relation of master–slave. This relation in turn is shown to be inadequate in the light of the same purpose. But what justifies us in imputing this purpose in the first place?

If we look at Hegel's most successful historical dialectics, the ones which are the most illuminating and convincing, we find that in fact they convince the way any good historical account does, because they 'fit' well as an interpretation.[1]

This is, what we know about a given period can be made sense of, can be made to cohere without implausibility on this account, or in any case with less implausibility than other rival explanations. But the point about these interpretive explanations is that they have no absolutely certain starting point. The original imputation of a certain purpose to the actors, or a certain bent to events, or a certain logic of the situation is quite ungrounded on its own. It is only when it has been followed out, and connected with all the other imputations which go with it, and when these have been seen to fit the facts with plausibility, and to make over-all sense, that we feel confident about accepting it.

Thus Hegel's account of the breakdown of the Greek city state turns on the

---

[1] I am here of course taking sides in the debate about explanation in history, for an interpretive view and against the 'covering law' model. For brevity's sake, I cannot undertake to argue my position here although I have tried to argue something like it in my 'Interpretation and the Sciences of Man', *Review of Metaphysics*, xxxv 3–51, #1, Sept. 1971. But the same point about Hegel's historical account could probably be made from the other perspective as well.

underlying purpose of realizing a consciousness and way of life which is universal. The polis both fulfils this purpose and at the same time frustrates it because of its parochial nature. But what will convince us to accept this imputation of purpose to man (or *Geist*) as the mainspring of events? Only the sense which it enables us to make of the events of the period, the way it relates the vogue of the sophists, the development of Greek literature and culture, changes in Greek religion, the decay of the city state, and so on, into a whole which is both plausible and makes sense of what happened. The enduring interest of many of Hegel's historical interpretations lies just in the fact that they do illuminate the interconnection of events enough to induce us to take them seriously, even if we have to transpose them (as most notoriously Marx did). But the imputation of purpose can never be self-authenticating as a starting point.

This problem besets Hegel's historical dialectic in general. The ontological ones start with a realized goal or standard. The initial task is to show that the object in question is to be understood in terms of the realization of a goal. Once this is secured, the dialectic can proceed to define the goal. Since we know that the standard is met, we can set aside any conception of the goal which shows itself to be unrealizable. We can start with any definition, and, by showing how it conflicts with its own fulfilment, move to more adequate conceptions until we reach the fully adequate one. Or to put the point another way, from the nature of the object under study we know certain of its criterial properties. We have only to learn what more exact specification of the purpose will in fact exhibit these properties.

But this cannot be the case with our historical dialectics. Prior to the total unfolding of history we have *ex hypothesi* no realized purpose before us. So we cannot treat any tract of history as a fulfilment whose operative standard we have to discover. Nor can we read from any tract of history with certainty even a general description of what man is ultimately aiming at. We cannot be sure of having gleaned even some criterial properties of man's ultimate fulfilment.

Thus it seems that just as we distinguished between ontological and historical dialectics as two kinds of dialectical development, so we have to distinguish two ways in which a dialectical exposition can command our assent. There are strict dialectics, whose starting point is or can reasonably claim to be undeniable. And then there are interpretive or hermeneutical dialectics, which convince us by the overall plausibility of the interpretation they give. It would seem that while Hegel has some candidates for the first category – most notably, as we shall see, the *Logic* – his historical dialectics fall in the second category. They do not convince by strict argument, but by the plausibility of their interpretation.

What would Hegel say to this? Would he admit a distinction of this kind? Certainly not in the form presented here. And Hegel would never have agreed that any part of his system reposed on plausible interpretations as against strict argument, for this would be to abandon the conception of *Geist* as total rationality. But in another form, I believe the distinction does find a place in Hegel's system. Leaving aside the *PhG* for the moment, the final system of the Encyclopaedia starts with a strict dialectic, the Logic. This establishes that there is no independent finite being, but that all is held together in the Idea, the formula of rational necessity which creates its own external manifestation. This conclusion is then available for the succeeding dialectics of the philosophies of nature and spirit. And Hegel does in fact draw on it in these dialectics.

Hence we could say that for Hegel, certainty about the purposes of history, which could not be drawn in any form from its earliest periods, and which could only be gleaned with greater or lesser plausibility from the entire drama, can nevertheless be gained even for our examination of its beginnings, because these purposes are established previously by a strict dialectic. They are thus available as certain starting points for our understanding of history, and the ensuing dialectic can be said to flow with absolute certainty.

Thus in his introductory lectures to the philosophy of history, Hegel speaks of the principles 'that Reason rules the world' (*VG*, 28) and that the final purpose of the world is the actualization of freedom (ibid., 63), as having to be presupposed in the study of history, but as having been 'proved in philosophy' (*VG*, 28). It is clear that Hegel is referring here to the Logic, since the theses which are deemed to be proved concern the Idea, the culminating concept of this work. Its results are thus an 'input' into the philosophy of history. They are the presuppositions which enable it to begin.

But immediately after this passage, Hegel says of the belief that there is Reason in history that 'It is not simply a presupposition of study; it is a *result* which happens to be known to myself because I already know the whole. Therefore, only the study of world history itself can show that it has proceeded rationally, that it represents the rationally necessary course of the World Spirit' (*VG*, 30).[1] And he goes on 'History itself must be taken as it is; we have to proceed historically, empirically.'

This passage implies that there is another way of showing that Reason is at work in history than the strict conceptual proof of the Logic. And this is by examining the whole of history, 'as it is...empirically'. Is this perhaps a partial recognition that there are two different kinds of proof of a thesis, one a strict proof which builds from an undeniable starting point, and the other an 'empirical' one which draws it from an examination of the whole as the only conclusion which makes sense of this whole?[2]

---

[1] *Reason in History*, translated by Robert Hartmann, New York, 1953, p. 30. I have slightly amended the translation.

[2] This is perhaps what was meant in the sentence in the introduction of the philosophy of history (*VG*, 29), which says that the presence of reason in world history is a truth which has its 'proper proof [eigentlicher Beweis] in the knowledge of reason itself', whereas 'world history only gives a

Phenomenology

The strict philosophical proof would then be a presupposition for the study of history in this sense, that it makes us look at history with the eye of reason. And this is necessary, because in order to know what is substantial in history

one must bring to it the consciousness of reason, no mere physical eye or finite understanding, but the eye of the Concept, of reason, which presses through the surface and struggles through and beyond the manifold, motley tumult of events. (die Mannigfaltigkeit des bunten Gewühls der Begebenheiten, *VG*, 32).

But once we look at it in this way, we have a coherence, a convincing explanation of history's course, which provides independent proof of the thesis that Reason rules the world.

If I am right that Hegel draws on the conclusions of the Logic for the dialectics which come 'after' it in the system, then we still have to distinguish in his work between dialectical arguments that are self-authenticating and stand on their own, because they start from an undeniable beginning; and those which are dependent on others, which have to make use of the conclusions of others to authenticate their readings. What we have called 'strict' dialectics would be self-authenticating in this sense, and what we have called 'interpretive' would be dependent. And what we have called 'historical' dialectics, (as well as the philosophy of nature) would fall into the dependent category.

What does this tell us about the argument of the *PhG*? The greater part of the book is taken up with historical dialectics, hence arguments which are not self-authenticating. But, in fact, these only start after the strict dialectic with which the work opens, that of consciousness. The dialectic of self-consciousness, with its underlying notions of life, human self-consciousness and the desire for recognition, builds supposedly on the results of the first part. In this respect the *PhG* resembles the system laid out in the Encyclopaedia.

But when we look at it in this light, we can see that the first three chapters are much too weak and sketchy to support the rich superstructure of historical and anthropological interpretation that Hegel has erected. It is these interpretations, of course, which *persuade*, which give the work its power and fascination as a statement of Hegel's vision. But as strict argument, its success must turn in the first place on the solidity of the first chain of arguments, whereby consciousness turns into self-consciousness, that is, whereby our perception of a world, which seems at first other, turns into knowledge of self. Or as Hegel puts it

Consciousness of another, of an object in general, is in fact necessarily *self-consciousness*, reflectedness in self, consciousness of oneself in one's other-being. (*PhG*, 128, italics in original.)

convincing exposition of it' (in der Weltgeschichte erweist sie sich nur). But we cannot build too much on this passage. It is drawn not from Hegel's own notes, but from those taken by hearers at his lectures.

But as I indicated in the second section, the argument here does not really measure up, if indeed, any argument can. Nor is this surprising. If it is possible at all to establish Hegel's central contention that the world of things only exists as an emanation of *Geist*, and therefore that spirit knows itself in knowing it, then surely the argument which does this will be a long and difficult one, and will marshall an encyclopaedic set of considerations. The mature Hegel probably thought so. That is why the work which stands as the foundational strict dialectic of the final system is in fact long and difficult.

The *Logic* is in fact, once we set aside the *PhG*, the only strict, self-authenticating dialectic of Hegel's system. That is why it has to be presupposed in the philosophies of nature and spirit. On it the claim of Hegel to have grounded his vision in strict argument stands or falls. Small wonder that he devoted the attention to it that he did. Let us now turn to examine it.

PART III

LOGIC

CHAPTER IX

A Dialectic of Categories

The Logic exists in two versions, the *Science of Logic*, which Hegel first published in 1812–16 and partially revised for a second edition just before his death; and the first part of the system of Science, often called the Encyclopaedia, published first in 1817 and afterwards revised as well. I shall draw on both of these (respectively *WL* and *EL*) in what follows.

The *Logic* is the second of the great derivations of Hegel's vision, and a crucial one as we have seen, because it is the only real candidate for the role of strict dialectical proof. If the real exists and has the structure it has by conceptual necessity, then the task of the *Logic* is to show this conceptual structure by pure conceptual argument.

This may sound mad to ordinary consciousness and indeed to most philosophers. For we think of our concepts as instruments of our thought which may or may not apply adequately to reality. We start off, that is, with a notion of thought as over against the world about which we think. This dualism is linked to another; since a concept or a category is thought of as a universal which can apply to many contents, we are tempted to think of it as an abstract form over against the sensible contents to which it applies.

This double dualism naturally leads us to think that a study of concepts is quite distinct from a study of reality; and more particularly, that the necessary relations between concepts which we may discover from such a study in no way allow us to conclude to necessary relations among the things to which they apply. Logic, as a study of these relations is thus necessarily formal, touching our way of thought, and not the contents that we think about.

But Hegel as we see does not accept this notion of the concept and the two dualisms it entails. Thought and the determinations through which it operates (the *Denkbestimmungen*, or categories) are not the apanage of a subject over against the world, but lie at the very root of things. For the reality which we perceive as finite subjects is the embodiment of *Geist* or infinite subject. But the life of *Geist* is rational thought, a life which is carried in our own thought, i.e., that of finite subjects, and is adequately expressed in so far as we think rationally. The rational, truly universal thought which is expressed in our categories is thus spirit's knowledge of itself. Since the external reality to which these categories apply is not only an embodiment of *Geist*, but is posited by *Geist* as its embodiment, and hence reflects the rational necessity of thought, in grasping the categories of thought about things, we are also grasping the ground plan or essential structure to which the world conforms in its unfolding.

So much for the first dualism, that which opposes our concepts and the world to which they apply. On the contrary, the ultimate understanding of the world of things comes when we see it as existing in order to embody the rational structure which is expressed in these categories. But this also puts paid to the second dualism; for once we see the world as posited by *Geist*, a spirit whose life is thought, then we see the categories of thought as necessarily embodied, as 'going over', as it were, into their embodiment. So that the idea of opposing concepts as forms to the things they apply to as contents turn out to be profoundly mistaken.

Hence the Hegelian notion of concept, which as we have seen is not just a descriptive notion applying to things but that which posits the things to which it applies. So that the concept is ultimately assimilated by Hegel to the subject, a spiritual being which posits its own embodiment. In fact, the concept is just spiritual subject when we see it in its aspect as rational necessity.

Hegel makes clear in the introduction to the *Logic* that he is not treating concepts as they are normally treated, but rather in his sense, as straddling the opposition between subject and object. That this opposition must be overcome he takes as the already established conclusion of the *PhG*. In this latter work we showed that the 'opposition of consciousness' (sc. between subject and world) is overcome (*WL*, I, 30, 32). Pure knowledge 'contains thought in so far as it is itself just as much the matter thought about [die Sache an sich selbst], and the matter thought about in so far as it is just as much pure thought' (*WL*, I, 30). It teaches us 'that what exists *an und für sich* is the known Concept, while the Concept as such is that which exists *an und für sich*' (*WL*, I, 30–1).

The title 'Logic' is therefore very misleading if we have in mind the formal logic with which we are familiar. But in fact Hegel is using the title here in the sense of Kant's 'transcendental logic'. Beside 'general' (i.e., formal) logic, which 'treats of the form of thought in general' (*Critique of Pure Reason*, A55, B79), Kant elaborated a transcendental logic which 'concerns itself with the laws of understanding and of reason solely in so far as they relate a priori to objects' (*CPR*, A57, B82). This logic brings to light certain necessities of our thought, which are not just concerned with its formal consistency but with the conditions of its empirical validity. The transcendental logic thus defines what Kant calls the categories, the necessary and inescapable conceptual structures which the world of experience must exhibit if we are to have any experience at all.

But then a transcendental logic comes very close to being an ontology. To say that certain conceptual structures must apply to the world is surely to say something about the nature of things. Kant avoids this conclusion by distinguishing between phenomena, the objects of experience, and things as they are in themselves, beyond our experience. The categories tell us only about the world as it must be for us, but justify no conclusions about the world of things in themselves.

But Hegel as we know emphatically rejects the Kantian distinction between phenomena and noumena. In the introduction to *WL*, as also to *EL*, he inveighs against Kant for propounding the idea of an unknowable *Ding-an-sich*. True, Kant deserves some credit for having gone beyond formal to transcendental logic. But he spoiled it all by restricting its conclusions to the world-as-known-by-us in contrast to the world as it is in itself. Hegel is going to offer us a transcendental logic which will also be an ontology. He will do away altogether with the epistemological beyond which the *Ding-an-sich* inhabits.

Thus in discovering the necessary relations between the categorial concepts of a transcendental logic, we will also be discovering the necessary structure of reality. But one might reply, this just displaces the problem; granted that knowing the necessary relations among categorial concepts is knowing the necessary structure of things, how do we go about establishing these necessary relations? Where do we start? What can we select as a categorial concept in the meaning of the act?

But in fact, Hegel would reply, this last is not a problem. Start anywhere. Take as category any one of those very general terms by which we try to designate a pervasive aspect of reality – 'being', 'cause', 'substance', 'quantity', etc. In fact Hegel starts with 'being' the category of 'simple immediacy' (*WL*, 54), because it seems the emptiest and poorest; it thus presupposes nothing but that there is thought of reality. And it is for this reason also the farthest from the terminus he is heading for, the notion of spirit; he will thus pass through all the other categories on the way.

So starting with 'being'. we have to show the necessary relations among categorial concepts. But how do we proceed? By showing the dialectical movement in these concepts. Dialectical movement is based as we saw on contradiction. So what we have to show is that our categorial concepts as we ordinarily understand them, unrelated by rational necessity, are in some way contradictory; and that this contradiction can only be resolved (or, in fact, reconciled) by seeing them as linked in a rational structure.

So we start with a single concept, for instance 'being', and our task is to show that taken on its own, it generates a contradiction. This of course does not leave us nowhere; being a specific contradiction it will call for some specific change or enrichment of the concept, and we will thus arrive at a new category. And from this point a new dialectic can start. We are already familiar with this aspect of the Hegelian dialectic where each contradiction has a definite result (*WL*, I, 36–7).

But how does one show a contradiction in a single categorial concept? How do we show that 'being' or 'quality' or 'cause', for instance, are incoherent? It is clear that we are not talking about empirical conflict with the facts. And nor are we talking about a simple contradiction within the meaning of an expression, such as we have with 'round squares', for instance. Rather we are concerned with a contradiction which shows up when we use the concept as a categorial one, that is, as a concept which applies to reality in general.

Once more we see a precedent for what we are trying to define in Kant. In the Kantian antinomies we find contradictions which arise when we attempt to apply certain concepts in a pervasive way, that is, to the full extent of their possible application. The logic of these concepts seems to licence two contradictory assertions. Thus in applying the notions of division of space and time in a systematic way, or in applying that of limit to the whole, or in using the related notions of causation and freedom to their full legitimate extent, we seem driven by our understanding of these concepts to make two utterly unreconcilable assertions, which both seem equally well founded.

Kant, says Hegel, deserves our gratitude for having laid bare these antinomies, but he drew totally the wrong conclusions. For he still shared the error of understanding in opposing thought to reality, and out of a misplaced 'tenderness for wordly things' (*EL*, §48) he sought the basis of these antinomies in the limits of our understanding, and not in the real nature of things. Hegel adds that Kant only scratched the surface in designating four antinomies (loc. cit., also *WL*, I, 183–4). In fact our categorial thought is shot through with them. 'Becoming, Determinate Being, etc., and every other concept could each provide its particular antinomy, and as many antinomies could be set up as concepts were brought forward.' (*WL*, I, 184).

The Kantian antinomies are thus just examples of something more pervasive in Hegel's eyes. Our categorial concepts when we consider them as descriptions of reality as a whole or of pervasive aspects of this reality show a crucial inadequacy. And this lands us in a contradiction. For these categorial concepts are inescapable; they are meant to designate indispensable aspects of reality if there is to be a reality for us at all. If then these concepts portray a reality which is in some sense impossible or incoherent, we are caught in a contradiction: the seemingly indispensable descriptions of reality portray a reality which cannot be.

This is the process operative in the Kantian antinomies Hegel thinks, and he holds that it has much wider application. So portrayed the Hegelian dialectic of categories seems to require two separate lines of argument: the first showing that a given category is indispensable (as Kant does in the transcendental logic), the second showing that it leads us to a characterization of reality which is somehow impossible or incoherent. But in fact Hegel fuses these together. Here we see from another angle the advantage of starting with 'being'. No one can deny that this concept must apply to anything which can be a reality for us. Then our dialectical argument by showing a contradiction in 'being' deduces the next category (in this case, 'determinate being'). This new category is thus shown to be indispensable, since it is introduced as the only way to resolve the contradiction in the earlier category, 'being', which was taken as indispensable. In other words, if 'being' must apply, then 'determinate being' must as well, since it is the only way of making sense of 'being'. So the dialectical argument in deducing a definite outcome to each contradiction doubles up as a transcendental logic: in showing the incoherence of one concept, it demonstrates the indispensability of the next.

But how do we show that a given concept portrays an impossible reality? What gives us the inner complexity which we have seen is essential for the dialectic? What is the 'standard' against which we can measure the concept? The answer is that we know certain criterial properties which any conception of reality as a whole must meet, e.g., that we be able to distinguish reality from non-being, that reality sustain itself against what negates it, and thus be capable of continued existence, that reality as a whole be self-subsistent, etc. We thus have the same three-termed relation that we saw in the last chapter was essential to the Hegelian dialectic: a concept of reality comes into conflict with the criterial properties of such a concept when we try to 'realize' it, that is, apply it systematically to the world. Qua concept of reality, it conflicts with its own criterial properties. And hence any reality which meets this concept must be in conflict with itself.

Now the contradiction in Hegel's Logic comes from the fact that certain concepts are both indispensable *and* incoherent: that is, as concepts of reality they are in conflict with their own criterial properties; and yet being indispensable they must be instantiated. This is the key to Hegel's enterprise and it is worth looking at a little more closely.

If a concept were just incoherent, then it could be set aside in favour of a more adequate one. Or if while indispensable, it was just inadequate as against incoherent, there would be no conflict in *complementing* it with a fuller one. Now some of Hegel's transitions seem to be based on simple inadequacy, for instance that which occupies the first chapter of the *Logic*, from Being to Determinate Being. The contradiction is between the concept's claim to adequacy and its de facto inadequacy (or so one can plausibly argue; Hegel sees more in it than this). There is no claim that the concept must be realized precisely in the respect in which it is inadequate, i.e., that there must be a reality which conflicts with the adequate conditions of its existence, that is, a contradictory reality.

But this stronger claim is made in other transitions, for instance that between Determinate Being and Infinity, in Chapter II of the *Logic*, which plays a key role in the argument of the whole work. Here it is not just that determinate Being as limited is inadequate as a concept of reality and requires to be completed by a notion of the whole. Hegel also will try to show that this inadequacy is an inner conflict, in which determinate reality will not accept its inadequacy, its defining limits, and in struggling against them, fights against itself. We might say that in this case the criterial properties of reality are in conflict with each other. Reality is in contradiction.

But how can reality be in contradiction? How in other words can concepts be both incoherent and instantiated?

For Hegel, this poses no problem, as we are now aware. For reality is incoherent, that is prey to contradiction. What the inadequate categories correspond to is inadequate, partial reality, which both necessarily exists (hence the categories are indispensable), and yet being contradictory necessarily goes under (hence the categories are incoherent). We are thus not dealing with a dialectic of illusion where we cut through false conceptions which are justly consigned to oblivion once we arrive at the truth; but rather with a dialectic of reality. It follows that our finally adequate category, which Hegel calls the Idea, will not be beyond the earlier categories, making no reference to them, but will incorporate them. This category will rather exhibit the necessary connection of the whole ascending chain of categories, whereby the lower as indispensable and incoherent can only have application in relation to the higher, because the reality they designate can only exist as a necessary but self-cancelling embodiment of the Idea.

This then is how we exhibit a necessary conceptual structure of things. We show that our indispensable categorial concepts are contradictory. But as contradictory each is necessarily related to another which resolves the contradiction at its level. Hence we have a necessary relation founded on a contradiction. And this suits Hegel's ontology perfectly. A given categorial concept is indispensable yet incoherent. This means that the partial reality it designates both must exist and yet destroy itself. But this can only be because the higher reality, designated by the higher category which resolves the contradiction at this level, also exists, and this partial reality is kept in being by its inherence in this higher reality. A partial reality which continually destroys itself can only go on existing if it is continually posited by the larger order of which it is part. Thus the fact that we move through the chain of conceptual necessity by contradictions and their resolutions means that the lower terms are related to the higher as posited by them (because they depend on them to exist), yet necessarily posited (for these terms are indispensable), and just as necessarily disappearing, (because they are contradictory). But this exactly mirrors Hegel's ontology, where the larger whole, or absolute, necessarily issues in partial, external reality, which qua expression of the absolute is contradictory and must go under.

Does Hegel in fact make good this claim to show reality as contradictory? The reader will have to judge in studying the *Logic*. I do not believe so. But this is not to say that the arguments of the *Logic* fail altogether. On the contrary, the work is a tissue of powerful arguments which show the weakness of other philosophical positions. But Hegel tries at crucial moments to force them further, to make them yield his ontological vision. And it is here that they fail as arguments. What Hegel does succeed in doing is to portray the structure of things as offering 'traces and hints' of his vision of embodied spirit. The suggestion is sometimes powerful, but at the crucial points it falls short of conceptual proof.

The *Logic* thus presents the chain of necessarily connected concepts which give the conceptual structure of reality. This allows us to answer more satisfactorily the question posed above of what Hegel considers a categorial concept. Starting from the poorest, most general and most irrecusable general concept, 'being', the chain of concepts which is generated in the dialectical movement will constitute the list of categories, i.e., those general concepts indispensable for a description of reality. That seems to be the idea. In fact the practice is somewhat different. As in other dialectics, Hegel is anxious to take in all the terms which could plausibly be thought of as categorial and others besides which are essential to his ontology. The dialectic moves in such a way as to link these into its conceptual chain, which means that the transitions are not always compelling, and there are many detours to take in essential matter, where one might have expected an immediate leap to a higher category.

The *Logic* shows a necessary conceptual structure of reality based on contradiction. It shows that contradiction belongs to the very nature of our categories (Denkbestimmungen, *WL*, I, 38). They move themselves, and thus show that they are at base concept (Begriff) in the full Hegelian sense, i.e., self-embodying subjects. What the *Logic* gives us therefore is the basic formula of rational necessity which embodies itself and thus is manifest in the universe.

Thus the formula presented in the *Logic* is in a sense the inner kernel of *Geist*'s self-knowledge, God's inner intellectual life, or as Hegel puts it somewhat misleadingly (*WL*, I, 31) it is 'the presentation of God...as he is in his eternal essence before the creation of nature and finite spirit.'[1] If we disregard the interpretation of this 'before' as temporal, which would clash with what we have seen to be the essential notions of Hegel's ontology, we can see this as another expression of the idea that the *Logic* provides us a picture of the conceptual formula of rational necessity that is the essence of *Geist*, or God. It shows us God in his inner nature, as it were, rather than as we may see him reflected in nature and history. An essential vision, but not sufficient by itself.

[1] 'Die Darstellung Gottes..., wie er in seinem ewigen Wesen vor der Erschaffung der Natur und eines endlichen Geistes ist'.

CHAPTER X

Being

I: DASEIN

The first movement of Hegel's logic, if one can use this musical expression, runs through the first two chapters of the first part of Being, Quality. After this, in the third chapter, Hegel takes another tangent in order to link this first study with Quantity; but the first two chapters form an unquestioned unity of development.

The guiding thread of this movement is the notion of determinate being. In it Hegel manages to express his basic ontological vision of finite being as the necessary and yet inadequate and hence vanishing vehicle of infinite being. He establishes this vision in an argument about Being.

The germ of the whole thing is contained in the first famous argument in the opening lines. Let us start with the simple notion of being and we shall see that it is inadequate. Nothing *is* simply without having some determinate quality. Simple being which was nothing but this, i.e., was neither animal, vegetable, nor mineral, etc., would be nothing. And this is the famous first argument of the logic: pure being turns out to be pure emptiness, nothing; and reciprocally, this nothing which is purely indeterminate is equivalent to pure being. Hence the notion of pure being frustrates its own purpose. We cannot characterize reality with it alone, and we are forced to move to a notion of being as determinate, as having some quality and not another. Being can only be thought as determinate.

But this means that being and non-being are joined together; for the only way to characterize determinate being is in terms of some property, and property terms can only be made intelligible by being opposed, contrasted to each other. In this sense Hegel takes up the Spinozan principle that all determination is negation. The upshot of this first dialectic of being and non-being is thus the synthesis of the two in *Dasein* or Determinate Being.

In Hegel's exposition, however, we do not arrive immediately at *Dasein*; the first synthesis of Being and Nothing is Becoming, which also can be said to unite the two: what is coming to be or passing away is moving from not-being to being or vice-versa. It is clear why Hegel wants to bring in becoming here: for it is central to his ontology: *Geist* can only be embodied, and yet the embodiments are all inadequate, and hence disappear to give place to others;

232

Being

the being of *Geist* is thus a perpetual movement, a perpetual coming to be and passing away.

But the derivation of Becoming here is not as solid as that of *Dasein*. This is the first, but not the last place in the *Logic* where Hegel will go beyond what is strictly established by his argument, because he sees in the relation of concepts a suggestion of his ontology: here the universality of movement and becoming in the relation of Being and Non-Being. But of course as probative arguments these passages are unconvincing. They fail, as strict conceptual proof, however persuasive they are as *interpretations* for those who hold Hegel's view of things on other grounds. Thus, in this case, the notion of becoming imposes itself supposedly because of the passage from Being to Nothing and back; but this is a passage which our thought is forced to when we contemplate either. Of course, as we know, this distinction between thought and reality is ultimately untenable; but we cannot trade on this principle at this stage.[1] We are dealing with Kantian-type categories, categories in which we think about things; what we have to show is not that in our thought about things we move from one category to another, but rather that things cannot be thought in certain categories unless others also apply. And this is what we do show when we establish that *Sein* (Being) can only be applied as *Dasein* (Determinate Being), whereas we have not yet shown the objective necessity of Becoming. This will come when we examine *Dasein* further and see that it is a prey to contradiction and hence movement.

Dasein

This is the basic thesis which the second chapter attempts to establish and here is the crux of the argument. Contradiction is attributed to *Dasein* or Determinate Being via the notion of negation. We saw above that *Dasein* is a marriage of being and nothing, Hegel will say here: of reality and negation. Let us look at this more closely. In the complex argument which follows, Hegel weaves a number of separate strands together without clearly distinguishing them.

We can think of determinate being as a marriage of reality and negation first because of the Spinozan principle mentioned above that all determination requires negation. It is essential to the meaning of our descriptive concepts that

---

[1] Of course, if we allow ourselves to use the conclusions of the *PhG*, that knowledge is one with its object, then there is no problem with this derivation. But this would turn the whole *Logic* from a strict proof to a mere exposition of an already established principle. It would put it on the same level as the dependent dialectics which follow it. In view of the gaps in the *PhG* as a strict dialectic, it would be fatal to Hegel's system.

In spite of certain references to the conclusions of the *PhG* as the starting point of the *Logic* (e.g., *WL*, I, 30, 53), it is doubtful that Hegel actually wanted to trade on these conclusions, as against just seeing them as defining the *task* of the *Logic*. But it is possible that he had not fully clarified his thought on this point, which may explain why he permitted himself to pass off these passages of suggestive interpretation as argument.

they be contrasted with others. We cannot have the shape concept 'square' without other shape concepts, like 'round', which can be contrasted with it; we cannot have 'red' without 'yellow', 'green' or 'blue' or some such. To enrich our colour vocabulary is to add to our available stock of colour distinctions. Thus because all the property-terms by which we can characterize determinate being are essentially contrasted with others, and because we can only grasp being as determinate, that is, as having some property or other, for otherwise we fall into the emptiness of pure being, the characterization of *Dasein* as possessing a quality is at the same time its characterization negatively as not possessing others. The red object is also essentially not-blue; it can only be grasped as red if it is grasped as not-blue.

So far so good. What may worry us is that Hegel seems to move from this unexceptionable point that all reality must be characterized contrastively, that in this sense determinate beings negate others, to the notion of determinate beings in a kind of struggle to maintain themselves in face of others, and hence as 'negating' each other in an active sense. And this connection is essential to his argument, as we shall see. Hegel's reasoning is not entirely clear here, and the argument is differently laid out, with many more stages in *WL* than it is in *EL*. But I think we can attempt an interpretation of the underlying argument.

Although the quality by which we characterize a given *Dasein* may be defined in contrast to imaginary properties, that is, properties which are not instantiated, some of the contrasts on which we base our descriptions must be instantiated. In these cases, the contrast between *Daseine* as qualities is a contrast between distinct things: Hegel uses the word 'something' here (*Etwas*) – '*Ding*' is reserved for a later stage. But when we talk of 'something' and not just qualities, we can see that they are not just related contrastively in our characterization of them, but that they also enter into a multiplicity of causal relations with each other, relations which form the causal background to their maintenance, their alteration, or their eventual disappearance. As being in causal interaction with other things, some of which are potentially destructive, a 'something' can be thought rather figuratively to be maintaining itself against the pressure of its surrounding, as a rigid body, for instance, maintains its shape against (some degree of) pressure and impact from surrounding bodies.

It might be thought, however, that the argument is getting a bit loose here, for we seem to be bringing in facts which may be well-attested by common sense, but which are not shown to be necessary features of being. Everybody knows that things in the world are in causal interaction, but we cannot claim to have derived this at the present stage. What is more embarassing, we could not claim to have done so explicitly, for the categories connected with cause are reserved by Hegel for a later point in the Logic, in the part on Essence. In fact, however, there appears to be an implicit set of considerations here, which being implicit are very unclearly expressed. They can perhaps be spelled out as follows:

Not only are the properties by which we characterize things defined contrastively, but it is also an essential part of their meaning that they characterize what they apply to in part in terms of its potential causal interactions with other things. To qualify something as hard is to say something about its penetrability, malleability, etc. in contact with other things; to qualify it as square is to say something about what it can fit snugly alongside of, and so on. This notion of our empirical property-language flies in the face of the Cartesian–empiricist tradition which from a basically contemplative picture of perception derived the model of purely phenomenal properties. The paradigms which seemed to fit best this model were properties available to only one sense, of which the most oft-quoted example was our set of colour terms.

Now it is very dubious if we can abstract purely phenomenal colour-terms from the web of properties by which we describe what we perceive. One can argue plausibly, for instance, that red looks different when it is seen as the colour of a Persian rug or of a vase, that in real perceived space, the visual cannot be disintricated from the tactile. But even if this point is left aside, it is clear that we cannot take our abstracted colour terms as the model for property terms in general, and that at least the great mass of these are understood in part by the type of interactions they attribute to what they are applied to.

Starting from this point, we can see another sense in which the quality of determinate being involves the negation of others. Not only is it defined contrastively, but it is also defined in part by the type of causal interactions with others which beings of this kind enter into, in which interactions the maintenance, alteration or destruction of the thing concerned is always at stake. With just a little bit of poetic licence, therefore, we can speak of its quality as defining the way in which a thing maintains itself or ultimately goes under in its environment, the way in which it 'negates' the potential 'negations' of others.

I believe that Hegel has both points in mind, both the contrastive and the interactive 'negation', perhaps undistinguished when he speaks of Something as the 'the first negation of the negation' (*WL*, I, 102); in this way adumbrating already with simple *Dasein* the principle of return to self in the other which comes to its fullest realization in the subject. This, of course, is central to Hegel's ontology, that the lowliest form of being must be understood as an imperfect proto-form of the highest, which is subject (loc. cit.).

And both points seem to underlie the treatment of *Etwas* in the *WL* (I, 103–16). Hegel first makes the point that Something is necessarily in relation to another Something, in other words, that there must be some real contrasts. Indeed, we can say that each something is the other of some other. From this he moves to the view of Something as in interaction, and hence as having two aspects, what it is in itself (Ansich) and its being in relation to others (Seinfüranderes). Hegel's point is that the two are inseparable, and he pauses to take a swipe at the Kantian notion of a *Ding-an-sich* (*WL*, 108), that is, an entity which would be out of relation with others, and particularly, with our knowledge of it. Here Hegel seems to rely on the interaction point, as he seemed also earlier in the *PhG*.[1] Something which is meant to be characterized in abstraction from all interaction with others must remain for us utterly blank, undetermined, a nothing. To characterize Something must be to talk of its style of interaction with others.

How does Hegel come to establish that *Etwas* is in contradiction? By basing himself on this notion of negation; a Something can only be defined by reference to another with which it is contrasted. This other is its negation. And this negation is to be understood not simply in the contrastive sense, but in that of interaction: the other is the causal context against which Something must maintain itself, hence it is that which negates Something in the strongest sense, that which tends to suppress it. But then this means that Something is in essential relation to, can be thought in this sense to have within it, its own negation; it is hence in contradiction and doomed to disappear.

This argument arouses our suspicion, and rightly so. For it trades on a number of confusions. First the two senses of negation, the contrastive and the interactive, are elided in the term 'frontier' (Grenze). Something only has determinate being through its contrastive frontier with others. Its frontier is in this sense constitutive of it. 'Something [Etwas] is only what it is in its frontier and through its frontier.' (*EL*, §92, Addition). The frontier is not to be understood in a quantitative sense as at the edge of an area. Rather the qualitative frontier 'goes right through its entire existence' (geht vielmehr durch das ganze Dasein hindurch, loc. cit.).

But this frontier is common with the other contrasted properties. It also defines and is constitutive of them. Hence in containing it each contains what negates it as well as what essentially constitutes it.

If we now shift to the other sense of frontier, that of interaction, we can give this 'negation' a concrete as well as just a contrastive logical sense, and it looks as though each entity essentially contains the seeds of its own destruction. But of course however much we may be tempted to speak of something containing its negation in the contrastive sense, when we move to the frontier at which things 'negate' each other by interaction, it is just false to say that each contains its own negation. Quite the contrary, to the extent that they maintain themselves, they hold their 'negations' off. If they fail to do so, of course, they go under, but they are not essentially determined to do so by the very way in which they are defined.

[1] Ch. II. I could not discuss these passages adequately in Ch. IV above. But see my 'The opening arguments of the *Phenomenology*' in Alasdair MacIntyre (Ed.) *Hegel*, New York, 1972, 151–87.

236

Being

A field to use Hegel's example (in *EL*, § 92) is contrastively defined, say, with a wood and a pond. It is also capable of being transformed into wood or bog through the seeds which are carried onto it or the water which drains onto it, and it only maintains itself thanks to its inhospitability to tree growth and its own drainage properties. But the sense in which wood or pond are essentially related to the meadow in its definition has nothing to do with their having gained or not gained a real foothold in it.

It certainly is bound up with the principle that things are necessarily in causal interaction with each other that they are always in principle open to alteration and destruction. In this minimal sense everything is mortal. But Hegel wishes to have more. He wants to show from conceptual necessity what we know from experience and from a deep intuition only, viz., that all things not only can in principle but do effectively pass away. He wants to show this because it is essential to his ontology that all finite things are in contradiction, in being finite embodiments of the infinite, and hence that they *must* go under. And it is this notion of contradiction and necessary demise which he draws as conclusion from the essential relation of Determinate Being to its other.

And in preparation for the ontological conclusion of this whole movement, Hegel calls this condition of mortal self-contradiction 'finitude'.

When we say of things that they are finite, we mean thereby not only that they have a determinateness, that quality is reality and determination existing *an sich*, that they are merely limited – and hence still have determinate being beyond their frontier and their being. Finite things are; but their relation to themselves is this, that being negative they are self-related, and in this self-relation send themselves on beyond themselves and their being. They are, but the truth of this being is their end. The finite does not only change, like Something [*Etwas*] in general, but it perishes; and its perishing is not merely contingent, so that it could be without perishing. It is rather the very being of finite things, that they contain the seeds of perishing as their own being-in-self [Insichsein]: the hour of their birth is the hour of their death.   (*WL*, I, 116–17)[1]

We have here a second and much more important case in which Hegel forces his argument beyond what it can strictly yield, and ends up with what is really an interpretation of things powerfully suggestive of his ontology, rather than a strict demonstration of it. The fact that everything passes away can be seen as the manifestation of an inner self-negation. We can draw on this and other facts about the world to suggest Hegel's vision of things.

But Hegel is aiming and must aim at much more. Not only is the contradiction, as with all stages of the dialectic, meant to be the object of a strict proof. But as a contradiction in the very concept of Determinate Being, it shows the demise of finite things, as well as their dependence on a larger whole (which Hegel will call the 'infinite' as we shall see in a minute), to be a matter of

---

[1] Translation by W. H. Johnston and L. G. Struthers (slightly amended) in *Hegel's Science of Logic*, London, 1929, vol I, 142.

Logic

conceptual necessity. For both the passing away and the ontological dependence of the finite exist to resolve a conceptual contradiction, and hence obtain
of rational necessity.

The necessity in Hegel's system, as we saw in the last chapter, is powered by
contradiction. And that is why this discussion of *Dasein* as finitude plays a
crucial role in the whole argument of the *Logic*. It is the charter of the
necessary inter-relation of things. We can think of the structure of the world as
necessary, because finite things being contradictory are linked to the whole of
necessity.

The contradiction in the finite is meant to be based on this: being must be
determinate, as we saw in the opening dialectic. To exist is to exist with a
certain determinate nature, as against other possible ones. Determinacy is a
criterial property of reality. And since there is no doubt that there is reality (of
some kind or other), there must be determinate being. Or to put it another way,
since 'being' must have application, and since it can only apply as determinate, then 'determinate Being' must have application.

But then we discover that to be determinate is to contain one's negation
within oneself. And whatever contains its own negation cannot survive. Thus
the very determination which reality must have in order to be tends to annul it.
It is contradictory; and this contradiction affects its very concept. We are not
just talking of some accidental conflict of requirements where, e.g., some
medicine I must take for one malady tends to aggravate another. This is a
conflict of requirements which obtains in virtue of contingent facts about me.

But here we are talking about a conflict of criterial properties of 'reality' or
'being', a concept which *must* apply. Being must be determinate, and at the
same time it must avoid annulment. So that the conflict is conceptual,
necessary, that is, a contradiction in the full sense; and it is also in things. That
is why the movement it powers in finite things is conceptually necessary, as is
their relation to a larger whole.

An indispensable concept has an incoherent application. We can see now
why Hegel looked on the Kantian antinomies as examples of a pervasive
conflict which his *Logic* would lay bare. But he will not take Kant's line that the
incoherence is in our way of representing reality rather than in the things
themselves. And indeed, Kant's line is unavailable here. For we are not just
dealing with concepts like 'divisibility' or 'limit' which we could plausibly argue
pertain to a representation of things in time and space which is all we mortals
can attain to. The contradiction we have uncovered touches 'Being', that is, the
concept of reality in general.

Hegel's argument here is thus of ontological import. It would be of
immense consequence if valid. But unfortunately in linking determinateness to
self-annulment it builds, as we saw, on an equivocation on the concept of
negation, and this is fatal to the argument. What Hegel in the end gives us is

rather a portrayal of the mutability of all reality as springing from an inner conflict, a negation of self. But powerfully suggestive though it is the language of self-contradiction is not established by a strict proof. The only status it can successfully claim is that of a more or less persuasive gloss on the facts of finitude.

Hegel goes on to discuss the contradiction in things as 'finitude'. And in taking up this notion he presents another account of their necessary demise, which is the obverse of the earlier one. In striving to maintain themselves, things struggle to overcome their negation. Now its frontier, as we have seen, is the negation of a finite thing; it therefore strives to go beyond its frontier. But since the frontier is also that which defines it and hence constitutes it, its over-stepping of the frontier is its dissolution, or its transformation into something entirely different. This way of putting it, of course, trades on the same confusion as the above: the sense in which a thing in developing or maintaining itself might be thought to be pushing back a frontier of interaction has no intrinsic connection whatever with the abolition of a qualitative frontier. But this way of putting things presents the drive towards destruction as coming from the thing itself, and from its striving to realize itself fully; and this, of course, is a way of putting it which suits the underlying ontological conclusions which Hegel is edging towards, that finite things disappear precisely because they are attempts to embody the infinite, that death is thus their fruition.

Hegel puts this latter account of the contradiction in other language; the frontier (Grenze) here is called a 'limit' or 'barrier' (Schranke), and the inner drive to fulfilment is called 'ought' (Sollen). These particular terms are of course introduced to allow a reference to the errors of Kant and Fichte, whose ethics and metaphysic is bound up with the notion of a goal which we are bound to seek but can never realize. In particular, Hegel's criticism of Kant's ethic, as we have seen, is that Kant is thought to have presented an opposition between nature and obligation such that men must ever attempt to make the former correspond with the latter, to make the world over and their own sensibility in line with the moral law and the dictates of conscience; but that they cannot succeed on pain of collapsing the distinction between the two and hence doing away with the moral law and with duty.[1] This dilemma of Kantian morality is much commented on by Hegel, and it obviously provides the model for the depiction of the contradiction between *Sollen* and *Schranke* here, an 'ought' that must destroy the distinction on which it is founded in order to realize itself.

---

[1] Cf. the discussion in Chapter VI, 3.

Logic

Infinity

The use of the word 'Sollen' is enough to warn us if we did not know already that we have not reached the end term of this movement. For the type of finitude which is bound up with the 'ought' is the kind that breeds as a corresponding term the 'bad' infinite, by which Hegel means a form of infinity which is not encompassable, which is not held together in a coherent structure, hence boundless in another sense. We can remind ourselves here that the Hegelian notion of infinity is of a whole which is not conditioned or bounded by something else; but this does not mean that the infinite has no structure or shape; it means only that there is no relation to anything outside. An infinite universe is thus not necessarily boundless, rather it can be an ordered whole whose elements are only related to each other. This is indeed for Hegel the true notion of the infinite, the notion ontologically founded in the nature of infinite spirit. It is opposed to the infinite as simply the limitless, the indefinite extension which has no inner unity.

The true infinite for Hegel thus unites finite and infinite; and this in two ways. First he refuses to see the finite and the infinite as separate and over against each other, for in that case since they cannot fail to be related, the infinite would be related to something which was not itself, and hence would not be infinite. The infinite must thus englobe the finite. At its most basic level this reflects Hegel's option for an absolute which is not separate from or beyond the world but includes it as its embodiment.

But secondly, the infinite cannot just include the finite as the endless progress includes the individual terms which make it up. In Hegel's sense this too would be a failure to unite finite and infinite, since the unity could never be consummated. However far one takes an infinite progress, there is always more to go. On this model the infinite can never be an ordered whole in which the various finite elements have a necessary place.

The Hegelian notion of the infinite is therefore that of an infinite life embodied in a circle of finite beings, each of which is inadequate to it and therefore goes under, but is replaced in a necessary order by another, the whole series not being boundless but closed on itself in a circle. Such is the circle of categories which make up the logic, the circle of levels of being which make up the philosophies of nature and spirit, the circle of roles which make up the state. Such ordered wholes are not related to anything outside themselves. The elements are indeed finite and perishable, while the whole is infinite and eternal. But there is no separation between the two, because the infinite only exists in the necessary order of the finite.

This is the conception of the infinite to which Hegel will now take us. *Dasein* as determinate being which necessarily goes under is finitude. The determinate thing is related to others outside it both statically, in contrast and

Being

interaction with other finite things, and dynamically, in that it goes under and is replaced by others. But this calls for another category. The finite as so defined cannot subsist on its own, for finite being always refers us beyond itself. We need another category to encompass the whole of reality, or reality as self-subsistent.

Let us call this new category 'infinity'. We will then agree that it cannot be thought of as something which exists beyond the finite. First because we have seen that non-finite, non-determinate being is equivalent to nothing, and so such an infinite would be empty. Secondly because this empty infinite would have something outside itself, as we have just argued, and hence would not be the true infinite, and not a concept of the whole. This infinite would be finite. But nor can we think of it as the merely boundless. For this too would fail to give us a concept of a self-subsistent whole. The finite is dependent on other things, both at any moment of time and also in that it issues out of other finite things. But relations of dependence cannot stretch on forever for otherwise nothing would ever come to be. As we trace out relations of dependence we must eventually come to a whole which is self-subsistent, which is not dependent on anything outside.

The concept of the infinite must thus be that of the whole system of finite things and their relations which is not itself dependent or limited by anything else. This infinite includes the finite, it is in a sense identical with the finite, but it is also an encompassable whole.

I take this to be the nub of Hegel's argument, although it is not set out in these terms, and it is not entirely clear what he means. The argument against the empty infinite beyond is clear enough, but the crucial transition in both versions of the logic is that from the bad infinite of endless progress to the true infinite. The bad infinite presents us an endless series of finite things, each of which disappears as it must and is replaced by another. The passage to the true infinite comes when we see that each something which disappears is replaced by another finite something. There is identity in the change: 'it follows that Something [Etwas] in its passage into other only joins with itself'[1] (so geht hiermit Etwas in seinem Übergehen in Anderes nur mit sich selbst zusammen, *EL*, §95). This is 'true infinity' (die wahrhafte Unendlichkeit).

I understand this transition as follows: if we contemplate the succession of finite things where each passes and is succeeded by another, we are eventually forced to shift our central point of reference from the particular ephemeral finite things to the continuing process which goes on through their coming to be and passing away. This is the identity in difference. But the locus of this process is not any particular finite thing, but the whole system of limited, ephemeral things.

[1] William Wallace translation, in *The Logic of Hegel*, Oxford, 1874.

241

This passage from a notion of a limited, dependent reality to the complementary notion of a self-subsistent whole is a step which Hegel will take a number of times in the course of the *Logic*. It is a crucial weapon in his armoury. And he uses it here to good effect. But Hegel's category of infinity which he derives here is considerably richer than we may be willing to warrant on the basis of his argument. That the notion of the finite and dependent requires a complementary notion of the whole may be readily granted. But Hegel's 'infinity' is not just the notion of a whole but of a whole whose inner articulation and process unfolds of necessity.

Thus Hegel speaks of this insight of the unity of finite and infinite as the discovery of 'Ideality' (*EL*, §95). We come to the fullest understanding of things when we relate them to a necessity whose formula is expressed in Idea, in something close to the Platonic sense. Hence 'the truth of the infinite is...its ideality', and 'true philosophy therefore is always idealism' (jede wahrhafte Philosophie ist deswegen Idealismus, *loc. cit.*)

What licences this stronger conclusion is the earlier argument we examined above which shows the finite as the locus of contradiction. If the infinite is the whole system of changes which the finite undergoes, and if these changes are powered by contradiction, then the inner process of the infinite is governed by necessity.

Let us examine this a little more closely. A finite thing goes under of necessity. But in going under it does not simply disappear. The negation from which it suffers is itself a determinate one, and hence in breaking up it is replaced by another determinate thing – e.g., wood which is burnt becomes smoke and ash. In any case, we cannot think of determinate things as just disappearing, because being as we saw must be determinate, and since Being is an indispensable concept, so is *Dasein*.[1]

Thus the demise of one finite thing is the birth of another. This is where ordinary non-speculative thought tries to evade the issue. When it rises to an intuition of the inescapable mortality of finite things (even though it does not see the contradiction), it naturally thinks of the finite as sustained by an infinite being who is beyond finitude. This being would replace finite things as they go under. But this kind of infinite being is impossible on Hegel's argument. First of all he could not be without being finite, i.e. determinate. And secondly, he is really surreptitiously defined as determinate since he is *contrasted* to the finite. The notion of such an infinite being is a contradiction.

[1] We can put this point another way: if we think of finite things as just disappearing, then we are back in the category of Nothing. But Nothing in the context of the *Logic*, where we are dealing with categories, i.e., concepts which bear on some reality, cannot be absolute non-being, whatever that might be. It must rather be thought of as a reality which is not this, not that, in short not any determinate thing. It is thus equivalent to Being, our starting point, and as such it generates Determinate Being once more. Thus Dasein cannot disappear. Cf. *WL*, I, 118–19, where Hegel alludes to the parallel between the dialectic of Nothing and that of the finite.

Hence infinity, the self-subsistent whole which we are forced to assume once we grasp the mortality of the finite, can only be the whole system of changing determinate beings. There is no foundation for finite things outside the system of the finite. Hence there is no source outside the system on which we can draw to explain the coming to be of new finite things. Their coming to be is just the passing away of their predecessors.

But the predecessor goes under of conceptual necessity. For its demise is the resolution of a contradiction. Hence the successor comes to be of conceptual necessity. But all finite things are the successors of some others. So that not only the passing away but the coming to be of finite things happens of necessity.

Thus the infinite as the whole system of changing finite things is the unfolding of conceptual necessity, for these things change and deploy themselves in a perpetual attempt to resolve contradiction. Contradiction is the motor of things. And it touches everything, so that everything is swept along in a perpetual becoming (*WL*, I, 138). The infinite can only be the whole, and what remains identical is the formula of necessity which runs through the whole circle of changes.

Because of this inner necessity, the infinite is not just the whole in the sense that it is a collection of finite things from which nothing has been left out, or a group of finite things which are in contingent causal interaction. It is a totality, a whole whose parts are intrinsically related to each other, that is, where each can only be understood by its relations to the others. For these parts, or finite things, arise and succeed each other by conceptual necessity. Thus Hegel's conception of the contradiction of the finite, which we saw went beyond what his argument could sustain, is already having important consequences. It makes all the difference between seeing the whole as a contingent grouping of finite things, and seeing it as a totality which deserves to be called 'infinite' in Hegel's sense of the term, and in which the finite is seen as having its truth in the Idea.

Because of this Hegel's notion of infinity already contains the essential character of his ontological vision and of the final category of the *Logic*, the Idea. It is a self-subsistent system whose structure is determined by conceptual necessity, and which is embodied in finite things.

But Infinity is still a poor and abstract version of the Idea. For we only know that it has a necessary structure deployed in space and time. We have not yet been able to define the articulations of this structure. This will come with further and richer categories of the *Logic*.

In moving from *Dasein* to Infinity, we have shifted the centre of gravity of reality. Instead of seeing it as simply one particular thing, we see it rather as centred in a process which runs through the transformations, the coming to be and passing away of many things. And this is in line with the whole development of the logic, whereby each stage takes us further towards inwardness, that is, further towards a notion of being as centred on itself, as inwardly articulated and deploying its autonomous activity, in short as closer and closer to the model of the subject. The first notion of *Etwas* as a negation of negation, as a self-maintaining being, already set us on this path; now we take a further step, we uncover a deeper centre whose activity is deployed not just in the maintenance of this thing, but in the ordered series of transformations, comings to be and passings away. We have a negation of negation at a deeper level, a more all-embracing unity, and hence a greater degree of inwardness; or otherwise put a deeper level of connection between things, now underlying not just the maintenance of disparate things but the transformations from one to the other.

Hence the first movement of the logic closes with Hegel having established (to his own satisfaction) his basic ontological vision of finite being as the vehicle for an infinite life which is not separate from it, and this from the basic starting point that being must be determinate to be. The dialectic of Being engenders *Dasein*, and *Dasein* as a mixture of reality and negation, being and non-being, is interpreted as inherently contradictory, hence as containing its own destruction. This contradictory self-destructive nature is finitude, but the drive to dissolution is interpreted as a transcending of the barrier and hence as a drive to infinity, which is then seen as the life inherent in the coming to be and passing away of the finite. Hence Being and Non-being not only unite in *Dasein*, but also in Becoming as was intimated perhaps a little prematurely in the first dialectic.

II: QUANTITY

In the last chapter of 'Quality', entitled '*Fürsichsein*', Hegel makes the transition to quantity. This transition may seem a little strained, which in fact it is. It offers another example of a twist we have often noticed in the Hegelian dialectic: where Hegel 'goes back' from the advanced point he has reached in order to take up and 'feed into' his dialectic some other important range of concepts or transitions.

This would seem to be the case here, for what has arisen out of *Dasein* is as we saw a notion of infinite life which continues in the coming to be and passing away of *Dasein*, of reality as related to 'ideality'. Hence we have the idea of a being which survives the demise of this quality. To use more Hegelian language, we have a being which negates its particular determinations, or which returns to itself out of the other by which it is determined ('unendliche Rückkehr in sich' *WL*, I, 147), or which is 'simple relation to itself' (einfache Beziehung auf sich *WL*, I, 147).

This is the Hegelian notion of *Fürsichsein*, Being-for-self, the stage we have now reached, and not surprisingly Hegel cites the 'I' of subjectivity as a paradigm example. For the subject as consciousness has a certain object before him, and as self-consciousness has a certain set of characteristics, but he 'returns to himself' out of these in the sense that he cannot be identified with them, that objects and characteristics change through the life of this identical person. Of course the human subject eventually goes under himself, and the highest example of *Fürsichsein* is the absolute subject whose life continues through the entire range of changes in external reality.

All this may be clear enough in Hegelian terms: we seem in *Fürsichsein* to have derived the notion of the subject as life vehicled by the coming to be and passing away of its external embodiment. But this is not where we want to get at this stage of the *Logic*; rather this will come in its proper place in the third book. What we want to derive at this stage is simply Quantity.

Hegel therefore steps in to direct the traffic. He reminds us that we are still at the level of Being, that it is we are still looking on reality as undimensional simple being, not that is, as emanation or manifestation of something. This will come only in the second book, on Essence. Hence it cannot be a question of entertaining the notion of the subject here. But if we transpose this fuller notion into the poorer context of simple being, we do derive a new form which can be the starting point of a new dialectic.

This new form is simple being, but what it retains of the subject, what justifies its being called '*Fürsichsein*', is its negation of its specific determination. It is a being picked out as such without any specific quality. But this is not a return to the indeterminacy of pure Being from which the Logic started, claims Hegel, for this indeterminacy is posited by the self-relation of *Fürsichsein*, it has arisen out of the dialectic. In this of course, Hegel seems to be having his cake and eating it, retaining those prerogatives of the subject he needs for his argument, while remaining in the sphere of Being; but let us waive this objection in order to follow his argument.[1]

Now this being, Hegel calls 'the one'; and we can see the underlying logic of this, even if Hegel's derivation seems much more fanciful. For a being of this kind can only be picked out, that is, distinguished from others, by some numeration-like procedure. In other words, we can only identify a particular being of this kind by attributing to it some number in a series, or some ordinal position. For all beings of this kind are identical in being without determinate quality, they can only be distinguished numerically.

Of course, in this argument I am taking for granted that identifying 'the one' is the same as distinguishing it from others, that a being of this kind is only conceivable as one among many. How else can a being without internal differentiation be identified, except in contrast with others? The absolute spirit

---

[1] Cf. dissatisfaction on this point expressed by Jean Wahl: *Commentaires de la Logique de Hegel.* 'Les Cours de Sorbonne' Paris n.d., p. 95.

in his full manifestation is, indeed, must be identified without contrast; but his life is the necessary inter-relation of rich and varied realities, whose identification in contrast to each other poses no problem. But what has no internal differentiation cannot be identified by what it contains or includes: it can thus only be picked out by what it 'negates'. This was the case with *Dasein*, which being identified with a simple quality was undifferentiated, and hence had to be contrasted to others to be determinate. But here, the one is not only undifferentiated but without specific quality; it cannot be contrasted qualitatively to others, only numerically. 'The one' must exist as one among many.

This argument brings us to Quantity. But although it might be thought to underlie Hegel's reasoning here, his derivation of Quantity takes quite another form. It passes rather through the notions of repulsion and attraction, which Hegel following Kant thought were essential to physics (and hence worth while deriving as stages in the *Logic*).

This is another example of a detour to take in what Hegel judges to be essential notions. The derivation of repulsion, which we cannot go into here, turns on the idea that the one in negating its own qualitative determination has a 'negative relation to itself'. Hence the one must become many. But at the same time the many which spring from the one are after all identical, homogeneous. The relation of each to the others is also a self-relation. Hence there is attraction as well.

Before deriving repulsion (in the *WL*) Hegel connects the idea of the one with the philosophy of atomism, as put forward by Democritus. Atoms are indeed, 'ones' in this sense, for they are internally undifferentiated and quite qualityless, in that they offer absolutely no qualitative contrast to each other. Hegel tries to account for the idea that atoms are in a void in terms of his notion of the one: the one is quality-less, is empty, is itself in that sense void; it remains only to separate the two moments of the one, its affirmative being and its emptiness, in order to posit atoms in a surrounding void.

But atomism offers us an inadequate notion of the ones, because it conceives their relation to each other, their combination, as purely contingent; as a contingent fact, some atoms 'swerve', and hence encounter others; whereas in reality, the ones can only exist in relation to each other. It is this necessary relatedness which Hegel tries to make explicit with the notions of repulsion and attraction.

But I think that the crucial transition to Quantity is best put in the more general terms that I introduced above, of distinction and homogeneity; and Hegel himself introduces general terms which are not far removed from these in his own treatment of quantity, viz. continuous and discontinuous. For to see things as made up of distinct and homogeneous elements is to see them as measurable, as quantifiable.

Thus for Hegel, Quantity is defined as 'pure being, in which the determinateness is no longer posited as at one with the being itself, but rather as annulled or indifferent' (*EL*, §99). The crucial word here is 'indifferent' (gleichgültig): qualitatively considered, the determinateness or limit of a thing is not a matter of indifference; if we alter the limit, we alter the nature of the thing; but considered purely quantitatively, the limits of a thing can be altered without changing its nature; it is 'indifferent' to them. It is thus a mark of the quantitative, says Hegel, that we are dealing with such indifferent limits, that the things can increase or decrease in extension without changing their nature.

Now this presupposes that we can treat the reality thus dealt with as homogeneous, that is, not partitioned by qualitative differences, and also as divisible into units, i.e., into distinct 'ones'. Hence in deriving the distinction and homogeneity of the ones, we have derived the category of Quantity.

This double feature of reality considered quantitatively, which I have called homogeneity and distinction, and which Hegel discussed at the end of the last chapter in connection with attraction and repulsion, he introduces here in the first chapter on Quantity as continuity and discreteness. These are both 'moments' of Quantity, for reality quantitatively considered must be homogeneous (that is continuous), and yet we must be able to draw a line at any point and measure it up to there; that is, it must be capable of being cut up (in our measuring procedures if not in the flesh) into discrete units.

The problem is just that reality considered purely quantitatively can be carved up in a number of ways. In purely quantitative terms, there is no ground for dividing it in one place rather than another. Hegel makes it clear that merely quantitative, mathematical terms are inadequate to express any philosophical truth. And we can see why: to see things in quantitative terms is to see them as homogeneous and particulate; whereas for Hegel speculative truths concern articulated wholes; their basic stock in trade is conceptual opposition. Hence the belief that we can understand the world in quantitative terms is bound up with materialism; for only matter is appropriately understood in terms of quantity (as well as time and space, of course). But materialism is bound to miss all the important connections which express the necessary structure of the world.

Hegel hence has a low view of mathematics as a philosophical language, Mathematics takes us beyond merely sensible observation; but it gives us only the most external, i.e. non-conceptual, relations.

But even granted the poverty of mathematics, how does the characterization of things in quantitative terms lead us to a contradiction, and hence to higher categories? Hegel comes to this in the third part of the second chapter on Quantity. Here he takes up the feature we mentioned earlier viz., that quantitatively considered, things are indifferent to their limits, there is no ground for dividing them in one place rather than in another. In the section considered here, Hegel puts this point in a way reminiscent of the discussion of

Quality: a quantum cannot but alter its limit, it unavoidably becomes greater or smaller, and hence another quantum. But this process has no natural stopping place, hence the self-alteration of the quantum is an endless progress, just as the self-othering of *Dasein* was. And like that latter process, Hegel seems to consider this one as contradictory, as requiring some resolution.

But one might think that Hegel is a little cavalier in his transitions here. Granted that Quantity is the realm in which things are indifferent to their limit, how does that show that quanta must go beyond themselves, and change? (whatever this means). And even if they do so endlessly, even granted Hegel's dislike for the 'bad' infinity of the endless progress, does this show a contradiction requiring resolution by a higher category?

One can perhaps make sense of this Hegelian way of putting the matter, if we recall to mind that we are dealing here with categories of transcendental logic, that is categories by which we can grasp reality; and we are testing them to see if they can offer us a way of grasping reality coherently. It will be remembered that it was against this yardstick that pure being failed, and showed itself to be synonymous with nothing. And the same requirements, we might argue, show purely quantitative characterizations to be radically inadequate.

The argument might go something like this: to characterize things purely quantitatively would be to be able to describe everything in terms of combinations of homogeneous, i.e. qualitatively indistinguishable units. This is the dream of atomists, be they physical or logical. But even this dream in any conceivably realizable form would have to re-introduce quality. For there must be some grounds for picking out one set of combinations of units rather than others. Let us say I pick out object A which contains, say, 100 units and object B which contains 50. Now what reason did I have for drawing the limits here, for delineating an object grouping these 100 units together, and not, say, rather 101 or 99? These reasons, the criteria for 'A' and 'B', cannot be stated in terms of numbers of units, for the question concerns the grouping of units into aggregates of a certain number, viz. 100 or 50. We have to introduce some other range of descriptive concepts in order to express the criteria; let us say, that this group of 100 is *bunched together* away from the rest, or that 50 forms a certain *shape*.

This point is unaffected by the consideration that we may characterize the world in an indefinite number of different ways, and hence in our imaginary situation, groups units in an indefinite number of ways: our A, for instance, might also be described as an M and an N grouping respectively 88 and 12 units; and so on. For in any case, if there are any reasons for carving the world up in any given way, they can only be given by introducing other ranges of descriptive concept than that of units and aggregates of units. Rather, this point of the plurality of ways of characterizing things re-inforces the argument. For the distinction between two different ways of characterizing things can only be given in terms of the different ranges of concept appropriate to each.

Hence it is that any thoroughgoing conceptual atomism, to give a name to the view we are considering here, must burke the issue of how we characterize things, that is, group units. It must imagine a phenomenal world in which there are no groupings at all, or what is the same thing, in which any groupings we make are utterly arbitrary in the sense that nothing at all can be said concerning the principle of such grouping – a sort of super-nominalist doctrine. But this is plainly impossible. For unless the only things we allowed in this strange imaginary phenomenal world of the conceptual atomist were those consisting of single units, in which case there would be only one kind of thing, hence no qualitative concepts at all (because no contrast), and hence *no kind* of thing, (i.e. we fall back into the emptiness of pure Being), we would have to allow entities which were aggregates of units. But then there would have to be some criteria for singling out aggregates of n units as a given kind of thing, other than their simply having n units. For there could be no sense to recognizing, say, a thing of 100 units, and saying 'there's an A' unless As had other properties than just that of containing as aggregates 100 units, e.g. that As grouped these units in a certain way, or a certain shape. For in anyone's field at any time there would undoubtedly be hundreds, if not thousands of such units, on any plausible interpretation of a universal atomic element, and hence if A just meant 100 units, it could never fail to be given.

Of course, this imaginary phenomenal world is rather weird, so far removed is it from our actual one, which is full of qualitative diversity, so that we find it very difficult to imagine such a reduction of all things to a single type of element. Even the reductions achieved by the more successful sciences, the real atomism of physics, say, have no relation to an atomism of aggregation out of homogeneous units, even though they may reduce seemingly diverse phenomena to a single explanatory base. The aim of the above excursus was just to show how the characterization of things in purely quantitative terms, that is, without introducing any qualitative distinctions, or plurality of descriptive concepts, is impossible.

And the motive for this rather far-fetched demonstration is that I believe something of this underlies the Hegelian argument here. In the argument as we have seen Hegel moves from the thesis that reality quantitatively considered (for short, the quantum) can alter its limits arbitrarily, to the thesis that it must do so; and he sees in this a contradiction. 'According to its quality, therefore, a quantum is posited in absolute continuity with its externality and otherness. Thus it not only *can* go beyond every determinate magnitude, it not only *can* be altered, but it is posited that it *must* alter' (*WL*, I, 221, italics in original). And a little above, Hegel speaks of 'contradiction' (Widerspruch).

Now this move from 'can' to 'must' is comprehensible if we understand that what we are seeking here is a set of categories which will allow us to grasp things coherently, and if as we have seen a purely quantitative characterization cannot give us an adequate specification of a thing. In purely quantitative terms, there is no reason to place a limit anywhere. Now we can put this by saying that quanta *can* see their 'size-determination' altered, in the sense that there is no reason to stop this. But we can just as well say that there is no basis to speak of fixed quanta at all; any given size we attribute to a quantum is totally arbitrary. We might just as well pick any other. Hence to say that quanta *can* change is misleading; for it implies that there are quanta which also can perhaps remain the same; whereas in fact there is absolutely no ground to single out any fixed quanta at all; *there is no sense to the idea* that a quantum remains the same. And this point can be expressed (misleadingly, it is true, but not more so than in the 'can' formula) by saying that the quantum must change, that 'it is now posited in itself to refer beyond itself and to become another' (*WL*, I, 222).[1]

The contradiction can also be understood if we put this discussion in the basic context of the *Logic*, which we recalled above: our aim is to grasp some reality, to give an adequate specification of a thing, here in quantitative terms; and the specification we give, the quantum, turns out not to be one, turns out to be quite indeterminate in its limits. Intended as a specification, the quantum can never succeed, and hence is doomed to defeat its own purpose. Like 'being' (and ultimately for some of the same reasons) quantitative concepts have to be supplemented by other categories if they are to be applied to reality.

My interpretation could seem wide of the mark. For Hegel uses a quite different idiom in speaking of this transition. He speaks of the quantum being driven beyond its limits to another quantum, and this quantum in turn suffering the same fate, so that it is involved in an endless progress. But I think that this image (how Hegel would have disliked this word, but no other seems appropriate) itself can be understood in the light of the interpretation: what drives the quantum on to its endless alterations is the search for an adequate specification in purely quantitative terms, a search whose object always eludes it, and which for this reason is endless.

The fact that he puts the contradiction in the form of an endless progress enables Hegel to present his solution in a familiar mould. After launching a broadside against those who see something sublime in the quantitatively endless e.g., astronomers who contemplate the heavens (and of course, Kant comes in for more punishment for a passage about the heavens in the *Critique of Practical Reason* and even more for his application of the idea of endless progress to the sphere of morals), and after a critique of the Kantian first

---

[1] Johnston and Struthers translation I 240.

Being

antinomy, Hegel then comes to a solution similar to the one he found to the endless progress of *Dasein*: for quantum is always moving on into another one; it must therefore find a way of returning to itself in this other; and this it can do if we conceive it as the term of a relation between two quanta.

Hegel here comes to the solution which he develops through the third chapter of this section, and which fully developed is the object of the third part of Being, Measure. Measure is the return of quantity into quality at a higher level, a level which involves the synthesis of the two. The idea is that although a thing cannot be specified in terms of a single quantum, it can be in terms of a relation between quanta. Hegel is thinking, as is evident in the later discussion on measure, of the functional laws of natural science, linking two or more variables. We can return to a specification of a thing's quality or nature, in a much fuller and richer form, when we can characterize it in terms of some functional law or relation. We achieve in this way the synthesis of quality and quantity; we achieve quantitatively defined quality.

But the point to be made in relation to the above interpretation is that in introducing the relation between quanta, we have gone beyond the homogeneous universe of conceptual atomism. The two or more quanta which are related are measurements of two or more different things, properties or dimensions, that is they are distinguished by more than having a different number of units (if indeed, they have a different number of units – the length and depth of a square are equal in extent, but distinct). It is this escape from unidimensionality which allows the quantum to fix on a determinate size. To return to our above example: we pick out these 100 units as an *A*, because the units are at distance *d* from each other. Hence we have a reason for grouping these 100 units as an *A*, because 100 is the number of units which are grouped together so as to be distance *d* from each other. *A*s are then defined by a relation between quanta, as aggregates of units which are all a certain distance from each other; and the quantum 100 is fixed here because it is one term of a relation of which the other is *d*. The introduction of a second dimension (which here is also quantified, but that is not essential) allows us to motivate our grouping of the units in our original dimension. I believe that it is this important property of pluri-dimensionality – operating with more than one dimension – which accounts for Hegel's solution of the infinite progress here: 'The quantum is thus posited as self-repelled; there are thus two quanta, which are however cancelled [aufgehoben] and exist only as moments of one unity, and this unity is the determinateness of the quantum' (*WL*, I, 239). But of course, I need hardly repeat that this is not his argument as we see it in the text: rather he reaches this by the familiar argument that the quantum returns to itself, and hence finds its own moment in its beyond, i.e., the other quanta into which it is constantly turning: and this self-identity in other quanta is quickly

251

re-interpreted as the unity of two related quanta mentioned above, which forms the basis for the third chapter and the entire synthesis between quantity and quality that we find in the section on Measure.

Understanding reality in the category of Measure is thus understanding qualities which are founded on certain quantities or relations between quanta. As a very simple example, we have water which must have a temperature between 0° and 100° C, turning else into ice or steam. We have here the simple unity between quality and quantity which defines measure, the quanta 0° and 100° C are picked out as significant because of the qualitative changes which occur at these limits, and these qualitative changes are accounted for by the changes in temperature. We have thus the relation between two property dimensions, the state of the substance and its temperature, which we saw in the above discussion to be essential to quantitative characterization.

We have thus in a sense returned to quality in this third section of the Logic of Being, but on a higher level on which it is united with quantity; for we see properties as reposing now on quantitative values. This category of Measure is also of universal application: 'Everything which exists has a measure' (Alles was da ist, hat ein Maß, *WL*, I, 343). We are reminded of the Greek preoccupation with measure, but also of modern physics and chemistry which has uncovered in a host of fields the limits within which things must remain to retain the same qualitative character.

But this category, too, while universal is radically inadequate. Hegel cannot accept that the quantitative characterization of things, even united as it is with quality in Measure, touches more than the surface of things. It cannot penetrate to the core of reality. And to penetrate to the core is to enter into the dialectic relation of inner and outer, both identical and yet opposed to each other, which is central to Hegel's ontology. We make the transition to this type of characterization in the present section, introducing us to the Logic of Essence where we shall no longer be dealing with the one-tiered categories of Being, but with two-tiered ones.

The argument in *WL* is very complex and is closely tied in detail to the sciences of Hegel's day and his view about them. It touches on themes which will re-appear in the Philosophy of Nature. But in *EL* the argument is very economically set out. It is simply a continuation of the considerations under-lying the transition from Quantity. Measure is the immediate unity of Quality and Quantity (§ 108), as such it is also simple quantum, and hence susceptible to increase and decrease. But beyond certain limits this increase or decrease abolishes the quality, it pushes us beyond into the 'measureless' (das Maß-lose). This new state is, however, itself a new quality; so we return to Measure.

But this new measure can again be overstepped, and so forth in a (potentially) endless regress (§ 109) (e.g., ice changing to water, changing to steam). But since we always return to quality and measure, albeit a different one, we shouldn't look on this change as an endless progress of new terms, but rather as an identity in difference. 'But Measure shows itself...to remain just as much together with itself in its transition.' (Das Maß zeigt sich aber...eben so sehr nur mit sich selbst zusammenzugehen, § 110).

We recognize here the same argument-type as underlies the transition from all three sections of the Logic of Being. First the finitude of the entity under consideration (*Etwas* in the first section, quantum in the second), i.e., the fact that it goes under if taken beyond a certain limit, is presented as an inner necessity; but its going under is the birth of something else (the other in the first section, a new quantum in the second). This yields the prospect of an endless progress of terms. This (to Hegel) unacceptable result is avoided by recognizing a unity in difference between the different phases of this necessary change.

But this conception of things gives birth to a two-tiered notion of reality, of a substrate which underlies changing states. It is the variants of this conception which we are to explore in the second book. In a sense we were already there with the derivation of true infinity in the first section; but we put off entering the promised land because we had to integrate Quantity into our synthesis, for the encyclopaedic reasons already discussed. We thus took as it were a sideways step, via *Fürsichsein*, to Quantity.

The dialectic of Measure, by contrast, is continuous with that of Quantity, it is the prolongation of it, through the same considerations – the instability of Quantum, the resulting endless progress, and the solution of identity in difference – to the ultimate resolution in a two-tiered conception of reality.

With Measure we have a characterization of things as of a certain quality which is grounded on their falling within certain quantitative limits. The introduction of this quality-concept gives the reason for our fixing on the particular quanta which define the limits, while these quanta account for the thing's having the quality it does. But Hegel seems to say, quanta thus linked with qualities in Measure are themselves driven beyond themselves just as simple quanta were. How are we to understand this?

In somewhat the same way, I would suggest: the characterization in terms of Measure is also in a sense inadequate, not quite in the same way as the above, that it falls below the minimum complexity required to have a world at all of which we can be conscious, but rather in this way, that the characterization in Measure terms necessarily goes along with another, deeper one, which goes beyond Measure. For we are speaking of things which have a certain quality while they remain within certain quantitative limits; but this means that we are no longer talking only of entities which are identified by a certain property such that if this property ceases to hold they cease to be; we are also talking of entities of which we can say that they lose what we have up to now thought of as defining properties and gain others. The category of Measure is what makes the transition: for in it we see what was hitherto a defining property as grounded on the entity concerned being within certain limits. We see water, for instance, (H_2O in its liquid state) as grounded on the temperature's being between 0° and 100° C. But once we think of the entity as having to remain within certain limits, then we have introduced a new notion of the entity, viz., that of an entity of which it can be predicated that it is within certain limits, and therefore of which it can be predicated as well that it is beyond these limits. We have introduced a notion of an entity which is deeper than any of the hitherto defining properties, an underlying substrate which can be in a number of states (Zustände), which states are defined by these properties. Thus to follow our above example, once we say of the water of everyday perception that it must remain within 0° and 100° C, else it becomes ice or steam, we are introducing a more fundamental entity, let us call it H_2O, which while it is within these limits is in such a state that we call it water, and when it is beyond these limits is in the states we call ice or steam.

Thus the characterization of things in Measure terms refers us beyond to a characterization of reality in terms of substrate entities which can be in a number of states, that is, the measure characterization only makes sense if this deeper one does too. This is how I propose to interpret the Hegelian argument that quantitative characterization in measure 'is itself as such the act of stepping beyond itself' (das Hinausschreiten über sich selbst, *EL*, § 109, Addition), the thesis of the inherent necessity to overstep the limit. And if this interpretation is correct, then we can undertand at the same time why this stepping over the limit is also an identity in difference, a 'joining with itself' (zusammengehen mit sich selbst); for the deeper substrate entity is just that which is identical through the changes in state.

In being led to introduce the substrate entity which can enter and leave many states we have taken the major step which leads out of Being into Essence. The categories which Hegel groups in the first book, on Being, all characterize things simply, in one-tiered concepts: *Etwas* is identified with its defining quality, the quantum with its degree. In Essence on the other hand, we will have to do throughout with two-tiered concepts of an underlying reality and its manifestations. In thinking of reality as a substrate which can enter many states we have already left the domain of the one-tiered.

It is of course essential if we are to reach Hegel's ultimate destination that we leave the realm of the one-tiered, for the concepts of Being in suffering transformation can only go under and give way to others – *Etwas* disappears and is replaced by another, the quantum changes ceaselessly into another. It is only with the two-tiered concepts of Essence that we can allow for the maintenance of identity through change which is essential to Hegel's ontol-

Being

ogy. The categories of Essence are not single concepts, but essentially related couples, (*EL*, §111, Addition) appearance and reality, thing and properties, etc. And even though one term may be defined as the more 'essential', they are both necessary to characterize reality, and one cannot be posited without the other. Hence in positing one we are led necessarily to posit the other, but without the first being suppressed, as happens in the categories of Being.

But two-tieredness is not all there is to Hegel's notion of the categories of Essence. There is also this feature of essential relation on which we have just touched. The substance must issue of necessity in the external manifestation, and this in turn refers us necessarily to the substrate. Now we cannot establish this element of necessity from the argument which takes us to substrate from Measure, as we have set it out. But necessity is already established in the category of Infinity. As we move beyond the endless progress of Measure, we rejoin the category which took us beyond the endless progress of determinate Being. There as we saw we were ready to step beyond Being. The centre of gravity shifted from determinate things to the whole system of which they are passing parts or phases. We were thus ready then to step to the categories of Essence, that is, to two-tiered concepts which relate the underlying whole and its passing phase. We put off taking this step in order to take in Quantity, but now that we are ready to go over to Essence, we have a much richer conception of this whole. By showing all qualities as founded on relations of quantity, Measure has given us a language in which to speak of the limits of different qualitites and of the underlying process which carries us from one to another.

But in moving beyond Measure we are still dealing with Infinity, that is, with a self-subsistent system of mutable finite things, the order and successive changes in which occur of necessity, powered by their internal contradiction. So in going beyond Measure we are not just showing that things must inhere in a substrate, but also that they are related in this substrate by negation, i.e., by mutual exclusion, (for each is defined by its other). And moreover, that this negation by the other is internal to each, so that each must necessarily go under and be succeeded by another.

The substrate or whole in which things inhere is thus one whose necessary deployment is powered by contradiction. Its structure and deployment over time is determined by negation or self-exclusion. Hegel speaks of it as a 'negative totality' (*WL*, I, 397). It is a totality because it is not just a collection whose parts are indifferent to each other, but in which each is what it is only in virtue of its necessary relation to the whole. It is negative because

it is simple and infinite negative self-relation, the incompatibility of itself with itself, repulsion of itself from itself. (loc. cit.)[1]

1 Amended Johnston and Struthers translation I 403.

because this necessary relation, in other words, issues from contradiction.

In *EL* Hegel simply states the identity of the present category with the Infinity which issued from *Dasein* (§ 111). In *WL* he undertakes a derivation of Essence which forms the last chapter of Measure. It begins with the notion of a mere substrate which is 'indifferent' to the different states in which it finds itself, whose change therefore from one state to another must be explained by external factors.

The word Hegel uses here, '*Indifferenz*', cannot but refer us to the Schelling of the early 1800s, from whom Hegel broke away. Schelling's *Indifferenz* was the supposed point of unity of subject and object, which Hegel came to see as untenable precisely because it swallowed up the difference in the unity. And there is a reference in the Remark to Spinoza (*WL*, I, 396), whose absolute is like an abyss in which differences disappear.

These solutions all suffer from the same disability, that they cannot explain how differences arise. If the changes in its states cannot be explained by the substrate, but only by external factors, then we have not yet arrived at a self-sustaining system. If we do arrive at such a self-subsistent system, then its changes must be explained out of itself, and its different states cannot be thought of as just affecting it externally. The idea of an indifferent substrate is itself a contradiction.

Hence we move from the categories of Being to those of Essence. We see determinate beings as necessarily inhering in a whole or substrate which persists through their coming to be and passing away. But thanks to the category of Infinity we see this substrate not as some self-sufficient reality beyond the finite, but as one which necessarily issues in finite beings, which deploys finite beings according to a necessity which itself is grounded in the very contradiction of the finite. What we heretofore saw as just being there (Dasein) we must now see as 'posited' (gesetzt), as deployed by a process of necessity.

> The determinations...now no longer belong to themselves, they do not emerge in independence or externality, but belong as moments first to the unity existing *an sich*; they are not released by this unity but are carried by it as a substrate and receive their content only from it ...Instead of *beings* as in the whole sphere of Being, they are now simply *posited* reality, with just this determination and meaning, that they are related to their unity and hence each to its other and to negation... (*WL*, I, 398)

We saw in Chapter III how important this notion of reality as posited is for Hegel.

We thus enter the realm of two-tiered categories, those of Essence, which Hegel will also call determinations of reflections ('Reflexionsbestimmungen'). There is quite a rich set of references in this term. First, as we remember, Hegel used 'reflection' from quite an early date to designate concepts of division, separation or duality, the concepts of the understanding which are prepotent between the first primitive unity and the final higher one. The determinations of reflection thus fit in the *Logic* between the immediacy of Being and the higher unity of the Concept.

But the term also refers us to the reflective understanding, which is trying to go beyond a mere grasp of things in their immediacy to understand them as mediated. This brings us to an important feature of Essence, that its categories all make implicit reference to a subject of knowledge. Throughout the Logic, of course, we are dealing with categories by which the world can be known. We are throughout in the domain of transcendental logic. But in Being, we have categories which provide no hint of reference to a subject of knowledge; they characterize reality simply. In Essence, however, the distinctions made between the two terms, e.g., in a pair of related categories such as Appearance and Reality, refer us implicitly to a subject of knowledge; they are made, as it were, from the point of view of such a subject.

The categories of Essence are thus determinations of reflection because they are categories of relation and mediation, and also categories of reflecting understanding. But thirdly, and most fundamentally, they deserve this name because they are both at once; because as grounded in conceptual necessity, the inner structures which mediate external reality are ultimately understandable as structures of thought (and hence as one with our reflective thought). Hence what we will follow in the dialectic of Essence is not the external reflection of the subject trying to understand, but the inner articulations of Essence itself, which however will be expressed in the concepts of reflective understanding. Or rather, we will be following both at once, for as we move to more and more adequate conceptions of the inner articulation of essence we will at the same time be breaking away from inadequate notions of the relation of Essence to the subject of knowledge, as a merely external one. Movement on these two fronts is inseparable, since as we saw above the categories of Essence all refer implicitly to the subject of knowledge and hence posit a certain relation to this subject.

In other words, the reflection of Being back into the underlying reality of Essence can only be for the reflecting subject who is distinguishing appearance and reality; essence and outer manifestation. To follow the contradictions of and transformations in Essence is to follow the contractions of and transformations in the subject's relation to known reality. The two reflections are thus at first symmetrical, each following its own path. But in the end they become one when we see that the ultimate structure of reality is a structure of thought, and hence that knowing spirit is perfectly at home in, is no longer separated from the inner core of things.

CHAPTER XI

Essence

I: FROM REFLECTION TO GROUND

Essence is the domain in which we see things not just by themselves, 'immediately', but as founded on an underlying basis. This is the realm of mediacy, for the notion of essence is inescapably mediate in Hegel's sense, that is, we can only get to it via another: we come to Essence by reflecting on Being, seeing that it does not suffice to itself, and hence referring back beyond it to what underlies it. Essence thus always refers us to a starting point, to Being which is negated (as self-subsistent). This, says Hegel, is what is expressed in the rather odd etymology of the German word for Essence, 'wesen', which is reminiscent of the past participle of the verb 'to be', 'gewesen': 'Essence is Being which has passed away, but passed away non-temporally' (Das Wesen ist das vergangene, aber zeitlos vergangene Sein, *WL*, II, 3).[1]

It is this movement back which also gives foundation in part to the image of reflection which plays such a large part in this book. But Hegel first wants to make clear the nature of the Essence he will discuss. It cannot be understood simply by the one-way movement mentioned in the above paragraph, where we start from Being and realizing its inadequacy move to the underlying substrate. This is a movement of 'reflection' in one sense, the external reflection of the subject of knowledge who postulates some inner reality to make sense of what he sees. We must also understand this external observable reality as emanating from Essence. The one-sided view which takes into account only the movement to Essence from external object is an account which takes the observed properties of this external reality as simply given. Reflection is external, subjective, because it works on a datum which must just be accepted, which cannot be seen in any way as determined by thought; and hence this reflection, not discovering any necessity in what it observes, must just postulate an underlying reality which it cannot observe.

But as we know already, this is not Hegel's notion of reality. On the contrary, what exists is not to be seen as simply there, as merely contingent, but rather as the manifestation of a thoroughgoing systematic web of necessary relations. Just as the basic theme of Being was the breaking out of Determinate Being into its other, its necessary self-transcendence and hence demise,

---

[1] Johnston and Struthers translation II, 15.

which was always shown to be ultimately a return to self; so the basic theme of Essence is going to be the progressively more clear and articulated revelation of necessary connections in the phenomena, until finally these are seen as nothing but the adequate manifestation of thought or inner necessity, and we will have arrived at the concept. This is why in this book the focus of application of the categories will shift (without Hegel taking the trouble to announce it) from the particular thing which it was in Being and can still be seen as in the first parts of Essence to the system of interconnected things, ultimately to the whole system of reality as a totality, of which we had a foretaste in Infinity. For it is finally only the whole which reveals self-sufficient necessity.

Hence Hegel sees Essence not just as that which one gets to from the external observable which is shown to be non-self-subsisting. It is also the underlying necessity which makes the observed what it is. So it must be understood not just in a movement of reflection from the external which is seen as given, and hence presupposed, to a posited substrate; but also in a movement from the underlying necessity which can thus be thought of as 'positing' the external observable. Moreover the underlying necessity 'posits' (setzt) this observed as something external, hence in a play on words in German we can see this positing as 'voraussetzen' which is the German word for 'presuppose': the presupposition of external reality in the first movement is the positing which we grasp in the second. This expresses the unity of the two movements, for the inner reality which the external is founded on is nothing but the necessity which posits it. As grasped intellectually, the dependence of external reality on the essential underlying substrate just is the fact that this external reality is posited by the substrate; whereas the real 'return' of the external reality, its demise, whose necessity is grasped in our conceptual understanding, is one with the positing of the next term in the necessary sequence.

In the light of this double movement, 'reflection' is to be understood not only as external reflection, that which follows the first movement, but also as an internal, objective reflection, a self-unfolding into external reality, which external reality nevertheless remains identical with Essence. Or in other words, our external reflection is not just dealing with something given, and positing something behind it, rather it is following the real underlying necessity, and hence is no longer a simple external reflection.

Now Hegel thinks himself justified in starting the Book on Essence with this conception of Essence as defined by these two related movements. He does this because as we saw the derivation of Essence is from the demise of Being, a demise which is the necessary positing of another particular being; hence the notions of necessity and positing are there from the start. Indeed, they have been with us in a sense since the category of Infinity, which showed deter-

Logic

minate beings to be linked in a process in which they came to be and passed away of necessity. Thus what the book of Essence is about is not the derivation of this inner necessity but the development of richer and richer concepts of it until we come to the full adequacy of external manifestation to inner necessity which will allow us to go over into the Concept.

In the *EL*, therefore, Hegel starts right off with Essence as Ground, and this is the first triad of the book. In the *WL* version, however, which is earlier, Hegel spells out the duality of the movement further, without however really deriving it, since he draws throughout on what he has already shown. This preliminary takes up the first chapter of the triad, Show (Schein).

In this first chapter of *WL*, Hegel makes the basic point of the two-directionality of Essence in two ways. First in a discussion of the idea of external reality as simple Show, that is, as something simply inessential, as a curtain of the unreal which has to be got behind in order to reach the really self-subsistent reality (whether or not we believe that this reality can be observed or reached – we may believe with Kant that the thing in itself is unknowable). This view cannot be maintained once we see that this external observed is not just given, but emanates from Essence, it is not just a barrier, a curtain before reality, but what is necessarily posited by reality, hence it is not separate from but integral to Essence itself. This shows that external reality is not mere Show, but the word Hegel uses here, 'Schein', enables him to maintain the same term, for this word is reminiscent of reflection; so he can speak of Essence as a 'Scheinen in ihm selbst' (reflection into itself).

The second way in which he makes the two-directional point is in a discussion of reflection, where his point is that the type of reflection which is central to Essence is a synthesis of outer and 'positing' reflection. There are references in this discussion to Kant's distinction between reflective and determining judgement. To mark the essential nature of reflection Hegel calls the category which issues from this dialectic 'determining reflection'.

With this basis, the dialectic of Essence begins, immediately in *EL* and after the introductory chapter in *WL*, to develop the vision of the systematic necessary connection of things.

Identity and Difference

We start first with the most elementary inadequate notions of reflective understanding, in which the persistence of posited being is thought of under the category of Identity and the connected ones of Difference, and non-contradiction. Hegel is here going to set aside the false reifications of the understanding which cannot accept that contradiction is inherent in reality and which thus shows that 'customary tenderness for things' (*WL*, II, 40) which is anxious not to attribute contradiction to them but rather to the understanding. For the understanding informed by this spirit, it seems the most elemen-

260

tary truth of logic that everything is identical with itself, and different from everything else: the 'Everything is what it is and not another thing' of Bishop Butler.

But for Hegel things cannot be so simple. True, everything is identical with itself, but it is also so that it is different from itself. The subject of identity, what remains identical through change, is now no longer the simple quality but the underlying essence. But Essence we have understood as the inner necessity which first posits one property, then cancels it in favour of another, and then still another, and so on. Hence, in Hegelian terms, the underlying identity is the difference, the self-differentiation, that which deploys the different properties in their necessary relation to each other. The nature of Essence is to manifest itself in these properties as necessarily related. It is the 'repulsion' (Abstoßen) of itself from itself, which at the same time is the reflection back into itself. Hence the identity of a thing with itself – so long as we are not talking about an entity which is defined in terms of a single property, but rather about something which can bear many properties[1] – properly understood bears on the underlying substrate which not only can undergo change, but is the necessary source of change itself. This identity thus has difference as an essential moment, and difference as reflected back into itself (through the necessary relation of the two terms) is also one with identity.

On this basis, Hegel moves in this section from the categories of Identity and Difference, through that of Diversity to the category of Opposition. There is not space to go into the detail of the derivation here, which in any case draws on the arguments deployed in the logic of Being. The upshot of this dialectic is that a characterization of things as merely diverse is shown to pass over into a characterization in which things are in essential, or polar opposition to each other. In polar opposition, each term is such that its interaction with another opposed entity is constitutive of its own reality. This is the case, for instance, with positive and negative electricity, or the north and south poles of a magnet. In addition to these examples, Hegel also mentions: light and darkness, virtue and vice, truth and error (*WL*, Remark 1 to the section on Contradiction, II, 55–6); organic and inorganic nature, and nature and spirit (*EL*, Addition 1 of § 119).

But it is not Hegel's intention to claim that the notion of diversity is without application. Of course, there is a diversity of things in the world. What he does have to claim, however, is that seeing things in the world as simply diverse, involving as it does seeing them as being merely contingently related to each other, is a superficial view. Understood at a more fundamental level, each thing is what it is only in a relation of contrastive and interactive opposition with another, which is thus 'its other' (*EL*, § 119).

---

[1] This alone provides the basis of informative identity statements, as Hegel points out in the second Remark to section A of this chapter (*WL*, II, 30).

Logic

Having drawn polar opposition from diversity, Hegel then goes on to draw out Contradiction, which of course was in there all along. For what is in opposition is founded on what negates it, and is thus in contradiction with itself and must go under. It is dependent on excluding what is an essential part of itself, its opposite. It cannot stand; both sides 'thus fall to the Ground' (gehen hiermit zu Grunde, *EL*, § 120).

Ground

On this pun we turn the corner to a new dialectical development. The discussion of identity and contradiction led us to look on Essence as the underlying necessity which determines the unfolding of external reality. We thus come to look on Essence as the ground of this reality. Later we shall see that it is of the essence of this inner necessity to manifest itself in what it deploys so that the division between Essence and external reality will be overcome again. But for the moment the division is there and the focus of our interest has shifted to the inner ground.

We have in a sense only now come to the dialectic of Essence, after a lengthy introduction. After approaching Essence through Being, and thus seeing Essence as postulate, we have at last completed the switch whereby we think of Essence as primary, and external reality as simply emanation from it.[1] Having taken Essence as our theme in Ground, we can then focus on the real purpose of this book which is to show that the underlying reality is nothing but self-manifesting thought as necessity.

The derivation of the category of contradiction gives the occasion for a couple of Remarks. One contains a blast against the principle of the excluded middle, which again seems utterly foolish taken on its own, but makes sense as an aside to the ontological views developed in the central text. The other Remark (no. 3, *WL*, ii, 58–62) expresses a central idea of Hegel's philosophy, the necessity of contradiction as the source of all life and movement. A basic prejudice of logic and common sense is

that contradiction is not as essential and inherent a determination as identity; but indeed, if it were a question of rank and the two determinations were to be held separate, we would have to take contradiction as the deeper and more essential. For as opposed to it identity is only the determination of the simple immediate, of dead Being; while contradiction is the root of all movement and life; only insofar as it has a contradiction in itself does anything move, or have impulse and activity.   (*WL*, ii, 58)

Hence all is in contradiction, and this sends it to ground, the pun whereby Hegel refers both to the demise of all finite things, and their necessary reference to an underlying ground, a necessity which deploys them. For contradiction means not just demise but necessary development. Contradic-

---

[1] This is the kind of switch we shall see later in the proofs for the existence of God, where what is second in ratio essendi is primary in ratio cognoscendi.

tion and necessity are closely linked. The whole point of this section can be seen as a rising above mere contingency to the point where the search for necessary relations can start with the dialectic of Ground. This is the properly philosophical task: 'The goal of philosophy is...to banish indifference and apprehend the necessity of things, so that the other will appear as standing over against *its* other' (*EL*, § 119, Addition 1).

With the category of Ground we come to look on reality not just as being there, but as grounded. Everything that exists has a reason, is the principle which underlies the concepts of this category; and Hegel quotes here the principle of sufficient reason of Leibniz. To accept this principle is to see that whatever is 'must be seen not as an immediate existent but as something posited' (*WL*, ii, 65). So with this category we have really passed beyond the sphere of Being: we now see everything as emanating from its ground. Hegel adds here, on mentioning the name of Leibniz, that this philosopher was quite right not to seek for sufficient reasons in mere mechanical, efficient causes, but rather in final causes.

And this, of course, expresses Hegel's goal as well; as we have seen in the above paragraphs and all along, the aim is to bring us to a vision of reality as the manifestation of necessity. It was the necessary links between opposites which brought us into the category of Ground, and it is the same necessary interconnectedness between elements of a system which will emerge from it. Hegel is here, once more, immersing himself in a certain range of generally accepted concepts, in order to show how they feed into his own ontological vision, and in the process enrich further our idea of this vision. In a sense, therefore, we will emerge from the discussion on Ground with the same basic notion of reality as necessary interconnection with which we entered, having added another range of ordinary concepts to those which have been shown to be properly understood only in the light of Hegel's ontology. But in another sense, this vision is further developed in this section; for it becomes clearer that we are dealing with a system of related beings, a totality of external being which is systematically and necessarily related.

This comes out in the argument.[1] Starting out simply with the concept of ground or sufficient reason, we explore the contradiction implicit in its application. The contradiction consists in this: in order to have a really sufficient reason for something, we have to outline conditions which are identical with or which entail the event or thing to be explained. But a reason which amounts to the same thing as what is explained is not satisfactory as an explanation: it fails to be informative. Hegel takes to task in his comments here empty explanations, like that which attributes the effects of opium to a *virtus dormitiva*, although some of the examples he picks hardly seem to fit this

---

[1] I am following the line of thought in *WL* here, that in *EL* is somewhat different but turns on the same basic contradiction.

particular criticism. To be informative an explanation must give us a ground which is not identical with what we are explaining. But in doing so, we lose the sufficiency of the reason; for ground and grounded are now no longer the same, and hence they are only contingently linked. It cannot be sufficient to give *A*, the contingent cause of *B*, as its ground; for *A*, by itself, is not sufficient for *B*, but only *A* in combination with the causal connection by which it brings about *B*.

The dilemma, or contradiction, in which we find ourselves with the notion of ground is thus this: to the extent that our citing of a ground is informative, it will be distinct from the entity to be explained (Hegel calls this 'real ground'), but then it will be insufficient; on the other hand, if it is sufficient, it will no longer be distinct from the explicandum, and then it will be empty and uninformative (what Hegel calls 'formal ground').

This dilemma does not seem difficult to resolve for contemporary thinkers, in so far as it can be recognized at all. There do seem to be points in common with the notions of explanation current in contemporary philosophy of science: a valid explanation must be one in which the explicandum can be deduced from the explicans; while at the same time, Hume's dictum of the contingency of the relation between cause and effect must be adhered to. But these two requirements can be met by the standard form of explanation according to many writers in the philosophy of science, where we explain *B* by the combination of two premisses: that *A* occurred, and that *A* is followed by *B*. This satisfies both the condition of sufficiency, which here is interpreted as requiring a deductive relation between explicans and explicandum, and the condition of informativeness, that the cause and effect be contingently re-lated. The latter is satisfied in so far as the major premiss, the general law, is contingent.

But this modern interpretation of the requirements of sufficiency and informativeness is not Hegel's. If this were not already evident, it would certainly become so in the discussion of the relation of condition to ground, which is somewhat similar to that between particular condition and general correlation in the canonical explanation, and which provides the transition out of Ground. For the canonical explanation of today's philosophy of science is still radically incomplete in Hegel's eyes; and this precisely because it is contingent. Because '*A* leads to *B*,' is contingent, it calls for a further explana-tion: why does *A* lead to *B*?; And a canonical explanation of this will call for a further such explanation and so on ad infinitum; And a similar infinite regress opens out behind the condition *A*, once we ask why it occurred. (Cf. *WL*, ii, 96.)

Hegel is looking, as we have seen before, for an explanation which is complete in a sense that is thought impossible by contemporary philosophy of science, a deduction of necessity which is not grounded on what are ultimately

Essence

contingent premisses, but which is necessary through and through. We have seen the idea of this as that of a circle of necessary connections, in which the starting point, which at the beginning is just posited and hence unsupported, ends up being derived. This is obviously the vision of reality as thoroughgoing necessity which is being forged out of the dialectical transitions of the *Logic*, and it is this which gives Hegel his criterion of sufficiency. This, of course, seriously weakens his argument from the point of view of a contemporary reader, for it amounts to assuming a crucial aspect of what he wants to prove, but it seems difficult to deny that Hegel is proceeding on this criterion here, as he does in similar passages elsewhere.[1]

But while it might appear gratuitous to assume a criterion of this kind if we raised the issue of scientific explanation out of the blue, as it were, there is some justification for it in the context of Hegel's argument in the *Logic*. For we have supposedly already established that reality forms a system of changes which are powered by necessity. But if changes come about by necessity, a fully adequate account of their grounds must show the necessary connection. This is what justifies us in demanding something more than the deducibility from general law of the canonical theory of explanation.

And once we grant the legitimacy of this demand we can appreciate the dilemma; if complete explanation must be complete in the sense that one can no longer ask why?, and if this, as is evident, is incompatible with our relying on unexplained contingent premisses, then it does appear that the two criteria, of sufficiency and informativeness, are in a head-on clash.

And in fact the only way of solving this dilemma, if it can be solved at all, is by some solution along the lines that Hegel proposes: contingent relations can be observed to hold between particular things and events whereby some can be picked out as grounds for others, but the whole system of which these form part is structured by necessary relations.

Contingency can be thought to exist in the interstices of necessity in one of two ways: either we think of the contingency as just apparent, the result of our looking at just these two things or events, whereas when we see the whole we can see why they must be related that way – analogously the correlation of two features in an organism may be just brute fact as long as we concentrate on these two features alone, but may receive a fuller explanation (albeit, of course, still not one of thoroughgoing necessity) if we look at them in the context of the whole organism. Thus we would claim that the fact that animate beings are mortal might appear as just a contingent correlation if we focus simply on these beings, but can be seen to flow of necessity from the nature of things once we grasp the correct ontological vision.

Or else, contingency might be thought to be real, but contained: the

---

[1] E.g., the discussion in Chapter III of the *PhG*.

general furniture of the world, that there is matter, body, gravity; that there are different kinds of animate being, that men exist, that human history takes the general lines that it does; all this is so of necessity. But particular facts: that there are islands half way across the Atlantic, or that the value of G is 32 feet per second per second; these matters of detail could be different.

Hegel seems to have held to the existence of both kinds of intersticial contingency. The two can be brought together under the general formula which would consider the basic structures of the universe, what is described by categorial concepts and their connections, to be necessary; while descriptions couched in other, less general terms either relate features of this structure in ways which obscure their necessity, or apply to detailed aspects of reality which can vary relative to the structure.

If this second kind of contingency seems difficult to reconcile with the thesis of thoroughgoing necessity, the answer is that the structure of things is such that *all* the categories of the Logic have application. Things can be described as Determinate Being, as Quantity, and so on. The dialectical passing beyond these categories does not show them to be empty, but to be inadequate, to call for supplementation by others. And hence they apply. Reality is also made up of determinate beings, quanta, and so on. As such reality also has its contingent aspect. This can be reconciled with thoroughgoing systematic necessity by the thesis that such contingent facts and relations hold within a certain framework which itself is necessary. And it must be so reconciled once we see that all the categories must hold. For then contingency, inseparable from determinate being, quantity, and so on, exists of necessity.

Now in relation to the solution of the dilemma of sufficient reasons, these two notions of intersticial contingency would involve either the view that the contingent relation of particular ground to particular grounded can be transposed into a necessary one by supplementing it with an understanding of the system of which it is a part, or else the view that the grounds of particular details must remain contingently related to them, but that the realities concerned characterized in their essential properties are grounded in necessity. In either case, we move from a superficial contingency to an underlying necessity as we move from detail to system.

And this is Hegel's solution to the dilemma of Ground. There are particular relations of ground to thing grounded which taken on their own are contingent, but underlying them is the systematic necessity of the whole. As long as we remain thus at the level of the particular details, we are necessarily dealing with insufficient grounds. The principle of sufficient reason, however, is satisfied in the fact that they take their place in the whole by necessity. Hence the only sufficient explanation which is based on thoroughgoing necessity is one which refers us to the whole system. And in this case explicandum and explicans are no longer identified on their own as particular elements, but are related to the whole. The explanation of these elements is by the whole of which they are parts. So that the explicandum ceases to be distinct from the explicans, rather it is incorporated in it.

Thus the mortality of men may seem at first contingent to us. But when we see it as grounded in the contradiction of spirit, which must be embodied in finitude, and yet must go beyond it, we see its necessity. But at the same time the necessary process of spirit by which we explain mortality is not distinct from it. Mortality, as well as birth, is one of its phases. [1]

But nevertheless this explanation has none of the vices of *virtus dormitiva* explanations for to grasp this global necessity is to grasp a system of differentiated elements which are related to each other. It is thus richly informative, and includes a number of particular relationships, which taken on their own appear as contingent. In this way, the necessity required by the principle of sufficient reason is combined with the real differentiation of terms in the relationship of ground to grounded without which explanations are uninformative.

The notion of reality as a total system of necessarily related elements gives another aspect to the dialectic of identity and difference above. As a whole (ein Ganzes) the system of related elements is one, it reflects identity, and the explanation of the whole by the whole is one in which ground and grounded are identical. But as a system of different elements, and moreover elements which are separately existing objects, the system has otherness, difference; ground and grounded are different entities which are related in this way. Reality is necessarily both. Without the necessary link which is identity, what exists would have no ground, it would be without foundation, hence would not exist. But without difference, real differentiation of elements, there could also be no existence, because pure being as we saw is equivalent to pure nothing. And difference requires real separately existing objects, external reality, objects which exist apart from each other, hence in time and space. Without difference, there would be no real independent existence (Bestehen).

We can look at this whole also through the concepts of mediation and immediacy. Unlike the sphere of Being, the elements of this system are all mediated; each is posited, brought about, grounded by the others. Mediation

---

[1] In ordinary life says Hegel in *EL* (§ 121, Addition) we often use explanations which fail to distinguish explicandum and explicans, as for instance, when we explain some electrical phenomenon by reference to electricity. Nothing is wrong with these explanations in the context of ordinary life. But this kind of reason is unsatisfactory for philosophy, because the ground is not yet articulated in a whole whose structure is necessary. Ground has as yet no 'an und für sich bestimmten Inhalt'. We have not yet really got to what is active (thätig) and productive (hervorbringend, cf. § 122). Hence at this ordinary level anything goes. A reason can be found for anything.

The argument is different in *EL* than in *WL*, and the transition turns rather on the unsatisfactoriness of this ordinary giving of reasons in which good grounds can be found for and against anything depending on which description of it you select.

Logic

is thus universal. But the system as a whole is not mediated, it is the locus of all mediation, but it depends on nothing outside itself. It is thus immediate. But its immediacy is not like that of the first categories of Being. This is an immediacy which is founded on mediation, which has overcome mediation in the sense that it closes the circle of a set of mediations back on itself. It is an immediacy of a self-subsistent system, which suffices to itself. Thus Hegel speaks of it as 'grundlos' (*WL*, II, 99–100). It is 'the restoration of immediacy or Being, but of Being in so far as it is mediated through the suppression [Aufhebung] of mediation' (*EL*, § 122).

This says Hegel is the category of Existence. The use of this latin-derived word is designed to trade on the etymological reference to externalization. For what Hegel wants to emphasize in this solution to the dilemma of Ground is that this category is not to be seen as designating something inner and hidden which lies behind reality. When we think of reality as grounded, we think of it as reposing on something else; and this may lead us and has often led men to think of that on which they are grounded as some hidden inner basis. This is the more likely, when they reflect that particular external events and things which are candidates for ground are insufficient. Hegel's point is that what is lacking in the particular conditions of an event to make the sufficient reason is not something behind this event and hidden, but the necessity of the whole system of which it is a part. Or to put the point differently, the inner basis of things is not some entity behind, but a necessity which finds its full and only expression in external reality, precisely in the necessary connections of this reality as system. The full understanding of Ground shows us that there is nothing behind external reality. But this is not to say that we are at the starting point where we confront simple being. By the fact that we have grasped the pervasiveness of necessity we now see what is out there as posited, as brought about by this necessity. Hence we see things not only as external reality but as coming out into external reality, as unfolding, coming to be in their externality in conformity to the inner formula of necessity. And this is what gives force to the notion of *Existence*.

Hence with the transition to existence, Hegel has taken the crucial step in the task of this book, which is to make us see Essence, as that which underlies external reality, not as something hidden behind, but as fully manifest necessity. It will remain in the following sections of this book to enrich this notion of systematic necessity, but the problem here has been posed. In this sense, the dialectic of Ground represents an advance. True, this notion of the necessary relation of elements was present before, and was essential to earlier arguments of this book, and especially to the derivation of Ground. But in this section there has emerged more clearly the idea of a whole of systematically related elements, and the accompanying idea of an inner basis whose nature it is to be fully manifest externally. These are crucial themes which need and will

Essence

get a lot of further development, but which are here adumbrated. Hence Existence

is the indefinite multitude of existents as reflected into themselves, which at the same time equally throw light upon one other – which, in short, are relative, and form a world of reciprocal dependence, and of infinite interconnection between grounds and consequents.[1]   (*EL*, § 123).

But this mass of existents, though related to each other in a whole, is not yet the full manifestation of necessity which alone is an adequate ground of things. This is what now must be derived.

In this motley play of the world, if we may so call the sum of what exists, there is nowhere a firm footing to be found; everything bears an aspect of relativity, conditioned by and conditioning something else. The reflective understanding makes it its business to elicit and trace these connections running out in every direction; but the question of a final end remains unanswered through all this. Thus the demand of conceiving reason takes it beyond this position of mere relativity with the further evolution of the Logical Idea.   (loc. cit.)[2]

In the section on Ground in *WL* Hegel takes up the discussion of the distinctions between form and essence, form and matter, form and content. The latter two are discussed at a somewhat later point in *EL*. But this is not a substantial revision, for Hegel's task here as usual is to show how his basic idea emerges out of an examination of these distinctions, and in the process to break down the fixed oppositions of the understanding. There is as such no single point at which these distinctions must be taken up.

Hegel will go on to develop the idea of manifest necessity through the category of Appearance. This is understood, like Existence, as a verbal noun rather than a simply adjectival one: appearance is that which appears, that which steps out into exteriority. It will not therefore be contrasted with a reality which is more essential and which is hidden.

Thing

But before going on to this discussion there is one more important category of common sense and traditional philosophy which Hegel has to have it out with, that is the Thing. We are speaking here of the thing which possesses properties, which is the bearer of properties. We had not come to it in the sphere of Being, for there we had Quality which was one with Being: the Something ceased to be once the quality changed. So that the relation of 'having' could not be ascribed there.[3] But here we have come to the idea of a

---

[1] William Wallace translation.   [2] William Wallace translation (amended).

[3] (*EL* § 125) Hegel cannot resist remarking here that in many European languages 'have' is used to form the past tense, hence is connected with 'aufgehobenes Sein', and hence with *Wesen*, which as we saw is also related to the past participle of to be.

Logic

totality of interconnected elements, a multiplicity of properties bound together, hence of a unity which has properties, but can survive alteration in them, hence to the relation of having.

Not the notion of the thing which has 'properties' (which word also is resonant of the having relation, and in German as well as English with the word '*Eigenschaft*') is a conception of totality which Hegel must oppose. And this for two reasons.

The first can be put in three related ways: first, Hegel's idea of totality as we have seen is of elements which are inseparably related and yet in opposition, but the ordinary notion of thing with properties is rather that of the peaceful coexistence of different properties in the thing. Secondly, Hegel sees contradiction, that is the opposition within the inseparable, as necessary as the source of movement, becoming, while the notion of thing with properties is rather that of stable co-existence. Thirdly, the fact that the different elements of a totality are related by contradiction which is in turn the ground of necessary relations is what warrants our seeing the world of real existent things as grounded in thought, as ultimately emanating from subjectivity, whereas the model of thing with properties offers us a view of external, material reality as reposing ultimately on itself, as not requiring appeal to something other than itself to be consistent and self-subsistent.

The model of thing with properties is thus an alternative model to Hegel's whether it is applied to particular things or extended to the whole universe, which in this sense can be seen as a single thing with different aspects. It is one in which external, material existence suffices to itself, since all its different aspects can be seen to fit together coherently in a unity which is simply external material reality writ large. Whereas for Hegel the truth that this was not so, that external material reality emanates from thought and hence spirit, that it cannot be understood as self-supporting but really is grounded on thought, this appears in, indeed *is* the fact that it is not self-consistent, that it is a relation of aspects which at once require and oppose each other. This is what makes it contradictory, and hence destined to go under, and undergo perpetual change. And this is why reality can only coherently be grasped as a necessary chain, or circle of beings through which alone this contradiction can find resolution. In other words, the problem posed by the contradictoriness of external reality can only be solved by seeing this reality as part of a larger whole, as the manifestation of an inner necessity, hence as not self-dependent, but dependent on thought, which Hegel identifies with this inner necessity, and on what later in the Logic will be seen as spirit.

In a sense, therefore, the issue about the coherence of our conception of the thing with properties, is the issue about idealism. But only in a very special sense: for there are lots of non-materialists, like Kant, who are attacked in this dialectical dissolution of the thing. And moreover, Marxism on the other side is a doctrine which while it claims to be anti-idealist builds on this Hegelian insight of universal contradiction and hence movement. The conception of the thing with properties is the quintessence of stable, identical thought, which cannot grasp things in their essential movement, and which for Marxists is at its height in the bourgeois era, the era of maximum 'reification'. Perhaps there is after all more than a bad pun in the fact that this category makes such use of the relation of having and the notion of 'property'.[1] But the idealism that is being defended here is clearly not a dualistic kind, nor one that would resolve dualism by affirming spirit alone, but rather the absolute idealism of Hegel. It is clear that this form of idealism cannot consort with the conception of totality which is implied in the thing with properties, as a stable, self-subsistent ensemble.

The second reason why Hegel must take up the cudgels against this notion is that it tends to solve the problem of the unity of the object over against its multiple properties, by seeing this unity as a substrate, moreover as one which is unknowable. It seems a plausible argument of traditional philosophy that whatever we observe, we are always observing properties. The unity which ties them all together is a *je-ne-sais-quoi* underlying them, not itself observable. This notion of an unknown substrate develops into the *Ding-an-sich* in Kant's philosophy, and it is in this form that Hegel takes it up in this section. But what all other forms of substrate concept share with Kant's, and which Hegel objects to, is the aspect of unknowability, which puts some of reality effectively beyond the reach of spirit, and hence accepts an unabsorbed dualism. This is, of course, against the most basic motivations of Hegel's entire philosophical endeavour. Hence his (as one might have thought) rather excessive barb against Kant (*WL*, II, 111–12) that this notion of the distinction between thing in itself and phenomenon contradicts the consciousness of freedom.

But Hegel seems to think that this recourse to the unknowable substrate comes naturally out of the conception of the thing, as an attempt to solve the problem of its coherent unity. For Hegel there is such a problem as we saw above in the discussions of the second chapter of the *PhG*, and indeed, an insoluble one. And this is just the essence of his case, for in Hegel's view such an insoluble contradiction holds precisely between the elements which are united in a totality, as we have just seen. Hegel's claim that there is an unavoidable contradiction in the notion of a thing with properties is no stronger than his thesis that finite things in general are contradictory. We cannot follow out his argument here, which covers some of the same ground as the second chapter of the *PhG*, and relies in part on certain current notions of the time, e.g., a physics founded on the notion of various kinds of 'matters'.

Where Hegel does uncover contradiction is in the various ways in which the

[1] Cf. Eugene Fleischmann, *La Science Universelle*, Paris, Plon, 1968, p. 166.

Logic

unity of the thing has been conceived in the modern epistemological tradition which starts with Descartes and continues through the empiricists, and from which Kant only partly freed himself. In this too contemplative tradition in which the subject was not seen as being at grips with the world, but just as being affected by it, the unity of the thing was always in danger of flying apart into a number of separate data of sense. So that it was either conceived as an unknown substrate, or as something constructed; but never as really experienced.

Hegel's basic *démarche* in both versions is to trade on the incoherencies of the notions of the thing derived from this modern epistemology, very much as in the *PhG*. The *Ding-an-sich* is first considered: it is the unity which is reflected into a multiplicity of properties in its relation to other things, principally the knowing mind. But its properties cannot be separated from the thing in itself, for without properties it is indistinguishable from all the others. We might therefore say that there is only one thing in itself, but then it has nothing with which to interact, and it was this interaction with others, which gave rise to the multiplicity of properties. If there is only one thing-in-itself, it must of itself go over into the multiplicity of external properties. If we retain the notion of many, however, we reach the same result, for the many can only be distinguished by some difference of properties, hence the properties of each cannot be separated from it, it cannot be seen as simple identity.

Thus the notion of a *Ding-an-sich* as unknowable, simple substrate, separate from the visible properties which only arise in its interaction with others, cannot be sustained. The properties are essential to the thing, whether we look at it as one or many. And so Hegel goes over to consider the view which makes the thing nothing but these properties, which sees it as the simple coexistence of the properties. Here is where the theories of reality as made up of 'matters' naturally figure in Hegel's discussion.

But the particular thing cannot just be reduced to a mere coexistence of properties. For each of these properties exists in many things. In order to single out a particular instance of any property, we have to invoke another property dimension. If we want to single out *this* blue we have to distinguish it from others, identify it by its shape, or its position in time and space, or its relation to other things. But to do this is to introduce the notion of the multipropertied particular, for we have something now which is blue and round, or blue and to the left of the grey, or blue and occurring today, or something of the sort.

The particular is necessarily multipropertied, and this multipropertied particular is essential to our experience. For otherwise the only entities which could be distinguished would be properties themselves, these would become in effect the things of our universe. But properties cannot be distinguished without occurring in contrast, and to occur in contrast means to occur in

272

particulars; either as blue and green occur in different patches, or as shape and colour can be distinguished because they are contrasting dimensions of particulars. A world of qualities without particulars is inconceivable because there would be no communication between these qualities, they would not exist in the same world, hence could not be contrasted, hence would not be qualities, which requires determination through the negation of others.

Hegel uses this necessity of contrast to bring the argument back to the initial and he thinks insoluble problem, how to think together the thing and its properties without incoherence. The 'this' cannot be done away with, but nor can the multiplicity of properties. The thing is thus in contradiction with itself. 'The thing is nothing else but this contradiction itself; that is why it is Appearance' (*WL*, II, 121). Hence Hegel has vindicated his basic idea of the contradictory nature of a reality which is a totality of elements which require each other, and yet are in opposition to each other: here properties which must exist together (for the thing cannot be done away with) and yet which cannot cohere. He has vindicated it against the static, reified view of the thing as self-subsistent ensemble. And hence he has shown that the material thing is essentially that which breaks up (sich auflöst), and goes over into appearance. By this he means that the thing is not self-subsistent entity, that it is not only mortal, but that its existence is the unfolding of a totality which can only exist as the manifestation of inner necessity, not as an ensemble of elements on its own. That is, the elements only fit together, because they are opposed and contradictory, as the unfolding moments of a totality which is ruled by necessity. Hence the break-up of the thing is not just its impending, necessary demise, but also reflects its non-self-sufficiency, the fact that it is the manifestation of something else, inner necessity. And this means that it is not just there, but is deployed. It is made to *appear*. This is what underlies the transition to Appearance.[1]

II: APPEARANCE

In Appearance the principal development is of the idea of relation. The force of 'appearance' here is that we see things as appear*ing*, as posited, as coming to manifestation through necessity, rather than as just being there 'immediately'. To see things as appearance is to see them not as just reposing on themselves (auf sich selbst beruhend), but as moments of a larger whole (*EL*, § 131, Addition), and hence to see them as in necessary relation to others.

Reality seen as appearance is something higher than immediate, independent beings. This comes as a surprise to ordinary consciousness, but that is because it understands appearance as a screen before reality. In fact there is

[1] This is already made in *WL*, where Ding is the first part of the second triad, rather than the last part of the first, as in *EL* – another sign of the essential looseness in the links of the Logic.

nothing behind. To say that Essence is appearance is to say that it *must* appear, 'that essence does not remain behind or beyond appearance', but goes out into existence. (*EL*, § 131 Addition.)

Hegel's use of 'appearance' thus expresses the exact opposite of Kant's. Instead of pointing by contrast to the essential hiddenness of the trans-cendent real, it rather expresses the essential manifest-ness of all reality. Seeing reality as Appearance for Hegel is seeing it as the *appearing* of inner necessity, as deployed in order to manifest a necessity which is deter-mined by nature to become fully manifest. Thus the point of this category is the central Hegelian one that the real is not 'just there' but is posited, deployed in fulfilment of a rational formula. Thus what is afoot here is the development of a notion of Essence as a necessity which must come to full manifestation in external reality. This will come triumphantly to light in the third section of Essence, which Hegel calls Reality (Wirklichkeit). Here we will be laying the groundwork for it through the idea of necessary relatedness.

The relatedness discussed is between two kinds of terms: first, relatedness between the different elements of the totality, which must ultimately come to exhibit necessity; and second the relation between the underlying reality and the external totality of elements. These two forms of relation develop to-gether, in that the less necessity appears in the totality of external reality, the more we must distinguish this external reality from the underlying essence, in which all things are in unity. In other words, since we are ultimately dealing with a necessarily related totality, the non-manifestness of this necessity in external reality must go along with a distinction between this external reality and the underlying essence. Conversely, the greater manifestation of the necessity will go along with a fuller identification of reality and essence. These two developments will occur together in this section.

With Appearance, we start again from a putative distinction between essence and manifestation, and overcome it. But unlike in earlier phases, we are now dealing with reality as totality, and as related totality, and as a totality which is not simply stable coexistence of elements, but undergoes change, development, has inner opposition. So the inner essence is not any longer a thing-like reality, as with the thing in itself. It is rather an inner formula of relatedness. But as inner it is still separate from external reality, and hence is an *inner* formula, not yet the manifestation of essence in the system of reality, which we shall see in *Wirklichkeit*. We have to overcome this opposition of inner and outer, which will in fact be the last opposition of the section, but everything else builds up to it.

In order to set the stage for the consideration of necessary relatedness, Hegel takes us through a preceding dialectic which is different in *WL* and *EL*. In the latter, he leads up to it by a discussion of content and form, the substance of which comes earlier in *WL.* In this earlier work, the lead-up is through a discussion of laws.

In both cases, the relevance of the lead-up is the same: appearance for traditional philosophy is in contrast with something more fundamental. But at this stage, as we have seen, this more fundamental cannot be thing-like, but must be the underlying relatedness. What we are dealing with at this stage therefore is a pair of alternative ways of conceiving this relatedness as beyond or underlying the external reality. One such way is to contrast the manifold of heterogeneous external reality, with the inner relatedness of laws which underlie it. We see the realm of laws as 'the tranquil image of the existing or appearing world' (*WL*, II, 127). Another way is to contrast the content of intuition with the form in which the heterogeneous manifold of intuition is seen as related. The former is the way of the *WL*, the latter of the *EL*.

In both cases, the task is to show that this distinction cannot stand up: that form and content are inseparable, that each turns into the other, or that the inner identity or relatedness of the law cannot be separated from the real external manifold. In the first case, the Hegelian reading of these terms 'form' and 'content' is enough to ensure the transition. In *WL* reference is made to another Hegelian theme, the inadequacy of contingent laws.

For considered as a 'calm reflection' of the world of phenomena, laws do not have the same content. The real events which happen in conformity with law have a host of other particular characteristics which the law does not explain. There is thus a gap between the two. In addition, in the law itself, there is only a contingent relation between the two terms: for instance, in the law of falling bodies, there is no necessity linking distances to the square of the times. But, on Hegel's view, the point of the law is to explain, and the explanation is not complete as long as there is any contingency in it, as we saw. Thus speaking of the law of falling bodies:

The law governing this is known empirically, and in so far it is merely immediate; and a proof is still required, that is, a mediation for cognition, that the law not only operates but is necessary. The law as such does not contain this proof and its objective necessity.[1]
(*WL*, II, 129)

In both cases, the law is unsatisfactory as a candidate for the underlying reality behind the Appearance; for it neither really underlies everything, nor does it achieve the inner relatedness which it is supposed to. It is both too inner (because not having the full content of the outer) and too outer (because not rising to necessity).

Just as in the *PhG* (Chapter III) we can note that this kind of necessity is not what we demand of our scientific laws, and it is no objection to the law of falling bodies that it does not achieve this. But Hegel is here frying other fish. For we have already deduced necessary relatedness in the previous phases.

---

[1] Johnston and Struthers translation II, 134.

Hence law is seen against this background, as a way of conceiving the necessary relatedness underlying the phenomena. As such it fails. Of course, it may be perfectly valid as a tool of empirical science. All we know is that it cannot be the final word and stopping point of our quest for a valid ontology.

What emerges out of this dialectic in *WL* is the unity of the underlying relatedness expressed in the law and the external reality of which the law is true. And this gives us the idea of a totality of elements which while separate from each other are essentially related. The distinction between essence and externality thus becomes rather one between the elements of this external reality and their relatedness. The dialectic of Relation (Verhältnis) allows Hegel to go through a series of conceptions of this relatedness and show their inadequacy, and at the same time to underscore the unity between elements and relatedness which is also a unity between inner and outer.

The section therefore goes back and forth between dualisms which contrast inner and outer, and dualisms which contrast elements and the necessity binding the elements. At first we have both, with a dualism between the external world of the manifold and the inner law, which is a connection between the elements of the manifold. Now the emphasis shifts to the dualism: elements/necessity, only to end up once more with a pure opposition of inner and outer which cannot but collapse.

Whole and part

The first stage of the opposition elements/connection is the relation of whole and part. Hegel plays a dialectic with this by showing that each requires the other, in the sense that the whole is only whole if in relation to parts, and the parts only parts if in relation to a whole. If the parts are seen on their own, they are no longer parts, but become wholes. This, he says, (*WL*, II, 143–4) is one way of looking at the Kantian antinomy of endless divisibility: we take the parts, and by looking at them on their own make them into wholes, which in turn must be divided, and so forth endlessly. But we should rather realize that parts are only parts in relation to the whole.

Yet, on the other hand, parts and whole are not identical, each only exists in opposition to the other, and each in order to exist for itself, must as it were reduce the other to satellite status, dependent on itself: the whole must hold the parts as subordinate elements to be self-subsistent, the parts have to break free to be self-subsistent. But then each in achieving success would negate itself: the whole would melt its parts into one, and thus not be a whole (which it only is in contrast), the parts would break free and hence not be parts.

So whole and parts are each as terms related essentially to their other. Each is only itself in relation to another which is its negation. Each refers us to the other. This inner relation of the two takes us beyond a simple conception of the part–whole relation where we think of the whole and the assemblage of parts coexisting peacefully as two ways of looking at the same thing. Looked at either way, we have a contradiction, says Hegel, in which both terms are involved. The idea that there are two optional ways of looking at the same reality really supposes that this reality is stable, and simply admits of two descriptions; whereas the contradictions in it that we see by looking at part and whole show that it is in movement, that it is constantly going over from unity to multiplicity and back again. But this relation of exteriorization is that of force and its manifestation. It is the whole seen dynamically as inner force which produces external reality as its manifestation.

This transition to force reminds us of that in the *PhG* which also came from an attempt to unify two opposites into a stable view of the object. Hegel's argument is that if the wholes are really out of subsistent parts, then the whole is just our reading of the ensemble of parts, but then there are no real parts. And similarly, if we think of the whole as real, then the parts are just our abstraction, and then there is no real whole. For there to be real wholes out there which nevertheless have parts, there have to be elements which are bound together by interaction. Interaction itself will come up later in the next section, but the idea of a dynamic reality, in which different external elements are really linked into a unity outside our own subjective grouping is what is at stake here.

This brings us to force and its manifestations, whereby we can see the external manifold as issuing from some underlying force; so that it is not only unquestionably manifold, but unquestionably also bound together in a totality.

But the notion of force is inadequate in its turn to the vision of totality we are looking for. Force, as Hegel reminds us sternly, is inadequate as a way of representing *Geist* (this is directed, inter alia, against Herder). It proceeds blindly, and not as purpose does, towards a rational end. And it is bound up with this that forces are limited, they have particular contents and particular conditions. Thus we can think of a given force, like magnetism, but this presupposes specific kinds of substrate, like iron (*EL*, § 136, Addition 1). And iron has a host of other properties which are not essentially related to magnetism. Similarly, forces require certain conditions to manifest themselves. Hegel calls this the requirement of another force to 'solicit' the first; and we have a dialectic which is again reminscent of Chapter III of the *PhG*.

Thus to see the world as the manifestation of forces, is to see it as the joint product of many forces, which are complexly related as 'soliciting' or triggering each other. Hegel as in the *PhG* goes through an involved dance with the forces which are solicited and yet soliciting at the same time. The background of this dialectic is a terminology which had some currency at the time. But the basis of the transition is more fundamentally that we have got to a stage where we cannot allow a diverse multiplicity of forces any more than we could allow a diversity of qualities earlier, in the opening phases of Essence. We have reached a point where we are dealing with essentially related totality, and any category which cannot cope with this has to be gone beyond. Hence the relation of force to the 'soliciting' force, which is its precondition, is essentially that for Hegel force itself as a thrust towards some external manifestation can be seen as determining in turn its own triggering conditions. Instead of just being the impulse behind a given manifestation it must be seen as that which brings this manifestation out of the conditions which determine it, it is the inner link between conditions and manifestation.

But putting together this idea of totality and the newly arrived at notion of force, we have a new way of looking at the totality, viz., as the manifestation, the external expression, of an inner link. It is this notion of deployment outwards of reality which was present in Existence and Appearance, but which has now a much more adequate expression in a category which incorporates the notion of force. External reality is expression, a manifestation of essential connection.

Inner and outer

This effectively puts an end to the duality posed in terms of elements and their link, for now the elements only exist as expression of the linkage. But it remains to do away with the last possible semblance of duality, between the inner necessity and its manifestation. This would be a pure distinction between inner and outer in that, unlike with the case of law above, there is now absolutely no difference in content between inner and outer, for the latter is nothing but an expression of the former. They have the same content.

But this kind of duality is untenable on Hegel's terms, and we have now got to the point where he can show us this. As we saw in Chapter III, the conception of reality as manifest necessity makes it such that there is a link of equivalence between the state where reality is purely inner, in the sense of hidden, and reality is purely outer, in the sense of external to itself, not inwardly related by any link of necessity. The more that the essence is hidden (inner), the more reality is purely externally related (outer). This is what Hegel calls the immediate unity of inner and outer. Conversely, the more essential reality is externalized in the sense of expressed, the more the relatedness of reality is developed, and the more inwardness it has. This is the mediated unity. Hegel gives other examples of the immediate unity. A child is one in which humanity is merely inner, undeveloped; and for that reason he has to receive his humanity in training from the outside. This relation of inner and outer is predicated on the Hegelian idea of reality as manifestation of necessity, relatedness.

Hence any attempt to separate inner from outer cannot but make the outer external in the sense of no longer intro-reflected, and hence open a rift

Essence

between the two. Once there is a rift between the two, we are in the realm of the immediate unity in which one simply goes over impotently into the other. But if they are really the same, if they have the same content, then there can no longer be any distinction between them.

Hence in this realm where inner is really one with outer, the inner is such that it must express itself. Its nature is to reveal itself (sich offenbaren), to make itself evident. To say that inner and outer are the same is to say that reality is essentially self-manifesting. And this is what Hegel means by Reality (Wirklichkeit), that which is a union of Essence and Appearance, which is external and yet fully manifestation of the essential. Reality is now such that

since its content and its form are completely identical, it is nothing else *an und für sich* but the fact of its self-externalization [sich äußern]. It is the revelation of its essence, so that this essence simply consists in this, that it is that which reveals itself.   (*WL*, II, 155)

III: REALITY

With *Wirklichkeit* we get to an important category of Hegel's philosophy. It is external reality which is fully expression of the essence, and external reality which has nothing hidden behind it, because it is full manifestation of what is essential. It is the unity of Being and reflection, Being and Essence. Existence was in a sense already this, as appearance, but this says Hegel was only their immediate unity; for it was mediated out of Ground, and we had yet to show the dialectic of outer reality and inner relatedness. Existence 'comes from the ground and falls to the ground' (kommt aus dem Grunde und geht zu Grunde, *EL*, § 142).[1] But *Wirklichkeit* is the posited unity of Being and Essence, it is the relation which has developed to identity (das mit sich identisch gewordene Verhältnis). 'It is thus exempted from transition [dem Übergehen entnommen] and its externality is its energizing [Energie]. In that energizing it is reflected into itself; its determinate existence [Dasein] is only the manifestation of itself and not of something else' (loc. cit.).[2]

The Addition to the same § of the *EL* goes on to excoriate the common sense way of talking of *Wirklichkeit* as separate from the idea. On the contrary, *Wirklichkeit* is the unity of inner and outer and is hence the really rational.[3]

The section on *Wirklichkeit* develops this idea of manifest necessity, manifested essence, through two main dialectics which are common to both versions: the first is a study of modal terms, of necessity, actuality and possibility. This is

[1] William Wallace translation. Wallace has managed to capture Hegel's pun here: 'gehen zu Grunde' ordinarily means to collapse or go to ruin. But in Hegelian terms the demise of a thing is also its return from particularity to the life of the totality which sustains it, i.e., to its ground.
[2] William Wallace translation (amended).
[3] p. 321, cf. famous quote about the rational and the real.

279

Logic

destined to vindicate for actuality the status of manifested necessity, and also at the same time to explicate the relation of necessity to contingency. We finally, therefore, come to grips here with the notion of necessity which has been underlying Essence all along. The time has come now to take these modal categories into our system. We must show that they can not be seen as with Kant as touching not reality but just its relation to our faculty of knowledge. Nor can possibility be allowed the last word as with Leibniz for whom this world was only the best of all possible, and was hence in an important sense contingent.

The second dialectic is one which finally goes into the three substantive relations which Kant singled out for a special role in the analogies of experience, substance–accident, cause–effect, and interaction, in order to derive them as having their place in the reality which has been shown to be a totality governed by necessity, and which yet points beyond to subjectivity, and hence to the Concept. The main transition which is afoot in this whole section is that which moves through completed necessity to freedom, and hence the activity of the subject. Real necessity which depends only on itself is the same as freedom, as self-development, which we think of as an attribute of subject. Fully developed necessity is therefore freedom, and since in Hegel's terminology the fully developed is the true, we can say that the truth of necessity is freedom, as we shall see by and by.

But before both of these dialectics, we have in the *WL* a first phase concerning the absolute, which is in fact a critique of Spinoza and a situating of Hegel's position vis-à-vis Spinozan monism.[1] Although not essential to the dialectic, this raising of Spinoza is not a departure from the central theme. Spinoza is an important philosopher for Hegel, and this not simply in the sense that all past philosophy was important for one who was the first major thinker to express his position as essentially an *Aufhebung* of all previous thought. Within this general importance of all the philosophical past, some philosophers stand out: Aristotle, of course; and Kant as the indispensable starting point, the definition of the dualities which Hegel is trying to overcome. But Spinoza is important for the opposite reason to Kant, viz., that he believed in the unity of everything in the absolute which was both God and also the whole. Everything is linked in a totality which is dependence on the Absolute which is God. Spinoza thus comes very close to the Hegelian position, and now when we have got to the stage of seeing reality as totality expressive of essence is the time to take our position vis-à-vis Spinoza.

For close as Spinoza is to Hegel, there are important differences. The point is that because Spinoza is close, the expression of these differences is one of the best ways Hegel knows of making clear his own position. Hence he does so frequently.

---

[1] The reference to Spinoza is relegated to the Addition to § 151 in *EL*.

Essence

The difference can be summed up in categories which only will come clear at the end of this section, that for Spinoza the absolute is only substance and not subject. The absolute is what lies behind, and cannot be equated with any particular thing in the world. All determination is negation, the principle of Spinoza which Hegel makes his own, but from this Spinoza holds that the absolute is beyond determination, is beyond negation. But this Absolute is one in which particular things sink without trace, it is simple self-identity. And for this reason, it remains a pure hidden inner reality; and hence it is a reality without inner movement, which is not conceived as such that the external determinate things can be deduced from it, or flow out of it in virtue of its own nature.

The Hegelian absolute, on the other hand, contains negation, it is determined to go beyond itself, to go into its other, determinate being. Hence for Hegel but not for Spinoza, the external reality of the world is not just there, not simply something found, but an order which manifests an inner necessity. Spinoza's God being pure and beyond determination is a pure inner, and hence the reality of the world is a pure outer in the Hegelian sense. Hegel likens this notion of the emanation of particulars from the absolute to that we find in some eastern religions, in which the Absolute is light which streams forth, gradually losing its nature as it issues in lower and lower beings. Hegel seems to think that some such idea underlies the religion of the ancient Persians, but something of the same notion is found in Neo-Platonism. Hegel rather sweepingly calls this an oriental cast of thought, and connects Spinoza's adoption of it with his Jewish origin, for it is 'in general the oriental way of seeing things, according to which the nature of the finite world seems frail and transient, that has found its intellectual expression in his system' (*EL*, § 151 Addition).[1]

Reciprocally, the particular is thought of as disappearing, but not as inwardly related to the absolute as it is with Hegel, where the nature of the absolute can be read out of the contradictions in the particular. What we lack in Spinoza is thus the idea of contradiction, of the unity of opposites, which is the source of movement, and which affects the absolute, God himself. Spinoza's philosophy lacks the contradiction of an absolute which is the source and fount of all particular, and yet which has particularity in it; which is over and against the particular and which nevertheless contains it. Hence the world which we see as emanation from this absolute lacks necessity. There are all sorts of particulars. The absolute has an undetermined number of attributes. Although Spinoza only names two, extension and thought, he does not see that these are the only two and that they are related by the necessity of being the two contradictory sides of the absolute, whose contradiction is the source of

[1] William Wallace translation.

281

movement. They are united, but without their opposition being seen, hence they are immobile, and without necessary connection.

Because Spinoza's absolute is immobile in itself, we have to think of its modes as arising from its contact with an understanding, which does not really have a place in the system. Spinoza's is still a system where a pure inner is balanced by an outer. But the distinction between inner and outer refers to an observer which is still unintegrated in the system. It is relative to him that modes exist. In contrast, Hegel's is a system in which the observer is integrated, and in which ultimately, as we shall see, the duality between observer and reality is overcome.

The defects of Spinoza's system are matched by defects of his method, which proceeds *more geometrico*. For this involves taking certain definitions as starting point; but as starting point their inner necessity is not seen. The Hegelian system by contrast, claims to be thoroughgoing, seamless necessity.

At the end of the Remark where he discusses Spinoza in *WL*, Hegel takes up Leibniz, who is guilty of an opposite error. Leibniz has in the monad the notion of a subjectivity which is such that it manifests itself in its properties. It issues necessarily in its properties and is conscious of them. But this is compensated for by Leibniz' idea of a multiplicity of such monads which see the world from different points of view. This multiplicity is not derived, so that it cannot be seen as the manifestation of necessity. Rather Leibniz has recourse weakly to God who is thought to have made a system of pre-established harmony out of them. But they are not harmonized out of themselves. It is not immanent in them that they are in harmony. This harmony is something purely external, and hence is also something internal, hidden in the designs of God.

Spinoza's notion of the absolute as without contradiction, and hence movement, is what makes his absolute just substance and not subject. For the subject is what moves itself, and what is conscious of itself, hence is necessarily other than itself, in Hegel's view.

So much for Spinoza. Hegel thus rejects the notion of an undetermined Absolute. But this of course was already rejected with the distinction between outer and inner, for an undetermined absolute is a pure inner. We come back thus to Reality as manifestation, and we take up the dialectic of contingency and necessity.

Possibility, reality and necessity

Hegel starts off his discussion of these modal concepts with the concept of possibility. In its lowest form this is often taken as bare possibility, as simple non-contradiction. (This, of course, Hegel hastens to add, amounts to a contradiction, since everything which is real – and hence also possible – is really in contradiction with itself.) But the purely possible, as what is not contradictory, includes just about anything. Things seem non-contradictory

Essence

when we take a partial view of them, as we saw earlier in the discussion of identity. So anything can be seen as possible under some frame of abstraction. For instance, the moon could fall on the earth this evening, or the Turkish sultan can become Pope (*EL*, § 143, Addition, 324).[1]

But this is a thoroughly uninteresting notion of possibility. We can think of it as covering a wider scope than the actual, but it only does in a rather Pickwickian way. We move therefore to a fuller, more grounded sense of 'possible', what is really possible. But the really possible is related to the actual. Something can only be judged as really possible against some background of presumed reality; this is what makes a given outcome possible or impossible. Whether something is possible or impossible 'depends on the content' (loc. cit.).

This conception of possibility thus is applied only in relation to a system of reality, it is not a simple concept like the previous one which was supposed to repose only on the non-contradictory nature of the content considered. Now a content is possible because it can be grounded in what is real. The relation of grounding comes back, though not in the same terms. The possible in this sense is thus not simply opposed to the real, but related to it. More, we can say that the real and the possible are one, for what makes content *A* possible is a state of affairs *B*, which can permit it to happen, which might ground it, which is latent with the potentiality for *A*. Thus Hegel moves with real possibility to the Aristotelian notion of potentiality. *B* is the potentiality of *A*, when realized in *A* it is actual. Hence the 'possibility of *A*' is also a reality, viz. *B*.

Contingency is the category which first arises from the relation of reality to possibility. The contingent is something real, but considered against a field of possibilities, of which others could have been realized. If it was the only possible outcome, then it is not contingent. In the light of bare possibility, everything is contingent. But when we begin to consider real possibility, then not everything is contingent. On the contrary, some outcomes are ruled out, and others are unavoidable, given the surrounding conditions. In other words, some outcomes are necessary.

Hence the notion of real possibility brings us to the notion of real necessity. Real necessity is still not absolute necessity which no longer reposes on any contingency; for it is circumscribed. A given outcome is only necessary, i.e., inevitable, given certain conditions. But these conditions being given is contingent. Nevertheless, we see that with the idea of realities conditioning each other, which was introduced with real possibility, we necessarily introduce real necessity. Hence this too arises from a combination of possibility and actuality. It is what adheres to a certain actual states of affairs, seen against the background of possibles, as the only possible outcome. (*EL*, § 147.)

[1] This also reminds us of the discussion of Ground, where Hegel points out that a reason can be given for anything, just by considering it under some abstracted aspect.

Logic

Hence real necessity and contingency are both concepts which can be applied only on the basis of some application of 'possible' and 'actual'. If we do not want to deal with an empty sense of contingency, linked to bare possibility, we have to consider the contingent as the actual which could have been otherwise, that is, where the conditioning actuality would have allowed another outcome. And the real necessary is what could not have been otherwise. In both cases, we are dealing with reality as systematically related, as conditioning and conditioned. Thus real necessity is still inseparably linked with contingency. What is really necessary, is also from another point of view contingent. B follows from A, but A might not have happened. And reciprocally contingency is also from another point of view real necessity. We say A is contingent when A' could also have followed from B. But what made A and not A' happen was differential factor F, and A is a real necessity given B and F. Thus Hegel calls this natural or real necessity 'relative' (*WL*, II, 179) or 'outer' (*EL*, § 148). For it depends on something else.

But we also know that things are bound together by a kind of necessity which is absolute or unconditioned. 'The absolutely necessary is only because it *is*; it has beyond this neither condition nor ground' (*WL*, II, 182). It is causa sui. For the system of necessary changes as a whole reposes on nothing outside itself, no foundation which would be outside the web of necessity.

What then is the relation of these two kinds of necessity? It is absurd to deny contingency any place, and to consider it just a 'subjective representation'. (*EL*, § 145, Addition.) In this paragraph, Hegel admonishes those philosophers who would try to do away with it altogether and deduce everything. Sciences which try this become merely 'empty juggling and wooden pedantry' (eine leere Spielerei and ein steifer Pedantismus, loc. cit.). So much for a proceeding which is often attributed to Hegel by his critics!

On the contrary, as we have seen earlier, contingency has its place of necessity. Its relation to necessity is what we described earlier, in the discussion on Ground, as 'intersticial'. But we could also describe it as 'superficial'.[1] The basic categorial structure of the world is of necessity. But by the very fact that this must be embodied (the categories of embodiment and exteriority also must have application), it must exist in a form which is 'external', that is, not all of whose aspects exhibit perfectly the inner connection of necessity. The surface, or detailed aspects of things are thus, indeed *must be* contingent.

Now things exhibit connections which are merely of real necessity when we single them out by these surface or detailed aspects. My car is smashed because of my driving over the icy road. This is indeed a contingent event. It could have been other, were it not for certain differential factors (e.g. my deciding to go out on this day). But this contingency is evident because I single

---

[1] Hegel himself uses this image when he speaks of contingency having free play 'on the surface of nature'. (loc. cit.).

284

out the entity concerned as 'a car', or even more particularly as 'my car'. If I consider it as a finite thing, then I see that it *must* go under, although the day and manner of its passing is contingent. Or as Hegel puts it, we see conditions and conditioned reality as separate, independent (selbständig) existents over against each other because of the 'limited content' of the matter we are considering (*EL*, § 148). But on a deeper level, conditions and conditioned are inwardly linked, they are identical as well as different. The form which is evident on this deeper level is that of necessary connection: the car as a finite thing must break up some day. But on the superficial or detailed level the content does not exhibit the form. Hence there is contingency: that this accident comes today.

> Thus in fact real necessity is *an sich* also contingency. – This becomes evident first in the following way: the really necessary is indeed necessary in its form, but in its content it is limited and it has its contingency through this content. (*WL*, ii, 180)

Since the content is external to the form, it is 'external' to itself, i.e., contingent (*EL*, § 148).

In this section Hegel is not really deriving absolute necessity out of real necessity. Rather unconditioned necessity has already been established, for we know we are dealing with a self-subsistent system of necessary relations. What he does show is the relation between the two, the manner of their coexistence, one might say. And here there is a crucial point in the transition from real to absolute necessity. Real necessity was united with contingency, but just immediately. At this stage 'necessity has not yet determined itself out of itself to contingency' (*WL*, ii, 179).

This is what is achieved by absolute necessity. It shows how contingency must exist, it as it were produces it out of itself. But then the two do not just coexist. Necessity has the higher place. Real necessity shows us necessary consequences of contingent conditions. Necessity is an island in a sea of contingency. But in the category of absolute necessity the position is reversed. Contingency is rather the ornament borne by the necessary structure of things.

Thus necessity shows itself as self-conditioned, as dependent only on itself. But this means that necessity is ultimately the same as freedom. We ordinarily complain that necessity is the opposite of free purposeful action. Necessity is blind, while free purposive action sees its end (*EL*, § 147, Addition).[1] But necessity is only blind when it is thus joined with contingency, so that we cannot see the connection between the terms it joins. We have seen however, that this contingency is a mere surface on necessity. Properly understood, this underlying necessity, seen as really reposing on itself, is fully transparent. Moreover, we will not just mean transparent to us or some observing consciousness, but

---

[1] Cf. also 'die absolute Notwendigkeit ist daher blind' (*WL*, ii, 183).

transparent as the emanation of reason which produces the totality of the real. Hence it will be transparent to an underlying reason. But this is the formula for self-consciousness, for purposive action: that what exists is transparent for that which posits it. Hence the truth of necessity, what it is basically, is what Hegel calls the Concept (*EL*, § 147 Addition, 332). And the structure of the world and history should be seen as the result of purpose.

This is what makes sense of the notion of divine providence. Certain philosophers and ordinary men believe that divine providence has no room for necessity. But this is to reduce providence to 'a blind, irrational caprice' (einer blinden, vernunftlosen Willkür, *EL*, § 147 Addition, 332). For Hegel God is *Geist*. He is the subject which is at the same time the rational structure of the whole. Hence necessity is his trade mark, not a limitation on him.

Hegel takes the occasion to make a comparison with the ancients' idea of fate. This was really external necessity, one which seemed to contradict freedom. But providence is not to be contrasted with fate in that it no longer partakes of necessity. Rather the difference is that fate took no account of men as subjects – or even of Gods – whereas in the Christian religion is the idea that the absolute is subject, and that in going over into something else, in death, we are united as throughout life with the life of absolute subject. Hence all adversity has this consolation, that we are in a sense always one with ourselves, once we see ourselves as emanations and vehicles of absolute subject. This is the 'consolation' of the Christian religion, and it is as consolation that providence is to be distinguished from fate, not by the absence of necessity. Our fate thus partakes of necessity, but not of a foreign or inscrutable one, rather of a necessity which expresses rational subjectivity in which we partake, and hence we are never in exile, but always *bei sich*.

More precisely, the consoling power of the Christian religion lies in this, that because in it God himself is known as the absolute subjectivity, and subjectivity in its turn contains the moment of particularity, it follows that *our* particularity too is recognized as something which is not just to be abstractly negated, but which at the same time is to be preserved. (*EL*, § 147, Addition, 334)

Substance

From absolute necessity Hegel goes over to the last and culminating triad of the Book on Essence, which he calls absolute relation. We already saw in the relation between absolute necessity and freedom, that we are about to step over into the categories of the Concept. But Hegel first wants to develop further the relation of the totality to its elements, and in so doing he will deduce and incorporate into his system the Kantian analogies of experience, with the concepts of substance, causality and interaction.

We started the book of Essence with the conception of a self-subsistent system of necessary changes which we established basically with Infinity.

Essence

Throughout this book Hegel has been spelling out the implications of this notion. He showed first that a system of this kind is a totality of necessary connections where each element must be explained out of the whole chain. For an adequate explanation must exhibit its necessity, but its necessity only flows out of the whole system of necessary links. Thus we learnt in the dialectic of Ground that the necessary derivation of things from sufficient reason could only be satisfied by relating them to the whole of which they are a phase. The task from then on till the end of Essence is one of relating this whole with the multiplicity of its elements.

Through the dialectic of things and properties, of law, of form and content, of whole and part, and finally of inner and outer, we discover that the whole of necessary connection cannot be seen as some force separate from and/or behind the external manifold. For contradiction which is the motor of necessary movement affects all reality. Thus the inner connectedness of things, or the totality, cannot lie behind but must be immanent to external reality. This is what is expressed in the category of *Wirklichkeit*. Necessity flows out of things themselves, and is thus manifest in them.

But at the same time, just because the inner unity is not separate from the outer elements, it can be thought of as all-embracing, all-powerful. To the extent that it were separate, the uniting power it wielded would not be total because some aspect of the external elements would escape it. If it shaped external reality from outside, then the original existence of this reality would be presupposed, not derived from necessity, But if the uniting power is fully immanent in things, then they are entirely under its sway; their unfolding is simply the manifestation of this power.

Further, a necessity which is all-embracing is absolute or unconditioned in the sense of relying on no merely given premiss. And indeed, that the necessity is absolute follows from the fact that we are dealing with a *self-subsistent* system of changes, powered by contradiction, and hence coming about of necessity.

Reality is thus deployed by an all-embracing and unconditional necessity. This necessity can be seen as a substance underlying the 'accidents' of external reality, more, a substance which deploys these accidents. It is a substantial power (Macht). We thus come to the vision of Spinoza, which is really what Hegel builds on here to write the finale of Essence. The substance which is the totality of its accidents, and which is this totality as deployed in a certain order or structure, is the power which underlies this deployment. The totality, which is present in our dialectic since the exit from Ground, now comes to have the quality of agency, comes to be seen as what actively posits the external reality, a feature which was implicit in it all along.

This substance is already referred to in the Absolute which opens this last division of Essence in *WL*. But in both logics, substance comes out clearly in the first term of the last triad.

For having arrived at Actuality, Hegel now has to make clearer what this unity between the inner cohesion of the totality and its external multiplicity amounts to. He did this first in setting out the relations of contingency and necessity, and showing that contingency itself emanates from the necessary structure of things, and is not outside it. But this relation was laid out in the abstraction of modality, as it were, in the phase discussed above. It remains to be vindicated in the concrete form which should be evident in our most concrete terms for relatedness, causality.

Hence the last phase is concerned mainly with causality. But the causality is seen within the context of a vision of the unity of everything in substance. Hegel throws in interaction and hence can set up this last triad as a kind of reminiscence/commentary on the Kantian analogies. But this is rather misleading and unfortunate. Interaction turns out to be a rather inexact term, as Hegel is forced to say in *EL* (§ 156, Addition).

The beginning point in substance is not at all artificial, however. We have the Spinoza-derived vision of everything as posited by substantial power. Absolute necessity is absolute relation (*WL*, II, 185). This is being which is because it is, which is absolute mediation of itself with itself. The 'accidents' are independent realities, which nevertheless are inwardly related, they are the potentiality to each other's actuality, and therefore have the determination to go over into each other. The inner is now no separate entity, but a power over them, which is also their power. It is the power to create and to destroy, and in destroying to create afresh. Substance is thus the power which deploys and hence does away with real external subsistent entities, which are therefore seen as its 'accidents'.

But substance is the necessity, the power which is fully manifest. Hence it is entirely deployed in the creation and destruction of accidents; and these 'accidents' are subsisting entities. Hence this same power must also be seen as the flow of necessitation which runs between the entities; but this is the relation of cause to effect.

Causality

When we look at this relation, the basic relation which we are trying to understand comes out again, the problem to be reconciled is again posed: how to put together inner necessity with real subsistent difference? Taking this basic relation as one of substance–accidents we accentuate the processual unity. But we are immediately reminded that the accidents are self-standing; and hence that they must be seen as in causal relation to each other. And thus the problem arises of finding our way back: of showing through the causal relation itself, that is the relation of the accidents among themselves, their inherence in the self-generating totality, which is defined as causa sui, being which is because it is.

This is not easy, and it is not clear how Hegel thinks he has done it. The nature of the relationship is perhaps a little clearer than the transition. In fact causality is seen as one of these imperfect manifestations of the underlying necessity of things, a manifestation which is affected with externality. This external causality is thus seen as referring beyond itself to its inclusion in a deeper, more essential relatedness of the totality.

Causality is external in the sense that it lies between terms which are only contingently related. There is no necessary relation between cause and effect, as we have learnt from Hume. But while for empiricist consciousness this is the end of the matter, for Hegel the externality of causality is just the reflection of a deeper link of necessity which is fundamental to things. Its being fundamental to things is the fact that the very structure of things follows a necessary order of deployment. Things are connected of necessity, but this necessity also calls for an externality where this connection is looser, is not purely transparent or entirely reflected in things. This is what we see in causality.

In both logics Hegel starts off by laying out two aspects of causality which seem to reflect its nature as the trace of some deeper unity. On one hand, cause and effect are thought of as joined in necessity, and they are certainly correlative terms: no cause without effect and vice versa. We can even see a single content which joins them, which is the point of their meeting. Thus when we say that the rain wet the grass, the wetness appears in both terms. This reflects the inner unity of the two. But this is of course not the whole story. The identical term, here wetness, is embedded on both sides in different terms which each have other properties, not inwardly related to wetness or each other. That the rain wet the grass tells us that wetness in the form of water which fell from the sky is what is responsible for this state of wetness of the lawn. This is what is informative, and not the tautological reference to wetness. Explanation by cause thus must go beyond this tautology, and this is its externality.

Hence we have in cause/effect a relation which reflects an inner identity, yet projected into mutual exteriority. This reading of causality is further reflected in Hegel's dealing with the potential infinite regress of causes and progress of effects. Efficient causation being never complete calls always for further terms, both to explain the transition between cause and effect, and to explain the occurrence of the cause itself. Hence every effect is also in another aspect a cause, and every cause an effect. This, Hegel comments, shows the identity of cause and effect. But because this identity is here affected with exteriority, it comes in the form of an endless series. Each cause is effect but only of something else, not of itself; and similarly each effect is cause.

Having reached an endless progress, we can see that it is time as far as Hegel is concerned to transit to a new plane, and this is what Hegel proceeds to do through the rather inadequate term of interaction. The argument is that each effect also helps to determine itself, and helps to determine the cause as well; so that there is not only action but reaction. But the action and reaction of Newton are not really what Hegel has in mind as the synthesis here. And this he makes clear in *EL* (Addition to § 156) where he points out that ordinary reflection often has recourse to this category of interaction when it wants to explain a kind of causation from totality which is much deeper.

The examples he takes are rather revealing of what this causation from totality is. They are the relations between organs and their functions in an organism, and the relation between a people's laws and customs on one hand, and their constitution on the other. The remarks in this Addition are clearly to be put in relation to the passage in *WL* (II, 193–4) where Hegel says that causal relations can not be applied globally to relations in the organic or spiritual realms. Speaking of the laws of the Spartans in relation to their constitution in the Addition mentioned, Hegel points out that they cannot be treated just as independent terms of a causal relation, but each must be seen as moments of a third, higher entity, their 'Concept' (Begriff).

What Hegel is referring to is what I have just called causation out of the totality. We encounter this in fields where we apply teleological explanations (in the sense of inner teleology), or where we invoke relations of meaning. Thus we might explain a given note in an étude or a given brush stroke in a painting by their role in the whole structure of music or visual tableau they help constitute. Or – more controversially – we might seek to explain a given practice or institution of a people (the Spartan constitution) by its place in their whole way of life of which it is part expression.

It is obvious here that we are dealing with totality in a strong sense, i.e., one whose specification could not be given in terms of descriptions of particulate elements, but on the contrary where we cast light on the nature of these elements by revealing their relation to the whole.

It was this kind of explanation which provided the sufficient reason by which we resolved the dilemma of Ground. And we can see that it cannot be understood as a unilateral causal relation between particular features. On the contrary, it accounts for a given feature by reference to the totality; a totality, moreover, of which this feature is an essential part, so that the explicandum in this mode of explanation is not distinct from the explicans. But even an account in terms of reciprocal causation, action and reaction between elements in a system, is not adequate, since it misses the crucial factor, recourse to the totality.

This is the kind of explanation, Hegel claims, which is suitable for organic and spiritual life. But it is also the kind of causation implicit in his Spinoza-derived vision of the universe as substance. Substance is power deploying the particular entities in the world. It is a totality which can be thought of as causa sui because it unfolds according to an inner necessity. The existence of particular elements is explained out of the global necessity. We can see this more clearly by referring back to what we know of Hegel's vision. The structure of the world, that it contains matter, time and space, life on all levels, finite spirit, all this can be seen as existing of necessity following the requirement that *Geist* be. But then the existence of any of these features must be explained by the whole formula of necessity of which it is an essential part.

Part of what is shown to be necessary, however, is precisely reality which is partes extra partes, which is external to itself; where the links of all reality to all reality are no longer fully transparent, or transparently reflected. But if there is to be real externality, it is not enough that these links be not visibly necessary, i.e., that they be fully necessary in fact, only just not transparently so. They must also be real links which are less than fully conceptually necessary. These are really links and hence necessary in a sense, but this necessity is 'real', not absolute. It is dependent, and hence bound up with contingency. In other words, there must be contingency, as we saw above. And these contingent links will hold between entities (e.g., slippery roads and crushed fenders) which are really independent of each other in the sense that their entering into these relations is not part of their concept.

These are causal relations. They correspond to a certain way of looking at things, but also to a certain level of reality. In some aspects, things are just to be understood as linked by causal relations. But once we move to another level, we have to go beyond this relation between independent terms, and understand them out of totality. We have to go beyond causality. This is what ordinary understanding has the greatest difficulty doing, and when it is really stuck with what is obviously a system, it has recourse to interaction, which is simply the reciprocal relation of particular terms.

Hence we come to the most concrete representation of totality, one which is nevertheless made up of independent realities. In a sense, as we progress through Essence, the external realities take on more independence, more reality (more *Selbständigkeit*). With Ground, they were still just opposed properties which went to ground. What came out of Ground, were or could be entities but in Thing, we were still dealing with properties. From Appearance on it has been clear that we are dealing with separate entities, and hence the aspect of their exteriority has always been kept in view. And as we move into *Wirklichkeit*, we stress this independence all the more in that this external reality is not any shadow of some truer reality behind, but really has the solidity which it appears to have. Hence we reach here the fullest solidity of external being. And this is necessary for the system, since we have seen that it is one in which the inner, *Geist*, can only exist in external reality; hence the reality of the inner depends on the solidity of the outer.

But for this very reason inner necessity and outer reality cannot be reconciled at the expense of the latter. The reality of externality must be maintained. So for this reason, the totality of Ground wherein sufficient reason could be found for everything had to go along with the real difference of particular ground and grounded; the system of absolute necessity not only had to go along with contingency, but produced it necessarily out of itself. This relationship of opposition and necessitation, of presupposition which is taken back in subordination, is expressed or struggling to be expressed in the dialectic of modality.

But it comes to its fullest, most concrete expression in the dialectic of causality. For here we can see a real exteriority of particular causes and effects, a multiplicity without number of such relations, but which are part of a system which can only be explained in its structure out of totality. Moreover, this totality, being ruled by necessity, and requiring that there be exteriority, necessarily posits causality as an external kind of necessity, one which unites necessity with contingency.

Hence we have the ascending and descending relation: external causality cannot suffice to explain the whole, it runs simply to endless regress, and it refers us beyond itself to explanation out of totality. This totality once understood shows us the necessity of this external causality. We thus have the concrete expression of the kind of totality relation we have been heading for, one which fills out the more abstract discussion of modality above.

The transition out of causality shows the ascending movement. As I mentioned above it is not clear whether this is meant to stand as an independent argument or simply to apply the conclusions of the earlier argument to causality. Certainly the transition both in *WL* (II, 198–202) and in *EL* (§ 154) resembles much more a reading of the causal relation in terms of his ontological vision.

Hegel does not even invoke the endless regress as an argument. He presents it rather as a result of the exteriority of the finite (*EL*, § 153, Addition). Cause and effect are really one 'in their concept', but in finite reality a given cause is an effect only in another relation. Thus the slippery road, cause of my dented fender, is an effect, but of something else, e.g., the freezing rain.

The transition is *WL* draws on what we have learnt in the earlier categories of Essence. Cause seems to work on effect as on another, passive substance. But the passive substance, which suffers external force, is really such that its nature is to be posited by something else. 'The passive substance is, through the operation of force, only *posited* as what it *in truth is*' (200). So that the effects turns out to be something which it works on itself. But then this reacts on the first substance, which no longer can be seen as simply active substance, as sole cause. We thus come to action and reaction; and from there Hegel moves on to totality. In this way the endless progress of finite causation is 'bent back' on itself into an 'infinite interaction' (202).[1]

[1] The involved discussion of this passage (*WL*, II, 198–205) is much easier if we read it with one of Hegel's paradigm examples of causation out of totality in mind, e.g., the relations between the customs and constitution of a people; and also if we read it together with the recap at the beginning of Book III, (*WL*, II, 214–16).
  Substance splits into two, into articulation. So the spirit of a people has to be embodied in an articulated whole of constitution, customs, way of life, etc. Hence the Spartans have laws and customs, and a constitution. We take the example of the causality between customs and constitution. Here we have two terms, and there must be this duality. There must be external constraining law, to express the necessity of a certain *Geist* against the weakness and caprice of individuals. But at the same time, without a certain spirit expressed in the customs this law would be corrupted, it would become an outer shell. Thus there is duality, but also a profound unity between the two.
  If we turn now to see these two as in causal relation, we can notice that the constitution affects the customs, and vice versa. Each is external to the other. Hence we have what Hegel calls the condition, or pre-supposition of causation (198–9), that the cause presupposes some other substance outside of it to work on. It becomes really cause only in working on this. There is an active substance, e.g. the constitution, and a passive substance, e.g., the customs. So the customs are thought to be presupposed, to have to be already there, for the constitution to work on them.
  But in a second moment, we notice that the customs are such that they can only be customs of a people which is organized with a constitution of this sort; there could not be such customs among people who, say, were organized under an oriental despotism, or a loose tribal system. So that what seems to be presupposed is also really posited by its relation to the constitution (and, of course, all the other aspects of the society's life – in causality we are just *isolating* certain elements). Thus

'The passive substance is, through the operation of force, only *posited* as what in truth it *is*; that is, because it is simple positive or immediate substance, it is just for that reason only something posited; the prior existence which it has as a condition [das Voraus, das sie als Bedingung ist] is the show of immediacy which operative causality strips away from it.'   (*WL*, II, 200)

Immediately before Hegel says 'what has force over the other only has it because it is the latter's power, which manifests in this both itself and the other'.
  Thus instead of seeing the passive substance, say the customs, as just there waiting to be worked on, as in the first moment, we now see them as such that they are necessarily emanations from this influence, really the inner spirit that flows through both constitution and customs in their mutual relations. We see them for the first time in their truth, viz, this *Geist*. Hence we see them for the first time in their truth, viz. as emanations of this something deeper, for this is their nature, to be posited by this deeper reality, which works through all the mutual influences of the different aspects of society, including that influence we are now looking at, viz., that of constitution on customs.
  But then in a third moment, we find that having admitted that only in being worked on by the other aspects of society (here the constitution) is the passive substance (the customs) what it really (*an sich*) is, we can turn this around and say that this being worked on is the realization of the passive substance's own *ansich*. In other words, being worked on in this way is a realization of what these customs really are, they of their own nature call for being held in place by such a constitution. Hence they are not just passive substance, but themselves cause.

'Thus on one hand the passive substance is preserved or posited by the active one...on the other hand, it is the operation of the passive substance itself to join with itself [mit sich zusammengehen] and thus to make itself original and cause.'   (*WL*, II, 201)

But then two things follow from this. First, the second substance can not only be considered in a sense the cause of itself to some degree, but the nature of its relation with the first is reciprocal. It is not just the cause of itself, but also conditions the first. The point is that once we have admitted that this second side, the customs, has as much as the first side the right to be called cause, then we have to admit that it also works on the first, because the reality is that they are complexly

Logic

This latter image hints at some of the underlying considerations of this transition. The row of causes in an efficient causal chain simply form a cut in reality. To single them out presupposes that one could also take a broader sweep and look not just at term *A* producing *B*, but at the system formed by *A* and *B* together, or *A* and *B* and other terms together. But when one does this, then one is bound to rise to a view in which one sees things in interaction.

This is undoubtedly well founded. When one shows the pressure of a gas to be a function of its temperature, this is a cut in a system of interacting elements which relates pressure, temperature, and other properties. We reach a more complete explanation by rising to this more systematic level.

But, of course, rising to the point where one sees the system in interaction does not entail that one arrives at the point where we explain the features of the system out of totality. We may remain within the bounds of good old efficient causality, as in the theory of gases example above. The necessity to move to causation out of the totality is something that must be established independently of the necessity to move to the perspective of systematic interaction. Hegel clearly admits this in the Addition to § 156 of *EL*.

In fact, we seem to have once more a case where Hegel is sure of an ascending transition because he is already sure of it; where he gives us what are only hints and traces of the higher reality which the lower is meant to be an emanation from, and takes these for a proof. The necessity to move to interaction or to the systemic perspective, can indeed be seen as a trace of the Concept; but it does not establish it. This conviction reposes rather elsewhere. The transition from interaction to causation out of totality is already there and is grounded on the whole earlier argument of the *Logic*, on the very conception of Essence as totality whose parts follow one on another of necessity.

Anyway, with this most concrete expression of the vision of necessity positing contingency, we come to the full expression of objective logic. Essence is now one with Being, for it is fully manifested in Being. What does not directly manifest necessity, viz. contingent relations, still is its manifestation,

intricated together, each works on the other. The customs are what they are only as held in by these laws, but at the same time these customs help to maintain the laws that so hold them in.

Hence we have action and reaction. But this stage in turn must be rapidly by-passed, for we realize that we are not dealing with mechanical action and reaction of separate terms. The truth is that the terms are *not* separate, that each is internal to the other. Each in going into the other 'joins with itself' (geht mit sich selbst zusammen), or 'the cause...stands related in the effect to itself as cause' (*WL*, II, 203). Or each remains identical with its other (216).

In other words, what we have seen from this is that each term is in a sense internal to the other, that we cannot get to a proper conception of each term without seeing its relation to the others, seeing how the others enter into what it is. What we really have thus is a whole, a spirit of the people, which exists through all these varying aspects and their relation. It is this which re-appears in the definitions of each of these aspects, and hence which makes it such that each is internal to the others. This is the substance.

294

since this contingency itself is necessary. Hence we have a set of relations between things, which are relations to self. We have what amounts to immediate being, that of the whole system, which is mediation with self. We have subsistent realities which are nevertheless involved in an infinite self-relation, an identity (*EL*, § 157).

Substance thus as the inner necessity which posits outer reality is really the Concept. The Concept is an inner conceptual necessity that produces, or issues into an external reality which expresses it. The final development of Substance – or the truth as Hegel calls it – which is in turn the truth of Being and Essence – is the Concept.

> The truth of Substance is the Concept – the independence which is a thrusting of itself off from itself into distinct and independent units, and which as this repulsion is identical with itself; a reciprocal movement which remains self-present [bei sich selbst bleibend] and interacts with itself. (*EL*, § 158)

But the Concept as an inner conceptual formula which produces a world according to its own inner necessity, has taken us beyond the realm of blind necessity into that of subjectivity, of freedom. We have a necessity which is all-embracing and absolute, which reposes only on itself, which is fully transparent; it produces an order out of itself out of a necessity which is its own nature; what can this be but freedom? Hence 'The truth of necessity is...freedom' (loc. cit.).

In the Addition to this paragraph Hegel returns to the relation of necessity and freedom. Ordinary consciousness sets them against each other. Necessity seems hard because it decrees that what I am immediately must go under. But real freedom is not crushed in this, only the false arbitrary will (Willkür. 'the freedom which is as yet without content and merely potential', § 158 Addition). But true freedom is attained by penetrating to the inner identity underneath the enforced transformations of necessity. The freedom of a civilized man is not to be found in defiance of the laws which necessitate his being other than he immediately is, but rather in his finding his own identity in this change, in this transformation of himself. He then understands and lives the rational necessity which corresponds to his own nature, which came first in the guise of external necessity, but which as rational, and his own, is freedom. Freedom is in living in rational, i.e., one's own, necessity. But this calls for the transformation of what one is immediately. Hence it may appear to the undeveloped man like an external imposition, a restriction of freedom. Such a man is living on the level of contingency, of pure externality, as though he were a thing. But the nature of man as *Geist* is to live the negation of his immediate nature which things only suffer; hence to negate this immediacy and make himself over, and to find his freedom in the necessity.

Necessity is thus the outer form of freedom. And since we live the outer before we live the inner it is the presupposition. 'Freedom has necessity as its presupposition, and contains it as cancelled [aufgehoben] within itself' (loc. cit.). Those who have not grasped this inwardly will not understand. The criminal sees his punishment as restriction of his freedom: but his punishment is not a foreign force, but the manifestation of his own action. Once he recognizes this, he comports himself as a free man (loc. cit.). This is what Spinoza called the amor intellectualis Dei.

It is having arrived at this freedom which takes us now to the subject, so that the next book of the *Logic,* dealing with the Concept, will be the subjective logic. This freedom which is at one with reality, as existent is the 'I', 'as developed to its totality it is *free spirit,* as feeling, *love,* as enjoyment, *bliss* [Seeligkeit]' (*EL,* § 159).

CHAPTER XII

The Concept

Having reached the subject, Hegel is now in a position to spell out what has only been implicit in the earlier books. We saw that the categories of Essence as against those of Being make implicit reference to a subject of knowledge. This reference is now made explicit. And this consciousness that the real is for a subject will no longer be lost sight of in the *Logic*.

This is the first justification for calling this section the book of the Concept. That the world is for a subject means that the world-as-object-of-knowledge is structured by concepts. This was intrinsic to our starting point in the Logic, which is a dialectic of categories, but it is now to be examined explicitly. And it shows Hegel's debt to Kant. But while Hegel's notion of the Concept owes a lot to Kant, it involves a profound transformation of Kant's basic ideas.

Hegel takes the basic Kantian idea of the original unity of apperception which he says 'belongs to the deepest and most accurate insights that can be found in the critique of reason' (*WL*, II, 221) and gives it a twist which Kant would have received with horror. This original unity is what unites the different representations, and it is this unity which gives them objectivity, i.e., relates them to an object. As just intuitions, the contents of our experience have no objectivity, but as brought together by the 'I', and brought together under concepts, they achieve objectivity. Through being conceived, they become posited reality, and not simply immediately given.

All this is Kantian. But Hegel gives it a totally different meaning. Where Kant went wrong, he says, was that he thought of this unity of the object in the thought of transcendental apperception as simply phenomenon, as set over against the thing in itself, which was unknowable. And in line with this basic idea, the Kantian notion of the category was of a simple form, which without content would be empty. This form thus had to be filled with external intuition in order to generate real knowledge, knowledge of (phenomenal) objects.

For Kant, therefore, the operation of the Concept had to wait on the reception of intuitive filling. It presupposed sensible intuition; it operated on this intuition, which had to be given beforehand. In Hegelian terms, we have here an ascent which has not yet turned around and recognized that the lower is produced out of the higher, that it is not self-subsistent.

The issue between Kant and Hegel is this: Hegel takes up Kant's idea that

297

reality or objectivity is only where the stuff of sensible intuition is structured by thought. But whereas for Kant this principle was valid only for our knowledge of the world, i.e., for phenomena, and not for things in themselves; for Hegel this is valid ontologically; For the inner truth of things is that they flow from thought, that they are structured by rational necessity. What for Kant just happens to be true of our faculty of knowledge is for Hegel an ontological fact which finds its reflection in our faculty of knowledge. All this he feels he has shown in the preceding parts of the Logic. For these have demonstrated that the conceptions of reality as separate from and over and against thought, as simple being, as hidden essence, as just given, etc. are all inadequate, and all go over into substance whose truth is manifest necessity, or freedom, hence concept.

But then the other side to knowledge besides the concept, viz., its intuitive filling, is not given separately, it is produced out of, posited by the Concept. This is where Kant went wrong. But all that he said about objectivity, its dependence on thought and the unity of the 'I', which he intended only for phenomenal objectivity, turns out to be right of reality as such.

So obviously we are dealing with Concept in a very different sense than in Kantian philosophy, or indeed, common sense. For the latter, the concept is a tool of our knowing, a way we have of grasping reality. Our use of it is, as it were, without prejudice to the nature of reality itself. For Hegel, on the other hand, the Concept is an active principle underlying reality, making it what it is.

The second connected difference is this: that for common sense, the concept is an abstraction. Its universality is bound up with this. We find a word which applies to a host of similar instances, and the concept does this by abstracting from their particularities. But on Hegel's view, the Concept is such that it develops the reality which corresponds to it out of itself. For it is not just a content in our minds, but the principle underlying the real. Hence it is a universal, but one which has the difference within it. As Hegel puts it, it produces the particularities which are its manifestations out of itself 'the Concept [is] ground and source of all finite determinateness and multiplicity' (*WL*, II, 227).

Hence for Hegel, the best representation of the Concept in the furniture of the world is the 'I'. I may have particular concepts, 'but "I" is the pure Concept itself, which as Concept has come to existence' (Dasein, *WL*, II, 220). For 'I' as Hegel explains is a unity which is self-identical, and can abstract from all particular determination in order to concentrate on its self-identity. It is thus universal. But at the same time, it is particularity, different from others, individual personality. The point is that the particular characteristics of the 'I' are not merely given, but belong to a being who is also capable of abstracting from them and making them over, who is free in the sense of having an identity which is beyond any of them. Hence these characteristics can be seen

298

as affirmed by this universal self-identity. At the same time, while free from any of these characteristics, the 'I' is not free from having some; it cannot be without affirming some character or other, hence the universal must issue in the particular.

Finite spirit is thus the clearest readily available manifestation of the Concept. But it is not the highest. For a particular finite spirit cannot disengage itself from its characteristic and change them totally. In Hegel's own theory, the only really adequate representation of the Concept must be infinite spirit, as represented in the whole system of reality. However, among finite entities, finite spirit is obviously the best, followed later by living beings.

The Concept is thus the universal which develops particularity out of itself. This development is contrasted with the simple transition (Übergehen) of Being, or the reflection (Scheinen) of Essence. In the first, the first term disappears to make way for the second. In Essence, the first refers us to a second which is not itself; but in the Concept, the new terms developed out of it remain fully identical with it. The image Hegel uses in the *EL* (§ 161, Addition) is that of a plant growing. This develops and articulates itself. It is at first simply the undifferentiated source of the later unfolding. This is Concept in the other Hegelian sense of the germ or undeveloped form. This undifferentiated source is hence like the universal, which is abstract, undifferentiated. But it contains the power, indeed the necessity, to grow and develop and to produce the particular out of it.

The question naturally arises, and Hegel takes it up in *EL* (§ 160, Addition), why we even use the same word here for what we ordinarily call concept, and for Hegel's Concept. Does this not simply invite misunderstanding and confusion? The short answer is that the two notions, the ordinary language and the Hegelian specialist one, are not as far apart as we might think. But the deeper answer which comes in the sequel is that the Hegelian Concept will be shown to develop out of the ordinary one in the course of the dialectic to follow.

For in the book we are now starting our task will be to move in the opposite direction to that of objective logic. There we started with the poorest, least contentful notion of external reality and led it through Essence up to a vision of this external reality as manifestation of the Concept. But if this is so, if everything really does issue out of the Concept, like the plant out of the seed, then we should be able to show this by examining the Concept itself. Of course, the Concept which is the source of all is the fully developed Concept, the Idea, which we shall come to at the end of our search. But if this is really the source of all, we should be able to get to it starting from the concept in something like the ordinary sense, the subjective concept which is the stuff of thought.

Our basic ontological vision is that the Concept underlies everything as the inner necessity which deploys the world, and that our conceptual knowledge is derivative from this. We are the vehicles whereby this underlying necessity comes to its equally necessary self-consciousness. Hence the concept in our subjective awareness is the instrument of the self-awareness of the Concept as the source and basis of all, as cosmic necessity. But if this is so, then the concept in our minds must on closer examination turn out to function like the Concept at the root of reality. This latter produces reality out of itself, it is the universal which goes over into the particular, it is the inner formula of necessity which generates an external reality which, as external, both negates and manifests this necessity; it posits its own opposite with which it remains inseparably united. It is the totality which moves by contradiction. Unless the concept in our minds turns out on deeper examination to function like this, unless it too goes over into opposition and an identity mediated by its other, unless indeed it turns out ultimately to link up with the thought underlying reality, then Kant and the dualists are right: there must in fact be an unbridgeable gulf between our thought and the foundations of the real. The conceptual necessity underlying what is would not be within the grasp of subjective thought, but only at best through an intuition beyond thought, in image, hint, symbol. *Geist* as reason would never come to self-consciousness.

In a sense, we have been showing all along in this examination of our categorial concepts that they generate contradiction and are linked to their opposites. But we should be able to show this in the very concept of a concept itself.

This is what we are going to do in the first part of this third book of the Logic. We are going to look at our thought, that is, at concepts, and what we make with them, viz. judgements and syllogisms. In short we are going to look at much of what usually is studied under the head of formal logic. This is the point where Hegel's Logic (which we must remember is principally a transcendental logic) is congruent with what usually goes under the title. And we have seen why in the strategy of that transcendental logic this matter has to be taken up here.

But it also follows from the foregoing that Hegel cannot really accept the idea of a formal logic, that is: a study which would claim to be of the form of thought in abstraction from content. The whole Hegelian message is that 'form', or the nature of thought itself, goes over into its opposite. Concepts reveal on examination inner contradictions; as universals they show them-selves necessarily related to particulars which nevertheless negate them. And in showing these inner contradictory relations they are really showing forth the nature of things, for our concepts behave like this because they are the vehicles of self-consciousness of the inner necessity of the cosmos. Hence a study of concepts as pure forms generates the basic structure of things, or the content. Reciprocally, of course, a study of content, of things, reveals the inner conceptual necessity, or form.

Hence a purely formal logic is a chimaera. In a crucial passage (*WL*, II, 229–34, also *EL*, § 162), Hegel expresses this point through a discussion of his notion of truth. The usual (and Kantian) idea of formal logic is that it treats of concepts and propositions in abstraction from their (substantial) truth. That is, they may have logical truth, but not truth in the ordinary sense of adequacy to the facts. Truth requires two terms. But if our study of forms shows them as issuing in an inner development which reflects the structure of things, then the question of substantive truth arises within so-called formal logic itself. In other words, there is no separate domain of forms which are only susceptible of being judged as coherent or incoherent, as we judge a proposition as making sense or not, abstracting from all questions of truth as concerning only the agreement of this form with a quite independent empirical content. Rather, because the forms themselves undergo inner development out of their internal contradictions until they come properly to reflect the structure of things, the question of their truth necessarily arises. They are in truth only in their fully developed form. In any earlier form they are inadequate, untrue.

Substantive truth thus cannot be excluded from the domain of formal logic, which is another way of saying that formal logic fits into transcendental logic, which itself is ontology. The truth of something is within that thing, or within the concept of the thing. For everything is an emanation of Concept, hence it is either in agreement or disagreement with it, hence either true or false. Truth in the sense of Hegel's absolute Idealism is the form of something when it is fully developed, for then it is in full agreement with its concept.

This whole section expresses once again the profound difference from Kant; that Kant accepted the duality of knowing mind and ultimate reality; that ultimate truth, truth in the sense of adequacy of thought to ultimate reality, remains beyond our reach. Whereas for Hegel, truth is within our grasp, because reality is not foreign to thought, rather it develops out of thought itself. For Kant categories are finite because they are subjective, for Hegel they are finite because they are partial, they have their place in the whole process, and have to go under each in their turn.

Finally what Hegel reproaches Kant for is not having cleaved to the notion of an intellectual intuition, which he himself invented. This would be an understanding which unlike ours did not have to depend on external reception, on being affected from outside, for its contents, but created them with its thought. This archetypical intellect Kant attributed to God; it was quite beyond us. But God's intellect is ultimately revealed to us for Hegel, it only lives in our thought. Hence we can participate in an intellectual intuition. God's thought is ours.

I: SUBJECTIVITY

The first division of the subjective logic is called 'Subjectivity', and its aim is to lead us through the concept considered as subjective grasp of things to the notion of a self-articulating world. Rather, we are already there, for we have achieved this notion through the development out of Essence. But we are going to show that we get to the same spot by going in the other direction, and starting with the concept by which we know things, as we did starting with the being known.

In the course of doing this, we will come to grips with some of the notions of formal logic, and in the process transpose the whole set of ideas connected with this discipline. We shall take the fixed distinctions and set them in motion. In the general introduction to this book, the part in which he gives its division (Einteilung), Hegel tells us what we shall be dealing with in this division: (*WL*, II, 236).

Starting off with the Concept *an sich*, we see it as something purely inner, and hence as simply outer. We start off thinking of the concept as the property of subjective thought only (as inner); and for this reason it is thought of as only outwardly related to what it is a thought of. And the various elements of this thought (the particular concepts) are only outwardly related to each other. But the identity of the Concept will set them in dialectical movement, and will overcome their fragmentation and the division of Concept from reality (Sache).

This first segment of the Logic of the Concept goes through three parts, the Concept as such, judgement, and syllogism. These are the stages on the road which will lead to objectivity, that is, will take us beyond subjective Concept once more to the self-articulated totality of the real.

The best way to expound what goes on in this first chapter on Concept is to set out the articulation of the Hegelian notion, and see how the ordinary subjective one fits in. This is close to Hegel's own procedure, at least in the fuller exposition of *WL;* (except that Hegel considers the two frequently together without distinguishing them for long passages, which hardly adds to clarity).

The exposition of this chapter goes by the deployment of the well known distinction between universal (Allgemeines) specific (Besonderes) and particular (Einzelnes) which obviously gets a special twist at Hegel's hands.

Concept

First, let us take the Hegelian Concept. This is a universal, a self-identical inner principle of a diversified totality. But it is also sundered into many, for there must be differentiation for there to be totality. This sundering is the specificity which falls under the universal.[1]

[1] The German word 'Besonderes', cognate with our English word 'sunder', carries this sense of self-diremption as well as the ordinary logical meaning, giving Hegel that speculative play on words he so enjoyed.

The Concept

But then, thirdly, this totality has to have real, external existence, and as such to be a real particular thing, *Einzelnes* (sometimes better translated 'individual').

Unlike the earlier spheres, the development here is purely intrinsic. Each of these three moments is itself the whole totality, as Hegel says. That is, one cannot give an account of it without mentioning the others as well. Thus in starting off with the universal, we had to mention that it was the inner principle of a diversified totality, and hence refer to the other two 'determinations' (Bestimmungen). All three are inseparably linked.[1]

But now, as we have seen earlier, this ideal scenario is not everywhere embodied as such. It is in the whole which is the embodiment of infinite spirit. And it is in those particular entities which are closest in nature to infinite *Geist*, viz. Life, the 'I', finite spirits (*WL*, II, 244). But even in these particular entities, it is not realized as it is in the whole, for here its self-specification flows from its 'creative power' (schöpferische Macht, 244–5), and is thus unconditioned by anything else.

Another image of the Concept is the genus, which specifies itself in its species. But already here, we are coming to an example of less perfect realization. For the ordinary genus groups a diverse set of species which does not follow any necessary articulation which can be deduced from its Concept. The genus of birds includes a whole row of species neither whose number nor whose differentiae show any necessity whatever.

This contingency finds a place in Hegel's system, as we have seen, for on his view the lower realizations of the Idea contain this kind of imperfection, of looseness of fit, which is from another point of view contingency. Thus speaking about the contingency of species Hegel says

This is the impotence of nature, not to be able to hold fast to and present the rigour of the Concept, but rather to disperse [verlaufen] into this concept-less and blind multiplicity. (*WL*, II, 247)

This falling into simple diversity of nature is matched by a similar production of diversity in the representations (Vorstellungen) of finite spirit. Both the manifold natural genera and species and the arbitrary ideas (Einfälle) of the mind

show indeed everywhere traces and hints [Spuren und Ahnungen] of the Concept, but they do not present it in its true image, because they are the side of its free self-externality... (*WL*, II, 248)

But this contingency is itself contained in the Concept

it is absolute power precisely because it can leave its difference free to take the shape of independent diversity, external necessity, contingency, caprice, opinion; all of which, however, must not be taken for anything more than the abstract side of nullity (Nichtigkeit, loc. cit.)

[1] Cf. e.g., *EL*, § 164.

303

Imperfection thus takes this form, that the universal, which is here the genus, does not issue necessarily in its specification, that this specification has a great deal of the arbitrary, of the simply contingent, in it, around the basic structure of necessity. And this lack of necessity can be seen in another way as well, that the different species, the different parts of its specification, are not internally related as opposites to each other. They show no necessary articulation, as we saw above. Necessary articulation for Hegel can only be the essential relation of opposites, whereby each reposes on its other, so that each cannot be without the other, which is in this sense *its* other. As contradictory they become a whole in movement, whose necessary articulation these parts are. This for Hegel is the true Genus, which would have thus only two species which would be essentially related opposites. Such is the absolute which necessarily sunders itself into spirit and nature, which in turn while opposed can only be conceived in relation to each other.

Hence the imperfection of the embodiment can be seen as a contingency in the issuing of specification from the universal, or as a contingency, a lack of opposition, in the mutual relations of the specified elements. But it can also be seen from the point of view of particularity: that the genus as a whole does not make an ordered particular; rather a contingent number of particulars fall under it.

Contrast again the absolute and the genus of birds, if this does not sound too ridiculous. The former is an articulated sundering into a totality which is also a real, self-moving external existent, or individual. Finite spirits approach this, but they do not suffice to themselves, rather the spirit which underlies them is embodied also in an ordered society of such spirits. But here enters an element of contingency in that the number of human beings is not fixed by necessity; only the society is a self-subsistent whole whose number is fixed at one (for any given stage). The contingently numbered particulars fit into a larger, and necessarily articulated particular.

But with the different species of birds, not even this is the case. There is an 'undetermined multitude' (unbestimmte Menge) of them, that is, both species and specimens, and yet the whole which is the Genus does not even make an articulated totality. As a particular, the genus of birds is an utterly ungainly entity. So that the unitary, articulated existent falls out of close inner relation to the universal under which it falls: the whole extension of the universal no longer qualifies, and what does qualify exists in undetermined number, and with much contingent articulation.

Now as we saw earlier, Hegel puts the imperfect embodiment of the Concept in nature into parallel with the contingent representations of the mind. And, as we shall now see, the purely subjective concept suffers from the same disabilities as the imperfectly embodied Concept. In this sense it has a certain justification, which it loses, though, when it claims to be the whole truth

The Concept

of Concept, which is what happens with common sense and philosophies of the understanding.

Let us see this by looking now at the subjective concept in relation to the three terms above. The subjective concept is a universal, in an unproblematic sense: it is indeed that for which 'universal' was first coined. But it also has specification, that is, there are criteria by which it is applied, it has some content, in this sense. The idea of a simple concept, one with no further criteria, Hegel rejects out of hand. It is to confuse representation with conceiving. There can be simple representations which swim before our minds. Even the richest realities, Spirit, nature, the world, even God, can be represented in the mind as utterly simple; that is, we can avoid going into their articulation. (*WL*, II, 255, also *EL*, § 164). But if we talk seriously of conceiving, then surely we cannot accept these as *concepts*. They are simple representations in which the universality is thought in abstraction from the specificity and particularity (loc. cit.).

Translating Hegel out of his own language, we come to a thesis which would be widely accepted today:[1] a concept is necessarily bound with other concepts: no concept can be introduced on its own. We cannot be said to have a *concept* of a thing if we can say nothing about this thing except to apply this concept to it. This is the point behind Wittgenstein's argument against a private language:[2] the sensation '*E*' would have to be such that at least we could say that it was a *sensation*, and hence link it to the rest of our language. There is no concept we can deploy which is not so linked and hence which cannot in some way be explicated by others.

The belief in the simple concept belongs to another theory of meaning, that in which words were given significance simply by linking them to sense contents. Then the word which was linked to an utterly simple sense content would itself be incapable of further articulation. But Hegel points out that this kind of distinction confuses psychology with logic. There can perhaps be simple sensuous presentations, even representations in the mind: as a matter of autobiographical fact, I might see that I had not noticed before the articulation of a given scene, or even a given idea. But when one comes to concepts, this notion of simplicity is totally misplaced.

Thus the universal (concept) must have a specification (its criterial explication). But as with the imperfect embodiments above, the merely subjective concept will be such that there is no necessary link between the two. Of course, there will be a purely analytic link, in that this concept's meaning is what is given in the criterial explication. But there will be nothing necessary to the articulation of this explication; its elements will be quite contingently linked. In giving

---

[1] The point was anticipated by Herder in his *Essay on the Origin of Language*. To have linguistic consciousness of something is to identify it by a criterial mark (Merkmal).

[2] *Philosophical Investigations*, I, paras 258 ff.

the explication of 'parrot', we will speak of a bird, which has certain colours, a certain kind of beak, which can 'talk', etc. But all these characteristics are quite contingently linked together. There is no necessity in their being the articulations of a single thing; they do not form a totality.

Thirdly, the universal concept with its specification is used to designate particulars. As in the exposition of the ontological Concept, the moment of particularity is the moment where we come to external, real existence. But in the case of the subjective concept, the step into reality is one that goes beyond the subjective, it is the reference to things in the world.

Thus universal, specific, particular are present in the subjective concept, its specification, and the things to which it can be used to refer.

And as in the case of the explication above, the purely subjective concept shows the same contingency or externality of relations between particular and concept, as between concept and explication. It is part and parcel of the same contingency. This contingency is analogous to the imperfect embodiments of the Idea in Nature which we discussed above. The perfect embodiment is one which has a necessarily articulated totality as its specification, and this is thus necessarily a particular which properly understood goes back of itself into its universal qua articulated. The imperfectly embodied Concept has no necessary articulation. Its extension is thus not a particular, and the particulars which fall under it are of contingent number and variety. Reciprocally, this whole extension does not show of itself the universal to which it belongs and nor do the constituent particulars.

Similarly, the simply subjective concept is only contingently, or analytically, united to its explication; and it is only contingent that it has particulars which fall under it, or how many. Reciprocally, these particulars are not such that they essentially must be characterized by this universal, they can be subsumed under a host of different, unrelated concepts. The parrot is also a blue object, one which makes noise, etc. On the other hand, the spiritual entity deploys all its different properties so that all are manifestations of the same inner necessity. Whatever term one chooses to start with, one is referred beyond to the whole.

In Hegel's terms, the subjective concept is such that its form and content are not united, (*WL*, II, 261), or else we can say that they are just immediately united. The latter expression perhaps best describes the relation between concept and specification. For these are analytically united, hence represent no conceptual unity in the strong sense. There is no mediation in this link, simply a spelling out what is involved in the concept.

But the former expression perhaps best suits the relation between concept and particular. The concept is the form, the particular thing the content; and they are contingently or externally related in so far as the concept does not itself determine its particulars, and these do not of themselves prescribe their characterization.

The Concept

This is the purely subjective concept, as it is seen by common sense and philosophy of the understanding. It is a mere form which is separate from content; and which is obtained by abstracting from the content, that is, from the difference that different particulars have which fall under it. The concept is thus seen as containing simply the common elements among the things that fall under it.

In part this notion of the common element (das bloß Gemeinschaftliche, *EL*, § 163, Addition 1, also *WL*, ii, 263) stems from a false notion of the concept as the product of abstraction, fruit of the same psychologizing theory of meaning which yielded the idea of the simple concept. But in part it corresponds to a real distinction; for the inessential characterizations of things or the characterizations of inessential things yield the simply common. It is common to all men that they have ear-lobes, but this does not give their essential characterization. We need to distinguish the universal Concept, that which really produces what falls under it, from the simply common, which has no intrinsic relation to the things it relates, does not produce them, and is simply noticed by external comparison.

In the first Addition to *EL*, § 163, Hegel gives two important instances of this distinction. The Greeks he claims did not really have a concept of the universal of either God or man. Hence they could believe that Hellenes were radically different from barbarians, and that some men were naturally slaves. Christianity brought the principle of the universal to its full recognition, which is why there is no slavery in modern Europe.

Secondly this can also illuminate Rousseau's distinction between *la volonté generale* and *la volonté de tous*: the latter is the simply common, the former would better be called the concept of will.

The point of all this, as Hegel explains in Addition 2, is that the Concept comes first, as we understand in the ontological version, and as is always overlooked in the subjective version. This is the truth behind the idea that God created the world ex nihilo.

It is clear from the foregoing that the subjective concept as understood by common sense is not just wrong. In its inessentiality, its purely contingent relation to what it covers, which could as well not have existed, or could have been easily subsumed under other concepts, it corresponds to much that is contingent and inessential in the world; the contingent in the imperfectly embodied (ontological) Concept. Where this subjective view is hopelessly wrong is in not seeing that this inessentiality is itself posited by the essentially creative Concept. And this is to say that its failure is to ignore the very existence of the ontological Concept. Hence it believes that all concepts are subjective, that they are all forms which are separate from content.

We want to show now that this subjective version of the Concept transcends itself by the force of its inner contradictions. But as often in crucial transi-

Logic

tions, Hegel seems to be assuming what he means to prove. For the basic contradiction here is the 'incommensurability' (Unangemessenheit) of the universal and its specification (*WL*, II, 252). But this inadequacy only holds if we assume that the lack of inner connection constitutes inadequacy.[1] Understanding, says Hegel, manages to achieve the fixity of the universal out of the flux of the changing sensible. This is quite an achievement; it is too much to expect of it that it go beyond this to see that its own fixed universal concepts are themselves in dialectic flux. But these fixed notions, these particular determinate concepts, which are held to be separate from each other, go themselves over into dialectical movement from the force of their own inner contradictions. But these contradictions turn on the incommensurability of determination to universal, which itself is a requirement of the system. Ordinary understanding is quite satisfied with determinate concepts, where there is no essential relation in the articulation or to the particulars which fall under it, and cannot be made to feel the contradiction.

But Hegel's derivation of objectivity is not just based on the simple fact of incommensurability (Unangemessenheit). It takes off from the concept to pass through a long development by means of other logical notions. The first is judgement. The transition comes out of this conclusion that in Subjective Concept, the particular which falls under it is external to it. And yet it is not without relation. We are not back in the sphere of Being, where we were dealing with simple entities on their own, and which simply went over into another. Nor are we in Essence where we were dealing with hidden reality. We are in the Concept where the particular has been derived as coming out of the Concept, as that which is referred to by the Concept. Hence we are thinking of the particular here as the object of reference. And as such, though separate from the Concept, it is also inseparably connected to it. Thus particularity 'excludes the universal from itself, but since this is a moment of itself, this universal is also essentially related to it' (*WL*, II, 264).[2]

Judgement

Thus the subjective concept, by referring to particulars which are not produced out of it, essentially refers us to the judgement. A concept can have no use except in the making of a judgement. This is the short way to this conclusion which dispenses with the whole argument of this section, except of course that this argument is essential to the Hegelian purpose which is to see the subjective concept against a background of requirements which are posed by the ontological Concept. From this point of view, it is not only important that we could not have concepts without judgements, that concepts are essentially

---

[1] Why Hegel feels entitled to make this assumption, we shall discuss below.

[2] As a a matter of fact, this section has a lot in common with Essence, since we have the relation of two moments which are not really shown as identical, until we transcend this part to Syllogism.

what we use to make judgements, that they are not entities like stones which have a reality outside their use. Rather what is important is that the judgement is born out of a division, a diremption, where the two sides are not in full agreement, for this is what will power the development of the judgement as we see in the next section.

Judgement is joined to the idea of division for Hegel, of a splitting apart of the two terms which are joined. And this is aided and abetted by another word-play which the German language offers him on a platter. The movement of particularity is the original separation of itself ('die ursprüngliche Teilung seiner'), and this is judgement (Urteil). The movement of diremption, or *Entzweiung*, which underlies everything, and which is later matched by the return to unity, is what underlies the judgement, where different things are declared the same. This we shall follow in detail in the dialectic which now ensues.

The discussion of Judgement helps to make clearer what for Hegel is the relation of formal logic to his kind. The usual idea of common sense is to see judgements as activities of our (finite) minds, in which we attribute some property to an object. We join two concepts in our minds; and the judgement is correct if the things we talk about with these concepts are really joined in fact. But for Hegel, judgement is first and foremost an ontological reality. In *EL*, § 166, Addition, he cites the favourite example of the plant: this comes from the seed and unfolds out into root, twigs, leaves, etc. This external unfolding into differentiated reality is the equivalent as we saw above to the universal which sunders itself into its specifications. But this sundering is the judgement (Urteil = ursprüngliche Teilung), as Hegel reminds us again. Hence this unfolding is to be seen as 'das Urteil der Pflanze' (366). Judgement is thus, first, the ontological reality whereby the Concept sunders itself and issues in particular realities.

This is what underlies the judgement in our minds and speech. We might think of judgement thus as a putting together (Verbindung) of two separate concepts, but this is quite wrong; it fails to take account of the fact that judgement is at bottom separation, partition of the unity.

There is, of course, another view of judgement as the separation of unity, which is also current in common sense. When we judge that the rose is red we cut apart in our minds by abstraction what in reality is the indivisible reality red-rose and think it in two parts or aspects which we join by judgement. But this view too errs by subjectivity. It is not totally wrong, but it misses a crucial dimension, that we do this act of separation as the inner reflection of the ontological act which is original (*ursprünglich*).

But of course not all judgements are really true to this ontological act. Hence there are different types of judgement. But it is important to realize that it is not just various forms of subjective judgement which are not true to ontological judgement; Reality, too, as we have seen, is more or less truly a reflection of the basic ontological sundering of concept. The more external it is, the more approximate, inexact, the more mixed with contingency. Hence there will be imperfect, 'untrue' judgements, which correspond to untrue realities. 'Untrue' is the word to use here, for we have seen that truth in Hegel is correspondence to the idea. Hence we shall be concerned throughout this section with something quite different from what is ordinarily called the truth of judgement, viz., its correspondence to the (often quite contingent) facts. This correspondence Hegel calls 'Richtigkeit', rightness, correctness. A judgement can thus be correct, but what is applies to untrue: e.g., that someone is sick, or someone has stolen something (*EL*, § 172, Addition). This content is untrue, because in both cases the reality fails to conform to its concept; it is as it should not be.

But just as some contents can be characterized as untrue, so we can characterize judgements which bear on them as true or untrue, not in virtue of their correctness, but in virtue of their kind of object. And we can go further and distinguish different judgement-types, by their capacity to convey truth, that is, to bear on true objects. This will be a formal study, in that we will be dealing with judgement-classes, abstracting from their determinate content. But it will most emphatically not be formal in the usual sense as abstracting from the *type* of content, for the different judgement-types will be discriminated precisely on the basis of what they can *say* about the world.

We can thus think of a categorization of judgements on a scale which represents a successive approximation to judgements which have true objects, that is, objects which are in conformity with their concepts, and which state this conformity. To begin with, judgements will be declared untrue because, regardless of their correctness, they cannot state this adequacy, for the reality concerned will not admit of it.

Hence we have a categorization which is both one of judgements in the usual sense and one of levels of reality.

This will perhaps make more easily understandable the motor of the dialectic in this division. A judgement has the basic form '*S* is *P*', which Hegel further specifies as linking an individual term to a universal term, hence saying 'the (particular) is (universal)'. The motor of the dialectic is the lack of commensurability of these two terms.

For it is clearly not true that the individual is the universal. Hence there is something contradictory in the judgement, and it must be transformed. This dialectical movement, which was taken up in essentials by the British Hegelians, has been often laughed at and thought to be based on a simple mistake: the confusion of different kinds of 'is'; between the 'is' of predication, the 'is' of existence and the 'is' of identity.

In order to see how the accusation of trivial confusion can arise, and also to

310

The Concept

answer it, we should start the movement of this section. We start off with the most lowly and simple kind of judgement which attributes a universal to a particular, e.g., the rose is red. We can think of this with an emphasis, as it were, on either side: either the rose as something rich containing many determinations, of which redness is one; or redness as extremely rich, instantiated countless times, of which this rose is only one example. But in either case, there is an incommensurability between the two, they are not equivalent; they are two incommensurable realities which touch only at this point, that the rose is red.

The incredulous reader is excused for believing himself the witness of a simple confusion between the 'is' of predication and the 'is' of identity. Of course, when we say the rose is red we are saying nothing about what entities the rose is identical with. The impression of confusion is increased by the emphasis Hegel puts on the copula. It carries the burden of expressing the ontological *Urteil*, that which underlies the very existence of external reality, hence the copula is linked at the same time to the 'is' of existence. So that this seems confounded in the general confusion as well. But what seems confusion here is nothing but a reflection of Hegel's ontology. For if we are looking at judgement forms for their truth, that is, adequacy to express the basic truths of ontology, then we have to look at the terms they link from this point of view of their commensurability. At the root of everything is an idea which sunders itself into external reality, which reality nevertheless remains identical to the idea. Subjectivity must be embodied so that it both is and is not its external embodiment. Really true judgements are those which can capture this truth. But then they must be such that the terms they link are candidates for this kind of identity relation. In other words, to the extent that judgement can capture the ontological basis of things (and a *single* judgement cannot really do so), it must be inter alia a judgement of identity, one in which the terms it links are in an important sense identical. This we plainly do not have in judgements of quality like 'the rose is red'. Hence they still suffer from incommensurability.

Does this mean that Hegel is assuming his ontology for the purpose of the argument in this segment, possibly because he thinks that it is already established in the earlier books of the *Logic?* It might sometimes sound like that, since Hegel's discussion of subjective concept is shot through with terms which he has developed in the earlier books. One cannot be quite sure what, if anything, Hegel intended to borrow from the argument which precedes this book. But it seems unlikely that he was simply feeding the conclusion of his earlier argument into the dialectic of the Concept.

Rather what seems to underlie the motor of this dialectic is the attempt to reach a standard of really adequate thought of the object. Really adequate thought would not just relate some superficial aspect of its object, but would lay bare its essential structure. It is in virtue of this requirement that we can reproach perfectly ordinary, correct judgements of quality with being untrue

311

Logic

because of the impossibility of relating their terms in an identity ('Such a single quality is not congruous with the concrete nature of the subject' *EL*, § 172).[1]

The basic property of really adequate thought for Hegel is thoroughgoing necessity. This requirement will be the real basis of incommensurability as we shall see clearer later on. Of course, this requirement, too, is bound up with Hegel's ontology, and is unlikely to be held to by one who did not share it. But Hegel probably did not see it as a corollary to be deduced from his vision of things, so much as an inescapable requirement of thought on any theory. We shall return to this below.

Hegel starts the section of qualitative Judgement with statements like 'the rose is red' which he calls positive. But the incommensurability forces us to recognize that particular is not really related to universal. Each is really for itself, identical only to itself; the particular is the particular, the universal is the universal. And this evocation of identity brings us to the next category, reflective judgements.

We cannot follow the detail of Hegel's exposition here which takes us through a number of different forms of judgement – judgements of reflection, of necessity, of the concept. The continuing theme is the incommensurability of the two terms. Later stages of this dialectic make the connection even clearer between this notion of incommensurability and Hegel's ontology. For instance, judgements of 'necessity' – such as, e.g., 'man is an animal' or 'gold is a metal' – are necessary in that they align a species to its genus. But they are still incommensurable because they do not reflect the movement in the other diection whereby the genus determines itself to species. Gold is necessarily a metal, but there is no necessity that metal should have gold as one of its species, i.e., that gold should exist.

The basic incommensurability of the terms in Judgement could also be described as the inability of the copula 'is' to unite two really commensurable terms. The resolution of this contradiction comes only when we replace the simple copula with an inference; we then have no longer just '*S* is *P*', *but* '*S*, qua *X*, is *P*'. Only a judgement of this complexity, which Hegel calls apodictic, can really show the link between *S* and *P*.

In other words, throughout Judgement the 'is' has not expressed the full reality of the ontological relation. It is the link between two terms, but it has not expressed the full richness and concreteness of this link. Now this comes out in the apodictic judgement, but it comes by a transformation of this link from a simple 'is' to a mediating specification. For instance, instead of just saying 'the house is good', we now say 'the house, as built in such and such a way, is good'. But this filling out of the copula makes it into an inference. We thus transcend the sphere of Judgement and enter that of inference, or as Hegel calls it, Syllogism.

[1] William Wallace translation.

The Concept

Syllogism

Syllogism unites Concept and Judgement. And it too must be seen first as ontologically grounded. As Hegel says in the note to *EL*, § 181 'Everything is a syllogism.' Judgement is ontological because the concept always goes out into external embodiment. But we come to a truer, completer picture of reality with the ontological version of Syllogism.

The unversal is united through its sundering with the fully external existent, the full reality of the particular. Thus we really need three terms to grasp reality. There is (1) the inner unity of things, which may be taken as the universal; there is (2) the sundering, but this is always into two opposed terms, whose relation constitutes (3) a totality which is the exteriorization of the at first undifferentiated universal. Each of these terms can then be taken as our starting point, and as such is related to another through the third.

Thus in the Addition to § 187 of *EL*, Hegel takes as example the Idea, Nature and Spirit. The Idea is the formula of necessity underlying all reality: it must externalize itself in nature, and also come to self-knowledge in spirit. Now these three are such that each is related to one of the others through the third. Nature is what by externalizing the Idea makes possible spirit, which is internalized exteriority or nature. But nature can only rise to full manifestation of the Idea through spirit. But thirdly, the Idea is the whole which is exposed and manifested in the sundered totality of *Geist* and nature.

The sense in which everything qua rational is Syllogism is therefore some quite transposed sense. Syllogism Hegel takes here in the sense of that which unites two terms through a third. The real is Syllogism because it is of itself diversified, and yet the elements of this diversity are internally related, so that they unite themselves. But what is more, the division can be expressed in three terms, whereby each is connected with another through a third. The reality is a whole which can be seen first as self-identity; but which second exists as two systematically related and opposed realities; realities which each can only be through their other. Hence each of these realities is related to the whole through the other; and to the other through the whole. So that all three terms can be thought of as middle term in its turn.

The analogy of Syllogism is (1) thus the unity of each to the other through a third, (2) the fact that this can be seen as in some sense a rational, necessary, conceptual unity, and (3) the triplicity of the relationship.

But where it is dissimilar from Syllogism is in this: that the relationship is wholly symmetrical. Each one of the terms can be the middle. The nature of this unity is one which goes beyond what can be captured in a single syllogism. It can only be captured in three, and then, we would still be lacking the unity of these three formulations. In fact ontological reality shows a unity that can only be hinted at in the syllogism; as becomes clearer at the end of this section,[1] but which Hegel fails to mention at the outset. It follows from this symmetry that it can appear rather arbitrary to attribute the logical terms universality, specificity, particularity to the terms of the Hegelian ontology. There is necessary triplicity, necessary conceptual unity of each to every other through the third, but the step further into the language of universality–specificity–particularity does not always fit.

Hegel in both logics is rather harsh with the ordinary sense of his age (and ours), which might accept the syllogism, as the soul of reasoning, as a subjective activity, but does not see it as an ontological property of those great objects of reasoning, (*EL*, § 181 note, also *WL*, II, 308-9) God, freedom, the infinite, etc. But everything is Syllogism because the underlying reality is ultimately such that it can only be understood as a triplicity of terms, one of which is the unity of the whole, while the other two represent the reality of this whole as sundered in two opposed, yet mutually dependent terms, which together as totality make up the whole. In fact, it is truer to say that every thing is a system of three syllogisms – or everything that is *wirklich*, that properly reflects the concept.[2]

So the truth of Syllogism is that each term is really the whole, is really the inner connection of the other two, not just externally in our reflection, but in itself.

The different forms of syllogism are laid out by Hegel with the double claim to deduce the usual table of distinctions, and to move through them as truer and truer forms to the final transition out of subjectivity. Once again, we cannot follow the detail of the development through the different forms of Syllogism. The motor of development here, the lack in each successive form that impels us on to a higher form, is the absence of necessity. A syllogism or inference claims to show a connection between two extreme terms, and if this connection is merely asserted, if the premisses are contingent, or rely on further reasoning, or worse, if they presuppose the conclusion, the inference is pro tanto imperfect.

Now what is being demanded of the syllogism here is something we do not usually ask of our inferences: not just that the conclusion follow from the premisses, but that these too be grounded in necessity. What is being sought – and what Hegel claims to find (rather implausibly) in the 'disjunctive' syllogism – is a form of self-subsistent necessity, a necessity of reasoning which requires no postulate, where whatever is given at the beginning must be shown out of the system. By this criterion even judgements of the kind 'man is a

---

[1] *WL*, II, 351; also *EL*, § 192.
[2] Of this we shall see examples later in the next division, e.g., the note to *EL*, § 198: The individual (particular) is connected through the system of needs, civic society (specificity) with the state (universal). But at the same time the individual will is what actually relates the two, which satisfies needs in the society, and gives the Right of this society reality. But thirdly the state is the substantial middle term which holds both individuals and their civil society in a coherent whole.

mammal' fail to provide adequate premisses, for – as we saw above – while it is not to be questioned that man is a mammal, we could not have this judgement unless man existed.

But to achieve a self-subsistent necessity in our thought is the same as winning through to a vision of necessity in things. To the extent that the necessary connections we are aware of are just between concepts *as against* in reality, to that extent we can only generate true factual conclusions if we start with a contingent postulate about reality. If we wish to use the necessary truth that the angles of a triangle = 180°, we have to be *given* the premiss that X is a triangle to be able to derive that X's angles = 180°. Conversely a necessary reasoning about reality which was self-subsistent, i.e., did not need a contingent premiss, would have to be grounded on truths about reality which could not be otherwise, that is, a necessity in things. But of course, it is this vision of necessity that we are aiming at. That is why mere conceptual necessity without existential implications is no use to us.

Now of course we have already seen this ontological necessity, manifested in the development of our indispensable categories of Being and Essence. What we have been doing in this first segment of the Logic of the Concept is showing how the same vision arises out of an examination of the categories in which we describe thought. Just as the categories of reality on examination move towards a manifestation of inner necessity; so the categories of thought on examination strive towards the corresponding culmination of self-sufficient necessity.

Thus from the stage at which Concept sundered itself into Judgement, by referring to particulars in the world, we have been following the development of thought about reality. And this development was sustained by the aim of achieving self-sufficient necessity. This then has been the real basis of that incommensurability which was the motor of the dialectic. It is why the non-identity of subject and predicate in the simple judgement of quality made them incommensurable (since identity in some sense is thought by Hegel to be involved in necessary connection). This is what forced us up through the different levels of judgement, and beyond these to syllogism.

Hence this development can be seen as powered by contradiction. For if we think that the goal or standard which thought aims at is absolute necessity, then all contingent judgements and reasonings are self-defeating. This is undoubtedly how Hegel does think of it. The essence of thought is rationality, and rationality comes to full expression in necessity. Once this is accepted, the dialectic of Concept, Judgement, and Syllogism has some chance of standing up as a strict dialectic.

But the question is whether one can accept this standard as the defining one for thought. And on the strength of what should one accept it? In the case of the *Logic* it could be justified as flowing out of the earlier books. This may have been Hegel's justification. But I do not think this question was all that clearly answered in Hegel's mind; and I believe that he at least half thought that rational self-sufficient necessity was one of the criterial properties of thought. And in this case, of course, the dialectic of subjective concept would be a self-authenticating one quite independent of what precedes it in the *Logic*. Hegel would be encouraged in this belief by the reflection that our thought is not easily satisfied with purely contingent correlations, that it looks everywhere for a reason.

But whatever the grounding of its principle, the dialectic of this segment moves towards a culmination in rationally necessary thought. And since this culmination is inseparable from a vision of rational necessity in things, this is the point at which we can say that subjectivity goes over into objectivity.

'Subjectivity' has two applications in Hegel. The absolute is subject, and one which posits its own embodiment. In this sense reality is ultimately subjectivity and this is an ultimate category. It is in this sense that the whole third book of the Logic is also called 'Subjective Logic'. But the word can also be used in something like its ordinary sense, in which we contrast what is 'merely' subjective with the reality over against it. This is the sense that the term has in this first segment of the third book, whose title is 'Subjectivity'.

This second sense in which what is subjective is less than, is inadequate to the real, has a perfectly legitimate use. Throughout this first segment we have been looking at modes of thought which are subjective in this inadequate sense. Corresponding to this imperfect thought is, as we have also seen, imperfect reality, which also fails to exhibit thoroughgoing necessity. But when thought rises to perfect necessity, and hence to a vision of the ontological foundation of things, it ceases to be one-sidedly opposed to reality. It becomes one with cosmic subjectivity which is so far from being devoid of and less than the real, that it actually produces the world out of itself.

Subjective thought goes over at its perfection into objectivity not only in that it ceases to be distinct from reality because inadequate to it; but also in the stronger sense that it rejoins absolute subjectivity which 'goes over' in the sense of positing reality.

This sounds awfully reminiscent of the ontological argument. And Hegel is the first to recognize and welcome this rapprochement, which he raises in the text. For of course, the ontological argument is really founded, if we give it the right form. We have here the right form. The absolute, as Concept – not just in someone's mind, here Anselm is still inadequate – must go over into existence. For the Concept, properly understood, is a self-subsistent conceptual necessity and this requires instantiation in reality. And to understand the Concept is to understand that it can only be this kind of conceptual necessity. But of course this only applies to the Concept, the absolute, the concept of the whole, or the idea of God in traditional language. This necessity of existence does not cancel contingency as we have seen, and hence whole lots of things are quite contingent and their existence is not contained in their concept, like the hundred dollars in my wallet, which is of course without necessary connection with the hundred dollars in my mind.

And even for things whose existence is necessary, features of the universe, like man: their necessity only flows from the whole, not just from *their* concept, if we think of this as the particular concept in the whole system which designates them. We can prove the necessity of finite spirit (men), but this follows from the whole system, not just from the concept of man taken on its own, as, e.g. rational life. Hence the Kantian objection weighs for such particular elements, and particularly for those which are contingent. It weighs for particular elements in so far as they are taken in abstraction, and for the contingent, for it is what takes itself as an abstraction, that wherein the concept is separate from the existence. But the objection totally misses the point applied to the ontological argument, the proof of the whole.

On the other side Hegel cannot just accept the formulations of Anselm, Descartes, Leibniz *et al.* For one thing they would be horrified to see the kind of 'God' whose existence is here proved, for this existence is inseparable from that of the world as ordered whole, and this is not the God worshipped by Christians. But Hegel specifically points out that the whole probative centre of the argument is left out and the conclusion just given in the Anselmian premiss that existence must belong to the most perfect. Or if it is argued for it is on the grounds that existence is in general a perfection, which invites the Kantian riposte. What is needed is to give the concept of the infinite whereby it must necessarily exist in a way which does not apply to the finite. This is connected with the other failing of the traditional proof which is to start with a concept in our minds. The proof really follows the unfolding of existence out of the ontological concept. Hence in the ratio cognoscendi it presupposes the other proofs for the existence of God, while it is really primary in the ratio essendi.

This last reflection enables us to see even more clearly how Hegel is at cross purposes with formal logic as this is usually understood. The 'forms' of thought are classified in terms of their functions in reasoning by both types of study. But for Hegel reasoning reaches its culmination in self-sufficient necessity, which is the same as the vision of a necessity in things. Hence the basic *démarche* of formal logic is *not* to abstract from content. On the contrary, it is the distinguishing mark of imperfect forms that form and content are not united, that they are 'just formal'. As we ascend the scale to more and more adequate forms, we move away from what ordinary formal logic would accept as formal criteria of distinction. We are no longer dealing with propositional functions which could take just anything as their arguments. Rather the search for an adequate 'form' in Hegel's sense (rational necessity) requires that we put restrictions on the concepts which can serve in it. Thus the judgement of reflection, or the syllogism of necessity are partly defined by their objects. And the final perfectly adequate form is only instantiated in Hegel's ontological vision itself.

Thus the 'formal' part of his logic and the usual science of formal logic are on utterly different tracks. But this is not to say that they can peacefully coexist as two quite independent enterprises. There is a philosophical issue involved. First, Hegel's enterprise is only given viability, even sense, by his ontological vision. It is because form is already immanent in content (necessity is in things), that it makes sense to try to draw content out of form (develop by formal criteria a thought adequate to reality). And reciprocally, Hegel while not denying the validity of ordinary formal logic cannot but depreciate its importance. It is *not* the science of reasoning at its highest. Hegel in fact would have been delighted with the modern developments in which logic has been shown to be continuous with mathematical thinking, since he always classed mathematics as the most external form of thought, incapable of really grasping the conceptual structure of things.

Thus in the dialectic of the subjective Concept we have come to the same conclusion as arose out of the dialectic of Being and Essence, the vision of a totality of the real which is manifestation of rational necessity. We had to prove this out of subjective thought also. Because if we were right that reality comes to exhibit conceptual necessity, then our conceptual thought should point towards a completion in unconditionally necessary reasoning. This has now been done and we return to a self-subsistent totality, an immediate reality

which has emerged through the cancellation [Aufhebung] of mediation, a being which is also identical with mediation, and [which] is the Concept which has constructed itself out of and in its otherness. This Being is therefore a reality [Sache] which is *an und für sich* – Objectivity. (*WL*, ii, 352)

II: OBJECTIVITY

The Concept thus goes over into objectivity. The search for self-subsistent necessity only reaches its end in a vision of reality as a necessary totality. We have thus in a sense returned to the vision of things which we had at the end of Substance. But we are now in a position to draw a much richer and fuller portrait of it.

What we learnt through Being and Essence was that reality constituted a totality governed by necessity and which manifested this necessity. But we learnt very little about the concrete articulation of this totality. We know only, through the dialectics of inner and outer, and necessity and contingency, that the whole must display contingency on its surface, as it were, since this is inseparable from exteriority.

The Concept

What we did glean from this, however, was that reality as absolute or unconditioned necessity is structured by concepts. This led us to examine subjective conceptual thought, and we found that it, too, was driven by an inner standard to what is now self-consciously a vision of a self-sufficient necessary totality. But now that we know that subjective thought reaches the same culmination as reality, that the concept in the mind is fundamentally one with the ontological concept, we are able to draw on what we have learned about the articulations of subjective concept to derive some of the necessary articulation of the real.

This is what Hegel now proceeds to do. What previously we knew only as totality governed by necessity is now seen as a structure with levels. Reality necessarily manifests different levels of being. The dialectic of Objectivity derives these in ascending order.

The stages by which we pass are called by Hegel 'Mechanism,' 'Chemism', 'Teleology'. But we must not assume from these titles that we will be concerned with an examination of mechanical and chemical theories. These are treated in the philosophy of nature. Rather we are dealing with certain very general ways of conceiving objectivity which have application respectively in the mechanical and chemical spheres, but also outside. Thus the mechanical also applies to certain functions of the mind, as when we learn by rote; and the 'chemical' in this sense is visible in the attraction between the sexes.[1]

The whole movement of this division is from externality of connection to the kind of intrinsic necessity which we have with life. For this section will end with Internal Teleology which is the category by which we understand life, and the next part opens with life. But Hegel wants to take in on the way different ways of conceiving objectivity which also have their obvious place and which were present in the sciences of his day. Some of these ways seem a little odd to us because they belong to the science of his day, or one school of speculation within it, but not in ours.

The motor of this development is the 'absolute contradiction' (*EL*, § 194) which consists in the fact that the real is at once a totality, whose parts are thus inwardly related, and yet also made up of parts which are integral and independent (*selbständig* and *vollständig*). For as well as having mediation and relatedness, it also has objectivity, immediacy, externality. In order to satisfy fully both these opposed descriptions reality has to articulate itself into different levels.

We start off with things as purely external and independent. Each thing is external and indifferent to the others. But this means that it is a mere aggregate in itself, for there is no reason to draw the boundaries of a thing or

---

[1] The notion of affinity belongs here, which played a certain role in the literary life of the period. Cf. Goethe's novel, *Elective Affinities.*

319

object at any given level. Hence each object is itself an aggregate of objects without intrinsic connection.

Mechanism

This is the level of mechanism. On this level of immediacy and externality, the thing is indifferent to its own characteristics, or put another way, its characteristics hang together in it without any internal necessity. It is because of this that we have to explain these characteristics by something else; the relations of causation which explain what it is are external, foreign to it (*WL*, ii, 360). Hence mechanism recognizes only efficient causation, which is always causation between terms which are merely contingently linked and identified, as Hume showed. Even causation 'within' an object turns out on examination to be a causal relation between separable parts of this object.

This yields the vision of determinism, in which the characteristics of one object are explained by another, and this in turn by another, and so on to the bad infinite.

But this level of purely external, contingent relations cannot be the whole story. For we know that things are also internally related, by necessity. Hence this level cannot subsist alone but requires others at which the relation is progressively interiorized. The object must become more of a centre. It must develop greater internal coherence, and demand according to its nature to be related in a certain way to others.

In the course of this interiorization Hegel takes us through a number of stages, each of which correspond to an obvious aspect of reality according to the science which he took as valid. Thus we move from the object which is purely indifferent to its characteristics, which thus offer no resistance whatever to the communication of such imponderable properties as movement, heat, magnetism, electric charge,[1] to the object as having a certain definite character and hence offering resistance to influences from outside, which thus appear as external force.[2] And from here we move to a further interiorization where an object is intrinsically related to others, as in a solar system for instance, which is not just a bunch of indifferent objects, but of objects which are ordered in definite roles vis-à-vis each other; sun, planets, satellites.[3]

[1] Analogous influences are communicated in the spiritual sphere between persons, as in a resistanceless medium, e.g., ideas, styles. *WL*, ii, 365–6.
[2] In the human realm this takes the form of fate: Cf. *WL*, ii, 370, where Hegel points out that natural objects go under in an external and contingent manner, because externality and contingency is their own immediate nature. But men have a fate because they act out of their universal nature, and yet inevitably sin against this nature, fate being the retribution of the genus on the particular acting man. Thus for man what happens to him, what undoes him has meaning for him; hence he has a destiny, which things do not.
[3] Hegel speaks of the relations between these as exemplifying three syllogisms wherein each is in turn the middle term; this is analogous to the individual in civil society and the state.

The Concept

But the intrinsic relation to others is still not in the very stuff of the object at this stage: true the earth is held in orbit by the sun, but this is dependent on its being in this spot, its very matter is not of itself and alone related to this centre. So that if we hauled it into outer space it would no longer be so related. Hence we step to the stage of Chemism where we see different substances as intrinsically related to each other, 'tensed' towards each other with the nisus to combine, to overcome their one-sidedness and become a single neutral substance. The dialectic of Chemism which is the middle chapter of this second division is pretty heavily indebted to chemical speculations of the time as they were taken up in contemporary philosophies of nature. Hence this chapter is both hard to follow, and unconvincing. It ends with a transition to Teleology.

Teleology

We come here to the highest level of reality which the world must exhibit. For in teleology we have the fullest embodiment of internal necessity. We are thinking, of course, of the notion of internal teleology, derived from Aristotle.[1] For this is the notion of a sense or purpose which is inherent in the object itself. The purpose is its essence, its most profound characterization. Internal Teleology is thus the category we need to characterize the system of absolute necessity, which we have had before us since the end of Essence.

Although Life is the category which comes after, and out of Teleology, living things – conceived outside of a possible reduction to mechanism – provide the best example of Hegel's category here. For living things have a form which is inherent in them. That is, the form is not imposed by the hazard of outside efficient causes, but is one which they realize themselves as they grow. This form is inseparable from their matter, it is the form inherent in a physical organism.

Their form is also a necessity, as it were, in that they cannot help trying to conform to it. But at the same time it is their own necessity. It is what defines them and is not something foreign. To conform to it is freedom for them.

The requirements of the whole life form can explain partial acts or processes in the organism, as what is needed for the whole. But this explanation does not just account for a fact by relating it to another, as with accounts in terms of efficient cause. It relates this fact to a purpose; it gives the reason for it. It gives the sense behind things.

Teleological explanation is explanation out of totality. The partial pro-

---

[1] Hegel gives credit to Aristotle; but also to Kant. For Kant had the idea in his third Critique of a unity between concept and intuition in which the two were not separated, but fused. The content is not just an example subsumed under a general concept, so that the two remain separate, but the form is somehow intrinsic to the content; it would not be the same without this particular content. But Kant is berated, of course, for holding his reflective judgement apart from determining judgement, and for refusing teleology a place – and indeed, the place of honour – in the order of things.

cesses are explained by their role in the whole. And in this way, also, explicandum and explicans are not really distinct, since the process explained is part of what explains it.

Teleology is thus the category in which we can account for the kind of totality Hegel envisages. For it is made up of independent, external realities, whose deployment nevertheless follows a necessity, but which necessity is not imposed from outside but inheres in the external reality itself. This necessity is, as it were, the life form of the whole. Internal teleology is thus the highest form of inner connectedness which external reality can exhibit. It is therefore the culminating term of this development which started with the pure external indifference of mechanism. The gamut of levels of being which the universe must contain runs from this formal mechanism to teleology.

The necessary instantiation of this highest level is what lies behind the fact that there are living beings in the world. But this category is also instantiated by the whole itself. Only, of course, the whole or absolute, unlike any living being, does not have a life-form which is just given, but rather one which it develops fully out of itself, as Reason. Its life's blood is reason, and the heart which pumps it is contradiction.

But in talking about life, we are running ahead of Hegel, who takes up this category at the beginning of the next and last segment of Concept. And Hegel, moreover does not step right from Chemism into the proper conception of teleology. Rather he makes one more transition, in which he starts from the conception which is current for common sense and philosophies of the understanding.

This inadequate notion is External Teleology – which of course is also instantiated as a subordinate level of reality. This is a category in which we look at things as the fulfilment of ends which are external to them. External teleology has its place, for instance in the artefacts and doings of man. We build houses to live in, grow food to eat, and so on. The 'teleology' of a house, a car, a field of corn (their *Zweckmässigkeit*) is outside of them; it must be referred to another agent.

Now Hegel believes as always that the basic principles of his ontology have been there in a confused form in people's minds for a long time. And one of the confused views, which puts together both the sense that teleology is an important category with which to understand the whole, and the common sense view shared by the philosophy of the understanding that form and content must be separate, is the view of the world as the product of an external teleology, that of God.

Hegel inveighs against this notion of providence, particularly the variants current in a certain facile, optimistic Deism of the eighteenth century, and prefers to take the side of mechanism against it. In actual fact, he explains, it leads to the attribution of all sorts of quite ridiculous particular purposes to

The Concept

God in the attempt to account for the detail of the world. It ends up with a whole set or bundle of unconnected ends ascribed to the deity; whereas the demands of reason are for a connected whole. At least mechanism tries to give us this (*WL*, II, 385–6). Moreover, it does not really lead to a fully necessary explanation by reasons, because God's reasons remain unknown. Hence contingency has the last word. In this, mechanism is no better; but it makes no claim to real explanation by reason. Hence External Teleology is worse because it lets down the side as it were, occupying the place of reason without being able to deliver the goods and do better, or even as well, as mechanism. 'External teleology is the stage immediately before the Idea, but what thus stands on the threshold is often precisely the least adequate' (*EL*, § 205, Addition).

Hegel wants thus to transcend External Teleology to Internal. External Teleology still maintains the separation of content and form (*EL*, § 205). The whole interest of Internal Teleology was that it really united the necessity with that which it operates in, that the form was inherent in the matter, as we saw with the analysis of the living thing. But this feature which gives it a place in Hegel's explication of the absolute is lost in External Teleology. On this view, I stand over against an external world. I have at first a purely subjective goal, and I put it into effect. So External Teleology presupposes at the start a separation between matter and the form which is to be fulfilled. And this separation is not really overcome, since the form is just something I impose on a pre-existing matter, it does not come from that matter itself. Thus let us say I build a house. The materials which go to make up the house are formed by me, but this form remains external to these materials; it is not a self-formation on their part, as the growth of a living organism is. My interaction with these materials is purely external, it belongs to the domain of mechanism and chemism; they are formed from outside, and remain 'indifferent' to this form.

This is not only true of our external teleology, that of our finite goals, but also of the teleological explanation of things by God's intentions. For the objects which God makes to serve a certain purpose remain in this sense 'indifferent' to this purpose. It does not come from them. This is why the purpose remains hidden unless we come to understand the being who made them. And since on this view we cannot understand God, the purpose remains forever hidden; something Hegel cannot accept.

In our particular purposes, the end is finite in another sense as well. It is a particular end, not the end of the whole; and therefore not something that justifies itself. It is a purpose which I impose on things, but not one which springs from them themselves. It is arbitrary. It is this, I think, which Hegel is saying where he claims that the product of a finite goal is itself a means, and that this is the root of an endless regress. (*WL*, II, 397). As long as we are dealing with externally imposed goals, with goals which presuppose an independent object

323

Logic

to be worked on, what is end and what is means is something arbitrary and subjective, depending on the agent who is acting. We grow grain in order to make bread, and eat bread to live; and live to? Living is the end, perhaps; but then is eating just a means to it, or is it part of it? Or to put the point another way, whatever we decide is the end can itself be questioned in its turn. Why seek this? We do not come to a final end which springs from the very nature of things, as with internal teleology.

But alongside, or underlying the external teleology of everyday life is an internal teleology of the whole; one which englobes our activity, which we understand in terms of finite ends. This transition is of course, powered by the need to grasp in objectivity an inherent necessity, which we can ultimately only find in internal teleology. Hegel makes the transition through the use of the concept of means.

Finite agents use means to accomplish their finite ends. That is, they take up a bit of the external world, and turn it on other bits to fulfil their purpose. They use tools, for instance. In this way, some part of the world becomes incorporated into their activity, it becomes swept up in action (Tätigkeit). The fulfilment of a finite end is like a syllogism in which the agent is related to the object through the means.

Now the relation of agent to means is at first just external and mechanical; but it eventually must point to a more inner relationship. Part of what Hegel seems to be hinting at is this: there is a certain incoherence in the idea of means as external to the agent if we want to push it to the very end and class everything as means which serves the end. For in order to use mechanical means in the world the agent must himself be a body. But we cannot understand this body just as a tool, and all that it does as simply means, for then there is nothing left of the agent. For instance there are certain primitive actions which cannot be further broken down, cannot be understood as performed by the performance of other actions. These can be seen as means, but not as means separate from the agent. He is not manipulating these actions; his manipulation of things just *is* these actions. This and related points have been explored in contemporary philosophy. Moving outward we can see that some of these primitive actions include our skilled manipulation of certain tools; so that in this sense our interaction with the means-object we are employing cannot be thought of as just mechanical.

Thus the first 'premiss' of our syllogism can be seen as mediated. But the second seems still quite external. When I work with an axe on a tree, the relation between me and the axe has to be understood in terms of skilled performance; the axe is integrated into my skilled performance. But the relationship between axe and tree is fully mechanical. But, says Hegel, these mechanical processes 'return of themselves, as has been shown to the goal' (*WL*, II, 397). In other words the whole movement of this chapter, rather than any examination of the particular phenomenon of subjective end-activity, requires that we go to a higher standpoint. We may see some unity between agent and means by examining external purposive production. But what is needed is a change of standpoint altogether, whereby we see the whole as purposive.

The switch of perspective to the whole brings us back to Internal Teleology. We must now see the activity of man, and the course of the world, which is the backdrop to it and which it affects, as one great course of life; as forming itself. But in this vision, all the oppositions fall away. What is worked on is no longer separate from the agent. The forming agent is internal to the formed.

Hence in Inner Teleology all the terms which are held apart in Outer Teleology come together. In the organism, to take this example again, everything is means to its life, but its good functioning, of liver, heart, etc., is also the end, for this is part of the organism. The organism again, in its adult healthy state is the realized end, but this does not prevent it from being always in the process of realization. Hence it is as it were, a standing intention, or *nisus* towards its own realization Hence *nisus*, means, realized end all come together. But all these aspects are not just collapsed. They remain as real aspects of the object. In order to understand it we have to see it as realized and realizing, see the end-means relations in it.

In this ascending dialectic, therefore, mechanism, and the pursuance of finite ends by finite spirits, point towards a fuller, all-embracing teleology of the course of the world; one which is always both realized and being realized, which is always at the end and the beginning; in which everything is means and yet part of the end. But mechanical relations and finite purposive activity are not cancelled or annulled. They remain real; only their action is in some way taken up and is grist to the mill of the infinite purpose.

The underlying conception here is one of different levels of being, the necessary articulations of a universe which must exhibit both independent externality and inner connectedness. Because there are different levels of being, there are also different levels of explanation. Mechanism can thus provide adequate explanations on its level (and the different stages of mechanism each on its own sub-level), while the phenomena it explains are incorporated in more complex beings which must be accounted for in higher categories, and ultimately in a whole which can only be understood teleologically.

We saw in Essence how the necessity of the structure of things went along with, indeed required contingency on their surface. Now the relationship between the two is fleshed out in the vision of a universe which exhibits different levels of being. The necessary structure of things manifests itself in a vision of the universe as the unfolding of an inner purpose. But the unfolding of this purpose requires its embodiment in external, material reality, and this is subject to mechanical and chemical forces and laws. The interstitial or superficial contingency of things, which always remains within the bounds of rational structure and plays its part in the perpetual realization of this structure, can be studied and mapped by laws of these lower levels, of Mechanism and Chemism.

Hegel is nowhere very clear about the way these different levels relate to each other. But he invokes here, as elsewhere, his famous image of the 'cunning of Reason', by which the higher purpose makes use of lower level principles in encompassing its end. Rather than working directly on the object, the higher purpose slips another object between itself and what it wants to transform. If it were to enter directly into the interaction of things, it would be a particular thing itself and would go under like all such things. But it cunningly saves itself from this fate by having its work done for it by the mechanical interaction of things in the world. (*WL*, ii, 398.)

This image may not be totally clarifying. But it reiterates the Hegelian idea that the infinite life of the world goes on through and beyond the demise of finite things. It only lives in these finite things, and hence through them, but it perpetually survives their necessary end. More, the play of contingency itself serves to realize the necessary plan of things. This is the full meaning of Hegel's image. If we ask how things work out this way, the answer is that contingency itself is part of the necessary plan. Within the play of contingency I may die today or forty years from now. But in either case my demise, as my life, expresses the necessary structure of things by which *Geist* must be embodied in finite spirits which as finite contradict his infinity and hence must die. I die in the end because of some footling mechanical failure: e.g., my heart fails as a pump. But then it is in the nature of the finite subject as a materially embodied being to be subject to the play of mechanical forces, and hence exposed to such failures. If it had not been this one it would have been another.

But Hegel's image of the cunning of Reason is also, and especially, related to history (cf. reference in *EL*, § 209, Addition). In this sense God's providence is the absolute cunning because he lets men follow their own passions and interests, but what happens is nevertheless the fulfilment of *his* intentions. We may find this relation harder to understand and credit than that between Mechanism and Inner Teleology. We will return to it in the next part.

Thus the universe has many levels because it is the unfolding of an inner necessity in external reality. The infinite end is realized through finite ends. And that is why we can see the end of Reason both as always realized and as always having to be realized.[1] The experience of finite subjects is that the plan

---

[1] This notion of a goal which is always realized and yet to be realized is the basis of the crucial concept of Hegel's political philosophy, as we shall see in the next part. This is the notion of ethical life (Sittlichkeit). It is what takes us beyond a mere morality of what ought to be, a striving

of Reason has yet to be fulfilled. They strive towards it. But if we rise to a vision of the whole we can see that this very striving is part of the plan and that as a whole it is already realized (*EL*, §212, Addition). The appearance of unrealizedness is an error, a deception; and yet this deception itself is brought about by the Idea, as is the overcoming of this error by ourselves.

Thus the necessity which we followed through the book of Essence emerges here as purpose. The necessity inherent in reality is an unconditioned one, as we saw. This means that the course of things is not determined by merely given antecedents, it does not exhibit the ineluctable consequences of certain given premises. On the contrary, nothing is merely given in the system of unconditioned necessity. Everything which happens issues from necessity. Hence what follows from the conception of the universe as the locus of unconditioned necessity is a vision of things in which purpose is paramount.

We can speak of a purpose when for some reason a goal can be thought of as at work in events prior to its fulfilment, bringing these events about, so that they occur, as we say, 'for the sake of' this goal. But this means that the notion of purpose was already implicit in the idea that changes in the world come about of conceptual necessity. Thus when we explain the changes in finite things, as we already did in Infinity, as powered by contradiction, we are saying that the cycle of changes in the world comes about in a perpetual attempt to resolve contradiction. Or in other words, we explain these changes by a norm they are striving to meet.

But the conception of the purposiveness of things is taken to a higher power when we come to see the necessity as absolute. To see events as directed towards a norm or end is to see them as offering an answer to the question, why do they happen? But normally we think of the search for reasons as coming to an end somewhere, at a goal which just has to be taken as given. When we have described the life form of a finite living thing, in terms of which we explain aspects of its structure and activity, there is no further answer to the question, why? The life form just is as it is.

But absolute necessity does not repose on some given premiss which would be beyond explanation. Necessity is absolute because everything can be derived from Reason. Hence the question, why? never reaches a barrier in the merely given. Or if one prefers this formulation, the ultimate goal is just that *Geist* or Reason be, i.e., that there be a rational structure all aspects of which yield an answer to the question, why? in which nothing is given as a merely 'positive' fact. In this world purpose is supreme or absolute, purposive explanation is ultimate in a radical sense.

Hence the universe is to be seen as the unfolding of a purpose. Moreover the purpose must be internal. For an unconditional necessity, as we saw at the end

after which never is fulfilled because it is not grounded in the nature of things, which is thus the particular goal of External Teleology.

327

of Subjectivity, must be in things. If we were dealing with external teleology, a purpose imposed by a transcendent God, then the necessity would not be absolute. The shape of things would repose ultimately on divine fiat. The whole must thus be seen in the category of Internal Teleology. The all embracing purpose inheres in the universe itself. This is what underlay the Substance, Cause, Interaction of the later phases of Essence. For to explain by the inner purpose of the whole is what we called there explanation out of the totality. The universe which unfolds according to its own purpose is causa sui. The purpose is a cause but no longer an external one. Purpose remains in its result ('it is not transient in its agency but maintains itself', *EL*, §204).

Hence at the end of Objectivity we come to a view of the universe as unfolding in fulfilment of an intrinsic purpose. But we are not just dealing with a living thing. We know that this objectivity has been posited by the Concept, by thought seeking necessity, seeking the fully rational. So it passes to a new ontological category, that of a reality which only exists to fulfil a formula of Reason; whose only existence is to fulfil an Idea. This is a unity of the objective and the subjective. But it is not a simple identity. Rather they must also be in a sense distinct since one posits the other and determines it to be what it is. They are one, but also in relation. As in a subject, their unity is not only *an sich* but also *für sich* (*EL*, §212). Objectivity not only fulfils the ideal formula of thought; but is made to do so by this formula. Hence the two are joined and yet forever over against each other (as the purpose in inner teleology is always fulfilled and being fulfilled). For this relation, the term which irresistibly springs to mind is Plato's Idea. Kant first borrowed the term. Now Hegel follows suit.

III: THE IDEA

So we begin the Idea, Idea is to be understood in the Platonic sense. It is the inner reason which makes the external reality what it is. Hence it is to be understood in connection with the Hegelian idea of truth, the unity of concept and objectivity. 'The Idea is the true which is *an und für sich*' (*EL*, §213). For truth as we saw is that reality be in agreement with its concept, with the concept which produces it. But the concept producing a reality and bringing it into agreement with it, this is the Idea.

Kant was right thus to think of the Idea as something unconditional, transcendent, of which we could make no adequate empirical application (*WL*, II, 407). But as usual, he drew the diametrically wrong conclusion. Instead of concluding that the Idea has no ontological status but is just regulative of our thought, he should have seen that this inadequacy of the empirical reality is not a lack in the Idea but in empirical things. This is why they are finite. 'The individual on its own does not correspond to its concept; it is this limitation of its existence which constitutes its finitude and its demise' (*EL*, §213).

The Concept

Nevertheless, however imperfect, the particular thing only exists at all because it to some extent expresses the Idea. Even bad states, men, etc. that is, untrue states, men, etc. only exist because they are not entirely so. For everything that exists comes out of the Idea. The totally untrue, a reality which would in no way correspond to the Idea, would be nothing (*WL*, II, 309).

In this third part, we are going to bring this conclusion of the whole *Logic* to its full development. We started off in the category of Infinity, which was our first category which presented the whole as totality, with the idea of a self-subsistent system of necessary changes. Through Essence we developed this further and saw that this necessity was inherent in external reality itself; but that this reality as external also exhibited contingency. But this contingency was not independent, rather it was posited by necessity. The necessity in things was thus absolute, that is, not conditional on anything merely given.

Absolute necessity brought us to the Concept. With what we gained from this we returned to examine the totality of the real and developed its articulations much further. So that we now see it as distributed on a hierarchy of levels of reality, of which the lower, starting with the mechanical, are incorporated in greater, more intensive unities by the higher. The highest level is that of purpose, and it is instantiated by the whole. So that we not only see the whole as governed by necessity, but as exhibiting purpose.

It is this ultimacy of purpose which has been drawn out explicitly in Objectivity. And this is what has led us to the higher category of the Idea. For if absolute necessity means that purposive explanation is ultimate, then we must see the whole world as there for a purpose, as there in order to manifest this necessity. So that we are no longer envisaging it as a whole which is given, and which as a matter of fact is governed by necessity, as we have an animal species which is given and which as a matter of fact is shaped by a given life-form. This whole which manifests necessity exists for a purpose, so that we can say that it exists in order to manifest necessity. The formula of this conceptual necessity is the Idea, hence the world exists to realize the Idea.

Now we can see the whole as the locus of a double movement. There is the movement of finite things which go under and succeed each other in an effort to overcome the inconsistency of finitude, to attain the self-coherence of rationality. But there is also the movement of the Idea of rationality itself, which goes out and posits a world of finite things. The duality of worlds, or the duality in the real which we constantly had in Essence could never sustain itself, for reality is one. But the duality of movements which we have now arrived at is consistent with the unity of the real, for these movements form a circle. We have not added something but enriched our understanding of the one self-sufficient totality.

But if the Idea itself goes out and posits a world, which is external and thus only imperfectly exhibits its inner connections, then it too contains difference and division within it. For it must posit its opposite, what negates it, in order to be. Hence corresponding to the contradiction in the finite and grounding it is as it were a contradiction in the infinite, which lies in the fact that the infinite only achieves its identity by reconciling contradiction, by finding itself in its other. This central position of contradiction follows once we accept absolute necessity. For if the world of contradictory, finite, things exists of necessity, if that which being external and indifferent cannot fully embody the formula of necessity exists according to that formula, then this Idea itself contains its own opposition.

The Idea is thus a process of positing its other and then recovering its unity with itself in its other (*EL*, §215, *WL*, II, 412). This process is a dialectical one. It is a struggle, and any conception of the Idea which omits this is radically faulty.

the thought which frees reality [Wirklichkeit] from the show of purposeless mutability and transfigures it into the Idea must not represent this truth of reality as dead repose or a mere picture, lifeless, without impulse or movement...; the Idea, by virtue of the freedom which the Concept attains in it, has also the *most stubborn opposition* within itself; its repose consists in the security and certainty with which it eternally creates and eternally overcomes this opposition, and comes together with itself in it [in ihm mit sich selbst zusammengeht]. (*WL*, II, 412)

The whole system hangs together by contradiction and struggle. The Idea puts forward reality in order to be. But were this reality not contradictory, and hence transient and in movement, it would not show forth necessity, and hence the Idea would not be. So the Idea has to put forth a world which is in contradiction to itself, as well as being its own other.

This process can only be grasped by reason, the thought which thinks the oppositions in their movement, whereby they come to be and are overcome. Understanding which tries to fix the opposition is impotent here and is doomed to distort reality. (*EL*, §214.)

It follows from this that the final category, the Idea, is not just the result of the previous stage of the *Logic*. It in a sense includes them all. For the Idea issues in the particular realities which are captured by the other categories. And at the same time it links them all together so that they come back to itself. It thus englobes all that has gone before.

The absolute is the universal and one Idea, which sunders itself in the act of judgement into the system of determinate ideas; which in turn by their very nature return to the one Idea which is their truth. (*EL*, §213)

This division will articulate what it is to see reality as posited by the Idea, by a purpose. First, of course, it is to see the whole as analogous to a great process of life, as we saw in the last division. The first category taken up will therefore be Life.

But if we think of the whole as emanating from conceptual necessity, then this necessity has to be for a subject. Hegel now adds a crucial dimension to the picture of reality he is drawing. Of course, the existence of the subject has been implicit all along for we have been dealing with categorial concepts, concepts with which the subject thinks his world. But this was just part of our given starting point. Now Hegel shows it to be a necessary feature of the universe that the world appear to a subject.

The underlying reasoning seems to be this: conceptual necessity means a necessity of thought and this presupposes a thinker. To say that the world is posited by conceptual necessity is to say that thought is at its foundation. And thought necessarily appears to itself. So that a universe posited by conceptual necessity must be aware of itself. But this awareness could not remain merely implicit and semi-conscious, for the thought at the basis of everything is conceptual necessity, and this can only be exhibited in the explicit clarity of conceptual thinking. True necessity can only be properly aware of itself in concepts. So that if the process of thought at the base of things were to remain merely implicit, it would paradoxically remain outside the system of thorough-going necessity which it posits. It would violate its own essential requirement.

Hence if necessity is to be all-embracing, if it is not to leave something outside it as merely given, it must appear to itself. Hegel sees these two requirements, for the omnicompetence of the Idea and for its self-consciousness, as inseparably linked. The link was already present in the notion of reality as Appearance, of necessity as manifest, which we saw in Essence. For the claim was first that necessity as manifest is really in things, not imposed from some other, hidden source, and hence that it is total, i.e., it does not presuppose a reality on which it works and whose original existence is outside its scope. But Hegel was also claiming in the same breath, as it were, that a necessity which is intrinsic to manifest, external reality must itself be made manifest, that is, it must appear to a subject. A necessity which could not be made manifest, one which was hidden and unknowable, and in that sense merely inner, would also be 'outer' that is, it would not fully bind reality. Thus conceptual necessity to be absolute, to penetrate reality without remainder, must become manifest in thought.

That is why the winning of clarity in philosophy is itself part of the realization of the Idea in the world. And that is why this third book of the *Logic* has explicitly envisaged reality as for a subject.

Thus the unity of Idea and reality cannot be simply *an sich*, as it is in Life, it must also be *für sich*. So that Knowledge is a fundamental category of the *Logic*. We must accept that 'absolute truth is the object of the logic and *truth* as such is essentially *knowing*', (*WL*, ii, 413–14).

But then knowledge requires consciousness, the structure in which a subject is over against an object. In other words, there must be finite subjects, both because as consciousness they must be over against a world of objects and because as really existing subjects they must be determinate. And this introduces another division in the world, or rather shows us the basic division of Idea and reality from another angle. The Idea must go out into its other, external reality, in order to return to itself. But its return is just the making manifest of this necessity in reality. Hence the return is complete when this necessity is fully grasped by the subject. But subjectivity is necessarily finite, and hence the struggle to return can be seen as the struggle to overcome this finitude and come to a grasp of the infinite, the whole, the absolute.

Beyond Life, therefore, the Idea must generate the category of Knowledge. But knowledge, too, as the consciousness of finite subjects must be transcended. Since this is a struggle of finite subject to transcend himself, it concerns not only knowing but also willing. And the transcending of finite knowledge brings us to an infinite knowledge, that knowledge of the whole by the whole, which is the Absolute Idea.

This then will be the plan of this last segment. It will take us from Life, to Knowledge, which in turn will be divided into a discussion of knowing and willing, to the Absolute Idea.

We start with Life, both because it is the immediate unity of Idea and reality, and also because knowledge presupposes life. For the kind of unity between Idea and reality which knowledge is presupposes an immediate unity, one in which reality is actually in conformity with the Idea. Consciousness, as we saw, can only arise in living beings. So this immediate unity is derived in the Logic both for itself, out of the category of Teleology, and as a presupposition of Knowledge which is the necessary following category (*WL*, II, 414).

Life

Hegel understands life very much as Aristotle did. The living being is the locus of inner teleology; he is both means and end. He cannot be understood as just composed of parts, but of members, that is his parts are essentially related to each other in their role in the whole life-process. Each is both means and end. Thus Hegel quotes Aristotle with approval, that a hand which is separated from the body is still a hand in name only (*EL*, 216, Addition). Life realizes the immediate truth of the Idea because it illustrates the unity whereby the purpose or form is intrinsic to the content, the matter itself. A living being is an objective totality, intrinsically bound together in a single process of life which is always realized and always being realized. Life thus transcends mechanism and chemism which are held in subordination as long as life continues. They start to take over as soon as death occurs; 'the elemental forces of objectivity ...are as it were continually ready to pounce [auf dem Sprunge], to set their process going in the organic body, and life is a standing fight against them' (*EL*, §219, Addition).

But the objective does have its day, for death is essential to the living. Here Hegel states again one of his basic theses (*EL*, §216). As unity of the Idea and objectivity, Life must be embodied, hence must be embodied somewhere, hence must be particular living thing. But as particular living thing it can never really conform to the universal idea, it is contradictory and so mortal. It must go under.

But as particular living thing, it is over against inorganic nature (*EL*, § 219). This is the 'Urteil' of the concept; that is, the concept of life necessarily sunders itself into living thing and world which stands over against it. He has to maintain his life over against this reality. Hence life is a standing activity, a struggle (beständiger Kampf) against its opposite. Life is a process which must always be creating itself out of its opposite. For life is particular living things. These are distinguished and hence opposed to the outside world. They have to maintain themselves by assimilating this outside world. This is the dialectical derivation of the assimilative interchange of animals with the environment.

This struggle is a reflection of the struggle that is inherent to the Idea which must realize itself against its own external self. This struggle is a contradiction and so is it in the animal world. The animal needs something; it knows that this something outside it should be part of it and is not. It feels this in impulse, or sometimes pain. Pain is thus the 'privilege' of living things, it belongs to them only as the existing concept (*WL*, II, 424). This is the living contradiction, which is the answer to all those who claim that contradiction is unthinkable (loc. cit.).

The contradiction is resolved by the animal incorporating what it needs. This it can do because external reality is already *an sich* the idea. It thus becomes incorporated to the organic. The organic can work on the inorganic mechanically, but not vice versa. The inorganic can only stimulate (erregen) the living. (*WL*, II, 425.)

Thus the living individual comes to produce himself, to cancel the 'presupposition' of an inorganic opposite him and incorporate it in himself. In doing this he becomes substantial universal, what Hegel calls 'Gattung' (genus). This means that he undergoes another kind of sundering, now into two individuals. This is the dialectical derivation of sexual differentiation. The living thing is an embodiment of the Idea which must sunder itself into particular elements and then maintain its unity through them. Thus the separate individuals strive to unite. But they cannot succeed, or rather they do succeed, but only in a third individual, their child. This then steps forward as a new individual, while they, as all particulars, the contradiction of individual embodying universal, die.

The living thing dies because it is the contradiction of being *an sich* the universal or the genus while yet existing immediately as only a particular.   (*EL*, § 221, Addition)

Thus Hegel sees living things as an imperfect realization of the Idea. They are life, purpose intrinsic to matter. But they do not succeed in maintaining the unity or the eternity they seek. Unity and eternity here are linked, since eternity is unity over time. They achieve this thus only in a broken-backed way, an endless regress of succeeding generations. We have first the living thing deduced from the Concept, then we see it producing itself out of the inorganic. So we see that the Idea which produced it is really in it; it is Concept, Genus. As such it sunders itself and gives itself differentiated existence in the world. But it cannot come back from this and maintain its unity; or it can do this only in the broken-backed way of reproducing its kind, and then undergoing death, being succeeded by others.

But this unity is broken-backed because it is only *an sich*. It points beyond itself to the necessity of a unity *für sich*. There must be a way in which we can escape from the separation in particular beings, from being strewn in exteriority, to inwardness and unity. This step beyond the finite, which is realized *an sich* by death of particulars, the cancelling of their exteriority, is realized *für sich* by self-consciousness, by knowledge. Hence the rise of consciousness is related to death; it is the dialectically higher form of which death is the lower.[1] It is the real immortality of living in *Geist*. And it is the next stage which is ineluctably pointed to by the consummation of life in the Genus.

The Idea of life has...thus freed itself not just from some one particular immediate 'this' but from this first immediacy as a whole; it thus comes to itself, to its truth; with this it steps out into existence as free genus on its own. The death of the merely immediate individual living being is the coming to be of spirit. (*EL*, §222)

Knowledge

So Life as immediate unity goes over into what Hegel calls Knowledge. This is really the subjectivity of the Idea, that wherein it shows itself not just as the inner rational formula of everything, but as a subject, which knows its own external reality; and which can thus be thought of as positing it as a subject does. That is why this section will deal not just with knowledge in the narrow sense, but with will as well.

In short we are showing how the category of consciousness or self-consciousness has a necessary application, because it is integral to the Idea. And because consciousness is necessarily finite, we are proving out of the Idea another feature of the world which was implicit in our starting point; the world of Being is for finite subjects, it is grasped in categories.

In the introductory passage in *WL* (II, 429–39) Hegel naturally cannot resist referring once more to Kant; and as usual with a mixture of plaudits and condemnation. Kant was certainly right against the former metaphysic, which wanted to understand self-consciousness as a soul which was necessarily simple. On the contrary, we see that consciousness is necessarily diremption, that

---

[1] Death is the natural *immediate* negation of the particular. We need a *standing* negation, self-consciousness. Cf. the dialectic of master and slave, *PhG*, 145.

which posits objectivity over against it; and which is in essential relation to objectivity.

What is basic is thus the polarity between subject and object. This Kant saw and made basic. But he drew from it the conclusion that subjectivity could never be understood, that it was merely the everywhere present unity of apperception which could never be an object of knowledge. The 'inconvenience' (Unbequemlichkeit) of the 'I think' that it is always subject and never object; so that we are objects to ourselves only as empirical selves, not as the original subject; this Kant takes as a bar to knowledge of self-consciousness. But for Hegel this attitude was inexcusable. For in seeing that subject is necessarily polarization, that it necessarily must be subject confronted by object, far from having a bar to knowledge, we have a basic grasp of its real nature. This is what distinguishes it from a stone (WL, II, 432). We can only consider ourselves barred from knowing it if we take the basically Humean attitude that the subject is what must be known in inner intuition. Then of course, the 'I think' escapes characterization, because it is the presupposition of all content. But if we try instead to *conceive* the subject, we have here the basic clue to its nature; self-diremption, that which gives itself a content; that which becomes for itself.

But this self-distinction must take two forms. The Idea is both self-knowledge in other, and self-creation in other. Hence its subjectivity has to be thought under two modes. It is both knowledge of itself as other; and also realization of itself as something independent of itself. In the absolute Idea, these two aspects are one. But this life has to be lived through finite subjects, for infinite subject can only be real through embodiment in finite subjects. This necessity of embodiment is what introduces opposition, opacity in the absolute subject. For finite subjects have to struggle to recover the transparency of the self-identity of the Idea. Or in other words the opacity which comes from the necessary external embodiment can be seen as the opacity inseparable from the thinking of finite, embodied subjects.

Hence the two aspects which are one in the Idea are separated in the life of finite subjects. These subjects have to win through to the difficult grasp of their unity, whereby at last the Idea has produced integral truth, a reality which is in conformity to it. This separation takes the form of a separation within each of the aspects. Finite subjects know the world, but they know it normally as separate, over against them. This is connected with their perceiving it as contingent, for they do not penetrate to its inner necessity, which is nothing other than the Concept, hence the very stuff of their thought.

At the same time finite subjects have a sense of the good. Hegel is here talking not just about some finite end, such as we discussed in external teleology, but about the absolute justified end, the creation of a world of truth, of conformity to the Idea, which is also the good. Now men have an inkling of this, too, as well as the idea of knowledge. But here too they misconstrue it as a merely finite end; one which is absolutely justified, but nevertheless the end of a finite subject, to be wrought *ab extra* on the world. (*WL*, II, 479); 'here [the content] is indeed finite, but it is as such also an absolutely valid one'. Hence they oppose their activity to the as yet untransformed external world.

In other words the Idea yields the necessity of a unity in difference which is both a production of external embodiment and a knowledge of self in this external embodiment. So that finite spirit, as its vehicle, must know and strive; it has an Ideal of knowledge, and an Ideal of Good (which Hegel calls the 'Ideas' of knowledge and the Good respectively in *WL*). But as finite it has both these ideals as perpetually unrealized ideals. Knowledge cannot come to full necessity; and striving always sees itself as unfinished.

Hegel puts it also this way: for knowledge, the important side is the objective side; the point is to conform our knowledge to the outside reality. For striving the important reality is subjective; it is the good which has to be realized in the world. The outside as yet untransformed reality is known by the striving subject as the '*an sich* null' (nichtig, *EL*, §225).

This leads to contradictions on both sides, which take the form of endless incapacity to reach the goal. In the theoretical domain, we never arrive at the necessity of things without transcending the partial, finite point of view. In the practical, the contradiction is even more marked.

As long as we remain finite agents of the good, then the good we achieve is open to all the accidents of fortune. It is a finite content, which can be destroyed by outer contingency or by evil. And worse, its conditions of realization can enter into conflict with each other (*WL*, II, 479–80).

But this is not yet contradiction. This comes to light when we see that the finite good will cannot reach full success. For if the world were quite transformed to conform with the good, then there would be no more striving. For the good will, by its very definition as finite will over against a world to be acted on, would not exist. (*EL*, §234, Addition.)

Hegel is here once more criticizing Kant and Fichte, as he makes explicit in the Addition to the paragraph just quoted. The notion of morality as simply *Sollen*, as not being capable of fulfilment because then it would cease to exist as morality, is one of the basic oppositions which Hegel bent himself to overcome. But he now sees this contradiction of the endless progress of an 'ought' that never reaches fulfilment as intrinsic to the notion of a finite good will as such; since the idea of a finite good will is that of a will over against an external reality which it must be exercised on. What would become of morality if everything good were integrally and definitely realized?

The answer can only be a conception of the realized goal of morality which incorporates as an essential element our moral activity. This means a course of the world which is realized goodness, but which exists not in abstraction from our activity, but includes and is predicated on this activity. But this means a view of the good in which moral action is not necessarily the struggle against the im- or amoral reality which waits to be transformed; but can be the response which completes a context of realized goodness. This is of course a view of morality which must break with the Kantian opposition between the good will and inclination.

But this vision can be seen as the dialectical synthesis between the stance of cognition and the stance of will. As we saw above the former is the view that the external world is the essential, whereas we have to conform our minds to it in knowledge; the latter is the view that our project is essential, to which the world as the inessential, the 'null' (nichtig) must conform. The true solution which solves the contradiction is one which unites these two; which retains the essentiality of our project, and does not fall back into the error of knowledge which was to feel that we are out of the truth; while adding the truth of knowledge that the object or the world also is essential embodiment of the Idea.

We then have a notion of a course of the world which is the fully realized good – this we get from knowledge – but we do not think of ourselves as separate from this, so that we just have to try to conform ourselves in knowledge. An integral part of the world's goodness, of its being the realized good, is that it incorporates our action for the good, our striving. The idea of the good as finite will retained the basic inadequacy of finite cognition that it held subject and world separate. Hence the subject could only be the good will by opposing itself to, working on, an unregenerate world. This is the subject defined by irreconcilable opposition to, difference from the object – the abiding sin of Kantian philosophy. This must be overcome.

And we know this must be overcome because we have understood that reality must issue from a conceptual necessity which is a subject, that therefore everything must be in its truth, i.e., conformity to the Idea; and hence that such a separation is nonsense, blind, obstinate nonsense. This is what mediates the transitions here. For Hegel the finite will just has to come to see that it is operating in a world in which the good is realized. In *WL*, Hegel makes use of the dialectical conclusion of the phase of External Teleology: that the means is the end, in order to show here that the means-activity that is the striving of the finite agent to the good, is not separate from the good, but identical with it. This unity is there *an sich*, it simply has to become *für ihn*. What is needed is to see this striving in perpetually unrealized causes, this imperfection constantly trying to rise above itself, as the realized goal of goodness itself.

For as we have seen, from the highest standpoint, imperfection, evil, opacity, separation, have their necessary place in the Hegelian course of things. Only by this exteriority, and hence division, opacity, suffering, can the good be realized. This is the vision which we finally climb to. 'The null and the transitory constitute only the surface not the real essence of the world.' (*EL*, § 234, Addition.)

In *EL*, §§ 233 and 234, Hegel presents the contradiction in a slightly different way. Finite will is the contradiction which holds that the world over against it is inessential, 'nichtig', and yet it is also essential, for without it this good will would not be.

We have seen how the dialectical synthesis of both attitudes, cognition and will, solves the problems of will as finite. This is, of course, a familiar theme with Hegel; it is one of the central ones, if not *the* central one of the *PhG*, under another name. Here it was a matter of the relation between consciousness and self-consciousness; the first being the attitude that set us opposite an essential world we have to conform to, the second being the certainty of self that sought to make good against an inessential world.

But we should also see how the synthesis solves the problems of finite knowledge. As long as the subject is over against a world from which he is forever separate because he cannot in any sense penetrate or be part of it, then the problem of knowledge is insoluble. We are forever shut out from the depths of things, from things as they are in themselves. We can only register certain facts, which remain for us contingent, brute facts, of which we cannot give the why? What enables us to go beyond this is that the world is not other to mind, to reason, to our reason; and it is not other because it is posited by that reason. Hence the finitude and limits of knowledge, too, can only be over-come by fusion with the other stance, that of striving, of the will to realize the good, which is the intelligible plan of things.

Of course, on the level of finite spirits, these two cannot coincide, for we only know in part, and we can only effect part of the whole plan; hence the two remain separate. We know much more than we can effect; and this we know externally. And we effect things which we do not really understand; and in this respect we act in the dark not seeing the real cosmic significance of what we do. But when we rise to the unconditioned, absolute subject then we see that the two come together and are both whole; as they must be.

This is the major drama of this chapter, which therefore culminates in Absolute Idea. But there is also a lot of detail. The chapter starts first with the Idea of the true (just 'knowledge' in the *EL*) and goes on to develop the idea of the good ('willing' [das Wollen] in *EL*). Cognition passes first into willing, and then the transition out of willing to the next section takes place with the synthesis of the two.

We cannot go into the detailed development of cognition, which Hegel uses as a springboard to discuss analytic and synthetic knowledge.[1] It culminates in

---

[1] In the discussion on analytic knowing in *WL*, Hegel returns to a discussion of the famous Kantian claim that mathematical propositions such as $7+5 = 12$ are synthetic (446–9). For Hegel they are analytic; and cannot but be because they involve no 'conceptual' element at all; they are purely

The Concept

the notion of a purely abstract necessity, one which is outside of the content of the world, or purely inner. Cognition is before a simply given world, one just 'come upon' (vorgefunden). The necessity is subjective, (*EL*, § 232); and this is what makes the transition to willing. We have seen how this in turn leads to a synthesis between the two; and so we climb to the speculative or absolute Idea (*EL*, § 235).

This [essence of the world] is the Concept existing *an und für sich* and so the world is itself the Idea. Unsatisfied striving ceases when we learn that the final purpose of the world is accomplished, even as it is perpetually accomplishing itself...But this agreement between what is and what ought to be is not torpid and without inner process; for the good, the end of the world, has being only while it constantly produces itself, and this difference remains between the spiritual and the natural worlds, that while the latter moves only in a recurring cycle, in the former at any rate progress takes place.

(EL, § 234, Addition.)

We have an 'objective world whose inner ground and real subsistence is the Concept. This is the absolute Idea'. (*WL*, II, 483.)

Absolute idea

Thus we reach the absolute Idea which can be seen as the synthesis of knowledge and life, the unity *für sich* and the unity *an sich* of Concept with its object. It is soul, free subjective Concept. 'All else is error, confusion [Trübheit], opinion, striving, caprice and transitoriness; the absolute Idea alone is being, imperishable life, self-knowing truth, and is all truth' (*WL*, II, 484).

It is a self-determining (Selbstbestimmung) which sunders itself and comes back to unity with itself. Art and Religion are modes of its grasping of itself and its giving itself an adequate existence. But philosophy is the highest, purest way; for it is the way of the Concept itself. The Logic seizes the Idea in a pure and transparent way.

Thus logic presents the self-movement of the absolute Idea only as the original *Word*, which is an exteriorization or *utterance* [Außerung], but one which in coming to be has immediately vanished again as outer; the Idea is therefore only in this self-determination, that it *apprehend itself*; it is in *pure thought*, in which difference is not yet *otherness*, but is and remains perfectly transparent to itself. (*WL*, II, 485)[1]

---

abstract like all quantity. Hence it is quite inappropriate to ask whether '7+5' and '12' have the same or different content. But Hegel is not just deducing his conclusion here out of his prejudice against mathematical philosophy. His argument is interesting.

When we say 7+5 = 12, we are saying that if you take seven, and add ones five times to it, then the answer is twelve; '7+5' is thus not a description which could contain '12' or not, it is simply a set of instructions (an Aufgabe) to add five to seven. These instructions presuppose a set of accepted operations by which they are to be carried out, which are simply those involved in counting; to follow these instructions correctly is to get to 12. There is nothing synthetic here in the Kantian sense because there is no predication, indeed no description in the normal sense. We have here no theorem, only an *Aufgabe*.

[1] A. V. Miller translation (amended), in *Hegel's Science of Logic*, London, 1969, 825.

The Logic is the science of the Idea as the pure inner formula of necessity of the world, which thinks itself and produces a world which is in conformity with it. If this is the ontological truth, then it follows that we can follow this through the study of the different concrete dimensions in the world, the structure of nature, of spirit, in politics, history, the structure of the mind, and so on. All these must reveal the basic form of the Idea, that they are posited by the Idea. And this is what we shall discover in the other sciences which make up the Encyclopaedia, the philosophies of nature and spirit.

But there also must be a science which takes the inner formula not through its concrete outer embodiment, but through its inner conceptual structure; which deals therefore not in concrete descriptions but simply in categorial concepts, and which shows how these are bound together. Such a science is the *Logic*, and we have just gone through it. But it is not abstract, against the concreteness of other sciences. For it is concrete in the sense of presenting us with a self-sustaining whole; it presents us with the necessity that the Idea go into external reality, and come back to itself. Hence it presents us with no vision of the concept as abstract, but rather as fully concrete. But as the derivation of the structure of the universe in pure thought, in categorial concepts, it is a pure vision. It is as Hegel says ideally transparent, because it is nothing but thought of thought whereas all the other sciences are thought of some particular matter, which has contingent and not totally transparent content to it. The logic is pure thought. It is the inner life of God before the creation of the world, in the famous image which Hegel uses in the Introduction to *WL*.

In both Logics, Hegel terminates by a discussion of the 'method', which is a kind of recapitulation of the whole procedure followed. In *WL*, this takes up a great deal of space, and is worth commenting on.

The method is the basic procedure; but we now know enough to know that this method is not externally chosen or applied to what we are studying; it is the internal movement of the categorial concepts. It is the movement of the Concept itself (*WL*, II, 486). It is not some kind of tool which can be separated from the knowing subject and the object reflected on.

We have to start with something immediate; but it must not be an immediacy of sense or representation, but of thought, hence a categorial concept (488). We need something which does not have itself to be derived, for otherwise we would never get started. The obvious candidate is 'being' itself, for we have here a categorial concept which all others seem to presuppose if they are to have any application at all; for if they are to have application, then there must be some object to which they apply.

Hence 'being' is a kind of absolute beginning, which does not seem to repose on anything else, as they all do on being. Of course this does not mean that our beginning is without presupposition, for it is not shown as a matter of necessity yet that things must be; this will come at the end when we close the circle. But we have a concept such that if anything is to be assumed, it is the one to start with. In a sense we can say of 'being' that it sums up, englobes within it all the other categories, it is their universal; but only in the abstract sense that it is what is common to them all in abstraction from their differences.

It is the whole in this abstract sense; and as the whole is not related to any other concepts outside it; it does not presuppose any others, as 'cause' for instance requires 'effect', or 'essence' requires 'manifestation'. This Hegel sums up in the expression that 'being' is the abstract self-relation (die abstrakte Beziehung auf sich selbst). It is self-relation, because related to nothing else, but abstract because it is this only by being the abstract universal; without internal differentiation.

But as self-relation it is already implicitly totality, it is already the germ of the real infinite of self-related totality in system which the absolute will reveal itself to be. The absolute *an sich* is already there, what is going to follow is an inner development whereby it will get internally richer, and become the articulated absolute, or the absolute *für sich*.

But now as we have seen this simple universal goes over itself into differentiation, sundering, judgement. From the point of view of finite knowledge, the additional specific content which we have to add to the universal is found, or observed in reality. But we see that it comes out of the universal itself, that the universal itself goes over into its other. This is the dialectical movement in it. We saw that Being goes into the differentiation of *Dasein*, that *Dasein* goes into its other, and is contradictory, and so on in perpetual becoming and change.

Now this dialectic has usually been taken to show the nothingness either of the objects which it affects (as with the Eleatics for instance), or of the thought which encounters it (as Kant held, for instance). But both these views are mistaken. The result of the dialectic is not just negative, not just nothing, so that we have to go back to square one. Because the contradiction is a determinate one, the result is a new form. Hence Being becomes Determinate Being, which in turn as contradictory refers us to others, which are bound to follow it because of its inherently contradictory nature. This it is senseless simply to give up and conclude to Nothing. Moreover Nothing itself as we saw is not a stable stopping point, because being is inescapable. Nothing is only comprehensible as the negation of Being.

Thus the ordinary reaction before contradiction, to conclude to nothingness, will not work. It fails to work in both its forms. We cannot conclude to the nothingness of reality, without landing in the absurdity of Nothing. And we cannot conclude to the simple error of our thought, for we have seen that this contradiction is implicit in being itself. Our thought is neither just analytic nor synthetic, but both.

The contradictory is real, or the real (Being) with which we started is

Logic

contradictory. This is what we are forced to accept. But if the contradictory is real, reversing the first development, then it must somehow be self-related, and not simply be dependent on others and still others in endless regress whereby we come to no firm basis. The second term, difference or contradiction or fragmentation, issues out of the first term, unity or Being, by a necessary movement. It is the other of the first. But it contains this first in itself, because it issues from it. If the positive or unity contains necessarily the negative or division in it, by a necessary movement, then the reverse is also true. Division must also come to unity (*WL*, II, 495–6).

In other words, being, real being turns out to be contradictory; but then contradiction must be real. Hegel speaks of this as a conversion or turning point (496, 497). It comes when we see the contradiction which strikes being not just privatively, as a disaster. But seeing that there must be some reality – else how could we be undertaking this enquiry? – we conclude that contradiction cannot be its demise or the proof of its impossibility, but rather its basis. And since contradiction is necessary becoming, inner conceptual necessity governing change or unfolding, we see this inner conceptual necessity as that which underlies all reality. In other words, we reverse the proposition, as we saw above, and in doing so substantialize the second term. Contradiction is now not just a predicate implying non-existence; but is itself a reality, a subject, an operating principle. Contradiction as necessary movement posits, or deploys Being.

So being *is* in contradiction. Because being cannot but be, therefore contradiction has reality. This, on closer examination, turns out to form a circle. Contradiction is that which dissolves, destroys being. But if being is and contradiction is nevertheless essential to it, then contradiction must also create being. So contradiction, necessary movement, deploys being.

We thus reach a third term (497) which is the restoration of the first. The negative is negated and comes back to the positive. We have once more Being, self-related, in this sense immediate, but now having contained and cancelled mediation in itself. It is 'the immediate, but through cancellation [Aufhebung] of mediation, the simple through cancellation of difference, the positive through cancellation of the negative' (*WL*, II, 498). We have a return to self.

But this return can be seen from two sides. It can be seen as the return of pure Being to itself through the overcoming of mediation. That is, we can start with Being, see it break up into determinate beings, and then see these come back to unity through being linked in a necessary movement powered by contradiction. But in the course of doing this we discover that everything is as it is of necessity, following a necessary formula or Idea. And so we can also start with the Idea. We can see this go over into objectivity, hence exteriority and indifference; and then see the return as the recovery of unity with subjectivity, where the inner connection nevertheless becomes manifest.

The Concept

These two ways of putting it correspond to the path of discovery, and the real ontological order, respectively (*EL*, §242). In other words, the reversal of proposition by which we make the contradiction itself subject brings us to the true order of things. This contradiction properly understood will turn out to be the inner necessity, which is Concept, Idea, absolute subject.

This contradiction or negativity is

the simple point of negative self-relation, the innermost source of all activity, of living and spiritual self-movement, the dialectical soul which everything true has in itself and through which alone it is true. (*WL*, II, 496)

The third term is then this subjectivity embodied; it is 'the individual, the concrete, subject' (*WL*, II, 499).

This basic necessity of return to self, or reversal, is the motor of the whole dialectic, its inner formula. But the science of Logic is not reached in one step. This necessity was discovered at the very beginning, as we saw, with the Infinity of *Dasein*. But although we then knew that reality had to be such a self-returning circle, that it had to be inner necessity of movement which is one with being, we had not yet got an adequate way of conceiving this reality. The one-storied categories of Being did not suffice; nor did the not properly unified categories of reflection. We knew that we were dealing with external reality, which is also inwardly bound by necessity; but we had yet to put these together in an adequate concept. In other words, we had only the formula of an adequate ontology; we had yet to work it out.

This dialectic is what we have followed through the various stages of the Logic, particularly Essence and the Concept. We find in the end that only a subject, a self-thinking rational necessity which posits necessarily an external world which it governs and in which it recognizes itself, that only this meets the bill; this is the Idea. But in the meantime we shall find that all the various other ways of conceiving it; as ground and grounded, appearance and law, cause and effect, force and expression, whole and part, inner and outer, all these show themselves to be inadequate. They do not meet their concept, and have to go under.

But each of these stages is in a sense the absolute. It is a manifestation of the whole system. It is an attempt to grasp the whole system which reverses on itself. And because the inner cohesion of the Idea also requires externality and division, each of these imperfect stages has a certain relative truth. Each 'is an image of the absolute, but at first in a limited mode, so that it is driven onwards to the whole...' (*EL*, §237, Addition).

So the progress from stage to stage is a progress from totality to totality where each succeeding version is richer and more concrete, is closer to a real image of what the totality is. It is an enriching of our concept, in which greater extension means higher intensity. (*WL*, II, 502). We start off with simple

Being, in which we have in a sense an image of the totality, for it is self-related. It suffers diremption into *Dasein*, but returns to itself in Infinity and *Fürsichsein*. This is richer inwardly. Finally we get to the Idea which is the richest of all. But in achieving this inner complexity we have also achieved greater inwardness, greater intensity of inner unity, hence in a sense greater interpenetration and hence higher simplicity. When we come to the end we have subjectivity, self-consciousness, which is the most complex unity, but at the same time the most simple, because it is totally transparent. It is a unity where the separation of parts, the mutual exteriority (Auseinandersein) is totally overcome. We come to the greatest articulation of our concept, but also the most intense unity and hence clarity and simplicity.

This is the point where we return through this great simplicity to Being again. Whereas each of the stages is a return, in the sense of being a model of the great necessary return, with the Idea we really bring it off. We have an adequate model of this return; and hence a real derivation of this simplicity of Being. With this we really close the circle. We not only show the necessity of a return which flows from the postulate of Being and the discovery of contradiction, but we achieve this return, with the idea of a necessity which must posit its own existence, a subject which must posit its own embodiment.

We only achieve the return of Being to itself with the Idea, that is, with the understanding that reality is the locus of a double movement, only one of which starts from Being. The other, which is the more fundamental one, starts from the inner necessity, from the Idea, itself. Thus being only returns to itself at the price of being dethroned or displaced as the real starting point of things.

Being breaks up into the complex multiplicity of determinate things. What we call its returning to itself is the recovery of the simplicity and unity of the category 'being' in spite of, or through this complexity. But this comes about through our seeing that the multiplicity of determinate beings is bound together by necessity. The real return to unity comes when we see this necessity as absolute. But if necessity is absolute, then everything that exists, all being, exists for a purpose. So that the starting point is really this purpose itself, the inner formula of necessity, or the Idea. The whole third book of the Logic shows that this reversal is essentially involved in the notion of absolute necessity, and hence it culminates in the Idea.

So Hegel has established his ontology. What is primary is subject or reason or conceptual necessity. These terms are inseparably linked. The essence of subjectivity is rational thought and the essence of rational thought is conceptual necessity. Or, alternatively, reason requires conceptual necessity. And so sovereign reason requires absolute necessity. But if necessity is absolute, then it must posit all reality to conform to it. It is thus purpose. And as thinking (conceptualized) purpose, it is subject.

This primary term, which can also be called the Concept or Idea, produces out of itself a real world. And this it does of necessity, since subjectivity, hence thought, reason or conceptual necessity, can only exist embodied. This embodiment has a necessary structure, that is, a structure it must have if it is to embody the Concept. Hence both *that* the world exists and *what* it is like are necessary, given that reason, subject, necessity must be. This embodiment as external negates the Concept, and hence negates itself since it only exists as posited by the Concept. This is why it is mortal, in perpetual movement, and in this movement returns to the Idea.

Thus what emerges from the *Logic* is Hegel's vision in which the whole structure of things (including what is contingent) flows necessarily from the one starting point, that Reason (or spirit, or the Concept) must be.

But we have seen that in order to close the circle of necessity, in order to show that this ontology was not just an interesting and perhaps persuasive interpretation of things (another argument from design: things are just as they should be, if...), Hegel had to demonstrate this starting point itself, show it to arise inescapably out of the scrutiny of the finite. And this proof was doubly necessary: not just to convince others, but to fulfil one of the requirements of his ontology itself, which called for Spirit to return to full rational knowledge of himself through man.

It is this titanic, incredible task which Hegel has been struggling with in the Logic, and which he thinks himself to have realized. For in starting with Being, the simplest, emptiest, most inescapable postulate, that there is (some kind or other) of reality, he claims to have shown that the dependence of everything on reason or the Idea follows inescapably. Hence the circle is closed. Being, our starting postulate is swallowed up, in the sense that it is shown to exist necessarily. With this reversal, Hegel has established the circle of seamless necessity of which we spoke in Chapter III.

This concept of necessary existence, of course, will be hotly contested, and it is impossible to give a justification of it which is distinct from the entire argument of the *Logic*. But perhaps it is now a little clearer what it means than it was in Chapter III. Necessary existence means first existence for a purpose, in order to fulfil a plan. That things exist necessarily means to begin with that they are posited. But it requires also that the plan or purpose be itself necessary, and this for Hegel means that it be derived from the notion of necessity, together with the related ones of reason, concept, subjectivity. To this we must add a third condition, that the plan or purpose is not that of a subject who exists separately from the world governed by it. The teleology is internal.

Now the ontology of necessary existence is one in which nothing is merely given, except that necessity must be. There is no being which is given, since everything which is derives from the necessary plan. The content of the plan is not simply given, since it derives from the nature of necessity. Everything that is, one might say, exists for the sake of necessity (or Spirit, or reason). And so

345

at the foundation of all is a requirement, that conceptual necessity, or the subject, or reason be. Thus this necessity inheres in things. It is the intrinsic purpose of the whole.

Not only does reality exist of necessity, the ascending movement by which we rise from an external understanding of things to a vision of the Idea is itself part of the plan. A world issuing from rational necessity must be known rationally. Since the subjects who know are finite, they have to ascend in knowledge from a finite point of view which sees contingency to a vision of necessity. And in order that this ascent be fully rational, it has to be made throughout of necessary inferences. If it were not, then finite minds could never rise to rational certainty (through necessary argument) of rational reality (the necessary in things). But it is integral to the realization of the Idea that they do so. So that the rational inferences of the ascending movement are part of the necessary existence which the Idea deploys for us.

And this is another reason why the Idea as the final category includes all the earlier categories within it. Not only because they correspond to levels of being which issue of necessity from it, but because they are also stages of imperfect insight on the road of its return to itself out of finite consciousness. The error in these imperfect ways of seeing is thus not absolute, but simply consists in not seeing their partiality; not seeing, in other words, that what they apply to is itself partial, and an outwork of perfect necessity.

The Logic is thus meant to be the ascending movement which takes us from finite consciousness to the vision of things as issuing from the Idea. It is, once we have eliminated the *PhG*, the only serious candidate for this function in Hegel. Does it succeed?

It is evident from the above that a crucial factor in the answer will be what one thinks of Hegel's proof of the contradictory nature of the finite which comes in the second chapter, on *Dasein*. For it is this contradiction on which Hegel's attribution of necessity to the real is grounded. It is this which allows him to derive the category of Infinity as a self-subsistent whole whose deployment is governed by necessity. And at this point the decisive step has been taken, since the whole rest of the work can reasonably be regarded as a development of what is implicit in this notion of necessary totality, one in which the necessity is in things.

For this allows us to show that the various conceptions of Essence, which project some underlying foundation behind the external phenomena, are untenable, since they would separate the inner necessity from things. We derive from this that necessity must be manifest; and later that it must be absolute. And from the absoluteness of necessity, we derive that the totality is there in fulfilment of a purpose, that it is a subject which knows itself, and hence that it is grounded in an absolute Idea. In other words, quite early on in

The Concept

the *Logic*, with Infinity, we establish necessary connectedness as a criterial property of adequate categorial thought about the world. This then provides the motor for the dialectic which takes us through the rest of the work, and by which the higher categories are made in the end to reveal their dependence on the absolute Idea.

This means in practice that the Hegelian dialectic does not function throughout according to the formula described above in Chapter IX (and earlier in Chapter IV), whereby each term shows itself to be in contradiction, the attempt to resolve which generates a new term which reveals a fresh contradiction, and hence generates still another term, and so on. The opening passages do indeed follow this formula: the dialectics of Being and Nothing and of *Dasein* in the *Logic*, of consciousness in the *PhG*. Thus Being suffers the contradiction that it turns into its opposite, Nothing, and this forces us on to *Dasein*. To be, Being must be determinate. But then we encounter a fresh contradiction, which tells in the opposite direction, as it were, that Determinate Being contains its own negation and hence necessarily goes under. Under the impetus of these two opposed requirements – that Being must be determinate, and yet that its determinacy is mortal to it – we are pushed on to Infinity, the immortal, self-subsistent system of mortal dependent finite beings. But with Infinity we reach a term which does not suffer (although it contains) contradiction; rather it is a formula whose implications only need to be fully drawn out to bring us to the final reconciling synthesis.[1]

At this point there is still a lot to be done: much is implicit which has to be spelled out, and a host of categorial terms have yet to be considered. But the procedure from now on is not really that these new terms, once generated, reveal each a *fresh* contradiction which pushes us on to the next, as Hegel seems to have thought. It is much more that these higher categories are brought before the bar of Infinity and its successor terms, that is, before the concept of a self-subsistent chain of necessary changes, and shown to be inadequate. In the process the vision of self-subsistent necessity is enriched from Infinity up to the absolute Idea.

What from time to time appear like fresh contradictions and hence independent bases of argument, other than this development of the implications of necessary totality, such as the conflict between sufficiency and informativeness

---

[1] Similarly, in Chapter I of the *PhG*, Hegel showed that there is no pure awareness of particulars, but that we always designate by universals. But then in the dialectic of Perception he shows that the universal cannot be designated independently of the world of particulars. The difficulty of combining these two requirements, i.e., of combining the particular thing and its properties, is what pushes us on to force, and eventually to the self-repulsion of the identical, and hence self-consciousness. The rest of the *PhG* as a largely interpretative dialectic 'coasts' on this initial set of transitions.

In comparing the two works we can see that the weakness in the opening arguments of the *PhG*, mentioned at the end of Chapter IV, that it seems to assume the requirement of necessary explanation, is at least meant to be repaired in the *Logic* by the capital transition to Infinity.

in Ground, or the 'incommensurability' of ordinary judgement and reasoning to self-sufficient necessity as a criterial property of thinking in Subjectivity, turn out on examination to be dependent on this main line of argument. It is quite likely that Hegel did not think they were so dependent. This seems quite plausible in the case of the ascent through Judgement and Syllogism in Subjectivity. But it may have been as well that many transitions, e.g. from Measure to Essence, from Cause to Interaction, from Possibility and Reality to Necessity, were understood by him as semi-independent of this main conclusion of necessary totality, that they fed into it without relying on it. But this independence would be very difficult to sustain. In fact most of these arguments collapse ignominiously without the underlying premiss of ontological necessity.

If this interpretation is right, then the crucial support for the whole edifice of Hegel's system reposes on the argument in *Dasein* on the contradiction of the finite. For those who like myself find this argument unsuccessful, Hegel's demonstration of his ontology can only have the force of a more or less plausible interpretation of the facts of finitude, the levels of being, the existence of life and conscious beings, the history of man, as 'hints and traces' of the life of an absolute subject, deployed in the world.[1]

---

[1] Hegel throughout the Logic faces the difficulty that the basic ontological structure he means to establish is more readily visible 'high' in the scale of being – e.g., in living beings, or conscious subjects – while his enterprise demands that he establish this ontology first at the lowest level, with simple Determinate Being. So that the examples he needs to give his thesis plausibility are in a sense not apposite when he really needs them.

Thus Hegel from time to time finds himself drawn to illustrate a category with an example from a much higher sphere. In discussing Being-for-self, he refers us to the 'I'; in talking of polar opposition, he not only cites the examples of the magnet and electricity, but also of virtue and vice, truth and error, nature and spirit.

The dilemma Hegel finds himself in can be put in this way. On one hand he holds that the lower forms of simply material reality are imperfect manifestations of the basic ontological reality which comes out most clearly in spirit. Hence the centring of the solar system around the sun is a reflection of the centring of subjectivity, but imperfect in the sense that it is a centring in external space, not conscious of self. Similarly, we might think of the struggle between fire and water as the imperfect manifestation on their level of the struggle between opposites which comes out best in the spiritual realm.

But on the other hand, it is not enough just to hint at the truth in a sort of hermeneutic of natural science, one in which we point to the 'signs' in natural things of their ontological relation to the Idea. Rather to have to *demonstrate* this ontology. And the demonstration has to be made at the level of the lowest categories, those which apply to everything, and not just to animals, men, society. For otherwise we will not have shown the categories which Hegel draws from the life of subjects to have truly universal, cosmic application.

Thus, for instance, with material oppositions like fire and water, we have imperfect, unclear manifestations where the basic ontological structure is not transparent. And this opacity is what makes it difficult if not impossible to demonstrate this structure in lower, material things. And yet it must be demonstrated here, if we are to prove that nature is an emanation of spirit and hence that we are *justified* in explicating virtue and vice, or body and soul, or birth and death in terms of this structure as Hegel does. The Hegelian ontology is easy to *expound* in relation to spiritual beings, but has to be *proved* first in an ascending dialectic which starts with mere determinate beings, where on Hegel's own theory it is imperfectly and unclearly manifested.

This poses a dilemma for Hegel's enterprise, which he hopes to avoid by the proof of contra-

But although this might be satisfactory for a Romantic view it was radically insufficient for Hegel. Spirit must come to full rational self-knowledge in man. And this means that man must come to rational certainty about the absolute. If this kind of certainty, founded on rigorous argument, is not possible, but only an interpretive vision, then Hegel's synthesis breaks asunder.

Either God does not come to full rational self-knowledge, but only a profound and not fully articulable intuition of his nature, and we slide towards a Romantic pantheism. Or God comes to rational self-clarity but beyond man and hence beyond the world (since man is the only worldly self-consciousness); and we slide towards orthodox theism. In one case we sacrifice the principle of rationality, in the other the principle of embodiment. They can no longer be held together.

But even those who draw this dismaying conclusion will find in the *Logic* an immense tissue of restless argument, which even though it does not reach its appointed conclusion, leaves no reference point of the European philosophical tradition untouched, unexplored, unshaken. The enormous energy of thought, struggling with the raw material of argument to make it yield an impossible conclusion, has generated a profusion of unforeseen lines of reasoning which have yet to be properly explored.

diction in finite being. If this proof is unconvincing, then there is a gap in his argument which he can only make up by borrowing, as it were, on his later ontological conclusions. But this loan is from a bankrupt bank, for these conclusions are themselves founded on the supposed pervasiveness of contradiction in finite being.

CHAPTER XIII

The Idea in Nature

We have in the logical Idea the pure inner thought of the world. But the truth of this entails that it go over not just in inner necessity but in reality into a world. And hence the Logic ends by deducing the fact of nature. In other words we have just shown that everything emanates from an inner necessity and thus that Being is self-related as a totality, and hence immediate. But this as Hegel says, is no transition, or becoming; it is not like the moving from a less perfect to the more perfect form. These transitions were between levels within the totality. Here we have nothing but the totality itself as we have already shown it to be.

The point is that real self-subsistent necessity has to inhere in an independent reality. It must be a free necessity, that is, must emanate from the reality itself as its own. And this means that there must be a free self-subsisting being which has its own necessity. Hence says Hegel the freedom of the Idea entails that it 'leaves itself free' (*WL*, II, 505); that it must issue in, *be* a reality which is not held in the lead strings of the Idea as an external source of control, but which itself has this necessity. But to be is to be determinate. Determinancy implies that things are really external to each other; and this means that they exist in space and time.

Hence this existent totality in space and time must be what has the necessity in itself. Freedom, that is, self-necessitation of the real, since the real requires existence in time and space, implies a totality in time and space which secretes its own necessity, whose necessity is not external to it, as it still was in the forms of subjective concept, and cognition. Thus the very attainment of the Idea as the fullness of internal necessity, requires that this be fully external. The fully inner is the fully outer; in both good and bad sense these coincide, as we saw.

Thus there is really no transition here but an equivalence. The Idea leaves itself free, as we saw. 'Because of this freedom the form of its determinateness is also completely free – the externality of space and time existing absolutely on its own without subjectivity' (*WL*, II, 505).

The underlying image here is that a subjectivity before a world without inner necessity can only retain necessary order by thinking the world himself. He must perpetually watch it and keep it in the tutelage of his thought lest it fall into mere contingency. But if we are really dealing with free necessity, then the world can be left free, and will exhibit this order itself. So the freedom of the

Idea entails that it 'resolves to let the moment of its particularity, of its first determination and other-being, the immediate Idea as its reflection, to let itself as *nature* go forth freely from itself'. (*EL*, § 244.)

Nature thus issues from the Idea. This is the starting point of the philosophy of nature and the entire set of dependent, interpretative dialectics which make up the philosophy of spirit. We cannot unfortunately follow them all here. In the *Encyclopaedia*, which Hegel published in 1817 and which went through three editions before his death, Hegel lays out his whole system in compact form. The *Logic* is succeeded by the Philosophy of Nature, and this in turn by the Philosophy of Spirit, which in a sense completes the triad by mediating the Idea and Nature.

The Philosophy of Spirit is itself divided into three parts. The first, Subjective Spirit, deals with what can roughly be called psychology and man's powers as a thinking (individual) being. The second, Objective Spirit, deals with spirit as embodied in human society, and is Hegel's philosophy of history and politics. The third, Absolute Spirit, touches on the absolute's knowledge of itself, as couched in the three great media of art, religion and philosophy.

The latter two parts were of course the object of other works of Hegel's mature years, the *Philosophy of Right*, which he published himself, and the lectures on the philosophy of history, aesthetics, philosophy of religion and history of philosophy, the notes for which were published shortly after his death. These were the domains of Hegel's richest interpretative dialectics, about which he thought deepest and in which his originality came most to the fore. We shall take them up in the next two parts.

Hegel's philosophy of nature was a somewhat more derivative work. He drew greatly on the earlier speculations of Schelling and the Romantics. We saw in the first chapter how the idea of a poetic physics, which would show traces of the divine in nature, greatly excited the Romantics. And it was a preoccupation which they shared with Goethe. Hegel, off on his own eccentric path in the 1790s, seems to have come late to this preoccupation.[1] He was concerned rather with the religious history and destiny of man. Schelling was the philosopher who cashed in on this vogue of spiritualized physics, as it were, and supplied the philosophical vision of nature the age hungered for.

Hegel's first steps in philosophy of nature were taken under the influence of Schelling. But his own system required a philosophy of nature. For all being issued from the Idea, and it must be possible to show this by examining reality at all levels. Hegel's final philosophy of nature is thus a transposition of

---

[1] The only sign of Hegel's interest in this area in the 1790s is the unpublished MS which has been entitled 'The earliest System Programme of German Idealism', where Hegel speaks of 'giving wings back to our physics which advances slowly and laboriously by experiment' (Hegel's *Werke*, Suhrkamp edition, Frankfurt 1971, Vol. 1, p. 234). This text was long attributed to Schelling.

Schelling's in which the structures of the Idea, as Hegel understood them, are shown to be embodied in the natural world.[1] The philosophy of nature is therefore really what we called a hermeneutical dialectic. Hegel would probably not like this term, with its implication that final certainty always eludes us. But it is in any case clear that this dialectic is a dependent one. It does not start from an undeniable point of departure and move thence by strict argument. Rather it presupposes what has been proven in the *Logic*, and also what has been shown by natural science and shows how one reflects the other. Rather than a proof, it provides an exposition of the agreement of nature with the Idea.

The philosophy of nature thus comes after natural science and must agree with it. Or as Hegel puts it

> It is not only that philosophy must accord with the experience nature gives rise to; in its formation and in its development, philosophic science presupposes and is conditioned by empirical physics. (*EN*, § 246, Remark)[2]

But at the same time, it must seize the inner necessity of nature. It sees nature in 'its own inner necessity according to the self-determination of the Concept' (*EN*, § 246).

Necessity belongs to the Concept. We have to show its traces in nature, and this presupposes the empirical results of natural science. But it is not an appeal to experience, for the structure of necessity comes from the Concept. We deduce its stages and then recognize them in empirical nature. Hegel reminds us that

> in the course of philosophical knowledge the object not only has to be presented in its determination according to the Concept, but the empirical appearance corresponding to this determination also has to be specified, and it has to be shown that the appearance does in fact correspond to this conceptual determination. But this is, in relation to the necessity of the content, not an appeal to experience. (*EN* § 246, Remark)

Later on, he says that natural philosophy takes the stuff that physics prepares for it out of experience at the point where physics has brought it, 'and reconstitutes it' (*und bildet ihn wieder um, EN*, § 246, Addition, p. 44). It gives the findings of physics its form of necessity as something which 'as an intrinsically necessary whole proceeds out of the Concept' (loc. cit.).[3]

The trouble with the findings of physics as they are is that they lack this necessity. The universals are just formal, abstract, that is, without inner relation to their particular embodiment. Which means that they are also

---

[1] Naturally Hegel wants sharply to differentiate his philosophy of nature from that of the Romantics, which he considers largely arbitrary and gratuitous, based as it is on intuition, which is really only a 'Verfahren der Vorstellung und Phantasie (auch der Phantasterei) nach Analogien...' (*EN*, § 246, note).
[2] M. J. Petry translation, in *Hegel's Philosophy of Nature*, London 1970.
[3] M. J. Petry translation, in *Hegel's Philosophy of Nature*, London, 1970 (amended).

contingent, for they are discovered by examining this embodiment which is without inner relation to them. And so the determinate content is outside the universal 'split up, dismembered, particularized, separated and lacking in any necessary connection within itself, and so is only finite' (*EN*, § 246, Addition, p. 45)[1]

Our job is to take this back to unity. But here is where we run into a lot of resistance. Some believe that the universal, thought, the subject, is forever cut off from the particular existence, reality, the object. We can never pierce the veil. But in fact this absolute division is denied every day in our practical activity. Even animals have this intuition of the nothingness of what opposes us. Against those metaphysicians who claim that we cannot know things, 'because they are absolutely fixed over against us', we could say 'that even animals are not as stupid as these metaphysicians, for they fall to and grab, seize and consume things' (loc. cit. p. 42).

And in fact what underlies things is the Idea, the Idea in the Platonic sense, thought, the Universal. For this universal has to go out into existence, God has to create the world.

This is sensed by some. They see the world of abstract universals of physics as not satisfactory. But they despair of reason, and talk about reconstituting the unity of things through simple intuition. Hegel is here referring to the Romantics. They have a premonition of the universal, he says, but the appeal to intuition is an 'impasse' (Abweg, p. 46). For we must seize thought with thought. This kind of flight is also related to the phenomenon of primitivism.

The vocation of natural philosophy is to realize the goal of *Geist* to recognize himself in nature, to find there his 'counterpart' (Gegenbild). *Geist* has the certainty of Adam before Eve: 'this is flesh of my flesh; and bone of my bone' (loc. cit. p. 48).

Later Hegel says again that we must set up a comparison to see whether our definition of nature out of the concept 'corresponds to our ordinary thinking about nature' (der Vorstellung entspricht, *EN*, § 247, Addition, p. 51), for in general the two must agree.

Nature is the Idea in the form of other-being. It is not only external to the Idea, but is externality itself. (*EN*, § 247). God must go out and become other: As Idea, this is the Logos, the eternal son of God. He also goes out to finite Spirit, which is also Geist as 'other-being' (Anderssein). But Nature is the Idea, the son of God, as

abiding in otherness, in which the divine Idea is held fast for an instant outside of love. Nature is self-alienated spirit; spirit, a bacchantic god innocent of restraint and reflection has merely been *let loose* into it; in nature, the unity of the Concept conceals itself.   (*EN*, § 247), Addition, p. 50)[2]

---

[1] Petry trans. (amended).
[2] Petry trans. (amended).

But estranged (entfremdet) from the Idea, 'nature is merely the corpse of the understanding'. It is the Idea frozen or turned to stone. But this it cannot remain because God is subjectivity, infinite actuosity. (pp. 50–1).

Nature does not conform to its Idea. It is the 'unresolved contradiction'. (*EN*, §248, Remark.) Matter is that which is external to itself (*EN*, §248, Addition, p. 56). So it is blind necessity, not yet freedom, necessity which is one with contingency. Because necessity is the relation of seeming independent entities, nature is not free, but necessary and contingent.

For necessity is the inseparability of terms which are different, and yet appear to be indifferent. The abstraction of self-externality also receives its due there however, hence the contingency or external necessity, contrasting with the inner necessity of the Concept.   (*EN*, §248, Addition, pp. 56–7)[1]

Nature is a system of levels (Stufen) where each goes necessarily into a higher one. But the higher is not generated out of the lower. It is the work of the Concept. (*EN*, §249). Hegel here refuses any truck with evolution. The only thing which can really develop is the Concept. Hence development exists in its manifestation in *Geist*, but not in nature. Nature is that which is external to itself; its principle is the Concept; but this is purely inner. 'The Concept in a universal manner posits all particularity into existence at once.' (*EN*, §249, Addition, p. 59). The essence of Nature is exteriority, so that the differences which makes up its whole concept must fall outside each other as 'indifferent existents' (gleichgültige Existenzen, *EN*, §249, Remark). The argument seems to be that if nature were to develop to the fullness of its required moments out of itself, to be first inorganic then organic, etc.; this would confer the power of the Concept in nature itself, for it would be able to unfold. But the concept is only innerly embodied in *Geist*, which thus alone has history.

This paragraph is disastrous. In the Addition, Hegel not only argues further against evolution, but also against understanding differences in a series, in which the higher are produced out of the lower recursively by some formula. Nature does make jumps, because the Concept moves by qualitative differences. Thus Hegel also rules out the periodic table, Mendeleyev as well as Darwin.

Because nature is just inner necessity, it has lots of contingency in it. Contingency is for Hegel the same as determination from outside. Particular concrete things are full of such contingency and determination from outside. This is 'the impotence of nature that it only maintains the determinations of the Concept in an abstract manner and exposes the realization of the particular to determination from without' (*EN*, §250). This sets limits to what philosophy can deduce; and this is the answer to Herr Krug who asked natural philosophy to deduce his pen. We see in the particular only 'traces of

[1] Petry trans. (amended).

354

determination by the Concept' (Spuren der Begriffsbestimmung, *EN*, §250, Remark). This is why natural classes have lots of arbitrariness and disorder in them; not to speak of the problems created by monsters, etc.

There are three big stages. (*EN*, §252). These were already adumbrated in the Objectivity section of the *Logic*. First we have nature thought of as mass. This is the sphere of mechanics, and its highest realization is the solar system. This reveals the form of Being-for-self (Fürsichsein) in this sphere in the form of a drive (Trieb) towards the centre. The system is ordered, and turns around a central point. But this form is still external matter; the different bodies which have different roles are indistinguishable in their substance, only differentiated in their role.

We thus go to the next stage, where the form-differences become internal to matter; and here we have matter differentiated into different kinds of substance. The different roles called for by the Concept in order to make ordered unity are in the matter itself. But this stage is still one of immediate unity of form with its matter. They are united just positively. A matter is identified with its quality. It is not an inner identity which posits this property. It ceases to be itself when it loses this property. In this way it is like the *Dasein* of the first book of the *Logic*.

But with the organic we have *fürsichseiende* Totality, which develops itself to its differences. The life of these differences is now gathered into a natural individual and becomes one with his inmost nature. So that this inner necessity is now outwardly expressed and is intrinsic to a natural being. Life will now multiply into separate totalities, not just properties. These are specimens and also members. But they are produced and held in relation by one process of life.

I

Mechanics starts with the derivation of space, time, matter and motion. Then the second chapter 'Finite Mechanics', deals with gravity. The third chapter 'Astronomy' deals with the realization of mechanics in order, the solar system. This is the 'absolute mechanics' of the Logic.

Space is exteriority itself; the first, abstract, basic determination of nature, that it is external to itself. It is homogeneous, yet interruptible at any point. As pure exteriority it has no inner differentiation. Hegel thus, like Kant, rejects both the classical theories. Space is not just a property of things, because it is there even if you take them away. But nor is it a substantial reality itself; it has no reality on its own. (*EN*, §254, Addition). Kant is right in his own way that it is a simple form. But he is wrong as usual to think of this in a subjective manner. Space is not just subjective; but it is a form in the sense of a pure abstraction, the pure abstract reality of the natural, the external; hence it must be filled (*EN*, §254, Remark). It is a 'non-sensuous sensibility and a sensuous insensibility.

355

Logic

The things of nature are in space, and as nature is subject to the condition of externality, space remains the foundation of nature'. (*EN*, §254, Addition)[1]

Hegel also deduces the triplicity of dimensions from the Concept, and their lack of difference from the externality of this realization (*EN*, §225).

But this immediate external existence has negativity in it because it cannot exist as just external, hence it is in contradiction. Hegel sees negation first in the point (*EN*, §256), the attempt to get out of externality to singular self-identity. But the nature of space is such that this is a negation of it, to have no extension, so the point goes into the line, the line into the surface, and this into the whole space.

But this negativity has real existence as time. So space is no longer at rest, its parts just coexisting. Now it is in movement. Time is the side of Nothing, of becoming. It is the negation of the exteriority of space, but also in a purely exterior way (*EN*, §257). So time too is a pure form of sensibility, a 'non-sensuous sensibility' (unsinnliche Sinnlichkeit). It is the principle of subjectivity, hence movement, but remaining external, and hence as simple becoming (*EN*, §258). It is not a container either. We should not say, everything comes to be and passes away in time, but rather time itself is the becoming, the coming to be and passing away, 'the Chronos which engenders all and destroys that to which it gives birth' (*EN*, §258, Remark). The natural falls under this becoming because it is not in full agreement with its concept.

So space and time are not containers, but they are not just properties of things; they are conditions of things, since they are the exterior forms without which things would not be. 'Time is merely this abstraction of destroying... Things themselves are what is temporal. Temporality is their objective determination. It is therefore the process of actual things which constitutes time' (*EN*, §258, Addition, pp. 80–1).[2]

But the negation of space through time is not going to be satisfactory, we still have nothing but flowing away. As well as their unity in Becoming, time and space have to have a subsisting unity, analogous to *Dasein*. Hegel derives this through place, movement, and finally matter. The point was a first stab at some subsistent centre, which failed. But now out of the movement of space to time and back again, we have the point attaining greater concreteness as the place. In other words time cannot just be the negation of space, and space of time; but they have to unite. And this unity is place. This is the enduring (Dauer, das Dauernde); that which remains through time. There must be something enduring. All cannot simply flow away; this would not yield any existence. The enduring is place as here and now (*EN*, §260).

But place goes through the same dialectic as point. It is negative in itself. It

[1] Petry trans.   [2] Petry trans. (amended).

356

is thus indifferent to itself; there is nothing to distinguish it from all others; or it is only distinguished from outside. As space and time it is boundaryless, continuing into other. It requires a reference system outside itself to be determined. So it is external to itself; and we are once more in change. But now we have place changing, and this is movement. (*EN*, §261).

But we cannot just go back; this is not just the abstract negation of space; It is actual change of place, and this requires that there be some unity between the two places. For there to be motion, there must be matter (*EN*, §261).

So for there to be real unity of time and space, there must be matter; a reality which is *partes extra partes*, and yet has some unity. It is identity and yet difference. But since it is not simple self-identity, it must be in motion. Matter and motion are correlatives. Both are to be seen as the unity of space and time. Motion relates space to time. 'Its essence is to be the immediate unity of space and time; it is time realizing itself and subsisting in space, or space first truly differentiated through time.' (*EL*, §261, Addition, p. 91.) Time first has reality when there is something changing; and space is first really differentiated when something moves from here to there. In other words, the negation of space through time becomes real only through matter in motion; for matter gives reality, and its motion is the cancellation of its exteriority which time was trying to be.

Hegel then goes on (*EN*, §262) to deduce gravity. Matter is both attraction and repulsion, for the same kinds of reasons as we saw in Quantity. As negative unity of these moments it is a particular, a centre but which is still separate from the exteriority of matter. This is gravity. We have the beginning of subjectivity, but it is still always outside itself. The middle point to which it strives is always outside it.

So we go naturally to the total system of these bodies; here we have absolute mechanics – the solar system.

But this brings us to the unity of form and matter. The form has found itself in matter. Or matter in its totality has now found the centre it was looking for. So we get to the next step up on the scale, which is qualified matter; not just homogeneous gravitational matter; but matter with a specific substantial nature (*EN*, §271).

In other words, we started with just exteriority. But exteriority cannot stand by itself; and it comes through attraction and repulsion to gravity; and this develops to system; and from this we go beyond to see matter as differentiated. 'Its abstract, dulled being-in-self, general weightedness, has been resolved into form; it is *qualified matter.*' (*EN*, §271.)[1]

---

[1] Petry trans. (amended).

357

Logic

II

This second sphere corresponds to Essence. Now the form differences differentiate matter itself. And so they are related to each other; but still externally, or by a merely hidden unity.

This sphere falls into three parts which are not easy to understand in their articulation. Hegel admits that this is the hardest part of the *Naturphilosophie* (*EN*, § 273, Addition). The following seems to be the gist.

First we have the simple differentiation of physical qualities. They are taken as simple qualities. Each is internally unarticulated as formerly matter itself was. They have no inner centre, but are still taken as bodies related to a centre by their gravity, which takes the role in this dialectic of relatedness to others.

This first chapter takes these simple physical qualities through three phases. First we see them in different heavenly bodies, the sun as the source of light, the moon, comets, the planets. Secondly, we see these qualities in the elements, where Hegel takes up the four classical ones, air, fire, water, earth, and attributes certain properties to each, and certain conceptual affinities. Thirdly, we see all these in process, in interaction, in the meteorological process.

This gives us a picture of the unity of a system as negative unity, and hence real individuality (*EN*, § 289). We achieve here a self-like nature ('Selbstisch-keit'); and this is now seen in matter, in objects. This means that they are seen as having an inner unity, and inner process, or life other than their relation to others in gravity. They are not simple physical qualities, but are objects which are the locus of inner activity, or of inner force.

The account of this stage is in four parts. First we see the 'selfishness' in the property of specific gravity. In this way the body gives itself its specific 'Being in Self' (Insichsein). In other words, we begin to account further by internal parameters for the properties of the body. We then go over into cohesion. But we reach higher inwardness with Sound (Klang). This is a kind of ideal cancellation of the exteriority of the thing in different parts; it is the expression of its inner vibration. It is thus a kind of gathering up into ideality of its material existence, of spatiality into temporality. It is rather like the soul of its body. It rings out when it suffers violence and quivers (erzittert) in itself; or when it triumphantly maintains itself. Fourthly, the kind of unity which the *Klang* represents ideally comes materially in heat, which melts and dissolves inner difference.

So, thirdly, this takes us to a higher form of inwardness, where objects have not only an inner unity, but are seen to produce themselves out of an inner process. We have not only stepped from the simple quality to an internal articulation which underlies it; but we are now going to see the form as fully embodied in it, the object with its specific quality is produced by the form. Thus although in the second phase the object had its own individuality over against the relation to a centre (gravity); now it steps right out of the relation, in that we see it as an inner process with its own centre (as every process must have). We are needless to say on the threshold of life.

In this chapter, Hegel tries to derive, *inter alia*, magnetism and electricity, and takes us up through the transition to chemism. Chemism shows us the relativity of immediate substances and properties. And seeing these deployed by a visible, unified life-form is the next stage, life.

III

Life is recounted in three parts. First we have the world as a whole which is in a sense an organism, but not really a living one, 'only the corpse of the life-process' (*EN*, § 337). It does not really return to itself. It is external to itself. It really belongs to the previous forms in its detail; but as a whole it shows an order which is that of the Concept, and therefore deserves consideration here. Hegel considers under this head: the history of the world and its geographical lay-out, geological phenomena, and the operation of atmosphere, sea and land.

But as Life world has to go over into real life. So there has to be the real living individual. Real life is where this inner necessity is manifest in the reality concerned; where the unity of the Concept is essential to the explanation of what goes on. The living organism as matter operates by the laws of the Concept and does not just end up presenting an order which is ultimately related to the Concept but which can also be understood by laws which make no reference to this inner unity itself. The living are such that what they do and are can only be explained as coming about for the sake of their form.

So there must be living organisms. The organic is related in three ways to its inorganic base (*EN*, § 342). First it is one with the organic, for the living being has its own inorganic in itself, in a sense. It is constantly making itself one life, through a digestion process of itself, as it were (*EN*, § 342, Addition, pp. 492–3). It articulates itself into members and holds these in the same life process. Secondly, the organic individual must be over against the inorganic, it feeds off it. It knows the inorganic is inessential; but this represents a reversal, because it is also sustained by the whole which is largely inorganic. Then thirdly, we have the reproduction process which we have already seen. The individual becomes two, and goes under in the production of a new individual.

The second chapter treats then of the lowest form of real organic life – plants. These, says Hegel, grow out and unfold themselves, but lack the element of return to themselves. They grow out indefinitely. They grow to manifold, but cannot gather this up into unity. They have no real differentiation of an inner kind, for instance, entrails. Without this differentiation and

Logic

without the moment of unity which goes with it they cannot move, they have no self-feeling (Selbstgefühl), and they are related only to elements, not to things. Their self is not really objective. They are inner, and so outer. Hegel then takes plants through the three processes defined above: the formation-process, the assimilation-process, and the generic- or reproduction-process.

On the other hand the animal is a self reflected in himself, the unity comes to subjective universality (*EN*, § 350). The animal organism retains the unity in the articulation of its members. So animals have self-movement (*EN*, § 351). An animal has a voice which expresses its soul and presents a free 'quivering in itself' (Erzittern in sich selbst). It has animal warmth, as the continuous dissolution-process of its own cohesion and new production of its members. It can break off feeding; and above all it has feeling which is its simple individuality. It is also related to objects, not elements. So the beast also has a theoretical relation to things, and also a unity of theoretical and practical in his drive to shape things (*Bildungstrieb*).

Hegel then goes through the three processes with animals. As usual sensibility, irritability and reproduction have their place. But one important theme is the close relation between the reproduction process and death. What animals seek in the other sex is the Genus (Gattung); they sense their insufficiency, and it is this which brings them down. The Genus is thus the death of individuals, and lower organisms often die directly after the act of reproduction (*EN*, § 369, Addition). Only Spirit can carry the burden of the Genus without going under.

And hence the *Naturphilosophie* ends with a passage to Spirit out of the death of the animate. 'The original disease of the animal, and the inborn germ of death is its being inadequate to universality' (*EN*, § 375)[1] The individual is trying to embody the universal in itself, but can only do this in an abstract way, as a simple habit, as the sinking to regularity. But life requires that we constantly overcome difference. With the disappearance of diversity into regularity goes the end of the tension which sustains life and hence old age and death. Sickness itself (*EN*, § 371) is really a part of the system which, triggered by conflict with the outside, becomes fixed in its own activity and works against the whole. So sickness is nothing but the first source of death, for death we have seen is just such a hardening against the tension of life.

Spirit thus comes out of nature. The animal got away from gravity in moving himself, in sensation he felt himself, in voice he hears himself. But still the full process, the Genus only exists in the endless progress of individuals. So 'the idea has to break out of this sphere, and draw breath by shattering this inadequate existence' (*EN*, § 376, Addition).[2] The next step is Spirit, as consciousness that can carry the whole idea in unity. The goal of nature is to die, to burn itself as Phoenix, so that Spirit can rise.

[1] Petry trans.   [2] Petry trans.

360

Spirit comes out of nature. It is also prior to it, but it lets itself come out of nature. Its infinite freedom leaves nature free to operate by its inner necessity (loc. cit.), as we saw at the end of the *logic*.

But *Geist* wants to come to freedom by recognizing himself in nature. And this is the work of the philosophy of nature. Our aim is to force the Proteus of nature to show in exteriority only the mirror of ourselves, to be a free reflection of *Geist*. This was not easy because the Concept is sunk in a lot of refractory (widerspenstig) detail. But reason has to have faith in itself. We cannot deduce everything; 'thus we must not seek determinations of the Concept everywhere, although traces of them are everywhere present' (*EN*, §370, Addition, p. 680). But we can hope to find 'the real shape of the Concept which lies concealed under the mutual externality of infinitely numerous forms' (*EN*, §376, Addition).

With this derivation of Spirit, the philosophy of nature ends. Let us turn now to domains where the work of the spirit is more transparently evident; and first to history, spirit's unfolding in time.

.

PART IV

HISTORY AND POLITICS

CHAPTER XIV

Ethical substance

1

Hegel's philosophy of history and politics belong together, and form the sphere of what he calls 'objective spirit'. In the system, this comes after subjective and before absolute spirit. Just as we saw that the underlying rational necessity expresses itself in the general structures of the natural world, so it expresses itself even more in the phenomena of the human world. These phenomena, in so far as they have to do with the existence of individual consciousness, are the matter of the sphere of subjective spirit, and in the Encyclopaedia this recapitulates and takes over some of the ground covered in the *PhG*. But beyond this realm is the whole domain of the public, social, political reality in history which must now be reclaimed for the Concept.

This domain is discussed in the Encyclopaedia §§ 468–535, and also in the famous cycle of lectures on the philosophy of history, published after Hegel's death from his notes. Chapter VI of the *PhG* is a summary version of the philosophy of history. Finally, it includes Hegel's work of 1821, the *Philosophy of Right*, which is taken as the major mature statement of his political philosophy. Certain works of the early 1800s are also useful here, and will be referred to below from time to time.

Hegel's philosophy of history and politics has to be seen in three related frameworks. We should see it as an attempt to resolve in the sphere of politics what we have identified as the basic dilemma of this generation, how to combine the fullness of moral autonomy, with the recovery of that community, whose public life was expressive of its members and whose paradigm realization in history was the Greek polis. In this respect Hegel's work is of continuing relevance today, as we shall see.

Secondly, since Hegel believed himself to have resolved the dilemma in his ontological vision, we must look at his political philosophy in this framework as well. And thirdly, we must see it in relation to the political problems and crises of Hegel's time, which was dominated by the French Revolution and its aftermath. These events greatly contributed to shaping Hegel's outlook, but they were also read by him through the categories of his philosophy, so that in fact the three frameworks have to be seen as forming a closely connected structure.

Let us start out by looking at Hegel's political philosophy in the framework of his ontological vision. The goal towards which everything tends is the self-comprehension of Spirit or Reason. Man is the vehicle of this self-comprehension. Hence that Spirit know itself requires that man come to know himself and his world as they really are, as emanations of Spirit. This self-knowledge is expressed in art, religion and philosophy, which constitute the domain of absolute Spirit, which the mature Hegel designated as higher than that of politics.

But of course the full realization of absolute Spirit presupposes a certain development of man in history. Man starts off as an immediate being, sunk in his particular needs and drives, with only the haziest, most primitive sense of the universal. This is another way of putting the point that Spirit is initially divided from itself, and has yet to return to itself. If man is to rise to the point where he can be the vehicle of this return, he has to be transformed, to undergo a long cultivation or formation (Bildung).

But this cannot just be an alteration of his outlook. Since following the principle of embodiment, any spiritual reality must be externally realized in time and space, we know that any spiritual change requires a change of the relevant bodily expression. In this case, Spirit can only return to itself through the transformation of man's form of life in history.

What then is the form of life which man must attain in order to be an adequate vehicle of Spirit? First of all, this must be a social form. We saw above in Chapter III how the existence of finite spirits, in the plural, was part of the necessary plan of *Geist*. To be embodied means to be at a particular time and place, and hence to be finite. But finite spirit must go beyond an identification of himself as a particular, and this is why the existence of many men and their life together in a society plays an essential part. Man is raised to the universal because he already lives beyond himself in a society, whose greater life incorporates his.

Thus in order to know itself in the world, Spirit has to bring about an adequate embodiment in human life in which it can recognize itself.

The goal of world history is that Spirit come to a knowledge of what it truly is, that it give this knowledge objective expression [dies Wissen gegenständlich mache], realize it in a world which lies before it, in short, produce itself as an object for itself [sich als objectiv hervorbringe, *VG*, 74].

That is why the state as the highest articulation of society has a touch of the divine in Hegel's eyes. In order to realize God's (Spirit's) fulfilment, man has to come to a vision of himself as part of a larger life. And that requires that as a living being he be in fact integrated into a larger life. The state is the real expression of that universal life which is the necessary embodiment (it would not be inappropriate to say 'material base') for the vision of the Absolute. In other words, it is essential to God's progress through the world that the state be, if I may be permitted to render the spirit of that famous line of *PR* whose mistranslation has caused so much trouble.[1]

But of course, the state as it starts off in history is a very imperfect embodiment of the universal. Not just any state will do. The fully adequate state which spirit needs to return to itself must be a fully *rational* one.

It is worth stopping to examine this in some depth. For the requirement that the state be rational may not strike us as having any clear sense. Indeed, the very invocation of reason as a criterion for moral or political decision has long been suspect to an important strand of anglo-saxon philosophy, nurtured on empiricism. But of course, this invocation of reason has recurred in different ways throughout the European philosophical tradition. Hegel's use of it was quite original, and it will help to make this clear if we try to situate it in relation to the important landmarks of the tradition of practical reason.

One recognized form of the appeal to reason is that which goes back to Plato. Here 'reason' is understood as the power by which we see the true structure of things, the world of the Ideas. To act according to reason is to act according to this true structure, and was equivalent to acting according to nature.

Now this view was based on the idea that there is a larger rational order to which man essentially belongs. For if man is rational life, and to be rational is to be connected to this larger order in having a true vision of it, then man can only be himself in being so connected to this order. But as we saw in Chapter I, an important aspect of the seventeenth-century revolution was its rejection of this conception of the order in which man inheres in favour of the idea of a self-defining subject.

But this new view gave rise to a new conception of order, and hence a new kind of appeal to reason and nature. Man was now defined as a subject capable of rational thought and decision, and also as the subject of certain desires. An important strand of modern thought, in contrast to the tradition from Plato and Aristotle, takes these desires as given for moral reasoning; they cannot themselves be judged at the bar of reason. One of the most important early protagonists of this view is Hobbes, and it is continued in the utilitarian thinkers of the eighteenth century. Reason now comes to mean 'reckoning' and practical reason is the intelligent calculation of how to encompass ends which are beyond the arbitration of reason. This is of course the historical origin of the view mentioned above, according to which reason cannot provide a criterion for moral decision.

This was one side of Hobbes' legacy. Reason and nature were dethroned as

---

[1] 'Es ist der Gang Gottes in der Welt, daß der Staat ist.' Addition to *PR*, §258. This was first mistranslated as 'The state is the march of God through the world', and this has been frequently quoted as a *pièce à conviction* in the indictment of Hegel as an anti-liberal apologist of 'Prussianism'. For the mistranslations and their effect, see W. Kaufmann's introduction to the book he edited, *Hegel's Political Philosophy*, New York, Atherton Press, 1970.

the ultimate criteria. There was no longer a normative order of things evident in nature of which man was a part, such that the ground of obligation could be found in nature. Rather, political obligation was grounded in a decision, to submit to a sovereign, dictated by prudence (calculating reason). For a self-defining subject obligation could only be created by his own will. Hence the great importance of the myth of the original contract.

But this new view could also be presented in another way. Man as a subject of desires had one great second-order goal, that the first-order desires be satisfied. Their satisfaction was what was meant by 'happiness' (Hobbes' 'felicity') which was therefore given a quite different meaning than it had in the Aristotelian tradition. But then, whatever effect education (artifice) had in shaping the detail of our first-order desires, one could say that by nature and inescapably men desire happiness.

Now if intelligent calculation can show how to shape men and circumstances so that men achieve happiness, and all of them achieve it together and compatibly with each other, then is this not the highest goal, and one that is according to reason (intelligent calculation) and nature (the universal desire for happiness)?

There is a new conception of order here. Instead of seeing nature as expressing a meaningful order, one which has to be accounted for in terms of ideas, we see it as a set of interlocking elements whose relations can be explained in terms of efficient causation. The order (as against disorder) in things does not consist in their embodyng the underlying ideas, but rather in their *meshing* without conflict and distortion. Applied to the human realm, this means that man comes to realize natural order, when the company of desiring subjects comes to achieve full satisfaction (happiness), each compatibly with all the others. The perfect harmony of desires is the goal which nature and reason prescribe to man.

But a third conception of reason as criterion of action arose to challenge the utilitarian view in the late eighteenth century, and that was the radical moral autonomy of Kant. This view starts in a sense with Rousseau, to whom Hegel gives credit for it. It is a reaction against the utilitarian identification of good with interest and of reason with calculation. It wants to found our obligation on the will, but in a much more radical sense than Hobbes. Hobbes grounded political obligation on a decision to submit to a sovereign. But this decision was dictated by prudence, so that we can see the ground of obligation in Hobbes as the universal desire to avoid death. Hence the 'first law of nature', which is 'to endeavour peace'. In the end certain natural facts about us, our desires and aversions, have a decisive part in deciding what we ought to do, as far as the utilitarian tradition is concerned.

The aim of Kant was to cut loose altogether from this reliance on nature, and to draw the content of obligation purely from the will. This he proposed to do by applying a purely formal criterion to prospective actions, which was binding on the will as rational. Rationality involves thinking in universal terms and thinking consistently. Hence the maxim underlying any proposed action must be such that we can universalize it without contradiction. If we cannot do this, then we cannot as rational wills conscientiously undertake this action. A will operating on this principle would be free from any ground of determination (Bestimmungsgrund) in nature and hence truly free.[1] A moral subject is thus autonomous in a radical sense. He obeys only the dictates of his own will. Reason, as rational will, is now the criterion, but in a third sense, one opposed to nature.

Now Hegel builds on the whole development which we have sketched here. He will reconstruct the notion of a greater order to which man belongs, but on an entirely new basis. Hence he fully endorses the modern rejection of the meaningful order of nature, as seen in the Middle Ages and early Renaissance. These visions of order saw it as ultimately just given by God. The hierarchy of beings was an ultimate which could not be further explained or justified, and it was incumbent on man to take his proper place in this hierarchy. But the Hegelian notion of spirit as freedom cannot accommodate anything merely given, as we saw. Everything must flow of necessity from the Idea, from Spirit or Reason itself. Hence Spirit must ultimately rebel against anything merely given.

For this reason, Hegel sees the modern affirmation of a self-defining subject as a necessary stage. And he sees its necessary culmination in the radical Kantian notion of autonomy. Autonomy expresses the demand of Spirit to deduce its whole content out of itself, not to accept as binding anything which is merely taken up from outside.

In order to know what is truly right, we have to abstract from inclination, impulse, desire, as from everything particular; we must know, in other words, what the will is as such

(an sich, GW, 921)

and further

the will is only free, in so far as it wills nothing other, external, foreign – for then it would be dependent – but only wills itself, the will. (loc. cit.)

He takes up the radical contrast between nature and spirit. The 'substance' of material nature is gravity, but that of spirit is freedom (*VG*, 55).[2] Its freedom is to be centred on itself (in sich den Mittelpunkt zu haben).

The very notion of will is bound up with that of freedom. First, thought is

---

[1] *Critique of Practical Reason*, §5.
[2] Of course, 'nature' can also be used in a different sense, in which we mean the concept of a thing, in which case, there is a 'nature' of spirit. Hegel uses this expression in the passage just referred to: 'Die Natur des Geistes...' This shows the filiation of Hegel's thought to Aristotle's, in spite of, or rather beyond his espousal of the modern radical autonomy.

essential to the will. It is its 'substance', 'so that without thought there can be no will'. (*EG*, §468, Addition.)

It is because it is the practical expression of thought, that the will is essentially destined to be free.

Freedom is precisely thought itself; whoever rejects thought and speaks of freedom doesn't know what he's saying. The unity of thought with itself is freedom, the free will...The will is only free as thinking will. (*SW*, XIX, 528–9)

In *PR* he takes up the same theme, and characterizes the will as 'self-determining universality', and hence as freedom (§21). It is 'thinking getting its own way in the will'. Hegel here repeats that 'it is only as thinking intelligence that the will is genuinely a will and free'. In the course of the same note to this paragraph, he takes a swipe at Romantic theories of freedom who 'would banish thought and have recourse instead to feeling, enthusiasm, the heart and the breast'. This free will is also truly infinite, since its object is not an other or a barrier for it (§22). It is 'released from every tie of dependence on anything else' (§23), and it is universal (§24).

This will, which is determined purely by itself, and hence by thought or rationality, is the ultimate criterion of what is right. It is designated the 'ground of right' (der Boden des Rechts) in *PR* (§4). And therefore it is the basic principle of the fully realized state. Rousseau is given the credit for having been the first to seize this crucial principle

by adducing the will as the principle of the state, he is adducing a principle which has thought both for its form and its content, a principle indeed which is thinking itself, and not a principle, like gregarious instinct, for instance, or divine authority, which has thought as its form only. (*PR*, §258)

But while building on Kant, Hegel gives this principle of autonomy an entirely new twist. He generates out of it a new variant of the larger order which this modern consciousness started off by rejecting. In this way, he believes himself to have overcome the grievous dilemma which Kant's theory runs into.

The problem with Kant's criterion of rationality is that it has purchased radical autonomy at the price of emptiness. Once it is explained to us, we can see how the Platonic criterion of reason works to select some things as right and others as wrong, even though we may disagree with it, and reject its whole ontological base. The same goes for the utilitarian criterion. But Kant attempted to avoid any appeal to the way things are, either to an order of ideas, or a constellation of de facto desires. The criterion of the right is to be purely formal. Kant believed that this gave him a viable theory because he thought that the formal criterion would actually rule some actions in and others out. But the arguments to this effect are very shaky, and once one loses faith in them, one is left with a criterion which has no bite at all, which can allow anything as a morally possible action. Moral autonomy has been purchased at the price of vacuity.

This is a criticism that Hegel never tires of addressing to Kant. We will remember that his argument in Chapter VI, section 3 of the *PhG* turned partly on the vacuity of the Kantian criterion. But the point crops up elsewhere. In a work of the early 1800s 'Über die wissenschaftlichen Behandlungsarten des Naturrechts', Hegel takes issue directly with the example Kant uses in the *Critique of Practical Reason* (§4, Remark), that of a deposit which a dead man has left me. If there are no written instructions, so that no-one can find me out, am I justified in just appropriating it? Kant asks. Surely not, for a general rule to the effect that anybody can deny holding a deposit, when no-one can find him out, would destroy itself as a law, since it would end up destroying the practice of leaving deposits with others.

Hegel argues[1] that there is no contradiction whatever here. Supposing that my action generalized would do away with the practice of leaving deposits, in what way does that contradict the rule of stealing them while I can? If the rule also enjoined me to preserve the practice, there would be contradiction, but it does not. We end up with a simple 'tautology', something like 'generalized stealing of deposits is incompatible with the practice of leaving them', or 'generalized theft is incompatible with property'. But the problem remains entire whether we want to affirm property as a value, or generalized theft, or thorough-going communism.

The Kantian principle if it is to work in this and other cases is rather something of this kind: no maxim is acceptable, if general obedience to it would make it inapplicable by doing away with the reality it bears on. But this would make us reject as immoral such maxims as 'help the poor', 'defend your country against its enemies', and so on (op. cit. 345–5).

Hegel returns to this point in *PR*, § 135. The Kantian criterion can lead only to an 'empty formalism'. There is no contradiction in the proposition that property should not exist. The right to property must be more concretely grounded.

Now Hegel claims to resolve Kant's dilemma, because he will show how the concrete content of duty is deduced from the very idea of freedom itself. We already have a general idea of what he means by this, but before going on to see it in greater detail, we should note how this reproach of vacuity was central to Hegel's critique of Kant, and of the whole revolutionary age.

Because he only has a formal notion of freedom, Kant cannot derive his notion of the polity from it. His political theory ends up borrowing from the utilitarians. Its input, we might say, is the utilitarian vision of a society of

[1] *Schriften zur Politik und Rechtsphilosophie*, ed. Lasson, Leipzig, 1923, 349 ff.

371

individuals each seeking happiness in his own way. The problem of politics is to find a way of limiting the negative freedom (Willkür) of each so that it can coexist with that of all others under a universal law. In other words Kant's radical notion of freedom being purely formal and therefore vacuous cannot generate a new substantive vision of the polity in which it would be realized, one founded on goals derived intrinsically from the nature of the will itself, ('der Wille...als an und für sich seiender, venünftiger...') which would thus be unconditionally valid for men. So Kant's political theory has to borrow its content from nature, as it were. It takes its start from men as individuals seeking particular goals, and the demands of morality and rationality, i.e., universality, only enter as restrictions and limitations (Beschränkungen) imposed on these individuals from outside. Rationality is not immanent, but an external, formal universality which demands only that the negative freedom of all individuals be made compatible (*PR* § 29).

Thus although Kant starts with a radically new conception of morality, his political theory is disappointingly familiar. It does not take us very far beyond utilitarianism, in that its main problem remains that of harmonizing individual wills.

This is undoubtedly a little unfair to Kant, as we shall note later on. But it seems even unfairer to Rousseau who is lumped together with Kant as the target of the same criticism, both in this paragraph (§ 29) and elsewhere.[1] In § 258, Hegel complains that Rousseau sees will still as individual will, and thinks of the general will not as 'the absolutely rational element in the will' (das an und für sich Vernünftige des Willens), but only as the common element (das Gemeinschaftliche) which emerges from the conscious individual wills. The result is that the state is ultimately based on arbitrary decisions and consent (Willkür, Meinung und beliebige, ausdrückliche Einwilligung).

As it stands this certainly fails to do justice to Rousseau. His *volonté générale* was certainly meant to be more and other than the common element of everyone's particular will, and the task of the contract was not to bring these particular wills into agreement. But a clue to what Hegel is driving at is provided by the reference in both paragraphs (§§ 29 and 258) to the fearful destruction wrought by the French Revolution, which here as elsewhere Hegel sees as following logically on the principles of Rousseau.

For in fact, the vacuity of formal freedom can have another quite different outcome than the one ascribed above to Kant. There we saw the theory of autonomy having to fall back on utilitarianism to define the problem of political life. But it is possible for theorists of radical autonomy to feel this lack themselves, and to yearn for a society which would go beyond the struggle and compromise of particular wills and attain an integral expression of freedom.

---

[1] Cf. *PR*, § 258; *SW*, XIX, 528.

This is the drive for 'absolute freedom' which Hegel described in the *PhG* and which he saw in the Jacobin period of Revolutionary terror.

But as we saw, the curse of vacuity haunts this enterprise as well. Its aim is to found society on no particular interest or traditional positive principle, but on freedom alone. But this, being empty, gives no basis for a new articulated structure of society. It only enjoins to destroy the existing articulations, and any new ones which threaten to arise. The drive to absolute freedom thus becomes the fury of destruction, 'and the experiment ended in the maximum of frightfulness and terror' (§ 258).

It seems strange, however, to link this Terror, which sacrificed the individual to the general will, to a theory which is said still to define will as individual. But I think what Hegel was really driving at was something else, which was not very perspicuously put in these passages. It is that Rousseau, Kant, both revolutionary and liberal protagonists of radical autonomy, all defined freedom as *human* freedom, the will as *human* will. Hegel on the other hand believed himself to have shown that man reaches his basic identity in seeing himself as a vehicle of *Geist*. If the substance of the will is thought or reason, and if the will is only free when it follows nothing else but its own thought, the thought or reason in question turns out not to be that of man alone, but rather that of the cosmic spirit which posits the universe.

This transforms the situation. The vacuity which bedevilled the theory of radical autonomy is overcome. The dilemma of radical freedom can be restated succinctly as follows: if freedom is to renounce all heteronomy, any determination of the will by particular desires, traditional principle or external authority, then freedom seems incompatible with any rational action whatsoever. For there do not seem to be any grounds of action left, which are not wholly vacuous, that is which would actually rule some actions in and others out, and which are not also heteronomous.

But everything changes if the will whose autonomy men must realize is not that of man alone but of *Geist*. Its content is the Idea which produces a differentiated world out of itself. So that there is no longer a lack of determining grounds of action.

To put this less succinctly, Hegel's free rational will escapes vacuity because unlike Kant's it does not remain merely universal but produces a particular content out of itself. But this is its prerogative not qua human only, but rather that of the cosmic subject. It is the absolute Idea which deploys a differentiated world. Human rational will finds a content not by stripping itself of all particularity in the attempt to attain a freedom and universality which can only be formal, but by discovering its links to cosmic reason, and hence coming to discern what aspects of our lives as particular beings reflect the truly concrete universal which is the Idea. What reason and freedom enjoin on man's will is to further and sustain that structure of things which so reveals itself to be the adequate expression of the Idea.

This means first, as we saw above, that society must be such that men relate to it as to a larger life in which they are immersed. In other words, the demands of freedom on this reading take us beyond the atomistic forms of liberalism where the individual and his goals are of ultimate importance, and the task of society is to permit their fulfilment along with those of others.

And this in turn dictates a certain structure of society. It must be such that the various moments of the Concept, immediate unity, separation, and mediated unity, all reach full and compatible expression. We shall see later how Hegel gives concrete content to this seemingly abstract requirement, which is made the ground for the essential articulation of the state into 'estates' (Stände) and into levels of society (family, civil society, state).

The demands of reason are thus that men live in a state articulated according to the Concept, and that they relate to it not just as individuals whose interests are served by this collectively established machinery, but more essentially as participants in a larger life. And this larger life deserves their ultimate allegiance because it is the expression of the very foundation of things, the Concept. Freedom has been given a very concrete content indeed.

But in this Hegel has brought off an extraordinary tour de force. For this relation of man to society is parallel to the pre-modern one. Before the revolution of modern subjectivity men were induced to revere the structures of their society: monarchy, aristocracy, priestly hierarchy, or whatever, on the grounds that these reflected the will of God or the order of being, in short, the foundation of things to which man owes ultimate allegiance. The king was to be obeyed because he was God's anointed, more, he was the expression in the polity of what God was in the universe. Now this mode of thought returns in the most surprising way, growing out of the most extreme expression of modern self-defining subjectivity, the radical notion of autonomy.

No wonder Hegel has been difficult to classify on the liberal/conservative spectrum. For he rehabilitates the notion of a cosmic order as a cornerstone of political theory, e.g., he speaks of the state as divine. And this kind of thing we think of as the hallmark of conservative, even reactionary thought. But this order is utterly unlike those of the tradition. There is nothing in it which is not transparently dictated by reason itself. It is thus not an order beyond man which he must simply accept. Rather it is one which flows from his own nature properly understood. Hence it is centred on autonomy, since to be governed by a law which emanates from oneself is to be free. The order thus gives a central place to the autonomous, rational individual. Hegel's political theory is quite without precedent or parallel. The attempt to classify it by picking out liberal or conservative shibboleths can just lead to laughable misinterpretations.[1]

Thus Hegel's answer to the vacuity of Kant's moral theory is to deduce the content of duty out of the idea of freedom. But this is a feasible operation because he is not talking of the idea of merely human freedom, but rather of the cosmic Idea. From this he can derive the notion of the kind of society that men should belong to. It is this vision of society which then can give concrete content to moral obligation which enjoins us to further and sustain its structures and live according to its precepts. Morality is only given a content via the notion of a whole society. Thus

An immanent and consistent 'doctrine of duties' can be nothing except the serial exposition of the relationships which are necessitated by the Idea of freedom, and are therefore realized across their whole extent, that is, in the state.   (*PR*, § 148)[2]

Hence rationality becomes a substantive criterion for Hegel both in morals and politics, and this in a manner original with him. His conception has some affinities with Plato, since it does involve the idea of a cosmic order. But it also owes a great deal to Kant, since it is built on the requirement of radical autonomy, that the will should obey nothing but itself, its own immanent rationality. It manages somehow, as we saw, to combine both, and in this its striking originality consists.

As the criterion of rationality actually applies to Hegel's politics, it is quite complex. It has some of its applications in common with Kant's. For in fact this latter is richer in its consequences for political theory than Hegel sometimes allows.[3]

First of all, rationality requires that man be treated as a rational subject, as, in Kant's formulation, an end, and not only as a means. And in political terms, this means that the modern state must recognize the rights of the autonomous individual. It cannot accept slavery. It must respect property, conscience (*PR*, § 137), the free choice of a career (*PR*, § 206), religious confession (*PR*, § 270), and so on.

Secondly, rationality, even in its formal Kantian definition, requires that the state be ruled by law (*PR*, preface), and not by arbitrary caprice; and that the law treat all alike, which means that to the extent that it emanates from men at all, it must in an important sense emanate from all alike.

These are the corollaries which flow from the liberal, Kantian criterion of

---

[1] These unfortunately abound in the anglo-saxon world. The latest one has been perpetrated by Sidney Hook. Cf. his contributions to the volume edited by Walter Kaufmann, *Hegel's Political Philosophy*, New York, Atherton Press, 1970.

[2] Knox translation slightly amended.

[3] Kant's theory can in fact largely compensate for the vacuity of the universalizability criterion by certain other consequences of the aspiration to radical autonomy. For this also says something about the way men should be *treated*, and the kinds of rules they should be subject to.

rationality. Hegel adds to them his own, that political society should realize and express the Idea.

But we can still see the justice in Hegel's claim that Kant's criterion does not take us very far beyond the utilitarian Enlightenment. The first two principles tell us how individuals should be treated, and give us a general, formal characterization of the good society, that it should be based on law. But only the third, Hegel's criterion, enables us to derive the actual shape this society should take. Kant's moral theory remained at the edges of politics, as it were, setting limits beyond which states or individuals should not tread. For Hegel, in contrast, morality can only receive a concrete content in politics, in the design of the society we have to further and sustain.

This set of obligations which we have to further and sustain a society founded on the Idea is what Hegel calls '*Sittlichkeit*'. This has been variously translated in English, as 'ethical life', 'objective ethics', 'concrete ethics', but no translation can capture the sense of this term of art, and I propose to use the original here. '*Sittlichkeit*' is the usual German term for 'ethics', with the same kind of etymological origin, in the term '*Sitten*' which we might translate 'customs'. But Hegel gives it a special sense, in contrast to '*Moralität*' (which of course has a parallel etymological origin in 'mores', although being Latin it would not be so evident to German readers).

'*Sittlichkeit*' refers to the moral obligations I have to an ongoing community of which I am part. These obligations are based on established norms and uses, and that is why the etymological root in 'Sitten' is important for Hegel's use.[1] The crucial characteristic of *Sittlichkeit* is that it enjoins us to bring about what already is. This is a paradoxical way of putting it, but in fact the common life which is the basis of my *sittlich* obligation is already there in existence. It is in virtue of its being an ongoing affair that I have these obligations; and my fulfilment of these obligations is what sustains it and keeps it in being. Hence in *Sittlichkeit*, there is no gap between what ought to be and what is, between *Sollen* and *Sein*.

With *Moralität*, the opposite holds. Here we have an obligation to realize something which does not exist. What ought to be contrasts with what is. And connected with this, the obligation holds of me not in virtue of being part of a larger community life, but as an individual rational will.

Hegel's critique of Kant can then be put in this way: Kant identifies ethical obligation with *Moralität*,[2] and cannot get beyond this. For he presents an abstract, formal notion of moral obligation, which holds of man as an individual, and which being defined in contrast to nature is in endless opposition to what is.

---

[1] Cf. *Schriften zur Politik und Rechtsphilosophie*, ed. Lasson, Leipzig, 1923, p. 388.

[2] Once again, this is Hegel's term of art; Kant himself used the usual word '*Sittlichkeit*' in his works on ethics.

Ethical Substance

We can see how all of Hegel's reproaches against Kant's moral philosophy are systematically connected. Because it remained with a purely formal notion of reason, it could not provide a content to moral obligation. Because it would not accept the only valid content, which comes from an ongoing society to which we belong, it remained an ethic of the individual. Because it shied away from that larger life of which we are a part, it saw the right as forever opposed to the real; morality and nature are always at loggerheads.

The doctrine of *Sittlichkeit* is that morality reaches its completion in a community. This both gives obligation its definitive content, as well as realizing it, so that the gap between *Sollen* and *Sein* is made up. Hegel started off as we saw, following Kant in distinguishing will and freedom from nature. But the fulfilment of freedom is when nature (here society, which started in a raw, primitive form) is made over to the demands of reason.

Because the realization of the Idea requires that man be part of a larger life in a society, moral life reaches its highest realization in *Sittlichkeit*. This highest realization is an achievement, of course, it is not present throughout history, and there are even periods where public life has been so emptied of spirit, that *Moralität* expresses something higher. But the fulfilment of morality comes in a realized *Sittlichkeit*.

This is the point where Hegel runs counter to the moral instinct of liberalism then and now. Between obligations which are founded on our membership of some community and those which are not so contingent we tend to think of the latter as transcending the former, as the truly universal moral obligations. Hegel's reversal of the order and his exalted view of political society is what has inspired accusations of 'Prussianism', state-worship, even proto-Fascism. We can see already how wide of the mark these are. We tend to think of *Moralität* as more fundamental because we see the moral man as being ever in danger of being asked by his community to do the unconscionable. And particularly so in an age of nationalism. We are probably right in feeling this in our age, but it was not what Hegel foresaw. The community which is the locus of our fullest moral life is a state which comes close to a true embodiment of the Idea. Hegel thought that the states of his day were building towards that. He was wrong, and we shall discuss this more later on. But it is ludicrous to attribute a view like 'my government right or wrong' to Hegel, or to think that he would have approved the kind of blind following of orders of German soldiers and functionaries under the Third Reich, which was a time if ever there was one when *Moralität* had the higher claim.

We should not forget that two of Hegel's 'heroes', i.e., pivotal figures, in history are Socrates and Jesus, both of whom undermined or broke with the *Sittlichkeit* of their people, and struck off on their own. Hegel's point is, however, that man's (and *Geist's*) true realization cannot come like this. No matter what great spiritual truths a man discovered, they could not be made

377

real, i.e., embodied, if he remains on his own. As an individual he depends on his society in a host of ways, and if it is unregenerate, then he cannot realize the good. If he does not want to compromise his truth and corrupt his message, then he must either withdraw, and/or offer a challenge to his society which will earn him the fate of Christ or Socrates.

Full realization of freedom requires a society for the Aristotelian reason that a society is the minimum self-sufficient human reality. In putting *Sittlichkeit* at the apex, Hegel is – consciously – following Aristotle. And in following Aristotle, the ancient Greek world. For the last time that the world saw an effortless and undivided *Sittlichkeit* was among the Greeks. Hegel's notion of *Sittlichkeit* is in part a rendering of that expressive unity which his whole generation saw in the Greek polis, where – it was believed – men had seen the collective life of their city as the essence and meaning of their own lives, had sought their glory in its public life, their rewards in power and reputation within it, and immortality in its memory. It was his expression for that *vertu* which Montesquieu had seen as the mainspring of republics. In common with his generation he recognized that this *Sittlichkeit* was lost forever in its original form, but along with many of his contemporaries he aspired to see it reborn in a new way.

2

The idea that our highest and most complete moral existence is one we can only attain to as members of a community obviously takes us beyond the contract theory of modern natural law, or the utilitarian conception of society as an instrument of the general happiness. For these societies are not the focus of independent obligations, let alone the highest claims which can be made on us. Their existence simply gives a particular shape to pre-existing moral obligations, e.g., the keeping of promises, or the furtherance of the greatest happiness of the greatest number. The doctrine which puts *Sittlichkeit* at the apex of moral life requires a notion of society as a larger community life, to recall the expression used above, in which man participates as a member.

Now this notion displaces the centre of gravity, as it were, from the individual onto the community, which is seen as the locus of a life or subjectivity, of which the individuals are phases. The community is an embodiment of *Geist*, and a fuller, more substantial embodiment than the individual. This idea of a subjective life beyond the individual has been the source of much resistance to Hegel's philosophy. For it has seemed to the common sense at least of the Anglo-Saxon world (nurtured by a certain philosophical tradition) as both wildly extravagant in a speculative sense, and morally very dangerous in its 'Prussian' or even 'Fascist' consequences, sacrificing the individual and his freedom on the altar of some 'higher' communal deity. Before going further, therefore, we should examine this

378

notion of the society and the relation of individuals to it. We shall see, indeed, that Hegel's notion of objective *Geist* is not without difficulty; but the extravagance is not where the atomistic mentality of the empiricist world thought it was.

Hegel uses a number of terms to characterize this relation of man to the community.

One of the most common is 'substance'. The state, or the people is the 'substance' of individuals. This idea is clearly expressed in the *Encyclopaedia*.

The substance which knows itself free, in which absolute '*Ought*' is equally well *being*, has reality as the spirit of a *people*. The abstract diremption of this spirit is the individuation into persons, of whose independent existence spirit is the inner power and necessity. But the person as thinking intelligence knows this substance as his own essence – in this conviction [Gesinnung] he ceases to be a mere accident of it – rather he looks on it as his absolute and final goal existing in reality, as something which is attained in the *here and now*, while at the same time he *brings it about through his activity*, but as something which in fact simply is. (*EG*, § 514)[1]

We can notice here at the end a reference to that basic feature of *Sittlichkeit*, that it provides a goal which is at the same time already realized, which is brought about, and yet is. But what is worth noticing here is the set of related concepts which help to explain 'substance'. The community, says Hegel, is also 'essence', and also 'final goal' for the individuals.

The notion behind 'substance' and 'essence' is that the individuals only are what they are by their inherence in the community. This idea is put in a passage of *VG*.

Everything that man is he owes to the state; only in it can he find his essence. All value that a man has, all spiritual reality, he has only through the state. (*VG*, 111)

Or more directly

the individual *is* an individual in this substance...No individual can step beyond [it]; he can separate himself certainly from other particular individuals, but not from the *Volksgeist*. (*VG*, 59–60)

The notion behind 'final goal' (Endzweck) seems to be more sinister, for it seems to imply that individuals only exist to serve the state as some pitiless Moloch. This seems even more clearly to be the message of *PR*, § 258

this substantial unity is an absolute unmoved end in itself, in which freedom comes into its supreme right. On the other hand this final end has supreme right against the individual, whose supreme duty is to be a member of the state.

But this reading is based on a serious misinterpretation. Hegel denies that the state exists for the individuals, in other words he rejects the Enlightenment

---

[1] Cf. also *PR*, §§ 145, 156, 258.

utilitarian idea that the state has only an instrumental function, that the ends it must serve are those of individuals. But he cannot really accept the inverse proposition.

> The state is not there for the sake of the citizens; one could say, it is the goal and they are its instruments. But this relation of ends and means is quite inappropriate here. For the state is not something abstract, standing over against the citizens; but rather they are moments as in organic life, where no member is end and none means...The essence of the state is ethical life [die sittliche Lebendigkeit].　　　　　　　　　(*VG*, 112)

Rather we see here that the notion of ends and means gives way to the image of a living being. The state or the community has a higher life; its parts are related as the parts of an organism.[1] Thus the individual is not serving an end separate from him, rather he is serving a larger goal which is the ground of his identity, for he only is the individual he is in this larger life. We have gone beyond the opposition self-goal/other-goal.

Hegel adds to this notion of the community as living that of the community as 'self-consciousness'. And it is this, together with the use of the words '*Geist*', '*Volksgeist*' which has given rise to the idea that the Hegelian state or community is a super-individual. But in the passage of *VG* where he introduces the terms 'self-consciousness', Hegel makes clear that he is not talking about it in connection with *Volksgeister* in the sense that it applies to individuals. Rather it is a 'philosophical concept' (*VG*, 61). Like any *Geist* larger than the individual it only has existence through the vehicle of individual concrete subjects.[2] It is thus not a subject like them.

But why does Hegel want to speak of a spirit which is larger than the individual? What does it mean to say that the individual is part of, inheres in, a larger life; and that he is only what he is by doing so?

These ideas only appear mysterious because of the powerful hold on us of atomistic prejudices, which have been very important in modern political thought and culture. We can think that the individual is what he is in abstraction from his community only if we are thinking of him qua organism. But when we think of a human being, we do not simply mean a living organism, but a being who can think, feel, decide, be moved, respond, enter into relations with others; and all this implies a language, a related set of ways of experiencing the world, of interpreting his feelings, understanding his relation to others, to the past, the future, the absolute, and so on. It is the particular way he situates himself within this cultural world that we call his identity.

---

[1] In the language of the *Logic*, the category of External Teleology is inadequate here. The state can only be understood by Internal Teleology.

[2] Thus in *PR*, §258, Hegel speaks of the state possessing 'the actuality of the substantial will...*in the particular self-consciousness* once that consciousness has been raised to consciousness of its universality' (my italics).

But now a language, and the related set of distinctions underlying our experience and interpretation, is something that can only grow in and be sustained by a community. In that sense, what we are as human beings, we are only in a cultural community. Perhaps, once we have fully grown up in a culture, we can leave it and still retain much of it. But this kind of case is exceptional, and in an important sense marginal. Emigrés cannot fully live their culture, and are always forced to take on something of the ways of the new society they have entered. The life of a language and culture is one whose locus is larger than that of the individual. It happens in the community. The individual possesses this culture, and hence his identity, by participating in this larger life.

When I say that a language and the related distinctions can only be sustained by a community, I am not thinking only of language as a medium of communication; so that our experience could be entirely private, and just need a public medium to be communicated from one to another. Rather the fact is that our experience is what it is, is shaped in part, by the way we interpret it; and this has a lot to do with the terms which are available to us in our culture. But there is more; many of our most important experiences would be impossible outside of society, for they relate to objects which are social. Such are, for instance, the experience of participating in a rite, or of taking part in the political life of our society, or of rejoicing at the victory of the home team, or of national mourning for a dead hero; and so on. All these experiences and emotions have objects which are essentially social, i.e., would not be outside of (this) society.

So the culture which lives in our society shapes our private experience and constitutes our public experience, which in turn interacts profoundly with the private. So that it is no extravagant proposition to say that we are what we are in virtue of participating in the larger life of our society – or at least, being immersed in it, if our relationship to it is unconscious and passive, as is often the case.

But of course Hegel is saying something more than this. For this inescapable relation to the culture of my society does not rule out the most extreme alienation. This comes about when the public experience of my society ceases to have any meaning for me.

Far from wishing to deny this possibility, Hegel was one of the first to develop a theory of alienation. The point is that the objects of public experience, rite, festival, election, etc. are not like facts of nature. For they are not entirely separable from the experience they give rise to. They are partly constituted by the ideas and interpretations which underlie them. A given social practice, like voting in the ecclesia, or in a modern election, is what it is because of a set of commonly understood ideas and meanings, by which the depositing of stones in an urn, or the marking of bits of paper, counts as the making of a social decision. These ideas about what is going on are essential to define the institution. They are essential if there is to be *voting* here, and not some quite other activity which could be carried on by putting stones in the urns.

Now these ideas are not universally acceptable or even understandable. They involve a certain view of man, society, and decision, for instance, which may seem evil or unintelligible to other societies. To take a social decision by voting implies that it is right, appropriate and intelligible to build the community decision out of a concatenation of individual decisions. In some societies, e.g., many traditional village societies throughout the world, social decisions can (could) only be taken by consensus. An atomistic decision procedure of this kind is tantamount to dissolving the social bond. Whatever else it is it could not be a *social* decision.

Thus a certain view of man and his relation to society is embedded in some of the practices and institutions of a society. So that we can think of these as expressing certain ideas. And indeed, they may be the only, or the most adequate expression of these ideas, if the society has not developed a relatively articulate and accurate theory about itself. The ideas which underlie a certain practice and make it what it is, e.g., those which make the marking of papers the taking of a social decision, may not be spelled out adequately in propositions about man, will, society, and so on. Indeed, an adequate theoretical language may be as yet undeveloped.

In this sense we can think of the institutions and practices of a society as a kind of language in which its fundamental ideas are expressed. But what is 'said' in this language is not ideas which could be in the minds of certain individuals only, they are rather common to a society, because embedded in its collective life, in practices and institutions which are of the society indivisibly. In these the spirit of the society is in a sense objectified. They are, to use Hegel's term, 'objective spirit'.

These institutions and practices make up the public life of a society. Certain norms are implicit in them, which they demand to be maintained and properly lived out. Because of what voting is as a concatenating procedure of social decision, certain norms about falsification, the autonomy of the individual decision, etc. flow inescapably from it. The norms of a society's public life are the content of *Sittlichkeit.*

We can now see better what Hegel means when he speaks of the norms or ends of society as sustained by our action, and yet as already there, so that the member of society 'brings them about through his activity, but as something which rather simply is' (*EG*, § 514). For these practices and institutions are maintained only by ongoing human activity in conformity to them; and yet they are in a sense there already before this activity, and must be, for it is only the ongoing practice which defines what the norm is our future action must seek to

Ethical Substance

sustain. This is especially the case if there is as yet no theoretical formulation of the norm, as there was not in Hegel's view in the Greek city-states at their apogee. The Athenian acted 'as it were, out of instinct' (*VG*, 115), his *Sittlichkeit* was a 'second nature'. But even if there is a theory, it cannot substitute for the practice as a criterion, for it is unlikely that any formulation can entirely render what is involved in a social practice of this kind.

Societies refer to theoretical 'value' formulations as their norms rather than to practices, when they are trying to make themselves over to meet an unrealized standard; e.g., they are trying to 'build socialism', or become fully 'democratic'. But these goals are, of course, of the domain of *Moralität*. *Sittlichkeit* presupposes that the living practices are an adequate 'statement' of the basic norms, although in the limit case of the modern philosophy of the state, Hegel sees the theoretical formulation as catching up. Hence we see the importance of Hegel's insistence that the end sought by the highest ethics is already realized. It means that the highest norms are to be discovered in the real, that the real is rational, and that we are to turn away from chimaeric attempts to construct a new society from a blue-print. Hegel strongly opposes those who hold

that a philosophy of state...[has]...the task of discovering and promulgating still another theory...In examining this idea and the activity in conformity with it, we might suppose that no state or constitution has ever existed in the world at all, but that nowadays...we had to start all over again from the beginning, and that the ethical world had just been waiting for such present-day projects, proofs and investigations.

(PR, preface, 4)

The happiest, unalienated life for man, which the Greeks enjoyed, is where the norms and ends expressed in the public life of a society are the most important ones by which its members define their identity as human beings. For then the institutional matrix in which they cannot help living is not felt to be foreign. Rather it is the essence, the 'substance' of the self.

Thus in universal spirit each man has self-certainty, the certainty that he will find nothing other in existing reality than himself.   (*PhG*, 258)

And because this substance is sustained by the activity of the citizens, they see it as their work.

This substance is also the universal work [Werk], which creates itself through the action of each and all as their unity and equality, because it is Being-for-self [Fürsichsein], the self, the act of doing [das Tun].   (*PhG*, 314)

To live in a state of this kind is to be free. The opposition between social necessity and individual freedom disappears.

The rational is necessary as what belongs to substance, and we are free in so far as we recognize it as law and follow it as the substance of our own essence; objective and subjective will are then reconciled and form one and the same untroubled whole. (*VG*, 115)

But alienation arises when the goals, norms or ends which define the common practices or institutions begin to seem irrelevant or even monstrous, or when the norms are redefined so that the practices appear a travesty of them. A number of public religious practices have suffered the first fate in history; they have 'gone dead' on subsequent generations, and may even be seen as irrational or blasphemous. To the extent that they remain part of the public ritual there is widespread alientation in society – we can think of contemporary societies like Spain, which remains officially Catholic while a good part of the population is rapidly anti-clerical; or communist societies, which have a public religion of atheism, even though many of their citizens believe in God.

But the democratic practices of Western society seem to be suffering something like the second fate in our time. Many people can no longer accept the legitimacy of voting and the surrounding institutions, elections, parliaments, etc., as vehicles of social decision. They have redrawn their conception of the relation of individual to society, so that the mediation and distance which any large-scale voting system produces between individual decision and social outcome seems unacceptable. Nothing can claim to be a real social decision which is not arrived at in a full and intense discussion in which all participants are fully conscious of what is at stake. Decisions made by elected representatives are branded as sham, as manipulation masquerading as consensus. With this redefinition of the norm of collective decision (that is, of a decision made *by* people, and not just for them), our present representative institutions begin to be portrayed as an imposture; and a subtantial proportion of the population is alienated from them.

In either case, norms as expressed in public practices cease to hold our allegiance. They are either seen as irrelevant or are decried as usurpation. This is alienation. When this happens men have to turn elsewhere to define what is centrally important to them. Sometimes they turn to another society, for instance a smaller, more intense religious community. But another possibility, which had great historical importance in Hegel's eyes, is that they strike out on their own and define their identity as individuals. Individualism comes, as Hegel puts it in the *VG*, when men cease to identify with the community's life, when they 'reflect', that is, turn back on themselves, and see themselves most importantly as individuals with individual goals. This is the moment of dissolution of a *Volk* and its life.

What happens here is that the individual ceases to define his identity principally by the public experience of the society. On the contrary, the most meaningful experience, which seems to him most vital, to touch most the core of his being, is private. Public experience seems to him secondary, narrow, and parochial, merely touching a part of himself. Should that experience try to make good its claim to centrality as before, the individual enters into conflict with it and has to fight it.

Ethical Substance

This kind of shift has of course been instantiated many times in history, but the paradigm event of this kind for Hegel occurs with the break-up of the Greek city-state. Thus in the Greek polis, men identified themselves with its public life; its common experiences were for them the paradigm ones. Their most basic, unchallengeable values were those embodied in this public life, and hence their major duty and virtue was to continue and sustain this life. In other words, they lived fully by their *Sittlichkeit*. But the public life of each of these poleis was narrow and parochial. It was not in conformity with universal reason. With Socrates arises the challenge of a man who cannot agree to base his life on the parochial, on the merely given, but requires a foundation in universal reason. Socrates himself expresses a deep contradiction since he accepts the idea of *Sittlichkeit*, of laws that one should hold allegiance to; he derives this from universal reason as well. And yet because of his allegiance to reason he cannot live with the actual laws of Athens. Rather he undermines them, he corrupts the youth not to take them as final, but to question them. He has to be put to death, a death which he accepts because of his allegiance to the laws.

But now a new type of man arises who cannot identify with this public life. He begins to relate principally not to the public life but to his own grasp of universal reason. The norms that he now feels compelling are quite unsubstantiated in any reality; they are ideas that go beyond the real. The reflecting individual is in the domain of *Moralität*.

Of course, even the self-conscious individual related to some society. Men thought of themselves qua moral beings as belonging to some community, the city of men and Gods of the Stoics, the city of God of the Christian. But they saw this city as quite other than and beyond the earthly city. And the actual community of philosophers or believers in which they worked out and sustained the language by which they identified themselves was scattered and powerless. The common life on which their identity as rational or God-fearing individuals was founded was or could be very attenuated. So that what was most important in a man's life was that he did or thought as an individual, not his participation in the public life of a real historical community. (This was not really true of the Christian church for which the Eucharist was of central importance, but certainly applies to the sage of the late ancient world.)

In any case, the community of the wise, as that of the saints, was without external, self-subsistent existence in history. Rather, the public realm was given over to private, unjustified power. This is Hegel's usual description of the ancient period of universal empires which succeeded the city-state, particularly the Roman empire. The unity and fulfilment of *Sittlichkeit*, lost from this world, was transposed out of it into an ethereal beyond.

What then is Hegel saying with his thesis of the primacy of *Sittlichkeit*, and the related notion of the community as 'ethical substance', a spiritual life in which

385

man must take part? We can express it in three propositions, put in ascending order of contestability. First, that what is most important for man can only be attained in relation to the public life of a community, not in the private self-definition of the alienated individual. Second, this community must not be a merely partial one, e.g., a conventicle or private association, whose life is conditioned, controlled and limited by a larger society. It must be co-terminous with the minimum self-sufficient human reality, the state. The public life which expresses at least some of our important norms must be that of a state.

Thirdly, the public life of the state has this crucial importance for men because the norms and ideas it expresses are not just human inventions. On the contrary, the state expresses the Idea, the ontological structure of things. In the final analysis it is of vital importance because it is one of the indispensable ways in which man recovers his essential relation to this ontological structure, the other being in the modes of consciousness which Hegel calls 'absolute spirit', and this real relation through the life of the community is essential to the completion of the return to conscious identity between man and the Absolute (which means also the Absolute's self-identity).

Obviously these three propositions are linked. The third gives the underlying ground of the first and second. If man achieves his true identity as a vehicle of cosmic spirit, and if one of the indispensable media in which this identity is expressed is the public life of his political society, then evidently, it is essential that he come to identify himself in relation to this public life. He must transcend the alienation of a private or sectarian identity, since these can never link him fully to the Absolute.

This is the complex of ideas which lies behind the Hegelian use of terms like 'substance', 'essence', '*Endzweck*', '*Selbstzweck*' in speaking of the community: First of all that the set of practices and institutions which make up the public life of the community express the most important norms, most central to its members' identity, so that they are only sustained in their identity by their participation in these practices and institutions, which in their turn they perpetuate by this participation. Secondly, that the community concerned is the state, that is, a really self-sufficient community. And thirdly, that this community has this central role because it expresses the Idea, the formula of rational necessity underlying man and his world.

Thus what is strange and contestable in Hegel's theory of the state is not the idea of a larger life in which men are immersed, or the notion that the public life of a society expresses certain ideas, which are thus in a sense the ideas of the society as a whole and not just of the individuals, so that we can speak of a people as having a certain 'spirit'. For throughout most of human history men have lived most intensely in relation to the meanings expressed in the public life of their societies. Only an exaggerated atomism could make the condition of alienated men seem the inescapable human norm.

Ethical Substance

But where Hegel does make a substantial claim which is not easy to grant is in his basic ontological view, that man is the vehicle of cosmic spirit, and the corollary, that the state expresses the underlying formula of necessity by which this spirit posits the world.

In other words, the idea of a ' Volksgeist', the spirit of a people, whose ideas are expressed in their common institutions, by which they define their identity, this is intelligible enough. And something like it is essential if we are to understand what has gone on in human history. What is harder to credit is the thesis that men – and hence in their own way these Volksgeister – are vehicles of a cosmic spirit which is returning to self-consciousness through man.

Thus there is no specially odd Hegelian doctrine of a super-individual subject of society, as is often believed. There is only a very difficult doctrine of a cosmic subject whose vehicle is man. This is woven into a theory of man in society which by itself is far from implausible or bizarre. Indeed, it is much superior to the atomistic conceptions of some of Hegel's liberal opponents.

But it is his ontological view which makes Hegel take a turn which goes against the mainstream of liberal thought. This latter tends to assume that individualism is the ultimate in human evolution. Even if civilized men are not alienated from the state, still their highest foci of identity are thought to be beyond it, in religion, or some personal moral ideal, or the human race as a whole. Thus the condition in which men identify themselves primarily in relation to the common life of their society must be a more primitive stage, and especially where this common life is thought to embody cosmic or religious significance. For this kind of society to *succeed* an age of individualism could only represent regression. And this is, of course, why Hegel has been harshly judged by those in this strand of liberalism (which does not exhaust what can justifiably be called liberal thought: Montesquieu, de Tocqueville, Herder, von Humboldt, and others have been concerned about the quality of public life, with which men must identify themselves).

But the attempt to understand Hegel within the terms of this liberal tradition has just led to distortion. A notorious example is Hegel's doctrine of the state. In the atomist liberal tradition, 'state' can only mean something like 'organs of government'. To talk of these as 'essence' or 'final goal' of the citizens can only mean subjection to irresponsible tyranny. But what Hegel means by 'state' is the politically organized community. His model is not the *Machstaat* of Frederick the Great, which he never admired,[1] but the Greek

---

[1] In a work of the early 1800s, which has been published since his death under the title, *The German Constitution*, Hegel expresses his opposition to the modern theory that a state should be a 'machine with a single spring which imparts movement to all the rest of the infinite wheelwork' (*Schriften zur Politik und Rechtsphilosophie*, ed. G. Lasson, Leipzig 1923, p. 28; *Hegel's Political Writings*, translated T. M. Knox, ed. Z. A. Pelczynski, Oxford 1964, p. 161). Prussia, as well as revolutionary France, is cited as an example later in this passage. (*Schriften* 31, *Political Writings* 163–4. Cf. discussion in Schlomo Avineri, *Hegel's Theory of the Modern State*, Cambridge 1970, 47–9).

polis. Thus his ideal is not a condition in which individuals are means to an end, but rather a community in which like a living organism, the distinction between means and ends is overcome, everything is both means and end. In other words the state should be an application of the category of internal teleology (cf. quote from *VG*, 112 above, p. 380).

Thus the state which is fully rational will be one which expresses in its institutions and practices the most important ideas and norms which its citizens recognize, and by which they define their identity. And this will be the case because the state expresses the articulations of the Idea, which rational man comes to see as the formula of necessity underlying all things, which is destined to come to self-consciousness in man. So that the rational state will restore *Sittlichkeit*, the embodiment of the highest norms in an ongoing public life. It will recover what was lost with the Greeks, but on a higher level. For the fully developed state will incorporate the principle of the individual rational will judging by universal criteria, the very principle that undermined and eventually destroyed the Greek polis.

This integration of individuality and *Sittlichkeit* is a requirement we can deduce from the Idea. But this is also Hegel's way of formulating and answering the yearning of his age to unite somehow the radical moral autonomy of Kant and the expressive unity of the Greek polis. Hegel's answer to this conundrum was, as we saw, an extraordinary and original combination of the ultra-modern aspiration to autonomy, and a renewed vision of cosmic order as the foundation of society; a derivation, we might say, of cosmic order from the idea of radical autonomy itself, via a displacement of its centre of gravity from man to *Geist*. This synthesis he saw as the goal of history. Let us turn now to see how it develops in history.

CHAPTER XV

Reason and History

1

The fulfilment of Spirit therefore requires the growth of a community which will fully express and embody reason. And since spirit posits the world of space and time in order to realize itself, this fulfilment and hence also the community of reason can be considered the goal of history. This is how Hegel speaks of it in *Reason in History:*

> The goal is that it come to be known that [Spirit] presses forward only to know itself as it is *an und für sich*, that it brings itself in its truth to appearance before itself – the goal is that it bring a spiritual world to existence which is adequate to its own [sc. the world's] concept, that it realize and perfect its truth, that religion and the state be so produced by it that it becomes adequate to its concept... (*VG*, 61)

In this passage, both sides of the goal of spirit in history are expressed: spirit is trying to come to an understanding, a knowledge of self. But in order to do this it must bring into existence a reality, a spiritual community which must also be a real community (the 'geistige Welt' must be embodied in a 'Staat') which is adequate to its concept. Or again:

> the goal is this, that Spirit come to consciousness of itself or make the world congruent to itself [die Welt sich gemäß mache] – for these come to the same thing... (*VG*, 74)

Thus history is to be understood teleologically as directed in order to realize *Geist*. What happens in history has sense, justification, indeed, the highest justification. It is good, the plan of God.

> The true good, the universal divine reason, is also the power to bring itself about. This good, this reason in its most concrete representation is God...The insight of philosophy is that no force prevails over the power of the good, of God, which would prevent it achieving its end [sich geltend zu machen]...that world history exhibits nothing other than the plan of providence. God rules the world. (*VG*, 77)

History is according to providence, and the true philosophy of history as Hegel says is a theodicy.

History thus reaches its culmination in a community which is in conformity with reason; or we could also say, one which embodies freedom, for 'the final purpose of the world is Spirit's consciousness of his freedom and hence the first full realization of this freedom'. (*VG*, 63)

389

This freedom is not, of course, individual, negative freedom, the freedom to do what I like. It is the freedom that man has in following his own essence, reason. On the other hand,

the arbitrary choice [das Belieben] of the individual is precisely not freedom. Freedom which is limited is caprice [Willkür] which relates to the particular element of needs.
(*VG*, 111)

But to follow reason is to participate in the larger life of the state, for 'In the state alone has man rational existence' (loc. cit.). But the fully rational state is not the first community with which men identify as their 'substance'. On the contrary, all important historical developments take place in such communities. Those men who live outside a state, in patriarchal tribal societies, for instance, are totally on the margins of history, either before it really starts or at its fringes. What comes at the end of history is not community as such, but rather one which from the first time is fully adequate to the concept, to freedom and reason.

Hence the march of history can be seen as the succession of such communities,[1] the earlier ones being very imperfect expressions of what the later ones will embody more and more adequately. Hegel calls these concrete historical communities or peoples which are (more or less adequate) embodiments of Spirit, *Volksgeister*. They are the subjects of history. 'The Spirit we have to do with here is the *Volksgeist*' (*VG*, 59).[2]

Thus the Idea is realized in history, but through stages, and these stages are historical civilizations, *Volksgeister*.

World history is the presentation of the divine, absolute process of Spirit in its highest forms, of this progress through stages whereby he attains to his truth and self-consciousness about himself. The forms of these stages are the world-historical *Volksgeister*, the character of their ethical life, their constitution, their art, religion, science. To bring each of these stages to realization, this is the infinite drive [Trieb] of the world spirit, his irresistible thrust [Drang]; for this articulation and its realization is his concept.
(*VG*, 75)

The last sentence points to the fact that this set of stages is itself necessary, according to the Concept. It is necessary to its self-realization that spirit move from the greatest outwardness to full self-consciousness. But in the same way the stages on the road are set by necessity; each must work itself out. The motor

---

[1] 'Völker, die sich vernünftig in sich organisiert haben, sind es, die wir betrachten. In der Weltgeschichte kann nur von Völkern die Rede sein, welche einen Staat bilden. Man darf sich eben nicht einbilden, daß auf einer wüsten Insel, überhaupt in Abgeschiedenheit solches hervorgehen könne.' (*VG*, 113.)

[2] Let me repeat that this notion of *Volksgeist* does not involve some special doctrine about a supra-individual subject of society. *Volksgeister* are historical cultures, but seen as embodiments of *Geist*, at a certain stage of its realization and self-knowledge. The basic difficulty, if there is one, concerns the relation of man to this cosmic subject of which they are the vehicles. There is no special problem about the historical configurations men adopt in order to embody Spirit.

force of movement is contradiction, that between the external reality and what it is meant to realize. The contradiction eventually brings any given form to dissolution. But the particular nature of the contradiction in this form determines the outcome, and hence from the collapse of the first form another specific one arises. Having resolved the contradiction of its predecessor, it falls victim to its own, and so on through the whole of history.

In this way history shows a dialectical movement, of the kind we described above in Chapter IV. But since the beginning point and the goal are set by the Idea, hence by necessity, so are all the intermediate stages necessary. For granted the starting point and the goal, the particular nature of the contradiction in the first form necessarily follows; and from its resolution arises the second form; from which and the goal the nature of the second contradiction must follow, and so on. History should thus follow a necessary dialectical plan.

The plan of history is that of the Idea, the philosophical understanding of which is presupposed by the philosophy of history.[1] Hence the dialectic of history is to be understood as reflecting the conceptually necessary stages in the self-unfolding of the Idea.

But as will surprise no-one there is in fact a looseness of fit between history and logic. The conceptual relations in their general form permit of too many combinations to form a very rigorous a priori framework; and the historical events permit of too many interpretations in such high level concepts as 'universal', 'particular', 'individual' not to allow a great deal of play. One feels that the system would allow of accommodation to very wide changes in the course of history if we were suddenly to discover that our knowledge of the past had been mistaken.

In spite of this, however, there is a very strong and even potentially convincing unity to the general plan of things. The higher one soars over the detail, the more persuasive the philosophy of history seems. Even though there are very often fascinating insights in Hegel's detail, it is the fit of the detail with the whole which raises doubts.

Stages of history, as the last quote above says, are represented by *Volksgeister*. Each stage is embodied in a certain people which labours to bring forth the idea of that particular stage. This is the common purpose of the people; they remain entirely captured by this common task, entirely identified with it, until it is achieved. Then things fall apart. Its members cease to give themselves totally, they turn to reflection, to an identity as individuals outside the public goal. They fall into 'political nullity' (*VG*, 68).

Hegel talks in this passage as though the transition from one stage to the next came about through the fruition and natural death of each world-historical people, rather than through an inner contradiction. But this is not really an incompatible view. Having developed its particular form to the utmost a given

---

[1] Cf. above Chapter VIII.

Volksgeist has also brought its inadequacy to a head. There being no further development of the Idea, only the inadequacy now stands out. Hence it is inevitable that men desert this state and dream of something else – desert it in their fundamental allegiance, that is, for they may go on living happily in it for some time. Somewhere else, however, a new force arises which bears the next stage.

But what men are doing in history, they do not fully grasp. Why they desert one standard and go to another is not clear to them. Or rather, they may have some clear idea, but this is not the deepest truth; since of necessity men in earlier stages of history cannot understand the plan of *Geist* as the philosopher now can (Hegel now can). This is where Hegel introduces his famous idea of the cunning of reason. Reason is represented in this image as 'using' the passions of men to fulfill her own purposes. Particular men and their purposes fall in the battle, but the universal purpose carries on safe above it.

It is not the universal idea which places itself in opposition and struggle, or puts itself in danger; it holds itself safe from attack and uninjured in the background and sends the particular of passion into the struggle to be worn down. We can call it the *cunning of reason* that the Idea makes passions work for it, in such a way that that whereby it posits itself in existence loses thereby and suffers injury.   (*VG*, 105)[1]

But this picturesque image is not meant to be taken *au pied de la lettre*, as though a super-individual subject was deploying tools to its own ends. Rather we have to take into account that even men at the earliest stages of history are the vehicles of *Geist*. They have some sense, however cloudy, however fantastically expressed, of the demands of spirit. Hence it is not just a question of men's individual ambition being used for a foreign purpose. Rather it is that those men whose individual ambition coincides with the interests of Spirit are filled with a sense of mission. They instinctively sense the importance of what they are doing, and so do the men around them, who flock to their banner; even though both the great man and his followers would be incapable of articulating the significance of what they are doing or of articulating it correctly. Hegel uses the word 'instinct' for this unconscious recognition of significance.

Thus in the passage quoted above about the cunning of Reason, Hegel cites the case of Caesar who in fact falls under the assassins' knives as soon as he has done the work of spirit in bringing the Republic to an end. This is an example of Reason using expendable instruments. But in an earlier passage (*VG*, 89–90), he says in connection with Caesar that the correspondence of his own goal with that of the World-Spirit (*Weltgeist*) was what gave him strength:

his work was an instinct which brought to fruition what the time called for *an und für sich*.

And Hegel goes on:

These are the great men in history, whose own particular purposes comprehend the substantial content which is the will of the world spirit. This content is the true source of their power; it is in the universal unconscious instinct of men. They are inwardly driven

---

[1] Cf. passage in the Logic, in the section on Inner Teleology, *WL*, II, 397–8.

to it, and have no further support against him who has taken up the fulfilment of this goal as his interest, so that they could resist him. Rather the peoples assemble under his banner; he shows them what their own inner bent [immanenter Trieb] is and carries it out.

Thus the work of the *Weltgeist* is felt as an 'immanenter Trieb' among men, one that is merely 'instinctual', that is, not understood; and this is why the work of reason gets done among the clash of individual ambitions in history.

Thus the greatness of world-historical individuals does not just lie in their being instruments of the World-Spirit. They are also those who first sense and give articulation to what must be the next stage. Once they raise this banner men follow. In a time when one form is played out, when Spirit has deserted the reigning form, it is the world-historical individual who shows the way to what all men in their depths aspire to. 'It is the world-historical individuals who first told men what they wanted' (*VG*, 99).

Once they do articulate this new form, it has an irresible force, even for those who are inclined by their own interest or judgment against it, because deep down they cannot help identifying with it.

For the spirit which has stepped on to the next stage is the soul of all individuals, but an unconscious inner sense which great men first bring to consciousness for them. It is nevertheless what they really want, and it thus exercises a force on them which they surrender to even against their own conscious will; thus they follow these leaders of souls, for they feel the irresistable force of their own inner spirit which confronts them.

(loc. cit.)

A category like the 'cunning of Reason', far from being another incomprehensible, 'mystical' Hegelian idea, is indispensable for any theory of history which wants to give a role to unconscious motivation.[1]

2

Let us now look at the main themes of the philosophy of history. The principal drama of the sweep of history is the one which builds towards the major crux of Hegel's philosophy of politics; how to reconcile the freedom of the individual who knows himself as universal rationality with a restored *Sittlichkeit*. The main drama of history is then opened by the breakdown of the perfect unity of *Sittlichkeit* in the Greek world, the birth of the individual with universal consciousness. It then follows the slow development through the succeeding centuries both of the individual (his *Bildung*) and of the institutions embodying *Sittlichkeit*, so that the two can eventually rendez-vous in the rational state.

---

[1] Avineri, cf. *Hegel's theory of the Modern State*, p. 233, finds that Hegel contradicts himself in his doctrine of the world-historical individual, since he seems to hold sometimes that he is fully conscious of the idea he is realizing, at other times only instinctively conscious, and in still other passages he is said not to be conscious at all. Avineri's quotes are from *Reason in History*, and it seems to me that with a little allowance for the unpolished nature of this text which Hegel never prepared for publication, the texts can fairly easily be reconciled around the notion that world-historical individuals have a sense of the higher truth they serve, but they see it through a glass darkly.

The version of the history in compressed form which we have in Chapter VI of the *PhG* starts with the Greek world. But the major version contained in the lectures on the philosophy of history starts earlier, takes us through Chinese, Indian, Persian, Phoenician, Egyptian civilizations in the run up to Greek. It also deals with the Jews. There are also differences in the way Hegel cuts into even the areas common to the two versions; as there are between different cycles of the lectures. This reinforces what was said above about the detail of Hegel's philosophy of history.

My aim here will be simply to give the general line of the dialectic of history, as a background to the main political problem mentioned above. In dealing with the pre-Greek civilizations, Hegel discusses their religious consciousness, and there are many elements here which reappear in the philosophy of religion. Their political structures and public life are closely bound up with this religious consciousness. As ever with Hegel the different aspects of a people's life are bound together in its *Geist*. But the religious consciousness for these early peoples offers the most striking expression of the stage they were at, of the way in which they tried to realize the ontological reality, *Geist*, and its relation to the world and subject.

Spirit is struggling to achieve an understanding of itself as spirit, that is, as free subjectivity, and to see this as the absolute. But with the pre-Greek peoples – except for the Jews – the absolute is still less than subject; it is still bound up with external, hence impersonal reality, nature, or the total abstraction of the void (one aspect of Indian religion). The Persians achieve a high form of this in that they see the absolute symbolized in light, which is the most spiritual among natural forms, but they are still not yet at the break-through point.

This comes in one form with the Jews. Here we suddenly come to the realization that God is pure subject, spirit. But this realization can only be won at that stage by a radical separation of God as spirit from all contamination with natural, finite reality. The Jewish spirit, thinks Hegel, is therefore one of separation, radical transcendence. Abraham starts off by leaving his family and home in Ur of the Chaldees to become a wanderer. The Jewish people wage a constant fight against idolatry, which amounts to a mixing of the divine again with the finite. But this solution can only be a stage on the way, for it is radically imperfect. God is spirit, but at the cost of being beyond the world, and above all beyond, above and over finite subjectivity, that of man. Man is not reconciled with God, does not see himself as at one with the absolute, as its vehicle, but rather the absolute is over against him, he is its slave, totally submitted to it. Similarly, the natural world is totally emptied of the divine. It is 'entgöttert', as Hegel puts it; Jewish consciousness sees only a world of finite things, which are to be used by man, not the embodiment of Deity. The world is totally under spirit, at our disposal, even as we are totally under God. Hegel

394

also speaks of this vision of God as of 'pure thought', which in Hegelian terms is closely linked with being pure subject. In this formulation he stresses again that the Jewish concept of the absolute is of something universal, totally without particularization.

The Greek solution is in a sense the opposite of the Jewish one. The Greeks, too, win through to a consciousness of God as subject. But it is not a subjectivity which is frighteningly beyond nature, which negates natural expression in the purity of thought. Rather the Greek gods are perfectly harmonized with their natural expression. But instead of this being something infra-personal, as with the earlier natural religions, the paradigm expression of these Gods is in the form of realized subjectivity, that is, in human form.

But the Greek God, unlike the Jewish, is parochial. And this same parochial nature is what we shall see reflected in the Greek polis, and will be the cause of its downfall. A similar advantage is won at similar cost. On one hand, the Greek concept of the divine is the charter of Greek freedom. It is the sense that the divine is not totally other, that finite subjectivity has its place in it. And this is the sense of freedom, that man is not the slave of the absolute, of something which is utterly foreign to his will. Hence the Greek polity will be the first home of freedom.

It was this which enabled the Greeks to build an embodiment of *Sittlichkeit* for which Hegel's day pined, one in which men were fully at home, in which their whole identity was bound up with the living public reality of their polis. The vision of God in human form was the foundation for a public life woven around this divinity, the God of the city, in which the citizens could fully recognize themselves. This public life was a reality which was fully theirs. Their activity kept it going, and yet it also represented what was of ultimate significance for them, an expression of the divine. Hence their realized public life was their 'substance', the basis of their identity. Their ethic was one of *Sittlichkeit*, where what ought to be also was.

But this was a limited freedom. Only those who were citizens, who were thus members of a certain polis and the servers of its God, were so reflected in public reality. Slaves, and in general outsiders, were not. Each state had its own God, own laws, with which its members were fully reconciled, but these were different from state to state. The reassuring form of the divine was reassuring only for some. It reflected only part of humanity. Hence the Greeks did not have the intuition that man as such is free. Freedom was the appanage of citizens; slaves and barbarians were outside its ban.[1]

---

[1] This is, of course, the background to the famous passage in which Hegel resumes the history of freedom (*VG*, 62): The oriental world knew only that one man was free – the king represented the absolute principle, e.g., the Persian despot (but of course in an important sense not even he was free, as a really rational subjectivity). The Greek world won through to an intuition of freedom, but saw only that some were free. Only with Christianity do we win through to the intuition that man as such is free.

Correspondingly, the identification with the city on the part of its citizens was not based on universal reflection, but was one of immediate unreflecting adherence. The laws must be obeyed because they are those of our city, *sans plus.*

In this world, democracy (direct democracy) is the most natural form of government. For all men are totally identified with the whole. They only want to live and die for it; they can thus be entrusted with running it. But it is a parochial democracy, it excludes slaves and metics; for the identification is parochial.

Hegel makes clear why in his view ancient democracy is inappropriate as a model for the modern world. Ancient, direct democracy was possible in part because societies were so small; all could really take part and be really present when decisions were taken. But this is not all. One of the essential conditions of Greek democracy was precisely its exclusiveness. All the menial economic tasks were taken over by non-citizens. This not only meant that citizens had in general more leisure than otherwise would be possible to attend the ecclesia and see to affairs of state. It also meant a homogeneity of the population which cannot be attained in a modern polity where all functions are fulfilled by citizens. But heterogeneity makes essential an articulation of the modern state which in Hegel's view excludes democracy.

But there is a third reason why ancient democracy is not an appropriate model for our time. The Greek state could work because men were immediately identified with it. Now while we hope to restore the integrity of *Sittlichkeit,* we can never restore this immediate, unreflecting unity. Modern man will also remain a universal individual. And this individuality will be reflected in the structure of modern society, and we shall see – in the form of civil society. This necessary articulation of the polity to take account of the greater complexity of man requires a balance between institutions which Hegel thinks is incompatible with direct democracy. More of this below.

This beautiful unity of the Greek state is doomed. It is doomed because of its limitations, its parochialness. The world spirit has to march on. Hence once the polis is realized the cunning of reason calls world-historical individuals to look beyond. Such a figure in his own way is Socrates. Socrates turns his allegiance to universal reason. And although he wants to remain obedient to the laws of his polis, he would like to found them on reason. Thus while he maintains his allegiance to Athens to the death, nevertheless his teaching cannot but corrupt the youth, for it undermines that immediate identification with the public life on which the polis rests. Men turn to a universal reason, turn their back on the parochial state and its gods. But this universal reason is not embodied in public life, it is the beyond.

The dissolution of the polity is the birth of the individual with universal consciousness. This is an individual who defines himself as subject of universal reason. But he can find no identification with the public life of his city. He lives in a larger community, the city of men and Gods of the Stoics, but this is unrealized. Hence the new individual is an internal émigré.

But this has the necessary consequence that the life goes out of the public institutions of the polis. It cannot but go under and gives way to the universal empire, a form of dominance from on top which is predicated precisely on their being no such identification. This universal empire is no more than the polis a realization of the universal reason which has now come to conscious-ness. It is the correlative in the sense that the individual of universal reason must bring about the collapse of the city-state, but it is not at all expression in public life of this reason. On the contrary, it is the expression of the fact that this reason is now felt as beyond the world. Thus the individual is cast into an external world which is ruled not by reason but by the arbitrary will of emperors, powerful despots. Internally he defines himself as universal reason, but externally he is a bit of flotsam on the huge flood of events, entirely at the mercy of external power.

In this diremption he goes even more to an inward definition of himself. This is the age in which Stoicism flourishes. But for Hegel, this cannot be a solution, for it is a completely unrealized figure of reason and freedom. Hence the individual cannot but yearn to go beyond this, to find realization. The ground is laid for the unhappy consciousness.

This is the era of the Roman Empire. Thus Roman society is the place of origin of the idea of the Person, an individual defined as a subject of rights in abstraction from his relation to the substance of *Sittlichkeit*. The Person is the bearer of 'abstract' right, right unconnected to social and political role; he is the bearer of right as property. This will be one of the dimensions of the modern state. It has its origins here.

The stage is set for the birth of Christianity. Christianity comes to answer the yearning of the universal individual, who cannot be reconciled with the universal in this political world, that nevertheless the finite subject and the absolute be fully united. And so they become so united once, in the person of Christ. There is no question of this happening many times, as with the avatars of Hindu religion. The absolute is one, and the paradigmatic founding unity can only be realized once. But this unity, as we have seen, must also be overcome in its immediate form. Christ must die. And he must rise again, go to the Father, and return in spirit to animate the community.

But with the birth of Christianity this unity is only realized in principle. It is still not fully realized in the world. The Church which is the external realization of the new community is thus in inner exile at first as well, just like the universal individual. The task of history now is to make this reconciliation externally, politically real; to make the church community in a sense one with the society. And this means a slow transformation of institutions, and a slow making over of men – *Bildung*. This is the task of the next eighteen centuries, and it will be undertaken by a new world-historical people, the Germanic nations.

The German nations Hegel means are the barbarians who swarmed over the Roman empire at its end and founded the new nations of Western Europe. There is no particular chauvinism in this use of the word German. Montesquieu and others also recognized that modern European polities had issued out of these Germanic barbarian kingdoms.

But these Germans were ideally suited to take history to the next stage – the *Weltgeist* always sees to such convergence of material and ends – because they were naturally very conscious of their individual independence from authority. They were only with difficulty, and then precariously, submitted to authority. Hegel pictures the early German as being loosely under leaders who, like Agamemnon, were barely primus inter pares. In this way, they were as it were pre-programmed to build a civilization which would be based on the freedom of the individual. But first this freedom has to be purified, it has to grow into and incorporate the rational inner freedom which was achieved by the ancient word and Christianity. The real, external independence of the German in the woods has to be united to this spiritual freedom, and this freedom given reality. But second, it is essential to this that the wild independent German must learn to accept rational authority, must accept to be integrated into a rational state.

The development of medieval and modern Europe is the working out of these two related processes. The feudal system in which the public realm is shot through with private relationships is the natural form in which these German tribes set up states. But then the process starts by which these loose skeins of private relations are united into the common overarching will which is inseparable from the state. In Europe this comes in the form of the growing power of the monarchy. Charlemagne represents a crucial phase in this process.

We have here the foundation of one of the essential features of a modern state for Hegel. It must be united at the top by a monarchy. Hegel seems to hold that this is essentially linked with the principle of modern individual freedom. The Greek city-state could be a republic since all gave themselves immediately to the state, they had no private will outside it. But the modern universal individual also has a private identity, he cannot be simply a member of the state. In order to be real as a common will, any state must however have this moment of immediate unity in it. At some moment, at some point, the will of the whole must be one with a real existent will. This not just in the sense that in order for the state to act, some men must act in its name. Rather Hegel is making the ontological point that there must be some place in which the immediate unity of concrete and general will is realized. The state cannot be for everybody just one dimension among many of their action and will.

What Hegel is presenting here, and later in the *PR*, is a renewed variant of the medieval idea of the representative individual, that is, an individual who bodies forth a basic principle of the common life. This is 'representation' not in the modern sense of standing in for someone else or being delegated by him, but of bodying forth, of incarnating an underlying common reality to which all show allegiance. The notion of kingly majesty, that the king is the point at which the majesty of the whole is manifest, belongs to this idea. In the ontological dimension of his political thought, where he is concerned to derive the structures of the state from the 'Concept', that is, from the ontological structure of things, Hegel has recourse to an idea of this kind. Different features of the constitution 'represent' in this sense different aspects of ontological reality.

Alongside the powerful monarch, who draws together the unruly subjects, there grow up the institutions known as estates, which in England became Parliament. These are the necessary mediating elements between the sovereign will and the particulars. And hence we have here another essential institution of a modern state, thinks Hegel. It is by the estates that the people as a whole take part in the life of the state. Here again we shall see that Hegel's notion of the participation of the people is not founded on the modern notion of representation, as it is in theories of modern representative government. It is not a matter of legitimating decisions, by leading them back to popular choices, but of establishing some kind of identification.

At the same time the state develops more and more towards impersonality, the dependence on law, and what Weber was later to call rationality. The kingly power becomes less and less a private appanage, and is seen as the public power of government. Service by magnates is replaced over the centuries by a trained bureaucracy. The state becomes more and more founded on general principles, on legal rationality.

As these institutions are developing – to what final fruition we shall discuss further below – the parallel process of spiritualization is going on, purification of the raw, primitive human material, and its formation (Bildung). One of the key stages in this is the Reformation. The Christian Church took over a good part of the task of forming the raw barbarians. But in the process it had to sink to some degree to their level. The higher spiritual truths of Christianity were united with gross external realities. Men tried to find God by the actual physical conquest of the Holy Land, the presence of God was reified in the host, and so on. This is Hegel's notion of what underlay medieval Catholicism. In order for the spirit to progress, there had to be a recovery of purity, a rediscovery of the spiritual meaning of the presence of the spirit in the world, a setting aside of the gross sensuous meaning this had with Catholicism. This is essential to the development of the modern state; so much so that Catholic countries are incapable of realizing this state integrally.

With the Reformation, and the freeing of spirituality from its imprisonment in gross external things, with the recovery of a sense of the presence of God in the community which was purely spiritual, the way was free for the task of making this presence objective and real in the external world, not in the gross and inadequate way of the external rites and hierarchy of Catholicism, but by building a real earthly community which would realize the universal, reason. The world was ready for a state founded on reason. In other words, the unity of God and man has to be externally realized. But we have to go beyond the primitive, purely external, and hence totally inadequate realization in host, sanctuary, relics, indulgences, etc.; we have to liberate the true spiritual dimension, if we are to achieve the adequate realization in a political community. Thus from the Reformed Europe comes the attempt to realize the rational state, to overcome the opposition of Church and state. The Protestant religion is at the foundation of this state.

The spiritualization process begun by the Reformation, however, carries on and brings about what we call the Enlightenment. More and more aware of themselves as at one with the universal, men come to recognize that they are inwardly free with the freedom of pure thought. The spiritualization brings them back to an understanding of their identity as resting in the freedom of universal thought. But this is not simply a return to the ancients. For these latter found themselves faced with a world which was totally refractory to reason; their sense of their identity as reason was a purely inner one, buffeted by the forces of the world; the world of reason was a beyond. But since then men have come to see that they are at one with the very foundation of things. Christian culture has wrought this. Consequently the modern Enlightenment does not just define man as thought, it is sure that the whole of external reality conforms to thought too. This is Hegel's reading of the new scientific consciousness which strives to understand the world as law-governed order.

In other words, thought and being are one. This is Hegel's rather idiosyncratic reading of the Cogito ergo sum of Descartes. The point is that man is reason, and he is as such one with the principle of things; so he will find reason in the external world if he only looks for it.[1]

This spiritualization completes the process of the desacralization (*Entgötterung*) of things. The world becomes a set of external realities simply laid out before human consciousness, transparent to it. But we might ask, why should Enlightenment mean *Entgötterung?* Surely religion too, of the purified kind, sees thought behind all reality. The answer is, of course, that at base the Enlightenment is at one with purified religion; its battle with religion is based on self-illusion, as Hegel tried to show in a passage of the *PhG* discussion. But this self-illusion is its crucial flaw. It sees itself as purely human. It comes to an

---

[1] This is also the line of Chapter v, *Vernunft*, of the *PhG.*

understanding of itself as reason, that is, of man's self as reason; to a vision of the world of external reality as subject to reason, but it loses its sense of the larger cosmic self, *Geist*, which is the fundamental locus of reason.

This Hegel sees as grounded in the fact that the Enlightenment remains at the level of *Verstand*, that is, at the level where thought clearly distinguishes things and separates them but without going beyond to the level of *Vernunft*, where we see the inner connections which link all separate realities, the dialectical life which engenders them all in a chain. Hence the Enlightenment distinguishes clearly and has a vision of men as individuals, independent of each other, but it loses sight of the community in which they are set. Its political theory is atomistic. Hence, too, the Enlightenment sees merely external, individual objects in the world that surrounds us; it does not also see the world as an order posited by God, *Geist* or reason. What the Enlightenment sees is true, but fatally partial. Thus it desacralizes, for it only sees the world as a heap of objects, open to human scrutiny and use; it does not see it also as manifestation, the emanation of reason.

This is the reason why the value theory of the Enlightenment is utilitarian. All objects are seen as lying to hand. The dimension in which they are manifestation of something higher which would require an attitude of respect is occluded. Their only value must lie outside themselves, in their use for subjects, for men. Consequently, the universal category of value is an extrinsic one, what is the utility of a thing, an action, a policy? What are its consequences for human desire?

In this way the Enlightenment inevitably comes into conflict with religion. Really the conflict as was said above is based on self-illusion on both sides. But this illusion is itself real and powerful. The only way the Enlightenment can accommodate *Geist*, the cosmic subject, is by emptying him of all content. He can no longer be a subject, and active; for there is only room for human subjects and law-governed nature. God thus must be reduced to the impersonal and colourless 'supreme being' of Deism. In other words, the principle of the totality becomes empty. And in this, Hegel argues, the materialist and the deist forms of the Enlightenment are not that far from each other. For the 'matter' of the materialists is also a purely empty, colourless category. It is indistinguishable from the *être suprème*.

Confident in himself as Reason and in reason as mastery over reality, the man of the Enlightenment rejects all authority and sets out to shape reality to reason, i.e., to himself. But this is where his onesidedness turns out to be disastrous. For once we lose sight of *Geist*, the form of reason remains but the substantive content is lost, that is, we have no longer a vision of the ontological structure of things, which all that we live in must conform to if it is to be adequate to reason. We are all ready to master the world, and to shape it, but we have lost the plan. In our desperation to find an alternative we tear things to pieces.

The lack of content of reason in the vision of the Enlightenment can be seen first if we probe its basic system of valuation, utilitarianism. The principle of utility assesses the value of things extrinsically, by how they serve the ends of man. But where should this process stop? With the de facto desires of man? But why should we stop here? Men with their desires, are themselves external facts in the world; why should not they too be evaluated extrinsically in the interest of 'society', or the future? We are in danger of falling into a senseless regress, what Hegel calls a 'bad infinite'. The point of this criticism is not just to lay bare a problem for the justification of utilitarian ethics, but to identify a real tendency in the system. Utilitarian thought can step over the brink in which man becomes means and not end, as for instance with reforms like the English Poor Law of 1834, which put the unemployed into work-houses for the sake of general utility. For it lacks a notion of intrinsic good.

And it is the more easy to step over this brink in that the criterion of de facto desire cannot work in practice. For desires are too varied and contradictory, between and within people. Moral conflict breaks out between desires, and some criterion of intrinsic goodness, that is, of what makes a desire good, has to be found.

In addition, in order to make our desires real in the world of history, we have to achieve common goals. For the only self-subsistent reality is a community, and any shaping of things which will be self-subsistent must be the shaping of a whole community. There must be a common aspiration.

Now this fact seems to provide the answer which we were looking for above, a criterion for judging between desires. Those desires are to be followed which are truly general, which are for the good of all, and not just of oneself. We have the basis here for the idea of the general will. This is the other great discovery of Enlightenment ethical theory. Man shapes his society according to right reason by founding it fully on the general will. For the rational is the universal, that which holds for all men and is binding on all men.

The step from utilitarianism to general will theory is an attempt, as we saw in the last chapter, to achieve a more integral realization of reason. The ethic of utility has to take an arbitrary final point in de facto human desire, something which is just given. The ethic of the general will promises to go beyond what is just given, what men happen to want, to ends derived from the rational will itself.

This is in any case how Hegel sees the step taken by Rousseau and later developed by Kant. But this new theory is as incapable as its predecessor of developing a content, a set of substantive goals out of the idea of reason, because as we saw it remains centred on the free, rational will of man. It remains like utilitarianism in the domain of 'understanding' (*Verstand*) which separates finite from infinite, and cannot see that finite spirits are linked into the larger reality of *Geist.*

The ethic of the general will, of formal universality, remained empty.

But it is one thing to weave empty ethical theories in one's study; it is another thing to try to put this empty general will into reality in history. The Germans only did the first; but the French tried the second, and the terrible, destructive consequences revealed what was implicit in this emptiness and showed the need to go beyond to another stage. This traumatic, climactic event was the French Revolution (cf. *PR,* § 258).

3

We come now to the great political event of Hegel's youth, the event against which all his generation had to think out their political philosophy, and had to rethink their stance to the Enlightenment. For Hegel, as we see, the disaster of the Jacobin Terror, the excesses of the Revolution as it went off the rails, are to be understood from the root inadequacy of the Enlightenment.

The aspiration to remake the world entirely according to the prescriptions of rational will is the aspiration to 'absolute freedom'. But this arises essentially out of the whole modern development of which Reformation and Enlightenment are phases. The basic insight underlying this development is that the world is posited by Spirit, that we are at one with the very foundation of things, or that thought and being are one. But thought or Spirit is identified simply with those of man. Hence the whole of society is seen as reposing on human will alone. To remake it according to reason is to rebuild it entirely according to the prescriptions of human will, and thus to realize an unrestricted, unconditioned freedom.

With this, Spirit is present as *absolute freedom*; it is self-consciousness which understands itself, and from this understands that its certainty of self is the essence of all the spiritual structures [Massen] of the real as well as the supersensible world, or conversely, that essence and reality are the knowledge of consciousness of *itself*.

(*PhG,* 415)

This aspiration wreaks terrible destruction. We saw in the discussion of the Terror in the *PhG,* that the root failure of the drive to absolute freedom is that it cannot accept the differentiation which is essential for society. Its vacuity condemns it to unmitigated destructiveness. But we were not in a position to understand then why differentiation is essential to modern society. We began to see the reason for this in the last chapter, in that the articulations of the Concept must be matched in the state. But in examining more closely why this articulation must be and why the aspiration to absolute freedom cannot provide it, we shall get to the heart of Hegel's theory of the modern state.

The society of absolute freedom must be entirely the creation of its

403

members. First, it must be such that everything in it is the fruit of human will and decision. And secondly, the decisions must be taken with the real participation of all.[1] This condition, which we can call universal and total participation, is one in which all have a say in the whole decision.

This contrasts with an arrangement whereby a group may distribute functions, so that one sub-group has the responsibility for determining one aspect of things, another the responsibility for another, and so on. We can say of this group, too, that the total outcome is determined by the will of the members; but it is not true of the individual members, perhaps of any individual members, that they took a decision concerning the total outcome, or had a voice in such a decision in the sense of voting on the total outcome along with others.

Thus an ideal free enterprise economy in which all men are independent entrepreneurs is one in which the outcome is determined by the decisions of members, but where no-one has taken a decision or participated in a decision about the total outcome. Alternatively a traditional society may have a structure with differentiated roles which is considered as outside the realm of decision. This structure in turn will determine how and by whom those matters are decided which remain within the realm of decision. In all like-lihood, this structure will relate different people differently to the decisions to be taken; so that some will fall to the chief, say, others to the elders, others to the medicine man, some to the women, others again will be the responsibility of the whole people. Perhaps, too, even when the whole people decide, the manner of the decision will be determined by the structure, say, they vote to accept or refuse proposals framed by the elders.

The society which aims at absolute freedom must be unlike both the free enterprise and the traditional society models briefly adumbrated. Unlike the latter, it cannot allow for structures which are beyond the reach of decision, which are supposedly rooted in the nature of things, the will of the Gods, time-hallowed law, and so on. It is the nature of the Enlightenment as Hegel saw not to accept any such authority. Everything must be thought out from the ground up by human reason and decided according to reason by human will. To use a term which Hegel employs in one of his early theological writings, the rational will cannot accept the merely 'positive', that is, institutions and structures which are simply there, simply in being, without being rationally justified, shown to be necessary or desirable by reason. Hence it is that the state founded on the general will contains no structures which are not themselves the result of decision, save simply those which are essentially part of the process of decision itself which yields the general will: that deliberation be in

[1] 'die Welt ist [dem Selbstbewußtsein] schlechthin sein Wille, und dieser ist allgemainer Wille. Und zwar ist er nicht der leere Gedanke des Willens, der in stillschweigende oder repräsentierte Einwilligung gesetzt wird, sondern reell allgemeiner Wille, Wille aller *Einzelnen* als solcher.' (*PhG*, 415).

general assembly, by free discussion, without factions, etc. But all else, the form of the government, who is to fill the roles of government, the rights of property, all these are decided. There are not even entrenched individual rights, matters taken outside the sphere of government, as there are with Locke.

Absolute freedom thus rejects structures which are not founded on will, the fruit of decision. But at the same time it rejects the other model, which is instantiated for instance in the free enterprise economy. This, too, be it noted, has broken with the traditional society. It is a child of the Enlightenment. It need have no 'positive'institutions, save the institutions of property, and those which go along with its exchange and alienation, contract, buying, selling, etc., in other words institutions which are essential to the type of decisions which it makes central, decisions of individual entrepreneurs concerning the disposal of their property. No structure founded on the authority of tradition, the divine the order of things, is to be respected or obeyed. Only those are taken as fundamental which are essential to the exercise of rational human will. In this way, the free enterprise society is similar to the society of absolute freedom. Where they differ profoundly is in their conception of the exercise of rational will. In one case this is expressed in the decisions of individuals about their good, in the other rather in decisions of the whole society about their common affairs. One is the realm of the particular, the other of the general will. The root structures of each are meant to make possible the respective paradigm decisions of each. But the general will model cannot accept the model of free enterprise, for even though this latter rejects the 'positive', it remains true that the total outcome is not the fruit of will and decision. Each man decides for himself, and hence the outcome in so far as it results from this decision is his own. But he has only a relatively minor effect on the whole outcome. For the rest he is faced by conditions which he did not make, which are the fruit of hundreds of other wills, each one of whom is in a similar predicament. The way these wills concatenate is a function of blind natural law, not will. But if the point of freedom is that what I live should be decided by myself, then to the extent that I live in conditions which are only partly the fruit of my decision, to that extent I am not integrally free.

Complete freedom would require that the whole outcome be decided by me. But of course, since the whole outcome is a social one, it cannot be decided by me alone. Or rather, if I decide it alone, then no one else who lives under this outcome is free. If we are all to be free, we must all take the decision. But this means that we must all take the whole decision, we must all participate in a decision about the nature of the total outcome. There must be universal and total participation. Participation must be not only universal, that is, involving everybody, but in this sense total, that all have a say in the whole decision. Of course, even this is not enough. If there are irreconcilable differences of view, so that some of us are voted down and forced to knuckle under, then we will be unfree, coerced. The theory of absolute freedom thus requires some notion of the unanimity of our real will; and this is what we have in the theory of the general will.

The aspiration to universal and total participation seems to be implicit in the formula in Rousseau's *Contrat Social*, where the aim is to find a form of association which man can enter, and yet while obeying only himself remain as free as before. The notion of 'obeying only oneself' requires that the laws under which one lives should result totally from one's decision. The only way to reconcile this with life in society is by the universal and total participation which is the formula of the general will.

But then it is clear that the aspiration to absolute freedom cannot consort with any articulated differentiation of the society. The only structures which can be accepted as untouchable are those which underlie the taking of decisions. But these have to be totally taken by all. Thus these structures have to be based on and ensure the maximum homogeneity of citizens. For if all are to take the total decision, then in this crucial respect all are to be seen as identical. Moreover among those institutions which are created by the society none can be allowed which would negate this fundamental likeness and equality of all in taking the decisions. For instance, if it turns out to be necessary to this end that property be equalized (Rousseau thought so), then this will have to be done. No differentiations can be allowed which entail different relations to the process of decision, not even those which would have this as indirect result, such as inequality in property. The society must be a homogeneous one. Under the sovereignty of the general will, differences are of course allowed and necessary. Some men must fulfill the roles of government. But this is seen on the Rousseauian scheme as simply carrying out the decisions made by the whole, the putting into practice of the general will. And this role-differentiation must on no account reflect back on the process where legislation is passed.

The demands of absolute freedom therefore rule out any differentiation of the society into estates, different social groups identified by their ways of living and making a living, who would be differently related to the government of the society. And they also rule out any differentiation of the political system along the lines of the division of powers. For here, too, different groups take decisions affecting only part of the outcome. Indeed, the presupposition of a division of powers which can be meaningful as a system of checks and balances is that each of the powers be exercised by different people, hence not more than one by the whole, and the others by less than the whole. But no decisions of significance can be taken by less than the whole if we are to keep to the exigencies of absolute freedom. We can allow for the delegation of purely executive decision, but not for any which affects the design of our society, or the laws we live under. The general will theory cannot admit of representative institutions, as we see with Rousseau.

Hence the aspiration of absolute freedom contradicts Hegel's notion of what is necessary for a rational state in ruling out differentiation. I have said above that we can find warrant for this belief in differentiation in Hegel's ontology. But this deeper ontological ground meshed with insights Hegel gleaned from the history of his time as he saw it. I mentioned above in connection with Hegel's discussion of the polis, that he held it to be no model for the modern state. Direct democracy was possible then because societies were small, because they were homogeneous by virtue of relegating many functions to slaves and metics, and because the individualism of modern times had not yet developed. All these changes in the modern world which mark it off from the polis make differentiation unavoidable in Hegel's view. And in some of this reasoning, Hegel is far from alone in contemporary thought and judgement.

It is now a commonplace that the size of the modern state makes it impossible for all to rule together under a system of universal and total participation. There must be representation. So that the contemporary protagonists of total participation – and they are perhaps more numerous today than ever before – follow Rousseau in opting for a radical decentralization of power as the only solution.

But although the size of the modern state may make some differentiation of political roles unavoidable, it does not show that there must be social differentiation and that this must have relevance for the process of decision. But this is the force of the Hegelian notion of 'estates' (*Stände*) into which society is articulated. For these have not only each a distinct economic base and mode of life, but are also related each in its own way to the process of government.

Hegel's account of the different estates differs slightly between his works in the early 1800s and the mature version of the *PR*, but basically he singles out the following groups: (1) the peasantry, (2) the land-owning classes, (3) the business class, and (4) the class of professionals and functionaries which could staff the administration of the modern state. He also observed the beginnings of (5) a proletariat, with misgivings, one might even say dismay. He saw this more as a catastrophe to be avoided than as a new group which had to find its own characteristic way of integrating into the state.

In order to understand Hegel's views, we have to remember that these social groups were much more sharply marked off from each other than the classes of contemporary society. Then the peasants on the land, the urban bourgeoisie, and in some countries the landed aristocracy, were indeed strikingly different in outlook, style of life, interest in politics, conception of political life, and so on. The development of modern society, partly under the impulse of general will theory and Enlightenment modes of thought generally, has been towards a greater and greater homogenization, and in this respect a modern

Western society would be unrecognizable to a man of early nineteenth-century Europe (though America at that time already gave a foretaste of what was coming, as de Tocqueville saw).

But faced with the differences he witnessed in his day, Hegel reasoned that the idea of universal and total participation was chimaerical. The modern state, as against the ancient polis, aims at universal citizenship. This means that all economic functions will be exercised by citizens. But visibly, Hegel thought, these different tasks go along with very different outlooks, modes of life, values and life-styles. So that, first of all, these different 'estates', would have to have an important life of their own which would not be under the jurisdiction of the state as a whole. (This only really had application for the land-owning and bourgeois classes; Hegel did not consider the peasants capable of self-government, nor the proletariat; but in this he was far from exceptional in the Europe of his day where these classes were almost universally without the franchise.) And secondly, because of this, they would require a different relation to the business of government. (We will see later how Hegel used this to justify legislatures on the model of the traditional European estates-general, where the nobility took part in person and the commons by representatives.) Both these requirements involve a breach in the principle of universal and total participation.

In this predicament of real-life differentiation, it was chimaerical to seek to place everyone on the same footing at the centre of the total decision-making. The groups would naturally want in some areas to take partial decisions on their own. And for the rest, their way of relating to and identifying with the whole would be profoundly different. The peasant class for instance in Hegel's view was steeped in an unreflective adherence to the *Sitten* of the nation; their basic reaction was one of trust (*Vertrauen*) to their natural leaders. They did not require to be at the centre of decision in order to identify with the result, to sense it as their own.

In a different way the burghers, given over largely to the pursuit of their private gain, production and exchange, have on the whole neither time nor inclination to give themselves over totally to the *res publica*. They are more happily and appropriately related to the process of government by representatives. The class of land-owners is, on the other hand, one whose whole life is meant to be given in service. It is no question of their being related at second hand to public affairs.

In talking of the burghers we touch on the third reason Hegel gave differentiating our predicament from that of the ancient polis. We have developed a consciousness of the individual which had no place in the ancient polis, which indeed brought about its demise. This consciousness of the individual as simply a man, and as significant for that reason, that is, neither as Athenian or Spartan, German or French, Jew or Gentile, is what is expressed in what Hegel calls 'civil society' which we can roughly think of as the bourgeois economy. Modern man has an extra dimension of complexity as compared to the ancients. He is not simply a citizen of his country, he also thinks of himself as a man *tout court*, and this is a significant part of his identity since man as such is a bearer of universal reason.

It follows that not all men can give themselves totally to the public life. For some of the energy of most men will be engaged by the private. But since the state can only be if some men identify totally with it and make its life their life, there must be a political division of labour. Hence once more universal and total participation is impossible. The class which most gives itself to the private is the bourgeois class; hence they are happy to be represented by some of their number in the direction of affairs. But there is another group, which in the earlier Jena variants of Hegel's theory is the aristocracy, and which later is the bureaucracy or universal class, which gives itself totally to the affairs of the state.

We might think of coping with this third difficulty by breeding a society of all-round men who could at once each have a full range of private occupations and also all participate fully in the life of the state. But Hegel rejects this possibility for two reasons. First, his theory of man's individual career is that we only achieve something significant by giving ourselves fully to it, and that means renouncing other things.[1] Those who pine after everything achieve nothing. The fully realized is the particularized. Hegel's ontology and worldly wisdom come together here.

But behind this notion of necessary specialization in society there are also the requirements of the Idea. These were that the different facets of the concept find embodiment in the state. But the fullest embodiment of an articulated whole is when its varied facets are realized in different parts or organs. To be mingled in undifferentiated form is a more primitive stage. Thus the fully developed state is one in which the different moments of the Concept – immediate unity, separation, and mediated unity – are realized in separate groups, each with the appropriate mode of life. This is the dialectical derivation of the estates of modern society from the Concept, which we shall examine in the next chapter.

Thus Hegel's understanding of the inescapable diversity of modern society converges with his ontological vision. They lead him to the conclusion that the real differentiation of economic, social and political roles which is unavoidable in a society which does not shunt menial functions off onto non-citizens brings with it inescapably differences of culture, values and mode of life. These in turn demand a certain measure of autonomous life within each estate, and even more, they make the way that each estate can and wants to relate to the whole

---

[1] Cf. *PhG* and *PR*, §207.

different. This is why the aspiration to absolute freedom is misplaced and vain, and this for reasons which are much more fundamental than those which relate to the size of the modern state, serious as these are.

We might be tempted to conclude that Hegel is just wrong and reactionary on this issue, and that developments since have shown this. Of course, his first argument about the size of a modern polity is well taken. And he is also right that modern man has a private dimension which makes it difficult if not unlikely that men can ever again all give themselves so thoroughly to the public life of their society as in earlier ages. But on social differentiation he has surely just been proved wrong. The great homogenization of modern society shows that however varied may be the functions performed by citizens they can develop to a unity of outlook and life-style which puts paid to any argument for different relations to the process of decision. The increasing 'classlessness' of modern society seems to point in this direction. Of course, Hegel was more realistic in his day than those who believed in what was then an 'abstract' equality. But they turn out to be more far-seeing in that they foretold the homogeneity which a society founded on this doctrine could bring about.

But if we abstract from the particular application of Hegel's theory to the 'estates' of his day, there is an important issue which is far from being decided today. What kind of differentiation can modern society admit of? There is a dilemma here which we have yet to resolve.

We can see the aspiration to what Hegel calls 'absolute freedom', or universal and total participation, as the attempt to meet an endemic need of modern society. Traditional societies were founded on differentiation: royalty, aristocracy, common folk; priests and laymen; free and serf, and so on. This differentiation was justified as a reflection of a hierarchical order of things. After the revolution of modern, self-defining subjectivity, these conceptions of cosmic order came to be seen as fictions, and were denounced as fraudulent inventions of kings, priests, aristocrats, etc. to keep their subjects submissive. But however much they may have been used, consciously or not, as justifications of the status quo, these conceptions also were the ground of men's identification with the society in which they lived. Man could only be himself in relation to a cosmic order; the state claimed to body forth this order and hence to be one of men's principal channels of contact with it. Hence the power of organic and holistic metaphors: men saw themselves as parts of society in something like the way that a hand, for instance, is part of the body.

The revolution of modern subjectivity gave rise to another type of political theory. Society was justified not by what it was or expressed, but by what it achieved, the fulfilment of men's needs, desires and purposes. Society came to be seen as an instrument and its different modes and structures were to be studied scientifically for their effects on human happiness. Political theory would banish myth and fable. This reached clearest expression in utilitarianism.

410

But this modern theory has not provided a basis for men's identification with their society. In the intermittent crises of alienation which have followed the breakdown of traditional society, utilitarian theories have been powerless to fill the gap. So that modern societies have actually functioned with a large part of their traditional outlook intact, or only slowly receding, as in the case of Britain, for instance. Or when some radical break is sought, they have had recourse to more powerful stuff, some variant of the general will tradition (Jacobinism, Marxism, anarchism) as a revolutionary ideology. Or modern societies have had recourse either in revolutionary or 'normal' times to the powerful secular religion of nationalism. And even societies which seem to be founded on the utilitarian tradition, or an earlier, Lockeian variant, like the United States, in fact have recourse to 'myth', e.g., the myth of the frontier, of the perpetual new beginning, the future as boundlessly open to self-creation.

This last is the greatest irony of all, in that the utilitarian theory itself leaves no place for myth of this kind, that is, speculative interpretation of the ends of human life in their relation to society, nature and history, as part of the justifying beliefs of a mature society. These are thought to belong to earlier, less evolved ages. Mature men are attached to their society because of what it produces for them. As recently as a decade ago this perspective was widely believed in by the liberal intelligentsia of America and the Western world, who announced an imminent 'end of ideology'. But they turned out to be latter-day, inverted variants of Monsieur Jourdain, who were speaking not prose, but myth without knowing it. It is now clearer that the utilitarian perspective is no less an ideology than its major rivals, and no more plausible. Utilitarian man whose loyalty to his society would be contingent only on the satisfactions it secured for him is a species virtually without members. And the very notion of satisfaction is now not so firmly anchored, once we see that it is interwoven with 'expectations', and beliefs about what is appropriate and just. Some of the richest societies in our day are among the most teeming with dissatisfaction, for instance, the U.S.A.

The aspiration to absolute freedom can be seen as an attempt to fill this lack in modern political theory, to find ground for identification with one's society which are fully in the spirit of modern subjectivity. We have grounds for identifying ourselves with our society and giving our full allegiance to it when it is ours in the strong sense of being our creation, and moreover the creation of what is best in us and mostly truly ourselves: our moral will (Rousseau, Fichte), or our creative activity (Marx). From Rousseau through Marx and the anarchist thinkers to contemporary theories of participatory democracy, there have been recurrent demands to reconstruct society, so as to do away with heteronomy, or overcome alienation, or recover spontaneity. Only a society which was an emanation of free moral will could recover a claim on our allegiance comparable to that of traditional society. For once more society

411

would reflect or embody something of absolute value. Only this would no longer be a cosmic order, but in keeping with the modern revolution, the absolute would be human freedom itself.

The aspiration to absolute freedom is therefore born of a deep dissatisfaction with the utilitarian model of society as an instrument for the furtherance/adjustment of interests. Societies built on this model are experienced as a spiritual desert, or as a machine. They express nothing spiritual, and their regulations and discipline are felt as an intolerable imposition by those who aspire to absolute freedom. It is therefore not surprising that the theorists of absolute freedom have often been close to the reactionary critics of liberal society, and have often themselves expressed admiration for earlier societies.

Hegel understood this aspiration. As we saw he made the demand for radical autonomy a central part of his theory. He has indeed, an important place in the line of development of this aspiration to absolute freedom as it develops from Rousseau through Marx and beyond. For he wove the demand for radical autonomy of Rousseau and Kant together with the expressivist theory which came from Herder, and this provided the indispensable background for Marx's thought. And yet he was a strong critic of radical freedom. This alone would make it worthwhile to examine his objections.

Disentangled from Hegel's particular theory of social differentiation, the basic point of this critique is this: absolute freedom requires homogeneity. It cannot brook differences which would prevent everyone participating totally in the decisions of the society. And what is even more, it requires some near unanimity of will to emerge from this deliberation, for otherwise the majority would just be imposing its will on the minority, and freedom would not be universal. But differentiation of some fairly essential kinds are ineradicable. (Let us leave aside for the moment the objection that Hegel did not identify the right ones.) And moreover, they are recognized in our post-Romantic climate as essential to human identity. Men cannot simply identify themselves as men, but they define themselves more immediately by their partial community, cultural, linguistic, confessional, etc. Modern democracy is therefore in a bind.

I think a dilemma of this kind can be seen in contemporary society. Modern societies have moved towards much greater homogeneity and greater interdependence, so that partial communities lose their autonomy and to some extent their identity. But great differences remain; only because of the ideology of homogeneity, these differential characteristics no longer have meaning and value for those who have them. Thus the rural population is taught by the mass media to see itself as just lacking in some of the advantages of a more advanced life style. The poor are seen as marginal to the society, for instance, in America, and in some ways have a worse lot than in more recognizedly class-divided societies.

Homogenization thus increases minority alienation and resentment. And the first response of liberal society is to try even more of the same: programmes to eliminate poverty, or assimilate Indians, move population out of declining regions, bring an urban way of life to the countryside, etc. But the radical response is to convert this sense of alienation into a demand for 'absolute freedom'. The idea is to overcome alienation by creating a society in which everyone, including the present 'out' groups, participate fully in the decisions.

But both these solutions would simply aggravate the problem, which is that homogenization has undermined the communities or characteristics by which people formerly identified themselves and put nothing in their place. What does step into the gap almost everywhere is ethnic or national identity. Nationalism has become the most powerful focus of identity in modern society. The demand for radical freedom can and frequently does join up with nationalism, and is given a definite impetus and direction from this.

But unless this happens, the aspiration to absolute freedom is unable to resolve the dilemma. It attempts to overcome the alienation of a mass society by mass participation. But the very size, complexity and inter-dependence of modern society makes this increasingly difficult on technical grounds alone. What is more serious, the increasing alienation in a society which has eroded its traditional foci of allegiance makes it harder and harder to achieve the basic consensus, to bring everyone to the 'general will', which is essential for radical democracy. As the traditional limits fade with the grounds for accepting them, society tends to fragment, partial groups become increasingly truculent in their demands, as they see less reason to compromise with the 'system'.

But the radical demand for participation can do nothing to stem this fragmentation. Participation of *all* in a decision is only possible if there is a ground of agreement, or of underlying common purpose. Radical participation cannot create this; it presupposes it. This is the point which Hegel repeatedly makes. The demand for absolute freedom by itself is empty. Hegel stresses one line of possible consequences, that emptiness lead to pure destructiveness. But he also mentions another in his discussion in the *PhG*. For in fact some direction has to be given to society, and hence a group can take over and imprint its own purpose on society claiming to represent the general will. They thus 'solve' the problem of diversity by force. Contemporary communist societies provide examples of this. And whatever can be said for them they can certainly not be thought of as models of freedom. Moreover their solution to the emptiness of absolute freedom is in a sense only provisional. The problem of what social goals to choose or structures to adopt is solved by the exigencies of mobilization and combat towards the free society. Society can be set a definite task because .t has to build the *preconditions* of communism, either in defeating class enemies or in constructing a modern economy. Such societies would be in disarray if ever the period of

413

mobilization were to end (which is why it would end only over the dead bodies of the ruling party).

But an ideology of participation which does not want to take this totalitarian road of general mobilization cannot cope with the complexity and fragmentation of a large-scale contemporary society. Many of its protagonists see this, and return to the original Rousseauian idea of a highly decentralized federation of communities. But in the meantime the growth of a large homogeneous society has made this much less feasible. It is not just that with our massive concentrations of population and economic interdependence a lot of decisions have to be taken for the whole society, and decentralization gives us no way of coping with these. More serious is the fact that homogenization has undermined the partial communities which would naturally have been the basis of such a decentralized federation in the past. There is no advantage in an artificial carving up of society into manageable units. If in fact no one identifies strongly with these units, participation will be minimal, as we see in much of our urban politics today.

Thus Hegel's dilemma for modern democracy, put at its simplest, is this: The modern ideology of equality and of total participation leads to a homogenization of society. This shakes men loose from their traditional communities, but cannot replace them as a focus of identity. Or rather, it can only replace them as such a focus under the impetus of militant nationalism or some totalitarian ideology which would depreciate or even crush diversity and individuality. It would be a focus for some and would reduce the others to mute alienation. Hegel constantly stresses that the tight unity of the Greek city-state cannot be recaptured in the modern world that has known the principle of individual freedom.

Thus the attempt to fill the gap by moving towards a society of universal and total participation, where it is not actually harmful in suppressing freedom, is vain. It can only aggravate the problem by intensifying homogenization, while offering no relief since absolute freedom by itself is empty and cannot offer a focus of identity. And besides, total participation is unrealizable in a large-scale society. In fact ideologies of absolute freedom only produce something in the hands of a minority with a powerful vision which it is willing to impose.

The only real cure for this malady, a recovery of meaningful differentiation, is closed for modern society precisely because of its commitment to ideologies which constantly press it towards greater homogeneity. Some of the differences which remain are depreciated, and are breeding grounds for alienation and resentment. Others in fact fill the gap and become foci of identity. These are principally ethnic or national differences. But they tend to be exclusive and divisive. They can only with difficulty form the basis of a differentiated society. On the contrary, multi-national states have great trouble surviving in the modern world. Nationalism tends to lead to single homogeneous states. Where nationalism is strong, it tends to provide the common focus of identity and to fend off fragmentation. But then it is in danger of suppressing dissent and diversity and falling over into a narrow and irrational chauvinism.

Hegel gave, as we shall see again below, little importance to nationalism. And this was the cause of his failure to foresee its pivotal role in the modern world. As an allegiance it was not rational enough, too close to pure sentiment, to have an important place in the foundations of the state. But it is also true that it cannot provide what modern society needs in his view. And this is a ground for differentiation, meaningful to the people concerned, but which at the same time does not set the partial communities against each other, but rather knits them together in a larger whole.

This in a single formula is what modern society would require to resolve its dilemma. It is something which traditional societies had. For the point about conceptions of cosmic order or organic analogies is that they gave a meaning to differences between social groups which also bound them into one. But how to recover this in modern society? Hegel's answer, as we saw it, is to give social and political differentiation a meaning by seeing them as expressive of cosmic order, but he conceives this order as the final and complete fulfilment of the modern aspiration to autonomy. It is an order founded on reason alone, and hence is the ultimate object of the free will.

We can see now more clearly how the two levels of Hegel's thought on the necessary differentiation of society meshed with each other. On one level, there is the set of considerations drawn from a comparison with the Greek polis: the size of the modern state, the great differences which a state must encompass once all the functions are to be performed by citizens, the modern notion of individuality. These will be generally accepted by everyone though their significance might be disputed. On the other level, there is the necessary articulation of the Idea which has to be reflected in society. In Hegel's mind these do not operate as quite separate orders of consideration, as I have set them out here. They are intricated in each other, so that Hegel sees the existing social differentiations of his time as reflecting the articulations of the Idea, or rather as preparing a perfectly adequate reflection as the Idea realizes itself in history. And that is of course why he did not see these differences as remnants of earlier history destined to wither away, as the radical thinkers of this time thought, but rather as approaching the lineaments of a state which would finally be 'adequate to the concept'.

We cannot accept Hegel's solution today. But the dilemma it was meant to solve remains. It was the dilemma which de Tocqueville tried to grapple with in different terms, when he saw the immense importance to a democratic polity of vigorous constituent communities in a decentralized structure of power, while at the same time the pull of equality tended to take modern society towards uniformity, and perhaps also submission under an omnipotent government. This convergence is perhaps not all that surprising in two thinkers who were both deeply influenced by Montesquieu, and both had a deep and sympathetic understanding of the past as well as of the wave of the future. But whether we take it in Hegel's reading or in de Tocqueville's, one of the great needs of the modern democratic polity is to recover a sense of significant differentiation, so that its partial communities, be they geographical, or cultural, or occupational, can become again important centres of concern and activity for their members in a way which connects them to the whole.

4

Returning now to Hegel's reading of the French Revolution, we can see how the drive to absolute freedom had to fail. Being hostile to *any* articulation, it was incapable of rebuilding a new society on the ruins of the old through which men could once more be linked with the universal. It could come

> to no positive realization [Werk], to no universal achievements [Werken] either in the domain of speech or in reality, neither to laws or universal institutions of conscious freedom, nor to deeds and achievements [Werken] of practical [wollenden] freedom.
> (*PhG*, 417)

But then its entire energy has to be spent negatively. Faced with the existing society, the ancien régime, the aspiration to absolute freedom was driven to destroy its institutions, to level its differentiation. But since it could not produce anything in its place, absolute freedom was stuck in this negative moment, its energy could only be spent in continued destruction.

> Universal freedom can produce no positive work or deed; only *negative action* remains to it; it is only the *fury* of destruction. (*PhG*, 418)

This is Hegel's derivation of the Terror. The Terror was not an accidental consequence of the aspirations of the Jacobins and the other radicals of the French Revolution. The vacuity of this demand for freedom as such, what Hegel calls (in *PR* § 5) 'negative freedom' or the 'freedom of the void', which flies 'from every content as from a restriction', we have seen on a philosophical level in the emptiness of Kant's criterion of universalization. Now it erupts onto the political scene in the fanatical refusal of any differentiated structure. The revolution may 'imagine that it is willing some positive state of affairs, such as universal equality...', but in fact it can realize nothing. For

> such actuality leads at once to some sort of order, to a particularization of organizations and individuals alike; while it is precisely out of the annihilation of particularity and objective characterization that the self-consciousness of this negative freedom proceeds. Consequently, what negative freedom intends to will can never be anything but an abstract idea, and giving effect to this idea can only be the fury of destruction.
> (*PR*, § 5)

But what can it destroy when the whole régime is in ruins? The answer is itself, its own children. For in fact the aspiration to total and complete participation is rigorously impossible. In fact some group has to run the show, has to be the government. This group is really a faction. But this it cannot admit, for it would undermine its legitimacy. On the contrary it claims to be the embodiment of the general will. All other factions are treated as criminal; and so they must be, since they seek to escape from and thwart the general will. They seek to separate themselves from the universal and total participation. They set themselves up as private wills, and therefore they must be crushed.

But actually participating in a faction is not necessary. Since the basic concept of legitimacy is the general will, even those whose *wills* are hostile and refractory, whether or not they act to oppose the revolutionary government, are enemies of freedom and of the people. In times of stress and crisis, these too must be dealt with. But of course contrary, ill will cannot be proved in the same way as counter-revolutionary activity. If we wish to strike at all the enemies of the will as well as those of the deed, then we have to go on the basis of reasonable suspicion by patriots.

Being *under suspicion* thus comes to take the place of being *guilty*, or has the same meaning and consequences. (*PhG*, 419)

Hegel thus derives the revolutionary *loi des suspects* of the height of the Terror; and at the same time he states the basis of future terrors for whom refractory intention has been made equivalent to criminal action ('objectively' although not 'subjectively').

The Terror also has a characteristic attitude towards its enemies and their liquidation. The essence of humanity is to be found in the general will; man's real self is there, the content of his freedom. What opposes the general will can only be the irrational, whatever there is in man of deformed misanthropy or perverse caprice. In doing away with such enemies one is not killing really autonomous men, whose opposition is rooted in their own independent identity, but empty, refractory, punctual selves which have no more human content. Their death is therefore

a death which has no inner scope and represents no fulfilment, for what is negated is a point void of content, that of the absolutely free self; it is thus the coldest, flattest death, with no more significance than cutting through a cabbage head or throwing back a draught of water. (*PhG*, 418–9)

In these prophetic passages, Hegel delineates the modern phenomenon of the political terror, which we have become even more sickeningly familiar with than the men of his time: a terror which sweeps aside 'enemies of the people' in the name of a real will which is definitive of humanity; a terror which thus escalates beyond active opponents to engulf suspects. This by itself is not new. The court of any tyrant has always known the execution of people on

417

suspicion. But in the modern political terror the suspicion is no longer based on any calculus of likelihood of hostile action. It escalates beyond this to punish the refractory or simply the lukewarm will for itself, because this is the essence of the crime against humanity, not to belong to its forward march. And with this the victims are read out of the ranks of humanity, so that they can be treated like vermin. So that highly civilized nations outdid the worst barbarisms of Genghis Khan and Attila. And the perversion of this ideology of the collective will through its mixture with racism surpassed all previous human criminality.

In Hegel's view, terror, or at least destructive fury, is endemic to the drive for absolute freedom itself. It cannot brook any standing structures, even its own past creations, which are not an emanation of contemporary active will. Consequently, it feels true to itself only in the work of demolition. 'Only in destroying something does this negative will possess the feeling of itself as existent' (*PR*, §5). We can readily imagine what Hegel would have thought of Mao's Cultural Revolution, and in general of the contemporary revolutionary's fear of bureaucratization. What Hegel did not foresee was how positive goals and structures can be imposed in the name of absolute freedom, and how very much more terrible that can be.

Hegel's analysis of the French Revolution sees it therefore as the final culmination of the Enlightenment, the climax of its inner contradiction. The Enlightenment is the apex of the movement of spiritualization of man in modern times. It is conscious of the fact that man is the bearer of rational will, and that nothing can stand in the way of rational will. It has disengaged itself from all the 'positive', from the acceptance of any simply existing institution and the irrational authority of the past. But blinded by the narrow focus of 'understanding' it cannot see that man is the vehicle of a greater subject. It defines man alone as the source of rational will. And as a result it can find no content for this will. It can only destroy. It ends up therefore destroying itself and its own children.

What happens then is that the state goes back to a rediscovered differentiation. But this is not just going back to square one. For something has been gained. There has been a sweeping away of the old positive structures, the irrational past, or rather one might say the past institutions which were only an imperfect embodiment of rationality. The institutions of the ancien régime had to go under, to make room for the new revivified structures which will replace them.

Thus the state which has truly incorporated the world-historical shift represented by the French Revolution is a restored differentiated state. It has some continuity as we shall see with the structure of estates which preceded it, but it is restructured and above all founded on reason. This is the state structure which Hegel delineates for us in *PR*.

418

But before we go on to look at this we should remark that this state's arrival on the scene of history, its realization, matches its nature. Just as it is not seen as an emanation of human will simpliciter, so it is not brought about by conscious human planning. True it comes about by men's actions in history; but what is going on here is always more than the men themselves expect. The French Revolutionaries left their skin in an attempt to do the impossible; yet they played their part in clearing the ground for the new state. Napoleon was driven to conquer Europe, to seize power for himself, and what resulted from this was the restored state. Even the disastrous consequences played their part, since the Terror had the effect Hegel attributes to any close brush with death. It brought men back to the universal, and hence facilitated the founding of the new state (*PhG*, 420). This is the cunning of reason.

Here we come to a crucial difference between Hegel and Marx. In Hegel's critique of absolute freedom, we see him squaring accounts with Rousseau and the French Revolution. But this was also a critique by anticipation of Marx.[1] For Marx also believes that in the end we come to a society of universal and total participation, that we win through by overcoming the division of labour to a new homogeneity. And Marx's refusal of Hegel's differentiation was based on precisely the issue which, as we saw, ultimately divided Hegel from the Revolutionaries: the freedom of the end of history is for Marx a purely human freedom, not the fulfilment of *Geist*. Consequently its realization is a conscious act.

Hence while Marx takes up Hegel's concept of the cunning of reason, this fails to apply to the last great revolution. In Marxist thought, the bourgeois, and earlier political actors cannot understand the significance of their acts; they do more and other than they think. But this is not true of the proletariat. These have in Marxism a scientific view of things. In this case the significance of their innovative action is understood by the actors.

In Marx the equivalent thesis to the cunning of reason is based on the notion of a species nature of man. What gives the hidden significance to men's actions in history is the as yet unknown nature of man. But with the breaching of the last contradiction, this comes to consciousness. Men see what they are, and since the agent is generic man, those who are capable of acting at the level of humanity as a whole, that is, the proletariat, can see clearly what they are doing. To put it another way, the unseen agent in history, what corresponds to Hegel's 'reason' is generic man. As long as generic man is in contradiction to his actual historical embodiment, in class society, then man cannot be clear what he is doing. But once this contradiction is overcome, as it is with the proletariat, his action is self-conscious.

For Hegel, on the other hand, man is never clear what he is doing at the time;

---

[1] Though Marx who has his own variant of the Hegelian principle of embodiment and sees man set in the matrix of nature in part escapes this criticism. See discussion below, Chapter xx, section 2.

for the agency is not simply man. We are all caught up as agents in a drama we do not really understand. Only when we have played it out do we understand what has been afoot all the time. The owl of Minerva flies at the coming of the dusk.

In an important way therefore the agency is not fully ours. We did not design and plan the rational state and will it into existence. It grew through history. It grew in the institutions which came out of the German forests and developed through the middle ages, the institutions of kingship and estates which become constitutional monarchy. These institutions needed to be altered, purified, rationalized. Even this was not done to plan, but rather arose through the cunning of reason out of the activities of revolutionaries and a great conquering general who had other goals.

If for Hegel's political theory the state must be made in conformity with reason, it follows from his philosophy of history according to which reason, i.e. Spirit, realizes itself, that this does not come about by some men seeing the blueprint of reason and building a state on the basis of it. That Reason realizes itself means that the outcome arises out of human action which is not really conscious of what it is doing, which acts while seeing through a glass very darkly, but which is guided by the cunning of reason.

Moreover, even if by some strange time-warp men could have got the correct formula of the state ahead of time, it still could not just have been applied. For an integral part of this formula is that men identify themselves with the realized public life. But this cannot simply be turned on at will, it is something which develops over time in the depths of our unconscious spiritual life. That is why Hegel says, one cannot just implant a good constitution anywhere – as Napoleon discovered in Spain. The *Sittlichkeit* of the Spanish people was uncombinable with that kind of Liberalism.[1]

And similarly, the *Sittlichkeit* of the right constitution grows slowly, and grows only in certain people and at a certain pace and in certain conditions. It is not just an unfortunate accident that the understanding of it does not come until it is there. Rather the understanding does not come because before it is there men are not yet grown up to this *Sittlichkeit*, and it is small wonder that they cannot conceive it. They have their own *Sittlichkeit*, but this has not yet attained the fulness of rationality. Its growth is not understood, because it involves a growth of reason, a growth in reason, and the higher stages of such a growth cannot be understood from the vantage point of the lower. The growth has to have taken place before we can understand it.

As a culmination of the growth of reason, the rational state cannot be fully understood before it is on the scene. And if one could have flashed it back to some men, they would have been powerless to effect it, for it could not have been understood, much less identified with by their contemporaries.

---

[1] *PR*, §274, Addition.

The idea of just designing a constitution and then putting it into practice is an Enlightenment idea. It treats the whole affair as an engineering problem, an external matter of means and design. But a constitution requires certain conditions in men's identity, how they understand self; and hence this Enlightenment idea is radically shallow. To try in philosophy to transcend one's age is like trying to jump over Rhodes. (Preface to *PR*, p. 11.)

5

Hegel's conception of the French Revolution has afforded us an opportunity of seeing how his philosophy of history interwove with his reading of the events of his day. And from this perspective we can see where he situated himself in the political disputes of his period. The Preface we have just quoted from is a good place to find this curtly expressed; because he uses it as an opportunity to lash out at his *bêtes noires* while deploying some of his philosophy of history.

Thus we have seen that Hegel cannot accept the vision of those *Aufklärer* who would design a rational state and they try to put it into operation like an engineering plan, be this a state on utilitarian principles or one founded on the general will. But in his preface he also lashes the main opponents of these rational planners, the Romantics, writers like Jacobi, Fries, Schlegel (though only Fries is mentioned by name),[1] who put little faith in reason to lead men to a higher political life. The Romantics rather put faith in sentiment, in the spontaneous love of good and of fellow, something which could not be grasped or planned by reason.

[1] Hegel has been strongly criticized for this attack on Fries. Fries was a professor who sympathized with the *Burschenschaften*, student fraternities dedicated to carrying on the spirit of the patriotic war against France, and bringing about a united Germany. Their Romantic nationalism was very much out of favour with the restored German state governments in the post-1815 period. Fries attended the Wartburg festival of the *Burschenschaften* in 1817 and gave a speech full of Romantic enthusiasm for the cause of a revivified Germany. For this he was later suspended. The *Burschenschaften* were subsequently suppressed by general agreement of the state governments.

Hegel's acton in attacking Fries at this point has been called ignoble. It seems like kicking a man when he's down, and moreover a man of the Liberal left. This seems to put the seal on Hegel's reputation as a conservative defender of the status quo, and a somewhat nasty one at that.

But this is not the only way we can look at it. The young men of the *Burschenschaften* were not just Romantic nationalists. There was a great deal of chauvinism and anti-Semitism in their rhetoric. The Wartburg festival featured a great book-burning of authors they opposed. One of their members murdered the poet Kotzebue on suspicion of being a Russian agent.

Then as now there were intellectuals who publicly condoned this kind of action, or ambiguously praised the pure intentions of the youth while avoiding endorsement of his action. In an age in which once more young people are egged on by their elders to a violence justified only by its exalted motivation, we cannot be so sure as we used to be that Hegel was sinning against liberalism, or against his duty as an intellectual, in denouncing this kind of frothy ethical subjectivism, and especially in tackling its most notorious exponent. Cf. the discussion in W. Kaufmann (Ed.), *Hegel's Political Philosophy*, between Sidney Hook and Schlomo Avineri. See also S. Avineri, *Hegel's Theory of the Modern State*, CUP, 1972, pp. 119–21.

History and Politics

Hegel is totally opposed to this line of thought and treats it to his battery of heavy irony. For politics must be founded on reason, even if not the shallow notion of reason of the revolutionaries. The Romantic school earn his hostility not only because they depreciate reason, but because the recourse to sentiment makes law of secondary importance. And these two errors are at base the same.

Right and ethics, and the actual world of justice and ethical life, are understood through thoughts; through thoughts they are invested with a rational form, i.e., with universality and determinacy. This form is law [Gesetz]; and this it is which the feeling that stipulates for its own whim, the conscience that places right in subjective conviction [i.e., Romantic conscience], has reason to regard as its chief foe. (PR, 7)

The purely subjective romantic conscience cannot be a guide. To rely on it is to desert thought and reason, and to fall into the purely arbitrary, the whimsical, This cannot be a foundation for political life.

A third, related fault of Romanticism is that it sees present reality as disorder, as God-forsaken. Romantic thought looks backward in nostalgia to ages of integration, or at least beyond the present dead, meaningless social world within which man cannot feel at home to an ideal of social brotherhood. But the point is not just that the state is founded on reason ideally, but that this reason is actualizing itself in history. So that reason underlies the world not only ideally, but must be found in the existing world.

Hegel launches here the much-quoted slogan 'what is rational is actual and what is actual is rational' (PR, 10) by which he expresses the ground principle of his philosophy of history. History is the self-realization of reason. It is a realization which goes through a number of stages, the less perfect to the more perfect. This means, of course, that at earlier stages reason will be imperfectly realized; in this sense the real will also be irrational, or not fully rational. But since these stages themselves follow necessity, since they are dictated by reason, we can say that the stage of relative imperfection that reason has reached at any given time is itself according to reason. The degree of reason's actualization in history at any given point is dictated by reason.

In short what is at work in history is reason. And therefore the real (wirklich) understood on the deepest level where we see the forces which bring it into being and shape it, this real is rational. On a more superficial level, where we concentrate on contingent variations it is not and is not meant to be. But these are not part of what Hegel calls 'Wirklichkeit'.[1] The wirklich is reality understood in relation to its underlying necessity. This is rational, because rationality is what posits the real.

Hence those who see the world as God-forsaken are blind. The job of philosophy is to uncover this rationality. But this brings us back to the

---

[1] Cf. Hegel's comment, added in a later edition of the Encyclopaedia, on this slogan from PR (EL, §6). Cf. also the Wirklichkeit category of the Logic, and the accompanying notion of superficial contingency, above Chapter XI.

objection above against rationalist reformers: we uncover the rationality not to plan the world, to remake it according to reason. To uncover reason is to uncover the force, the plan, already at work. We cannot plan because we cannot anticipate the realization of this reason in philosophy: 'philosophy...always comes on the scene too late to give...instruction as to what the world ought to be' (*PR*, 12). 'The owl of Minerva spreads its wings only with the falling of the dusk' (*PR*, 13). We have seen the reason for this above.

Thus 'to comprehend what is, this is the task of philosophy, because what is, is reason' (*PR*, 11). The aim of his book, Hegel says, is 'to apprehend and portray the state as something inherently rational' (*PR*, 11). But this not only breaks with the Romantic critics of the 'Left', and those who yearned for another society. It also involves a vigorous rejection of legitimist thought which based the right of monarchical power to rule on the pure right of possession, or on 'natural' grounds which could not be derived from reason. The most influential thinker of this sort in Berlin in the early 1820s was von Haller; and Hegel lights out after him, not indeed in this preface, but in the explication to §258 of *PR*. This form of thought is tarred with the same brush as Romantic rejection of the existing order; both cannot penetrate to the rational order of things.[1]

It should be obvious from this, that for all his critique of the French Revolution, Hegel is poles apart from Burke. True they agree that the Revolution was bent on a destructive course, and that from this nothing positive could be built. But the moral drawn by Burke was that men should remain within the spirit of their 'positive' institutions, there is no higher rationality by which these can be judged. While for Hegel the aim of philosophy is to discover the universal rationality in these institutions. But this rationality is developing, it is changing and transforming the positive institutions as it realizes itself in history. This is not something which is planned by man, but it is by Reason. And this plan may make use of, may *have* to make use of a Revolution.

In other words for Burke, men do plan change, do reform. But they should respect certain limits in this, the limits of their own institutional tradition, for otherwise they return to barbarism and destruction. Revolution of the French type is thus always destructive, it always sets one back. Hegel on the other hand insists how little men can plan, can consciously organize reform. He probably in the end is much more bearish about this than Burke. But against this, he does see a universal reason at work in history; and this reason may have to make use of revolution. For it uses men who do not fully understand its purposes. Thus the progress of reason may require a revolution, even though this is only clear afterwards, and what is gained is not what the revolutionaries aimed at. Revolution is thus not necessarily destructive, or a setback.

---

[1] Cf. Fr. Rosenzweig, *Hegel und der Staat*, München 1920, II, 190.

History and Politics

The French Revolution was certainly not a set-back in Hegel's eyes. It was a world-historical event which inaugurated the completion of the modern state. Late in life he could speak of it in these terms:

As long as the sun has stood in the heavens and the planets have circled around it, we have never yet witnessed man placing himself on his head, that is, on thought, and building reality according to it. Anaxogoras had said first that *nous* rules the world; but now man has come for the first time to recognize that thought should rule spiritual reality. This was a magnificent dawn. All thinking beings joined in celebrating this epoch. A sublime feeling ruled that time, an enthusiasm of the spirit thrilled through the world, as if we had now finally come to the real reconciliation of the divine with the world.

(*GW*, 926)

Not quite 'Bliss was it in that dawn to be alive', but hardly a statement that Burke could endorse. The two positions in spite of superficial similarities are really incommensurable.

It should be clear from this how little it really tells us about Hegel to class him as a conservative. First, the idea of seeing the rational in the actual is not necessarily conservative. Particularly when this rationality is an active one which is transforming the real. Thus the Hegelian notion of history as the realization of reason was easily transposable by Marx into a revolutionary theory, where the essentially rational is the revolutionary force which is transforming present reality, the proletariat.

Hegel was not a revolutionary. But the thesis that the rational became real made it impossible for him to accept the standard conservative position of that time or of any other, which cleaves to the ancient, the traditional, the long-established. Hegel constantly combatted this position, whether it came from the historical school of law, with its opposition to rational codification, or philosophers of the Restoration, who based the right to rule on prescription or the will of God (e.g., von Haller, attacked in *PR*, § 258), or the traditionalists of Württemberg who wanted to restore the pre-Revolutionary constitution intact.[1] His opposition to what was merely 'positive', just given and not deduced from rational will, remains constant from his earliest writings to the end, even though his notion of what it is to be deduced from rational will changes profoundly. This is why he continued to think of the French Revolution as the great crucible out of which alone the rational state could emerge. It posited the principle of reason:

thought, the concept of right, now asserted its power all at once, and against this the old frame of injustice could offer no resistance. (*GW*, 926)

What is conservative, or at least non-revolutionary, in Hegel has its source in the thesis that the rationality of the real is not that of man, but of *Geist*. This is

[1] Cf. his essay of 1815–16, *The Württemberg Estates*, in *Hegel's Political Writings*, Ed. Z. Pelczynski, Oxford, 1964.

what makes him oppose the unchecked supremacy of the principles of the Enlightenment and the Revolution, which would lead to a society of atomic individuals or a totally homogeneous general will state. This underlies the articulations of the rational society which we saw in the last section and will examine further in the next chapter.

And this view of cosmic spirit as the subject of history rules out the possibility of a revolutionary praxis founded on reason. Revolutions are only understood and justified by reason ex post facto. What human reason can do is only to grasp what has already been realized, to understand what reason has already achieved. In doing this, of course, philosophy defends the rationality of the real and purifies it, keeping it from the corruption which would beset it if it were to be generally misunderstood by the various merchants of irrationality, both Romantics and reactionaries. For a given level of realization of rationality in the state requires a given level of subjective understanding of rationality in the citizens. Hence Hegel takes his task in the *PR* to be expounding and making clear the rationality inherent in the state. He has to defend this vision against those who would muddy the waters, by turning men's gaze into the impossible beyond, or make men prize the actual for infrarational reasons, and hence deform it.

But should an actual breach in existing reality, a revolutionary transformation, be necessary for reason, and thus on the cards, philosophy could not know. It would go on expounding the rational in the current system, while revolutionaries without benefit of sound thought would launch themselves into action. Later a higher synthesis would show how both understandings were partial.

But this is obviously deeply unsatisfactory to the revolutionary. He must believe that he has grasped the nature of reality, that he sees the truth which is inaccessible to his opponent who justifies what is; not simply that they both have partial visions which some future Hegel will show to be strands in the great tapestry of Reason. This is why the young Hegelians and particularly Marx saw the rejection of Hegel's *Geist* as the essential step from his philosophy to theirs. The anthropologizing of Hegel does away with the cosmic subject of history, with the reason whose cunning is always beyond men's understanding at the time. By making man the subject of history it allows for a time when the transformations he is bringing about are finally fully understood by him. This is the epoch of the proletarian revolution.

But Hegel's philosophy of history is as it were a defense of the Revolution after the event. Hegel sets his face firmly against any further revolutionary transformations. Not that there are no further transformations to be made. For the fully rational state has yet to be completed. The theory that Hegel was an apologist for the existing Prussian state is a result of lamentable historical ignorance. It overlooks how many features of Hegel's rational state were yet to be realized in the Prussia of his day, as we shall see more clearly in the next chapter. The Spirit still has work to do. But revolution is most emphatically not the way to do it.

This 'conservatism' of the mature Hegel is sometimes attributed to his desire to preserve his position in the Prussian state university. But this is really quite implausible. The whole of Hegel's experience of revolution, and his judgements on the French Revolution indicate that his opposition to revolutionary methods springs from his central philosophical position and his judgement of the age. Nor is this opposition only an attitude of the later Hegel. It is continuous throughout his adult life.

What can be said of the mature Hegel, however, is that his rejection of further revolutionary change is not based just on his repugnance at the Terror, or just on the impossibility of a clairvoyant revolutionary action, but he rejected it mainly because he believed that history had come to some kind of plateau, on which the need for revolution was past. For the bases of the rational state were at last laid.

And indeed, something of the kind is implicit in the claim to have understood the rationality of history. For if this were not the case, if reason required some further revolutionary transformation of society, this could of course not be understood by those living now; and the higher synthesis which would come out of such a revolution would similarly not be understood. The claim to have grasped the rationality in history and politics thus carries with it the presumption that the major transformations are behind us. For if the owl of Minerva only flies at the coming of the dusk, then history can only be understood when its major transformations have been realized.[1]

This does not mean that the rational state is fully realized, as I pointed out above, or that history has reached an end. On the contrary, there is a great deal of further development required of the principle of rationality which was far from being embodied in all its ramifications. Indeed, it seems most likely that Hegel thought that it would never be embodied in an absolutely perfect exemplar. And even if those West European states which came closest to the Idea were perfect, history has a great deal yet to do in bringing other parts of the world up to scratch. (Hegel makes occasional, brief references to the future of Russia and America.)[2]

---

[1] It has been argued (E. Weil: *Hegel et L'Etat*, Paris, 1950) that Hegel's theory itself points to further transformations, to cope with the contradictions of civil society, and to bring a world state out of the existing sovereign states whose relations with each other are not *sittlich*. But I do not think this can be sustained in detail (cf. Franz Grégoire, *Etudes Hegeliennes*, Louvain 1958, IV); and above all, I do not think that the idea of such a further transformation can consort with the claim to have grasped the rationality in that state, not in some clouded form as 'representation' (Vorstellung) and religious thought achieves, but in the full clarity of philosophical thought. How could the full rationality of the state be evident, if it was meant to be superceded in reason's plan by a world-state?

[2] Cf. *Philosophy of History*, translated by J. Sibtree, Dover Edition, New York, 1956, pp. 82–7, 350.

But what remains to be done amounts to the working out of principles which are already come into their own. The new world has made that 'qualitative leap' into existence, of which the preface to *PhG* spoke (*PhG*, 15). But just as a new building is not ready when its foundations are laid, so a great deal remains to be done when the new world first establishes its general foundations (allgemeiner Grund, *PhG*, 16). This further work is of the utmost importance, but it neither admits of nor would be advanced by revolution.

What is this plateau which we have reached? We shall now see in a little more detail as we turn to examine the system of the *PR*. But in its broad lines it should be evident from the philosophy of history which we have been examining. It will be a state which somehow combines the universal subjectivity of Socrates and Christ with the *Sittlichkeit* of the ancients. It will be a state whose *Sittlichkeit* is such that universal individuals can identify with it.

The principle of modern states has prodigious strength and depth because it allows the principle of subjectivity to progress to its culmination in the extreme of self-subsistent personal particularity, and yet at the same time brings it back to the substantive unity and so maintains this unity in the principle of subjectivity itself.   (*PR*, § 260)

It will have achieved this because both sides will have moved to meet each other. The universal subjectivity will have come to see that it must find embodiment in a state; and will also have taken the further step of realizing that this cannot be a state founded simply on human will, but rather on man's will as an emanation of *Geist*. Hence that the individual must take his place in a wider order, with which he nevertheless identifies because it is the embodiment of reason.

The universal subjectivity will thus have understood that he cannot simply create the rational society, that he must also find it there as an order which unfolds in history. And when he does this he can step beyond individualism and once more return to the 'ethical conviction' (sittliche Gesinnung), the inner sense of being one with a realized order, where the highest form of freedom is found.

But at the same time the order itself had to evolve. It had to become in conformity with reason, so that the universal subject can be at home (bei sich), and identify with it as his *Sittlichkeit*.

This evolution, thinks Hegel, has now taken place. The strivings of reason to remake the world in conformity with reason have been ship-wrecked. But in the process they brought about a rationalization of the state which their authors did not yet properly conceive. They swept away the old positive, so that the state which arose after the cataclysm was not simply in continuity with the past but purified. Rational men, after developing their subjectivity to the full, are now ready to identify with this new state. The task of philosophy is to further this identification by laying bare the rational foundation of the real, and through this identification the rational state will come to completion. Let us now see this vision of the rational state as Hegel sets it out in *PR*.

427

CHAPTER XVI

The Realized State

1

PR explores what flows from the notion of rational will concerning human affairs. It goes beyond a simple political theory. It turns out to englobe also what Hegel calls civil society, and the family. But also it discusses the dimension of morality and private rights.[1]

Hegel intends to proceed from the most abstract to the most concrete. He will end with a picture of the state, because this is the highest embodiment of *Sittlichkeit*, which is implicit in the notion that man is the vehicle of rational will.

But we start off with the notion of private rights. Man is a bearer of private rights because he is essentially a vehicle of rational will. As such he commands respect. Man is a bodily existence who has to have commerce with the external world in order to live; he has to appropriate things and use them. But this fact becomes a value because man is the essential vehicle of the realization of reason or spirit, which is the same thing as saying that man is endowed with will. Hence man's appropriation is to be seen as in fulfilment of the ontologically grounded purpose. It is something infinitely worthy of respect. Thus the de facto process of appropriation becomes the de jure right to property. Man is a bearer of rights because as a will he is worthy of respect. An attack on his external bodily existence or his property is thus a crime, an attack against the very purpose underlying reality as a whole, including my own existence. The right of appropriation over things comes from the fact that these have no inherent ends; they are given to them by will. Will has the rights (*PR*, §44).

Hegel thus justifies the right to property. He sees this as a right to private property. For this right falls to man in the abstract, as an individual rational will. This is because it is on this immediate, individual level than man is related to things, that he is in interchange with nature.[2] Man is also part of a

[1] This scope was not, of course, entirely original. Standard treatises on law or right had to discuss private right and law relating to the family, marriage, inheritance, etc. And Kant in his treatise dealing with law, *Metaphysik der Sitten*, had also dealt with morality or a theory of duties (Pflichtenlehre) as well. What is new is the distinction of civil society and the state, and of course, the whole 'architectonic' of Hegel's system in which these different parts are deduced from the Idea.

[2] We can see the important differences from Marx. Although Hegel understood the importance of the division of labour, and was astonishingly prescient about the consequences of its extension in the industrial system, as we shall see, he did not see this necessary interdependence as an integral,

community of *Sittlichkeit*, but this touches him at another, higher level than this commerce with things. It touches his identification, his spiritual life, that for which he should be ready to give up life and property.

Hence in property we are dealing with the will of man as a single individual, as a person (*PR*, §46). Of course, this very basic consideration of man as a person, bearer of abstract right, although the starting point for the Logic-derived exposition of the *PR*, is not the point of departure, historically speaking. A long development was necessary before man was actually first considered in history as a person, as we saw in our consideration of the philosophy of history above. This occurred in the Roman world.

Hegel then goes on to consider a number of other matters related to rights, particularly property rights; for instance, contract, and crime and punishment. Crime, says Hegel, taking up a theme we saw in the Logic is a negative infinite judgement. It is not just saying, as it were, this particular thing is not mine, which my rival in a civil suit says; it denies the whole category of 'mine' and 'thine'.

Crime is an attack on the very purpose underlying things, the purpose even of the criminal, his will *an sich* (*PR*, § 100). Punishment has as goal to undo this rebellion against the purpose of things. This attack has come from a will which has set itself against the very principle of will. The undoing must therefore be a counter-injury against the particular will of the criminal

The sole positive existence which the injury possesses is that it is the particular will of the criminal. Hence to injure (or penalize) this particular will as a will determinately existent is to annul the crime, which otherwise would have been held valid, and to restore the right.   (*PR*, §99)

Hegel is therefore quite out of sympathy with the various liberal theories of punishment as preventive, deterrent, reformative, etc. And he opposes the softening of the penal code which springs from this kind of philosophy. In particular, he is opposed to the abolition of capital punishment. In an important sense if the punishment is to undo the crime it has to 'fit the crime'. To let someone off on the grounds that punishment is reformative is not to treat man with the full dignity of a bearer of will, whose will can thus incarnate wrong, and hence cry for punishment. It is treating him 'as a harmful animal who has to be made harmless' (*PR*, § 100). Punishment is a *right* of the criminal. He calls for it with his will *an sich*.

The exploration of what is involved in man's being rational will has led us first to see him as the bearer of rights, as such, as a person, outside of specific political contexts. But now we go farther. As will he not only has rights, but he

conscious expression of ethical substance. The domain of interchange with nature, or civil society, remains that of individual action and goals. The substantial element, which brings men to unity here, is quite unconscious. It is the operation of an 'invisible hand'.

429

has the duty to determine himself. He determines himself by giving a content to his will; and this should be a rational, universal content. This is the sphere of morality.

Man is a moral agent because as a bearer of will he ought to conform his will to universal reason. Man as a willing being is first of all a natural being, seeking the fulfilment of his own inclinations, needs, passions. But he has to purify his will and make the rationally conceived good his goal.

But as the subject of morality man still figures as an individual. The demand of morality is that I come to recognize that I am under the obligation of willing universal reason, simply in virtue of being a man. And this means as well that I come to this realization myself, by my own reason. The subject of morality is the universal subjectivity which rose on the ruins of the ancient city.

The demands of morality in other words are inner as well as outer. It is not enough that I do the right thing. If the requirement is that I conform my will to universal reason, then I must not only do what is right, but will the right as the right. In other words I have to do the right because it is the right; and it folllows from this that I have to understand the right myself. This is, of course, what Kant made central to morality, following a hint of Rousseau's: morality consists in the purity of the will, and this is considered by Hegel to be the highest expression of this category. Morality touches our intentions and not just our acts.

But this, of course, is radically incomplete for reasons which are now familiar to us. Morality needs a complement in the external world, a world of public life and practices where it is realized. For without this it remains a pure aspiration, a pure ought to be (Sollen) as Hegel puts it. It remains something purely inner. But there is more than that. The concept of rational will alone, as the will of an individual, is ultimately vacuous, as we saw in Chapter xiv. We cannot derive a content from the notion of duty for duty's sake (*PR*, § 135). It is only as ontological reason, which seeks its own embodiment in a community with a certain necessary structure, that rationality yields a criterion of the good. The content of the rational will is what this community requires of us. This then is our duty. It is not derived from formal reason but from the nature of the community which alone can embody reason.

Hence morality, the individual's search to conform his will to universal reason, refers us beyond itself both in order to complete its own attempt of deriving the right from reason, and in order to realize this right effectively. The demands on man as a bearer of rational will are thus that he live in a community which embodies reason, which is the fulfilled goal of reason. That is, what is implicit in the concept of man as a vehicle of rational will is only fully realized in such a community.

The two earlier stages thus refer us beyond to the concept of *Sittlichkeit* which is the third and major part of *PR*. Right is inadequate because it is simply the external expression of the fact that man is a bearer of will. It has no interiority. Besides it too requires to be defended by political power. By itself it is powerless. Morality shows a dimension of human life which answers one of the lacks of right; it shows human moral life as an inner purification of the will. But it cannot reach its goal of deriving the fullness of human moral duties from reason, nor realize these unless it is completed by a community in which morality is not simply an 'ought', but is realized in the public life. Thus right and morality find their place and are secured as parts of a larger whole.

But one essential feature of morality must be preserved in this community as it arises in its mature form in history. It must not as the earlier city-state have no place for moral man. On the contrary the basic freedom of moral man as man, the freedom to judge in conscience, must be preserved. This is an essential requirement of a *Sittlichkeit* which can incorporate modern man and with which he can identify himself. For the modern state, therefore, conscience is a sanctuary not to be violated (*PR*, § 137). Man retains this reflective dimension and this is why he cannot recapture the immediate unity and identity of the citizens with the state characteristic of the polis. But this is not to say that the modern or any state can allow men to decide by conscience alone whether to obey the laws. It means rather that freedom of conscience is an essential right in the modern state.

We thus come to *Sittlichkeit* which is substantial freedom in Hegel's terms. It is realized good. Men identify with it. It becomes their 'second nature' (*PR*, § 151), and they are its effective realization in subjectivity.

The *sittlich* is what has to do with a community in which the good is realized in a public or common life. Hence the category englobes more than the state. And Hegel will deal with three forms of common life in this section, which are also placed in an ascending order: the family, civil society and the state.

The first is an immediate unreflecting unity based on feeling. The second is society in so far as it conforms to the vision of the modern atomist theories of contract, a society of individuals who come together out of mutual need. Radically inadequate as a theory of the state, this vision is realized in Hegel's view in the modern bourgeois economy. Civil society is modern society seen as an economy of production and exchange between men considered as subjects of needs. This is at the antipodes of the family, for here there is no immediate unity but maximum consciousness of individuality in which men are bound together by external ties.

The state comes to complete this trio. For it offers once more a deeper unity, an inward unity, like the family. But it will not be just an immediate one based on feeling. Rather unity here is mediated by reason. The state is a community in which universal subjectivities can be bound together while being recognized as such.

First the family is a unity of feeling, of love. Men sense themselves as members within a family, not as persons with rights vis-à-vis each other. When rights enter into it, the family is dissolving. In this section Hegel deals with marriage, family property and the education of children. The main point of the family as *sittlich* is this fact that within it men see themselves as members of something greater, as having identity by their part in a common life.

But of course the family is quite inadequate alone as *Sittlichkeit*, for within it man is not really an individual and the allegiance to the common life is not founded on reason but on feeling only. Hence beyond the family, man is in another community in which he operates purely as an individual. This is what Hegel calls civil society.

Civil society is the society considered as a set of economic relations between individuals. Hegel had read and carefully considered the writings of the British political economists, most notably James Steuart and Adam Smith, whose works had been translated into German. His model of civil society owes a lot to these writers.

Civil society is the level of relations into which men enter not as members of family, nor as members of some ethical community, such as a state or a church, but just as men. It is a sphere in which men are related to each other as persons in Hegel's sense, i.e., as bearers of rights. In this sphere 'a man counts as a man in virtue of his humanity alone, not because he is a Jew, Catholic, Protestant, German, Italian, etc.' (*PR*, § 209 E).

In the level of social relations called civil society, men are thus individuals on their own; their relations to each other are founded on the fact that in fulfilling their needs they require each other. In other words, in this sphere we look at men as the subjects of individual purposes; they become related through these individual purposes whose fulfilment requires social co-operation.

Civil society can be thus looked on first of all as a system of needs. Men have needs which they try to fulfil by work and effort. But in so doing they need the work and effort of others. They have to enter into exchange. But this system of needs is not something static. The difference between men and animals is that the former go beyond a single set of species needs which are the same and remain the same for all specimens throughout time. On the contrary man exhibits his transcendence and universality (*PR*, § 190) in multiplying his needs and the means of satisfying them. This multiplication of needs is intensified by social comparison; men emulate others, and desire certain things because they come to be conditions of others' esteem. Here Hegel touches on a Rousseauian theme, but what for Rousseau was taken as the basis of decadence and evil in man is seen by Hegel as a necessary part of the development of reason. The Rousseauian view was indeed right in the ancient world where society could not cope with the growth of self-consciousness and the search for individual good. The simple unity with the whole was destroyed by this. But the modern state is capable of reconciling individual subjectivity and the universal. It does not therefore need to fear the multiplication of needs.

Needs can multiply without end. But in doing so they force an even more intense social co-operation. The greater production needed requires a farther-reaching division of labour. It also pushes man to greater work; and hence to work in more complex relations and systems of interdependence. This helps to form man, to educate him to the universal.

For the more intense and complex the social co-operation, the more man in working to satisfy his own needs is also working to satisfy the needs of all others. Hegel here (*PR*, § 199) takes up the famous Smith thesis of the invisible hand, and sees in it an example of the cunning of reason. It is a 'dialectical movement' which takes individual self-seeking and makes it into the fulfilment of others' needs. Smith's invisible hand thus represents the force of the universal here, and this is what Hegel means when he says that this sphere is the sphere of the individual in which universality is only abstract. It is not a living force in men's allegiance that binds them together in co-operation, but rather an external mechanism.

So far Hegel's portrait of civil society is closely based on the utilitarians and classical economists; and we can see already what part this plays in his system. This level of social life expresses the dimension of man as an individual, that which destroyed the old *Sittlichkeit* of the city-state. But it represents an incontestable advance and an essential dimension for men. For it is the level on which man stands as an individual seeking his own fulfilment, and yet as an individual he does not remain within narrow horizons. Rather he is swept up in the ever-widening system of division of labour and exchange. His wants are refined and cultivated in this society, and he learns to produce, within his speciality, not just for himself but for the world market. He is educated to universality. Civil society is the essential embodiment, one might say, material base, of modern universal subjectivity and is therefore ineradicable, even though as we shall see it is inadequate and has to be supplemented by a higher level.

But Hegel now goes on to develop traits of civil society (*PR*, § 201–7) which properly belong to his own ideas. He argues for the necessary articulation of civil society into classes or estates. The necessary division of labour gives rise to groups (allgemeinen Massen, *PR*, § 201) which have not just a different type of work, but also different life-styles and hence values. These are the Hegelian 'estates' (Stände). Hegel uses the older term, rather than class, and it is better to follow him here since these groups are not just differentiated by their relation to the means of production, but by their life-style.

Hegel singles out three: the substantial or agricultural class which lives close to nature and which is generally unreflective, living rather 'an ethical life which is immediate, resting on family relationship and trust' (*PR*, § 203); the reflecting or business class which really lives the life of individuality, that is which has the orientation to the fulfilment of individual needs through rationalized work. This is the class which is most saliently identified with civil society as a system of needs. Thirdly, there is the universal class; this is the class of civil servants which identifies itself with the interests of the community as a whole.

We see here Hegel's notion of the inescapable differentiation of society which underlay his critique of the French Revolutionaries and their attempt to abolish differences in a régime of total participation. Because men in order to fulfil their needs cannot but differentiate themselves in this way, a polity which tries to abstract from this is bound to come to grief. But the differentiation is not simply to be understood as a by-product of the division of labour; we can also see in it by anticipation the structures of rational necessity.

The three classes represent each a dimension which must be present in the modern state. There must be the sense of allegiance to a whole which is above and greater than oneself, the dependence on something bigger; this the substantial class has in an unreflecting way. There must be a sense of the individual as a universal subjectivity; this the business class has. There must finally be a reasoned identification with the universal in a will which embodies this universal; and this the class of civil servants has. These three classes can also be lined up against the three levels of *Sittlichkeit*: family, civil society and state.

One of the crucial points of Hegel's philosophy is his belief that these three cannot be brought to synthesis by being present in all citizens and harmonized in each of them. Rather the synthesis is achieved by a community in which the different dimensions are carried primarily by a specific group; but where these are bound together and live a common allegiance to the whole. A state in which everyone is immediately identified with the principle of common life in the same way, this was possible among the ancients, but not with the more complex moderns. Today, we unite individuality and identification with the state by an articulation into estates where these different dimensions respectively are preponderant, and yet where all have a sense of common life, and recognize that they are part of a larger whole.

What underlies this belief that each man cannot realize the total synthesis is on one level the Hegelian insight that in order effectively to realize a value a man has to be deeply immersed in it. 'A man actualizes himself only in becoming something definite, i.e., something specifically particularized' (*PR*, §207). He strongly endorsed Goethe's dictum: 'wer großes will muß sich zusammenraffen' (whoever would achieve something great must concentrate himself). The spiritual scope of modern society is too great for one man; he cannot fully realize it all in his life. Hence men must particularize: the synthesis must come from the fact that each in his particularization senses himself as part of a larger common life.

And here we meet the second level of Hegel's philosophical grounding for this belief: the whole must itself exhibit the ontological structure of reason. But for this it must be differentiated. For reason itself or the Idea differentiates itself in order to recover unity out of difference. Not to be differentiated is a primitive phase, like that of the seed, out of which flows a difference which returns back to itself. Thus the immediate unity of the Greek polis marks it as a primitive stage; the very differentiation of the modern state shows its maturity.

Thus society must be articulated into *Stände*. But in this the principle of the modern world, the freedom of choice of the individual must be respected. Within the bounds of external factors governing opportunity, the individual must have the right to choose his walk of life. (*PR*, §206.)

This of course sharply differentiates Hegel's 'estate' from those of traditional society. These usually defined a station into which men were born and to which they had to cleave throughout life. But Hegel rejects this immobile society, along with anything approaching a caste system. For this is incompatible with the principle of individual freedom, which is central to the fully realized state. This is generally overlooked by those who want to class Hegel simply as a conservative.[1]

Civil society as a system of needs is naturally forced to develop further beyond the simple set of relations of production and exchange. Since it is the sphere in which men are related as persons, it has to protect and maintain men's rights. Hence it is involved in the administration of justice. But beyond this, the operation of the economy for the good of its members is far from being entirely assured by automatic mechanisms, in spite of the good work of the invisible hand. Lots of things can go wrong; and in the name of the good of individuals public authority has to intervene.

Hegel thus takes us in the second and third sections of civil society beyond the level of economic relations to functions which are judicial and properly political. But we are not yet dealing with the state. The reason is that we are still dealing here with individual men, the subjects of needs, united together for their common interest. What we discover is that the exigency of this common interest takes us beyond relations of production and exchange; and requires as well the administration of justice and a certain amount of regulation of economic activity. But we are not yet at the stage where we are looking on the political community as the substance, that is as constituting itself the end. The goal of all the regulations spoken of in the third section of civil society is still the good of individuals.

Hegel sees the necessary regulation being done partly by public authority,

---

[1] But by the same token one cannot but doubt the viability of this system. Is it possible to sustain estates with really different modes of life in a society where there is real mobility, and where men are free to choose their profession? Does not for instance the unreflecting loyalty of the agricultural class presuppose a way of life into which one is born? So that entry could only be free into the other two estates. Generalized mobility is a powerful solvent. It would end up destroying estates altogether. Which is, indeed, what has happened. Although, of course, we benefit from hindsight in second-guessing Hegel on this.

partly by corporations which are representative of various groups and professions and which operate with a publically recognized status. But what is particularly interesting and worth pausing over for a moment is Hegel's insights into the problems of civil society. It is not just that many accidents of economic life, natural disasters, overproduction, etc., can reduce men to poverty and that society thus has to operate some kind of welfare state. It is also that there is an inherent drive in civil society towards dissolution.

If civil society expands in an unimpeded way, it grows indefinitely in GNP and population. This increases greatly the wealth of some. But it also leads to an intensification of the division of labour, the increasing subdivision of jobs, and the growth of a proletariat which is tied to work of this sort. This proletariat is both materially impoverished, and spiritually as well by the narrowness and monotony of its work. But once men are reduced in this way materially and spiritually they lose their sense of self-respect and their identification with the whole community, they cease really to be integrated into it and they become a 'rabble' (Pöbel). The creating of this rabble goes along with the concentration of wealth in a few hands (*PR*, § 244).

This in turn sets off a crisis of over-production. The under-privileged can be maintained on welfare. But this contradicts the principle of the bourgeois economy whereby men should work for their living; or they can be provided with employment by the state; but this will increase the crisis of over-production.

It hence becomes apparent that despite an excess of wealth civil society is not rich enough, i.e. its own resources are insufficient to check excessive poverty and the creation of a penurious rabble. (*PR*, § 245)

The explanatory note to this section mentions the situation in England and Scotland.

The inner dialectic of civil society drives it beyond itself in an attempt to solve this problem by finding overseas markets and by colonization (*PR*, §§ 246–8).

The passage reminds us strikingly of the work of Hegel's illustrious successor who was only three years old at the time. Nor is this just a superficial convergence. A study of some of Hegel's writings of the early 1800s shows that he had thought deeply about the connection between the growing industrial society and increasing material and spiritual impoverishment.[1] He had to a startling degree anticipated the young Marx's theory of alienation. For he sees the system of division of labour and exchange as taking on a momentum of its

---

[1] The works concerned are the *System der Sittlichkeit* of 1801–2 (published in G. Lasson (Ed.) *Schriften zur Politik und Rechtophilosophie*, Leipzig 1923), and two earlier attempts at a system, also of the Jena period, which have been called *Jenaer Realphilosophie* I and II (published by J. Hoffmeister, respectively Leipzig 1932 and Hamburg 1967). These works were unpublished in Hegel's lifetime, and were only given serious attention fairly recently. Cf. the interesting discussion in Avineri, *op. cit.* 87–98.

own. It becomes an 'alien power' (fremde Macht) operating by its own laws (of supply and demand), and disposing of people's lives as an 'unconscious, blind fate' (Bewußtloses, blindes Schicksal, *System der Sittlichkeit*, 80–1). This can enrich or ruin whole groups of people in a blind, unforeseeable way.

But further, it has its own dynamic. Wealth, abstracted from immediate possession of objects of use, tends to breed wealth (*Realphilo*, ii, 232–3), and this in turn becomes power (Herrschaft, *SdS* 83). So that extremes of wealth, and endless refinement of consumer taste go along with the relegation of masses to poverty and their condemnation to 'blunting, unhealthy, insecure and narrowing…work' (abstumpfenden, ungesunden, und unsicheren und die Geschicklichkeit beschränkenden…Arbeit, *Realphilo*, ii, 232). And this ramifying system constantly spreads itself through more and more branches of industry (*Realphilo*, ii, 233). In the process it deprives masses of men of all human culture. It reduces them to 'bestiality' where they cannot appreciate higher things (die Bestialität der Verachtung alles Hoen, *SdS*, 84). And it turns them against the whole system in indignation and hatred (die hochste Zerrissenheit des Willens, innre Empörung und Haß, *Realphilo*, ii, 233).

This extraordinary convergence[1] between Hegel and Marx allows us to see the contrast. For this clear-sighted view of the inherent tendencies of the economic system founded on the division of labour and exchange did not alter Hegel's conception of it as an essential dimension of modern society. Hegel goes on seeing the 'invisible hand' as an instrument of the cunning of reason even while grasping its appalling inadequacy to produce a just society, or even save society from dissolution. The division of labour, the refinement of taste, the economy of individual enterprise all were essential to the development of modern individuality and the specialization and differentiation which were inseparable from it, as we saw above. For Hegel there can be no question of abolishing the bourgeois economy. Rather its inherent drive to dissolution must be contained through its sub-ordination to the demands of the more ultimate community which is the state. This higher allegiance and the rules which flow from it must keep men from giving way to those extremes of the drive for self-enrichment which pull society into the slip-stream of uncontrolled growth.

In Marx's view, on the other hand, this solution was a chimaera. For the state itself was conditioned by the economy. Far from being able to control it, the state rather reflected its tensions and the relations of domination within it. The contradictions of civil society could neither be resolved, nor contained. It has to be abolished.

Of course, in respect of the possibility of controlling the bourgeois economy Marx was much more perspicacious than Hegel (he also had the advantage of

---

[1] It really is a matter of convergence, not of borrowing, since Marx never saw these early manuscripts. He only had available the condensed discussion in *PR*.

coming later). But the difference between the two was not just one of empirical judgement. The Hegelian synthesis as an ontologically grounded order which was embodied in differentiated groups necessarily contained within it controlled tension between opposites. Marx's perspective on the other hand, looks to the realization of man, not of *Geist*. The realization of *man* in freedom requires the universal and total participation which we saw as essential to a general will society. And this requires a homogeneous and united society, in which all differentiation is overcome. The quite different way of surmounting the strains in civil society, in one case by its sub-ordination, in the other by its abolition, are connected to the fundamental concepts of these respective thinkers.

For Hegel civil society is thus to be kept in balance by being incorporated in a deeper community. It cannot govern itself. Its members need allegiance to a higher community to turn them away from infinite self-enrichment as a goal and hence the self-destruction of civil society. Self-management through corporations can be seen as a stage on this road. It makes the individual member of a larger whole, and lifts him, as it were, toward the state. In the corporation he has the respect and dignity which he would otherwise seek, left as a simple individual, in endless self-enrichment (*PR*, §253 E).

2

We come now to the state which is the full realization of the Idea of *Sittlichkeit*, that is a community in which the good is realized in common life. The family and civil society were only partial, non-self subsistent realizations. With the state, we have a full and self-subsistent one. It is the manifestation of substantial will. It is the community in which the fullness of rational will is manifest in public life. The fully realized state reconciles the fully developed individual subjectivity and the universal. It is concrete freedom.

Concrete freedom consists in this, that personal individuality and its particular interests not only achieve their complete development and gain explicit recognition for their right (as they do in the sphere of the family and civil society) but, for one thing, they also pass of their own accord into the interest of the universal, and, for another thing, they know and will the universal; they even recognize it as their own substantive mind; they take it as their end and aim and are active in its pursuit. (*PR*, §260)

This is what is achieved in the modern state.

The state is to be seen as a realization of rational necessity, of the Idea. As such, its articulations are to be understood as self-articulations of the Idea. Hegel speaks of the state as an 'organism'. But it is an organism which is thought of as producing its articulations according to a necessary plan. These articulations are fixed by the Concept (*PR*, §269). They form the constitution of the state.

Hegel here has a note on the relations of Church and state. Religion contains the same truths as the state expresses in reality. True religion should thus support the state; it should cultivate the inner conviction that the state ought to be obeyed, supported, identified with. It is a deviation when religion either retreats into other-worldliness or turns around and sets itself up against the state. The state should afford help and protection to the Church, for religion is a form of spirit's knowledge of itself. But it cannot accept a claim by the Church to be higher, for this would imply that the state was simply an external authority, as association for utility, like civil society, and not itself an embodiment of reason (*PR*, § 270 E).

Because the constitution of the state is rational, that is, the state is articulated like an organism into its different members, we cannot think of the division of powers in a spirit of checks and balances. This assumes that the different powers are already self-subsistent and have either to strive against each other or reach a compromise. But this is contrary to the very principle of the state as an organic unity, a unity which articulates itself, and in which a common life flows through all the members. If we have got as far as to engage in the game of checks and balances 'the destruction of the state is forthwith a fait accompli' (*PR*, § 272 E).

There is an important general point here which is central to Hegel's philosophy of the state. The state as a community embodying reason has to be lived as an organic whole; it cannot be seen simply as an aggregation of its elements, be these groups or individuals. For in this case it could not be lived by its citizens as the locus of a larger life with which they identify. Hegel argues strenuously against the type of constitution or constitutional provision which is based on this atomistic or composite view of the state. This is the view of men in society as simply 'a heap', as against an articulated unity. If we start with men fractioned into individual atoms, no rational state or indeed common life will be possible.

The constitution into which the state articulates itself according to the concept has three members: the legislative power which determines the universal law; the executive which subsumes particular under the universal, and the power of subjective decision, the Crown. Hegel takes this latter up first.

We have already referred earlier to Hegel's argument for the necessity of monarchy from the Concept. The state as a whole has to have a will, that is, it has to decide things. The process of decision is one that may, and should involve many people, functionaries and representatives. But these are all operating in inter-dependence with each other, and in their official, not personal capacities. In order for the moment of decision as a single will of the state to have its own expression, as it must in a mature constitution, it must come to a head in a single person. The state's will then comes to actuality in the

'I will' of a concrete individual. For the state as subjectivity attains its truth only in a subject.

We may think that the monarch himself as so acting is also only acting in his official capacity. But the king is not an official like the others. For in him the office is not his in virtue of some mediation, choice by others, or certain qualifications he has achieved or whatever; but he acquires it in an immediate, 'natural' fashion, i.e., by birth. Hereditary monarchy provides us with an expression of the will of the state in an immediate individual, one who 'is essentially characterized as *this* individual, in abstraction from all his other characteristics' (*PR*, § 280). This is the real argument for hereditary monarch from the Concept. It is not justified simply by considerations of prudence, such that the throne in this way is above strife and faction, and so on.

In the ancient world, this 'moment of the final, self-determining, decision of the will does not come on the scene explicitly in its own proper actuality as an organic moment immanent in the state' (*PR*, § 279 E). Of course, the ancient democracies had leaders, and other ancient polities had kings. For practically speaking all social decision has to be inaugurated and completed by leaders. But what was absent was the idea of absolutely free decision. The power of the leaders was conditioned, they had to appeal beyond to fates, oracles, etc.

We recognize here Hegel's point that in the Greek world, the limited individuality of the Gods left over them, in the place of the absolute final mastery over reality, an impersonal fate. The ancients had no vision in the heavens of a subjectivity which had the final word over all reality. Subjectivity was always limited, in the grip of fate. As with the Gods, so with the states; these limited individualities felt that they also had to remit their power of final decisions over particular matters to the scrutiny of fate, through oracles or augury.

But in modern times, Christianity provides us with a vision of absolute subjectivity and hence in the modern age men no longer lack 'strength to look within their own being for the final word' (loc. cit.). The fullness of this self-determining will can only achieve an adequate expression if the society's decision culminates in a single consciousness.

This is one of those cases where the detail of Hegel's argument leaves one with a sense of the arbitrary. Granted that a social decision has finally to be promulgated by some person, it is not clear why the realization of the modern idea requires that this be a hereditary monarch, and not a president, or governor-general, or whatever, We might agree that the sense that a society is really deciding for itself, as against following some externally-derived rule or guidance, requires a political life which turns around leaders, representative figures, whose decisions and pronouncements count as ours. But that this must be a hereditary monarch is hard to credit, in spite of Hegel's persuasive deployment of the notions of immediacy and naturalness. One might think that the function of representative individual in this sense has been filled in our time just as well if not better by revered father figures like Eisenhower or Jomo Kenyatta, or 'charismatic' political leaders like J. F. Kennedy.

But it will not do to try to make Hegel sound less controversial here by claiming that the point really was more general, and concerned the need for a final pinnacle to the summit of the executive, whether this is filled by king, prime minister or president. Hegel knew this political necessity, that the buck stop somewhere. He recognized that it held in the ancient world too, in the passage I have just referred to. But he distinguished his point from this political necessity which he thought of as general and not specifically modern, and tied the modern sense of absolute decision specifically to the monarchy.

For in fact what is at stake here is not a practical necessity of politics at all, but the Hegelian idea of differentiation based on the Concept: the fulfilling of a necessary moment of the whole by a specialized person (or in some cases a group) who is nevertheless involved in a larger common life with the whole. He is an individual who can embody a moment of the whole because he is in this common life with the rest. Hence the modern monarchy must be a constitutional monarchy. For Hegel a unity is more developed the more its parts are articulated while still remaining in union with the whole. 'The realized freedom of the Idea consists precisely in giving each of the moments of rationality its own self-conscious actuality here and now. Hence it is this freedom which makes the ultimate self-determining certitude – the culmination of the concept of the will – the function of a single consciousness' (loc. cit.). The king is a truly representative individual, in the medieval sense, he bodies forth the moment of subjective free decision.

The prerogatives of the king are thus to be the apex of decision of the executive, to pardon criminals, and thirdly to embody the universal in his personal conscience – the universal which is also embodied objectively in the whole constitution.

The second part of the constitution is the executive power. This is charged with applying laws, which executing the law of the land, under the king. Hegel sees this as being entrusted to a class of civil servants whose lives are dedicated to this goal. In some cases, of course, the administration of the law will be in the hands of Corporations, but wherever this cannot be the solution, it must be in the hands of a civil service which is independent of the interests of society. This is an executive under the king which is made up of career, remunerated civil servants. The aim of making the civil service a career is to assure the maximum independence and dedication to the function itself, the maximum freedom from private interests. For the same reason and in order to secure the most effective service, the posts are filled on merit. Hegel accepts here *la carrière ouverte aux talents* (§§ 291–2 'Between an individual and his office there is no immediate natural link.')

441

The civil service makes up the greater part of the middle estate (§ 297) which Hegel has called the universal estate in the earlier discussion on civil society (the rest is presumably made up partly of officials of corporations and other professionals?). Here we have another application of the Hegelian principle of the articulation of the essential moments of the synthesis. The dimension of total identification with the life of the state, with public affairs, is not to be lived by everyone in the same way, but is the mode of life of a special group. This shares however with the others in the larger life of the whole state, and is an organ in a greater organism.

Thus the function of total immersion in the public, which was that of all citizens among the ancients, devolves on the universal estate in Hegel's mature polity. It is carried by a career civil service. This represents an interesting change from earlier variants of Hegel's theory in the Jena period. In his writings of the early 1800s, e.g., the *System der Sittlichkeit*, and also in his lectures, published in our time under the title *Jenenser Realphilosophie*, Hegel presents us another system of estates. The basic principle of articulation is the same, but its working out is interestingly different. The second estate in this system too is that of business, and it has the same political and ethical culture as its opposite number in the system of 1821. But the estate which represents the more immediate, unreflecting, ethical life, whose life is close to nature and whose deep sentiment is trust and loyalty, is represented not by the agricultural class as such, but only by the peasants. The landed aristocracy forms rather the background of the first, which Hegel calls here the absolute estate, and which fills the role of total involvement in the universal, public life of the state.[1]

What lies behind this change in the first two decades (really 15 years, for the Jena lectures are from 1805–6) from aristocracy to bureaucracy? In part it may have been Hegel's realization, under the impact of the Napoleonic state, of the importance and necessity of bureaucracy in the modern state, and the centrality of the principle of *la carrière ouverte aux talents*. In part, it may have been progressive disenchantment with the contemporary aristocracy. The landed privileged of Germany were generally dedicated, as soon as the Napoleonic hegemony was set aside, to restoring all the outworn and irrational privileges of the *ancien régime*.

This may also cast light on Hegel's emphasis on monarchy. In his home state of Württemberg, the monarch tried to set up a liberal constitution after the Restoration, and was bitterly opposed by the interests which dominated the old estates. This was the occasion of one of those occasional political writings of Hegel which are our main evidence for his political evolution. His commentary on the *Proceedings of the Estates Assembly* which appeared in 1817 shows him

[1] In the Jena lectures Hegel calls this 'the estate of universality' or 'the public estate'.

siding strongly with the king against the reactionary attempt to return to the practices of a quarter century earlier. The merely positive must be set aside and the state reformed to reflect reason. The position taken here in commenting favourably on King Frederick's constitution is in all essentials in agreement with the *PR*. But what is germane to our purpose here is that this and similar experiences may have helped convince Hegel not only that the aristocratic class was hardly a fit vehicle for the universal, but that the main instrument of reform without destructive revolution must be the monarchy. Just as early modern kings welded state power out of the warring chaos of their barons, so modern kings would help to embody the rational against the interests of the merely positive.

But it is unlikely that the model for this earlier version of the universal class was the aristocracy of Hegel's time, for whom he never had much use. It is rather to be found in the ancient polis. The absolute estate of the early 1800s is like the citizen class of the ancient republic in that it is also the class of warriors. Those who give themselves totally to the public life are also those who go to war for the state. The fact that monarchy plays no part in these early variants of the Hegelian state strengthens the likeness to the ancient polity. We have a picture of an aristocratic republic, which has incorporated the principle of articulated specialization and through this has taken account of universal subjectivity. In *SdS* there is even a kind of ephorate, a class of priest-elders above the estates who are charged with maintaining the purity of the constitution. The shift from this to the system of *PR* would thus represent a further maturing and working out of Hegel's belief that we cannot go home again, that much as he shared the immense nostalgic admiration and yearning of his generation for Greek *Sittlichkeit*, this was lost forever, and rightly so. The modern age could only remain true to its advances over the ancient through a representative monarchy served by a class of bureaucrats.

We come now to the legislative power. This must be made up of King, Ministers and Estates Assembly. In this latter we come to one of the cruces of the Hegelian system. The role of the Estates is to achieve the essential goal of the Hegelian state, to unite private individuals to public power, to make the former identify with and participate in this power.

> The Estates have the function of bringing public affairs into existence not only *an sich*, but also *für sich*, i.e., of bringing into existence the moment of subjective formal freedom, the public consciousness as an empirical universal, of which the thoughts and opinions of the many are particulars. (*PR*, § 301)

Thus the Estates are meant to be the locus in which there is crystallized, out of the maze of private wills of civil society, a common will which is one with that of the state. It is the place in which civil society achieves political expression, reaches a common political will.

Thus, says Hegel, the justification for representative institutions is not at all where it is commonly put, that the people or their representatives know their own best interests, or are more disinterested and dedicated to the general good. Indeed, these propositions are certainly more false than true when we compare deputies to civil servants. The real point of the Estates is to incorporate civil society into the political, by involving it in the common will of the state. It is to bring private will and private judgement to a political will and consciousness focused on the whole and its ends, and in this way to unite those who live in the private sphere to the public life of the whole, so that they identify with this life and its acts.

Hence the specific function which the concept assigns to the Estates is to be sought in the fact that in them the subjective moment in universal freedom – the private judgement and private will of the sphere called 'civil society' in this book – comes into existence integrally related to the state. (*PR*, §301 E)

And to drive home the point that this is no consideration of prudence, but ontologically grounded, Hegel adds

This moment is a determination of the Idea once the Idea has developed to a totality, a moment arising as a result of inner necessity not to be confused with external necessities and experiences. The proof of this follows...from adopting a philosophical point of view.

But the will crystallized out of civil society must not be one in opposition to the government. This idea of representative institutions as mainly revendicative, as existing to fight for society's rights against the state, which was quite widespread at the time, Hegel utterly rejects. A state in which this opposition arose would of course cease to be an organic unity, it would cease to have a common life and will with which all its members were identified. It would break apart into a sovereign governing will on one side, and on the other, over against it, into a fractioning of private revendications, 'the particular interests of persons, societies, corporations' (*PR*, §302).

This image of the dissolution of the organic into independent parts plays an important part in Hegel's discussion here, as a pendant to the image of the state as an organism. If the state is to realize *Sittlichkeit*, then it must constitute a common life in which all find their identity. But this cannot be if people mainly identify themselves by their private interests and see the state merely as the locus where these private interests have to come together to reach some kind of compromise essential to a functioning society. This is the kind of society which Hegel speaks of as a mere aggregate – a 'crowd' (Menge) or a 'heap' (Haufen) are terms Hegel uses (Cf. *PR*, §302) – and this means a state in dissolution. In this situation, government can only survive as a despotism over individuals crushing private wills under the yoke of a law with which no-one identifies.

Hence it is that the function of the Estates cannot be seen as one of opposition to the government, rather they are meant to be a mediating element, the middle of a Hegelian syllogism. This function dominates the whole Hegelian discussion of the Estates.

It means that the Estates as representative institutions must be based on the organic articulation of the estates of society. Hegel holds it to be far from arbitrary that the German word 'Stand' refers both to the social entity and its political expression (as does 'estate'). For only through its substantial articulations can the people be linked to government. These already have done part of the work of linking the individual will to the universal through his membership in a greater whole. The further step to political expression must build on this. This same principle is what underlies the important role of the corporation in public administration.

Hegel thus turns his face against what has become an absolutely fundamental principle of the modern democratic state, universal direct suffrage. The idea of direct suffrage is that people vote as individuals, they are not represented in their capacity as members of some estate or group or other articulation of society. Hegel calls this an 'atomistic and abstract point of view' (*PR*, § 303 E), it partakes of the vision of the state as a mere mass, an aggregate of individuals. To take this is to abandon any hope of a substantive common life, or indeed any hope of a common will. For the people, once it identifies itself as a mere multitude is 'a formless mass whose commotion and activity could therefore only be elementary, irrational, barbarous and frightful' (eine formlose Masse, deren Bewugung und Tun eben damit nur elementarisch, vernunftlos, wild und fürchterlich wäre', loc cit.). Even if we avoid upheaval and the dissolution of society, political life on this model becomes abstract, it is cut off from social life which is articulated whether we want to accept it or not. Politics thus becomes something in which men cannot recognize themselves (loc. cit.). Here we have a critique which will come back in a transposed form in Marx, where the alienation of citizen from bourgeois is one of the contradictions of capitalist society.

Thus the Estates are articulated into two houses, one of which represents the landed class, the other the bourgeois economy. These must be related differently to the universal because of their different forms of life. The landed class has a certain independence, at once of the Crown and of the vagaries of business fortune, in its landed property. It is 'independent of favour, whether from the executive or the multitude' (*PR*, § 306). And this peculiarly fits it for a role in public life. (Hegel here retains a vestige of his earlier view of the Jena time.) This class has a special vocation for public life, and thus is entitled to sit in the Estates through birth, and not election (*PR*, § 307). Its members present themselves in person, and not through representatives.

The upper house can itself perform a mediating function within the whole constitution of the Estates which is meant to mediate between society and the state. For they share something with the king, they too owe their position to the natural, to birth; but also they have needs and rights like the rest of society. They mediate between lower house and Crown.

By contrast the lower house is made up of representatives. But these are not to be elected at large; in keeping with the principle above, they are appointed by the various associations, communities, corporations which constitute civil society. In this way the individual is related to the universal not simply immediately, but through the specific moment of the articulated group to which he belongs. And Hegel makes his point again, that an atomistic state is without rational organization

To hold that every single person should share in deliberating and deciding on political matters of general concern on the ground that all individuals are members of the state, that its concerns are their concerns, and that it is their right that what is done should be done with their knowledge and volition, is tantamount to a proposal to put the democratic element without any rational form into the organism of the state, although it is only in virtue of the possession of such a form that the state is an organism at all.

(*PR*, § 308 E)

Men must relate to the polity not as individuals, but through their membership in the articulated components of the society. It is pure abstraction to demand that all men relate to political power in the same way.[1]

From the same principle that the Estates exist to mediate state and society, Hegel draws the conclusion that the deputies should not be seen as delegates of their electors. For the Estates, too, must function as an organic whole, bent on the common good, and not as simply an assembly of individual deputies.

And this principle also underlies Hegel's discussion of public opinion. Hegel holds that assembly debates should be publicized, and that the press and organs of opinion, within certain limits, should be free. But this is not because he believes in the central tradition of the Enlightenment, that public opinion, as formed through public discussion, is bound to be enlightened. On the contrary he sees it as a mixture of insight and particular prejudice. It is gold hidden in mud. It deserves as much to be respected as despised (*PR*, § 318), for essential truths are mixed up with raw confusions. By itself it is no criterion:

Thus to be independent of public opinion is the first formal condition of achieving anything great or rational whether in life or in science. Great achievement is assured, however, of subsequent recognition and grateful acceptance by public opinion, which in due course will make it one of its own prejudices.

Great acts need never bow to public opinion, they fashion its future form. The point of publicity is thus not to improve government, but as an essential part of the Estates' mediating function, to help the process of crystallization of a public

[1] Cf. also the discussion of the 'sovereignty of the people' in § 279 E.

political will out of the private, and one which will find itself in the actions of the state. The public is educated by the debates and forms itself up to the political in the development of public opinion.

We have looked at the essential features of the inner constitution of the Hegelian state. We can see why it has acquired the reputation of being reactionary. It is not just the stress on monarchy. It is much more that the key foundation of the modern democratic state is thought to be elections by universal suffrage in which men vote as individuals. Any other form of government we are convinced, must both neglect the interests of those not directly enfranchised, and also provide no possibility for the mass of people to educate themselves in the rights and duties of political citizenship.

Hegel's insistence that men not enter the political arena directly, but through their associations, corporations, etc., in a more organic fashion, strikes us as reminiscent of nothing so much as modern corporatism; which in Fascist countries has been used as a screen for dictatorial power, and which certainly did not provide a more meaningful participation. Even if corporatism were not controlled from on top, we tend to think, representation in legislative institutions which emanated from such associations would leave the people at the mercy of the élite groups which tends to control these. The ordinary people would live under a perpetual carve-up on behalf of the élites. In the eyes of many radicals our present society already resembles too closely this state of affairs. These radicals may even despair of Parliamentary government, but they turn rather to direct democracy, they are even farther from accepting some corporate solution.

Yet we must resist the natural tendency to understand and judge Hegel's work simply out of the experience of our own time. I fully subscribe to the above criticism of corporatism, but I think Hegel's work should be seen in another light.

I want to discuss this more fully in a minute. But first let us complete Hegel's vision of the state by looking at its external relations. Here, of course, we have another source of the deep disapproval with which many moderns regard him. For in the next section (*PR*, §§321–9) he rejects the two basic goals of liberalism in the international sphere, which had already been ably defended by Kant, peace on a permanent basis between nations and world federation of states.

The reason for his rejecting the latter is already implicit in the foregoing. The state must be the locus of a higher life with which men identify. But men cannot stretch their identification so wide as to include everyone. The state must be the object of a powerful feeling of identification, of patriotism, which Hegel calls '*sittliche Gesinnung*'. But this cannot just be stretched at will to cover the whole human race. It must on the contrary repose on the 'self-feeling' (Selbstgefühl) of a people (*PR*, §322 E). In other words, for Hegel, the project

447

of an international political entity makes sense on the liberal assumption that the state is just an external instrument for the well-being of individuals, or to further moral goals (Moralität). From this point of view a world state is a superior form. Hence we find Kant arguing for it. But once one understands that the state is the locus of an organic public life which is the focus of our identity, then we see that it must remain an individual against others.

But its individuality against others, its negative relation to others in Hegelian terms, is linked to its 'negative relation to itself', that is, its power as an individual to weld all its parts into a whole and even sacrifice them for the good of the whole. This relationship comes to its reality in war, where effectively the state calls on people to maintain this substantial unity 'at the risk and sacrifice of property and life' (*PR bee*, §209).

War is thus for Hegel in a pregnant sense the moment of truth. For it is the moment in which the true relation between the state and society comes to the fore. In peacetime the state has as one of its prime purposes to maintain and protect the property and other private interests of its members. And this is what leads to the mistaken view that political society simply exists to secure individual life and property (e.g., Locke). But in fact the state is the embodiment of the substantial, in fact it is the community in which men achieve their identity as bearers of rational will. *It* therefore is the end. And since its development is the goal of history, and civil society is one of its necessary component parts, we should think of the state as articulating itself into families, civil societies, spheres of right, etc., rather than these as constituting the state.

Now this real order of dignity and purpose only comes to the fore when the state is in danger and then shows its higher finality by commandeering property and calling its citizens to risk their lives and die for it.

But as a reflection of an essential moment of the state, according to Hegel's ontological principles, war has necessarily to occur. Whatever reflects an essential moment of the concept must achieve external existence. Hence, though it might appear as though wars were purely contingent occurrences, and often in their detail they are, war itself is necessary. War cannot either be considered as accidental, nor as absolutely evil. Its necessary function is to embody the primacy of the universal; and thus without it peoples would stagnate into the swamp of private interests. Hegel here quotes himself from an earlier work:

The ethical health of peoples is preserved in their indifference to the stabilization of finite institutions; just as the blowing of the winds preserves the sea from the foulness which would be the result of a prolonged calm, so also the corruption in nations would be the product of a prolonged, let alone 'perpetual' peace. (*PR*, §324 E)[1]

---

[1] Quoting the *wissenschaftlichen Behandlungsarten;* 'perpetual peace' is a dig at Kant.

448

The Realized State

Hegel also says in this section that death is the lot of the finite, of the particular anyway. This is assured by nature ordinarily; but

in the ethical substance, the state, nature is robbed of this power, and the necessity is exalted to the work of freedom, to be something ethical. The transience of the finite becomes a willed passing away, and the negativity lying at the roots of the finite becomes the substantive individuality proper to the ethical substance.   (loc. cit.)

Modern war since the invention of gunpowder particularly meets this function of war to the highest degree, for we have here a struggle not of personalities or inspired by personal hate, but general conflict, for large purposes and with the impersonality of distance (made possible by firearms). This aspect of the state as well is embodied in a particular group; a standing army is thus a necessity of reason and not just of prudence (*PR*, § 326). Power over war and foreign affairs is in the hands of the Crown.

In the next section (*PR*, §§ 330–9), on international law, Hegel returns again to the point that any world state or league of nations is a chimaera. There are norms of international law, but these must remain pure *Sollen*; they cannot be made substantial, part of a self-maintaining common life.[1]

There follows (*PR*, §§ 341–50) an account of world-history, along lines we have already seen.

3

How can we sum up Hegel's political purpose and vision? It must now be clear that the ordinary labels usually applied obscure much more than they clarify. Hegel has been called a conservative, and also a liberal,[2] an apologist of the Restoration Prussian state, and a proto-totalitarian who would sacrifice the individual on the altar of a state divinity. The latter two descriptions are quite wide of the mark. But the first two are not just wrong. They are fundamentally misleading just because of the elements of truth they contain.

It is not wrong to call Hegel a liberal because of the central place that he gave to the principles of 1789. First, that the state must be founded on reason, not tradition. Hegel consistently attacks the real conservatives of his day, who wanted to maintain the old, 'positive' constitutions and authorities just because of their venerable, prescriptive foundation. He attacks those who defend the patriarchal power of monarchs, or their divine right to rule.

---

[1] This reference to *Sollen* here is one of the considerations on which E. Weil bases his view that Hegel looked forward to a higher stage of history, one where a world state would be possible. Cf. *Hegel et L'Etat*, Paris 1950, pp. 75–9. But this is not very plausible, partly for the reasons mentioned above but also because of the point in § 322, viz., that as a locus of identification, the state cannot be superseded by some larger union.
[2] E.g., by Z. Pelczynski, who places Hegel on the liberal 'right', Cf. *Hegel's Political Philosophy*, Ed. W. Kaufmann, New York 1970, p. 85.

Secondly, the modern state must be built around the free, rational individual. It must respect his freedom of conscience, freedom to select his profession, the security of his property and freedom of economic enterprise. It must allow for the dissemination of information and the formation of public opinion. It must be founded on the rule of law.

We perhaps need reminding today that these were not principles of the 'Right' in the Restoration Europe after 1815 which was dominated by the Holy Alliance, however 'conservative' some of them may sound in Western democracies of the 1970s.

But Hegel decisively parts company from liberalism in that he believes that these principles are radically, indeed, disastrously inadequate as a foundation for the state. The label 'liberal' is uncommonly broad and loose, but there is a central tradition which has regarded individual liberty, equality (including the sweeping away of unearned privileges), and the responsibility of government to the governed as the three essential properties of a legitimate polity. Many thinkers we want to call liberal have wanted to mitigate the application of one or other of these principles: Locke did not think of the unpropertied masses as fit bearers of the franchise, and J. S. Mill thought that many peoples were not yet ready for representative government; but the thinkers we generally class as liberal did not recognize any other basic principle. (Unless, of course, we think of the rule of law as a principle independent of liberty and equality; in which case the trinity above should be a quaternity.)

The underlying belief of the liberal tradition is that these values were the sufficient basis for a viable society. That is, a society which embodied these should command the loyal co-operation of its members. It was believed either that men would be satisfied with the inherent justice of such an arrangement; or that enlightened men would see the utility of such a society and so play by its rules; or that men would identify with a society in which they were free and sovereign and consider it their own.

But whether for these reasons or others, the response of the liberal tradition to disaffection and break-up in society has always been to call for a further, more thoroughgoing application of the three principles; on the grounds that greater freedom, or the abolition of further inequalities, or fuller responsibility of government must be sufficient to overcome alienation or division.

In this sense, Hegel is most emphatically not in the liberal tradition. A society based on these three principles alone is one in which men are maximally free as individuals, with a homogeneous, undifferentiated way of life, and where government responds to the wills of these undifferentiated individuals. But this is just the kind of society which rather deserves to be called a 'crowd' (Menge) or a 'heap' (Haufen, *PR* §§ 302, 303). It is a 'formless mass' (eine formlose Masse, *PR*, §§ 279, 303).

450

Hegel's rejection of this model of society goes deep into the bases of his philosophical position and into the underlying motives of his thought. The ideal of the expressive unity of man and society, beautifully embodied by the Greeks, is radically denied by this atomistic model. If the state is to respond to the wills of independent, equal individuals, then it is nothing but an instrument in their hands. It cannot be the locus of a larger life. There is no room for *Sittlichkeit*. We are back to the issue we examined in the last chapter. If merely human will is central, then the state is reduced to the status of a tool. It cannot be a greater life-process of which individuals are members.

But without this, not only can man not return to unity with *Geist*, there cannot be a viable state at all. Without its necessary articulation (Gegliederung) a people falls apart as a state (*PR*, §279). Hegel seems to be borrowing Rousseau's idea of a people 'dissolving itself' – only for the opposite reason: for Rousseau it is the promise to obey a part of the whole which thus destroys the political bond. One might say that for him the creation of articulation is the mortal political sin, whereas for Hegel it is its abolition which destroys the state. Nor is this destruction thought of as merely metaphorical. A state so atomized must lose the allegiance of its citizens. It is paralyzed in inaction for lack of consensus, or else the plaything of the arbitrary will of factions.

Hegel thus cannot accept the usual liberal perspective on the principles of 1789, liberty, equality and popular sovereignty (if I may amend the Revolutionary trinity for the purposes of this discussion); that they only need to be integrally applied, to sweep all else before them, in order to achieve a rational and viable society, the summit of political perfection. On the contrary, Hegel combats the total implementation of these principles, in the name of what looks like a quite unrelated, conservative principle: that society must have an articulated structure, involving different relationships of different 'estates' to political power, which is ultimately justified as a reflection of cosmic order. But pre-modern theories also justified the structure of society by reference to the order of things, e.g., that the king was to society as God to the world, or that society was a body of which the king was the head.

Thus in the name of what sounds like a pre-modern principle Hegel severely restricts the application of the Revolutionary trinity. Freedom of economic action is not to go beyond certain limits set by a watchful state; and it is moreover to be carried on within the confines of corporations. Equality cannot be allowed to become homogenization and break down the distinctions between estates in their rights, obligations and way of life. Above all, men cannot be allowed to participate in forming the common will just as individuals, expressing their personal choices through a vote. They must take part through their role in a given estate or the corporation to which they belong. A fortiori this common will cannot be simply the emanation of individual

451

choices, but of deliberations which reflect the organic structure of the state.

No wonder, then, that Hegel has frequently been classed as a conservative. But this is just as unilluminating as to call him a liberal. For he in fact holds none of the pre-modern theories with their presumption of an order of things which is just given. Nor does he accept structures of subordination grounded in tradition or prescription. The only foundation he will accept is reason itself. The Hegelian tour de force is that he claims to deduce from reason and freedom a new articulation, so that this is held to be the true fulfilment of these central aspirations of 1789. The state of atomized, homogeneous individuals is not their logical fruition but a deviation, a monster produced by arrested development. For in fact the aspiration to reason and freedom comes to fulfilment by seeing the human subject as the vehicle of a larger Spirit. The proponents of homogenization, or limitless freedom, or universal suffrage democracy, have all failed to make this shift in the centre of gravity of their thought. They remain obsessed with the finite subject and his independence, and they are incapable of recovering a viable basis for the state. Thus Hegel does not see himself as arresting or limiting the realization of the principles of 1789 in the name of some extraneous principle of order. He sees the articulated state as their true, and indeed only viable fulfilment.

This original position is the ground for Hegel's judgements on the states and politics of his day. Hegel's widespread reputation as a conservative, even a reactionary, has been based on his supposed endorsement of Prussia as the fullest realization of the modern state. This view is based on lamentable historical ignorance. In fact the Hegelian state as portrayed in *PR* existed nowhere in totality, as I pointed out in the previous chapter. The new stage existed still only in general outline and was yet to be worked out. Contemporary Prussia (of 1821) evidently did not fill the bill. For instance there was no assembly of estates for the whole realm, but only for individual provinces; the debates in these were not public; trial by jury was not yet established; a rigid censorship prevented the formation of free public opinion; the Prussian monarchy was much more untrammelled than the constitutional monarchy portrayed in *PR*. No contemporary could have failed to notice discrepancies of this magnitude. Only later commentators who had forgotten or were uninterested in the history of the period could endorse this fable.

But once we have set aside the myth of Hegel as apostle of 'Prussianism', we have to understand the sense in which he saw Prussia as in the vanguard.

At least this was the case after the Restoration, when he overcame his admiration for Napoleon's work, and once more began to believe (if he ever stopped believing) that the state should be the sovereign cadre of spiritual life; or at least began again to believe that such a state could be built in Germany (but not a pan-German state; this was not at all a goal of Hegel's).

Now this seems grotesque to us because as believers in the liberal trinity we think of the good state as a polity based on representative institutions with universal suffrage. From this point of view, transferred back into the 1820s and early thirties, we give high marks among European states to France after 1830, to England particularly after 1832. Hegel died before 1832 (in 1831), but he read and wrote an article on the Reform Bill, and his criticisms seem beside the point and even churlish to a modern. It does not seem important to him that the Reform will broaden the franchise, but rather that it will end the abuse whereby a public role, that of deputy, should be in the gift of private persons almost as their property. But he has little confidence that this will lead to other such reforms for England seems to him as the principle of civil society run riot.

But this placing of Prussia ahead of England and France is very instructive. For these two Western nations represented two of the great disruptive forces which Hegel saw as endangering the unfolding of the modern state. The first was the kind of mob action inspired and controlled by revolutionary élites of which the Jacobins provided the paradigm example. The second was the force of private interest, inherent in civil society, which always threatened to overflow its limits and dissolve the bonds of the state. Both these were dangers implicit in the modern principle of free individuality, but corresponding to different philosophical stages. The first was in a sense Rousseau on the rampage, the second was utilitarianism run wild (Bentham gone berserk).[1]

France was peculiarly open to the first danger, largely because of her religious history. As we saw in the last chapter, the modern state develops partly out of the Protestant Reformation. This represents an important stage in the internalization of man's relation to the universal, which is no longer mediated through an external hierarchy and gross, sensuous forms. Hence in Catholic countries there cannot be a stable constitution based on a deep identification of people with the state. The Church is too powerful and stands in the way. The Catholic Church will not accept the role of a purely spiritual power. It will not admit that the unity between particular and universal reflected in Christian theology is meant to achieve its real, external historical existence in the state. Hence in these countries there is always division; the state cannot gain universal allegiance, the 'ethical conviction' (sittliche Gesinnung) which is possible in Protestant countries.

Now this disability affects France, which is thus disqualified for leadership in the development of the modern state. Because of this lack of 'ethical conviction', and the strength of ideas inimical to *Sittlichkeit,* France was prey to violent, sweeping changes and instability. As a natural consequence to Catholic rejection of the liberal state, one finds an ultra-abstract notion of this state among its followers, founded ultimately on the principle that Hegel combats,

---

[1] Of course, these dangers were not entirely separate. Civil society out of control can breed mob violence and revolution by creating an impoverished proletariat.

that the state unites and expresses the wills of individuals. The disorders of 1830 did nothing to change Hegel's judgement on France. And the enlarged electorate of the July régime naturally did not impress him as progress. But what about England? Here we have a Protestant country. Yes, but one which has succumbed to the second danger. The principle of the private, of individual property, has run wild in it, has even taken over many public functions. The English confuse freedom with particular rights. There is no real dominance of the universal, but only a chaos of negotiating private rights. And what is worse, the matter seems irremediable. For the only force which could cure this would be a strong monarchy, like those late medieval kings which forced through the rights of the universal against their refractory barons. But the English have crucially weakened their monarchy; it is powerless before Parliament which is the cockpit of private interests. Hence they are beyond hope of remedy. This is the ground for Hegel's pessimism which he expresses in his last occasional work, on the English Reform Bill.

However, one feels like asking, why does Hegel not see where the force actually was destined to come which brought (at least some of) these private interests to heel? I am speaking of the popular majority. In fact Hegel did foresee the danger of revolutionary action if the English did not sort out their problems quickly enough in an orderly way. And in general he sees this as a nemesis threatening a civil society out of control in the form of an alienated proletariat, the spectre which haunted Europe in 1848. And indeed, Revolution will be the fate of any society which will not do away in time with irrational and merely 'positive' privileges.

But for Hegel, Revolution was not a solution for the modern state; it was merely another form of disease. For the reasons outlined above, both in experience and theory, Hegel feared and distrusted popular power, change through mass force, either by Revolution or by popular pressure. Such struggle was incompatible with the achieving of unity around a substantial will. It could only be justified if society needed another revolution to complete the work of reason, and this Hegel did not believe.

Hence the vehicle by which the rational constitution could best be introduced and made real was a powerful modernizing monarchy. Admittedly the Prussian king left a lot to be desired in this respect. After undertaking to grant a constitution after the war, he welshed on this promise and did not like to be reminded of it by his subjects. The Crown Prince, the future Frederick William IV, was an outspoken reactionary. Nevertheless Hegel had hopes for the future based on the climate of the times. Germany had been shocked and swept into reform by the Napoleonic conquest. It consisted of societies founded on law in which the principles of rational Enlightenment had already gone some way and seemed bound to go farther. It had a Protestant political culture and hence could achieve a rational constitution unlike the benighted peoples of Latin Europe, and it was not too far gone in rot like England. It held to the monarchical principle and the monarchs retained some real power unlike England, and yet the societies were law societies. In a monarchy bound by law, but retaining the power of initiative, in a Protestant country in which philosophy had reached its peak, surely it was not too much to hope that some reforming King would move to embody the fullness of the rational state?[1]

But history, as we know, belied Hegel's hopes not only about Germany but about the development of the modern world. In fact the liberal trinity of individual liberty, equality and popular sovereignty have gone on apace, entrenching and extending themselves. Where they have been supplemented, or checked more than temporarily, it has not been by a vision of order based either on tradition or on reason, but by other, modern ideologies. For instance, the family of ideologies of total mobilization, of which Marxist-Leninism provides the paradigm for our century, but which has now been imitated and caricatured in every conceivable way, is the major contemporary rival of liberalism. And it is the linear descendant of that aspiration to absolute freedom which Hegel portrayed in so penetrating a fashion. It is powered by its own version of the three principles of liberty, equality and popular sovereignty.

But the most important force to fill the gap left by the decline of traditional allegiances has been nationalism. Indeed, much of the power shown by ideologies of mobilization has come from their marriage with national aspirations. And nationalism has been a force in liberal society as well. It has often been said of Hegel that he failed to appreciate the importance of nationalism for the coming age. But this was really just a corollary of his belief that the drive toward individualism and homogenization would be contained by a new vision of order. For it is the continued, unchecked operation of this drive, sweeping all traditional authority and social differentiation before it, which has opened the void that nationalism has been called on to fill. And reciprocally, the religion of nationalism, adopted by an élite which has broken free from traditional forms, has been a powerful instrument of homogenization. How many modern societies could command sufficient loyalty and civic spirit to carry on without a strong dose of nationalism? A clear-cut answer is hard to give, but one suspects the number is small.

[1] Perhaps understandably, this question seems to have been answered differently by Hegel the political philosopher and by Hegel the interested and committed observer of the contemporary political scene. Not that there was any difference in his conception of the vocation of the modern state, or of the obstacles and dangers in the way of its realization. But there does seem to be a difference in his confidence as to the outcome. The serene tone, certain of the triumph of reason, of the philosophical works contrasts with the realistic pessimism of the *English Reform Bill* and the anguish, even despair, of some private communications. As a concerned observer Hegel does not seem to have been as sure as his philosophical position might warrant that the various forms of irrationality – blind traditionalism, Romantic rejection of reality, revolutionary fanaticism – and the drives inherent in civil society to dissolution would not thwart the self-realization of reason and bar the way to the fulfilment of the rational state.

In other words, Hegel failed to identify the new age which was being forged in his time because he saw its driving forces, liberty, equality, popular sovereignty, as destined to be subsumed (aufgehoben) in a new rational order, grounded on ontological necessity. The shape of a world in which these forces would press ahead unchecked and independent of any order towards ever greater individual mobility and social homogeneity was something he never considered. It seemed a wildly unviable prospect.

But this does not mean that Hegel did not understand the nature of these (to him) disruptive forces. On the contrary, in a sense he understood them more deeply than his contemporaries. For he not only had a profound grasp of the two great clusters of ideas and images which have alternately shaped the drive towards liberty and equality, that is, utilitarianism and the aspiration to absolute freedom; he not only understood the inner dynamic of these as *ideas*.

He also saw the dynamic of modern 'civil society'. He saw, that is, how the manufacturing economy based on division of labour and exchange tended to extend itself endlessly, and in the process to prize men loose from any group allegiance, to accelerate their individual mobility while at the same time intensifying their reciprocal dependence in a vast, impersonal system. In other words, the modern economy, left to itself, would be a powerful engine of individualism and homogenization. The bourgeois economy would indeed generate differences, and extreme ones, of wealth and poverty. But these would be without rationale, unlike the estates of traditional (or Hegelian) society, and it would be left to chance, and the shifting sands of fortune, who ended up in which category, and for how long.

Hegel thus sees the drive towards modern homogeneity not just as residing in certain ideas, but as inherent in certain institutions and common modes of life. Indeed, Hegel understood as few other social thinkers how ideas are interwoven in practices and institutions, how the first are essentially involved in the identification of the second, and how the second in turn express and hence also define their constitutive ideas. This is the set of connections implicit in the Hegelian notion of institutions as 'objective spirit', as we saw in Chapter xiv. The bourgeois economy can be seen as modern individualism, in its utilitarian variant, expressed in a mode of life and set of practices. Its excesses breed alienation, a mass without identification with their society, and hence ready for a revolution. This in turn must be powered by the aspiration to absolute freedom, which represents the moderns' attempt to fill the void left by modern individualism, and recover a society expressive of themselves.

Hegel understood this whole dynamic well, uncannily well. He failed to *predict* it because he was confident it would be checked and subsumed in the rational order of the modern state founded on the Idea.

But because things did not turn out this way, intellectual history has been unavoidably unfair to Hegel. For his vision of order, which is neither

456

traditional (based on 'positive' authority), nor what we recognize as 'modern' (founded on the liberal trinity, or nationalism, or an ideology of mobilization) has quite naturally been lost to view. It is then assimilated to one or another of the above categories with which people are readily familiar.

This is the origin of Hegel's 'Prussian' reputation. Prussia went through a number of phases in the nineteenth century. Under the reactionary leadership of King Frederick William IV, it stood aside from the liberal nationalism of 1848. Then later, under Bismarck, it took the initiative in uniting Germany. This Hohenzollern Germany, of which the King of Prussia was Emperor, was a peculiar mixture of traditional allegiances and liberal practices, held together by the powerful fixative of nationalism.

As the actual content of Hegel's vision was progressively lost to sight, with ideologies of traditionalism or modernization dominating the scene, what came to be remembered of him was (a) that he thought that Prussia was on the right track, and (b) that he believed that the state was somehow divine and deserving of the individual's highest earthly allegiance. It was forgotten what track Hegel had thought Prussia to be on in the 1820s, and above all, what he meant by divinity and the state. So naturally both friends and enemies attributed to him the then current grounds for giving one's highest earthly allegiance to the Prussian German state, which were a mixed appeal to traditional authority and modern chauvinistic nationalism. That such an appalling salad of the merely positive and the sub-rational should be attributed to Hegel, the philosopher of a rational cosmic order, is one of the great ironies of modern intellectual history. Such are the penalties of too great originality.[1]

But does not the very oblivion into which his main ideas fell show the irrelevancy of Hegel's political thought? One might be tempted to think so since the forces of individualism and homogenization have pressed on apace. All social differentiation has come under attack, not only those forms which are based on birth or social position, but even the biologically based one, that between the sexes. The modern notion of equality will suffer no differences in the field of opportunity which individuals have before them. Before they choose, individuals must be interchangeable; or, alternatively put, any differences must be chosen. This emphasis on choice in the contemporary principle of equality reflect its marriage with a radical notion of freedom, as self-creation.[2]

Together these two have swept aside all the articulations of traditional

---

[1] The process of saddling Hegel with 'Prussianism' began even before the birth of Bismarckian Germany. Rudolf Haym's influential biography, *Hegel und seine Zeit* (1857), is probably its point of origin. But Haym identified Hegel with the Prussia of 1848, whose ruler was out of sympathy with everything he stood for.

[2] Hence contemporary demands for equality are made in the language of freedom, e.g., 'women's liberation'.

society, and have set themselves to combat the new ones which have arisen. As we look over the history of the last two centuries, there seems to be an unmistakable trend, in which stage by stage differences are set aside and neutralized, culminating in a society in which everyone (at least in theory) will stand equal with all others before a potentially limitless field of possibilities. In the name of this equality in freedom, we are now undergoing a profound revolution in the status of women, and even to some extent in that of minors (cf. for instance, the lowering of the voting age to 18, now almost general throughout the Western world).

Nor is this movement confined to liberal society. Contemporary totalitarian societies may restrict individual freedom, but they hold just as strongly to the principle of liberty as self-creation. And they have been even more determined agents of individual mobility, breaking individuals loose from their identification with primary groups and making them relate exclusively to the larger society. They too aim to create a society in which all men are equally master of their fate, interchangeable before a free choice in an expanding field of potentialities, even though they see this choice as necessarily a common, collective act, rather than a set of individual options.

What does Hegel have to say in the face of this development which he not only did not foresee, but arguably thought to be impossible? The answer is, in fact, a great deal. For although he did not foresee it, he understood a lot about its dynamic, as I argued above.

In fact the society of interchangeable free individuals is Hegel's 'heap'. He did not think such a society was viable, that is, it could not command the loyalty, the minimum discipline and acceptance of its ground rules, it could not generate the agreement on fundamentals necessary to carry on. In this he was not entirely wrong. For in fact the loyal co-operation which modern societies have been able to command of their members has not been mainly a function of the liberty, equality and popular rule they have incorporated. It has been an underlying belief of the liberal tradition that it was enough to satisfy these principles in order to gain men's allegiance. But in fact, where they are not partly 'coasting' on traditional allegiances, liberal, as all other, modern societies have relied on other forces to keep them together.

The most important of these is, of course, nationalism. Secondly, the ideologies of mobilization have played an important role in some societies, focussing men's attention and loyalties through the unprecedented future, the building of which is the justification of all present structures (especially that ubiquitous institution, the party).

But thirdly, liberal societies have had their own 'mythology', in the sense of a conception of human life and purposes which is expressed in and legitimizes its structures and practices. Contrary to a widespread liberal myth, it has not relied on the 'goods' it could deliver, be they liberty, equality or prosperity, to hold its members loyalty. The belief that this was coming to be so is what underlay the notion of the 'end of ideology' which was fashionable in the late 'fifties.

But in fact what looked like an end of ideology was only a short period of unchallenged reign of a central ideology of liberalism. Once it came again under attack, its lineaments were once more in evidence. An important support of the liberal consensus was the view of man as primarily a producer, that is, engaged in moulding the raw material of nature and environment to suit his needs. The liberal (as against Marxist) variant of this sees man as first of all an individual productive agent. He has to enter into co-operation with others in the division of labour, but this co-operation is thought to be constantly subject to re-negotiation. The society of producers was thought to be free and responsive to its members because its relations were perpetually being negotiated. It was deemed creative and productive because of the scope for individual initiative.

Some were ready to adopt a picture resembling this as a neutral description of society, which gave indeed, the basis for the impending atrophy of ideology. But it in fact is as 'ideological' as any other, not for the unimportant reason that it fails to take account of some important facts: inequalities, imperfections, exploitations, but really because to see social relations in this way, and hence to try to make them over on this model, presupposes a certain view of man and the ends of life which is as contestable as any other. For instance it supposes that man's primary relation to the world is as a producer, that the main importance of nature for him is as raw material, that men primarily define their purposes as individuals, prior to and relatively independently of the matrix of negotiation, that the future, as project, should always be more significant for them than the past.

That the liberal consensus depended, in some countries at least, on a complex of views of this kind became evident when an important part of the rising generation ceased to believe in them. The coming of a generation which is losing this allegiance to the goal of conquering nature and affirming man through work and production, has precipitated a crisis. We can now see how powerless and ineffective mere delivery of the goods is to keep a society from inner division, deadlock and possible breakdown.

This experience reveals that liberal society, like any other, cannot hold together simply by the satisfaction of its members' needs and interests. It also requires a common, or at least widespread set of beliefs which link its structure and practices with what its members see as of ultimate significance. The liberal vision of a society of producers is a far cry from the traditional conceptions of a cosmic order which human society reflected. But it is similar to them in this respect, that it interprets society's institutions and practices in the light of the important goals of human life, and this interpretation both helps define and justify these institutions. The modern view is as much, or as little, an 'ideology' as the traditional ones.

But in this respect a functioning liberal society was not entirely a 'heap' in Hegel's sense. For its members were drawn together by a set of common meanings, expressed in their common institutions. A liberal society which is a going concern has a *Sittlichkeit* of its own, although paradoxically this is grounded on a vision of things which denies the need for *Sittlichkeit* and portrays the ideal society as created and sustained by the will of its members. Liberal societies, in other words, are lucky when they do not live up, in this respect, to their own specifications.

If these common meanings fail, then the foundations of liberal society are in danger. And this indeed, seems a distinct possibility today. The problem of recovering *Sittlichkeit*, of reforming a set of institutions and practices with which men can identify, is with us in an acute way in the apathy and alienation of modern society. For instance the central institutions of representative government are challenged by a growing sense that the individual's vote has no significance.

But then it should not surprise us to find this phenomenon of electoral indifference referred to in *PR*.[1] For in fact the problem of alienation and the recovery of *Sittlichkeit* is a central one in Hegel's theory and any age in which it is on the agenda is one to which Hegel's thought is bound to be relevant. Not that Hegel's particular solutions are of any interest today. But rather that his grasp of the relations of man to society – of identity and alienation, of differentiation and partial communities[2] – and their evolution through history, gives us an important part of the language we sorely need to come to grips with this problem in our time.

That Hegel did not foresee the development of modern society is of no moment.[3] What matters is that he had insight into one of its perennial, recurring problems, one which the protagonists of the trinity of 1789, liberty, equality, popular sovereignty, whether in their liberal or revolutionary variants, have largely tended to deny. For they have seen the concern about *Sittlichkeit*, the identification of men with their society as a larger life of which they are a part, as essentially an affair for conservatives or even reactionaries. The full establishment of a society of free and equal citizens was to solve of itself all problems of alienation and division. But now that one of the bases common to both liberalism and Marxism, the apotheosis of man as producer, is beginning to falter under the impact of ecological disaster and the false

---

[1] Hegel remarks (§ 311) that this is especially evident in large states 'since the casting of a single vote is of no significance where there is a multitude of electors'.
[2] Cf. the discussion of the previous chapter.
[3] Hegel's work, of course, contains almost no forecasts, for prediction is an activity closed to philosophy. I am talking, however, about his identification of the emerging traits of the modern period, in which he was importantly wrong in the way described above.

priorities of uncontrolled technological growth, we are being forced to reassess the foundations of our civilization and re-interpret our history. We can now see that the free and equal society, far from being the antidote to alienation, rather presupposes some deeply held common conceptions about the ends of life, and our relation to nature and history.

This puts us in a dilemma, not unlike that of Hegel and the Romantic age. We need to combine the seemingly incombinable. Once more, as with the Romantics, restoring a society with which we can identify must go along with a new stance towards nature. But we have to combine this recovered common sense of a relation to nature which is not purely exploitative with the free, equal individual of modern society. We need at once freedom and a post-industrial *Sittlichkeit*. This dilemma may be as insoluble as its Romantic predecessor. But this should not stop us trying. And any serious attempt must incorporate the language and insights of those which have gone before. Among these Hegel's is a giant.

PART V

ABSOLUTE SPIRIT

CHAPTER XVII

Art

1

The state is the highest realization of the human community on earth. We can say that it is the highest form of human life, if we consider life-forms as a whole. But it is not yet the highest realization of spirit. For the goal of Spirit is to come to a full, that means rational, knowledge of self. We can see the state as developing in history in conformity with a plan which culminates in this self-knowledge of *Geist*. We saw in Chapter XIV how the basic structures of the state can be deduced from the requirements of this culmination.

But this final stage of Spirit's self-realization cannot be provided by the state. True, the state is in a sense an expression of the Idea. It is the Idea embodied in a common mode of life. It is objective spirit. But what we need now is another mode of expression which will be a vehicle of self-understanding, of pure self-contemplation. And this takes us beyond the state whose achievement is rather to realize the Idea in practices and institutions.

And the self-knowledge of Spirit must go beyond the state in another respect as well. The political community is substance of a certain people at a given epoch. But the cosmic spirit which must come to recognize himself underlies not just my own community but all of history, and beyond this the whole universe.

What is needed therefore is a mode of consciousness, which is a consciousness of the whole, the Absolute, or the very basis of things. As Hegel puts it in the *Encyclopaedia*,

The thinking spirit of world history, in that it strips off at once the limitations of particular *Volkgeister* and its own reality, grasps its concrete universality and raises itself to the *knowledge of absolute spirit*, as of the ever real truth, in which knowing reason is free *für sich*, and necessity, nature and history only serve to reveal it and as vessels of its praise. (*EG*, §552)

This will be, of course, a mode of human consciousness, but in this man will be the vehicle of *Geist*, and this will become clear as this consciousness reaches its highest forms. This self-knowledge of God through man, Hegel calls absolute spirit. It is 'absolute' because it is the final, highest realization of Spirit, that for the sake of which all the rest comes to be, and in this sense the foundation. (For the absolute is 'essentially result' – *PhG*, 21.)

Absolute Spirit

Absolute spirit takes three forms, which are, in ascending order of adequacy, art, religion and philosophy.

Absolute spirit is thus higher than Spirit's realization in objective reality which has not yet come to full self-consciousness. But this is not to say that it comes to fruition after the state in history. On the contrary, both the state and the forms of absolute spirit go through a historical development from the most primitive to the highest forms. And their development is intertwined. The forward movement of each requires that of the others. We saw in Chapter XIV how men's concrete modes of life in the world had to reach a certain stage of rationality before they could be fit vehicles of the self-knowledge of *Geist*. And reciprocally, they must have reached a certain stage of religious and philosophical development if they are to be capable of sustaining a rational state. Thus Europe had to go through the Reformation before the rational law-state could be built. The Catholic variant of Christianity was not yet purified of its intrication with external forms, with sacraments and priestly power. Thus the Catholic church is led to fight the state for earthly supremacy instead of accepting that the earthly realization of the Christian community is in the state. Hence Catholic countries remain unpropitious ground for the modern state.

This also means that the higher dignity, as it were, of absolute spirit as the highest realization of *Geist* takes nothing away from the supremacy of the state. For true religion does not oppose the state, rather it underpins its authority as the highest realization of the Idea in a whole life-form. Of course, obedience to the state is an old injunction in Christendom, in honour above all in the Lutheran countries. But here the idea is not that the Church underpins the state as the regent of a less important world, while it turns its attention to higher things. The state is the highest realization in external, historical life; and also the essential locus in which the internal life of thought and self-understanding of Spirit takes place. Where the state is raw and undeveloped, the church cannot substitute for it, for in those ages Spirit's self-understanding, i.e., religious life, is also raw and undeveloped. The blind cannot lead the blind. (Of course, it attempts to do so, as we saw with the Medieval church; and this turns the mill of *Geist*. But this is another example of the cunning of Reason.) In fact, *Geist's* self-knowledge must fit harmoniously into the highest form of life attained by his vehicle, man.

2

Absolute spirit has three levels. The only fully adequate self-understanding of *Geist* is one which is couched in pure conceptual thought. In thought, Spirit is fully at home, it is fully self-transparent. The divine is 'in its truest form, in the element which is most its own, in the form of thought' (*I & I*, 154).

Hegel has a notion of conceptual thought as self-transparent which we find it hard to share today. Much of contemporary philosophy has been concerned

466

with showing how the clarity of our most explicit conceptual formulations reposes on a background of which we are not fully aware and which we can perhaps never exhaustively explore. Much that is implicit, for instance, in the very system of concepts or classifications that we use to formulate our clearest thought remains unstated and possibly unstatable. In very different ways, Wittgenstein, Heidegger, Polanyi and Merleau-Ponty, for instance, have explored this avenue of the limits of the explicit or of clear explanation. The important issue which is at stake between Hegel and contemporary philosophy will emerge more clearly below. For the moment, I would like to take Hegel's notion of total clarity as a reference point from which to account for the lesser modes of absolute spirit.

The full transparency of thought is found in philosophy. But in default of such clear concepts, and while groping on their way to them, men use unclear modes of representation. This was the domain for which Hegel used the term 'representation' (Vorstellung), which he opposes to thinking (Denken). In order to avoid confusion with the usual, more general sense of the term 'representation', I shall use the German word ' *Vorstellung*' for Hegel's term of art.

The domain of *Vorstellung* is the domain of religious thought. Here men think of God not in clear concepts but in images. These provide, as it were, a partly opaque medium which prevent us from grasping God and his relation to the world in full clarity. Their opacity comes from the fact that these images have a primary meaning by means of which they refer us to their ultimate meaning. Since the properties of the primary domain are not the same as those of the ultimate domain, the images are never fully adequate. Either they are misleading, or we have to make allowances, to leave a margin of the unexpressed, or the mysterious.

As an example we can take the Hegelian interpretation of the story of the Fall of man in Genesis. The fall properly understood is the movement whereby man turns against the universal, and affirms himself as a particular. This is represented in religious imagery, or *Vorstellung*, as the fruit of an act, the sin of Adam, which might not have happened, and which occurred at the beginning.

Now the speculative truth we are trying to express here is that man, as a finite spirit, has to turn away and be cut off from infinite spirit; that the very assertion of self as finite spirit requires this 'fall' (cf. *PhG*, Chapter VII). In other words, this is necessary and fundamental to finite spirit. But this truth cannot be said in full clarity until one has the philosophical language of necessity, finitude, infinity, universal, particular, and so on. In the cruder medium of a *narration*, the necessary and fundamental comes out as something which happened temporally at the *beginning*, but which has great and lasting consequences. Given the properties of the primary domain here, which is a narrative of action, this is the only way we can render the insight that something is fundamental to the relation of man and God.

Of course, once Hegelian philosophy comes along to interpret Christian theology, we can distinguish clearly what the properties of this inadequate medium are and how much it distorts. But those who are entirely immersed in religious consciousness without benefit of philosophy cannot grasp its limits. Either they take it as undistorted truth (e.g., take the Bible literally), or they recognize that something is left unsaid, and conclude that God is to this extent unknowable.

Vorstellung is thus below thought, and religion is a less adequate level of absolute spirit than philosophy. But it is not the lowest level. For *Vorstellung* is still thought in a broad sense, that is, it is an inner representation in ideas of the reality, even if the ideas are interlaced with images and unclear. And in this way, it partially meets the demands of *Geist*, which as spiritual strives to know itself in the inwardness of thought. But there is a still lower level, where the images instead of being in inner thought, deployed in a discourse of myth or theology, are simply out there in the world, in sensuous form, as objects of intuition.

Now when the absolute, *Geist*, or the truth that the world emanates from Spirit, is presented out there in sensuous reality, we have the domain of art. This is what art is, in Hegel's view. No matter what the subject of a work of art is in the ordinary sense, the quality of beauty, that which draws us and delights us, comes from the manifestation of the Idea which it embodies in sensuous form. Beauty is the 'sensible manifestation of the Idea' (das sinn-liche Scheinen der Idee, *I & I*, 163). In its journey from unconsciousness to perfect self-knowledge, Spirit must start here, with a mode of consciousness which is purely intuitive, and bound up with the external and sensuous.

Now in speaking of art as a sensuous presentation of the Idea, or as the 'intuitive consciousness of absolute spirit' (*I & I*, 151), is Hegel returning to the traditional notions of aesthetic according to which art is primarily to be understood as mimesis, or imitation of the real? Most decidedly not. Hegel has in fact incorporated the aesthetic theories of Kant and Schiller, as well as the new departures of the *Sturm und Drang*, and builds his views on them.

Kant in his third critique strongly rejected the presumption of the Wolffian Enlightenment, expressed in the works of Baumgarten, that art is to be understood as a mode of confused (that is, non-distinct) cognition. Kant rejects both this intellectualist aesthetic and that of sensationalists, like Hume and Hutcheson, who would relate aesthetic experience to the human psyche and its capacities of sensation. The aesthetic experience, Kant argued, is the experience of pleasure which comes from the harmony between imagination and understanding when we contemplate an object. Certain objects by their form exhibit, as it were, an effortless accord with our understanding.

But against the intellectualists Kant holds that this accord is not accompanied by a concept; it does not involve subsuming the object under a concept. It is not a mode of knowing. Against the sensationalists he argues that this pleasure is not a satisfaction which relates to our de facto needs and desires. It is quite disinterested. It is not a pleasure we take in the possession, or even in the existence of the object, but purely in the play of our faculties of representation which it occasions. And it is valid a priori, for it relates to the a priori structure of the faculty of knowledge itself. The aesthetic judgment of beauty is paradoxically both subjective (not involving knowledge) and universally valid (a priori).

We have already seen how much Hegel's philosophy as a whole owes to Kant's third critique, both directly and via Schiller's work. It will come as no surprise that his aesthetics is particularly indebted to both. Hegel too sees beauty arising where the sensuous and the ideal come together. He too sees the work of art as exhibiting a finality (Zweckmäßigkeit), and he agrees with Kant that this finality cannot be explained by an external purpose, like well-being, that the work of art serves; nor can we impose on it a conceptual definition of the purpose, for this on Hegel's view would take us out of the domain of art. Hegel in other words has incorporated Kant's paradoxical formulation about the work of art as exhibiting a 'finality without purpose' (Zweckmäßigkeit ohne Zweck). Indeed, this formulation is one of the sources of the central Hegelian category of internal teleology.

For this is the idea of an entity exhibiting a purpose which is not external to it, but rather where the life of the whole is the purpose by which we account for any partial process. This internality of purpose figures in Kant's notion of the beautiful object, for it is beautiful not in virtue of any utility. This is part of what he means by 'finality without purpose'. It reflects his rejection of psychologistic theories and his defense of the disinterestedness of aesthetic experience. But Kant's phrase also contains the anti-intellectualistic point that no conceptual formulation of the finality of an object of beauty is possible. This idea re-appears transformed in the Hegelian category of Internal Teleology in the notion that Spirit only comes to an adequate definition of self through the perfection of its external embodiment. In other words no adequate conceptual definition can be given of the Idea which is not manifest in its embodiment. Thus the teleology of *Geist* is internal not only in the sense that no external purpose is served, but also in the sense that no prior external definition of the purpose is possible. *Geist*'s embodiment in a rational universe is not only the fulfilment of his rationally necessary plan, the Idea, but also the paradigm expression of what that purpose is, which cannot be pre-empted by merely conceptual formulation, but whose perfection philosophy must follow, as the owl of Minerva taking wing at dusk.

Hegel's category thus supplements Aristotle with an idea drawn from Kant, finality without purpose; and he supplements Kant with the expressivist theory, which we explored in the first chapter. So that finality without purpose becomes the 'self-purpose' (Selbstzweck) of Hegelian philosophy, which Hegel applies to those realities which must be seen as paradigm expressions of their own ends, which include the state as well as works of art.

Thus Hegel's ontology has one of its roots in Kant's aesthetic. And this while bringing him close to Kant's theory of art is the source of their divergence. For Hegel art is a vehicle of ontological vision. Kant most of the time[1] wants to see the beauty of objects as something quite unconnected with what we see in or through them.

But in this Hegel is not returning to the intellectualist tradition or the view of art as mimesis. Art is a *mode of consciousness* of the Idea, but it is not a *representation* of it. The distinction which comes to Hegel out of the expressivist revolution in thought underlies his theory of art.

Let us see more clearly what is involved in this distinction. We saw in the previous part how practices could be seen as the expression of certain ideas, unmatched by any parallel attempts at conceptual formulation. In this sense a certain practice of decision by voting and representative assemblies can be seen as embodying certain ideas about will, the individual and his relation to society, for which we might have no adequate theoretical formulation. It could thus be seen as a mode of (not explicitly formulated) consciousness of ourselves as individuals in society, which was not however a *representation*, that is, a description or portrayal of us as individuals in society, or indeed of anything at all.

But as we have already seen, these manifestations of objective spirit while being defensibly classed as modes of consciousness are not vehicles of understanding, or contemplation. The consciousness is one merely implicit in action and the norms of action. But at the highest level Spirit has to come to self-contemplation. Is there a mode of contemplative consciousness which is not representation?

The answer is that there is, and it is art. A Bach cantata, for instance, conveys a certain vision of God, of Christ and man's salvation. But it does not portray, describe or offer a representation of these. The only thing it might be

[1] This qualification is necessary, because Kant's third critique also flirts with another doctrine. Besides the central thesis that the judgement of taste tells us nothing about the world but is based on an accord of our faculties of representation, there appears towards the end of the discussion on aesthetics another view. Thus (§49) spirit (Geist) is defined as the capacity to present 'aesthetic ideas', and 'aesthetic idea' is explained as 'a representation of the imagination which gives much food for thought (viel zu denken veranlaßt), without any particular determinate thought, i.e., concept, being adequate to it; which thus no form of words can fully render and make understandable (die folglich keine Sprache völlig erreicht und verständlich machen kann). On this view, great art, art with spirit, would be prized for its depth of vision which goes beyond what words could express. These two doctrines can be made compatible, but the result is quite different from what Kant's central thesis is usually thought to be, and closer to Hegel.

thought to portray is a man praying. But this would be wrong too. It does not portray prayer. One might be tempted to say it *is* prayer. But this is not so either, however much it may owe its origin to prayer-forms (as more obviously, a setting of the Mass does). For we listen to it, and though we may be inspired by it to pray, and make of it a prayer, it can just be listened to. It is a kind of presentation of prayer, and through that of man's relation to God, which we can contemplate. If it were a prayer-form or a rite, the consciousness of God would be implicit in a practice, as with the manifestations of objective spirit above. But as a work of art, in the modern sense, it is offered as something to contemplate, in this case hear.

The fact that a cantata can only with difficulty be thought of as portraying *anything* is not the important point here. For a similar point can be made about, e.g., a painting of the Crucifixion, which clearly does portray something, viz., Christ on the Cross. It may be said of a given painting that it presents a vision of God or of suffering, but this is not what is portrayed in any straightforward sense. The only temptation to speak of these as portrayed comes from the fact that something is represented, the man on the cross, and the deeper vision can be thought of as shown through this. But this temptation disappears altogether with a work like a cantata.

An analogous point can be made about a novel, which narrates and hence portrays action and feeling, but which can present a vision which goes beyond these. Even if Tolstoy had not added passages of theoretical exposition to *War and Peace*, we would still take from it his vision that great men do not design and control history as their admirers think, that they are rather thrown up on the crest of deeper waves. But this is not described in the novel, as the actions and thoughts of the characters are.

This underlies the Hegelian view of the distinction between art and the higher levels of absolute spirit. Both philosophy and religious *Vorstellung* are representations (in the broad sense, not the particular Hegelian usage). They characterize the absolute in declarative sentences which are intended as correct description. On one level, at least, it is clear what they say, the level of the actual words they use, although their recourse to images may raise difficulties of interpretation when we want to go further – as we find in fact with religious *Vorstellung*.

By contrast the work of art does not 'say' anything in a straightforward sense at all. The message or vision is one we see in it, and any statement of its content is the fruit of interpretation and subject to challenge and perpetual reformulation.

The central contrast between conceptual description and artistic presentation of the absolute can thus be seen in this way: in philosophy my awareness of the absolute is couched in concepts, the inner, transparent vehicles of thought whose function is to point beyond themselves to a domain of objects they correctly portray or characterize. In art, my awareness is embodied in a work, an external, sensuous object, which by no means simply refers me beyond itself to something it describes, but rather lets us see the absolute only through its presence as a sensuous object. In descriptive discourse, we frequently remember what was conveyed while forgetting the words used or even what language was spoken. But the 'message' of a work of art does not survive the eclipse of its sensuous medium, or only in an emasculated way.

Religious *Vorstellung* would then be intermediate between the two extremes. Like philosophy it talks of God in declarative, descriptive sentences. But it uses images, like art, in which the absolute is portrayed only through the properties of another domain.

Hence art is lower than philosophy or religious *Vorstellung* because it does not characterize or describe the absolute, but only bodies forth an awareness of it which is non-representative. Hegel speaks of it not as ' *Vorstellung* ' (representation), but ' *Darstellung* ' (presentation), or as ' *Scheinen* ' (showing forth or manifesting) of the Idea in sensible form (Gestalt). The work of art has a certain inner luminosity, as it were. It manifests the spiritual at every point on its surface, through its whole extent. Everything in it is there in order to show forth the Idea.

That is why the work of art is incomparably higher than the works of mere nature however much we may have been misled by the theory of art as imitation to praise the works of nature as higher than those of man. It is true of course that nature is an embodiment of spirit in sensuous form. In particular a living being is such an embodiment, and at the summit, man is the highest. But this is still not the same as art. Even the most perfect human form still has much in it which is purely contingent, that is, not rigorously necessary to its vocation of embodying *Geist*. And even in regard to what is necessary, the necessity is not manifest, it is inner; that is, it is discovered by thought, but is not there on the surface of things. Before natural living beings, we come to a 'presentiment' (Ahnung) of the concept, but we have no clear manifestation of it (*I & I*, 168–86).

In order to have such a sensuous manifestation men have to create a work of art. This is thus not simply an imitation of nature, of which the most perfect realization would be simply another specimen of what is portrayed. Art leaves something out, but it does so with the aim of creating an object which in all its aspects makes apparent the necessity of *Geist*. A work of art is thus inhabited totally by an inner necessity; and Hegel speaks of it as *Selbstzweck*. The inner necessity means that all parts exist for the sake of embodying the whole message. But this message is not beyond it, but in it. We have thus a case of inner teleology; the art work is to be compared to the living being. And Hegel as we saw, adopts Kant's formula, in seeing in the work of art a 'finality without purpose' (Zweckmäßigkeit ohne Zweck). But unlike the organism, it is fully manifestation, it is nothing but manifestation of the Idea. It is free infinity (*I & I*, 166). What a living being is in reality, in itself, the art work shows forth. Its entire existence is to show this inner necessity forth. To see this fully manifest in the sensuous exalts us. It is the beautiful. And because the sensuous is here to manifest the Idea, art is 'disinterested', the sensuous in art is not an object of desire (*I & I*, 65, 167).

Because art is merely presentation and not a representation of spirit our vision in art will always defy exact definition. And for the same reason it will always lack the reflective clarity of the higher levels. When we describe by declarative sentences, we can reflect on the descriptive terms we apply, clarify their criteria, and hence our grounds for their use. But the artist cannot be that clear about why he uses this pattern, or tone or word. If he has articulated reasons for these, they will generally refer to the aesthetic force of this or that alternative, not to the truth of the embodied vision.

Thus in art we reach a vision of things which is maximally unreflective, unaware of what underlies the coherencies it embodies in the work. The artist follows a 'necessity' which he cannot grasp, and Hegel speaks of 'the inspiration of the artist' as 'a force foreign to him' (eine ihm fremde Gewalt, *EG*, §560). Considered a revealer of deep truths, the artist walks as though in a dream. He is a somnambulist. Reflective unclarity matches the enigmatic, disputable nature of what is said.

This lack of definition of the message is essential to art. Hegel points out that a work of art which is merely meant to say something which is already clear in thought is without interest. In other words, lack of definition and reflective unclarity are essential to art because it is a mode of consciousness embodied in an external work, rather than in the inwardness of conceptual description. Where we are conceptually clear, the work is superfluous. It becomes, as Hegel says, an empty husk (*I & I*, 44). Greek poetry and art is great because it was not rendering a teaching which was already abstractly formulated in 'universal religious propositions', but rather because the poets 'could work what fermented in them into external expression only in this form of art and poetry' (*I & I*, 152).

Because our awareness of the absolute is tied in this way to an external object, Hegel speaks of art as the 'intuitive' level of consciousness of Spirit (*I & I*, 151; *EG*, §556). And this is why absolute spirit must go beyond the level of art. It is still caught in external, sensuous reality. It is not yet fully '*bei sich*' in its own element, which is thought. In thought, one's ideas follow a necessity one understands, rather than one which is obscure and enigmatic. In this sense, thought is free, and man as a spiritual being is only free when he thinks (Im Denken bin ich frei, *PhG*, 152). For he follows a necessity which springs from itself. Spirit will thus have to go beyond art to a more 'spiritual' (geistig) unity with nature in thought (*EG*, §557).

473

This according of primacy to conceptual clarity is of course consistent with Hegel's basic ontology. But it gives a decisive twist to his theory of art. And this seems to align him again with the intellectualists. But Hegel as we saw was in no sense a protagonist of the kind of intellectualism we find with Wolff and Baumgarten. On the contrary he was the heir of both Kant and the *Sturm und Drang*. A work of art was not a confused representation, but rather a mode of consciousness which is not representative.

Hegel owed this idea to the developing expressivist current of thought. Prior to this consciousness was always thought of as representative. A good illustration of the shift involved in expressivist thought can be found in Herder's reflections in his essay *On the Origin of Language*. Previously, as Herder points out, the problem of learning language was seen as one of co-ordinating signs and things. But this is to take the relation of referring between signs and things for granted as something already understood. And this is precisely the most problematic thing in language.

So Herder turns his attention to the birth of linguistic consciousness, the kind of awareness of things which grasps them through signs. This makes us look on language in a completely new light. Instead of seeing it as an assemblage of signs co-ordinated with things, we see it rather as the necessary embodiment of a certain form of consciousness, which in this case is that form in which there are such things as signs for us.

But once one comes to see the external embodiments of thought not just as referential signs, but as vehicles of different forms of consciousness, there is no reason why one cannot see these forms as extending beyond representative ones, where we use terms to describe something. Hence we can come to see the work of art not just as obscure representation, but as the vehicle of another kind of awareness.

Now seeing the expressions of thought as embodiment of different kinds of awareness opens a second dimension in our consideration of language, and a second type of relation to the extra-linguistic reality it is meant to express. The obvious such relation is the representative one. Words describe or characterize something. They are faithful to this to the extent that they correctly portray it, that what we assert with them corresponds to what is the case.

But as an embodiment of awareness, a given formulation in words can also be related to the dim, pre-linguistic hunch or intimation which it is meant to express. Here, too, there is a question of fidelity to an extra-linguistic term. But this is not a matter of correct portrayal. We are not trying to describe the hunch – this would be very difficult, perhaps impossible – but to explicit faithfully and make clear what it intimates.

Now sometimes both these dimensions are relevant. Following an initially unclear intuition we elaborate a new descriptive language, and what we say in this corresponds well or badly, more or less with what is the case. But it can be that the descriptive dimension does not apply. And this is what we see with the work of art as understood above. For this, too, attempts to render faithfully an initially obscure inspiration. In doing so, it brings it to open expression and hence to a higher level of awareness. And yet it is not to be judged as description or portrayal.

The work of art renders something, is faithful to something. But what it is faithful to it does not describe. If this initial inspiration can be thought of as a sense of reality, or of the Absolute, then the work of art is a vehicle of higher awareness of reality or the Absolute. It is non-arbitrary, it results from a striving to render something faithfully and fully and in its entire depth. But it is not description. It is not to be judged by correspondence, since the initial dim, implicit sense is quite incommensurable with the articulate expression of insight.

This is the background on which Hegel draws for his conception of the work of art. But there is a crucial difference in the way he develops it from the way it has been developed in the post-Romantic period. Hegel insists on the primacy of clarity, which means ultimately of the descriptive dimension. This in a sense wins through to supremacy in the development of absolute spirit.

If we use the word 'disclosure' (following Heidegger) for the bringing to overt expression of what is at first merely intuitive intimation, then we can say that disclosure by itself, no matter how much it heightens awareness, is always surrounded with a horizon of lesser clarity. Perhaps our formulation is clear, or our work imposing, but the question remains, have we rendered the original inspiration faithfully? And to answer this we have to return to the half-light of our original, inarticulate intuition. Even the clarity of descriptive discourse is won initially through achievements of disclosure, in which we win through to a rigorous, adequate descriptive language. The question thus always remains, on its margins as it were, whether the way this language distinguishes and classifies things is really illuminating, whether it does not distort or occlude some important aspect of reality. If we focus on disclosure, we must see all clarity, all explicit, articulate thought, as surrounded by a horizon of the unclear, implicit, inarticulate.

This has been the turn of much contemporary philosophy, including the philosophers I mentioned above – though each would formulate things very differently. For Polanyi or Heidegger, for instance, even a clear descriptive language, in which our most explicit, distinct, unambiguous thoughts may be couched, has, as one way of classifying reality among others, as one among many possible 'grids', a host of implications of which we can never be fully aware. And these form the horizon of the unclear, the non-focal, which surrounds our explicit consciousness.

Of course, if we think of consciousness as only and always representative, then this whole dimension of disclosure and the accompanying horizon of the implicit is without meaning. This is the case with much empiricist thought, as with the intellectualist tradition of the Enlightenment. For both of these, descriptive discourse is not an achievement. Attaining clarity about the world involves only overcoming confusion in our representations.

But this was not Hegel's view. He took the essential notions of expressivist theory and built his philosophy on them. And yet he claimed that philosophy can and must attain to total clarity. This represents an important difference from the whole thrust of contemporary philosophy, which we shall discuss further in Chapter xx.

Hegel allows for the dimension of disclosure. He sees conceptual clarity as an achievement, won through the forging of a more and more adequate descriptive language, and the transposition into the clarity of representative thought of insights originally expressed in non-representative consciousness. Our consciousness of the Absolute is thus first of all obscure, enigmatic. It is a disclosure which is not sure of having rendered faithfully its original inspiration or intuition. But it climbs to the point where it is totally clear, where even the original horizon of unclarity is dissipated. And this it does because the zone of conceptual clarity extends itself and ultimately takes in even the original inarticulate intuition. For this is ultimately seen itself to be conceptually necessary. The Idea as result must grow out of the merely implicit and undeveloped. But this necessary unfolding is itself part of the formula of rational necessity which is the Idea. Hence the inarticulate beginning is itself shown in the end to be deduced from the Idea.

Thus in Hegel's system even the obscure and inarticulate is ultimately captured in the net of clear conceptual description. In the end description is totally victorious and swallows up the conditions of its own impure birth. The circle of necessity as we saw reaches back to recuperate its starting point. Spirit ultimately encounters only itself. This achievement of total clarity is essential to Hegel's ontology, and it is this which is finally at issue in the turn of contemporary philosophy, as we shall see in our concluding discussion below.

3

Art, as a form of absolute spirit, goes through its development in history. And here, its finest hour was the age of Greek civilization. For it was in this period when art first came to an adequate presentation of the Idea, while at the same time, no higher representation was yet attainable.

The only adequate sensuous form for the Idea is finally the human, for man is spirit. This the Greeks won through to, and their art is thus the art of the freedom of Spirit perfectly in harmony with its embodiment in man. This is the great period in which the Gods are understood in human form.

Before that men still struggled with a vision of the absolute as something sublime (erhaben) and beyond, something which could not really be given sensuous form. Hence the forms which were used – for instance, animal forms – were used as symbols, to hint at an absolute that could not properly be figured. And since the sense of the incommensurability of symbolic stuff and Idea symbolized was always pressing on them, the artists of pre-Greek religions distorted the forms they used, and created fantastic beings, e.g., half animal, half bird, giants and monsters, and so on, so that we are conscious of the boundlessness, measurelessness (das Maßlose) in the absolute. Hegel speaks of this 'symbolic art' as characteristic of oriental religion in general (*I & I*, 114–17), but what he is mainly thinking of here is Egyptian art. Hegel saw this as a struggle to win through to a vision of Spirit as free, a vision which finally comes triumphantly through with the Greek understanding of God in man-like form, of God thus as free subjectivity, and not simply sublime substantial force. This is the portrayal of Egyptian religion in the discussion in Chapter VII of *PhG*. But this struggle was a completely unreflecting one. It was a groping towards new art forms, and hence men were unconscious that what they groped towards was a higher vision of the Idea.

Men first win through to a vision of the absolute as free subjectivity, and hence as a reality in which man is at home, in Greek civilization, and this comes in the form of a presentation (Darstellung) of God in human shape. But this vision is won, not by the elaboration of a higher theology, but rather by groping through to an art form which for the first time is adequate to the nature of the absolute as Spirit, as subjectivity. We thus have an 'art-religion'. Hegel applies this term to Greek religion, not only because it is the first to find an adequate art-representation of the absolute as Spirit, but also because it is the last which relies principally on art. The religions that succeed the Greek will no longer consider art as the paradigm medium of their consciousness of the absolute. This will now be in 'religion', that is, theology and myth; art will be accorded only an ancillary role, a secondary illustration of what can only be grasped in spirit, in inward understanding. Indeed, some branches of this higher religious stream – Judaism and Islam – will refuse representational art altogether as idolatrous.

The fact that art-religion comes to its highest fruition with the Greeks is of course not unconnected with the fact that it is here on the verge of super-cession. This is the way the Spirit works, as we have seen. And we have already explored some of the inadequacies which make this supercession inevitable. The bringing of the Godly into harmony with the human is achieved at the cost of particularizing it, so that there are many Gods, and the absolute power over all remains behind them in the form of a fate to which even they are subject. On man's side, his sense of one-ness with the substantial comes through his identification with such a particular visage of the divine. Greek man is parochial. He has not yet attained reflection and universal subjectivity.

The universal reflective subject attains to a higher notion of the one absolute God as united to man, in Christ. But this unity is not immediate, rather it moves through the necessary suppression of the first unity in Christ through Resurrection/Ascension and return in the form of the Holy Ghost which dwells in the community. This dialectical unity cannot be fully manifested adequately in art, unlike the immediate unity of the Godhead with some particular form in Greek polytheism. Hence the absolute religion, Christianity, cannot be an art-religion. Art can have a part here, but it is subordinate to thought – thought, that is, in the general sense where it englobes both conceptual and imaged discourse. The absolute religion has to be inwardly understood in discourse.

Art again becomes symbolic, in the sense that it is once again not adequate to the Idea and knows itself as such. But whereas before it was the only medium which was struggling towards adequacy impelled by a dim inarticulate sense of the boundless, now we have an adequate vision of the absolute as subject in a higher medium than art.

Hence the new art is free as it formerly was not. It is free and can give itself over to the 'adventures of fantasy' (Abenteuern der Phantasie, *I & I*, 123). Since in the modern age, particular subjectivity attains to its full rights, and the absolute lord of all is known to be subjectivity, the actions of particular men win their significance for art. (This is a parallel point to that of the modern age having transcended the need for oracles.) This phase of art since the Christian era Hegel calls 'Romantic art'.

Thus the Idea shows us how art develops in history according to a necessary pattern. Its necessity can similarly be traced in the different art forms, which have an affinity to different stages. Architecture, being the wielding of the massive in non-figurative form, corresponds to the period of symbolic art. Here it is paramount. But then the preparation of the perfect temple calls forth the representation of the God. This, which comes to its highest point with the Greeks, corresponds to a paramountcy of sculpture.

So now the temple is erected for the God; his house stands ready, external nature has been wrought into shape, and suddenly it is pierced by the lightning bolt of individuality. The God stands there in nature, it exhibits him: the statue rises in the temple.

(*I & I*, 127)

Painting, music and poetry are more inward, they are not bound in the same way to three-dimensional external existence as their inescapable medium, as are architecture and sculpture. Painting deals in the 'abstract visible' (*I & I*, 131). Music is in sound which is already more ethereal; and poetry in words where sound rises to the spiritual reality of sign. These arts thus become paramount in the period of Romantic art.

Poetry is the highest form, where art is ready to go over into representation. The medium of poetry is language. Now when language ultimately attains to descriptive clarity, its properties as a physical medium cease to be important. It becomes entirely representative in the broad sense used here, that is, its function is only to focus our minds on the objects described and to characterize these correctly. Hence the actual sound or look of the word becomes irrelevant; whether we say 'chair' or 'chaise' or 'Stuhl', or any synonym in one of these or any other language, has no importance. All that matters is the descriptive meaning. The descriptive term becomes 'simply an indifferent sign without intrinsic worth' (gänzlich gleichgültiges und wertloses Zeichen, *I & I*, 133). The sensuous properties of our medium are no longer relevant, and we have transcended the domain of art.[1]

What can the place of art be in the new era? On one hand, the Romantic or Christian era has liberated fantasy; art can now portray the contingent, the subjective. But this is bound up with the fact that the Idea has found a higher mode of consciousness which art cannot match, religion and ultimately philosophy. So that art 'has ceased to be the highest need of spirit' (das höchste Bedürfnis des Geistes, *I & I*, 153). This applies to the whole modern era. But the situation of art will surely be aggravated when we win through in philosophy to a fully adequate expression of the Idea. Will art assume a secondary role, illustrating truths more clearly known in other media? Will it be to speculative philosophy what Church art was to Christian theology, with this major difference, that this theology never claimed to penetrate the mysteries of God or the Incarnation, and thus left art an endless frontier which the clarity of philosophy threatens to close?

The logic of Hegel's position seems to open this depressing prospect, on which he does not comment. Certainly this is not what he senses the future of art to be, as one can glean from his aesthetic writings. And here his instinct as a member of the Romantic generation was truer than his reason as a philosopher. For far from taking a second place in the spiritual life of modern man, art has taken over from religion in the lives of many of our contemporaries, in the sense that it is for them the highest expression of what is of ultimate importance, and/or the highest activity of man. And this by itself is an indication of how far we have moved out of the purview of Hegel's synthesis.

---

[1] What is why it seems strange that Hegel appears to attribute this transcendence of the sensuous medium to poetry, a view which is hard to credit not only in itself, but also in terms of Hegel's own theory. Cf. *I & I*, 133. It must be remembered that these are lecture notes, never prepared for publication by Hegel's own hand.

CHAPTER XVIII

Religion

1

And so we come to the second level, religion. This is the domain of *Vorstellung*, which is a more inward form of consciousness. It is in a sense an internalization of what is bodied forth in sensuous form in the arts. For *Vorstellen* makes use of images, of the sensuous and the pictorial.

But it makes use of them for a further purpose, that of portraying or characterizing the absolute. Religious thought is a representative mode of consciousness. It uses sensuous images, but not just to contemplate their sensuous referents, rather as symbols which strain to render a higher content. This description of a higher domain in images drawn from a lower one is typical of religious thought. For instance, the necessary self-diremption of the Idea or universal is rendered in theology by the image of begetting: God begat his Son before all ages. Of course everybody understands that this is not to be understood in the normal sensuous way, but rather that it is being used to refer beyond to something supersensible.

Vorstellung is thus a mode of consciousness which is freeing itself, as it were, from the merely sensible in order to reach the universal. But it has not yet fully succeeded, it is still caught in the sensible, and must use sensible images. Of course, religion also makes use of conceptual thought. We sometimes find fully worked out philosophies within a theological context, as for instance with the Church fathers or the scholastics (*GPhil*, 169). But almost always we find a mixture of sensible images and universal concepts, such as 'almighty', for instance (op. cit., 171).

But what religion lacks even in its purer formulations is the grasp of the inner necessity which unites the articulations of the Idea and brings them back to unity. It takes two essentially related determinations and simply narrates them as following each other in time – such as, for instance, the creation of man and his fall, or the different stages of the creation. *Vorstellung* simply *narrates* (erzählt, *BRel*, 297); it does not show the inner connections. This will be the task of thought.

But religion as a level of absolute spirit, that is, of *Geist*'s self-consciousness, is not simply a set of representations of the absolute, or of God. These are essential to it, and Hegel argues here against the Romantic spirituality of a Jacobi or a Schleiermacher, who wanted to displace the centre of religion onto the devotion of the worshipper, and stressed the unknowability of God. Hegel can understand this reaction to the Enlightenment – indeed, in a certain way he shared it in his early years, in the 1790s, as his writings of the time testify[1] – but he utterly rejects this flight into the subjective.

For Romantic faith remains caught in some of the central assumptions of the Enlightenment. It remains focussed on the finite subject and his freedom, and it accepts the conclusions of Enlightenment epistemology that nothing can be known about God. Hence it turns to a worship of God which is pure feeling, a God about whom nothing can be known but that he is. The entire accent of the faith is displaced onto the devotion of the worshipper. And this, argues Hegel, is outside the very concept of what religion is.

What is this concept of religion, why does it require a representation of God, and what does it require more? From a speculative point of view, religion is a mode of Spirit's self-knowledge.

God is God only insofar as he knows himself; his self-knowledge of himself is moreover his self-consciousness in man, it is man's knowledge *of* God that goes on to become the self-knowledge of man *in* God. (*EG*, § 564)[2]

In other words God comes to knowledge of himself through man's knowledge of him. Man is God's vehicle of self-consciousness. But then if God is *Geist* in the Hegelian sense, he is essentially determined to self-knowledge. And if this self-knowledge is vehicled by man's knowledge of God, then the idea of a religion whose God is unknowable is directly counter to the very essence of religion. Against the Romantic religion of devotion, Hegel will insist that God is essentially determined to manifest himself, or as in the quote above, 'God is God only in so far as he knows himself.'[3]

Of course, this process of self-knowledge is one which is slowly and painfully realized through history; for it is part of the self-realization of *Geist*. And in the early stages, God's self-consciousness will be very rudimentary and inadequate, very distorted one might even say. But even in this primitive form, it is recognizably a consciousness of God, and hence is more authentically religion than the Romantic aberration. It is essential, therefore, to religion to represent God. But this is not all of religion. For what is being represented is the absolute, the ground of all, including ourselves as finite spirits, and moreover an absolute which is not finally separate from us, but of which we are the vehicles. Now this understanding of our relation to the absolute, separate and yet in the end also identical, is not present in religious representation as such; in any event, not as a clear idea, for then we would be in the realm of

---

[1] Cf. Chapter II.
[2] Cf. *BRel*, 302–3. 'Die Religion ist das göttliche Wissen, das Wissen des Menschen von Gott und Wissen seiner in Gott.'
[3] This explains Hegel's seemingly excessive remark about Romantic devotion, that it was less worthy of being considered a manifestation of religion than a primitive nature-cult.

thought, and would have transcended *Vorstellung* and hence religion. But it must be there in some form. And in religion it comes in the form of devotion (Andacht).

The Romantics are thus not all wrong. They have left out an essential element, but they have hold of one of the dimensions of religion. For religious consciousness has to have a sense that this absolute is not just an object to which we are indifferent; it obscurely senses that this is a being with whom we are designed to be in some way united. Hence the believer not only has a vision of God, he longs for union with him. He is moved to devotion to the divine. Of course, the fact is that we are not only ultimately united with the infinite subject; it is also true that we are as finite cut off from it. The whole speculative truth is that the union is only made through a return out of division (Entzweiung). This is just what is sensed in religious devotion: that we are divided from God, from whom we should nevertheless not be divided; hence that we long to return to union with him.

Religion thus has two dimensions: a representation of God, and a powerful sense of separation from him which the believer longs to overcome. But there is also a third dimension: the cult. Religion is not just the locus of this consciousness and longing, but it also englobes the way that man strives to overcome this separateness. This is the essence of cult.

In cult, man overcomes his separation from God, his own subjectivity, the finite side of him which cuts him off from the infinite. He overcomes it by giving it up. Cult contains an element of sacrifice, and in many specific cults there is a real external sacrifice, something is really given up, or burnt. At the same time as man gives up his own separate subjectivity, and frees himself in sacrifice from his attachment to finitude, God becomes real in him: the sacrifice thus will often end with a communion meal, in which man is at last united with God.

Cult is thus the essential third dimension of religion: not only a representation of the absolute, not only an awareness of separateness and the vocation of unity, but a means of realizing this unity, even if only intermittently and never definitively. And this cult must not be seen as simply the act of man; God comes to self-knowledge through man, and man's unity with God is also God's returning to harmony with himself, Hence the work of reconciliation is not only man's but God's; and this not just in the sense that God also acts in response to man, but also that God himself lies behind man's act. In terms of the theology of the 'absolute religion', we are pushed to worship by the Holy Ghost. In the end, cult is not two acts, but a single act which unites two subjects. The contradiction of theology between salvation by God's grace and by human freedom is resolved, or rather, reconciled in the Hegelian speculative system.

It is because religion must be seen in these three dimensions that Hegel distinguishes his philosophy of religion from the old natural theology.[1] This latter was concerned only with our knowledge of God, that is, only with the first dimension. But, Hegel claims, we are led ineluctably to the wider study from the very idea of God itself, once we understand it speculatively. For God cannot be considered apart, on his own. To do so is to remain on the level of understanding. God must come to self-consciousness, and this he does only in the community of believers, the cult community.

The concept of God is his Idea, to become and to make himself objective for himself. This is intrinsic to God as *spirit*: God is essentially in his community [Gemeinde], he has a community, is an object for himself [ist sich gegenständlich], and is this truly only in self-consciousness; his highest determination is self-consciousness. The concept of God thus leads necessarily of itself to religion... *(BRel,* 156)

Religion is thus more for Hegel than a mode of consciousness of the absolute. This in a narrow sense only covers its first dimension. It is also a stance of the subject, and above all a praxis which has as goal to realize our unity with this absolute. This will raise a number of problems when we come to see how Hegel understands philosophy as recapitulating the content of religion in thought. For a question arises whether religion is really to be put on all fours with art and philosophy as ascending levels of consciousness of the absolute (and hence self-consciousness of the absolute), whether religion is not more than a mode of consciousness, or more than this in a sense which art and philosophy cannot match.

It is the dimension of cult which takes religion beyond simple consciousness. It is cult which realizes the unity, or restores the unity between finite and infinite spirit. But then this would seem to put it in the terrain of human practice, of the building of life-forms and actions which bring about reconciliation between man and *Geist.* In short it would seem to put it in the terrain of objective spirit as well. For we saw objective spirit as the domain of those collective life-forms and practices by which Spirit realizes itself, creates for itself a subject in history who will be capable of being vehicle of its self-consciousness; the actual self-consciousness achieved being the domain of absolute spirit. Religion seems to straddle this distinction, for cult is more on the side of life-forms and practices, and indeed in ancient civilization, cult was not separate from the other practices and institutions which were the polis.

If religion can be considered separately from the other institutions of objective spirit in the modern world, it is that it has itself introduced a gap. The locus of objective spirit is a people; it remains this in the modern just as much as in the ancient world. A people is gathered around its monarchy, its laws, its

[1] From the very beginning, of course, in his writings of the 1790s, Hegel was interested in religion much more as living piety than as theology. Hence the early distinction between subjective and objective religion (Cf. Chapter II). One might say that it was the mature Hegel who saw the importance of theology – suitably re-interpreted by philosophy.

representative institutions. But unlike in the ancient world, for the moderns, cult is not simply that of the people. It is in principle universal, and in practice goes beyond the boundaries of the state, while very often it fails to unite and hold all the citizens of any given political community. In this sense it stands somewhat aside from the institutions of the modern state. We shall see that while Hegel considers religion to have a crucial role in the rational state, he shies away from the idea of a confessional state. He takes the liberal line that men should take their place as citizens without regard to confession. He is even for giving full rights to Jews, which was very far beyond the conventional wisdom of his day. (*PR*, § 270). This principle of laicisation Hegel takes to be implicit in Protestantism. But this position also springs from the liberal-Enlightenment side of Hegel's thought, which looked to an ultimate convergence between faith and Enlightenment, a convergence to which the reinterpretation of religion in philosophy is essential. More of this later.

But if we think of the role of cult as that of bringing men back out of their finite subjectivity to unity with the universal, then this is not basically different from the institutions we saw under objective spirit. And thus it is not surprising to find Hegel saying

If heart and will are earnestly formed through and through up to the universal and the true, then we have in fact what we know as *Sittlichkeit*. To this extent, *Sittlichkeit* is the truest cult. (*BRel*, 236)

But Hegel goes on to add in the next paragraph: 'To this extent...*philosophy* is a perpetual cult.' (loc. cit.)

All this is very confusing. Of course, there is a clear sense in which philosophy is a way in which man returns to unity with *Geist*, through understanding. But Hegel's whole position is that this return in thought presupposes and demands a return in life and practice. The thought which returns cannot be disincarnate, but must be carried by a life which has been educated up to the universale. This life-form is that of developed *Sittlichkeit*. In this sense both can be thought of as cult, although the first presupposes and relies on the second. Philosophy, as inner understanding, is indeed thus a 'continuing cult'. It is not periodic and intermittent as the cultic practice of most religion. But in the sense of its being the central locus of man's effective union with the universal in life-practice, *Sittlichkeit* can indeed be called the 'truest' cult.

In short, the return of man to the universal must be accomplished in thought as well as in life. Indeed, it is not possible to return in life without one's thoughts being appropriately formed (gebildet). But reciprocally, this return in developed thought must be carried by a developed 'heart and will' and these are possible only in certain public institutions. Intellectual and life development are indissolubly linked.

But where does this leave religion? One can see a possible line of argument, based on Hegel's categories, which would leave it no place in the full flowering of Spirit. If religion is a union of man with the absolute, both in consciousness (via religious *Vorstellung*) and in effective practice (via cult), is it not surpassed in both its aspects, by philosophy (as a higher mode of Spirit's self-consciousness) and by the state (as a truly effective practice, a self-subsistent life-form, which no modern religious community can claim to be)? Would not the definitive human civilization substitute for the traditional amalgam of theology and cult a new combination of rational state and speculative philosophy?

Hegel in fact does not take this line. There are moments indeed, when he might seem to. For instance when he discusses the laicisation of the modern state, he takes a very tough line on the supremacy of the political society. Thus in *PR*, §270 Hegel makes clear that religion cannot see its vocation as in opposition to the truly rational state. For this is the real expression of right in the world. Rather religion should recognize that the state is a fulfilment of its fundamental idea, that it is 'the divine will, ...Spirit present on earth, unfolding itself to be the actual shape and organization of a world' (loc. cit., p. 166). The essence of what religion enjoins is given authoritative embodiment in the *Sittlichkeit* of the state. Without the concrete expression of ethical life in the state, the moral precepts of religion remain uncertain in their exact expression, underdetermined, and subjective in their application.

> In contrast with the church's faith and authority in matters affecting ethical principles, rightness, laws, institutions, in contrast with the church's subjective conviction, the state is that which knows. (p. 171)

Thus Hegel concludes that the state cannot be a confessional one. The state has to unfold its articulations out of its very concept. It has to be founded fully on reason, and hence cannot be grounded on mere faith in the truth, on a *Vorstellung* believed in by the instinct of reason only, which is all that even the fully true religion (Lutheran Protestant Christianity) can give. It must have an independent foundation in reason.

> If the state is to come into existence as the *self-knowing* ethical [*sittlich*] reality of *Geist*, it is essential that its form should be distinct from that of authority and faith. (p. 173)[1]

This secularization of the state Hegel remarks could only arise in history from the church's divisions, so that these far from being a misfortune provide another example of the cunning of reason.

But in fact Hegel does not think that religion is passé. Nor can this be simply dismissed as opportunism, a front designed to avoid the accusations of

---

[1] Knox translation amended.

atheism which had bedevilled Fichte and would certainly make an academic career impossible in the atmosphere of Restoration Germany. When Hegel claims to be a Lutheran Christian, one can certainly question whether his position really deserves this description, but not that he truly thought so himself.

We can see why religion has a continuing role if we remember that it has three dimensions, not only knowledge of God, not only cult, but also devotion, feeling. Religion unites man to the absolute in heart and sensibility. We recall that Hegel saw this as the vital function of religion at the very beginning of his intellectual career, in the Tübingen period, which is why he was looking for a religion which was not only rational but would also speak to 'heart, sensibility and fantasy'. And although he had come since then to see the crowning importance of philosophy, he never changed his mind about the irreplaceable role of religion. What altered rather was his appreciation of orthodox Christianity, which he now saw through the eyes of speculative philosophy as the absolute religion, rather than as a 'positive' aberration from the pure moral teaching of Jesus.

The reconciliation with the Absolute in philosophy pre-supposes one in life, as we saw. This is embodied in the state. But this cannot be achieved unless men are united to the Absolute in heart and feeling. Philosophy is, indeed, the late-comer. For although the properly articulated state is founded on reason, the final rational formulation of the Idea follows the entry onto the stage of history of the rational state (if only in 'general outline'; much of course remains to be done to complete it). But what the state inescapably requires, without which it cannot hope for effective reality (Wirklichkeit), is some instinctual sense of its rationality, of its irrecusable authority as founded on the Idea, in short some 'ethical conviction' (sittliche Gesinnung) on the part of its citizens. And this is grounded on religion.

The union with God which is philosophy thus requires the union with God in heart and feeling which religion provides; and this not just as a temporally prior stage which is destined to be left behind, but in a continuing way, since the union in thought can only continue if the union in life persists.[1] Thus while philosophy is higher than religion, in the sense that it understands both itself and religion while the converse is not true, it cannot replace religion as Hegel makes clear in this passage from the *GPhil*:

Philosophy is not opposed to religion; it grasps it in concepts. But for the absolute Idea, for absolute Spirit, the form of religion must be; for religion is the form of the consciousness of what is truly so as this consciousness is for all men. The cultivation of this consciousness [Bildung] involves: (1.) sensible perception, (2.) mingling universal form

[1] This is substantially the point made by Emil Fackenheim in his *Religious Dimension in Hegel's Thought*, Indiana University Press, 1967, 206–14, although my interpretation of Hegel's philosophy of religion differs from his.

Religion

with (1.), that is, reflection, thought, but an abstract kind of thought which still contains much externality. Then man goes over to the concrete mode of cultivation in thought, he speculates about what is truly so and becomes conscious of this in its true form. But this speculative activity which enters the process of cultivation at a certain point is not the externally universal form of thought which is common to all men. Hence the consciousness of what is truly so must [sc. also] have the form of religion.   (*GPhil*, 192)

What Hegel seems to be saying here is that the continuing necessity of religion is contingent on the fact that not all men can attain to full rationality. And this might tempt us to see religion as a kind of poor man's (or uneducated man's) substitute for philosophy, designed to keep the allegiance of those who cannot really understand. This is the impression one might glean from another sentence of the paragraph from *PR* quoted above (§ 270); 'since religion is an integrating factor in the state, implanting a sense of unity in the depths of men's minds, the state should even require all citizens to belong to a church' (p. 168. – Hegel hastens to stress '*a* church', since the state cannot interfere with the content of men's faith).

But to see religion as a means to keep the natives quiet would be seriously to misinterpret Hegel. The necessity of religion is not predicated on the inferiority of the masses, or their inability to attain the standards of rationality of an élite. On the contrary, differentiation is essential to the rational state as we saw, and every differentiated group is the vehicle of an essential aspect. Not all men can be philosophers because this requires dedication to a specialization which rules out other vocations and the development of other capacities. It is at base exactly the same exigency of specialization which prevents all men from being civil servants, or businessmen. Those who devote themselves to agriculture or trade cannot be specialist philosophers, any more than they can be functionaries of the universal class.

But this does not mean that the philosopher attains to a completeness which other men lack. This aristocratic ideal of all-round fulfilment is a mirage in the modern world, as Hegel keeps insisting. It died with the Greeks. The scope of modern humanity is too broad to be encompassed by a single man. Specialization is essential, and in a rational civilization, each speciality expresses an essential aspect of human life in which all others also participate in their way. Thus all men are in some way involved in the life of free individuality which is most fully expressed by the entrepreneurial class; all are related to the universal, although only one *Stand*, that of civil servants, devotes its career to this relation. Similarly, the non-philosophers have some inkling of the rationality that underlies things, and the philosophers also sense the absolute in heart and fantasy. As in the estates of political society, the development of each speciality is necessary to sustain the subordinate aspects of the other specialized modes of life. The philosopher's work is necessary if ordinary men are to have an inkling of the rational basis of things. And the un-

487

sophisticated religious devotion of the many is necessary if the philosopher is not to dry up.

In this sense the continued existence of religion is essential to man as such, philosopher and non-philosopher, in a fully developed civilization. And that is why 'in the nature of the case, the state discharges a duty by affording every assistance and protection to the church in the furtherance of its religious ends' (*PR*, § 270).

Religion thus remains essential as devotion to God. And we can readily understand from the foregoing how its mode of representation, *Vorstellung*, cannot be put behind us. But how about cult? Cult is essential to religion, because it is that by which I bring about the union with the divine which my devotion longs for. That is why it has always been so closely linked with sacrifice, since by sacrifice I surrender my particularity and unite with the universal. It is because cult is essentially this transcending of particularity and reunion with the universal that we can think of both philosophy and *Sittlichkeit* as a species of cult.

But it will now be clear from the above why there remains a place for religious cult beside or between these two. For the union with the Absolute in pure thought requires a union in heart and feeling as one of its standing conditions. But why can this need not be fulfilled by *Sittlichkeit?* Because man's reconciliation with the Absolute in the rational state is essentially parochial. He is reconciled with Spirit in its manifestation as particular *Volksgeist*. But man is called on to be the vehicle of a Spirit that strides beyond any particular *Volk*, that is master of all history and the necessity behind all nature. He must come to a sense of unity with Spirit at this level if this Spirit is to come to self-knowledge in man.

This shift to the universal, in the sense of cosmic, is one of the changes involved in the move from objective to absolute spirit as we saw in the last chapter. What I am suggesting here is that absolute spirit, man's relation to the cosmic *Geist*, requires a cult of heart, feeling and effective practice to underpin the cult of pure conceptual thought which is philosophy. This cannot be substituted for by *Sittlichkeit*. Rather, since our allegiance to the state is partly predicated on our sense that it is grounded in the Absolute, *Sittlichkeit* pre-supposes a healthy religious life, as we mentioned earlier.

Of course, in the ancient world the two cults, that relating to the polity and that relating to the divine, were fused. But that gives the measure of the parochial nature of ancient freedom. In the modern world with its consciousness of the individual as subject of universal reason, the two cults are necessarily differentiated. State and church can no longer be one. In a rational civilization the two cult-communities, if one can call them such, would not combat each other. On the contrary, each would sustain the other in the way Hegel describes in *PR*, § 270. But they would not be co-terminous. The church as universal would have members beyond the boundaries of any particular state. And since it appeals to free individual conviction, it would never command the unanimous allegiance of any given community. So that churches would be both narrower and wider than states.

Thus religious cult is not just a thing of the past. It retains its place in modern civilization. This is why Hegel defends (*AbsRel*, 210–15) the Lutheran view of the Eucharist not only against the Catholic interpretation but also against the conception of the Reformed Church. Against the Catholics, Hegel insists that God is not present in the host in a sensible, external, thingly way. Rather the transformation happens in the communicant as he communicates. God is present, but 'in spirit and faith' (Im Glauben auf geistige Weise, *AbsRel*, 214).[1] But against the Calvinists he insists that God is really made present, and not just remembered in 'a purely bodily form of remembrance of the past, devoid of spirit' (geistlose, nur leibhafte Erinnerung der Vergangenheit, loc. cit.). Hegel is not talking here about a rite of some past religion, but about the cult of the post-Reformation church to which he claimed to belong. The day of religion is far from past.

2

The religion which remains as the foundation of a rational civilization is, of course the 'absolute religion', Christianity. This is the culmination of the long, slow development of religion in history, which we shall examine in the next section. Christianity is the absolute religion because it presents the complete understanding of the ontological structure of things. It has the same content as philosophy; only its form is different, being that of *Vorstellung*.

Hegel will thus discover the principal tenets of his speculative philosophy in the major dogmas of Christian theology, thinly disguised by the images and symbols which are its medium of expression.

The dogma of the Trinity is ideal for Hegel's purposes. The Universal goes out of itself, undergoes self-diremption and engenders the particular (the Father begets the Son before all ages); and the particular nevertheless returns to unity with the Universal in a common life (the Holy Spirit proceeds from Father and Son and unites them). Thus Hegel sees deep speculative meaning in the notion of an eternal trinity, a play of love in the absolute itself. As against all previous religions of one god the trinitarian one grasps that God is movement, self-transcendence towards the particular, and return to unity; that his unity is fundamentally a return of diremption, that he is three-in-one. God does not remain immobile in himself.

Of course this is still in the mode of *Vorstellung*. Thus theology speaks of God 'begetting' his Son, and it represents the necessity of this begetting by

---

[1] Cf. also *GPhil*, 180.

putting it at the beginning (ante omnia saecula). But still it has the right idea.

The eternal trinity in its play of love corresponds to the Idea, as it is taken by itself in the Logic in abstraction from its embodiment.[1] But the Idea also must go out into external existence. This is what we have in the dogma of the creation. This creation must be ex nihilo, that is, all of reality must emanate from the Idea, Hegel cannot allow a beginning in brute fact, in the merely positive, as we have seen. Hence this dogma, too, is attuned to the speculative truth; except that once more its *vorstellende* form makes it portray the fundamentality of the creation in the language of temporal priority. The creation comes at the beginning of time. (In the beginning, God created...). And creation is seen as a free act of God in the sense of something he did not have to do. But this is wrong: the Idea issues in external reality of necessity (Cf. *BRel*, 146–8). For without this God cannot come to consciousness of himself which is his essential goal. He cannot really be God. 'God is not God without the world' (Ohne Welt ist Gott nicht Gott, *BRel*, 148).

The creation must not only issue in nature, but in finite spirit, hence man is created. But finite spirit qua finite is cut off from the infinite. It suffices for finite spirit to realize itself, to act in any way, and it inescapably asserts its finitude. Man in acting realizes his own intentions, goals, ideas, and hence realizes himself as something different from the universal. Hence the Fall.

But here too *Vorstellen* presents us with a contingent event at the beginning in order to communicate the necessary and fundamental. For man cannot remain innocent. The only way he could would be if he could avoid acting. Only inaction is innocent (*PhG*, Chapter VII).

But the Fall as necessary is not an unambiguous event. It is the rise of evil, as the division from God, the assertion of the creaturely will against God. But this is also the beginning of salvation, of reconciliation. Man's separation from God comes not just because he is a natural being and hence finite; it is because he is a finite *subject*, or *will*. Inanimate nature and the other animals cannot be evil. They do not reflect the fullness of God as *Geist*, because they cannot; but that is not evil. Man is evil because he opposes his will to God.

Hence this assertion of his will is also an essential step on the path to reconciliation. For in order to become the vehicle of true self-consciousness of *Geist*, man has to rise above his merely natural desires and goals. He has to develop his will. He has to oppose himself to nature. Thus what distinguishes man from the beast: his power to *assert* his finitude in will, is what cuts him off from the universal and is the origin of evil. But at the same time it is that which puts him in the category of a spiritual being, one who can be the vehicle for God's self-knowledge, and the assertion of his will is the first stage in a process

---

[1] Hegel thus refers to the Logic in its introduction as 'The presentation of God as he is in his eternal essence before the creation of nature and finite spirit', (*WL*, I, 31).

which will take him to being an adequate vehicle of God. Moreover there is no other road to reconciliation. In spite of the inference of the Genesis story, man could not have remained simply united to God before the Fall; for to do so would have been to remain as a beast. But then God could not be truly God, he could not come to self-realization for he would lack an adequate vehicle. God must have a finite spirit, a will, to come to self-knowledge in; but the birth of the finite will is the Fall. The Fall is thus necessary, an essential step to union with God. Or speculatively speaking, Geist is only *Geist* by returning to itself out of alienation from itself. O felix culpa.

Hegel takes warrant for this interpretation of the Fall as part of the economy of salvation, not only from the strain in Christian theology which insists that the salvation through Christ takes man higher than before the Fall, but also in the words of God in the Genesis narrative; 'See, Adam is become like one of us.' The Fall comes from eating the fruit of the tree of knowledge of Good and Evil, and hence becoming in this sense like God, a spiritual being (Cf. *AbsRel*, 102–9).

Man can thus only be with God by reconciling himself out of separation. The separation is man's finite existence as a finite spirit. Of course the first way in which this finitude is cancelled is death, and this is thus seen as a speculative necessity. And indeed, the Bible tells us that the wages of sin are death. Men die because of Adam. But men must find a way of cancelling their finitude without annulling their natural existence, which is the indispensable foundation for their existence as spiritual beings. Otherwise God cannot return to himself.

So man must develop a form of life in which the overcoming of finitude and the giving of self to the universal is built in. This comes to its apex, as we have seen, in the rational state, which is why *Sittlichkeit* is the 'truest cult'. But in the religious sphere, this return is reflected in the central Christian doctrines of the Incarnation and the Kingdom of God.

In order for the reconciliation to take place, man must come to sense in pain his distance from the infinite, and from this must come to see that *an sich* he is united to the infinite subject; and then he must form himself so that this unity is made real *an und für sich* in the human community.

But this speculative necessity is what is laid forth, albeit in the *vorstellende* mode, in the central doctrines of Christianity. In the fullness of time, when the appropriate point came in God's plan, God became man; the two natures were united in one person. But of course we can understand in the light of speculation that *Geist* cannot simply be united to a finite subject. If these two are united, they are also necessarily rent asunder again, for no finite spirit can realize the infinite.

Jesus thus dies. But this is not the end of the story. Something has definitively been changed. As a result of this Incarnation men are now capable of developing a life of union with *Geist* in a way which was not possible

491

before. And so the death of Christ is followed by his Resurrection and his Ascension or return to the Father (these two are never really treated separately by Hegel). And this return is the occasion for the sending of the Spirit, which dwells in the community and raises it to a life with God, so that the Incarnation is continued in the life of the Church, which is seen as the Body of Christ.

Christ's death is thus as necessary as the other great moments of orthodox theology, the Creation and the Fall. Christ had to go as a particular finite subject in unity with the infinite, so that this unity could go beyond the immediate and become universal. The Incarnation had to stop being a merely external unity and become interiorized or spiritualized. These two developments, spiritualization and universalization, are really one. To become part of all our lives, the Incarnation has to be spiritualized, to be wrenched free from a particular, external, natural reality. But the understanding of this spiritualization grows only slowly in the Christian community. We saw in *PhG* how Hegel interprets the Crusades as a (vain) attempt to recover contact with the historical Saviour.

These deep speculative connections are represented in religious *Vorstellung* by relations of time. Christ as cancelled (aufgehoben) immediacy is seen as in the past, for this is the time dimension which represents cancelled immediacy.[1]

At the same time the faithful know that the unity with God is not fully realized so they place it in the future, as the second coming. Speculative thought, of course, understands that separation is eternally and definitively a moment of unity; that the fullness of the Kingdom consists precisely in this, that separation from God is constantly arising and constantly being overcome. Hegel has managed to re-interpret a surprising number of orthodox Christian beliefs in his system. But the ordinary believer then as now cannot escape the feeling that the sense of his faith is being radically if subtly altered. This in spite of Hegel's protestations of orthodoxy.

The instinct of piety is dead right. Hegel is of course not in the direct line of succession of liberal 'de-mythologized' Protestantism. And this may throw us off the track. In fact with Enlightenment thinkers like Kant and Lessing, the process of throwing over dogmatic ballast had already gone quite far, in search of a religion in conformity with reason. A rational religion seemed to Lessing to be founded entirely on timeless truths. The great historical events in the relation of man and God, flight from Egypt, Incarnation, Resurrection, etc. turn out to be irrelevant. These stories were perhaps useful as divine pedagogy in an earlier stage of the 'education of the human race', just as we tell children cautionary tales before they can understand the general principles of morality. But with maturity we go beyond these tales to grasp the truth in

[1] Cf. Hegel's remarks on the relation between 'Wesen' and 'gewesen' in the Logic; (*WL*, II, 3).

rational concepts.[1] Hegel combatted this de-historicization of Christianity, which struck at the central teachings of Christian faith. For in Hegel's philosophy, the timeless truth itself unfolds necessarily in history. Historical events are not an irrelevant by-play, at best illustrating or dramatizing universal truth, but the inescapable medium in which these truths realize and manifest themselves. Hence Hegel's philosophy which claims to be an interpretation of Christian theology restores the decisive events of Christian faith to their central historical importance. Thus Hegel insists (*AbsRel*, 130–42),[2] that the Incarnation must be seen as a real historical event, and one which has played a decisive role in the history of Spirit. This coupled with the fact that Hegel incorporates into his philosophy the central and most mysterious Christian dogmas, like that of the Trinity, which the Enlightenment has a great deal of trouble with, and we can see how for some of his intellectual contemporaries he could appear as a restorer of orthodoxy against the 'rational theology' of the Enlightenment, which was pre-shrunk to meet the requirements of 'understanding'. And so he saw himself (*GPhil*, 198–9).

But these appearances should not deceive us. In fact the Hegelian re-write leaves out the very essence of Christian faith, or indeed, of any faith relating to the God of Abraham. The central tenets of this philosophy, that the only locus of God's life as spirit is man, and that this spiritual life is nothing but the unfolding of conceptual necessity, together rule out the kind of radical freedom of God to which faith relates. In Hegel's system, God cannot *give* to man – neither in creation, nor in revelation, nor in salvation through sending his Son. To see these as acts of God is to see them in the medium of *Vorstellung*, and what makes them acts is just what belongs to the inadequate narrative medium, which we transcend in philosophy. For to see them aright is to see them as emanations of a necessity which is no more God's than it is man's – except in the sense that God or the Absolute is in a sense the whole or substance, and man a part or accident. But the whole cannot exist without the part. God 'gives' me life, but it is also true that God can only be through this life, and that God must be of rational necessity. God 'reveals' himself to man. But this is also his revelation to himself, and this same necessary process could be called man's self-revelation as the vehicle of *Geist*.

Lacking the idea of God as giver, Hegel cannot accommodate the relations of God and man as they must be for Christian faith. He has no place for grace in the properly Christian sense. As Karl Barth puts it,

Hegel, in making the dialectical method of logic the essential nature of God, made impossible the knowledge of the actual dialectic of grace, which has its foundation in the freedom of God.[3]

---

[1] Cf. Lessing, *Die Erziehung des Menschengeschlechts.*   [2] Cf. also *PhG*, Chapter vii.
[3] *From Rousseau to Ritschl*, London 1959, p. 304. The chapter of this work devoted to Hegel is a penetrating study of the ambitions of Hegelian philosophy and its relations to theology.

And he has no place for divine love in the Christian sense, for God's love for his creatures is inseparable from its expression in giving.[1] And what can be said about God's relation to man must be said about the fully developed human relation to God, in which man comes to recognize his identity with the divine.

The creaturely response of gratitude and praise of God takes on a radically different sense in the rarified altitudes of the Idea. Both these responses transmute into a recognition of my identity with cosmic necessity and hence must cease to be gratitude in any meaningful sense (although something analogous to the glorifying of God remains, a sense of awe at the imposing architecture of rational necessity).

In short, how does a Hegelian philosopher *pray?* Certainly the prayer of petition has no meaning for him. Nor can he really thank God. What he does is to contemplate his identity with cosmic spirit, which is something quite different.

Kirkegaard was therefore quite right from a Christian point of view to protest against Hegelianism as an understanding of Christian faith, and to make the call of God to man something incommensurable with the universal demands of rational will (as when God commands Abraham to sacrifice his own son). And the question arises whether the claim to banish mystery altogether, to make the like of God fully open to reason, is not quite incompatible with faith in the God of Abraham. The ways of God who is the giver of life and author of man's salvation from sin must be beyond our ways. A God whose life can be fully comprehended by us would not be an interlocutor who was capable of inaugurating a radically new relation, of wrenching us from sin into a new life. God's salvation must be an 'incomprehensible reconciling' in Barth's phrase (op. cit., 302), or else lose its character as radical giving, free initiative.

Thus the Hegelian ontology itself in which everything can be grasped by reason because everything is founded on rational necessity is ultimately incompatible with Christian faith. Hegel's philosophy is an extraordinary transposition which 'saves the phenomena' (that is, the dogmas) of Christianity, while abandoning its essence. It is not a theism, but it is not an atheist doctrine either, in which man as a natural being is at the spiritual summit of things. It is a genuine third position, which is why it is so easy to misinterpret.

Once one gets the measure of the distance which separates the Hegelian system from orthodox Christianity, one begins to notice that not even all the dogmas are 'saved'. The doctrine of the Trinity is, of course, given pride of place. But the incarnation, although Hegel insists on its historicity, is really

---

[1] Here I part company with Fackenheim, *The Religious Dimension in Hegel's Thought*, Bloomington and London, 1967, with whose insightful interpretation I in other ways largely agree. But when Fackenheim attributes to Hegel's God 'a *total* and *gratuitous* divine Love *for the human*...by a Divinity *which does not need it*' (italics in original, p. 153), I cannot see the warrant in Hegel's work, or the whole structure of his system.

given an essentially different meaning. We examined above (Chapter VII, pp. 208–10) in what the Incarnation consisted as an historical event, and we saw that although Hegel probably continued to see in Jesus an exceptional individual who lived in harmony with God in a way quite without precedent or equal in his time, it could not be said of him that he was God in any sense other than that in which we all are identical with God. *An sich*, we are all the same in this regard. Jesus was special in that he lived this identity *für sich* in a way that no other men could at that time.

As for the Ressurection and Ascension, although Hegel never states anything one way or the other, the impression one gathers is that he really did not consider them as historical events. Their whole point is contained in Pentacost, the coming of the Holy Ghost to the apostles. On Hegel's view this fulfills the speculative necessity behind Christ's death: he had to disappear as a particular, external point of juncture between man and God, so that the Incarnation could be spiritualized and thus universalized. In Hegel's re-write it would have served just as well if the Gospel story had gone right from the Crucifixion to Pentacost, with the coming of the Holy Ghost carrying the whole weight of victorious dénouement to the Crucifixion which Christian theology attributes to the Resurrection. For this and the Ascension play no independent role in his interpretation. They belong to the level of *Vorstellung* purely.

Thus while Hegel is not in the main line of descent of liberal Protestantism, he is the point of origin of another important movement towards a de-mythologized, one might say, 'de-theologized' Christianity. Contemporary theologies of 'the death of God' are his spiritual grandchildren. The filiation is either direct, as with Paul Tillich who very much influenced the theologians of this school, or through the young Hegelian Ludwig Feuerbach. And in a sense, Hegel himself was the first 'death of God' theologian. For we have seen that Christ's death plays a crucial and necessary role as the indispensable basis for the coming of the Spirit and hence the Spiritualization of God's presence, which is the same as the building of this presence into the life of the community. Men must first of all see God concentrated in a single man. But this point of concentration has to disappear, if the fuller truth is to emerge that men carry God as a community, that God is in each and beyond each. God is like a flame which passes from mortal candle to mortal candle, each destined to light and go out, but the flame to be eternal.

3

Christianity as the true vision of the absolute as subject, albeit in the mode of *Vorstellung*, is thus the absolute religion. But it comes onto the stage only as the result of a long and strife-filled development in history. But if Christianity is the absolute religion it has to be shown to be the truth in Hegel's sense of all previous religions, that is, to develop necessarily out of them as their fruition. This Hegel tries to show in his lectures on the philosophy of religion. Let us now look at this.

Hegel's philosophy of religion is like all his work extraordinarily well-researched, and full of interesting detail. As a work in comparative religion it would not stand up today in most of its passages, but it was remarkable considering what was available at the time.

After a brief discussion of magic, Hegel starts human religion under the general category nature religion: here we have religion before man has come to the understanding of the absolute as free subjectivity. He covers here among others, the Chinese, Indian, Persian, Syrian and Egyptian religions. But the uniting point is not so much the role of natural reality or symbols in man's notion of God, but rather the fact that we are not yet at the stage of recognizing the absolute as free spirit. Thus in Indian religion, the absolute is conceived as a pure abstraction, as beyond all determination. But this is no closer to the vision of God as subject than the more naturalistic visions of God as the sky, or the earth.

Indeed, for Hegel there is a connection between this pure abstract notion of God and the most external, naturalistic conceptions of God. For his principle is that what is simply inner is also simply outer: that is, if the foundation of things is hidden, unknown, then the reality we know will be formless, inarticulated. The more we know the basis of things, the more we will recognize it in the articulations of the world; and the less purely 'external' these articulations will be seen to be. 'What is only inner, simply *an sich* and abstract, is only outer' (*NatRel*, 173). Hence it is no surprise that Hinduism is also a religion in which the divine is incarnate in a disordered multitude of external realities, cows, stones, trees, etc. The very abstraction of Brahma breeds this giddy tumult (Taumel) of divinity in nature.

Higher for Hegel is Zoroastrianism because this, while still a 'nature religion' has found a purer natural manifestation, light, and correspondingly has a higher ethical view. The crucial opposition is good against evil. But here we have not yet attained to an understanding of the unity of good and evil; each just stands over against the other. This overcoming of the opposition begins in the Syrian and Egyptian religions of the death and resurrection of Gods. And in the latter we get the fight towards a vision of God as free spirit which we find expressed in Egyptian art, and which we have already discussed in the previous chapter.

Out of this grow the two great religions which grasp in their different and opposite inadequate ways that God is free subjectivity: the Jewish and the Greek. (The lectures talk of three here, with the Roman as the third, but this really is a later development of the Greek.)

The first is described here as a religion of 'Sublimity' (Erhabenheit). God is

496

seen as spirit, as subject, and is finally grasped in his purity as thought. But this is at the cost of placing him way above the world of particular, natural things. God is above and the merely natural cannot reach to him. Rather the relation of God to the world is one of Lordship (Herrschaft).

Jewish religion therefore achieved for the first time a real desacralization (Entgötterung) of the world, and in this way originated one of the strands which is constitutive of modern consciousness. But this did not of course issue then in the Enlightenment notion of a world governed by impersonal law. Rather it opened the way for a belief in miracles, as the special interventions of God in an otherwise non-sacred course of things.

God is lord; as a subject he has goals; and creatures are meant to be his servants, to follow his goals. Thus the vocation of men is to serve God. The law of morality is presented as his command. Man is nothing before God, and hence he stands before him in fear.

But God as thus above the world is the subject of a universal goal, only this is still abstract and unarticulated. This is an inescapable feature of an absolute which is in no way connected with the articulations of the world; his purposes are unspecifiable, abstract. Now it is the fate of the abstract universal to go over into the rawest particular. Hence this sublime God ends up being bound to a particular tribe. This is his people; his purposes concern the fate and well-being of this particular people. They are in turn his servants, his slaves.

This particular derivation of the national affiliation of the Jewish God from his nature as sublime runs Hegel into trouble in his consideration of Islam. In general Hegel gives little consideration to Islam, for it was rather inconveniently placed, coming after the birth of the absolute religion. He chooses to consider it as a related phenomenon to Judaism. Islam is then seen also as the religion of a certain community, but directed outwards, a conquering religion. It is a religion Hegel thinks which is inherently fanatical.

To return to the Jews, the people of God are thus seen as chosen by God and having a vocation to serve him in absolute obedience. They serve, Hegel says in fear, in a kind of unreasoning slavery. But the very fact that they give everything over to God, that they give up all their particular being to God's service, puts them beyond fear in the ordinary sense, fear of loss through natural or human agency. On the contrary, they have a confidence that what God has given them cannot ultimately be taken away by others. They have confident certainty (Zuversicht) in God's purpose for them.

But along with this confidence goes the fundamental inadequacy of the Jewish religion in Hegel's eyes, that it shows us a God who is way above all particular things. These cannot return to unity with God, but remain unreconciled. Hence the Old Testament stresses the Fall as a turning away from God, not the aspect in which men also achieve the knowledge of good and evil. As a punishment men have to till the soil for their bread; but is this a punishment? Is it not work, the transformation of the world and thus self which distinguishes man from the beasts? This is what makes men free (*RelGI*, 87).

Hegel's very negative and sometimes caricatural picture of Judaism has often been remarked. But with Fackenheim I would maintain that the basic reason for this was his love for the Greeks. The rupture in the beautiful Greek unity of the Godly and the natural, which Hegel as a member of the Romantic generation felt so keenly and so painfully, is put to the account of the Jews. Judaism is the original religion of the unhappy consciousness. Later on Hegel will go beyond this Romantic regret at the passing of the Greeks; he will judge the Greek civilization as intrinsically inadequate, and he will see the unhappy consciousness as an essential step on man's road to universal rationality. This will change his view of orthodox Christianity (as he understood orthodoxy), but not of Judaism. We might say that the whole negative side of his judgement on the religion of unhappy consciousness is discharged onto Judaism.[1]

Nevertheless, Hegel does not let this feeling get in the way of his judgement of historical importance. Judaism is an essential phase, along with Greek religion, in creating the conditions, the fullness of time for the coming of Christianity. One might remark that it is already unorthodox enough to see Christianity issuing out of Greek and Jewish religion together and not just out of the latter; but this is related to the central unorthodoxy of Hegel's middle path.

Judaism prepared the road for the Incarnation, in that the utter sublimity of God, without hope of any union with man, comes ultimately to be lived as pain, a pain in which man senses his separation from the essential base of things, a kind of total absence of the very foundation. This pain cries for a saviour, for the coming of God in man. But at the same time this coming is prepared by another religious development which is in its inadequacies the complement of the Jewish.

This is the Greek religion of beautiful individuality, of necessity and beauty as Hegel calls it in *RelGI*. The Greeks won through to a view of the divine as free subject, in which man could be fully at home, and with which he could be one. Thus the paradigm representation of these Gods was in human form. But the price they paid for this was that these Gods were limited; that is, there were many of them, none was equivalent to the absolute which is the basis and substance of all.

Hence we have the complementary inadequacy to the Jewish. We can see it this way: men at this epoch are limited, they cannot rise to the notion of man as such, the universal subject who defines his identity by the human universal

---

[1] Cf. the discussion in Chapter II on Hegel's early works, especially 'The Spirit of Christianity', where he deals with the religion of Abraham.

Religion

of reason. These parochial men can therefore only feel united with a God who is himself parochial, who expresses their limited identity. But then there are many Gods and none is absolute. Or else they really do win through to the idea of an absolute God as single spirit above all, but then this God is way above them and there is absolutely no question of man being at home in him or feeling one with him; he remains insuperably above and beyond man. This God cannot be united with the world, for parochial men cannot understand a purpose in the world which would be commensurable with this God. His purposes remain inscrutable (abstractly universal). Hence they are (partially) identified with those of the most grossly particular, the chosen people. This is the only way parochial men can relate to this God. But because this God is really beyond and not capable of unity with men, belonging to him remains a servitude (Knecht-schaft), which it will not be for the Greeks.

Greek religion is that of the beautiful unity of man with God, his being at home with God. And this is tied up as we saw with his being parochial, with his not yet having a universal reflective consciousness. It goes along with his total identification with the customary law of his own polity (Sitten). A man is nothing but a bearer of this public life; and this public life in turn is identified with the God, the God who founded and who watches over the city, the God thus whose people we are, but in a happy unity, not in separation and transcend-ence. This unreflecting unity with city and God, the unity of a not yet reflective, and hence universal subjectivity, is what underlies the nature of this religion as an art-religion.[1] But in its parochialness it cannot understand that man as such is free, and is united with the divine; hence it is still a civilization with slavery.

As a religion of art, it has won through, past the dim perceptions of substantial power, of the divine in the natural which predominated in nature religions, to a luminous vision of the divine in human shape. The spiritual subjectivity triumphs over the natural, and achieves freedom. That this is the result of a struggle is reflected in the Greek myths. The Olympian Gods come to dominance through the conquest of earlier Gods who still represent intrication with nature or the sub-spiritual: with Uranos, the sky, and Kronos, time, with the Titans.

The cult of these Gods is one of union with the divine. Hence in the sacrifices we have not a renunciation (*RelGI*, 169–70), but rather the meat and offerings are enjoyed by the offerers. The God is made present in the community through his representation in human form, not only in statue, but in the ceremonial acts of living men. The great forces which surround men and with and under whom they live, the natural and societal (sittlich) powers, are brought by this cult to human shape, in which men feel at home. This shaping of the Godly makes this truly a cult of beauty.

[1] In *EG*, §557, Hegel relates the unreflecting nature of art as a mode of absolute spirit with the unreflecting nature of Greek *Sittlichkeit*, of the era of art-religion.

499

Greek cult also had a sense of the universal, however. This came out in the mysteries where man was united with the divine in a way which went beyond particular Gods. But here, Greek religion still remained with the symbols of the earlier nature-religions, it could not bring these cults up to the clarity of daylight. In these mysteries there began to evolve the idea of personal immortality.

Hegel once again takes up the connection of Greek religion with the notion of fate. Because the beautiful individualities are not the absolute, this universal power underlying everything remains in the dark in Greek religion. It is only dimly sensed as a fate, an inscrutable destiny that floats over the Gods as well as men. Each of these Gods is set in a sense in a matrix of unfathomable necessity which he cannot fully dominate.

Thus the contingent course of events in history is also seen as under the grip of inscrutable fate. The subjective freedom of a god only extends so far, it can go awry in the hands of fate. Free subjectivity which shapes and dominates nature, and hence raises us above nature religion, only extends to a certain point. Beyond is the matrix of fate, and this can annul the purposes even of the Gods. These are immortal, they remain personally inviolate, but not their favourites among men. What can be said of the freedom of the Gods goes of course for the human cities which are in unity with them, but this time redoubled, for man is not immortal.

Hegel thus makes a connection between finding unity with a parochial God and the necessary concomitant of the belief in fate. When man rise to a sense of union not with a parochial God but with one who is himself the absolute, the master of all, then the notion of inscrutable fate will go. For free subjectivity now controls all, and fate is replaced by the notion of providence. Then the whole course of things, even the contingent detail, is seen as part of the divine plan, as an expression of subjective purpose.[1]

From this Hegel derives a set of differences between ancient and modern consciousness. The ancient did not feel that he could make a particular decision, a decision about matters where the particular, contingent course of events could affect the outcome – whether to give battle now, to travel or marry today (*RelGI*, 187) – out of himself. He has driven to consult oracles, to take auguries, to try to coax some indication of the future out of the fates.

By contrast the modern is grounded in the notion of the absolute as subject; and moreover has achieved in the absolute religion a surety of union with this absolute. Hence there is no corner left for any inscrutable fate. In part the certainty of union with the ground of things has developed in the modern world into the faith in reason, the faith that human reason can understand

---

[1] Of course, this is not to say that there is no room for genuine contingency; we have seen that there is for Hegel; only that the plan of *Geist* is assured of going through whatever the contingent variations which it allows, also out of inner necessity.

nature scientifically; and hence decisions which can be affected in their outcome by the particular course of things are made on the basis of rational prediction. This aspect of inscrutable fate has been laid open to human gaze. In part, we moderns are certain that our decision is grounded in an absolutely valid purpose, and not one which is merely partial, that of a limited god, which as such may go awry or be set aside. Thus both as regards the absolute validity (and ultimate success) of our purposes, and with regard to the choosing of appropriate time and means, we have no need to have recourse to oracles, in an attempt to pierce the veil of destiny; we can decide out of ourselves. As for the element of ineradicable contingency in events, this sets a limit to prediction, but we understand this, and realize that this cannot be remedied by any oracle or augury. We decide to the best of our knowledge and for the rest we accept the risk. But our sense of risk is less for we know that the absolute being rational cannot but triumph, even if not quite in the way we plan. We know this through our belief in providence, or the Hegelian speculative re-write of it.

This power to decide out of oneself is thus based on the vision of the absolute over-arching power as subject and ourselves as in unity with it; which in turn requires of course that we come to define ourselves as universal subjectivity. And this is absent in Greece. The Greek was sunk in the public life of his city. Thus both the decisions of a particular kind which he took as an individual, and the decisions of a particular kind which the city had to take were felt to be beyond his unaided powers. It was necessary to consult the oracle. There was not the sense of inner confidence, of understanding and being at home in the course of events which would have made possible such autonomy of decision. Even Socrates took particular decisions on the prompting of his daemon.

But there was more than this. The purposes even of Gods were under fate, and could be annulled. Thus even purposes which were 'God-justified' (*RelGI*, 153) could go awry. In face of this, the Greek developed a reverence for necessity (*RelGI*, 150–4). He wept, but bowed to it, identified with it as his fate, and hence as part of it. He achieved reconciliation and hence a kind of freedom, by taking this necessity into himself and seeing this as part of his identity. His early death is *part* of Achilles, as much constitutive of his identity as his great prowess and invulnerability. There is something beautiful in this identification. Like all beautiful things in Greek civilization Hegel will try to re-integrate it in his system.[1]

The modern by contrast is sure that the absolute purpose must go through, will somehow triumph whatever the pattern taken by contingent events. But

---

[1] This Greek-inspired notion of reconciliation with fate goes back to the 'Spirit of Christianity' manuscript of the Frankfurt period. Only now it has been firmly relegated to an unrecoverable past, and replaced by a higher mode of reconciliation.

this makes modern man chagrined at the reverses of fortune. He cannot just take them and identify with them; he considers his goals absolute. But of course for Hegel this is not the height of wisdom either; when modern man does not simply take his own humanly defined goals as the absolute, but identifies with the goals of *Geist*, then he is ensured against reverses. Any reverses he suffers do not matter because they cannot upset the outcome as far as the purposes of *Geist* are concerned. The true and only way to recapture the beautiful ancient identification with necessity is to identify with providence. Then one is free and fulfilled whatever the course of things. One is reconciled to the course of events. But this no longer means as with the ancients that one has to witness the defeat of a divinely-warranted purpose. Between these two forms of wisdom, however, lies the kicking against the pricks of modern man. (*RelGI*, 152–4).

The Greek begins to get a premonition, a sense of the shape and the rational structure of necessity, in tragedy. This for Hegel is the way Greek consciousness came to awareness of the deep contradictions in its life-form. In the *Antigone*, 'for me the absolute example of tragedy' (*RelGI*, 156), we have the collision between the right of the parochial city represented in Creon, and that of a universal morality, in the form of the demands of family love, represented by Antigone. In tragedy what happens to people, their fate, begins to take shape. Here we have heroes who are identified with a substantial, God-backed purpose, and who go under (Antigone, Oedipus). But what brings them down is not just portrayed as inscrutable fate; there is a sense that the necessity of this defeat is intricated in the very purpose they espouse; for this is partial and must come into conflict with its counterpart. This immersion in partiality is their pathos.

Hence tragedy strengthens the sense that men should indeed find their identity in what happens to them, it portrays the counter-shock of events as intrinsically linked with what men have identified themselves with. But by bringing this play of fate closer to our understanding, by discerning the meaning in it, it prepares the moment when men can step beyond these partial identifications. To begin to grasp the necessary mechanism of their collision and hence of their fate is already to begin to grow beyond them. And once man grows beyond these identifications he has risen to a universal subjectivity; he has deserted the city, and hence ultimately its Gods.

We saw this process earlier with the fall of the Greek city. It is the same as the emptying of Greek religion; the two are the same process seen from different sides. Man can no longer identify with the parochial, either the city and its *Sitten*, or the Gods. The universal subjectivity rises, but in doing so drains of its lifeblood both *Sittlichkeit* and the beautiful cult of unity. The individual comes to himself, but he is in a world, a city and nature which are no longer in unity with him; he is in alien land. He pines with an immense sense of loss. Jewish pain comes to meet Greek loss in a God-forsaken world.

502

The locus of this late ancient loss of the divine, of the individual in alienation waiting as it turns out for the Incarnation, is the Roman Empire. This is a universal empire which matches the rise of the universal subjectivity. The collapse of the *poleis* from within through universal subjectivity is matched by their collapse outwardly as they fell under universal empires, of which the Roman is the culmination. The loss of contact with the Gods is also matched by their forceful uniting in the politically-motivated Pantheon of Rome.

And in both cases there is loss of union. The individual cannot be united with this abstract world state which is simply a power over him and with which he can in no way identify. It can protect him or snuff him out at will without rational ground or a purpose which he can feel as his own. At the same time the unity with the Gods is also lost. In the Roman Empire they cease to be the centre of autonomous goals and become means used for the purposes of the state. This comes to its culmination in the late Empire emperor-worship.

In the lectures on the philosophy of religion, Hegel presents this stage as a third term of a triad culminating the Jewish and Greek. This is by no means the only way he can pick his way through this material. Elsewhere he moves from Greek and Jewish religion right to Christianity as the synthesis. And this is evidently the more plausible order in Hegelian terms: the incarnate but parochial God and the absolute but separated God together issue in the supreme God incarnate.

But here there is a preliminary, very inadequate synthesis: the necessity of Greek fate comes together with the particularity of purpose of Jewish religion in a religion where the necessity above the Gods is a particular purpose, but one which claims to over-rule all others. This is the Roman drive to universal empire, to which the Gods in the end are impressed in service. This Hegel calls the religion of finality (Zweckmäßighkeit). But it is an outer teleology. The purposes of Athena were not to be realized by means of Athens; we have here the beautiful unity which we also find in the organism, or any entity with internal teleology. But the religion of Rome is that of external teleology, where everything serves an end outside of it, where means and end are external to each other.

The reader who has caught on to Hegel's shibboleths will already know that the Romans are not very *sympathiques* in his eyes. He will not be surprised by the detail. While having to give the Romans their world-historical due, Hegel plainly finds them very unpleasant. He represents this cold focus on external teleology not just as a late aberration but as basic to their religion from the beginning. The Romans had no idea of beautiful unity; everything was bent from the beginning to the purposes of their state. They gave themselves up for a goal which was not an absolute, universal one, but really limited, the universal empire of one people. Everything was grimly bent to this goal, and nothing had its purpose, its necessity in itself, which is the secret of beauty. They gave their lives in this external way, too. Gladiatorial combat was indeed reflective of this civilization, for death in this combat was a cold, senseless one, its entire meaning outside itself.

In any case, the ancient world reaches culmination in this sense of distance from God (Jews) and the loss of God (Greeks). The world pines for unity, and hence the fullness of time has come in which God acts in the Incarnation in the way described earlier.

The history of religion from then on is the history of the Christian religion. This we have already touched on from another side, that of the state – for the two became intertwined.

At first the union between God and man is only *an sich*; the Christian community feels itself to be a foreign body still in a yet Godless world. But this is not meant to be so forever, and gradually the Church builds itself into unity with the world. With the conquest of Rome by the barbarians this mainly occurs through the church acting as the tutor and civilizer of the barbarian kingdoms. But in the course of teaching these barbarians the church takes on some of their crudity; it becomes itself corrupted by the worldly power it is forced to assume to fulfill its task. It corrupts and reifies the Christian message by reducing the presence of God again to a gross external reality in host, relics, etc. And then it reacts to this corruption by the exaggerated other-worldliness of the monastic ideal.

But both this crude worldliness and its counterpart other-worldliness are incompatible with the full spiritualization of human life and community. A complete spiritualization of human life entails that man in his normal life become a fully adequate vehicle of *Geist*. Man must be such a vehicle as he is in the family, working for the means to life, and exercising his choice by reason. But the monastic vows of poverty, chastity and obedience go directly counter to these three dimensions of normal life. This spirituality is thus a deviant one. It is only understandable as a pendant to the crude reification of the spiritual which it accompanies.

But both these must be done away with. The spiritual must be rescued from its presence in the purely outer in order to infuse and transfigure life; and life as infused and transfigured must thus no longer be renounced by an other-worldly spirituality. The monk's life is against the true vocation of the Christian which entails family, work and responsibility. The monk must be made to wed, work, and choose for himself.[1]

Hence to the first stage of Church opposition to the world and the second stage of worldly power, must succeed a third stage in which the message becomes spiritualized again. This we have seen is the Protestant Reformation. But its momentum continues into the European Enlightenment.

[1] Hegel shares the liberal-Protestant lack of understanding of the basis of Christian monasticism.

Religion

The message of the Protestant Reformation is that the Christian faith must be followed in spirit, that is, built into and made to transfuse our life in the world. This means that the fullness of the Christian reconciliation of subject and absolute must be built into *Sittlichkeit*, the way of life of the sovereign, self-subsistent community. The state thus becomes the privileged locus for the institutional realization of the kingdom of God, and not as with Catholicism a church which by its separateness and opposition to the secular state proclaims the unredeemed and unredeemable nature of earthly power. The Catholic parallel power keeps the secular state in that condition of unredeemed refractoriness to spirit which justifies the finest aspirants to spirituality in taking the cowl. The principle of Protestantism is thus to accept the primacy of the state, to back it up and to push men into a full identification with their developing *Sittlichkeit*.

The first period of Christianity is one of opposition to the world; in the second the attempt is to hold the world in tutelage. But in the third men come to see that the world must realize spirituality freely in itself. And this, fully worked out, brings us to the Enlightenment. The principle that man, secular man, must realize the highest goals of spirit, that he already is master of the whole, reaches its fullest expression in a notion of the primacy of a reason which is purely human. Man identifying himself just as man hopes to realize the supremacy of reason on earth. God thus becomes simply an empty supreme being, without content or initiative or will, the God of deism.

But as we have seen, the Enlightenment which tries to draw all man's goals and purposes out of himself crucially lacks content. It cannot find a true objectivity. In order to do this it must rediscover man's link with the greater *Geist*, with God. It must become reconciled with a pure religion. This reconciliation is the task of philosophy. The emancipation of man, if pushed to its limits, brings the discovery of his true self as vehicle of *Geist*, and this is where philosophy unites religion and *Aufklärung*.

4

So we move to the highest form of absolute knowledge – philosophy. Philosophy when it reaches its fullest development expresses the same content as religion – the deep speculative truths we have found in the absolute religion – but in another form. This is the form of thought. Grasping the absolute in concepts, philosophy sees the inner necessity which underlies the content of revealed religion and makes this manifest. What is presented in a veiled form in *Vorstellen* comes here to explicit clarity, the thoroughgoing necessity which informs the whole structure of *Geist*. But the very nature of *Geist* is itself thought, rational necessity. Hence to grasp it in concepts is to grasp it in the final, totally adequate form, a form which is identical with the content, which itself determines itself to content, or produces this content out of itself. It is the elevation (Erhebung) of these forms

into the absolute form, which determines itself as its content, remains identical with this content and thus is the knowledge of that necessity which is *an und für sich.*
(*EG*, §573)

The believing worshipper senses that the *Vorstellung* of God puts him in contact with the absolute. This is the 'testimony of the spirit' which tells him that this content is spirit. But with philosophy this obscure sense is replaced by the certainty of reason.

This is philosophy at its apex. The whole history of philosophy is a development towards this, as we shall see in detail later. But at whatever stage, philosophy singles itself out as an attempt to capture the absolute in concepts. It cannot but be, of course, that in earlier more primitive stages its grasp is very imperfect, more imperfect than that of religion which since the coming of Christ at least presents the whole structure in the mode of *Vorstellen*. But philosophy in its final speculative development ultimately catches up and recapitulates the full content in thought.

Thought we have seen is the medium of total clarity, that where the maximum reflective clarity accompanies our awareness, and hence where it is maximally awareness. With total reflective clarity we have a complete transparency of thought. Whatever reason we have to doubt the possibility of this absolute clarity, it was Hegel's central claim.

This philosophy is thus the really adequate locus of the self-knowledge of Spirit. It is the medium in which it returns to self-consciousness as logical Idea out of its external realization in nature and finite spirit. It is the 'self-thinking Idea' (*EG*, §574). Thus the system closes with a reference to its starting point.

Now this philosophy as we have just seen reconciles the Enlightenment and religion. In the Enlightenment man frees himself from the external authority of the Church, and determines to entrust himself only to his own reason. But it pursues this emancipation one-sidedly out of a sense of rupture and opposition to authority, even ultimately the spiritual authority of God unmediated by man. But human thought which no longer identifies itself with the absolute, hence with the Idea which goes over into its opposite and return to itself, lacks the dialectical dimension; it is 'understanding' (Verstand) and not 'reason' (Vernunft). It pushes the clarity of thought to its extreme in marking and fixing distinctions, but it does not and cannot get beyond this to see that the distinctions overcome themselves, that the oppositions marked by these distinctions are not final but move to reconciliation, that each term reaches over into its opposite. The *Aufklärung* is the consciousness of *les idées claires et distinctes*, of the maximum rigidity and fixity of clear distinctions. It is incapable of understanding the dialectical truth in religion, and hence in real philosophy. 'The Enlightenment, this vanity of the understanding, is philosophy's most forceful opponent.' (*AbsRel,* 225)

Since it tries to understand everything by human reason narrowly understood, it sees God less and less as active spirit and more and more as an abstraction. Its incapacity to understand dialectical movement makes the Enlightenment move to this abstract view of God as an empty supreme being, with neither the power to intervene in nature, as rationally understood, nor the authority to command what is not already a law of reason.

The Enlightenment therefore turns against religion. But we have seen earlier that this very commitment to mere understanding and its insistence of defining man as simply man makes it incapable of doing the task of reason and generating an adequate content for its will. Once the Enlightenment has taken the part of man against authority, the divisive distinguishing tendency of understanding pushes it back to an atomistic picture of man. Man's goals are meant to be found in himself. But in himself he finds de facto merely a lot of desires which are not in agreement and which are not as such worthy of being made final purposes. So he attempts to rise above this to a moral view (Rousseau) in the notion of a general will. But this is still just a general will, i.e., one shaped by all the atomic subjects, not yet the will of a genuine subject which is their common substance. To grasp this we have either to make the transition to reason, to rise to speculative thought, or else remain in the confident relation to the absolute which religion still has. Without either of these Enlightenment man can generate no concrete content of action as good, and hence falls prey to the empty formalism of Kant and the destructive fury of the French Revolution.[1]

By its own contradictions the Enlightenment is destined to be forced beyond itself, to make the step which displaces the centre of things from the human self to the substantial subject. But in doing this it accepts the substance of the teachings of religion. Those who remain wedded to divisive understanding however, fight against this. Hence they oppose philosophy.

If philosophy brings the Enlightenment back to religion, it also re-expresses religion in fully rational terms. And this brings onto its head the opposition of many of the pious which is as bitter as that of the *philosophes.* They cannot recognize the content of their faith in Hegel's speculative reconstruction (and as we saw above, they are hardly to be blamed).

But what is worse, the two kinds of opposition can come together. This is what we find in a certain strand of Romantic devotion which takes off from Kant and Fichte, which we see reflected in Jacobi and Schleiermacher, and which is evidently Hegel's bête noire. Indeed the lectures on the philosophy of religion start in polemic against them, and it is fitting that they should finish with this polemic.

[1] Cf. above, Chapters xiv, xv.

These Romantics combine the oppositions of both *dévots* and *philosophes*, for they attack philosophy (i.e., Hegel) for the over-rationalization of faith; and appeal rather to intuitive devotion and faith. But at the same time they are not in the line of the orthodox, they have not even this excuse. They have been corrupted by the Enlightenment to the point of abandoning the hope of reaching knowledge of God. God is unknowable, beyond.

Along with the Enlightenment's doubts about our knowledge of the divine, this Romantic piety has also taken up its rejection of authority. It rebels against merely 'positive' religion, and insists on the worship of God which comes from the heart.

But then it falls into the same impasse as the Enlightenment. This man who cannot know God, or accept authority, is the same finite subject of 'understanding', who can only grasp his distinction from the infinite subject and is blind to the identity which overcomes separation. He suffers from the same incapacity as the *Aufklärer*. His faith cannot generate any content, a way of life which would express it. The law of the heart is just as empty as utilitarianism or Kantian formalism. By itself it comes to no determinate conclusion. In fact its content is dictated by caprice, or contingent desire. It remains simply arbitrary impulse masking as morality. Or else it shrinks away altogether from outer action to pure inner intention; and in this form volatilizes into nothing.[1]

The Romantics cannot get beyond themselves, their own élans of feeling, their own moral instincts, to the substantial subject which alone can give content to their ethical life. The truth that they are missing is man's rooting in this moral subject. And this is the truth that religion portrays. And yet they claim to be devout! We saw at the beginning of this chapter how this Romantic piety which renounces knowledge of God and takes refuge in feeling is in violation of the very concept of religion.[2]

Hegel finds this position particularly irritating not only because it obstinately would not lie down and be superceded as it should, but because it resembled too closely his own views of the 1790s, when he also rejected positive religion in favour of a spontaneous devotion of the heart. His criticism of the Romantic rejection of authority gives some measure of his own development in the intervening years. The Romantics have, of course, taken up the basic principle of Protestant Christianity, and hence of true religion, which must 'come out of one's own conviction and not simply repose on authority' (*GPhil*, 193–4). This principle Hegel held to all his life. But now he taxes the Romantics and *Aufklärer* with offering a caricature of the orthodox believer when they accuse him of blindly following external authority. For he

---

[1] Cf. the discussions in the *PhG* on the law of the heart, and the beautiful soul, respectively 266–74 and 445–72.
[2] Certain branches of Pietism also fall under this stricture. *AbsRel*, 226.

is rather moved by the 'testimony of the spirit' within him which is called forth by the absolute content of religion.

But if the ordinary believer is cleared of the charge of mere submission to positive authority, the only figure who is allowed fully to have escaped positivity is now the speculative philosopher. Certainly the Romantic free-thinker does not do so. All he does is canonize certain non-rational ideas and prejudices which come to him as spontaneous feeling. Really to think freely means more than just rejecting authority. It means being able to justify one's starting point. And this only philosophy can claim.

That philosophy is now free from all authority, that it has made good its principle of free thought, it owes to the fact that it has come to the concept of free thought, that it starts from free thought or that this is its principle. Hence that one's thoughts or convictions be one's own does not yet make it the case that one is free from authority. (*GPhil*, 169)

Thus philosophy has to fight a two-front war, against the devout and against the *Aufklärer*, and this to show that they are really *an sich* at peace, that they are on to different aspects of the same truth. They must be 'reconciled through the Concept'. This, says Hegel, is the aim of his lectures (*AbsRel*, 228). But it appears to have been tough sledding. And this may cast some doubt on how much the reconciliation has really been achieved *an sich*. For the strength of Hegel's polemic on both fronts rather reflects how the opposition was, and was to remain, widespread. The last pages of the lectures on the philosophy of religion (*AbsRel*, 229–31) even strike a rather despairing note. They see the fragmentation in contemporary times as almost analogous to that in the Roman Empire. At the end, there is an enigmatic reference to a possible retreat of the philosophers to sanctuary (231).

This may have reflected that pessimism which Hegel seems to have been prey to periodically in his mature years, when he reflected on the contemporary course of things, and which could not easily be reconciled with his system. Officially, this fragmentation is destined to be overcome by a philosophy which recapitulates and saves religion by giving it its true form in reason, and in so doing pulls the Enlightenment beyond itself.

CHAPTER XIX

Philosophy

1

This philosophy also has a history. Before examining this, it might be well to take stock, since we have been through a number of histories which are intricated into each other.

In fact there is only one history, that of Spirit, whose different aspects we have been following in examining the development of political society, art, religion and now philosophy. Any given stage in history is a totality in which the same spirit manifests itself in all these different modes. All the different forms (Gestaltungen) of an age belong together.

> The essential category is that of unity, the inner connection of all these diverse forms. We must firmly grasp this, that there is only *one* spirit, *one* principle, which leaves its impress on the political situation as well as manifesting itself in religion, art, ethics, sociability, commerce and industry, so that these different forms are only branches of one trunk.
> (*GPhil*, 148)

Philosophy is one side of this. It is a reflection of the spirit of the times. It cannot thus stand over its time. Or rather, in a sense it does, since philosophy always has the same basic insight.[1] So that it can sometimes be thought afterwards to have shown the world the way it had to go – as Neo-Platonic philosophy foreshadowed the reconciliation which Christianity would achieve (*GPhil*, 150). But on its own level of development, rather than seen in the light of the eternal truths it points to, a philosophy cannot step over its time.

> philosophy is at first only the thought of the substantial reality of its time; it cannot stand over its time, but only produces in thought the content of this time. (*GPhil*, 150)

But the philosophy of an age is not entirely contemporaneous with its other manifestations. 'Within a given form of Spirit philosophy comes on the scene at a determined time, not simultaneously with the other aspects' (loc. cit.). For thought is reflective. It stands over against and negates the immediate stream of life. 'Thus thought is the negation of the natural mode of life' (op. cit., 151). Thus philosophy does not tend to arise when an age is in its prime, in the bloom of youth, but rather when it has already started to grow old. And by taking a

[1] 'Daher gibt es schlechterdings auch nur *eine* Philosophie' throughout the whole of history, *GPhil*, 124.

Philosophy

reflective stance philosophy weakens the immediacy of commitment and helps along the process of decline (Verderben).

Thus if philosophy is to arise among a people, a breach must have been made in the world of reality. Philosophy is then the reconciliation to the ruin which thought itself initiated; this reconciliation occurs in the ideal world, the world of the spirit, to which man flees when the earthly world no longer satisfies him. Philosophy begins with the decline of a real world. When philosophy comes on the scene and – painting grey in grey – deploys its abstractions, the fresh colour of youth and vitality is already past.   (*GPhil*, 151)[1]

We see an example of this in the Ionians who start to philosophize when their states fall under Persian rule. The great age of Greek philosophy comes with the decline of the polis. The Romans properly come to philosophy with the demise of the Republic, and the greatest philosophical achievement of the Hellenistic and Roman periods, Neo-Platonism, comes when the Empire is on the way down (op. cit., 152).

Philosophy comes after life, and this seems to be true of the definitive philosophy as well, this reconciliation in thought of finite with infinite spirit, which as we saw in the last chapter, presupposes and builds on a real reconciliation in life. Although Hegel seems to have thought that the maturing of philosophy in this case would not be a signal of decline. Rather the new age still had a great deal – perhaps an endless task – to accomplish in order to work out its principle. Philosophy represents decline in earlier ages because their principles when adequately understood cannot be sustained.

But does this mean that we can attribute the famous Marxist slogan, that being precedes consciousness, to Hegel? Not at all. For Hegel reality cannot be divided up in this way. Any advance in men's form of life involves changes in their will, feelings, passions, their consciousness of themselves and their world. For the practices and institutions constitutive of a given way of life are bound up, as we saw in Chapter xiv, with certain ideas about man and his relation to society. Transformation in man's being and transformations in his consciousness are parts of a single totality, and cannot be put in a causal relation the way a certain oversimplified variant of Marxism is wont to do.

But it appears that for Hegel that particular mode of consciousness which is philosophy does follow after changes in life. The consciousness which is inseparable from life forms is carried by other vehicles. It is expressed in the practices themselves, in the way described above (Chapter xiv), or in art, or religion. Philosophy is special among the manifestations of an era in its tardy appearance and recapitulative role.

Why is this? It would appear to be because philosophy is purely a mode of consciousness in a sense which is not true of the other manifestations. We saw in the previous chapter how religion straddled the distinction between mode of

[1] This passage is reminiscent, even in some of the expressions used, of the famous lines of the preface of *PR*, p. 13.

511

Absolute Spirit

consciousness and effective practice, in that it combined a vision of God and a cult, bound together by the underlying stance of devotion. And art in the ages where it is fundamental to a civilization, e.g., among the Greeks, is inseparable from religion. The Greek art-religion had cults which were forms of art, e.g., festivals, tragedy. But philosophy by contrast is in the realm of pure thought. Its very clarity means that it is disintricated from the other levels of life and feeling, that it is purely contemplative and theoretical.

Thus unlike art in its crucial stages, unlike religion, philosophy is not the activity of a whole society. It is the property of single individuals, or very small communities (e.g., the Pythagoreans) who are not really understood by their time. The development of philosophy is thus not a factor in or vehicle for the real development of modes of life in history, as is the development of religion; which is why religious cult is still an essential part of that effective reconciliation of finite with infinite spirit in the modern world which has to be realized in life before philosophy can grasp it in thought.

There is one glaring, apparent exception to this rule of the historical inefficacy of philosophy, and that is Socrates, the only philosopher who was also a world-historical figure. But this is the exception, which in a sense proves the rule. For Socrates' world-historical efficacy was bound up with the collapse of the polis. The rise of universal subjectivity which he helped crystallize was precisely the inner decay of *Sittlichkeit*. And it issued not in a new *Sittlichkeit*, but in a reflection of individuals back into themselves.

The true birth of theory helps to shatter the unreflective unity with substance. But philosophy is impotent to bring a new world to existence. It remains the appanage of a few, disparate individuals, not expressed in collective practice. The birth of effective reconciliation and a new world has to await the coming of Jesus.

2

Philosophy is thus the perfect contemplative mode of consciousness; in thought, which is the true medium of Spirit, where Spirit is truly free and *bei sich*. The vocation of philosophy from the very beginning is to be the vocation of Spirit's self-recognition in everything that is. Hence from the beginning philosophy has the intuition that thought is not only its medium, but its object, that everything is at its base thought.

Thus the history of philosophy develops in a sense a single philosophy through different forms (*GPhil*, 124). But the basic insight is at first clouded. It has the right content, but an inadequate form (op. cit., 126), and it is forced to develop by its contradictions. Being a development moved by contradiction, its stages are necessary.

512

The progress of philosophy is necessary. Every philosophy had necessarily to appear at the time that it did; thus each philosophy appeared at the right time, none outleapt its moment, but all of them grasped the spirit of their time in thought.   (*GPhil*, 125)

But because we are dealing in a sense with the development of a single philosophy, nothing is lost. Earlier philosophies are retained in the fully adequate one as moments, for the true self-understanding of *Geist* is a return to himself out of alienation. The different philosophies are necessary stages on this return, and hence are legitimately part of the final synthesis.

The philosophies [sc. which have appeared in history] are absolutely necessary and hence imperishable moments of the whole, of the Idea; thus they are preserved, and not only in memory, but in an affirmative fashion.   (*GPhil*, 126)

In the Orient *Geist* is still absorbed (versenkt) in nature (*GPhil*, 229–31), thought is not yet really free. It is rudimentary, confined to a vision of the absolute abstraction of the universal in which everything is swallowed up. Hence philosophy proper starts with the Greeks. Even here it does not really get into high gear until the polis is on the decline with Socrates.[1]

The first movement of Greek philosophy reaches its culmination in Anaxagoras. It is a struggling through to the insight that thought is the basis of everything, thought, that is, as spiritual and self-moving. But at first with the Ionians this insight is still very imperfect, they are groping towards a basic principle, but it is still bound up with the material. It has not fully grown out of the consciousness of nature religion. And it lacks any principle of inner development.

Pythagoras thus is a step forward in these two regards. But he still has only the most external and unspiritual form of thought – number. Hegel as we saw throughout considered mathematical thought not the apex of rationality, as does the modern rationalist tradition, but on the contrary the most dead and external of all domains of thought. For the mathematical is the domain of understanding, of fixed distinctions and deductions which merely develop their implicit consequences. It lacks the distinctions of qualitative thought, the power to express a qualitative opposition, and hence the speculative, for only when the basic oppositions are seen in qualitative terms can one reach the insight that they go over into each other. Speculative reason cannot be expressed in mathematical terms.

The Eleatics come closer to the principle of pure thought. They also are the first to give dialectic its due: they show how the rival positions are not just set aside but refute themselves. But their dialectic remains subjective, it is a dialectic of refutation of false opinions, not in things. Heraclitus on the other

---

[1] For the connection between political freedom and philosophy, cf. *GPhil*, 225–8 and 232–5.

hand recognizes the dialectic in reality. He does not exclude non-being from being, and sees that the two together generate becoming. Hegel thus reads in Heraclitus one of the capital transitions of his Logic.

This dialectic is still, however, abstract. It is not concretely embodied in things. Empedocles by contrast has a view of the union of opposites which is fully concrete, his theory of elements, but it in turn lacks living unity. His notion of union is confused and involves recourse to images like religious *Vorstellung*.

The atomism of Leucippus and Democritus represents another attempt to see one of the important dimensions of the concept in concrete, objective reality. The theory of atoms and the void is a concrete representation of the relation of being to non-being; so that atomism, too, is in this way beyond the Eleatic One. This is in a sense a purer expression than Empedocles', but it remains tied to its material expression in the idea of a material atom. It is also too firmly fixed in the distinction of the understanding: atoms and void are external one to another. The principle of development whereby all the qualitative differences in things are generated remains unclear.

This atomism of course recalls another important passage of the Logic, *Fürsichsein*. Indeed this period is full of reminders of the Logic which in turn draws heavily in its examples on the philosophers of this period. The Logic provides the clue to their interpretation by Hegel.

This first movement of Greek philosophy comes to a head with Anaxagoras and his notion of *nous*. Now at last thought is recognized as the basis of things, not just abstractly, but as soul, the source of movement, in other words as the subject of purposes. Anaxagoras has the intuition that the world is to be understood teleologically. Hegel here follows Plato's account of what Socrates found in Anaxagoras. But Anaxagoras cannot really follow this through. The inner purpose remains over against the simply positively present stuff of the external world. It does not posit this out of itself. So we pass to the next movement.

The next movement is where the centre of interest shifts to the free thought of the subject. This is the period inaugurated by the Sophists. Man's thought is made the measure of all things and all fixed reference points outside are called into question. The laws which previously were unquestionably accepted must now be justified by Reason to man. This can lead to a dissolution of all standards and an exaltation of mere arbitrary will (Willkür), which it does with some of the Sophists.

But Socrates turns on the contrary to find universal criteria of reason in the depths of subjectivity. Socrates is looking for the universally valid norm, for the good. He is the founder of *Moralität*.

But there is a deep contradiction in Socrates' *démarche*. His dialectic shows, on Hegel's view, that we cannot generate concrete content for our ethical

514

norms out of the principle of rational subjectivity alone. We derive a content only when we see what the form of community is which reason requires to be fully embodied. In other words, reason can give us a real normative content only via the notion of a *sittlich* community which it requires for its realization. The concrete content of our duties can only be given in the concrete demands this community makes on us. If we try to derive a morality simply of general rules, without any mention of societal context, we will find that no rule will really stand up to examination; all must admit of exceptions, and the problem arises of judging when they really apply and when they do not. This Hegel holds is what the Socratic dialectic shows. This of course parallels the later point about Kant.

The great contradiction is that while the times are not yet ripe for the development of a fully rational *Sittlichkeit* out of the identity of the universal subject (they will not be yet for some 2200 years), Socrates' teaching helps to break down the only *Sittlichkeit* that then exists, the unreflecting one. There is a certain truth in the charge on which he is condemned to death: his reflecting consciousness is the death of Greek *Sittlichkeit*.

Then comes Plato. It is not possible to do real justice to Hegel's discussion of Plato, and even more Aristotle, which takes up a large proportion of his lectures. The reason is obvious: Hegel drew heavily on these giants of ancient philosophy, particularly Aristotle. I cannot claim to do more than briefly indicate how he sees the development of philosophy passing through them.

Plato unites the pre-Socratic and the Socratic. He sees thought not only as the essence of man, but as the ground of all things. The Idea of the Good is the root of everything; this is not just a supersensible reality, but rather an underlying rationality. This rationality is the ground of being. Thus Plato has grasped the basic truth of speculation. He has given *the* principle of philosophy, the principle of Idealism, a pure and lofty expression. The Idea is not secondary, predicate, but is what is substantive, the self-subsistent.

Secondly Plato grasps that knowledge must come from out of oneself. He thus has an insight into the speculative truth that the true knowledge of thought is not inculcated from outside, but must be inwardly developed. Ultimately thought must justify its own premises, and hence be totally self-dependent. Only of course, Plato does not grasp this in such a fully clear form. The truth rather comes in the cloudy form of the doctrine of reminiscence. Hegel of course cannot resist connecting this with his doctrine through a pun on the German word 'Erinnerung', 'memory', which as Er-innerung is resonant with the notion of interiorization.

Thirdly, Plato sees that the mortal is that which is inadequate to the Idea. His dialectic begins to show how the particular dissolves itself into the universal, which as that in which the contradictions resolve is the truly concrete. But Plato

515

does not fully dominate his own insight here, and the dialectic often leads to a simply negative result.

But of course, Plato could not have grasped the fullness of speculative philosophy at that stage. We can outline three, connected insights which are missing: the Idea is not really active, it does not generate its sensible content. Nor does the order of ideas have an inner principle of development, which generates all the ideas in their order. In other words, Plato's world of Ideas is not Hegel's logical realm. Thirdly, connected with this, God remains separate from the world of ideas, he is still 'represented' (vorgestellt).

Hegel cites a great many details in his rich discussion of Plato's work. Let me just mention the Republic which he sees as literally a reactionary work. Plato tried to deny the principle of subjectivity which had then broken out, and re-establish a *Sittlichkeit* which would have no place for it. But this was impossible. Modern *Sittlichkeit* must have a place for marriage and the family and property.

So great is Aristotle that he makes serious progress in two of the domains where we have seen Plato to be inadequate. For Aristotle the Idea is active, the Form is the formative principle in matter. Aristotle is the man who fully develops one of the most important principles of the Hegelian system, the principle of inner teleology. The Forms are not separate from things, but are the formative principles within them. The sensible is shaped by the Form.

Aristotle also has a more satisfactory idea of God as the unmoved mover whose pure activity was thought, and in whom Form and matter are the same. This highest activity of thought was thus not dependent on some prior existent matter in order to actualize itself. Hegel gives Aristotle high marks for this.

Aristotle's notion of virtue as an interpenetration of reason and desire is also another seminal basis of Hegel's thought, which is opposed both to hedonism, and the sharp distinction of duty and inclination which he finds in Kant.

But in the third respect above, it is obviously not possible to expect Aristotle to have achieved a contemporary insight: his world of Forms is still without inner principle of self-derivation. It is not the Logic. By contrast Aristotle is the father of formal logic, of the logic of the understanding. His grasp of speculative connections was so deep, however, adds Hegel, that his actual insights were often well ahead of his logical theory.

So what is lacking with both these giants is a notion of the universal which would develop all the particular out of itself in a whole system. The Idea in Plato is abstract. Even though with Aristotle it develops to the notion of a thought which thinks itself, it still does not have this character of generating all out of it. The level of culture and science is as yet insufficient.

This means that in this world, the particular is just subsumed under the universal without inner connection. Hence we have dogmatism, and its simple opposite: scepticism. Different schools simply assert that their favourite principles are the ground of everything: the Stoics make thought; the Epicureans make particular sensation, particular beings, atoms, the principle. But none of these are proven, as the sceptics rightly point out.

But all these schools have taken from their predecessors that the principle of things is to be found also in subjectivity. And this is the period in which the *sittlich* community has collapsed and man is thrown back on himself. The inability of the various universal principles to articulate themselves into the manifold of reality is thus parallel to the inability of the universal subject to articulate a *sittlich* world which would give content to his aspirations and in which he would be at home. These two dimensions are closely linked.

Hence Stoic morality ends up with an empty coincidence with self which abandons all claims on the external world: the Stoic sage can be inwardly free whether on the throne or in chains. The Stoic has a morality only of the abstract universal man, not of the concrete differentiated man who has some station in life and polity. Quite understandable one might think in an ethic founded on pure thought. But the Epicureans do not fare any better. For theirs too is an ethic of impotence. The goal is pleasure, but in the end the stress on self-sufficiency and inner satisfaction is such that only the most inward and thought-dependent pleasures are valued. They, too, make no claim on the external world. As for the sceptics, their position expresses a renunciation of the external. This discussion parallels in part the interesting derivation in *PhG*, IV.

But this then gives rise to the third movement of ancient philosophy, which we see principally in the Neo-Platonists. Hegel sees that the abstract universal of the second period now produces differentiation out of itself, but in a purely super-sensible world. The world of Plotinus is a return to the self-thinking thought of Aristotle but with a great speculative development, that all the forms which make up the intelligible world are now seen as emanating from the One. The principle of self-generating movement is there in the intelligible world. Of course it is still not properly worked out. It is still full of *Vorstellen*, and above all it is only the generation of an intelligible world, not yet fully articulated into the sensible world. The deep truth of reconciliation between the intelligible and reality is not yet present, the reconciliation between the Idea, the cosmic Spirit, and the real, concrete, finite spirit. This is to come in Christianity. But in a sense Neo-Platonism is a kind of adumbration of the speculative truth of Christianity in the still ineffective mode of a vision of the intellectual world. As such, it can be seen as the ancient world of philosophy coming to the historic rendez-vous with the new revealed religion.

Thus the first period of the ancient world was founded on an abstract principle (e.g. Eleatics); the second rose to the principle of subjectivity, of self-consciousness; the third becomes concrete, and sees a world generated out

517

of thought. But it is still supra-sensible, it has not yet come to the infinite subjectivity in finite subjectivity, to absolute freedom, to God in man.

The Incarnation must come. For the Neo-Platonists lack the point where the real opposites unite, where the intelligible world is one with the real outer one, the moment of a real particular 'this', of *Wirklichkeit*. This comes in the Incarnation, and the founding of the Christian community (Gemeinde). This takes man into a new religious development.

But this is a development in which man stands before a reconciliation which is already realized, which he has to interiorize. This reconciliation is a sensibly presented fact before him, as we saw earlier. It is a brute fact, not something which he can produce from his own thought, or yet understand fully by thought.

Man thus enters a period in which he must submit to an external crucial fact, and allows himself to be educated up to full interiorization of its significance. He enters a period of tutelage. But this is incompatible with true philosophical thought. Philosophy is by definition free thought, reposing on its own inner conviction of rational cogency. By contrast mediaeval thought is a period in which philosophy was in service, the handmaid of theology. Just as the Church had to take the barbarian nations into tutelage to train them up to the Idea, so it presses philosophy into service, and uses it to work out the fullness of its vision of God. Thus in a sense we can say that the Middle Ages is not a period of philosophy. Only the ancient and the modern worlds truly are. During the Middle Ages only the Arab East developed philosophy further in the pure Idea. But this does not mean that the Middle Ages is not full of interesting and important intellectual constructions, or that it will not importantly influence philosophy later on. It is far from being a blank page in the history of philosophy. Only men started then from given premises, the deliverances of revelation, not authenticated by philosophy itself. (But of course these theological premises were *an sich* speculative.)[1]

3

So we come to the modern world. Philosophy is reborn as an independent activity. For man once more turns to himself in self-dependence. The Reformation represents a refusal of the spiritual as something merely external, in host as a thing, in charismatic authority, in relic or sepulchre. Instead it seeks to find union with God in a spiritual, inner way. Thus man moves away

---

[1] One of these important ideas is the ontological proof of Anselm. This is the really speculative proof Hegel insists, because it starts with thought, the Idea, and goes over into existence, whereas the others move from existence, the contingent, etc., to God. Their form is thus inadequate to their content, because their form seems to imply that God is secondary to the world and not vice versa. Only the ontological proof is in the right order. But the proof as given by Anselm is in an inadequate form. Cf. discussion in Chapter XI.

from external authority to the inner testimony of his own spirit. At the same time, this spiritualization goes along with a greater interest in this world. The gross, reified sacred of mediaeval religion went along with an otherworld-liness as its natural pendant. The reified sacred expressed a condition of grossness and untamed naturality. In this world, the highest spirituality had to be flight. But the new principle of the Reformation, while spiritualizing the Christian presence tries to make it penetrate all of life. Hence secular life becomes important.

Thus the Reformation is part of the same basic movement as the Renaissance; which led to the great interest in exploration, the great burst of scientific effort, and so on. In this environment, philosophy as an attempt to think once more in free independence is naturally re-born.

So once again men take up the standpoint of the followers of Socrates, that we are certain of discovering the principle of things within our own self-consciousness, that by thought we can penetrate to the very basis of things. But this confidence now exists to a higher power. Where the ancients discovered the principle of the intelligible world in thought, but could never fully overcome the dualism with the sensible world, the moderns build on the certainty of Christianity that the Idea is fully reflected in the sensible world. The sensible world, in other words, is not just a cause of alienation and loss of the spiritual, it is posited by it. This is what is expressed in the Christian dogma of the creation of the world by God, who 'saw that it was good'. Thus Christians, even those influenced by Neo-Platonism like Augustine, cannot look on the sensible creation as negative, as a source of alienation.

The speculative instinct contained in this dogma lies at the basis of modern philosophy, though this is not clearly seen at the beginning. That is, there is a kind of instinctive certainty that rational thought will find itself expressed in being, even the most external and sensible being; that thought and being are one. There is a Christian-inspired absolute confidence in this reconciliation. 'The reconciliation...has occurred *an sich*' (*SW*, xix, 274). And this reason which is expressed in being is that which can be fully encompassed by the finite subject.

Thus the modern age has the boldness and courage to express the oppositions in their purest and most radical form, confident of their overcoming. And the principal opposition of the modern age is the most radical one, that between being and thought. But this comes out in other oppositions which are related, like that between freedom and necessity, soul and body, etc. Two basic approaches are taken to these oppositions; one starts from the natural (empiricism, natural philosophy, derivation of rights from nature), the other from the idea (various forms of idealism).

As a sort of hors d'oeuvre Hegel starts off by considering two rather ill-assorted philosophers, Bacon and Böhme. Bacon is taken up as the originator of empiricism, the enemy of scholasticism, and final causes. Hegel uses this as an occasion to show that empiricism prepares its opposite, that it discovers an articulation of things which prepare us later for a vision of how they developed out of the Idea, and indeed empiricism prepares some of the concepts for this, all unwillingly.

Böhme was, of course, an important figure for the Romantic generation. And Hegel sees prefigured in Böhme's figurative, mystical language, the central truths of speculative philosophy. Though why this should be considered philosophy is not entirely clear; unless it is that it is a theology which makes no attempt to base itself on any positive authority.

So we enter in the seventeenth century on the movement of modern philosophy proper. This unlike the ancients will give due honour to the empirical. It will take seriously and try to encompass the empirical and contingent, external reality. Hence modern philosophy gives rise to a burgeoning empirical science. But at the same time, it strives to overcome in thought the opposition between thought and being which it has the courage to push to its ultimate sharpness, a courage born of its deep instinctive confidence that this opposition is overcome.

Hence modern philosophy is marked both by a scientific movement and a metaphysical one, sometimes in intrication, sometimes in opposition. Descartes is the major opening figure of modern European metaphysics. Descartes brings us back to the full philosophical tradition of the Greeks; he is free from all authority. His questioning is radical. In this he may remind us of the ancient sceptics. But the difference, says Hegel, is that while these latter aimed to achieve a sense of their own freedom in this questioning, Descartes wanted to win through to solid knowledge of objective reality. For as a modern he is concerned with uniting thought to external reality.

But Descartes' *démarche* is thoroughly philosophical. He is determined to found all knowledge on the power of thought alone; no presuppositions are to be accepted. This is the point of methodical doubt. Thought is to be entirely *bei sich*, says Hegel, no matter foreign to it is to be accepted. But Descartes, in Hegel's judgement, does not manage fully to live up to this, as we shall see.

Hence his radical thought starts with the 'I', with self-consciousness as thinking. And from this Descartes derives his famous cogito. Hegel sees this, in line with his whole angle of vision on modern philosophy, as the assertion of an immediate identity between thought and being: cogito, ergo sum. The identity is immediate, because as Descartes insists there is not even an inference here.

But the thought here is pure and abstract. That is, none of the contents of my thought are englobed in this certainty, just the fact of thinking itself, with the inseparable concomitant of existing, is the turning point of doubt to certainty. Thought here is a universal, abstracted from all content. But of course this fits admirably with one of the Hegelian theses of the Logic: that thought which negates all its inner determinations returns to immediacy, and in its immediacy it is identical to Being, to the pure Being which is the starting point of the Logic. At the end of the Logic, thought goes over into being because its pure self-mediation is a kind of return to immediacy.

But of course he has not got it right, because he has no inkling of the immense inner self-articulation of thought and hence of being as truly developing out of it. His thought is thoroughly abstract and lacks all principle of development. Thus it is that when Descartes goes forward to establish the content of the empirical world against doubt he has to fall short of his promise and have recourse to presuppositions, to premises and elements which he merely accepts without being able to establish them by thought alone, to principles which are merely 'come upon' (vorgefunden). This is Hegel's judgement, for instance, on the recourse to God as guarantor of the veracity of my perceptions in the *Meditations*. And of course Descartes does not see that thought as such goes over into being. The thought which he is starting from is just the subjective thought of the I. That thought which is basic to all, God, is separate from and over against the I.

The result of this is that Descartes indeed ends up with an opposition between thought and being. Because their unity in the cogito is simply immediate, combining merely abstract thought with being, their true unity cannot be portrayed, and over against the being-which-is-thought, the cogito, is another mode of being which is radically non-thought, matter. Descartes thus poses a radically dichotomous opposition between thought and being, and in this he is a foundation thinker for the whole modern age, which as we have seen, has as its basic theme to push this opposition to its pure and radical form.

But the matter of Descartes which is in radical dichotomy with thought is itself very abstract and hence thought-derived. Its essence is extension, which is the property of matter which can be derived in pure thought, and not like other properties, smell, colour, etc., merely by the senses. This is a frequent theme with Hegel, that the pure matter of modern philosophy is so much a vision of thought and so little of sensuous experience that it constantly belies the role it is made to play. In accounting for reality in terms of matter, philosophers have often seen themselves as offering an explanation in radically non-spiritual terms, as developing a thoroughgoing naturalism. But in fact this pure matter is so rarefied by thought that explanations in terms of it might just as well be seen as having the opposite sense, as giving a basic ontological role to the spiritual, to thought. This matter is a *Gedankending*, but not in the usual dismissive sense, rather as such it touches on the deepest reality.[1]

[1] Cf. the discussion on equivalence of pure matter and thought in the passage of *PhG*, vi on Enlightenment materialism.

Descartes' matter is seen by Hegel as the transposition of abstract thought into external reality. Because the notion of thought is abstract and without rich internal development, so is the notion of matter. It is in the end simply extension, and because thought is essentially active, motion. All is to be explained in terms of extension and motion, that is everything in nature. Motion is the abstract, external transposition of the rich activity of thought. To explain everything by extension and motion is to explain it mechanically, and this becomes the main category of explanation with Descartes. He is thus the father of mechanism. But by the same token he cannot really understand life, and those domains of philosophy which can be called philosophy of spirit: psychology, politics, etc., are ill-developed in this thought.

By contrast, he develops a physics. But here Descartes and his age have not yet made the clear distinction in their physics between a science based on observation and one which develops its determinations purely out of the concept.[1]

Spinoza goes further. He takes off from Descartes, from the latter's opposition between thought and extension, and tries to unite these. This is an altogether more contentful and difficult enterprise than asserting the simple identity of abstract thought and being. In extension we have a less abstract, more developed determination of being and hence the problem of unity is greater and the notion of unity much higher, more developed.

Spinoza is in fact an important philosopher; one of the most important for Hegel's thought, along perhaps with Aristotle and Kant. Spinoza attempts to see the whole as system with God as its ontological base, a God who unites thought and being. Thus Hegel is always ready to rush to Spinoza's defense against the charge of atheism. Rather, as Hegel says, since God alone is the substance into which all determinations sink, we might more justly accuse Spinoza of the opposite fault, acosmism.

And this, indeed, is the burthen of Hegel's critique of Spinoza, who of course was a seminal philosopher for Schelling and for the whole Romantic generation.[2] Spinoza is thus one of Hegel's crucial landmarks, against which he defines his own position.

The trouble with Spinoza is that he has grasped the absolute as a single substance, but not yet as subject. He sees all the determinations of the world, including the 'attributes' of thought and extension as going back to a single substantial ground, to a basic unity. But this God of Spinoza lacks the movement in the other direction: he does not produce in turn all the articulation of the world by his own inner necessity, as Hegel has shown to be the case of the Idea. The God of Spinoza is thus not yet a living spirit, who must generate his own embodiment and return to himself out of it. In him, all

---

[1] 'Ableiten aus dem Begriffe, frei selbstständige Entwicklung des Begriffs.'
[2] Cf. Chapter I.

determinations are cancelled, annulled, but they are not generated by an inner necessity. In this sense, God lacks the crucial characteristic of the Hegelian subject. God is just substance, indeed he is merely an empty 'abyss' (Abgrund) in which all differences disappear, rather than the germinal centre from which they can all be seen to unfold by inner necessity. The actual determinations of the world are thus still not derived by necessity, but just 'come upon' (vorgefunden).

In this way, Spinoza, a Jew, remains with the Jewish absolute which is unreconciled with the articulated empirical world, and with finite subjectivity, who only exists still in the movement of negation of this finitude, without returning to be reconciled to it. But Spinoza's is of course a highly philosophically-transformed version of this vision. In this respect it can also be compared to the *to on* of the Eleatics, which also lacked the principle of inner development.

Hegel makes central use of the famous Spinozist principle: *omnis determinatio est negatio.* This is another way of expressing his debt to Spinoza. But here again we can see his basic critique. For Spinoza, this means that all the determinate realities of the world are carved out, as it were, from the whole. They are arrived at by selecting from the whole and negating the rest. The fully positive is thus that which is quite free of negation. But for Hegel the positive can only be the negation of the negation. It cannot exist without the negation of it which is its embodiment in the particular, with all the alienation, loss of self, and hence negation of its infinity which this entails. The positive, God, the infinite, the very basis of things, only can be by returning to itself out of these negations. Thus if it is true that determinate being is a negation of the absolute or infinite, it is also true that this infinite must issue in this negation. It must negate itself; and is only finally at one with itself by returning out of this negation.

We can also see the same difference from another angle in looking at Spinoza's theory of attributes and modes. These distinctions in the absolute substance are seen as introduced in it through subjective thought; the absolute refracts in that way into finite thought. The differences are not seen as integral to it.

This lack in the content of his philosophy is matched, says Hegel, by a lack in its form. Spinoza proceeds *more geometico.* We have already seen that for Hegel the mathematical is the poorest mode of thought and the farthest removed from the speculative. This naturally goes together with the failure to grasp the principle of inner development of the Idea. Hence we proceed from definitions and deductions from definition; we do not see how these notions so defined themselves issue necessarily out of the Concept, e.g., thought, extension, understanding, will, etc. We are still operating with presuppositions.

However, like Aristotle, the results are often much higher than the theory.

Some of Spinoza's definitions are full of deep speculative content. Hegel mentions, e.g., the notion of God as causa sui, Spinoza's notion of the true infinity of God who is unbounded totality. The latter is close to the Hegelian. But the distinction between thought and extension made by Descartes does not just disappear. The fixity of the distinction is defended against the Spinozistic 'abyss' (Abgrund) by another school, the empiricists. The modern world has as inner principle the unity of thought and being, but this means also that it really takes seriously external, empirical reality. These two concerns cannot be fully effectively united until the synthesis in true speculative philosophy. Until then they animate different philosophies with different priority weightings, and these philosophies are thus opposed. Hence while Spinoza gives primacy to the unity, Locke, and we shall see in a moment in another way Leibniz, give priority to the real independence of the external, empirical reality.

Hence the *démarche* of Locke is to start from the existent outside of consciousness, to take the Cartesian dichotomy and give the primacy to extention. The universal is not the root of all, thought is not substance. On the contrary the universal is derived subjectively out of the empirical object, ('entsteht subjektiv aus den Gegenständen' *SW*, xix, 419). This means that empirical thought has no use for a real essence, and hence never attains to the understanding of the essence as Genus (Gattung) which posits its empirical objectivity. Empiricism, just as much as Cartesianism, is dealing with a reality not derived from necessity, but just 'come upon' (vorgefunden). But now this is openly recognized, and indeed, seen as the principal value of this philosophy.

This path is a necessary phase. We have to gain greater knowledge of external reality through observation only before we can come back to discern in it the workings of the Concept. At this stage, both the empiricist and idealist sides of modern consciousness, those which stress unity and those which stress distinction, must proceed autonomously to their full development in order to prepare the ultimate rendez-vous. Hence the empirical efforts of Newton, or in another field Grotius, have a great importance. But it must be stressed that these thinkers often found themselves operating with a certain level of speculative concepts all unknowing. Newtonian science makes essential use of the concepts from the middle sphere in the logic, the sphere of reflection: e.g., forces. But the full significance of this only comes clear later. It all shows that the Concept is inescapable.

Leibniz too is a revendication of the differentiated reality against the Spinozistic *Abgrund*. But here the main point of rebellion is the individual, subjectivity. The Leibnizian monad is a deep speculative expression of the notion of a self; for it is a real unity of simplicity and difference, like the I. It contains the principle of movement in itself, the principle of negativity whereby it is not just unity but inherently differentiated. It is a 'simplicity in the multiplicity, but a simplicity which is at the same time change, movement of the multiplicity' (*SW*, XIX, 459). It is active and not just a subject of representation (*vorstellend*).

Hegel also lauds Leibniz's principle of the Identity of Indiscernables, which he takes over from him. But he gives it also a deeper speculative interpretation. It means, he says, that all things have the principle of their differentiation from others in themselves, that their difference from others is not just inertly there but something they actively assert and defend. That is why we find the defining characteristics of certain animals, for instance, in their claws, because that is what they maintain themselves by. Thus the frontier of differentiation is also a frontier of opposition, as we saw earlier in the Logic.

But the faults of Leibniz are closely linked with his achievements. He has wonderfully revendicated against Spinoza the place of subjectivity, of the actively self-differentiating and hence individual. This speculative principle achieves a deep statement in his doctrine of the monad. But the price he pays is that he cannot give an account of the unity of things. How do all the monads articulate together? There is no satisfactory answer to this in Leibniz.

The way the monads cohere together, their harmony, is not understood out of their own natures. Its inherent necessity is not made clear, but it is simply posited as coming to them from the outside, as 'pre-established' by God. The unity whose inner necessity we do not understand is thrown into God. It remains unilluminated. True, we supposedly know the goals of God's operation in establishing this world and its harmony, in that he is supposed to act so as to create the best possible world. But this remains purely formal. We cannot really understand why this is the best possible world.

This means for Leibniz that the evil in it is necessary for the good. But why this is so, or why evil is bound up with finitude, or why finitude is necessary, all this is not satisfactorily explained. Hegel, of course, will give the explanation.

Leibniz, in other words, cannot really penetrate to the inner necessity of connections. In keeping with this his notion of conceptual unity remains too close to the deductive. Even when we come to see all determinations as inwardly connected, as they are in the perception of a single monad which perceives the whole world from its point of view, this is just a reproduction in this monad of the uncomprehended coherence of things attributed to God's action. We cannot see the necessity of the connection as springing from the very inner nature of things connected. We remain with unconnected individual realities. We have indeed gained individuality, but have lost the whole.

Thus Leibniz, like Spinoza and Locke, and in his own way, cannot yet achieve the speculative vision of the concept developing reality out of itself by an inner necessity.

Hegel here has some unkind words for Wolff as an expositor of Leibniz in a particularly dead, pedantic way.

But at this point the modern thrust in philosophy becomes more radical. The modern certainty is that thought or the absolute is one with being, even the external, empirical reality of the world and of finite subjects. And this certainty is animating a philosophy, that is, it is not just accepted as the deep truth of revealed religion but it is meant to be grasped in human thought. Man, as it were, revendicates this right. There is in a sense a triangle: finite spirit, infinite spirit, world of things, which are in ultimate union, where spirit and matter are one. But finite spirit does not and cannot realize this unity alone, but only through infinite spirit. Descartes links our mind to the world in the certainty of perception through God; thought and extension meet in the Absolute for Spinoza; Leibniz's monads are harmonized by God.

But now human self-consciousness makes a more radical claim, to find unity with the world without the offices of God. Man as finite spirit can achieve this unity by plumbing the secrets of the world and reconstructing it according to human reason, so that it is fully pliable to his purposes. The reconciliation of thought and being, spirit and outer reality, will come through a domination of the second by the first, a complete conquest. But this is now to be achieved by finite spirit. We are entering the age of the Enlightenment.

To put it in another way, modern philosophy from Descartes to Leibniz is 'metaphysical', in the sense that it unites thought and being through postulating a supersensible order of being which sustains the empirical world. Now the radical self-confidence of human self-consciousness can no longer accept such speculations about a beyond. It directs against metaphysics a withering scepticism. And since this metaphysics is of the understanding, that is, has no idea yet of the development of reality out of the Idea, but just must state dogmatically the ontological primacy of thought, it is easy prey to this scepticism.

But this scepticism is not just despairing, or nihilistic, it springs from a profound confidence that finite human spirit can achieve reconciliation, is fundamentally in unity with external reality. It is a radical turn of the modern confidence that thought = being which attributes this achievement to finite thought. But of course this is as much a theory of the understanding as its metaphysical opponent; it too stops at fixed distinctions between things, and cannot see the inner connections. It too is one-sided. But it can make headway against metaphysics because the fault of the latter is that it *is* dogmatic.

The Enlightenment has two variants, which can roughly be identified as British and French. The British variant is more contemplative. A transition figure is Berkeley who collapsed external being into my representations. But these are still seen as produced by God. As Hegel points out, no speculative progress is achieved by this equivalence, for the inner necessity of the representations is just as little understood as when they were seen as things.

Hume represents a real radicalization of empiricism. The reference of everything to experience in a radical way does away with all necessity. Even causation is deprived of its necessity and reduced to a subjective connection. Hegel insists on reading the subjectivism of Hume not as a despairing confession of the impotence of human thought, but rather as expressing the deep sense that all that mattered concerning the basis of reality was available to finite self-consciousness.

Thus in the moral sphere, Hume's scepticism undermines all *sittlich* objective criteria. But the result of this is that we are thrown back on our own moral sentiment. And from Hume and other thinkers of the time there developed a theory of moral sense which expresses once again the principle of total confidence in self-consciousness. It shows, remarks Hegel, the stage of formation (Bildung) which Spirit has attained at this point.

With the French, the Enlightenment goes over onto the offensive, as it were. It strives after practical realization. It claims the right to reconstruct all of reality according to the dictates and norms developed by finite self-consciousness. It thus rejects all traditional morality, obligations to God, and any such norms not validated by self-consciousness.

God, if he goes on existing, is thus emptied and reduced to a pallid *être suprème*. Or else the Enlightenment takes the more radical step of denying anything except the finite. There is nothing except external, contingent being, which means ultimately, material being. Hence the radical Enlightenment goes to materialism; finite spirit is itself identical to matter. We come to another form of the equivalence of thought and being. But here again an immediate and stultifying one. Hence this Enlightenment science is just as incapable as its predecessors of explaining the inner articulations of things out of necessity, or of understanding the unfolding of things. This science is just crassly empirical.

The empty thought of the *être suprème*, and the inert abstract matter of materialism are not that far apart, as we remarked before. Both express the unbounded self-affirmation of finite self-consciousness, its refusal of an infinite, spiritual reality beyond. Hence we find the Enlightenment described as the absolute reign of the finite. Everything is finite, all the contents of the world, themselves finite, are laid before finite subjectivity. As finite, nothing has its raison d'être in itself. Hence this is the ideology of utility, universal utility. To see something under the light of utility is to see its raison d'être in something else, to see it as good for something else. The Enlightenment, taking the standpoint of the finite, is the age of utilitarianism.

But this confident self-consciousness steps over into action. The movement which began with Luther, and was carried forward in the modern period, has now come to an extreme form. There is no absolute beyond finite self-consciousness. The notion of Luther is that all men must interiorize the truth spiritually. There are no laymen, who must receive the sacred from outside, from priests. This principle is now about to be applied to the political world.

This leads to a negation of Spirit, of the larger order, and here of the real conditions of *Sittlichkeit*. We have already followed this disastrous movement. It comes to climax in the French Revolution. It has the essential idea of free will, or of thought making an external reality which is adequate to it. But it crucially fails to recognize the true nature of thought or *Geist*. It sees this as purely human, and can thus realize no adequate existence. Either we have the form of thought, but the content of ethics is given just by de facto desire (Trieb), or with Rousseau, we have the right content, the general will, but a disastrously wrong form – total participation and not the articulated, *sittlich* state. The disastrous consequences we have already seen.

This rage of subjectivity pushes us beyond. There is an absolute necessity to generate the concrete again, to come back to God. This is the task of the next and final cycle.

Hegel pauses for a consideration of Jacobi who as we have seen represents a Romantic streak of religion which has been infected by the Enlightenment to the point of denying knowledge of God. God is reachable only through immediate faith. But this religion which renounces thought is no answer to Enlightenment unbelief. Reason has to go beyond itself.

Kant who is the third great seminal figure for Hegel's thought takes another great step forward. He is fully in the line of the Enlightenment, whose principle is freedom. Thought must develop in complete autonomy, it cannot accept any external authority. And he goes along with the radical twist that the Enlightenment gives to this modern idea: thought can rely only on what can be made present in self-consciousness. Kant thus takes the side of Hume in rejecting the great metaphysical constructions of the second phase which were presented in Germany by Leibniz and Wolff.

But Kant took a tremendous step forward in that while remaining within self-consciousness he saw the real nature of thought as activity. He agrees with Hume that necessary connection is not in the matter of experience; but unlike Hume he goes on to recognize it in the very structure of consciousness, that is in the concept. The concept is not just that which is abstracted from experience, but rather what shapes it. Kant has thus discovered the real nature of thought; it is not passive, not simply what contemplates and draws inferences (for rationalists) or registers concomitances (for empiricists). It is the active principle which shapes the things of experience.

But Kant's great discovery is still incomplete. It lacks one thing. It still sees this thought, the active, shaping concept, as subjective, as the thought merely of self-consciousness; whereas in fact it is the ontological base of reality. And as a result, Kant sees conceptual form as having to receive its content from outside. It is ultimately passive in the sense that it needs to be affected from outside to function. But the truth of speculative philosophy is just that thought, the Concept, produces its own content out of itself. In the end all matter must be seen as posited by the Idea.

A crucial and hardly minor transposition; but one which provides the central access to the Hegelian system. Coming in from Kant, as it were, we enter through the front door. For many of the most important key Hegelian terms can only be understood as transposed from Kant. This is true of the Concept, which is the Kantian formative concept, given ontological status. It is true of the Logic, which can only be understood if we see it as a transcendental logic; it is true of the Idea, which derives not just from Plato but also through Kant as the completed form to which empirical reality tends. It is true of the distinction between 'understanding' (Verstand) and 'reason' (Vernunft). And so on.

But in all these cases, there is a systematic transformation. What for Kant is a structure of the mind is for Hegel an ontological foundation. The Concept is the basis of things, the Idea is that which posits reality. It is not simply an unfulfilled tendency; it *is* in a more fundamental sense than anything else. Hegel's philosophy can be seen as transposed Kant. What for Kant is merely a striving of the subject is for Hegel a completed self-subsistent totality.

Thus Kant sees the primacy of thought when he shows that the 'I think' must accompany all my representations. The only possible objectivity is one structured by thought. But he sees this as a demand of subjective knowledge, not an ontological principle. His notion of the schematism was a profound idea, the structuring of empirical reality by thought, but the same criticism applies.

Kant remains with the Enlightenment in the crucial respect that he holds to finite self-consciousness as an insurmountable standpoint. But within this he takes a giant step forward. He sees thought as active, shaping. And hence he begins to fill a lack which has been evident in philosophy since the ancients: he begins to order the categories not just empirically, but in a rational structure. His hitting on the form of triplicity for the categories reflects a 'great instinct of the Concept'. But of course he cannot push this insight right through to the full self-development which comes first in the Logic. Nevertheless, Hegel's 'category' is also a Kant-transposed concept.

But Kant's terrible shortcoming is to have accepted that the reality outside consciousness, the things in themselves, were beyond the reach of the Concept, and were to be distinguished from the appearances which the Concept shapes. This is an 'abominable distinction'. It underlies all the errors of his philosophy.

His crucial strength and his crucial weakness come out again in the Transcendental Dialectic. Here to his undying merit Kant has seen the deep contradictions in our basic categories. But characteristically, he fails to see that these contradictions are ontological, they are not just in our thought. Kant is 'too tender for things', as Hegel puts it. He is also wrong to restrict the antinomies to four; every category is the locus of an antinomy.[1]

In the field of moral philosophy the same basic error is visible. True to the principle of the Enlightenment, practical reason is to decide everything out of itself. It is to accept no external authority, not even that of God. It is to realize full autonomy. But once again this sovereign self-consciousness is set over against the world. The empirical domain, including the domain of my de facto desires, is refractory to practical reason. Reason cannot be integrally realized in it. If it were, and we were really inclined to the good by pure desire, the moral realm in its autonomy would disappear. Yet the very essence of the moral law is to be realized. Hence we have a law that is to be realized and can never be so integrally; and thus we are forever on the way. We are forever in the domain of the unrealized ought, of *Sollen*. We are in an endless progress and we only complete it in thought by the postulates of practical reason. This critique of the Kantian ethic of *Sollen* is one of the most oft-repeated themes in Hegel.

Connected with this is the fact that the ethic to be drawn from self-consciousness alone can find no content. It is forced back onto a purely formal criterion, for no particular content in the world can provide a standard, all are looked on as arbitrary. The true insight is to see that reason itself produces an articulated content, a community which is the locus of *Sittlichkeit*, and this gives content to our ethic. But as long as we determine to abstract from all this, as long as we rely simply on the resources of autonomous finite self-consciousness, we can have nothing but formal criteria: the Kantian criterion of a maxim not contradicting itself. We have already seen that this is empty; and Hegel repeats here the argument about theft and property (*SW*, XIX, 592).[2]

But for all this, if Kant had just written the first two critiques he would have an outstanding place in the development of speculative philosophy. But he went farther. He wrote the *Critique of Judgement*; and here he laid the groundwork for a synthesis which straddles the dichotomy of his philosophy. This *Critique* is even more crucial for understanding Hegel's philosophy than the rest of Kant's work. Indeed, it is the starting point for the whole post-Kantian development.

In the objects of reflecting judgement, the work of art and the living being, we have a unity of form and content, of inner law and outer reality, which we

---

[1] Cf. the discussion of the *Logic*, Part III, Chapter IX.

[2] This is like the argument in his article of the early 1800s. 'Über die Wissenschaftlichen Behandlungsarten des Naturrechts', discussed above in Chapter XIV. Basically the same criticism of Kant's moral philosophy, that in purifying the moral will and safeguarding its autonomy against any involvement with nature or dependence on God, Kant makes the demands of morality indeterminate in content and impossible of fulfilment, recurs throughout Hegel's work. Cf. also *PhG*, 301–12, 424–44, *PR*, § 135, and elsewhere.

are firmly denied in theoretical and practical judgement. For in these objects studied in the third *Critique*, matter and form are not separate. In reflecting judgement, we do not apply a universal form to a given content from outside. On the contrary, faced with a content, a particular, we look for a form which is peculiarly its. We discover a form which is thus immanent in the content, united with it, in the way that it never is in theoretical judgement. But this of course brings us back close to the Aristotelian idea of inner teleology, a necessity immanent in things themselves to assume their own shape. This inner necessity is of course for Hegel equivalent to freedom.

This is the inner teleology which we see in living organisms. And we have also seen how Hegel understands the work of art as inhabited by this same kind of inner necessity, one which unlike the living organism reveals itself, and exists only to show this free necessity. Because this is a manifestation of freedom, we feel free contemplating it, we are enraptured (entrückt). We saw how much Hegel's aesthetics owes to Kant.

Kant however cannot take the crucial step. This great insight of inner teleology remains a *façon de voir* for him; it is not a reality of things themselves. But he prepares the ground for the transcending of his own position.

It is also of a piece with the rest of Kant's position that he accepts the Enlightenment idea that God cannot be known. God is only an object of faith, and his authority over conscience is nil, unless it be simply to echo what rational will tells itself.

But Kant brought thought to such great heights that he awoke the irresistible urge to go beyond; and this in two directions: first, to complete the task of ordering the categories of thought in a consistent way, deriving from one another; and second, to overcome the Kantian dichotomy of form and matter; to derive reality from thought. The first craving was answered by Fichte, the second by Schelling.

The last eighty pages or so of the philosophy of history is taken up with Fichte, Schelling and various connected minor figures. It presents what Hegel sees as the immediate antecedents to his own philosophy. With Fichte, the attempt is made to develop all the categories out of a single principle in a systematic way. The starting point for Fichte is the I. Everything is to be developed from this. Fichte sees the I as under a necessity to posit a not-self, an opposed reality. Each of these can only be in relation to the other. There are two forms of relation: when the not-I is active, we have a theoretical relation, when the I is active, a practical relation. All the categories can be deduced from avatars of these relationships.

The I attempts constantly to abrogate and overcome the not-I. But this dualism is made ultimately insurmountable. So that Fichte like Kant has a philosophy of endless progress, of pure *Sollen*. In short, he has overcome one shortcoming of Kant, in that for the first time the categories have been fully and systematically derived and deduced. But he has not overcome the other shortcoming, which is to be still held at the standpoint of self-consciousness, of the I. His system therefore cannot be completed, cannot come to totality.

Remaining as he does at this standpoint of self-consciousness, of the individual will, Fichte's political philosophy is as unsatisfactory as Rousseau's and Kant's. The universal is not the true spirit, the embodiment of freedom of the individuals, but simply a negative force over against them. Fichte tries to ground the state on freedom, following Rousseau and Kant, but achieves the exact opposite.

Fichte's cult of the *Ich* resonates in certain strands of Romanticism, which cultivated inner feeling at the expense of reason and shrank away from external authority and action in history. Hegel mentions, e.g., Schlegel and Novalis. We have explored these connections.[1]

We turn now to Schelling who is the immediate ante-chamber to Hegel's system. Hegel only realized that he was on a different wave length than Schelling after some years collaboration with him, around the time of the *PhG*. Schelling finally sees that finite and infinite, subject and object are untrue alone. That the only concrete unity is the unity of these opposites, not just in simple identity but in living process and movement. Schelling thus develops a deep philosophy of nature – Hegel drew many of his ideas from it.

But his inadequacy is that he saw this unity as being accessible to intuition. He did not yet understand that the unity has to be grasped in thought, that it can be derived in the pure self-mediations of the concept. He grasped for the first time the concrete content but he did not see that its proper form of development was logical. His intuition was not susceptible to proof. For Schelling the highest manifestation of the Idea is thus in the work of art, where it is open to intuition. The work of art is the 'highest and only mode in which the Idea is for Spirit'. But for Hegel thought is higher, the Idea must yet come to itself in thought.

This inadequacy in form obviously repercusses onto the content of his system. Thus his philosophy of nature, while an attempt to show the progressively higher realization of the Idea, of concrete unity between subject and object, and while an immensely valuable beginning, is not really rigorously carried through. And this lack of rigor allowed Schelling's disciples to roam all over the place with arbitrary, irresponsible analogies, and give philosophy of nature a bad name.

To put it in another way, we can say that with Fichte we have the affirmation of the autonomy of self-consciousness which has been pushed to a delirious extreme. The I is no longer limited by another, it is infinitely

---

[1] Cf. Chapters I and VI.

self-realizing. It is no longer set over against a reality which it can never encroach upon. But precisely because it is still just an I, it *requires* always that there be something over against it. In order to be consciousness, and not to fall into the emptiness of I = I, it must always have the not-I to contend with. Hence its process of encroaching on the not-I is endless. It is the first true philosophy of infinite self-realization. But the infinite here is 'bad'; the process can never reach completion; it remains *Sollen*.

It is Fichte's radical affirmation of finite subjectivity which shows that this standpoint must be transcended. And so we have to go back to a content outside of finite subjectivity, and this can only be done by seeing the unity of subjectivity with objectivity in a living totality which is infinite subjectivity. This is what Schelling does. But he cannot demonstrate it; he does not give its place to thought.

We thus come to the end with Hegel, who does take this last step of demonstrating the absolute as identity of subject and object in self-developing life. He shows the absolute to be thought, which is ultimately grasped in thought. It comes to itself in its own proper medium. The 'intellectual intuition' of Schelling to be really intellectual must become thought. And in this consummation the world-spirit puts aside all foreign, external (gegenständlichen) modes of self-understanding, and grasps itself as absolute *Geist*. It shows that what is objective is generated (erzeugt) out of itself.

We can now see that there has always only been one philosophy. It now reaches final form, but it has been going forward from the beginning, even when for a time its development went underground and was not fully apparent. Thought is always trying to grasp itself as concrete. Aristotle saw that *nous* is the thought of thought.

But this progress has been by stages. Each stage showed us the highest form that this single philosophy could reach then. And even where there were different competing philosophies, they form a whole together as a single link in chain, though this may only be evident later.

But now we seem to have come to a climax. 'A new epoch has arisen in the world' (*SW*, xix, 689). Spirit at least seems to have come clear. What is objective to it, it produces from itself, and holds in its power peacefully. The struggle of finite self-consciousness with absolute self-consciousness seems to have come to an end. Finite self-consciousness is no longer finite, and so absolute self-consciousness has the reality it lacked. World history 'seems to be at its goal' (*SW*, xix, 690).

PART VI

CONCLUSION

CHAPTER XX

Hegel Today

1

This magnificent Hegelian synthesis has dissolved. After achieving an extra-ordinary ascendancy over the German intellectual world in the 1820s and 1830s, it began to wane a decade after his death in 1831. We think of the 1840s as the great age of rebellion against the Hegelian system, the age of the Young Hegelians, Feuerbach, Ruge, Stirner, Marx, the time also when Kierkegaard began his short, intense intellectual career.

But to be the object of virulent attack by a generation of young thinkers is still to be very much on the agenda. Much worse was in store for Hegel's absolute idealism. In the 1850s and 1860s it fell into virtual oblivion. Hegel was vaguely remembered in Bismarckian Germany as the state philosopher of 'Restoration' Prussia, and peripherally approved of or vilified in consequence. There is an amusing bit of correspondence between Marx and Engels of the 1870s in which they give vent to their impatience at the ignorance of the younger generation. The occasion was a footnote by a young Social-Democratic editor in which he referred to Hegel as the philosopher of the 'royal Prussian Idea of the state'.[1] The incident illustrates how much the Hegelian roots of Marx and Engels' thought came to be misunderstood even in their own movement.

Hegel, of course, made a 'comeback' in Germany towards the end of the century. Lasson's critical work in producing new, more scholarly editions of his work stimulated and was stimulated by this renewed interest. Dilthey helped to make Hegel an important reference point in the great German debate about the status of the *Geisteswissenschaften*, which influenced, among others, Max Weber. Dilthey started the inquiry into Hegel's development by re-examining his writings of the 1790s, an enquiry which continues to this day. At the same time, Hegel's influence began to spread abroad. 'Hegelianism', although of an oddly transposed variety, became important in England and America, through Green, Bradley, Bosanquet, Royce. For some decades it was dominant at Oxford. In the 1930s interest in Hegel, along with Marx, began to grow in the French philosophical world; while from the turn of the century, Hegel

---

[1] Letters no. 280 and 281, K. Marx, F. Engels, *Werke*, Berlin, 1965, v. pp. 32, 500, 503; quoted in E. Weil, *Hegel et l'Etat*, Paris 1950, pp. 15–16. The editor was Wilhelm Liebknecht. The footnote was appended by him to an article by Engels.

Conclusion

became an important pole of philosophical thought in Italy, mainly through the work of Croce and Gentile.

This renewed interest continues unabated to this day. Interrupted on the anglo-saxon scene by the reaction against the British 'Hegelians', it is nevertheless returning. But with all this attention focussed on Hegel, his actual synthesis is quite dead. That is, no one actually believes his central ontological thesis, that the universe is posited by a Spirit whose essence is rational necessity. Many men believe today that the world was created by God. Some hold as well to some 'de-mythologized' interpretation of this view. All the different types of materialist and naturalist views have their defenders. But no one holds the Hegelian ontology. Many much less 'relevant' thinkers (in the eyes of our contemporaries), such as the mainstream writers of the Enlightenment – Helvétius, Holbach, Bentham – or the 'reactionaries' such as Burke, can boast followers today in this sense, i.e., people who share their ontological or metaphysical views.

And in general it is true of the Hegelian revival which begins in the late nineteenth century that it is in no sense a revival of Hegel's central thesis. Croce in his famous work of 1907, *What is living and what is dead of the philosophy of Hegel*,[1] relegates the Logic and philosophy of nature to the latter category. Dilthey similarly tries to salvage the penetrating interpretation of historical forms while jettisoning the claims of the system to reach completion in a manifestation of rational necessity. History shows an open-ended series of transformations, forms whose significance is to be 'understood' (in the sense of 'verstehen'), but none of these give history its definitive meaning.

The British Hegelians do appear to be making stronger ontological claims, comparable to Hegel's. But on closer examination their views generally turn out to be significantly different. Bradley's dialectic, for instance, ends up showing how the only complete and undistorted truth, that of the whole, cannot be conceptually formulated. His conclusion is directly contrary to Hegel's logico-ontology.

Why is Hegel's central thesis dead? And why at the same time is his philosophy highly relevant to our time in a whole host of ways, as I have tried to show in the course of this work, and as current interest attests? I should like to try to adumbrate an answer to this double question in this concluding chapter. Normally one might expect the conclusion of a book on Hegel to dwell on the succession of influences his thought has had and new departures it has triggered. But the central items on the list – Marx, Kierkegaard, existentialism, etc. – are too well known, and the whole list is much too long[2] to make

---

[1] London 1915.

[2] Even if we do not go along with Merleau-Ponty, *Sense and Non-sense*, Northwestern U.P., 1964, 'All the great philosophical ideas of the past century – the philosophies of Marx and Nietzsche, phenomenology, German existentialism, and psychoanalysis – had their beginnings in Hegel' (63), the scope of Hegel's influence is beyond doubt considerable.

this a worthwhile undertaking. It would be more useful to try to account for his continuing relevance by seeing how the basic problems and aspirations underlying his philosophy have evolved since his day. For this is what we need to find an answer to our double question, how his thought can remain important while his conclusions are quite abandoned.

Part of the answer to the question, why Hegel's ontology was abandoned, lies in the development of modern civilization in an increasingly industrial, technological, rationalized direction. This civilization is in a sense the heir of the Enlightenment. Now while Hegel's philosophy claims to be the fulfilment of Enlightenment thought, he in fact tries to combine with this, and with each other, two strands of thought and sensibility which were as much reactions to as extensions of the Enlightenment. If we return to its basic intentions, which we explored in the first chapter, Hegel's philosophy can be seen as an attempt to realize a synthesis that the Romantic generation was groping towards: to combine the rational, self-legislating freedom of the Kantian subject with the expressive unity within man and with nature for which the age longed.

Hegel wanted to realize this synthesis in fully rational form, and that is what makes him an heir of the Enlightenment, and what marks him off from the Romantics. But it remains true that he was moved by philosophical purposes which went beyond and against the main trend of the Enlightenment, whether deist or materialist. I tried to characterize this roughly in the opening chapter in terms of the notion of a self-defining identity. Following on the seventeenth century revolution, men came to define themselves no longer in relation to a cosmic order, but as subjects who possessed their own picture of the world within them as well as an endogenous motivation, their own purposes or drives. Along with this new notion of subjectivity went what I called an 'objectification' of the world. That is, the world was no longer seen as the reflection of a cosmic order to which man was essentially related, but as a domain of neutral, contingent fact, to be mapped by the tracing of correlations, and ultimately manipulated in fulfilment of human purposes. This vision of an objectified, neutral world was, as we saw, valued as a confirmation of the new identity before even it came to be important as the basis of our mastery over nature.

The objectification extends beyond external nature to englobe human life and society and the result is a certain vision of man, an associationist psychology, utilitarian ethics, atomistic politics of social engineering, and ultimately a mechanistic science of man.

The conception of human life I have called 'expressivist', which develops with Herder and Rousseau among others, is in part a reaction to this. It is a rejection of the view of human life as mere external association of elements without intrinsic connection: of the human psyche as an assemblage of

539

Conclusion

'faculties', of man as a compound of body and soul, of society as a concatenation of individuals, of action as the fitting of means to external ends, of pleasure as the merely contingent consequence of certain actions, of right and wrong as residing in the external consequences of actions, of virtue and vice as the fruit of different concatenations of circumstances producing a different web of associations. Expressivism returns to the sense of the intrinsic value of certain actions or modes of life, to qualitative distinctions between good and bad. And these actions or modes of life are seen as wholes, as either true expressions or distortions of what we authentically are. It rebels against the dichotomizing of man into body and soul, spirit and nature, the conception of society as an instrument of independent individuals, the vision of nature as merely raw material for human purposes.

Similarly, the Kantian notion of rational autonomy was in part a reaction against the uni-dimensional utilitarian conception of man. It was a travesty to reduce the distinction between good and evil simply to the greater or lesser satisfaction of desires. What was at stake was rather a radical qualitative distinction, between self-determination as a rational being and heteronomy.

But the industrial, technological and rationalized civilization which has grown up since the eighteenth century has in an important sense entrenched in its practices and institutions the conception of man which belonged to what I called the main trend of the Enlightenment. And this, as it were, against the protests of Romanticism, which combined within itself in one form or another both the expressivist and the autonomist currents of reaction to the Enlightenment. The technology of industrial society pushes to a more and more extensive subjugation of nature. But what is much more important, industrial civilization enforced repeated re-organizations of society and men's way of life in the name of efficiency and higher production. Urbanization, factory production, depopulation of countryside and sometimes whole regions, mass emigration, the imposition of a rationalized, rigidly measured pace of life at the expense of the former seasonal rhythm; all these changes and others, whether induced by planning or arising through the hazards of the market and investment patterns, are explained and justified by their greater efficacy in meeting the goals of production. In this respect the utilitarian conception is entrenched in our practices and institutions, that is, a mode of thought in which different ways of living together are assessed not by some supposed intrinsic value, and certainly not by their expressive significance, but by their efficiency in the production of benefits which are ultimately 'consumed' by individuals. In this civilization, social relations and practices, as well as nature, are progressively objectified.

This instrumental mode of evaluation is endemic to the institutions of a modern industrial economy, that is, the activities which define these institutions relate them to an external purpose, e.g., profit, efficient production, or growth. And all advanced industrial societies are marked by this, even the Soviet Union, where consumer satisfaction is sacrificed in the name of some other extrinsic goal, such as national security, or 'surpassing capitalism', or future satisfaction. This may not have to be so, and China, for instance, may realize another model where economic considerations in this sense are not ultimate. But they have been in industrial civilization to date.

And in the West, many of complementary conceptions of society which have been invoked to mitigate the harsher consequences of the capitalist economy have themselves been off-shoots of the Enlightenment, e.g., notions of equality, of redistribution among individuals, of humanitarian defence of the weak. Of course, Romantic notions have also contributed to modern civilization. For instance the expressivist notion that each man's fulfilment is unique and cannot be foreseen, much less prescribed, by any other is an essential part of the contemporary belief in individual liberty. And we can see this connection in some of the recognized theorists of modern liberty, von Humboldt, de Tocqueville, J. S. Mill.

But the Romantic strain has been contained, as it were, in modern Western civilization. The major common institutions reflect rather the Enlightenment conception in their defining ideas. This is obviously true of the economic institutions. But it is as true of the growing, rationalized bureaucracies, and it is not much less so of the political structures, which are organized largely to produce collective decision out of the concatenation of individual decisions (through voting) and/or negotiation between groups. The major collective structures of an advanced industrial society tend to appear at best as instruments of production or decision (at worst, as threatening oppressors), whose value must ultimately be measured in what impact they have on the plight of individuals. The influence of Romantic ideas has largely been on the definition of individual fulfilment, for the sake of which these larger structures operate.

Modern civilization has thus seen the proliferation of Romantic views of private life and fulfilment, along with a growing rationalization and bureaucratization of collective structures, and a frankly exploitative stance towards nature. Modern society, we might say, is Romantic in its private and imaginative life and utilitarian or instrumentalist in its public, effective life. What is of ultimate importance in shaping the latter is not what its structures express, but what they get done. The bent of modern society is to treat these structures as a neutral, objectified domain, to be reorganized for maximum effect, although this may be held in check or even periodically over-ridden by powerful collective emotions, principally nationalism, which have their roots in the Romantic period. But the day-by-day predominance of these collective structures over private Romanticism is clearly evident in the exploitation of Romantic images of fulfilment to keep the wheels of industry turning, for instance in much contemporary advertising.

This is why those thinkers who stand in a Romantic or expressivist tradition of whatever kind, disciples of Rousseau, or of de Tocqueville, or Marx, whether they be socialists, anarchists, partisans of 'participatory democracy', or admirers of the ancient polis like Hannah Arendt, are all estranged from modern Western society. And those who feel fully at home in it are the heirs of the Enlightenment mainstream, who proclaimed recently (and somewhat prematurely) the 'end of ideology' and who accept models like that of the political system as a 'conversion process', popular among American political scientists of the last decade.[1]

From one angle we might see Romanticism as a crisis which occurred at the birth of modern industrial society, which parallels the deep social unrest of the transition and influences and is influenced by it. The crisis, like the social unrest, was overcome as the new society became established. Romanticism was absorbed by being encapsulated in private life, and thus allocated its place in the new society. Parallel to this social absorption was an intellectual one. The scientific outlook of the second half of the nineteenth century incorporated many of the insights of expressivist and Romantic thought, while setting aside the philosophical categories in which they had originally been couched.

Organic conceptions influenced a biology which once more became mechanistic in orientation. They underlie also the sociology of Comte, who nevertheless purges the categories of expression and final cause from science. Developmental conceptions become a central part of the canon of orthodox science with Darwin. And Freud himself pointed out how some of his key notions were anticipated by Romantic writers.

In a sense, therefore, the civilization which develops in Europe in the second half of the nineteenth century tended to entrench the Enlightenment conception of man, in its progressive transformation of nature, in its collective structures and in its most prestigious intellectual achievement, science. And this must provide us part of the explanation why Hegel's synthesis falls into eclipse around the half century. For it attempted to integrate the expressivist current in more than a subordinate way. The structure of the Hegelian state was to be understood and valued for what it expressed or embodied, the Idea, not for its consequences or achievements. The rationality of the Hegelian state was something quite other than the rationalization of bureaucratic structures. The modern mixture of private Romanticism and public utilitarianism is rather civil society run wild, a society which has become a 'heap'. The continuous transformation of industrial society under the dynamic or productive efficiency and the search for a higher individual standard of life has eroded

[1] Cf. D. Easton, *A Systems Analysis of Political Life*, New York, 1965.

the differentiations which were essential to Hegel's state, and prized the individual more and more loose from any partial grouping. It was in underestimating this dynamic that Hegel was most seriously wrong in his characterization of the coming age.

But this error, if that is the word, is directly connected with his ontology. Hegel thought that the forces of dissolution and homogenization of civil society would be contained because men would come to recognize themselves in the structures which embodied the Idea. Men would recover a new *Sittlichkeit* and identify with a larger life. The continued progress of these forces could only mean the progressive attenuation of this vision which must become every more unreal and improbable as the new society grows. If Hegel has been right, then men would have recognized themselves in the structures of the rational state, and industrial society would not have taken the path it has.

Parallel to the development of modern society which breaks the bounds of Hegel's state is a development of modern science. Empirical sciences were meant to be contained within the 'absolute science'. That is, the results of the empirical sciences should reveal the structure of the Concept, with the degree of approximation and inexactness appropriate to the level of reality concerned. But the sciences had already in his own day broken the bounds of the synthesis which Hegel's commentary imposed on them, and although the possibility always remains theoretically of recommencing a synthesizing commentary with each new important discovery, the development of the sciences has made the whole project of a philosophy of nature seem futile and misguided. The search for an underlying meaningful structure must seem arbitrary in an ever expanding and diversifying field of scientific knowledge.

Can we conclude then that Hegel's ontology is no longer a live option because modern civilization has made us all over into self-defining subjects with an objectifying stance towards nature and social life? Not quite. This explanation is too simple because in fact we have not been fully made over. There remains since the Romantic period a malaise around the modern identity. Certainly many of our contemporaries think of themselves primarily as individuals with certain de facto desires and goals; and of their society as a common enterprise of production, exchange and, ideally, mutual help, designed to fulfill their respective desires; so that the important virtues of society are rational organization, distributive justice, and the safe-guarding of individual independence.

But at the same time many – and often the same people – are moved by a sense of the profound inadequacy of modern society which has its roots in the Romantic protest. Since the end of the eighteenth century there has been a continuing stream of complaint against modern civilization as Philistine, productive of mediocrity and conformity, timidly egoistical, as stifling ori-

Conclusion

ginality, free expression, all the heroic virtues, as dedicated to a 'pitiable comfort' (erbärmliches Behagen).[1] Reproaches, or at least forebodings, of this order have come from the best and most sensitive minds, and across a broad spectrum, from very moderate and constructive critics, like de Tocqueville and J. S. Mill, to the wildest outsiders, like Nietzsche and Sorel, not to speak of the host of writers and artists who took a stance in opposition to 'bourgeois' civilization.

In different ways these critics castigate modern society as expressively dead, as stifling expressive fulfilment through the power of conformity, or through the all-pervasive demands of utility, of producing a world in which all acts, objects, institutions have a use, but none express what men are or could be. This stream of opposition has its source in the expressivist current of the late eighteenth century, and its continued force reflects the degree to which the modern identity has not become securely established.

We might be tempted to think that this current touches only a minority of intellectuals and artists, leave the majority of 'ordinary' men unaffected. But the wide resonance of this kind of critique has been shown if nothing else in periodic outbursts of unrest which have troubled industrial civilization. Deep expressivist dissatisfaction contributed to the success of Fascism, and underlies the revolt of many young people against the 'system' in contemporary Western countries.

Thus we cannot simply explain the eclipse of Hegel's ontology by the triumphant establishment of a modern identity which has relegated the Romantic protest to the past. Nothing of the kind has occurred. Rather the question is why the continued flourishing Romantic or expressivist protest can no longer find philosophical expression in Hegel's vision.

Part of the answer lies in the fact that it is a *protest*. Hegel's vision was of a world reconciled to the Spirit, but the Romantic spirit is conscious of being in opposition to modern society. It is a nostalgia for the past, the yearning for an as yet unfulfilled hope, or the determination to realize an unprecedented future, but certainly not the perception of the rationality of the real. And if men who longed for expressive fulfilment felt alienated from the course of modern history in the late nineteenth century, how much greater cause their successors have to feel this today. Prior to 1914, the Philistine society at least offered the solidity of a firmly established order destined to realize more and more fully its own limited, pitiable and unheroic form of good. But the upheavals since that time have called even this into question without setting Western civilization on a higher road of expressive fulfilment. The earnest search for 'a pitiable comfort' has been interrupted more by orgies of grotesque inhumanity than by departures toward a new and higher culture.

[1] F. Nietzsche *Also Sprach Zarathustra*, Zarathustra's Preface, §3.

544

And by a cruel irony, the Romantic protest itself has had its share of responsibility in these gruesome interludes. Various of its themes have been twisted to the service of Fascism, Stalinism, not to speak of the freelance practitioners of indiscriminate assassination of our day.

So that a contemporary is easily tempted to see history as a 'slaughter bench...onto which the fortune of peoples, the wisdom of states and the virtue of individuals have been brought to sacrifice'. (*VG*, 80). What he may find hard to understand is how Hegel after writing this line could nevertheless still see history as the realization of reason and freedom. What separates us from that age is the sense that the horrors and night-mares of history, the furies of destruction and cruelty which remain enig-matic to agent and victim, were behind us. This sense, which Hegel expressed in his philosophy – although he seems to have wavered at times in his private judgment – is just about unrecoverable even by the most optimistic of our contemporaries.

So that, whether as a member of a confident, growing modern society, or as a witness of this society's disintegration, the heir of the Romantics cannot but sense alienation. He cannot see history as the unfolding of spirit. And at the same time he can no longer see nature as the emanation of spirit. The growing control over nature of modern technology, as well as the ever-expanding frontier of science, has dispelled that vision of the world as the manifestation of spiritual powers or a divine principle which was the culmina-tion of the expressivist current of the late eighteenth century. That expressive pantheism, the 'Spinozism' of the *Sturm und Drang*, which tempted Lessing, all but conquered Herder, and was the common property of Goethe and the Romantics, ceases to be a live option as modern civilization entrenches itself. But Hegel's synthesis was built on this. Its aim, as I have tried to interpret it, was to combine this vision of nature as the expression of spirit, with the implied call to man to recover expressive unity with it, on one hand, with the aspiration to rational autonomy on the other. Spirit, the ontological foundation of the world in rational necessity, is meant to realize this synthesis. It guarantees that man can give himself to unity with the whole without losing his rational freedom. But if this vision of expressive pantheism wanes, if the aspiration to unity with the 'all of nature'[1] ceases to be meaningful, then the very basis disappears for the Absolute Idea, along with Goethe's *Urphänomene*, Novalis' 'magical idealism', and the wilder creations of the Romantics.

Thus Hegel's synthesis cannot command adherents today not only because it is built in part on the expressivist reaction to the modern identity which contemporary civilization has tended to entrench more and more, but be-cause it is built on an earlier and outmoded form of this reaction. It belongs to

[1] Hölderlin, *Hyperion*, Fischer Edition, Frankfurt, 1962, p. 9.

Conclusion

the opposition while claiming to give us a vision of reason triumphant; and it belongs moreover to a stage of this opposition which no longer appears viable.

2

Thus we can see, in rough outline at least, why Hegel's central thesis is dead, But why is it that his philosophy remains highly relevant? This will become clearer if we look at the forms of Romantic and expressivist opposition which have succeeded those of Hegel's time.

If the goal of a return to unity with the geat current of life is no longer plausible, even combined with the spiral vision of history where the restored unity incorporates subjective freedom; if the historial experience of objectifying and transforming nature in theory and practice is too powerful for it to survive as an interlocutor; then the expressivist current of opposition to modern civilization has to focus on man. That which is 'cabin'd, cribb'd, confin'd' by modern society, hemmed in by modern conformity, stamped out by the great machine of Utility, repressed by the 'system', is human nature, or rather, the creative, expressive potential of man.

But expressive fulfilment entails a certain integrity, a wholeness of life, which does not admit of division between body and soul, will and inclination, spirit and nature. If this fulfilment no longer means communion with nature as an embodiment of spirit, nature must still figure in it in some fashion.

Later forms of expressivism show this in two ways. Either the realized form of life is seen as expressing our deeper motivation as natural beings which is checked, frustrated or hidden by an artificial, divisive or repressive society. Modern society is seen as the oppressor of the spontaneous, the natural, the sensuous, or the 'Dionysiac' in man. In a sense, much of post-Romantic nationalism can be put in this broad category since it seeks to restore particular facts about men – their heredity, the land they live in, the language group they belong to – as centrally relevant motivations in a fulfilled human life, against 'abstract' 'cosmopolitan' ideals of man.

Or else, man is seen as achieving harmony with nature by transforming it. Philosophy, the contemplation of the Idea in nature and history, as a 'cult' which restores our unity to the whole, can have no meaning for those who have lost the sense of the divine in nature, and must seem obscene to those who are in revolt against an inert, oppressive, inhuman society. From within this horizon, the aspiration to expressive unity between man and the natural and social world on which he depends can only be fulfilled by his freely reshaping nature and society. In this kind of vision expressive unity is combined, as in Hegel's philosophy, with a radical notion of freedom, but in a fundamentally different way. Hegel's synthesis has been, as it were, anthropologized – transferred from *Geist* onto man.

This was, of course, the revolutionary transposition which was carried out by the Young Hegelians of the 1830s and 1840s. And it has been of considerable consequence. For the great expressivist protests against the course of modern civilization have incorporated this notion of willed transformation of nature, both human and external, as an essential part of man's fulfilment. Reactions to the expressive poverty of modern civilization have, of course, varied widely: 'Weltschmerz', a deep sense of the world as abandoned and expressively dead; or a nostalgia for an earlier, unrecoverable age; or an attempt to return to one such earlier time – the age of faith, or the primitive condition of balance with nature which many of today's 'drop-outs' yearn for – or again, the attempt to create a secondary world of art untrammelled by the work-a-day one. But the active protests have generally envisaged an active reshaping of human life and its natural basis. This has been true not only of the ideologies of the Left, like Marxism and anarchism, but also of those like Fascism which stressed as well the release of pent-up 'elemental' forces in man. Fascism in fact tried in a confused way to combine the above 'Dionysiac' alternative with this, 'Promethean' one.

Because of the importance of this Promethean aspiration, it is worth looking at its most influential formulation, in the theory of the man who was also the greatest of the Young Hegelians.

Many Marxists, and others, would object to an interpretation of Marxism which places it in what I have called the expressivist tradition. Of course, Marxism is more than this. But I do not think we can understand it and its impact if we try to abstract from this dimension.

Certainly few would want to deny that the young Marx is the heir, through Hegel, of the expressivist aspiration. And already in the early 1840s this is married with the thrust of the radical Enlightenment to produce the peculiarly powerful Marxist synthesis.

The young Marx is heir of the radical Enlightenment first in his notion that man comes to shape nature and eventually society to his purposes. He is its heir second in his critique of the inhumanity of the present order. The Enlightenment gave rise to a new kind of indignant protest against the injustices of the world. Having demolished the older visions of cosmic order and exposed them as at best illusion, and perhaps even sham, it left all the differentiations of the old society, all its special burdens and disciplines, without justification. It is one thing to bear one's lot as a peasant if it is one's appointed place in the hierarchy of things as ordered by God and nature. But if the very idea of society as the embodiment of such a cosmic order is swept aside, if society is rather the common instrument of men who must live under the same political roof to pursue happiness, then the burdens and deprivations of this station are a savage imposition, against reason and justice, maintained only by knavery and lies. They would cry to heaven – if heaven still existed – for redress and

Conclusion

even vengeance. The Enlightenment thus provoked a new consciousness of inhumanity, of gratuitous and unnecessary suffering, and an urgent determination to combat it. For if man is only a subject of desires who aims at their fulfilment (i.e., happiness), then nothing in heaven or earth compensates for the loss of this happiness. Unrequited deprivation is inconsolable, absolute loss.

Marx takes up this radical critique of inhumanity. But the principal justifying myth which he denounces as the alibi for exploitation and oppression is not the old religion but the new atomistic, utilitarian Enlightenment philosophy itself, principally as reflected in the theories of the classical economists. Indeed, orthodox religion comes off rather lightly in comparison. For it is 'the sentiment of a heartless world',[1] the flowers on man's chains, an almost indispensable consolation for men's suffering in an unjust world – an injustice which in the present phase of history is directly propped up by the bourgeois philosophy of utility.

But the tremendous power of Marx's theory comes from his joining this thrust of the radical Enlightenment to the expressivist tradition. In the theory as we have it in the *Economic and Philosophical Manuscripts* of 1844, which remained unpublished in Marx's lifetime, the transformation of nature is also a self-transformation. Man in making over his natural environment is reshaping his own 'inorganic body'. He suffers alienation because at first under class society his work and its product, transformed nature – which properly belong to him in the strong sense that they are part of him, his expression – escape from him and become an alien reality, with a dynamic of their own which resists and opposes him. This notion of alienation thus belongs intrinsically to an expressivist structure of thought. Man's work and its product, the man-made environment, is his expression, and hence its loss is not just deprivation, but self-diremption; and its recovery is not just the means to happiness but regaining wholeness and freedom. For man's production is his 'self-creation' (Selbsterzeugung).

Hence in his own way Marx takes up a common theme of virtually all expressivist critics of modern civilization, and denounces a society which makes possession the central human goal at the expense of expression. The drive for possession itself belongs to the alienated world where man's human powers are so detached from him that they can be transferred and circulate as property, a poor, distorted substitute for genuine recovery. 'Private property has made us so stupid and partial that an object is only *ours* when we have it, when it exists for us as capital, or when it is...*utilized* in some way.'[2]

This potent combination of the radical Enlightenment and expressivism comes from a transposition of Hegel's synthesis from *Geist* on to man. In

[1] Karl Marx, *Early Writings*, translated and edited by T. B. Bottomore, London and New York, 1964, pp. 43–4.
[2] Op. cit. p. 159.

Hegel's point of origin, as it were, the Idea goes out into nature and at first is lost there. That is, it has not yet an adequate expression, and hence there is division and separation within this world, and between the world and Spirit which cannot recognize itself. The development of an adequate embodiment, and hence the return of Spirit to itself is the work of history.

Now for *Geist* read man, not man as an individual, but as a 'generic essence' (Gattungswesen). At his point of origin man is a natural being, for Marx. He exists in nature and only continues through a constant process of interchange with nature. At first this natural matrix in which he is set does not express him at all. But because man unlike the beast can produce universally and consciously, this interchange with nature does not just renew the cycle but transforms it as well. Man makes over nature into an expression of himself, and in the process properly becomes man. Marx speaks of this self-creation of man through the fashioning of an adequate external expression as the 'objectification [Vergegenständlichung] of man's species life'.[1]

But the first attempts at a man-made world, carried out under the pressure of need, introduce division. Men can only achieve a higher type of interchange with nature, or mode of production, by reordering their social relations, and in the conditions of backwardness and indigence which prevail at the beginning, this means that some men must take command over, and hence exploit others. By a cruel irony, the first step towards a higher life, the true realization of man, takes men out of the paradise of primitive communism to the pain and cruelty of class society. We are forcefully reminded of Hegel's interpretation of the myth of the Fall. It is precisely man's primitive affirmation of himself as a subject, or spiritual being, which in the early condition of raw particularity cuts him off from the universal, and starts him on the long process of formation which will eventually make of him an adequate vehicle of Spirit.

But divided men cannot achieve an adequate expression, because the subject of the transformation is not the individual but the 'species being', human society set in the matrix of nature. Hence under class society men are not in control of their own expression. It escapes them and takes on a dynamic of its own. They suffer alienation in their lives. And this is matched by an alienated consciousness in which they take this estranged world seriously as though it were really the locus of an alien force; the divine in earlier epochs; or the iron laws of classical economics in the bourgeois epoch. Just as Hegel's Spirit in the period of unhappy consciousness, generic man does not recognize himself in his own objectification.

But if class division is ultimately forced by indigence, then once men have achieved sufficient mastery over nature, this division can be overcome.

---

[1] Op. cit., p. 128.

Conclusion

Generic man will return to himself in his own embodiment, will enter a realm of freedom, that is, integral expression, one which will belong indivisibly to the whole society, in which man will be reconciled with man. Communism will be the abolition 'of human self-alienation, and thus the real appropriation of human nature through and for man. It is, therefore, the return of man to himself as a social, i.e., really human, being, a complete and conscious return which assimilates all the wealth of previous development.'[1]

As an expressive fulfilment, communism will overcome the divisions and oppositions to which human life and thought has been prey.

Communism as a fully developed naturalism is humanism and as a fully developed humanism is naturalism. It is the *definitive* resolution of the antagonism between man and nature, and between man and man. It is the true solution of the conflict between existence and essence, between freedom and necessity, between individual and species. It is the solution of the riddle of history and knows itself to be this solution.[2]

In this list we see the Hegelian ambition attained in transposed form, the reconciliation of oppositions; and in particular the opposition between man's necessary objectification in nature, with which he must be in harmony, and the demands of his freedom which at first pit him in opposition against nature. Marx, too, in his own way unites expressivism to Fichte's radical freedom. For Marx's man creates himself. But in Hegel the reconciliation is achieved by a recognition of the embodiment of Spirit which is in large part already there. This recognition requires a transformation in the life form of man who is Spirit's vehicle in history, to be sure; but since the ultimate goal of this transformation is Spirit's self-recognition, even the transformed society reposes on a recognition: it requires that men see a larger order and identify with the differentiated structure of society as the reflection of this order.

For Marx on the other hand there is no recognition. The reconciliation is entirely created. Man is one with nature because and to the extent to which he has made it over as his expression. The transformation of human society is not aimed at an eventual recognition of a larger order but ultimately at the subjugation of nature to a design freely created by man.

The well-known short-hand formula differentiating the two thinkers, that Hegel speaks of contemplating the real while Marx wants to change it, is grounded ultimately in their different ontologies. Since for Hegel the subject is *Geist*, the Spirit of all, reconciliation must come through recognition, since a transformation of the whole universe is without sense. Marx's reconciliation on the other hand must come through transformation, because his subject is generic man; and man, unlike God, cannot recognize himself in nature until he has put himself there through work. Marx's reconciliation will, of course, always be incomplete; it never extends beyond the (always receding) frontier of

[1] Op. cit., p. 155.   [2] Loc. cit.

untransformed nature, But this is the price of his Promethean notion of self-creation.

Once one has made this transposition from *Geist* to man, then Hegel's whole differentiated structure must appear just like those of the *ancien régime*, as oppression and injustice masquerading as divine order. Hence Marx while acknowledging his debt to Hegel naturally released all the indignation of the radical Enlightenment at his conception of the state. The Hegelian synthesis is denounced as one achieved in thought only, masking the effective diremption of the real. In the polemic Marx inevitably distorted Hegel, speaking at times as though he was somehow concerned with 'abstract thought' alone, and not also the protagonist of another kind of praxis. But the debt is undeniable and comes through Marx's text even when he is not engaged in acknowledging it. In order to reconcile radical freedom and nature, Hegel developed his notion that radical freedom, as Spirit, was at the foundation of everything. At base everything is an emanation of freedom. It only remained to transpose this immensely activist conception onto man to generate the most powerful revolutionary doctrine.

Many commentators who would agree with this interpretation of early Marx, hold that his mature thought was quite different and that he jettisoned the Hegelian and expressivist formulations of the early 1840s in favour of a hard-nosed science of capitalist society which expounds the iron laws of its inner development and eventual demise. That Marx looked on *Capital* as a work of science, and that the term 'science' came to have for him very much the sense that it had for the later nineteenth century in general, seems to me correct. So that we might look at *Capital* as one of those great works of mature science, like Darwin's evolution theory, or later Freud's psychoanalysis, which incorporate the insights of the earlier Romantic period. But that this involved in Marx's view taking back anything of the position he held in 1844–7 seems to me a quite unwarranted conclusion. The position I outlined above is drawn from the Paris Manuscripts of 1844, complemented with a few details from the Manifesto. I see no evidence at all that Marx went back on this position in any essential respect, or felt that he needed to.

The conflict between the 'scientific' stance of mature Marx and his expressivist transposition of Hegel is in the mind of later commentators, and in this they are probably more clairvoyant than Marx. But it is an unjustified projection to attribute this sense of incompatibility to Marx himself. The fact is that from the beginning, his position was a synthesis between the radical Enlightenment, which sees man as capable of objectifying nature and society in science in order to master it, and the expressivist aspiration to wholeness. This is what he meant in speaking of communism as the union of humanism and naturalism. Expressive fulfilment comes when man (generic man) dominates nature and can impress his free design on it. But at the same time he

Conclusion

dominates nature by objectifying it in scientific practice. Under communism men freely shape and alter whatever social arrangements exist. They treat them as instruments. But at the same time this collective shaping of their social existence is their self-expression. In this vision, objectification of nature and expression through it are not incompatible, any more than they are for a sculptor who may make use of engineering technology in constructing his work.

In other words because expressive fulfilment came with the radical freedom to shape nature, it could be combined with the most far-reaching Enlightenment aspiration to dominate the natural and social world through science and technology.

What we see from the young to the mature Marx is not a change of view but a shift of emphasis within what to him must always have appeared as fundamentally the same position. In the climate of the late nineteenth century it was naturally the dimension of 'scientific socialism' which tended to predominate. And this orientation was finally sealed by the success of a Marxist revolutionary party in a backward country. For Marxism had to take on the role of a modernizing ideology. Socialism = soviet power+electrification, in Lenin's famous phrase. Both these goals required that the ruling élite adopt the stance of engineers relative to the at best inert, often refractory social matter they had to deal with. Marxist-Leninism began to be treated as a blue-print in the hands of master builders rather than the consciousness of a new age of freedom.

But official Marxism never simply rejected the expressivist elements of the synthesis. The vision of freedom and of the wholeness of communist man in the official Marxist movement remains in the expressivist tradition, as does much of their critique of bourgeois society. Indeed, this pretense of wholeness is what underlies the totalitarian tendencies of Soviet Marxism, e.g., the demands it makes on art and cultural life, a bureaucratic degeneration of the original claims made on behalf of communist man.

But the Soviet experience has just served to underline the weakness of Marx's synthesis between expressive fulfilment and scientific objectification. The example of the sculptor certainly shows that man can have both an expressive and an objectifying relation to nature at once. And we can imagine a harmonious group shaping and reshaping its social arrangements in order to meet standards of both efficiency and expression at the same time. But in these cases what men are relying on is an engineering technology or a technique of distributing tasks or something of the sort. They are not using a science of man in society which identifies the determinants of people's behaviour. For if this is being used then some men are controlling or manipulating others.

In other words a scientific objectification of man which identifies factors determining how men act and feel which are beyond the ken of most and/or the

552

will of all cannot really be the basis of the praxis of a communist society. This is not to say that a science of this kind must be used to ill purpose, or against the cause of freedom. On the contrary, psychoanalysis which claims to be an objectification of this kind, can be used by some men to cure others, and arguably increase their freedom. But the Marxist notion of communist society is that of men deciding together; the decisions represent in a sense a general will, not a concatenation of individual decisions but a genuine common purpose. This does not exclude the marginal use of technologies of human control, say, for the purpose of curing the sick. But the course which the society takes, as a conscious collective decision, cannot be an outcome whose determinants are encompassed by an applied science of this kind.

Now if *Capital*, or the corpus of Marxist-Leninism, gives us the 'laws' governing bourgeois society, and therefore tells us how best to go about abolishing it, the transcending of this society must also mean the suspension of these laws. For the science of bourgeois society shows how men are caught up in structures and a dynamic which they neither understand nor control. This science cannot remain the basis of the revolutionary praxis which supercedes bourgeois society or else this praxis will remain manipulative in contradiction to its central justification.

Thus at the revolutionary border between two eras there must be a jump, as it were, a shift in the laws which apply to society. And this is, indeed, provided for in the theory of alienation described above. The practices of bourgeois society which under alienation follow a dynamic of their own, which Marxist science will trace, are brought back into human control with communism, not to fall under similar external determinants but rather to be genuinely up for decision in a free society.

This transcending of external determinants in favour of free expression makes perfect sense, of course, in the categories of Hegelian philosophy. It is what we see when we ascend the levels of being in Hegel's philosophy of nature, e.g., from inorganic nature to life, or when we move from alienation back to *Sittlichkeit*. But it is foreign to the established tradition of science rooted in the Enlightenment. This can allow for man objectifying nature as a domain of neutral instruments on one level while he shapes an expressive object on the other. But it cannot admit of a shifting boundary whereby what is in the realm of objectification and natural law at one stage of history is pulled beyond it into the realm of expression at another. It makes no allowance for its laws being '*aufgehoben*'.

In epistemological terms, this is the ambiguity which the mature Marx never cleared up and probably never saw. This *Aufhebung* of the laws of society which occurs at critical turning points in history, so that the very terms necessary to explain one period are not applicable at another, this was certainly implicit in the original theory of the young Marx, as it had been in Hegel. It remained

553

essential to the logic of Marx's notion of revolution and the transition to communism. But it was not part of the model of science which Marx seemed to be appealing to in launching *Capital* on the world.

Marx never ironed out this wrinkle. No doubt if it had been pointed out to him it would have seemed impossibly precious and 'philosophical'. His scientific work was cut out by the urgent practical needs of bringing the revolution against capitalism to term. Speculation on the transition to communism was a luxury barely to be indulged in, much less on the epistemological problems raised by the existence of such a transition.

But if one probes deeper, it seems that the problem never arose for Marx because he had an extremely simple-minded view of the transition. The revolution would abolish bourgeois society and hence the laws of its operation, and a united class of proletarians would take over and dispose freely of the economy which it inherited. This kind of leap into untrammelled freedom is not really a dialectical *Aufhebung*, where the unity of the higher stage is always foreshadowed in the lower, and there is continuity as well as discontinuity between them. But nor is it very realistic. Marx seemed to have been oblivious to the inescapable opacity and indirectness of communication and decision in large bodies of men, the way in which the dynamic of their interaction always partly escapes men, even in small and simple societies, let alone those organized around a large and complex productive system.

The image of the leap, as much as the pressure of more urgent problems, dispensed Marx from having to think about the organization of freedom. It prevented him from seeing communism as a social predicament with its own characteristic limits, less confining and inhuman than those of capitalist society, but limits nonetheless. And thus the problem of the relation of these limits to those of capitalist society could not arise. Rather it is as though the laws of bourgeois society fall away with the abolition of this society the way the technology of carburetors would fall into irrelevance if we got rid of the internal combustion engine.

A shift of this kind can be understood by the most hard-boiled positivist, and it is some such conception which makes it appear that the *Aufhebung* of bourgeois society towards which *Capital* points can fit within the classical framework of science. But this compatibility with mainstream science is purchased by a wildly unrealistic notion of the transition as a leap into untrammelled freedom, which simply sets aside the old restraints.

The Marxian synthesis between Enlightenment science and expressive fulfilment is in the end not viable. To set out what is involved in a dialectical transition, to portray the relation between the 'laws' of society at one phase and those at a later phase, to give the social articulation of increased freedom, this would take us well beyond the confines of Enlightenment science. We would have to map the transition from a stage in which men's actions are governed by external laws, that is, follow regularities which are not desired or adequately conceived by anyone, to a stage in which they are limited by a situation which they (partially) understand and which orients their choices. But this kind of transition takes us beyond the boundaries of classical science. The step from a determination through external law to direction by a meaningful situation can be more readily accounted for in the categories of Hegel's dialectical transitions.

On the other hand, to make the transition comprehensible to mainstream science we have to think of it not as a step from blind law to meaningful situation, but as simple sloughing off of restraints. We leave the nature of the subject and his agency in the new social form as an unexplored point of complete spontaneity.

Later commentators have been right to point out the rift between Marx's expressivism and his scientism. But this is not a difference between the young and the mature Marx. Rather his inability to see this rift was already implicit in his original position, in the transposition onto man of Hegel's notion of a self-positing *Geist*. The powers of a Spirit who creates his own embodiment, once attributed to man, yield a conception of freedom as self-creation more radical than any previous one. It opens the heady perspective, once alienation is overcome, of a leap to a free self-activity of generic man limited only by the (ever receding) refractory bounds of unsubdued nature. The Marxian notion of the realm of freedom keeps us from exploring the area in which this rift appears.

But this was not a blind spot peculiar to Marx. It affects the whole communist movement. Just a few months before October 1917, in his *State and Revolution*, Lenin still expressed an incredibly simple view about the administration of communist society. The Bolshevik Party was thrown into the real history of state power with this simple image of human freedom as the unproblematic administration of things. And Soviet communist society has remained somehow fixated on it; so that it continues to resist the framing of any adequate conception of itself as a social form, even while it came to 'administer' men as things on a hitherto unprecedented scale.

The terrible history of Soviet communism has induced independent Marxists to rethink the theory, and this has led many to re-examine the more 'philosophical' works of the 1840s. The early Marx has offered a new point of departure for many 'revisionists', while these first writings are frowned on by official Communism as immature attempts, not yet entirely freed from Hegelian philosophy. This is not to say that official Marxism has sought to jettison the expressivist elements of the doctrine. Rather they have fought to keep Marx's unviable synthesis between expressivism and scientism from coming under close scrutiny. The appeal of Bolshevism is made up of the impossible combination of a promise of expressive freedom on one hand, and

Conclusion

the possession of 'scientific socialism' as an engineering blue-print for history on the other. It is in the interest of the movement to keep this contradiction from being exposed and resolved. When it is resolved, as in the work of Louis Althusser, who has tried to purge Marx of Hegelian notions in the name of a sophisticated form of scientism, the result is neither convincing as exegesis nor attractive as a political vision. The justification of élite rule by the Leninist party, in a supposed scientific objectification of the contradictions of society, does not suffer explicit statement without producing a malaise in the reader who has reflected on contemporary history.

The Bolshevik image of the proletarian party as 'engineers' building in conformity with the 'laws' of history combines two opposed pictures of the human predicament. It shows us man, on one hand, imposing his will on the course of history, even against odds and refractory matter. This is the 'heroic' image. On the other hand dialectical materialism sets out the laws which govern man and history with an iron necessity. These two pictures are not as such incompatible. But they cannot be combined in the way proposed. The laws which are applied by the engineers who impose their will on events cannot be those which hold with an iron necessity, if we mean by this that we can account for what happens by reference to them without invoking any human decisions. A true law of development of history would be one whose antecedents are not manipulable. It could serve us to adjust more harmoniously to the course of events, to smooth transitions, but not to impose our will. It would not be amenable to application by 'engineers'.

The Bolsheviks in fact imposed their will on events, not only in undertaking the Revolution in 1917, but much more in the drive to collectivize the peasantry after 1928. How much this was against the grain can be measured by the blood spilt, and by the state of Soviet agriculture almost half a century later. And it would seem that Stalin and his colleagues felt pushed by necessity: that either they brought the peasants to heel or the growth of the relatively free peasant economy under NEP would undermine the basis of their power. It was that kind of 'iron necessity', a matter of us or them, which indeed had something to do with the economic infrastructure of power, but nothing whatever to do with an inevitable direction of history. On the contrary, it was nip and tuck. The 'laws of history', which point to the inevitable triumph of communism, serve in the end as an alibi for a decision imposed on events. There can be regret but no remorse for blood spilt in the inescapable forward march of humanity to a higher civilization.

Marxist-Leninism has thus realized a marriage of incompatibles, a union first of an extreme voluntarism and scientism – the notion that the science of history objectifies society, as physics does nature, as a domain of potential manipulanda – combined then with the most thoroughgoing determinism. The first two are a natural combination for an élite which is imposing a new

556

direction on a refractory mass. But this practice cannot easily be squared with the Marxist perspective of expressive freedom. And so this massive social engineering is presented as the outcome of the laws of history, emerging from the masses as their inescapable will and destiny. There are colossal contradictions in this position: the laws of history cannot be the basis of social engineering *and* reveal the inevitable trend of events; the mixture of voluntarism and engineering allows no place for the growth of freedom. But the combination has been immensely powerful as a political rallying point in contemporary history.

Marxist revisionists have seen the links between these three terms. They have seen that the image of the revolution as imposed by will and the conception of it as determined by iron necessity paradoxically go together. They have tried to break from both these at once in a new reading of Marxism, by which we can trace the ripening of the conditions of revolution, which nevertheless 'can be translated into reality only through men's decisions between alternatives'.[1] The rediscovery, with the help of Marx's early vision, of the bent in things towards a revolutionary transformation is the guarantee against impotent preaching, a pure politics of '*Sollen*', on one hand, as well as against the attempt to impose communism by force against the grain, on the other. It is the guarantee that the liberation will be the work of the spontaneous activity of large masses of people and not just of a revolutionary élite, that the means used to achieve communism will be in conformity with the end.

At the same time, this bent in things is not an iron necessity, so that the paradox is avoided of a transition to freedom which is not itself mediated by free activity.

The revisionist attempt to rediscover the bent in things which 'inclines without necessitating', to use Leibniz's phrase, is rightly directed back to the formulations of early Marx. But early Marx is not enough. For Marx himself, early and late, held to a terribly unreal notion of freedom in which the opacity, division, indirectness and cross-purposes of social life were quite overcome. It is this picture of situation-less freedom which underlies the unviable synthesis of expressivism and scientism, and which allows Bolshevik voluntarism to masquerade as the realization of freedom. Whereas the bent of revisionism is to recover a notion of free action as in an oriented situation which the agent can either assume or refuse.

Now this freedom without situation is what Hegel called 'absolute freedom'. It was a conception of freedom which was sterile and empty in his eyes in that it left us with no reason to act in one way rather than another; and it was destructive, since in its emptiness it drives us to tear down any other positive work as a hindrance to freedom. I said above, in Chapter xv, that Hegel in

---

[1] Georg Lukács, as quoted in Istvan Mészáros, *Lukács' Concept of Dialectic*, London, Merlin Press, 1972, p. 44.

criticizing absolute freedom, while aiming at the French Revolutionaries, was also in a sense criticizing Marx by anticipation, while in another sense Marx as Hegel's heir in part escapes these strictures. We can now see more clearly how both these judgements are true, and how the early Marx is thus both a good and an insufficient source for the revisionist search for a definition of freedom in situation. Marx escapes Hegel's strictures because he does not start from the notion of a purely autonomous rational will, as Kant did. On the contrary man is in a cycle of interchange with nature: He does not gain freedom by abstracting from or neutralizing this nature, but by transforming it. And this sets him a very definite task; that of making nature over on one hand, and of overcoming the divisions and alienation which arise in the early stages of this transformation on the other. Man is thus in a situation, he is part of a larger order of things which sets him a task. In this way Marx's theory is like Hegel's, of which it is the transposition, as we have seen.

From the beginning man has to create the conditions of freedom. And this is what has given their direction to Marxist societies. They have to *build* socialism, develop the pre-conditions of communism. But once the conditions are realized, the Marxist notion of freedom is of no further help. It is not a matter of providing a detailed blue-print for a free society, a demand which has often rightly been rejected as contradictory. Rather it is that the overcoming of all alienation and division leaves man without a situation, and at this stage, the end of 'pre-history', the Hegelian point about the emptiness of absolute freedom begins to apply.

If it is absurd to ask for a blue-print of communist society, it is not at all malapropos to ask in general terms how we envisage men's situation will have changed, what constraints, divisions, tensions, dilemmas, struggles and estrangements will replace those we know today. Not only does classical Marxism have no answer to this; it implies that the answer is 'none': that our only situation will be that of generic man, harmoniously united, in contest with nature. But this predicament is not only unbelievable, but arguably unliveable. It would be an utterly empty freedom.

This situationless notion of freedom has been very destructive. Not quite in the way Hegel predicted. For Marxist societies have been very concerned with *con*struction, building the foundations of socialism. But Marx's variant of 'absolute freedom' is at the base of Bolshevik voluntarism which, strong with the final justification of history, has crushed all obstacles in its path with extraordinary ruthlessness, and has spawned again that Terror which Hegel described with uncanny insight.

3

We have looked at Marx's Promethean expressivism, because this is the most influential formulation of a widespread modern protest against the course of our civilization. The idea of overcoming the injustice and expressive deadness of our world at one stroke by recovering control and radically reshaping it according to a freely chosen design exercises a profound attraction well beyond the boundaries of official Marxism. We find it almost everywhere among the protest and liberation movements of our day.

And in its very ubiquity, we have the beginnings of an answer to our question above about the relevance of Hegelian philosophy. To the extent that these aspirations to radical freedom are influenced by Marx, they descend also from Hegel. But what is much more important, they encounter the same dilemma, which emerged from our discussion of Marxism. They face the same emptiness, the same temptation to the forceful imposition of their solution on an unyielding world, the same inability to define a human situation once the present imperfect one is swept away. The rebels of May 1968 were in this respect no different from the calloused commissars they so despised. The difference was that the latter had a programme, based on the disciplined building of the 'conditions' of socialism, while the former insisted quite rightly that the building had gone on long enough and it was time to enter the realm of freedom.

But this whole tradition, whether Marxist, anarchist, situationist, or whatever, offers no idea whatever of what the society of freedom should look like beyond the empty formulae, that it should be endlessly creative, have no divisions, whether between men, or within them, or between levels of existence (play is one with work, love is one with politics, art is one with life), involve no coercion, no representation, etc. All that is done in these negative characterizations is to think away the entire human situation. Small wonder then, that this freedom has no content.

In the heat of the struggle, behind the barricades, there is a real liberation of expression, a field for creative action, the breaking down of barriers, a real participatory democracy. But of course this arises in a very real *situation*, one of breach with the ongoing routines and structures, and of combat against the 'forces of order'. But in the image of the revolution triumphant, this situation too, along with all others, is thought away.

It is as though the rebels of May 1968 were sent by Providence out of a sense of irony to confront old revolutionaries with the logic of their position. This dilemma of absolute freedom is one that Hegel thought about, and that is one of the reasons why contemporaries will continually return to examine him. He is at the origin of an important modern cast of thought, whose basic dilemma he grasped more profoundly than most of his successors.

559

Conclusion

But this problem, which we have spoken of as that of relating freedom to a situation, affects more than the Marxist or even revolutionary tradition. It is a problem for all forms of modern expressivism, and in a sense also for the whole modern conception of subjectivity.

This modern notion of subjectivity has spawned a number of conceptions of freedom which see it as something men win through to by setting aside obstacles or breaking loose from external impediments, ties or entanglements. To be free is to be untrammelled, to depend in one's action only on oneself. Moreover this conception of freedom has not been a mere footnote, but one of the central ideas by which the modern notion of the subject has been defined, as is evident in the fact that freedom is one of the values most appealed to in modern times. At the very outset, the new identity as self-defining subject was won by breaking free of the larger matrix of a cosmic order and its claims.

This type of conception of freedom defines it as self-dependence, to coin a general description. It contrasts with earlier (and some later) conceptions which define freedom in terms of order or right relation. For instance, the notion of freedom implicit in Aristotle relates it to harmony, equilibrium, the mean, as against the disordered hegemony of the extremes.

This is in a sense a negative conception of freedom. But it is not equivalent to 'negative freedom' as this is usually identified.[1] Negative freedom usually means freedom defined as independent from external interference, whereas 'positive' conceptions define it rather as realized in action which comes from or expresses the true self. But even positive conceptions in modern times have been notions of self-dependence. Freedom is won by breaking the hold of the lower self or nature so that I may obey only my (true) self. Thus Kant, whose theory is at the origin of many positive notions of freedom, defines freedom as obeying a law made by the rational self, in contrast to dependence on the will of others, external authority, or nature.

This cast of thought, which sees freedom as self-dependence, has thus been a common basis underlying the revolutionary developments in the modern notion of freedom. It is common to the original 'negative' conception of classical liberalism from Locke to Bentham, to the Rousseauian conception of freedom as obeying only oneself, to the Kantian notion of autonomy, and its successors right up to the Marxian idea of the realm of freedom, where man having overcome all alienation and dominated the natural matrix in which he is set once more determines his destiny out of himself – though the subject of this freedom is here generic, not individual man.

But this basic idea has in fact undergone development. Its first empiricist or naturalistic versions saw the goals of the self as given by nature – as desires or

---

[1] Cf. Isaiah Berlin, 'Two Concepts of Liberty' in Berlin: *Four Essays on Liberty*, O.U.P., 1969.

drives. Later variants wanted to go beyond the given altogether. The watershed in this respect is perhaps Kant. As transposed by Hegel and again by Marx, the Kantian aspiration to radical autonomy turns into the idea that human nature is not simply a given, but is to be made over. To be integrally free man must reshape his own nature.

Now it is arguably this general conception itself, equating freedom and self-dependence, which generates the dilemma we examined above in connection with Marxism. For it is defined in such a way that complete freedom would mean the abolition of all situation, that is, a predicament which sets us a certain task or calls for a certain response from us if we are to be free. The only kind of situation which this view can recognize is one defined by the obstacles to untrammelled action which have to be conquered or set aside – external oppression, inauthentic aspirations imposed by society, alienation, natural limits. This kind of situation calls for 'liberation', a word which reappears today in every conceivable context. But liberation is understood as a process which *results* in freedom. On this view, there is no situation such that the response it calls for would *be* free action at its fullest extent as against just clearing the way to such action. Full freedom would be situationless.

And by the same token, empty. Complete freedom would be a void in which nothing would be worth doing, nothing would deserve to count for anything. The self which has arrived at freedom by setting aside all external obstacles and impingements is characterless, and hence without defined purpose, however much this is hidden by such seemingly positive terms as 'rationality' or 'creativity'. These are ultimately quite indeterminate as criteria for human action or mode of life. They cannot specify any content to our action outside of a situation which sets goals for us, which thus imparts a shape to rationality and provides an inspiration for creativity.

We might hope to fill this void by returning to the earlier variants of the modern conception of freedom as self-dependence in which our goals are supposedly given by nature. Freedom would then be the unchecked fulfilment of desire, and the shape of desire would be a given. But this is a very inadequate conception of freedom. For if free activity cannot be defined in opposition to our nature and situation, on pain of vacuity, it cannot simply be identified with following our strongest, or most persistent, or most all-embracing desire either. For that would make it impossible to say that our freedom was ever thwarted by our own compulsions, fears, obsessions; or to say that freedom widens with heightened awareness or awakened aspirations. And these are not only things that we feel inclined to say in our pre-philosophical reflections about life; they are essential to an expressivist perspective which is concerned to achieve full self-expression beyond the distortions of inauthentic desire and confined aspiration. We have to be able to distinguish compulsions, fears, addictions from those of our aspirations which we endorse with our whole soul, not just by some quantitative criterion, but in a way which shows these latter to be more authentically ours. That is what the radical conceptions of freedom as self-dependence have tried to do in seeing our authentic aspirations as *chosen* by us, as against simply given. But it is just this radical notion of freedom which runs into the dilemma of vacuity.

Hegel laid bare the emptiness of the free self and the pure rational will, in his critique of Kant's morality and the politics of absolute freedom. And he hoped to overcome this emptiness, to give man a situation, without abandoning the notion of rational will. This was to be done by showing man to be the vehicle of a cosmic reason, which generated its articulations out of itself.

But once this solution in terms of cosmic spirit became untenable, for the reasons we examined above, the dilemma recurs, and indeed all the more pressingly in that the notion of freedom has been intensified, made at once more urgent and more all-embracing in its passage through German Idealism and its materialist transposition in Marx.

One stream of expressivism turned to an idea of fulfilment as the release of the instinctual or elemental depths beyond the ordered limits of conscious rationality. But this in the end puts paid altogether to the ideal of freedom in either modern or ancient sense. This 'elemental' notion of freedom has no place for self-possession, hence for a specifically human sense of freedom.

Schopenhauer's philosophy was an important stage on the road towards this 'Dionysiac' expressivism. But his own theory was in a sense its pessimistic inversion. Schopenhauer's concept of the 'will' and of the body as its 'objectification' derive from the expressivist stream of thought, but there is no idea of fulfilment here. On the contrary, the elemental force of the will brings man only suffering and degradation. The only hope is in release from the will which Schopenhauer sees in an end of all attachment to earthly things, after the model of Upanishadic and Buddhist thought.

Schopenhauer's vision provides a model for a deeply pessimistic view of human freedom, based on the sense that man's instinctual nature is other than and uncombinable with rational freedom, and at the same time unconquerable. It is this latter point which differentiates Schopenhauer from his mentor, Kant.

This conception of man can lead to despair about freedom understood as self-dependence, either because the untrammelled 'freedom' of the instinctual self seems worthless if not loathsome, or because the self defined in opposition to the instinctual seems relatively powerless.

And 'despair' is the term Kierkegaard used in his *Sickness unto Death* for this inability to accept oneself. Kierkegaard makes this the point of exit, as it were, from which he steps altogether outside the tradition of freedom as self-dependence. Despair can only be overcome by relating oneself to the external

'Power which constituted the whole relation' (sc. of the self to the self),[1] i.e., God.

But the affirmation of freedom leads to a deeper dilemma, and it was Nietzsche who pushed this to its most uncompromising expression. If the radical freedom of self-dependence is ultimately empty, then it risks ending in nihilism, that is, self-affirmation through the rejection of all 'values'. One after the other, the authoritative horizons of life, Christian and humanist, are cast off as shackles on the will. Only the will to power remains. The power and impact of Nietzsche's work come from his fierce espousal of this destructive movement which he pushes to the limit.

And yet he also seems to have held that the will to power of self-defining man would be disastrous. Man as a purely self-dependent will to power must be 'overcome', to use Zarathustra's expression. Nietzsche had an idea of this reconciliation between man's will and the course of the world in his vision of eternal recurrence, which is not easy to follow. But his idea seems to have been that pure self-affirmation must lead to an impasse, that it has at some point to link up with a deep endorsement of the course of things. 'To redeem the men of the past and to change each "Thus it was" into a "Thus I would have it" – this alone I call redemption.'[2]

The modern notion of freedom is thus under threat from two sides. On one hand, there is despair about the realization of freedom, even doubt whether the aspiration to freedom makes any sense, in face of the irrational and elemental in man. On the other, the ultimate emptiness of self-dependent freedom seems to lead to nihilism. Thus much philosophical thought in the last century has been engaged with this problem; how to go beyond a notion of the self as the subject of a self-dependent will and bring to light its insertion in nature, our own and that which surrounds us, or in other terms, how to situate freedom?

This means to recover a conception of free activity which sees it was a response called for by a situation which is ours in virtue of our condition as natural and social beings, or in virtue of some inescapable vocation or purpose. What is common to all the varied notions of situated freedom is that they see free activity as grounded in the *acceptance* of our defining situation. The struggle to be free – against limitations, oppression, distortions of inner and outer origin – is powered by an affirmation of this defining situation as ours. *This* cannot be seen as a set of limits to be overcome, or a mere occasion to carry out some freely chosen project, which is all that a situation can be within the conception of freedom as self-dependence.

In this search for a conception of situated freedom, reductive mechanistic

---

[1] *Sickness unto Death*, Anchor Edition, New York, 1954, p. 147.
[2] 'Die Verganegnen zu erlösen und alles "Es war" umzuschaffen in ein "So wollte ich es!" – das hieße mir erst Erlösung.' Also Sprach Zarathustra, Part II, on Redemption.

theories of human thought and behaviour are of no avail. They do indeed place free activity within nature, since it is one possible output of a natural system. But they do this at the cost of returning to the definition of freedom as the unchecked fulfilment of desire, and we have seen that this is inadequate, that it does not allow us to make certain essential distinctions. The notion of a freedom rooted in our nature, and yet which can be frustrated by our own desires or our limited aspirations requires a more articulated, many-levelled theory of human motivation. It is very doubtful whether any theory which recognizes only efficient causation can do justice to it. We need the notion of a bent in our situation which we can either endorse or reject, re-interpret or distort. This not only must be distinguished from what we ordinarily call desire. But it is hard to see how a bent of this kind could be accounted for in mechanistic terms, not to speak of its relation to our desires.

Reductive theories claim to suppress the problem of relating freedom to nature. But in fact they cannot escape it. It returns, this time unadmitted, in that the scientific objectification of human nature presupposes a subject of science whose activity and judgments about truth and depth of explanation cannot be accounted for in the reductive theory. He remains the angelic observer outside the objectified stream of life.

The fact that this problem of situating freedom has become more salient is probably not unrelated to the political and social developments mentioned in the first section. In a smoothly running modern society, in which the exploitation of nature and the organization of society seem designed for the utility of individuals, it is quite natural for men to feel at home in a vision of themselves as autonomous subjects engaged in effecting their freely-chosen desires and purposes. In a scientific perspective, they may indeed see themselves as moved by drives, and their behaviour as part of a deterministic causal system. But although these two perspectives are probably incompatible, neither of them gives rise to serious question about freedom or about its relation to nature. The first is that of the subject which objectifies nature, who takes his own freedom for granted, while his goals are determined by the requirement that he play his part in the large productive enterprise in the search for individual happiness. On the second perspective, the problem of relating freedom and nature is suppressed from the outset, as we have just seen. Freedom is following the course of desire, itself determined by nature within us and without. And although these desires are not autonomous in the Kantian sense, they are clear and unambiguous and quite clearly mine as long as I identify with my own nature.[1]

---

[1] We can see why there is a certain link between the acceptance of reductive mechanistic theories of motivation and satisfaction with the atomistic, utilitarian, manipulative bent of our civilization. As we saw above, these theories are not really capable of coping intellectually with the self-thwarting of freedom through our compulsions or confined aspirations. Thus reductive theories are more

But when this society is challenged and its equilibrium lost, when the more radical expressivist aspirations to total freedom gain a wide hearing, when social and individual life seem to be the prey of irrational forces – either because the social mechanisms fail to function according to 'rational' prescription (for instance, in the Depression), or because desires and aspirations come to the fore which threaten the very framework of instrumentally rational collaborative action (e.g., chauvinisms, racism, war fevers) – then the notion of the autonomous self cannot but come into question. The demand for absolute freedom raises the dilemma of self-dependence in its acutest form. And the renewed saliency of irrational and destructive cravings makes us question the very idea of autonomy, and undermines the idea of an unambiguous attribution of desire, or alternatively of our unambiguous identification with the nature in us which desires. The course of modern history has made the perspective of Schopenhauer, as vehicled to us by Freud and others, very familiar and plausible.

The short history of the Phenomenological movement strikingly illustrates the turn in philosophy towards the attempt to situate subjectivity. Husserl starts towards the turn of the century defending the autonomy of the rational subject against psychologism, the reduction of logic to psychology. He then goes on to explore the structures of subjectivity. He still, even in the late 1920s with, for instance, the *Cartesian Meditations*, sees himself as in a sense the heir of Descartes. His last work, however, turns to deal with the 'life-world', the insertion of our subjectivity in our situation as natural, embodied beings. That is what is taken up and developed by his successors, e.g., Heidegger and Merleau-Ponty. Finally what survives are the insights about embodied thought; phenomenology itself, as a 'method' of 'pure description' of subjectivity, disappears from the scene.

One can perhaps see parallel developments in anglo-saxon philosophy, where in recent decades there has been a growing interest in tracing the conceptual connections between thoughts, feelings, intentions, etc. and their bodily expressions and antecedents.

But perhaps the most important development of twentieth-century philosophy is the focus on theories of meaning and the philosophy of language. I believe that this, too, reflects in part the desire to define a notion of subjectivity in situation, that this is one of the motivations for this new departure.

Of course, language as the vehicle of conscious, discursive thought can be studied by philosophy in all sorts of intentions. But it is a characteristic of twentieth-century discussions of language that meaning itself has been a

likely to gain acceptance where this problem is not salient, i.e., where the desires that men seek to fulfill through society seem normal and spontaneous. Correlatively, expressivist thought, from Rousseau on, has developed the theme of the self-thwarting of freedom.

problem, that is, they have focussed on the question; what is it for words, or language, or other signs, to have meaning?

As long as our activity as subjects, the fact that we perceive and think about the world, seems clear and unproblematic, as long as its relation to the rest of what we do and feel as living beings seems unpuzzling, the function of language also appears straightforward. Words refer to things, and we use them to think about things with. Words have meaning by pointing to things in the world, or in our thought. The unproblematic nature of the referring relation reflects the lack of question about subjectivity, about the fact that things appear for us as objects of the kind of explicit awareness in which we apply names and descriptions to them.

But our conceptions of language changes when this fact of explicit consciousness no longer seems something we can take for granted, seems rather an achievement and a remarkable one. For this achievement is only possible through language, which is its vehicle; and hence language becomes a relevant object of study not just as an assemblage of terms by which we designate things, but also as that by which there is such an activity as designating in the first place, as what underpins that field of explicit awareness within which it is possible to pick things out and fix them by words. In this perspective meaning is not simply a property which pertains to each word individually, but a fact about the activity of discourse as a whole which is in a sense prior to the individual terms.

Once we see language as the vehicle of a certain mode of consciousness, which we achieve through speech, then a whole host of questions can arise concerning its relation to other modes of awareness, to other functions and activities of life, in short its ' *Sitz im Leben*'. It ceases to be taken for granted that what we are mainly doing in language is designating and describing things, that this is the paradigm linguistic activity in relation to which all others are to be explained. On the contrary, other activities which also require linguistic consciousness to be carried through – invoking some power, performing a rite, bringing about certain states of affairs, clarifying our vision, establishing a sphere of communication – may be equally if not more primitive. That is, it may be that the meaning of certain terms and expressions can only be made clear if we understand them as occurring in the context of these activities. In these cases meaning can only be explicited by situating language in the matrix of our concerns, practices and activities, in short by relating it to our 'form of life'.

And if linguistic consciousness is an achievement to which we win through from less explicit modes, and if moreover the activities we engage in through language and symbols are various, then there are many types and levels of awareness of the world which can be embodied in words or signs. Men of any given culture may function on a number of such levels, e.g., in art, conversation, ritual, self-revelation, scientific study; and over history new conceptualizations and new modes of awareness emerge. It may be that our thought on any one level can only be understood by its relation to the other levels; in particular our 'higher', more explicit awareness may always repose on a background of the implicit and the unreflected.

We can easily recognize here some theses of contemporary philosophy. The later Wittgenstein has made commonplaces of the arguments for the priority of language over individual words in his discussion of the claims of ostensive definition. And he shows how the explication of meaning must end in a reference to forms of life. Polanyi has portrayed our explicit thought as an achievement, always surrounded by a horizon of the implicit, of subsidiary awareness. Heidegger speaks of linguistic consciousness as 'disclosure', as creating a field of awareness in which things can appear, and of our consciousness of things as shaped by our 'concern'. More recently, 'structuralist' thinkers have explored language as a 'grid' embodying a certain awareness of the world.

These ways of understanding linguistic thought situate this thought in 'nature', that is, in the life of man as an embodied, social being, while avoiding a reductive account of language and meaning through a mechanistic causal theory – like, e.g., behaviourism or psychologism – which suppresses all distinctions between different modes of awareness by making them unstatable. They go beyond the alternative between reductive, mechanistic theories and 'angelic' conceptions of subjectivity as disembodied thought. They open a view of subjectivity in situation. This is, of course, part of the philosophical intention of writers like Polanyi, Heidegger, Merleau-Ponty, and other 'continental' writers. But the connection has also come to the fore in the anglo-saxon world, since contemporary writers who have explored the theme of action and feeling as belonging to embodied agents have drawn heavily on the later writings of Wittgenstein.

What relation has Hegel's philosophy to this contemporary turn? Fundamental to Hegel's theory, as we saw, was the principle of embodiment. Subjectivity was necessarily situated in life, in nature, and in a setting of social practices and institutions. Hegel, as we examined in the Part v, saw language and symbols as vehicles of awareness,[1] and he saw different vehicles corresponding to different levels, in the various stages of art, religion and philosophy.

In a sense, Hegel can be placed in the line of development which leads up to the contemporary ways of understanding language. Its point of origin in modern thought is perhaps Herder, who made a radical shift of the kind

---

[1] A pithy formulation of this view of language as an embodiment of awareness rather than as assemblage of signs occurs in *PhG* (496): '...die Sprache, – ein Dasein, das unmittelbar selbstbewußte Existenz ist'.

described above. He ceased to take the relation of referring for granted whereby certain signs become associated with certain objects[1] and focussed on the fact that there were signs at all, on linguistic consciousness, as a remarkable human power that we are very far from adequately understanding. Language is no longer just an assemblage of signs, but the vehicle of this consciousness. As mentioned in Chapter I, Herder's reaction to Condillac and the established theory of language is reminiscent at certain points of the later Wittgenstein. By seeing language as an activity expressive of a certain consciousness, Herder situates it in the life-form of the subject, and hence develops the notion of different languages as expressive each of a vision peculiar to the community which speaks it.

This insight was developed in the Romantic period and by thinkers influenced by the expressivist current of thought, e.g., von Humboldt. But it seems to have gone somewhat into abeyance in the latter half of the nineteenth century, in the period in which the insights of Romanticism were being reincorporated into an expanded mechanistic science. The concern and puzzlement about meaning return towards the end of the century – through the new reflections on the sciences of man which start with Dilthey and make 'verstehen' their goal; as an inevitable by-product of Freud's revolutionary extensions of the notion of meaning; under the impact of the epistemological questions posed by new developments in physics and which were explored by Mach and his successors in Vienna.

Hegel can be placed in this line of descent, and yet in a sense he also departed from it, may even bear part of the responsibility for the hiatus of the later part of the century. This for the reason examined in Chapter XVII. The Herderian approach to language which has recurred in contemporary philosophy sees speech as the activity by which we gain a kind of explicit, self-aware consciousness of things which as such is always related to an unreflective experience which precedes it and which it illuminates and hence transforms. This is the dimension of language which I called 'disclosure' in Chapter XVII, which involves its own kind of fidelity to extra-linguistic experience. The view of language, on the other hand, which sees it as a set of signs, of which the most important are referential, makes the other dimension, the descriptive, the important, indeed the only relevant one.

Now Hegel unquestionably belongs to the first school. He sees the different 'languages', of art, religion and discursive thought as expressing an awareness of the Absolute which is not at first descriptive at all (in art) and which is never simply descriptive, since the revelation in religion and philosophy completes the *realization* of the Absolute and does not simply *portray* it. But nevertheless, his thesis that the Absolute must finally come to complete,

[1] Cf. above Chapter I.

568

explicit clarity in conceptual statement gives the primacy in the end to the descriptive dimension. Our explicit consciousness is no longer surrounded by a horizon of the implicit, of unreflected life and experience, which it is trying to render faithfully but which can never be fully, adequately, definitively brought to light. On the contrary, in the Hegelian synthesis the unclear consciousness of the beginning is itself made part of the chain of conceptual necessity. The unclear and inarticulate, just as the external and contingent, is itself shown to have a necessary existence. The approximate and incompletely formed is itself derived in exact, articulate concepts.

What makes possible this final victory of conceptual clarity is of course Hegel's ontology, the thesis that what we ultimately discover at the basis of everything is the Idea, conceptual necessity itself. Conceptual thought is not trying to render a reality whose foundations can never be definitively identified, nor is it the thought of a subject whose deeper instincts, cravings and aspirations can never be fully fathomed. On the contrary, at the root of reality, as in the depths of himself, the subject ultimately finds clear, conceptual necessity.

But once this ontology fades from view, what remains is the notion that descriptive conceptual thought is omnicompetent and ultimately self-sufficient, that is, that it does not in the end need to rely on a background of implicit understanding. And in this Hegel seems to emerge as the ally of those in the central tradition of modern subjectivity who take the existence of descriptive discourse quite unproblematically for granted. For they hold that the descriptive dimension alone has relevance for scientific or informative discourse, that the relation of explicit thought to unreflected experience has nothing to do with meaning, but can only be a problem for (a mechanistic, objectifying) psychology. Whereas those who are trying to relate linguistic consciousness to its matrix in unreflective life – once Hegel's logo-ontology is set aside – must necessarily see explicit thought as rooted in an implicit sense of the situation which can never be fully explored.

In other words, the new line taken by Herder, against the grain of the Enlightenment, opens the problems of the relation of our linguistic consciousness to deeper, unreflective levels of experience. Hegel in claiming the complete self-clarity of *Geist* in effect proposes to close this question as definitively solved. But as his solution fades, his far-reaching claims on behalf of conceptual thought separate him from Herder's heirs in our day, for whom the unreflective experience of our situation can never be fully explicited, and seem to align him with those for whom the problem should never have been posed.

569

Conclusion

4

Hegel's double relation to this tradition which descends from Herder, both an essential link in it, and yet at odds with it, illustrates his relevance for modern philosophy. As I said at the outset, his conclusions are dead, and yet the course of his philosophical reflection is very much to the point. We can now see more clearly why.

Hegel's philosophy is an important step in the development of the modern notion of freedom. He helped to develop a conception of freedom as total self-creation, which indeed was attributable in his philosophy only to cosmic spirit, but which only needed to be transposed on to man to push the conception of freedom as self-dependence to its ultimate dilemma. He thus had an important part in the intensification of the conflict around the modern notion of freedom. For absolute freedom has acquired an unprecedented impact on political life and aspirations through the work of Marx and his successors, whose debt to Hegel needs no underlining. And one of the sources of Nietzsche's thought, which drew the nihilist consequences of this idea, was the young Hegelian revolt of the 1840s.

At the same time Hegel was one of the profoundest critics of this notion of freedom as self-dependence. He laid bare its emptiness and its potential destructiveness with a truly remarkable insight and prescience. He has paradoxically helped both to bring this modern doctrine to its most extreme expression and to show the dilemma in which it involves us.

But most important of all, the contemporary attempt to go beyond this dilemma, to situate subjectivity by relating it to our life as embodied and social beings, without reducing it to a function of objectified nature, constantly refers us back to Hegel. In a sense, the modern search for a situated subjectivity is the heir of that central aspiration of the Romantic period which Hegel thought to answer definitively – how to unite radical autonomy with the fullness of expressive unity with nature.[1] Because nature cannot be for us what it was for

---

[1] Thus one of the deep motivations of Heidegger's thought is to take us beyond the adversary stance of domination and objectification towards nature which he sees implicit in our metaphysical tradition and its off-shoot, technological civilization, and inaugurate (or recover) a mode of existence in which the highest awareness is a way of 'letting things be', of disclosure. Heidegger claims to find his position foreshadowed in Hegel's friend and contemporary, Hölderlin, perhaps the greatest poet of the Romantic generation. (See following note.)

In view of this it is not surprising that Heidegger accords a pivotal position to Hegel. He sees him as the culmination of the tradition of 'metaphysics'. But he is more than just the paradigm of what Heidegger opposes. Plainly he has drawn a great deal from Hegel, and most notably perhaps the conception of authentic awareness as a return out of forgetfulness and error. (Cf. his discussion of the Introduction to *PhG* in *Hegel's Concept of Experience*, New York, 1970; translation of Chapter III of *Holzwege*, Frankfurt, 5th Edition 1972.) Hence his substantive philosophical thesis is as inextricably linked with a reading of the history of philosophy as is Hegel's. But Heidegger's reading is systematically different from Hegel's. For he rejects the Hegelian culmination in the total self-clarity of subjectivity. He sees in this rather an extreme, indeed insurpassable expression of the metaphysical stance of objectification.

570

that age, an expression of spiritual powers, the syntheses of the time can no longer command our allegiance.

But the problem which concerned that generation, the opposition they attempted to reconcile, continues in different forms to our day. It seems ineradicable from modern civilization, which as heir to the Enlightenment constantly re-awakens expressivist protest, and along with this, the claims of absolute freedom. The very urgency with which these claims are pressed makes the search for a situated subjectivity all the more vital. And the need grows more acute today under the impact of an ecological crisis which is being increasingly dramatized in the public consciousness. The fact that we are still trying to reconcile freedom and nature makes us still at home in the Romantic period. They speak to us, however bizarre their doctrines may appear to contemporary eyes.[1]

And in so far as this search for a situated subjectivity takes philosophical form, Hegel's thought will be one of its indispensable points of reference. For although his ontological vision is not ours – indeed seems to deny the very problem as we now understand it – Hegel's writings provide one of the most profound and far-reaching attempts to work out a vision of embodied subjectivity, of thought and freedom emerging from the stream of life, finding expression in the forms of social existence, and discovering themselves in relation to nature and history. If the philosophical attempt to situate freedom is the attempt to gain a conception of man in which free action is the response to what we are – or to a call which comes to us, from nature alone or a God who is also beyond nature (the debate will never cease) – then it will always recur behind Hegel's conclusions to his strenuous and penetrating reflections on embodied spirit.

[1] In the end, of all the members of the Romantic generation the most relevant may be Hölderlin, Hegel's friend and classmate at Tübingen. Hölderlin was also looking for a unity with nature which would preserve the clarity of self-possession. And his gods as well only came to themselves in human subjectivity. But they did not repose on a foundation of absolute spirit. Rather they were drawn from the primitive chaos of the elements into the light of measure and order by man, through the power of poetry and song.

Thus Hölderlin seems to open a perspective in which man's freest expression follows the prompting of nature, bringing nature in a sense into the light of freedom. But this nature is not and can never become an emanation of spirit. It remains inexhaustible and unfathomable, a constant invitation to the creative activity which brings it to light.

Hölderlin's position is not easy to interpret. In any case it may be inaccessible to philosophical statement. And one senses that madness overtook him before his thought came to mature expression. Hegel alone was left to give definitive shape to the thoughts and insights which they shared at Tübingen and Frankfurt. But to those who want to resume the task of Hegel's generation, his too-soon-silenced friend may point a surer way.

Biographical Note

Georg Wilhelm Friedrich Hegel was born in Stuttgart, 27 August 1770, son of a civil servant in the government of the Duchy of Württemberg. He was the eldest of three children, being followed by a sister, Christiane, with whom he remained close throughout his life, and a brother, Ludwig, who subsequently became an army officer. His mother died when he was in his teens, in 1784.

Hegel attended primary school in Stuttgart, and from 1780 the Gymnasium or secondary school there. He was a conscientious student, devoting himself a great deal to classical studies, and graduating first of his class.

In 1788 he went on to the *Tübinger Stift*, the theology seminary attached to the State University of Tübingen. This prepared young men for service in the government, church or teaching. Hegel as the holder of a ducal scholarship lived in the seminary. He studied philosophy and theology. It was here that he began to develop his ideas on *Volksreligion*. He formed friendships with Schelling and Hölderlin at the *Stift*.

On graduating from the seminary in 1793, he left to take up the post of preceptor with a patrician family of Bern. This was in fact normal for young graduates, and many famous university teachers spent their first post-graduate years in this manner (including Kant and Fichte). In Bern, Hegel managed to continue reading and thinking, but felt cut off from things, and in early 1797 he gladly accepted a similar post in Frankfurt which Hölderlin had secured for him.

The next years were spent in interchange with Hölderlin and others in the stimulating environment of Frankfurt. In 1799 his father died, leaving him a modest fortune. With this in hand, Hegel began thinking of a university career. At about this time he was coming to sense that philosophy was the indispensable medium of the reconciliation he was looking for. He approached Schelling, who helped him get established at Jena, which he did in 1801.

Jena had been Germany's most exciting university in the 1790s. Schiller, Fichte, the Schlegel brothers had been there. When Hegel came it was entering its decline. Fichte had left in 1799, Schelling himself was to leave in 1803. But Hegel's years at Jena enabled him to work out the bases of his own philosophical system and become known to the philosophical world through some of his minor publications.

Hegel at first was a *Privatdozent*, that is, an unsalaried lecturer remunerated by students' fees. In his lectures of this period he began to work out the early versions of what later became his logic and philosophy of politics, at first somewhat under Schelling's influence, but later more and more independently. In his early Jena years Hegel published his *Difference between Fichte's and Schelling's Systems of Philosophy* and *Faith and Knowledge* (*Glauben und Wissen*, a critique of Kant, Fichte and Jacobi), and a number of articles.

In 1805, he was finally appointed Professor *extraordinarius* (associate professor) at Jena, and began work on a major statement of his system, of which the first part became the *PhG*. But in October 1806, his life was rudely interrupted. Napoleon, after the battle of Jena, seized the city. In the ensuing disorder, Hegel had to leave his lodgings carrying the second half of the manuscript of the *PhG*. To cap this most turbulent period in Hegel's life, on 5 February 1807 the wife of his landlord in Jena bore him an illegitimate son, who was christened Ludwig.

Hegel was now looking for a job again, and his inherited fortune was spent. Although the *PhG* when it came out in 1807 began to make his reputation, there was little hope in those disordered times of another university appointment. Hegel's friend Niethammer found him a job editing the *Bamberger Zeitung*, and Hegel snapped at the opportunity. He enjoyed some aspects of newspaper editing, but it was not really his métier and he was glad when the following year Niethammer got him the post of headmaster and professor of philosophy at the Gymnasium of Nürnberg.

Questions of pride apart, Hegel was not too badly off at the Gymnasium. The budget was tight, and his salary was sometimes paid late, but the teaching of philosophy, even to high school students, obviously helped him to focus his thought. This period (1808–16) was very fruitful for him. It was during this time that he wrote and published the *Science of Logic* (*WL*, 1812–16).

His life was now reasonably stabilized; his work was approaching its mature statement; he continued to have hopes of an attractive offer from university. In 1811, at the age of 41, Hegel married. His bride was Marie von Tucher, 20 years old, daughter of a Nuremberg senator. They had two sons, Karl and Immanuel, and in addition took the illegitimate Ludwig into the household.

In 1816, Hegel finally got an offer which he had expected earlier on, to a chair of philosophy in the University of Heidelberg. At the same time, feelers were sent out from Berlin where the chair had been vacant since Fichte's death in 1814. The Berlin post was much the more prestigious and attractive, but Hegel opted for the bird in hand and went to Heidelberg. Hegel threw himself back with a will into university lecturing. In his first year at Heidelberg he prepared the statement of his whole system, the *Enclyclopaedia of the Philosophical Sciences* (*EL*, *EN* and *EG*), which appeared in 1817.

But in Berlin, the chair remained vacant, and in Germany, Hegel's reputation grew. The Prussian minister of education, von Altenstein came up with a firm offer, and Hegel accepted. In 1818 he took up the post of professor in Berlin which he held till his death.

In Berlin, Hegel came into his own. Berlin had become a major cultural centre, as well as being the capital of one of the two 'super-powers' of the German Confederation. To make an impact here was to exercise influence. And Hegel did make an impact. He rapidly grew to be the major figure in German philosophy, and the influence of his thought spread to other related fields, law and political thought, theology, aesthetics, history. Many came to his lectures, and a number became disciples. Hegel's thought more or less dominated German philosophy for two decades, the 1820s and 1830s. He was fortunate enough to die in the middle and not at the end of this apogee.

In his Berlin period, Hegel wrote the *Philosophy of Right* (*PR*, published 1821), and put together the great lecture cycles which were published after his death, on the philosophy of history, aesthetics, the philosophy of religion and the history of philosophy.

In 1829, at the height of his fame, Hegel was elected Rector of the University. But on 14 November 1831, he died suddenly and unexpectedly of what was diagnosed as cholera at the time, but was more likely a stomach ailment which had been giving him trouble in previous years. He was buried next to Fichte, accompanied on his last journey by a long cortège of students, colleagues and disciples.

Bibliography

I. HEGEL'S WORKS

Sämtliche Werke, Jubiläumsausgabe in XX Bänden, Ed. Hermann Glockner, Stuttgart, 1927–30.

H. Nohl, Ed. *Hegels Theologische Jugendschriften*, Tübingen 1907 – a collection of unpublished MSS of the 1790s; English translation (of parts): T. M. Knox: *Early Theological Writings*, Chicago, 1948.

Differenz des Fichte'schen und Schelling'schen Systems, Ed. G. Lasson, Leipzig, 1928 – Hegel's first published work in philosophy, Jena, 1801.

Glauben und Wissen, Ed. G. Lasson, Leipzig, 1928 – published 1802/3 in the *Critical Journal of Philosophy*, which Hegel edited with Schelling in the early Jena period. This work is a critique of Kant, Jacobi and Fichte.

G. Lasson, Ed. *Schriften zur Politik und Rechtsphilosophie*, Leipzig, 1923 – contains a number of Hegel's occasional writings on politics, including 'The German Constitution' and 'The English Reform Bill'. It also includes two unpublished theoretical works of the Jena period, 'Über die wissenschaftlichen Behandlungsarten des Naturrechts' and 'System der Sittlichkeit'. (This latter has also been published separately, Meiner Verlag, Hamburg 1967.) English translation of the occasional pieces by T. M. Knox, with introduction by Z. Pelczynski, *Political Writings*, Oxford, 1964.

Jenenser Realphilosophie, I, Ed. J. Hoffmeister, Leipzig, 1932 – edited lecture notes from 1803/4, unpublished by Hegel.

Jenenser Realphilosophie, II, Ed. J. Hoffmeister, Leipzig, 1931 (republished as *Jenaer Realphilosophie*, Hamburg, 1967) – edited lecture notes from 1805/6, unpublished by Hegel.

Phänomenologie des Geistes, Ed. G. Lasson/J. Hoffmeister, Hamburg, 1952 – published 1807, written at the very end of the Jena period; English translation by J. B. Baillie, *The Phenomenology of Mind*, London, 1931.

Another translation is in process by Kenley R. Dove. His translation of the introduction appears in M. Heidegger, *Hegel's Concept of Experience*, New York, 1970.

Walter Kaufmann's translation of the very important Preface to the *Phenomenology* appears in his *Hegel: Texts and Commentary*, Anchor edition, New York 1966.

Nürnberger Schriften, Ed. J. Hoffmeister, Leipzig, 1938 – includes the *Philosophical Propaedeutic* of the Nuremberg period.

Wissenschaft der Logik, Ed. G. Lasson, Hamburg, 1963 – published Nürnberg 1812–16. The first volume was revised for a second edition before Hegel's death. Often called 'Greater Logic'. English translations: by W. H. Johnston and L. G. Struthers, *Hegel's Science of Logic*, London, 1929, and by A. V. Miller, *Hegel's Science of Logic*, London, 1969.

Encyclopädie der philosophischen Wissenschaften im Grundrisse, published as *System der*

Bibliography

Philosophie in Sämtliche Werke, vols. VIII, IX and X, edited by H. Glockner, Stuttgart 1927–30 – first published in 1817 in Heidelberg, with second editions prepared by the author 1827 and 1830. Contains the Logic (the 'Lesser Logic'), Philosophy of Nature and Philosophy of Spirit. English translations: of the Logic, by William Wallace, *The Logic of Hegel*, Oxford, 1874; of the Philosophy of Nature, by M. J. Petry, *Hegel's Philosophy of Nature*, London, 1970; of the Philosophy of Spirit, by William Wallace and A. V. Miller, *Hegel's Philosophy of Mind*, Oxford, 1971.

Grundlinien der Philosophie des Rechts, Ed. J. Hoffmeister, Hamburg, 1955 – published Berlin 1821. English translation by T. M. Knox, *Hegel's Philosophy of Right*, Oxford, 1942.

Berliner Schriften, Ed. J. Hoffmeister, Hamburg, 1956 – lectures, articles, etc. of the Berlin period.

Posthumously edited lecture cycles

On the philosophy of History: in *Sämtliche Werke* XI, also edited by G. Lasson/ J. Hoffmeister in 4 volumes: *Die Vernunft in der Geschichte*, Hamburg, 1955; *Die Orientalische Welt*, Leipzig, 1923; *Die griechische und römische Welt*, Leipzig, 1923; *Die germanische Welt*, Leipzig, 1920. English translation: by J. Sibtree, *Lectures on the Philosophy of History*, Dover Edition, New York, 1956; of part of the introduction, by R. S. Hartman, *Reason in History*, New York, 1953.

On Aesthetics, in *Sämtliche Werke*, vols. XII, XIII and XIV, also Lasson, edition of the introductory part, *Die Idee und das Ideal*, Leipzig, 1921. English translation forthcoming by T. M. Knox, O.U.P. 1975.

On philosophy of Religion: in *Sämtliche Werke* XV and XVI, also edited by G. Lasson/ J. Hoffmeister in 4 volumes: *Begriff der Religion*, Leipzig, 1925; *Die Naturreligion*, Leipzig, 1927; *Die Religionen der geistigen Individualität*, Leipzig, 1927; *Die absolute Religion*, Leipzig, 1929. English translation: by E. B. Speirs and J. B. Sanderson, *Lectures on the Philosophy of Religion*, New York, 1962, 3 volumes.

On the history of philosophy: in *Sämtliche Werke*, vols. XVII, XVIII and XIX, also Lasson edition of the introductory part, *Geschichte der Philosophie*, Leipzig, 1940. English translation by E. S. Haldane and F. H. Simson, *Hegel's Lectures on the History of Philosophy*, London 1896, 3 volumes.

SUGGESTED FURTHER READINGS
(i) Biography

Fischer, Kuno, *Hegels Leben, Werke und Lehre*, 2 vols., Heidelberg, 1911.
Haering, Th. *Hegel: Sein Wollen und sein Werk*, 2 vols., Leipzig and Berlin, 1929, 1938.
Haym, R. *Hegel und seine Zeit*, Berlin, 1957.
Rosenkranz, Karl, *George Wilhelm Friedrich Hegels Leben*, Berlin, 1844.
Wiedmann, Fr., *Hegel: an illustrated Biography*, New York, 1968.

Bibliography

(ii) General commentary

Bloch, Ernst, *Subjekt-Objekt: Erläuterungen zu Hegel*, Berlin 1951.
Findlay, J. N., *Hegel: a Re-examination*, London, 1958.
Kaufmann, Walter, *Hegel: a Re-interpretation*, New York, 1965.
Kroner, R. *Von Kant bis Hegel*, 2 vols., Tübingen, 1921, 1924.
Marcuse, Herbert, *Reason and Revolution*, New York, 1955.
Mure, G. R. G., *An Introduction to Hegel*, Oxford, 1940.
The Philosophy of Hegel, London, 1965.

(iii) Collections

Grégoire, Franz, *Etudes Hegeliennes*, Louvain and Paris, 1958.
Henrich, Dieter, *Hegel im Kontext*, Frankfurt, 1967.
Hypollite, Jean, *Etudes sur Marx et Hegel*, Paris, 1955; English translation by John O'Neill, *Studies on Marx and Hegel*, New York, 1969.
MacIntyre, A., Ed., *Hegel*, New York, 1972.
Steinkraus, W. E., Ed., *New Studies in Hegel's Philosophy*, New York, 1971.
Travis, D. C., Ed., *A Hegel Symposium*, Austin, Texas, 1962.

(iv) Hegel's development and youth

Asveld, Paul, *La Pensée religieuse du Jeune Hegel*, Louvain and Paris, 1953.
Dilthey, Wilhelm, 'Die Jugendgeschichte Hegels' in vol. IV of his *Gesammelte Schriften*, Stuttgart, 1962–5.
Haering, Th., *Hegel: Sein Wollen und sein Werk*, 2 vols., Leipzig and Berlin, 1929, 1938.
Harris, H. S. *Hegel's Development*, Oxford, 1972.
Lukács, György, *Der junge Hegel*, Berlin, 1954; English translation by Rodney Livingstone, *The Young Hegel*, London, 1975.
Peperzak, Adrien, *Le jeune Hegel et la vision morale du monde*, The Hague, 1960.
Rohrmoser, G., *Théologie et Aliénation dans la pensée du jeune Hegel*, Paris, 1970.

(v) Phenomenology

Heidegger, M. 'Hegels Begriff der Erfahrung' in *Holzwege*, Frankfurt 1950; English translation: *Hegel's Concept of Experience*, New York 1970.
Hyppolite, Jean, *Genèse et structure de la Phénoménologie de l'Esprit de Hegel*, Paris, 1946.
Kojève, Alexandre, *Introduction à la lecture de Hegel*, Paris, 1947; English translation by Allan Bloom, *Introduction to the Reading of Hegel*, New York, 1969.

(vi) Logic

Fleischmann, Eugène, *La Science universelle*, Paris, 1968.
Hyppolite, Jean, *Logique et Existence*, Paris, 1953.
Mure, G. R. G. *A Study of Hegel's Logic*, Oxford, 1950.

Bibliography

(vii) History and politics

Avineri, Shlomo, *Hegel's Theory of the Modern State*, Cambridge, 1972.
Bourgeois, Bernard, *La pensée politique de Hegel*, Paris, 1969.
Fleischmann, Eugène, *La philosophie politique de Hegel*, Paris, 1964.
Hyppolite, Jean, *Introduction à la philosophie de l'histoire de Hegel*, Paris, 1947.
Kaufmann, Walter, Ed., *Hegel's Political Philosophy*, New York, 1970.
Kelly, George Armstrong, *Idealism, Politics and History*, Cambridge, 1969.
Marcuse, H. *Reason and Revolution*, New York, 1955.
Pelczynski, Z. Ed., *Hegel's Political Philosophy*, Cambridge, 1971.
Riedel, Manfred, *Studien zu Hegels Rechtsphilosophie*, Frankfurt, 1969. *Bürgerliche Gesellschaft und Staat bei Hegel*, Neuwied and Berlin, 1970.
Ritter, Joachim, *Hegel und die französische Revolution*, Köln, 1957.
Rosenzweig, Franz, *Hegel und der Staat*, Berlin and Munich, 1920.
Weil, E., *Hegel et l'Etat*, Paris, 1950.

(viii) Aesthetics

Kedney, J. S., *Hegel's Aesthetics*, Chicago, 1885.
Knox, Israel, *The Aesthetic Theories of Kant, Hegel and Schopenhauer*, New York, 1936.

(ix) Religion

Chapelle, Albert, *Hegel et la Religion*, Paris, 1967.
Christensen, Darrel, Ed., *Hegel and the Philosophy of Religion*, The Hague, 1970.
Fackenheim, Emil, *The Religious Dimension of Hegel's Thought*, Bloomington and London, 1967.
Iljin, Iwan, *Die Philosophie Hegels als kontemplative Gotteslehre*, Bern, 1946.
Léonard, André, *La foi chez Hegel*, Paris, 1970.

Analytical list of main discussions

Index

579

Index